Asian Security Order

Asian Security Order

Instrumental and Normative Features

Edited by

Muthiah Alagappa

Stanford University Press, Stanford, California, 2003

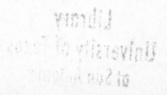

Stanford University Press
Stanford, California
© 2003 by the Board of Trustees of the
Leland Stanford Junior University
Printed in the United States of America

Library of Congress Cataloging-in-Publication Data

Asian security order : instrumental and normative features / edited by
Muthiah Alagappa.
    p.   cm.
Includes bibliographical references and index.
   ISBN 0-8047-4628-1 (cloth : acid-free paper) —
   ISBN 0-8047-4629-x (paper : acid-free paper)
1. National security—Asia.   2. Asia—Military policy.   3. Asia—
Strategic aspects.   I. Alagappa, Muthiah.

UA830 .A8553   2003
355'.03305—dc21   2002012941

This book is printed on acid-free, archival-quality paper.

Original printing 2003

Last figure below indicates year of this printing:
12 11 10 09 08 07 06 05 04 03

Typeset at Stanford University Press in 10/13 Minion

Contents

Part III. Management of Specific Issues

Part IV. Conclusion

Tables and Figures

Tables

Figures

Preface

When the Cold War ended, many Western analysts, especially of the realist persuasion, predicted dire scenarios for Asia. Deploying the general theories of neorealism and neoliberalism, drawing on the history of Europe, and emphasizing the institutional weaknesses and security challenges confronting Asia, they envisaged a dangerous region in which rivalry, power balancing, and conflict would be endemic. Specialists and policymakers in Asia, on the other hand, espousing the merits of the so-called Asian values, berating the decadent and declining West, assuming that Asia's economies would continue to grow at miraculous rates, and perceiving Asia to be radically different from Europe, envisaged a more optimistic future. In this view, although Asian states may be competitive and have a history of antagonistic relations, they also have a mutual interest in international stability and avoidance of war. Rather than suffer the dictates of the existing material and normative structures, they believed that a window of opportunity existed to build the necessary structures and institutions for peace and security and for a benign environment in which Asian countries could continue to develop. Much of the Western security analysts' prognosis for Asia was not grounded in solid empirical work. Lacking a good understanding of its history and complexities, many analysts simply deployed their concepts and theories to explain Asia and project its future. On the other hand, much of the security work by Asia specialists, dominated in large part by the Track 2 process, was highly empirical, lacked conceptual and theoretical bases, and was in many ways shallow.

It was in this context that the East-West Center launched a three-phase project on Asian security that would last almost a decade. Conceptually informed and empirically grounded, the first phase, which began in 1995, sought to understand and explain how sixteen Asian countries conceived and practiced security. Such an investigation, it was believed, would provide a solid foundation for understanding the security dynamics in Asia and for evaluating competing prognostications. Drawing on Asia's experiences, it also sought to weigh in on the then-ongoing debate over the definition of security. Much of the literature on this subject was grounded in the European and American experience. Happily Asia is now becoming more salient in conceptual and theoretical discussions of security. The findings of the first phase were published in *Asian Security Practice: Material and Ideational Influences*. The focus of the second phase was on understanding and explaining the security interaction dynamics at the subregional (Northeast, Southeast, South, and Central Asia) and regional levels. Unfortunately and much to my regret, for a number of reasons this phase, under the direction of my collaborator Yoshihide Soeya of Keio University, has not resulted in a book.

The third phase, which began in 1999, explored the existence and nature of order in the management of Asian security affairs. More than a decade has passed since the end of the Cold War, but the dire prognostications of certain Western analysts have not materialized. It is possible to argue that a decade is too short. But it is also not insignificant. It is important to specify a time frame for predictions. In the long run, all manner of things can happen, and we are all dead. Asia still faces serious security challenges, and the optimism of the Asia specialists has been undercut by the continuing economic stagnation in Japan and the 1997 financial crisis that tarred the miracle image of Asian economies. The rising concern with international terrorism further complicates the strategic situation in parts of Asia. However, the key point is this: although Asia still faces serious security challenges, it has enjoyed relative peace, security, and prosperity. Despite periodic crises, there has not been a major war since 1979. With very few exceptions, Asian states do not fear for their survival. Political differences and disputes are, for the most part, adjusted or managed in a relatively peaceful manner. Despite setbacks, international trade, investment, and production have flourished. In comparison with the first thirty years of the postindependence period, greater stability and predictability have characterized Asia's international relations in the last two decades. The existence of stability and predictability despite serious security challenges is the puzzle investigated in this study. Why has Asia become more stable? Does security order exist in Asia? What is the nature of that order? What explains the existence of order in the context of serious security challenges? How is the Asian security order likely to develop or alter? These are the questions investigated in this book, which advances five propositions.

Proposition One. Contrary to the assertion that Asia is a dangerous place, the study argues that security order exists in Asia. With very few exceptions states do not fear for their survival. International political interaction among Asian states, for the most part, is systematic and is conducted in observance of certain rules. States coexist; they coordinate and collaborate in the pursuit of national, common, and collective goals; most differences are adjusted in a peaceful manner;

and change, for the most part, is nonviolent. Asia is becoming a more stable and predictable region. Our contention that security order exists in Asia rests on the following: the existence of a widely shared normative framework; the growing salience of the principles and norms associated with this framework in ensuring state survival, easing the security dilemma, and sustaining normal political and diplomatic interaction among states that are part of the Asian security system; and the role of these principles and norms in facilitating coordination and cooperation in the pursuit of private and common security goals. The violation of the principles and norms carries a cost. Territorial disputes are being adjusted or managed in a peaceful manner. Even in the case of the acute conflicts (Taiwan, Korea, and Kashmir), certain basic understandings have been reached. Although still important, the role of force has become more limited. The extent and effectiveness of rules, however, vary by issue and by subregion.

Proposition Two. The prevailing security order in Asia is largely instrumental in character, but it also has important normative-contractual features. The primary purposes of order are mostly national: coordination and limited collaboration to facilitate coexistence, protect and improve national and regime security, enable the pursuit of national economic goals, increase national power and influence, and avoid undesirable outcomes, including misunderstanding and accidental war. There is virtually no commitment to a present or future collective political identity at the subregional or regional levels that would subsume or substantially modify national identity and interests. Power and force still play a key role in the interaction of the major powers, although their function is primarily in the defense, deterrence, and reassurance roles. There is growing acknowledgment in Asia that disputes should be settled without recourse to war and that the role of force in international politics should be constrained. However, the translation of such acknowledgment into concrete measures has been slow and difficult.

Proposition Three. Multiple pathways sustain the present security order. Hegemony, balance of power (including alliance), concert, global and regional multilateral institutions, bilateralism, and self-help—all play key roles, but with different functions. No single pathway is dominant in the management of Asian security affairs, although the preponderant power of the United States and the public goods it provides weigh heavily in the key security relationships and issues in the region. Nevertheless, the security order is not hegemonic—certainly not in the Gramscian sense—and Washington cannot manage security in Asia by itself. It needs the cooperation of the other Asian powers. The basis for sustained strategic cooperation among the major powers has yet to be forged.

Proposition Four. Security and stability in Asia rest on several pillars, not just the U.S. security role and forward military presence. Although important, the American role is not uncontroversial. It may also be retarding understanding and accommodation among the indigenous Asian powers. From the perspective of conflict management, the American role has been more significant in deterring the outbreak of war than in settling disputes. Three other key factors also underpin security and stability in Asia. One is the continuing consolidation of Asian countries as modern nation-states that has created the necessary conditions for rule-governed interaction. The second factor is the development of a normative structure that assures mutual survival and supports international cooperation. And the third is the rapid growth of the Asian economies and their growing integration into the global economy, which contribute to the consolidation of Asian states, strengthen their capacity to engage in rule-governed interaction, foster a shared normative framework, increase the incentives for cooperation and abiding by common rules, create a common interest in a stable environment, and increase the cost of using force to achieve political ends.

Proposition Five. The present security order is likely to persist for another decade or more. Change, when it happens, is likely to be gradual and occur both in the distribution of power and in the normative structure. The power and influence of Asian states, especially China, are likely to increase, but these countries are unlikely to be in a position to challenge the predominance of the United States in the foreseeable future. A hegemonic clash or a genuinely bipolar or multipolar Asia appears unlikely in the next decade. However, there may be spheres of influence in which certain countries like China, India, and Russia play key management roles with or without the support of the United States. For its part, the United States faces a number of challenges in converting its preponderant power into authority. Incremental change is also likely in the normative structure. Private economic activity and participation in the global capitalist economy have gained acceptance in Asia, although the negative consequences of globalization will have to be addressed. In the political arena, despite the resistance in certain countries like China, Vietnam, Pakistan, Burma, and North Korea, there is growing acceptance in Asia that sovereignty resides in the people and that public participation in a competitive political process with checks and balances is a must. Democracy, human rights, the protection of minority rights, and international involvement in these areas, which were hitherto solely under domestic jurisdiction, are likely to modify the regional normative structure.

Two other salient features of the larger project are noteworthy. One is the conceptualization of Asia as a single security region with several interconnected subregional clusters or complexes. The second is the role of analytical eclecticism in understanding and explaining Asian security behavior. Though it has been fashionable to use the term Asia Pacific and to delimit Asia to East Asia, it is becoming increasingly clear from conceptual and policy perspectives that Asia (not Asia Pacific) is the security region and that it should be conceptualized to include

Northeast, Southeast, South, and Central Asia. Our initial conceptualization of Asia as a single security region was based on security interdependence focused on China. Beijing's security concerns span all four subregions, and China is a primary concern of many countries in these subregions as well. Recent developments, including the nuclear tests in 1998, the rising concern with international terrorism, the growing salience of the Sino-Indian dimension, the burgeoning U.S.-India relations, the Chinese, Russian, and Indian interests in Central Asia, and the increasing American role in that subregion, are all testimony to the interconnectedness of the subregions and the analytical and policy value that can be had from an inclusive conceptualization of Asia. It is evident that no single general theory (neorealism, neoliberalism, constructivism) can fully explain the security concerns and behavior of Asian (and other) states. International social life in Asia is close to complex interdependence and is strongly influenced by historical memory, nation- and state-building processes, and concerns of political legitimacy. Accordingly, explanations of Asian security behavior must often draw on material and ideational factors at the unit and system levels. Insights from different theories and traditions are relevant. Dogmatic adherence to a single theory or tradition may misconstrue the issue or problem, and it may miss certain key dynamics. This is not the same as stating that everything matters or simply juxtaposing different insights. The significance of analytical eclecticism is in the interface of the different insights in framing and explaining an issue or problem. Analytical eclecticism is not a general theory or tradition but an approach to explanation that builds on the insights of other theories.[1] In the process it may create new insights.

The Asian security project as initially conceived comes to a close with the completion of the third phase. However, in light of the persisting salience of many issues investigated in the project and the new issues arising, the Asian security project is being continued at the East-West Center through two new publications. One is a monograph series entitled *Asian Security*. Initiated in 2002, this series is designed to promote scholarly analysis, understanding, and explanation of the domestic, transnational, and international dynamics of the security challenges in Asia, with the goal of reducing conflict and promoting a more robust security order in Asia. *Insight: Asia*, the second series, seeks to provide short, timely analyses of key issues in Asian security and defense, illuminating policy choices and their consequences. Also noteworthy are two related publications that resulted from

---

[1]See Peter J. Katzenstein, "The Case for Analytical Eclecticism," paper presented at the workshop on Asia Pacific Security, Cornell University, Ithaca, N.Y., Mar. 29–31, 2002; Rudra Sil, "The Questionable Status of Boundaries: The Need for Integration," in Rudra Sil and Eileen M. Doherty, eds., *Beyond Boundaries? Disciplines, Paradigms, and Theoretical Integration in International Studies*, Albany: State University of New York Press, 2000.

another East-West Center project (1998–2001) on the changing relationship of the soldier to the state in Asia. One publication, entitled *Coercion and Governance*, argues that the political role of the military in Asia, while still substantial in certain countries, from historical and comparative perspectives is on the decline. Such decline, the study argues, is a function of the reduced role of coercion in governance. The second publication, *Military Professionalism in Asia*, contends that military professionalism in Asia is shifting from "new" to "old" professionalism.

A project of this breadth and magnitude requires the participation and support of many people. I would like to express my deep appreciation to the contributors, senior scholars, discussants, readers, and reviewers of the manuscript in its various stages. Unlike my other projects, which were comparative in nature, the present study is a theory-informed study of regional security order. Contributors had to have both a good grasp of theory and sound empirical knowledge of the region. Scholars who combine such expertise are rare. The inclusive conceptualization of Asia made the task of contributors even more challenging, and many of them had to expand their geographical horizons to deal with issues, countries, and subregions they had not addressed before. Their tenacity and eventual knowledge of the region is remarkable, and their willingness to ground their inquiry in a common conceptual framework and to rework their contributions several times is admirable. I would like to express my sincere appreciation and admiration to them.

Barry Buzan, Sumit Ganguly, Takashi Inoguchi, Miles Kahler, Peter Katzenstein, and Yoshihide Soeya, as senior scholars, gave generously of their time and expertise. Participating in both project workshops, they read and reread several chapters. Venu Gopala Menon, Charles Morrison, S. D. Muni, John Ruggie, Akihiko Tanaka, Wang Jisi, Sastrohandojo Wiryono, and Wu Xinbo participated in one of the two workshops and commented on one or more chapters. Ezra Vogel, Marrack Goulding, Adam Roberts, Stephen Brooks, Daryl Press, Ernst Haas, Michael Brown, Ralph Cossa, Simon Dalby, David Dewitt, Khong Yuen Foong, and Tan See Seng reviewed certain chapters. Patrick Morgan read the complete manuscript. The insights and comments of these scholars added much to the project, and the contributors and I would like to express our deep appreciation to them.

On a personal level, my intellectual journey over the past decade has been a most fruitful one. It benefited enormously from interaction with established as well as younger scholars, policymakers, journalists, and graduate students in the United States, Asia, Australia, Europe, and Canada. It has been my privilege to work with a wide range of scholars in the comparative and international politics of Asia. Especially satisfying has been the opportunity to work with younger scholars. Recognizing the need to foster a new generation of scholars committed to high-quality scholarship on Asian comparative and international politics, beginning in 1993 I decided to invite mostly younger scholars to contribute chapters and papers, and to facilitate their interaction with leading scholars in the respective fields. Another goal was to bring together area specialists and theorists. In the present study a goal was to broaden the geographical perspective by encouraging contributors to work on subregions they had not worked on before. These efforts have been enriching and rewarding.

Thanks are due to the U.S.-Japan Foundation for providing funding support, the Center for Strategic and International Studies, Jakarta, for co-hosting the second workshop in Bali, Charles Morrison of the East-West Center for his support of this and other projects, Don Yoder for his copyediting, Yoshihisa Amae and Kevin Downey for their research assistance, Deborah Forbis, Paul Hazell, and Mrinalini Menon for proofreading, Carolyn Eguchi for so ably organizing the two workshops, and Lillian Shimoda for her secretarial support. Special thanks are due to Ann Takayesu, who word-processed and compiled the entire manuscript not only for this project but for all the projects I directed over the last decade. Muriel Bell, Caroline Casey, and John Feneron of Stanford University Press assisted greatly in shepherding the manuscript through the various stages at the press.

Finally, my deepest appreciation goes to my wife, Kalyani. Her unstinting support and forbearance through the different incarnations of my life have been crucial in all my undertakings—both professional and personal. Our move to Washington, D.C., in September 2001 to establish East-West Center Washington marks a new phase in my professional life and our family life. It is a joy to be geographically close to our children Radha, Shanthi, and Padma, as well as Adotei and especially Vikram and Arjun, whose intelligence and energy appear boundless. Finally I would like to dedicate this book to my late father, Alagappa Chettiar, and especially to my mother, Sigappi Achi, who has given so much to the family. I hope good health and peace of mind will mark her final years on this earth.

Muthiah Alagappa

Acronyms and Abbreviations

ABM	Antiballistic Missile
ADB	Asian Development Bank
AFTA	ASEAN Free Trade Area
AG	Australia Group
AMF	Asian Monetary Fund
AMM	ASEAN Ministerial Meeting
ANZUS	Australia New Zealand United States
APA	ASEAN People's Assembly
APEC	Asia-Pacific Economic Cooperation
APT	ASEAN Plus Three
ARC	Asian Relations Conference
ARF	ASEAN Regional Forum
ASEAN ISIS	ASEAN Institutes for Strategic and International Studies
ASEAN	Association of Southeast Asian Nations
ASEAN-PMC	ASEAN Post Ministerial Conference
ASEM	Asia Europe Meeting
BJP	Bharatiya Janata Party
BM	Ballistic Missile
BMD	Ballistic Missile Defense
BW	Biological Weapon
BWC	Biological Weapons Convention

BWC	Convention on Prohibition of the Development, Production, and Stockpiling of Bacteriological (Biological) and Toxin Weapons
CAEC	Council for Asia Europe Cooperation
CBMs	Confidence-Building Measures
CBW	Chemical and Biological Weapon
CCP	Chinese Communist Party
CD	Conference on Disarmament
CDCOM	Coordinating Committee for Multilateral Export Controls
CENTO	Central Treaty Organization
CFC	Combined Forces Command
CICA	Conference on Interaction and Confidence-Building Measures in Asia
CSBM	Confidence- and Security-Building Mechanisms
CSCAP	Council for Security Cooperation in the Asia Pacific
CSCE	Council for Security and Cooperation in Europe
CTBT	Comprehensive Test Ban Treaty
CWC	Convention on Prohibition of the Development, Production, Stockpiling, and Use of Chemical Weapons
DAC	Declaration of ASEAN Concord
DPP	Democratic Progressive Party
DPRK	Democratic People's Republic of Korea
EAEC	East Asian Economic Caucus
EALAF	East Asia–Latin America Forum
ECSC	European Coal and Steel Community
EEZ	Exclusive Economic Zone
EU	European Union
FDI	Foreign Direct Investment
FMCT	Fissile Material Cut-off Treaty
FPDA	Five Power Defense Arrangements
FUNCINPEC	United National Front for an Independent, Neutral, Peaceful and Cooperative Cambodia
G7	Group of 7 (heads of state and government of major industrial nations)

G8	Group of 8
GATT	General Agreement on Tariffs and Trade
GDP	Gross Domestic Product
GNP	Gross National Product
Golkar	*Golongan karya* [functional groups]
HPA	Hanoi Plan of Action
IAEA	International Atomic Energy Agency
ICBM	Intercontinental Ballistic Missile
ICJ	International Court of Justice
ICRC	International Committee of the Red Cross
IFI	International Financial Institution
IGO	Intergovernmental Organization
ILO	International Labor Organization
IMF	International Monetary Fund
INTERFET	International Force in East Timor
IPR	Institute of Pacific Research
IRBM	Intermediate Range Ballistic Missile
IWC	Inhumane Weapons Convention
JWG	Joint Working Group
KEDO	Korean Peninsula Energy Development Organization
KKN	[Bahasa Indonesia for] corruption, collusion, and nepotism
KMT	Kuomintang
KPRC	Kampuchean People's Revolutionary Council
kT	kiloton
LAC	Line of Actual Control
LWR	Light Water Reactor
MERCOSUR	Common Market of the Southern Cone
MILF	Moro Islamic Liberation Front
MIRV	Multiple Independently Targetable Reentry Vehicle
MRBM	Medium Range Ballistic Missile
MRV	Multiple-Reentry Vehicle
MT	megaton
MTCR	Missile Tech Control Regime

MW	Megawatt
NAFTA	North American Free Trade Agreement
NEA	Nuclear Energy Agency
NEACD	Northeast Asian Cooperation Dialogue
NEAD	Northeast Asia Dialogue
NFU	No-First-Use
NGO	Nongovernmental Organization
NMD	National Missile Defense
NNWS	Non-nuclear Weapons State
NPC	National People's Congress
NPCSD	North Pacific Cooperative Security Dialogue
NPT	Nuclear Non-Proliferation Treaty
NPWG	North Pacific Working Group
NSA	Negative Security Assurance
NSG	Nuclear Suppliers Group
NTW	Navy Theater Wide Missile Defense System
NWFZ	Nuclear Weapon–Free Zone
NWS	Nuclear Weapon State
NZ	New Zealand
OAS	Organization of American States
ODA	Official Development Assistance
OECD	Organization for Economic Co-operation and Development
OIC	Organization of the Islamic Conference
OPCW	Organization for the Prohibition of Chemical Weapons
OSCE	Organization for Security and Co-operation in Europe
OST	Outer Space Treaty
P-5	Permanent Members of the UN Security Council
PAFTAD	Pacific Trade and Development Conference
PBEC	Pacific Basin Economic Council
PD	Preventative Diplomacy
PECC	Pacific Economic Cooperation Council
PKI	Partai Komunis Indonesia (Communist Party of Indonesia)
PKO	Peacekeeping Operation

PLA	People's Liberation Army
PLAN	PLA Navy
PNE	Peaceful Nuclear Explosion
PNG	Papua New Guinea
PNTR	Permanent Normal Trading Relations
PPP	Purchasing Power Parity
PRC	People's Republic of China
PRK	People's Republic of Kampuchea
PTBT	Partial Test Ban Treaty
RCSS	Regional Centre for Strategic Studies
RMA	Revolution in Military Affairs
ROC	Republic of China
ROK	Republic of Korea
SAARC	South Asian Association for Regional Cooperation
SAM	Surface-to-Air Missile
SARA	*Suku, Agama, Ras, Antar-golongan* [ethnicity, religion, race, intergroup relations]
SBT	Seabed Treaty
SCO	Shanghai Cooperation Organization
SDF	Self Defense Forces
SEANWFZ	South East Asia Nuclear Weapon Free Zone Treaty
SEATO	Southeast Asia Treaty Organization
SLBM	Sea-Launch Ballistic Missile
SLOC	Sea lines of Communication
SLV	Space-Launch Vehicle
SMEs	Small- and Medium-Scale Enterprises
SRBM	Short Range Ballistic Missile
THAAD	Theater High-Altitude Area Defense
TMD	Theater Missile Defense
U.S. DOE	U.S. Department of Energy
U.S.	United States
UAV	Unmanned Aerial Vehicles
UN	United Nations

UNAMET	UN Assistance Mission in East Timor
UNCAR	UN Conventional Arms Register
UNCHR	UN Commission on Human Rights
UNCLOS	UN Convention on the Law of the Sea
UNDP	UN Development Programme
UNGOMAP	UN Good Offices Mission in Afghanistan and Pakistan
UNMOGIP	UN Military Observer Group in India and Pakistan
UNSF/UNTEA	UN Security Force in West New Guinea (Oct. 1962–Apr. 1963)
UNTAC	UN Transitional Authority in Cambodia
UNTAET	UN Transitional Administration in East Timor
UNTAG	UN Transition Assistance Group—Namibia
UNTCOK	UN Temporary Commission on Korea
USSR	Union of Soviet Socialist Republics
WAAS	Waasenaar Arrangement on Export Controls for Conventional Arms and Dual-Use Goods and Technologies
WMD	Weapons of Mass Destruction
WTO	World Trade Organization
ZAC	Zangger Committee
ZOPFAN	Zone of Peace, Freedom and Neutrality

Contributors

AMITAV ACHARYA is currently Professor of Strategic Studies, Nanyang Technological University, Singapore, on leave from York University, Toronto. He received a Ph.D. in international relations from Murdoch University. His areas of research interest include Asia Pacific regionalism, Southeast Asian affairs, regional institutions and world order, and Third World security.

MUTHIAH ALAGAPPA is Director, East-West Center Washington. He received a Ph.D. in international affairs from the Fletcher School of Law and Diplomacy at Tufts University. His research interests include international relations theory, international politics in the Asia Pacific region, and comparative politics of Asia.

DEWI FORTUNA ANWAR is Associate Director for Research at the Habibie Center and Deputy Chair for Social Science and Humanities at the Indonesian Institute of Sciences (LIPI), Jakarta. She received a Ph.D. in politics from Monash University, Melbourne, Australia. Her research interests include Indonesian foreign policy, Indonesian domestic politics, and ASEAN political and security issues.

JEAN-MARC F. BLANCHARD is a Lecturer with the International Relations Program and an Associate with the Center for East Asian Studies at the University of Pennsylvania. He received a Ph.D. in political science from the University of Pennsylvania. His research interests include territorial and maritime issues, subnational actors, multinational economic arrangements, Chinese foreign policy, Sino-Japanese relations, and the political economy of national security.

VICTOR D. CHA is Associate Professor of Government in the Edmund Walsh School of Foreign Service at Georgetown University. He received a Ph.D. in political science from Columbia University. His current research projects investigate strategic culture, military modernization, and the future of American alliances in Asia.

CHAESUNG CHUN is Assistant Professor of Political Science at Sookmyung Women's University. He received a Ph.D. in international relations from Northwestern University. He is currently working on two projects, one on emerging security order in Northeast Asia, and the other on formation of national identity in East Asia through the prism of diplomatic history.

ROSEMARY FOOT is currently Professor of International Relations and John Swire Senior Research Fellow in the International Relations of East Asia, St. Antony's College, University of Oxford. She received a Ph.D. in international relations from the London School of Economics and Political Science. Her main research areas include security relations in the Asia Pacific, U.S.-China relations, and human rights diplomacy.

JOHN GERSHMAN is a doctoral student in political science at the University of California at Berkeley and the Asia Pacific editor for *Foreign Policy in Focus* (www.fpif.org). He received an M.A. in political science from the University of California at Berkeley. His research interests include the politics of multilateral development banks and self-determination movements in Southeast Asia and China.

AVERY GOLDSTEIN is Professor of Political Science and Chair of the Political Science Graduate Program at the University of Pennsylvania and also Director of the Asia Program at the Foreign Policy Research Institute in Philadelphia. He received a Ph.D. from the University of California at Berkeley. He specializes in international relations, security studies, and Chinese politics.

BRIAN L. JOB is Professor of Political Science and Director of the Institute of International Relations at the University of British Columbia, Vancouver. He received a Ph.D. in political science from Indiana University. His teaching and research interests are in international relations, international security relations (especially in the Asia Pacific region), and Canadian foreign and defense policies.

DAVID KANG is Assistant Professor of Government at Dartmouth College. He received a Ph.D. in political science from the University of California at Berkeley. His areas of research interest include East Asian politics, international relations of Asia, and political economy.

MICHAEL MASTANDUNO is Professor of Government and Director of the Dickey Center for International Understanding at Dartmouth College. He received a Ph.D. in political science from Princeton University. His areas of research interest include international relations theory, international political economy, and U.S. foreign policy.

CHUNG-IN MOON is Dean of the Graduate School of International Studies and Professor of Political Science, Yonsei University. He received a Ph.D. in political science from the University of Maryland at College Park. He is currently working on a book-length manuscript on power, interests, and identity in East Asia.

ARUN R. SWAMY is a Fellow at the East-West Center, Honolulu. He received a Ph.D. in political science from the University of California at Berkeley. His research interests include the relationship between democratic competition and the politics of developing countries.

MING WAN is Associate Professor in the Department of Public and International Affairs, George Mason University. He received a Ph.D. in government from Harvard University. His research interests include international political economy, East Asian political economy, East Asian politics and foreign policy, Sino-Japanese relations, and human rights in international relations.

JIANWEI WANG is Associate Professor of Political Science at the University of Wisconsin–Stevens Point. He received a Ph.D. in political science from the University of Michigan. His research interests include Sino-American relations, Chinese foreign policy, and East Asia security affairs.

Asian Security Order

Introduction

Predictability and Stability Despite Challenges

MUTHIAH ALAGAPPA

Taiwan is a part of China, not a protectorate of the United States.
Foreign forces should not make irresponsible remarks, still less take
actions to intervene and interfere in our internal affairs.
—Qian Qichen, 1996

Peking should know and this [American armada] will remind them
that, while they are a great military power, the premier, the strongest
military power in the Western Pacific is the United States.
—William Perry, 1996

The Chinese people are ready to shed blood and sacrifice their lives to
defend the sovereignty and territorial integrity of their motherland.
—Zhu Rongji, 2000

The United States has an obligation to defend Taiwan and the Chinese
must understand that. The U.S. would do whatever it took to help
Taiwan defend itself.
—George W. Bush, 2001

Kashmir is in our blood. No Pakistani can sever his relationship and
link with Kashmir. . . . The armed forces of Pakistan are fully deployed
and ready to face any challenge to the last drop of their blood.
—General Pervez Musharaf, 2002

We don't play soldiers' games on the border. I have to be ready to defend my country. . . . Nuclear weapons are not meant for war fighting.
If India is the victim of a nuclear attack, the perpetrator of that attack
will be punished severely.
—General Sunderajan Padmanabhan, 2002

As indicated by the epigraphs to this Introduction, Asia still faces serious security
challenges. Termination of the Cold War ended some conflicts and localized others, but Asia is not free of dispute and conflict. In anticipating the post–Cold War

security situation, the numerous security challenges confronting Asia have led several analysts to project a dangerous region in which rivalry, power balancing, and conflict will be endemic, especially if the United States withdraws from the region. Aaron Friedburg (1993–94: 7) asserts that in the absence or weakness of the "soothing forces" present in Europe, Asia "in the long run seems more likely to be the cockpit of great power conflict." While "the half millennium during which Europe was the world's primary generator of war is coming to a close," he says, "for better or worse, Europe's past could be Asia's future." Similarly, Barry Buzan and Gerald Segal (1994) believe that "'back to the future' [instability and classical balance of power] is a distinct possibility in Asia." Writing five years later, Thomas J. Christensen (1999: 49; 2000: 196) asserts that whether "one looks at variables favored by realists or liberals, East Asia appears more dangerous [than Western Europe]." He bases this assessment on major shifts and skewed distribution of power among East Asian states, low levels of economic interdependence, anemic security institutions, historic antagonisms, and the widespread presence of territorial disputes. Christensen continues: "If security dilemma theory is applied to East Asia, the chances for spirals of tension in the area seem great, particularly in the absence of [the traditional deterrence and reassurance role of the] U.S. military presence." In a similar vein, Charles A. Kupchan (1998: 44–45) contends: "America's military presence continues to hold in abeyance the competitive jockeying that would otherwise emerge. . . . East Asia has a long way to go if it is to construct a consensual regional formation capable of overcoming its dangerous multipolarity."

The characterization of Asia as a dangerous place gained greater currency among analysts in the wake of the 1997 financial crisis. Dibb et al. (1999: 5) note: "In just two years, the strategic outlook for Asia has changed dramatically—the glittering visions of a forthcoming Asian century have given way to insecurity." Security planners, they say, should prepare for "alternative, less benign, security futures in Asia." Manning and Przystup (1999: 43, 65) think that the region's "economic crisis and protracted recession" are compounding the "risks of spiraling insecurity" and warn that "the dangers of renewed strategic competition and rivalry in East Asia should not be underestimated." Despite the powerful economic integrating forces and the compelling patterns of both intra-Asian and transpacific commerce, they say "there are reasons to be wary of Asia's future." Though less emphatic, Cheesman (1999: 333) asserts that "the direction of change overall is more backwards than forwards, favoring traditional rather than new or critical security approaches."

It is undeniable that Asia faces serious security challenges and that some rivalry and competition feature in the still-evolving strategic picture. It is not a foregone conclusion, however, that Asia is a dangerous place characterized by capricious interaction and instability. Contemporary Asia is a far more stable and predictable place than during the early postindependence era that coincided with the height of the Cold War. That period witnessed, among others, the Korean War (1950–53), the French (1946–54) and American (1964–75) wars in Indochina, the Indonesian confrontation against Malaysia and Singapore (1963–65), Soviet-, Chinese-, and Vietnamese-supported communist insurgencies in several Southeast Asian countries (approximately 1948–81), North Vietnam's conquest of South Vietnam (1975), Vietnam's invasion and occupation of Cambodia and Laos (1978–89), the three Indo-Pakistani wars (1947, 1965, 1971), the Sino-Indian border war (1962), and the Sino-Soviet military confrontation (1969) over their disputed boundary. For the better part of three decades, Asia was truly a region in turmoil.

Asia has now enjoyed relative peace for more than two decades. There has been no major war since the Vietnamese invasion of Cambodia in 1978 and the Chinese punitive attack on Vietnam in 1979. Despite periodic tensions, there has not been a war across the Taiwan Strait or in the Korean peninsula. The Kashmir conflict has witnessed much greater military activity and casualties, and the probability of overt military clash is higher than in the other two acute conflicts. However, even here, despite and in some ways because of the acquisition of nuclear capabilities by India and Pakistan, the actual use of force has been limited and confined largely to the areas adjacent to the line of control in Kashmir. Although it had the potential, the 1999 Kargil conflict did not escalate to full-scale war, let alone trigger a nuclear exchange. The crisis precipitated by the December 13, 2001, attack on the Indian parliament by militant Islamic groups based in Pakistan, continued Pakistani support for militant infiltration and terrorist activities in India, and the resulting massive Indian and Pakistani military mobilization along the line of control have generated much tension between the two countries, moving them to the brink of war. While a war cannot be ruled out, it is equally important to acknowledge the increasing constraints on the unlimited use of force. In the event that a war does occur, it is likely to be limited and confined to the conventional level. The many other territorial disputes on land and at sea in Asia have resulted only in occasional military clashes. The nuclear crisis in the Korean peninsula was defused through an agreed framework in 1994 to freeze North Korea's nuclear development. The Indian and Pakistani nuclear tests have not had the feared chain reaction, and despite the periodic crisis between these two states, the nuclear threshold has not been breached. The apprehensions among the Asian powers (rooted in old memories and contemporary concerns), as well as widespread concern with the predominant position of the United States and the rise of China, have contributed to the development of certain military capabilities (both conventional and nuclear) and redeployment of forces, but they have not resulted in unrestrained competition and arms racing. Asia has not become an arena of incessant rivalry. Nor has it become a hotbed of wars where the survival of states is deeply problematic and states are constantly jockeying for power.

With very few exceptions, Asian states do not fear for their survival. Even when survival is at stake as in the case of Taiwan, international interaction is not always governed by considerations of survival and threat of force. The international political, economic, and social interaction of most states occurs in the context of a stable and predictable environment and generally is in accord with internationally accepted principles and norms. International power and position are important, but these are long-range considerations, not immediate triggers of behavior. Contemporary Asia is much more stable than the Asia of the past and indeed more stable than several other regions of the world today (Eastern Europe, the Middle East, Africa). There is little likelihood that such stability will be undermined quickly.

Not only has Asia experienced relative peace and stability, but it also has prospered. Japan's continuing economic stagnation and the 1997 financial crisis that infected Thailand, South Korea, Indonesia, and Malaysia have tarred Asia's "miracle economy" image. Notwithstanding this sobering development, it is important to acknowledge that the spectacular growth enjoyed by the East and Southeast Asian countries for over twenty years has transformed their economies, which continue to grow at slower but respectable rates. China's economy continues to grow at a fast pace while India's has picked up. Indeed Asia has emerged as one of the three centers of the global economy. The regionalization and globalization of Asia's economies have also resulted in substantial flows of international trade, capital, and investment across the region and with the United States and Europe. Although they confront major challenges and there may be further setbacks, in the long term the strength of the Asian economies is likely to keep growing and become more integrated into the regional and global economies.

Predictability and stability in Asia are all the more remarkable in light of the persistence of acute conflicts involving the major powers, the spread of nuclear weapons and missile systems, the lingering suspicions and animosities, the internal political and economic challenges confronting several major Asian countries, and the region's weak institutionalization. Of the continuing security challenges, the long-standing identity and sovereignty conflicts involving Taiwan, Korea, and Kashmir are the most acute (Alagappa 1998b). With their roots respectively in the Chinese civil war, in liberation from Japanese colonial rule and the onset of the Cold War, and in the partitioning of British India, these three "intractable" identity cum sovereignty conflicts could escalate into open wars. The dispute across the Taiwan Strait is the most serious because of its potential to draw China, the

United States, and possibly Japan into a major war.[1] Beijing's determination to unify Taiwan with the PRC, by force if necessary; Washington's resolve to prevent the forceful absorption of Taiwan by the PRC, manifested in the deployment of two American carriers off the Taiwan Strait in 1996 in response to the Chinese missile firing and restated in a firm manner by President Bush in April 2001; Japan's refusal to affirm that the revised guidelines for Japan-U.S. defense cooperation exclude the Taiwan contingency—all are clear indications of the conflicting interests of the major powers in the dispute as well as its escalation potential.

Although the Korean conflict has become more localized since the termination of the Cold War, it could still flare up and involve the same powers and possibly Russia too. Major-power involvement in a war over Kashmir is less likely, but India and Pakistan now are nuclear-weapon states. Escalation to the nuclear level was an international concern during the 1999 Kargil conflict and the crisis precipitated in 2001–2 by cross-border terrorism. Of lesser intensity but not insignificant are the numerous long-standing bilateral and multilateral territorial disputes on land and at sea—some of which have led to full-fledged wars in the past. Several of these disputes involve China, India, Russia, Japan, and Vietnam.

Of great concern as well is the spread of weapons of mass destruction and their delivery systems. North Korea's development of nuclear capability led to a crisis in 1993–94 when the United States sought to impose sanctions and, according to some reports, contemplated a surgical strike to destroy suspected nuclear facilities in that country. Pyongyang's test of the Taepo-dong missile in August 1998 over Japan's main island created much consternation in Tokyo and Washington. The 1998 Indian and Pakistani nuclear tests and their subsequent self-declared nuclear status dealt a severe blow to the Nuclear Non-Proliferation Treaty (NPT) regime and heightened the specter of nuclear war in Asia—which is now home to five nuclear powers (the United States, Russia, China, India, and Pakistan) with widely differing capabilities and cross-cutting lines of amity and enmity. North Korea is on the borderline and may already have a rudimentary nuclear capability; several other states (Japan, Taiwan, South Korea) could develop such a capability relatively quickly if the strategic need arises and the political will is present. Most of these countries already have (or are in the process of developing) short-, medium-, and intercontinental-range missiles, some of which have the potential to carry nuclear warheads. The American proposal to build and deploy national and theater missile defense systems—ostensibly to counter nuclear threats from rogue nations—and the negative Russian and Chinese reactions to this proposal

---

[1]On the tension in the Taiwan Strait since the mid-1990s and its implications, see Roy (1994, 2000) and Ross (1999, 2000).

further complicate the strategic picture.[2] Indeed some observers claim that it could ignite a new arms race in the region. And there is also the danger of nuclear accidents and meltdowns in Russia and the new nuclear states.

Security concerns also arise from the changing distribution of power among the major players, including the perceived negative implications of American hegemony, the perception of a China threat (and, to a lesser degree, an India threat), and the fear of a remilitarized Japan as it becomes a "normal" power. With serious misgivings about America's strategic and political vision for the global and Asian order, as well as Washington's dominant influence in conflict management in Asia, China and to a lesser degree Russia oppose what they perceive as America's hegemonic designs. Beijing is particularly concerned that American dominance frustrates its key goal of unifying Taiwan with China and prevents it from assuming its "rightful" position in the region and the world. The eastward expansion of NATO, the reinvigoration of the U.S. alliance network in Asia, and the American proposal to develop and deploy national and theater missile defense systems are perceived by Beijing and Moscow as diminishing their strategic capabilities and influence. The United States, Japan, India, and Vietnam, for different reasons, are concerned with the rising power of China. Some South Asian states (especially Pakistan) and China are concerned about the growing power of India. China, South Korea, and North Korea are apprehensive about Japan becoming a "normal" country. Historic animosities that linger on—especially in Northeast Asia (between Japan, China, and the two Koreas; between Japan and Russia; between Vietnam and China) and in South Asia (China and India; India and Pakistan)—aggravate several of these disputes, conflicts, and apprehensions. Asian governments devote substantial revenue to developing military capabilities.

Several Asian states also confront internal conflicts that can bring about revolutionary political change, substantially alter their physical and ideational configuration, and, in some cases, even lead to the collapse of the state and internal turmoil. Certain minority groups challenge the present construction of nation-states in India, China, Pakistan, Sri Lanka, Burma, Indonesia, and the Philippines. In several countries the legitimacy of authoritarian political systems and incumbent governments has been severely challenged—leading to system changes in the Philippines (1986), South Korea (1987), Taiwan (1988), Bangladesh (1991), Thailand (1992), and Indonesia (1998). In several of these countries the democratic system is still in a transitional phase; in Indonesia it is under serious chal-

[2]In his State of the Union address on January 29, 2002, President George W. Bush identified Iraq, Iran, and North Korea as the "axis of evil" countries bent on exporting terrorism and developing weapons of mass destruction and missile systems.

lenge. Though China, Burma, and Pakistan have temporarily thwarted the forces for change, they are not free of political challenges. All three countries face the possibility of serious internal turmoil. Indonesia is the most vivid case right now, but this danger is also present in North Korea, Pakistan, and, to a lesser degree, China.

Internal conflicts threaten not only the survival of states but also the security of individuals and minority groups. Instead of providing security and welfare, several states are now perceived by segments of certain minority groups as oppressors (Indonesia in Aceh and West Papua, and previously in East Timor; China in Tibet and the northwestern provinces of Xinjiang; India in Kashmir and the northeastern states; Burma in nearly all minority regions, Sri Lanka in the North and Eastern Tamil regions, and the Philippines in southern Muslim provinces). Tens if not hundreds of millions of people still live in fear and abject poverty. Human security is a major concern throughout Asia. Although internal and international security may be distinguished for analytical purposes, in practice they are often fused. Several internal conflicts have transnational, subregional, and broad regional consequences.

Not only does Asia face serious security challenges. It is weakly institutionalized as well. Asia does not have the equivalent of a multilateral collective self-defense arrangement like NATO, a comprehensive multilateral institution for cooperative security like the OSCE, or unifying institutions like the European Union. And the institutions that do exist have very limited power and authority and meager resources to manage security in the region. Observers often cite weak institutionalization as a key reason why Asia is prone to conflict, power balancing, and instability. In some ways this observation confuses symptom with cause.

Viewed through the ahistorical realist lens, the contemporary security challenges could indeed suggest that Asia is a dangerous place. But a comprehensive historical view would suggest otherwise. Although Asia still faces serious internal and international challenges, there are fewer challenges than before and most of the region's disputes and conflicts (including the three acute ones) have stabilized. An outbreak of war cannot be completely ruled out, but the likelihood has diminished considerably, and there is greater predictability in the interaction of the parties to the conflicts in Asia. Over the years, Asian states have reached certain understandings and developed formal and informal forums and rules to manage their differences. For example, the border dispute between China and India, which precipitated a war in 1962, is now discussed at regular bilateral meetings. The dispute is still far from settlement, and China and India still have misgivings about each other. Nevertheless the two countries have instituted confidence- and security-building measures to prevent misunderstanding and the deterioration of bilateral relations. Although Asian countries are developing military capabilities, for the most part their purpose is defensive—to offset perceived technological weaknesses (the Kosovo effect on the Chinese military), ensure a certain minimum level of deterrence (the Indian and Pakistani nuclear tests), or achieve specific political objectives (unification of China). It is pertinent to note here that while force is still an important instrument of policy for Asian states, its function increasingly is in the defense and deterrent roles. Force is also becoming less salient in the interaction of certain states like the ASEAN Six (Malaysia, Indonesia, Singapore, Brunei, Thailand, and the Philippines), which have been characterized by several observers as constituting a nascent or quasi security community (Alagappa 1991; Acharya 2001). Military buildups, when they occur, are often undertaken with due regard to other national priorities, especially economic development. There is no significant arms race in the region, and arms acquisition is not always security driven (Ball 1996).

Over the last two to three decades, Asia has become a more stable and prosperous place in which, with a few exceptions, state survival is not problematic and international interaction, for the most part, is conducted in the context of internationally recognized principles, norms, and rules. Differences and disputes over territories are being settled through negotiations, or shelved in the interest of promoting better bilateral relations. The disputes between Russia-China and Vietnam-China have been settled, those between Indonesia-Malaysia and Malaysia-Singapore have been submitted to the International Court of Justice, and those between China-India, Russia-Japan, and Malaysia-Philippines are being discussed in bilateral forums. Though settlement may be far off, there is little prospect that these disputes will lead to military clashes. The actual use of force has been limited even in the case of the acute conflicts. Despite the fundamental issues in dispute, a minimum degree of understanding exists. This has prevented the eruption of full-fledged wars in the Taiwan Strait and the Korean peninsula. The rules of the game are less clear in the more volatile Kashmir dispute because at least one party (Pakistan) appears to believe that it can still benefit from supporting covert and terrorist activities in the pursuit of its political objectives. Nevertheless, it is pertinent to observe here that in January 2002, when India and Pakistan imposed sanctions on each other and undertook a massive mobilization of troops along their common border, the two countries exchanged information on their nuclear facilities in accordance with an agreement reached in 1989 "to keep each other informed of their nuclear installations and not to attack each other's nuclear facilities" (Dixit 1998: 198).

In the economic arena, international trade, investment, and production have flourished, particularly in Northeast and Southeast Asia. On the socioeconomic front, subjugated peoples are being freed, and there has been substantial increase in human dignity and welfare. And ten years into the post–Cold War era, Asia still has not become the dangerous place predicted by many analysts. Even the 1997 economic crisis has not undermined national and regional stability. The capacity of the Asian states to cope with the crisis, including the initiation of tough reforms, and the exploration of regional cooperation (ASEAN Plus Three) to avoid and deal with future crisis situations demonstrate the national and regional resilience of the Asian states. Admittedly regional institutions are few and weak when compared with those of Western Europe. However, when compared with those of Asia of the past and of other developing regions, they are relatively plentiful and play an important role in fostering intersubjective understanding and norm creation and in blunting the rough edges of the hegemonic and balance-of-power pathways in the management of security affairs in the region. The strategic picture and the management of security affairs in Asia, complex and still evolving, display characteristics of multiple paradigms. They are closer to complex interdependence than hard realism. Much of the interaction of the Asian states, including that in the security arena, is governed by formal and informal understandings and implicit or explicit rules of the game.

The existence of predictability and stability despite serious security challenges is the puzzle investigated in this study. Does security order exist in Asia? What is the nature of that order? What explains the existence of order in the context of serious security challenges? How is the Asian security order likely to develop or alter? What is the connection of the security order in Asia to that at the global level? These questions are investigated in this book. This investigation was conducted not only with due regard to the circumstances prevailing in Asia but also in the context of change in the larger international system.

International Systemic Change

A fundamental change in the organizing principle of the international system (anarchy/hierarchy) or in the distribution of power makes it necessary to construct a new international order. Such fundamental change, characterized as system and systemic change respectively, and building of a new order have usually followed victory in a major war (Gilpin 1981; Ikenberry 2001). Depicted variously as a grand transformation, sea change, and turning point, the termination of the Cold War, the victory of the West in that war, the subsequent collapse of the Soviet Union in 1991, and its succession by a weak Russia together constituted a fundamental change in the global distribution of power (not in the organizing principle) and the dynamics of international politics, creating the opportunity and necessity to construct a "new world order." The United States emerged as the sole superpower. Structural realist predictions that countervailing powers would emerge and that the world would soon become multipolar have not been borne out (Layne 1993; Mearsheimer 1990; Waltz 1993). Rather than compete, Germany and especially Japan have sought closer relations with the United States. For the first time in modern history the world is witness to a "unipolar moment" in which one state is far superior to all others in all indices of power and has the capacity to affect outcomes of major issues and conflicts in nearly every corner of the globe. This fundamental change in the material structure and in the dynamics of international politics (termination of the zero-sum competition between the two superpowers) effectively ended the bipolar order that had governed most aspects of international politics since 1946.

Another key development, the consequences of which are still unfolding, is the September 11, 2001, terrorist attack on the United States. In the immediate aftermath of the attack, American leaders and officials depicted that event as having fundamentally altered the world. They asserted that the global struggle against terrorism would be the defining feature of the new era. Nations were warned: "Either you are with us or you are with the terrorists" (Bush 2001). Reminiscent of the early days of the Cold War, neutrality is portrayed as immoral and out of place in the global struggle against terrorism. Comparing it to the war against communism, some observers portray the war against terrorism as a second cold war. This analogy has several limitations (McDougall 2001). Communism was the ideology of a rival global power (the Soviet Union). Moreover, the socialist system, at least in the early years, was attractive to a relatively large number of national elites, including some groups in the West. Radical Islam, mostly the ideology of extreme Islamic nonstate groups waging a terrorist war against the United States, the West, Israel, India, and certain incumbent governments in the Arab world among others, is not an attractive ideology even in the Islamic world. National and regime interests, rather than considerations of Islamic ideology and community, informed the reaction and behavior of the Islamic states in the wake of the September 11 attack. Elsewhere and certainly in the United States and the West, Islam, especially of the radical type, has no significant adherents.

In the unlikely event that the war against terrorism is transformed into a war between the West and the Islamic world, the struggle can become a war among states espousing different value systems. Such a war may take the line of a "clash of civilizations." For the present, the war against terrorism is neither a clash of civilizations nor a competition between two rival ideologies. Radical Islam is not propagated by any significant state. Even where it holds sway, as for example in Iran, the weaknesses of radical Islam are becoming apparent. Nevertheless, it still has the potential to undermine and overthrow corrupt and illiberal regimes in the Islamic world. The attack also highlights the vulnerability of open societies, including the most powerful state, to such attack in their homelands. Homeland security has become a key concern of the United States. However, international terrorism has not had any effect on the global distribution of power. The United States is still the only superpower. The threat of terrorism and the war against it have not resulted in significant realignment among the major powers. In terms of both power and ideas, the war against terrorism does not compare to the Cold War.

Nevertheless, because terrorism has become a high-priority concern for the United States (the world's most powerful state) and for a substantial segment of the international community, it has the potential to affect certain aspects of the international normative structure and foster international cooperation, possibly in the form of a grand coalition or a concert of major powers, to fight the threat of terrorism on a global scale. If carried to its logical conclusion, the war against terrorism can outlaw the possession of force by nonstate actors, reinforce the state and the interstate system, and increase state accountability by reinforcing the norm that the enjoyment of state rights in the international system is contingent on not harboring and supporting terrorist organizations, and that the principle of noninterference cannot shield governments engaged in such activities. It may also temper and make international support for minority rights and the principle of national self-determination more discriminating. This may have the unfortunate consequence of suppressing individual liberties and minority rights, as well as legitimate protest. Failure in the war against terrorism can undermine the interstate system, with the actions of terrorist and criminal organization and networks complicating international order.

The war on terrorism, if embraced by most major and medium powers, can also facilitate the development of a grand coalition or concert. The war has provided an opportunity for improvement in Russo-American and Sino-American relations. This improvement, however, has not been consequential in other substantive areas like the future of the ABM Treaty. Despite a cordial summit meeting with Russian President Vladimir Putin, U.S. President George W. Bush gave notice of the U.S. intent to withdraw from that Treaty. And Moscow is unhappy at the prospect that Washington will decommission but not destroy the surplus warheads under a plan to drastically reduce both their strategic nuclear arsenals. Similarly, while the war on terrorism has tempered the tension in U.S.-China relations, it has not significantly altered the mistrust between the two countries or the dynamics of the Taiwan conflict or of other issues of contention between them. Nevertheless, the war against terrorism appears to be moving U.S. policy toward China from the notion of "strategic competitor" to that of a "constructive, cooperative, but candid" relationship (Goldstein 2001). It is unclear whether the present improvement in bilateral relations is durable.

Notwithstanding these changes, the war has not affected the geopolitical interests of these and other powers in a significant manner. Failing the development of widespread international concern, especially among the major powers, international terrorism does not appear likely to become the defining feature or strategic overlay that affects conflict and cooperation in every corner of the globe. Terrorism is a major concern only in regions like the Middle East, Southwest Asia, Central Asia, and South Asia. In these regions the dynamics of international politics has been substantially altered. And the U.S. interest in and commitment to these subregions has increased considerably. Elsewhere terrorism is a lower priority. Further, the present international coalition against terrorism is a loose collection of states, some of which harbor terrorist movements under the guise of supporting liberation struggles. The United States with Britain (and with limited support from certain other NATO countries) have borne the brunt of the war in Afghanistan. The commitment of the other countries to the anti-terrorist cause is uneven and likely to be tested if the war expands to include targets like Iraq, Iran, and North Korea. Moreover, the war on terrorism is not a clear guide to the determination of friend and foe, and in the management of tensions among certain states, for example between India and Pakistan, both of which support the U.S. war against terrorism.

For the war on terrorism to significantly affect the international normative structure and foster international cooperation, the sights of the United States have to be raised beyond the immediate battle in Afghanistan. There has to be a comprehensive, long-term international plan to deal with terrorism throughout the globe that should be connected to other goals and concerns. However, thus far the impact of the war against terrorism on the dynamics of international politics has been limited and expedient. It has upgraded realpolitik, downgraded the goal of promoting human rights and democracy, and increased international tolerance of authoritarian regimes and of internal repression of minorities and dissent in countries like Russia and China. To assemble an international coalition and to gain access to staging facilities in geographically proximate countries like Pakistan and Uzbekistan, the United States has entered into expedient arrangements with authoritarian governments, which in an earlier context it had sought to isolate and castigate. The net effect of September 11 is that it adds a new security dimension. International terrorism is a key consideration that will inform the construction of order in the early decades of the twenty-first century. But by itself it does not constitute a sufficient basis for the construction of a new international order. The concern with terrorism has to be connected to other goals, values, and concerns of the United States and the other major countries to provide a more comprehensive basis for the construction of a new international order.

Constructing International Order

Emerging triumphant not only from the Cold War but also from the Gulf War (the first post–Cold War conflict in which Washington successfully orchestrated an international collective action to reverse the Iraqi invasion of Kuwait), the United States has been engaged in the last decade in constructing a new international order. The construction of the post–Cold War order has been more complex because unlike in 1918 and 1945, the United States is not writing on a blank slate. The widespread belief in the early post–Cold War years that unipolarity would be short-lived, that the economic and political center was shifting to the Pacific or Asia, and that the new order would have to accommodate the values and interests of the rising Asian powers further complicated the task of order building (Gilpin 1997). However, by the turn of the millennium it is clear that unipolarity is here to stay for some time and that although Asia's importance will rise, an Asian century is unlikely in the foreseeable future.

As envisioned by the senior Bush and later the Clinton administration, the new order, with the United States at the helm, would preserve American supremacy and embody the "universal" values of capitalism, democracy, and the protection of human rights. To prevent the rise of rival powers in critical regions (Europe and Northeast Asia), Washington reinvigorated relations with key allies like Germany and Japan and has attempted to circumscribe and accommodate the interests and aspirations of nonallied states like Russia and China. In the security arena, Washington adapted and strengthened American-led institutions like the NATO alliance and the U.S.-led bilateral alliances in Asia, especially that with Japan; supported the deepening and widening of the European Union (although it has been ambivalent about a European defense effort independent of NATO); opposed the creation and development of regional multilateral institutions in Asia that excluded the United States or were deemed hostile; has sought to reassure Russia (through such arrangements as the NATO-Russia Council, participation in the meetings of the heads of state of the major industrial democracies (G8), economic assistance, and the development of cordial personal relations with Russian presidents); and engaged the PRC in a strategic dialogue. While strengthening multilateral and bilateral institutions and engaging in dialogue with nonallied states, the United States has consciously preserved its flexibility to act unilaterally when it deems this necessary. Washington views the many institutions, including those under its leadership, as enabling and enhancing, not constraining, the exercise of the preponderant power it commands. Institutional restraints have not been irrelevant, but they have not prevented unilateral action on the part of Washington.

Although the United States has from time to time organized international co-alitions that go beyond a specific region as for example during the Gulf War and more recently in the war against the Al Qaeda terrorist network and the Taliban regime in Afghanistan, its security order–building effort has been largely regional. Regional order building in the security arena stands in sharp contrast to the economic arena, where Washington has engaged in both global and regional efforts. It did initially accord a key place for the United Nations (the only truly inclusive global institution) in the construction of the new world order. In his address to the 45th session of the UN General Assembly in 1990 President George H. W. Bush stated: "Not since 1945 have we seen the real possibility of using the United Nations as it was designed: as a center for international collective security. . . . We have a vision of a new partnership based on consultation, cooperation, and collective action, especially through international and regional organizations" (Bush 1990). However, the early promise of the UN and the U.S. attraction to that institution were short-lived. Member states, including and especially the United States, failed to endow the UN with the necessary authority and resources. The effort to reform the UN, especially the Security Council, stalled. With the failures in Somalia, Rwanda, etc., confidence in the UN plummeted. It continues to exist as an adjunct institution (rather than the primary institution for maintaining international peace and security as envisioned in its charter), serving useful normative, legitimating, and voice functions for the great and lesser powers. There is no other global organization dedicated to international peace and security. Recognizing this, and also the weakness of the UN, several observers have argued the case for a great power concert (Rosecrance 1992), for enlarging the out-of-area role of NATO (Lugar and Biden 2001), and for broadening the responsibility of the G8 to include security affairs (Allison et al. 2001). The prospects for realizing such suggestions, like that for reforming the UN Security Council, are not good.

Security order building at the regional level suits the United States. In addition to considerably enhancing its flexibility, regional order building enables it to isolate the different regional efforts and tailor its approach to a specific region based on its own strength and circumstances in that region. This divide-and-rule policy has been feasible and also necessary because of the absence of an overarching security dynamic that emanates from ideological or power competition among the major powers or agreement among them on the goals and norms that should inform the new world order. The clash of values (Western versus Asian values), clash of civilizations, and clash between dominant and ascending powers have not generated a dominant dynamic, although they may affect security calculations in varying degrees. The lack of an overarching dynamic complicates and regionalizes security order building. The post–Cold War security players (with the exception of the United States), their concerns, and the dynamics arising therefrom are in the main regional. Even the security concerns of key second-tier powers like China, Russia, and Germany are regional and local, and their capacities to affect outcomes in other regions are limited. Responsibility for international peace and security has increasingly shifted to regional arrangements and agencies, with the United States playing a key role, especially in Europe and Asia (Alagappa 1995b, 1998a: 3–5).

In Europe, the initial hope that the European Union (EU) and the Organization for Security and Cooperation in Europe (OSCE) would assume primary responsibility for security in that continent was dashed by their inability to respond effectively to the crisis in Bosnia-Herzegovina. Nevertheless, despite its shortcomings, the EU provides the crucial political and economic foundation for security in Europe. In addition to deepening and broadening that institution, there is renewed interest in beefing up the Western European Union, the fledgling security arm of the EU, so that Europe can assume greater responsibility for its own security. However, NATO has emerged as the key peace and security institution for Europe. In the process of adapting itself to the new circumstances, NATO is becoming less a threat-based alliance and more a modern concert of Europe to manage international change as well as ethnic conflicts in Central and Eastern Europe. Attention in Europe has been focused on the expansion of NATO to Central and Eastern Europe, the management of tensions with Russia created by such expansion, and the new roles and tasks of NATO such as those in Kosovo. In the wake of the September 2001 terrorist attack on the United States, which the NATO members judged to constitute an attack on NATO, that institution's out-of-region role is extending beyond Europe. Despite shortcomings, Europe has an extensive and well-developed network of institutions to manage security in that continent and in the adjacent areas.

By comparison, the post–Cold War security order in Asia is less developed, and the modest regional arrangements that do exist are not integrated into a coherent framework. In the absence of EU and NATO equivalents, the United States has projected its bilateral alliance system and forward military presence in East Asia as the crucial pillars of regional security (Baker 1991; DOD 1995; Nye 1995; Kelly 2001). Washington supports regional multilateral institutions like the ASEAN Regional Forum (ARF) but only as a supplement to its alliance system and forward military presence. Some Asian states, especially China and North Korea, view the U.S.-centered alliance system as anachronistic and detrimental to their security (Christensen 1999). Even those states that are not opposed to the American alliance system are uneasy about accepting it as the primary pillar of regional security. Asia is home to several subregional (ASEAN, SAARC, SCO) and regional (ARF, APEC) associations and forums. While not unimportant, commitment to these organizations is uneven, making for rather modest institutions in terms of authority, resources, scope, functions, and enforcement. APEC, for example, is limited to the economic arena, and because economic regionalism in Asia is market-induced, regional economic organizations do not have the political will or capacity to play an active role in shaping the regional and international order. The ARF has an explicit security focus, but because it is led by the Southeast Asian states, it cannot become the fulcrum of security management. The formation of ad hoc groups, sometimes of an informal nature, to address specific situations and issues like that in the Korean peninsula and in the South China Sea, as well as second-track meetings, have become relatively common in Asia. There is still a strong preference in the region for national self-help and bilateralism in managing security affairs. These various approaches to national security and regional security order—self-help, bilateralism, the American-centered alliance systems, and regional and subregional multilateral organizations—are only loosely connected, and their interface is at times productive of tension, especially among major powers. There is still much contention in Asia on the appropriate ideas, values, arrangements, and agencies for managing regional security affairs.

Purpose and Propositions

Despite such contention and the many security challenges, Asia has enjoyed relative peace, stability, and prosperity for over two decades. This suggests that although it may be less developed and certain features may be contested, security order is not absent in Asia. The nature of this security order, which of its features are contested and why, in which direction the present order is likely to evolve or radically alter, why, and how the regional security order in Asia is connected to the global level are questions explored in this study. Specifically it investigates the following:

1. The problem and nature of security order in Asia with particular reference to convergent and competing goals, principles and norms;

2. The roles of the different approaches and pathways to order and the effectiveness of the related institutions that have arisen spontaneously or have been consciously constructed;

3. The management of specific security challenges (disputes, conflicts, destabilizing developments), with particular attention devoted to how the different pathways and institutions complement or conflict with each other;

4. The role of global institutions in the management of Asian security affairs and their relationship to regional institutions; and,

5. The trajectory of security order in Asia.

The study advances five propositions. First, contrary to the widespread assertion that Asia is a dangerous place, the primary contention of this study is that international political interaction among Asian states is, for the most part, rule-governed and that Asia is becoming a more stable and predictable region. Except in very few cases, states recognize each other as sovereign states and, in large measure, manage their interaction in accordance with internationally accepted principles, norms, laws, and rules, some of which have also been codified in regional and subregional instruments. Rule violation like the Vietnamese invasion and occupation of Cambodia has been resisted by the regional and international communities and ultimately reversed. Although formal regional dispute settlement arrangements like the ASEAN High Council have not made much headway, peaceful adjustment of disputes is becoming more common through bilateral negotiations and the good offices of third parties.[3] Increasing use is also being made of international institutions like the ICJ. The three acute conflicts still defy settlement, and their consequences for regional order are significant. However the systemic consequences of such conflicts are more limited in the era of unipolarity. Moreover, a necessary minimum degree of understanding has been reached among the parties to the conflicts, except perhaps in the Kashmir conflict, that makes the outbreak of full-fledged war less likely. Although still a crucial instrument of national policy, the role of force in Asian international politics is in the midst of change, with its utility becoming more circumscribed. Asian states like China and India are beginning to adopt a more positive approach to international arms control regimes. Competition is still a strong feature of the Asian strategic landscape, but international coordination and collaboration in the pursuit of private and collective political, economic, and sociocultural goals are also on the rise. These developments have made for a stable and predictable environment in which international trade, investment, and production have flourished. The depth of order, however, varies by subregion. The Southeast Asian countries have developed a relatively deep understanding and a fairly robust framework for peaceful interaction, while order in South Asia is still shallow.

Our second proposition: The prevailing Asian security order is essentially of the instrumental type in a defensive-realist mode but with certain features of the normative-contractual order that is elaborated in Chapter 1.[4] Though relatively basic and expedient in several ways, a shared normative framework exists. Its primary purpose is coordination and limited collaboration to facilitate coexis-

[3]Although the High Council has not been realized, the 1999 ASEAN Informal Summit approved an ASEAN Troika comprising the past, the present, and the next chairman of the ASEAN Ministerial Meeting (AMM) as an ad hoc body to more effectively address issues affecting regional peace and security.

[4]On the difference between offensive and defensive realism, see Lynn-Jones (2001).

tence, protect and enhance national and regime security, enable the pursuit of national economic goals, increase national power and influence, and avoid undesirable outcomes, including misunderstanding and accidental war. There is virtually no present or future collective political identity at the subregional or regional levels that would modify or subsume national identity and interests. The nascent ASEAN identity frayed in the aftermath of the 1997 economic crisis.

Though basic, the normative framework is quite robust. There is growing acceptance in the region that the standard international rules associated with political independence, territorial integrity, noninterference in internal affairs (codified in the UN Charter and reproduced in certain regional and subregional instruments) should be observed, and that violations should not be tolerated. Although instrumental considerations may underlie the attachment to these principles, the norms associated with them are becoming important in their own right. They govern much of the international political interaction. However, there is still no durable understanding among the major powers to govern their interaction and to resolve serious conflicts like those across the Taiwan Strait, in the Korean peninsula, and over Kashmir to which they are parties. Although certain bilateral understandings have been reached (U.S.-Japan, China-Russia), others (U.S.-China, China-Japan, China-India, U.S.-Russia) have been difficult to forge.

Power and force still play a key role in the interaction of the major powers, although their function is primarily in the defense, deterrence, and reassurance roles, not in conquest, domination, and territorial annexation. There is growing acknowledgement in Asia that disputes should be settled without recourse to war and that the role of force in international politics should be constrained, but the translation of such acknowledgements into concrete measures has been slow and difficult. There are few bilateral arms control agreements and virtually no significant regional arms control accord. However, Asian countries are parties to several global arms control regimes, and there is evidence of change in the attitude of the major Asian powers like China and India toward global missile and nuclear arms control regimes. Nevertheless, the overall record is quite poor, and the same story goes for transparency and accountability in matters of defense.

Our third proposition is that the present security order in Asia is sustained by several pathways. Hegemony, balance of power (including alliance), concert, global and regional multilateral institutions, bilateralism, and self-help: all play key roles but with different functions. Hegemony and balance of power are crucial in managing major power relations and acute conflicts in Asia; concert is relevant in the management of specific issues like the nuclear crisis in the Korean peninsula; the UN has been the key player in peace building in Cambodia and East Timor; and regional institutions play an important role in the socialization of the policy elite and in the development and modification of intersubjective understandings. No single pathway is dominant in the management of Asian security affairs, although the preponderant power of the United States and the public goods it provides weigh heavily on the key security relationships and issues in the region. Nevertheless, the security order is not hegemonic in the Gramscian sense, and the United States cannot manage security in Asia by itself. It needs the cooperation of the major Asian powers. A durable basis for such cooperation has yet to be forged. As with the pathways, all three instruments of order—law, diplomacy, and force—are relevant in the management of Asian security affairs. Principles, norms, and rules govern much of the routine interaction. The adjustment of disputes, when they occur, is primarily through diplomacy backed by force. Only rarely is international law the basis for settlement of disputes. The role of war in the management of order has become limited. It is legitimate in very few cases. Force is still important, but in the deterrence and reassurance roles.

Our fourth proposition is that security and stability in Asia rest on several pillars, not just the U.S. security role. We concur that the United States plays a key role in preserving and enhancing security and stability in Asia. However, the American role is not the only factor. Equally important and in some ways more fundamental are three other factors: the continuing consolidation of Asian countries as modern nation-states which has created the necessary conditions (coordination and collaboration) for rule-governed interaction; the development of a normative structure that assures mutual survival and supports international cooperation; and the rapid economic growth and development of the Asian countries through participation in the global economy which contributes to the consolidation of Asian states, strengthens their capacity to engage in rule-governed interaction, fosters a shared normative framework, increases the incentive for cooperation and for abiding by common rules, creates a common interest in a stable environment, and increases the cost of using force to achieve political ends.

Through its alliance network, forward deployment, and the extended deterrence provided by its nuclear capability, the United States plays an important role in the management of the three serious security conflicts and in stabilizing relations among major powers. Washington deters war on the Korean peninsula and across the Taiwan Strait, and American leadership has been crucial in defusing tensions in these conflicts as well as the Indo-Pakistani conflict over Kashmir. Because of the mistrust among Japan, China, Russia, and the two Koreas, it is often argued that only the United States can play a stabilizing role in Northeast Asia—by binding Tokyo and preventing the development of a militarily powerful Japan, and by checking the growing power and influence of China that is feared by several Asian countries. By providing access to its markets, capital, technology and educational facilities, the United States also plays a crucial role in the economic development of the Asian countries. These claims have merit but, as the discussion in the final chapter of the book will show, they suffer certain weaknesses as well. The U.S. security role in Asia is not uncontroversial and also has downsides. Further, the United States cannot and does not want to be the manager of all security affairs in Asia. And, even if it so desires, the United States cannot create a stable environment if the conditions in the region are not ripe.

Of crucial importance in creating the necessary preconditions for order is the consolidation of Asian countries as modern states. Though some still face severe challenges, over the last several decades considerable progress has been made in many Asian countries in building nations, constructing viable political systems, and strengthening state capacity. Most Asian states are no longer quasi-sovereign states.[5] They now have the capacity to defend their internal and international sovereignty. The net effect has been to reduce their internal and international political and security vulnerabilities and prevent the overt and massive external interference in their domestic affairs that was common in the early postindependence era. State consolidation has helped reduce the number of internal and international conflicts and, with few exceptions, has created a common interest in mutual survival. Cooperation, especially in the economic arena, but also in the political and security arenas, has become an attractive option to further consolidate the nation-state and the incumbent regime and government. Asian states now have the confidence and capacity to enter into and honor international agreements.

Only cohesive nation-states with sufficient state capacity will be in a position to create the minimum conditions for coexistence and to prescribe and enforce the appropriate rules in the pursuit of the elementary or primary goals of order: maintenance of the external sovereignty of individual states, international peace, limitation of violence, keeping of promises, and stabilization of territorial possession (Bull 1995). External powers may assist in the development of appropriate conditions for the development of order, but in the final analysis such conditions have to be created by the states in the region themselves. Asian countries appear to have made considerable progress on this score. Further, increased interaction among Asian states (especially since the mid- to late-1980s) in bilateral meetings and subregional and regional forums has contributed to greater sensitivity to mutual concerns and has facilitated the development of shared understandings and frameworks to govern their interaction. This development has been most significant in Southeast Asia since the disengagement of the United States from

---

[5]On the concept of the quasi-state, see Jackson and Rosberg (1982).

that region. It is possible to argue that the prominent U.S. role may be inhibiting such development in Northeast Asia.

Although many Asian countries have made considerable progress in state building, several qualifications are in order. First, several countries still confront major internal challenges over national identity and political legitimacy (Alagappa 1995a). Instead of abating, in certain cases these challenges have become more acute. Second, while it strengthens the state in several respects, the consolidation process can be and has been productive of internal and international conflict as well. Third, consolidation is not a one-way street. There can be and have been reverses. These observations are especially pertinent since most Asian countries are relatively new as modern nation-states. State and nation building are long-term processes (they may take several decades or even centuries), and there is no certainty of "ultimate" consolidation. Nevertheless, when one takes a historical look over the last fifty years, it is evident that considerable advances have been achieved in many Asian countries.

State consolidation in Asia has been facilitated to a significant extent by the focus on economic development since about the mid-1960s. Combined with the growing acceptance by Asian states of the concept of comprehensive security, the emphasis on economic development has blurred the traditional hierarchy of issues, created common interest in cooperation for mutual gain, and facilitated the development of regional institutions and regional commercial and production networks (Katzenstein and Shiraishi 1996). Market-based economic development and participation in the global capitalist economy have created further convergence in national goals and strategies that bind the Asian states to specific international norms and rules. This is not to say that there are no differences and disagreement. But today there is much greater convergence than when states embraced rival capitalist and socialist models of development. Convergence has become even more marked in the wake of the 1997 financial crisis, which appears to have discredited the Asian developmental state model.

Concentration on economic development attaches a high premium to international stability and has tempered the pursuit of traditional security goals—even the PRC's vaunted goal of unification. As common interest in mutual survival and economic development through regional and global arrangements gained ground, an international society began to develop in Asia, the depth of which, as noted earlier, varies by subregion. This development is most evident in Southeast Asia but has recently emerged in East Asia as well. The consolidation of Asian states and their economic development through participation in the global economy have benefited from and contributed to the growing salience of international norms associated with sovereignty and private economic activity and have increased the restraint on the use of force. Internationally recognized principles (sovereignty, noninterference in internal affairs, nonuse of force in resolving political disputes) have enhanced the international survival even of small and weak Asian states. As noted earlier, the Vietnamese invasion of Cambodia and the Indonesian annexation of East Timor, for example, were resisted by the Asian and global communities and eventually reversed. With the exception of Taiwan (and possibly South and North Korea), no Asian state is in danger of disappearing from the political map in the foreseeable future. Territorial expansion and annexation are not the objectives of any Asian state.

Although force is still a key instrument of national policy in Asia, its role is increasingly limited to defense and deterrence. The actual use of force to achieve political ends has declined dramatically. Even in the cases of the acute conflicts, despite the rhetoric, force has been deployed essentially as a deterrent (preventing the independence of Taiwan, preventing the PRC's forceful absorption of Taiwan, deterring North and South Korea). The actual use of force has been limited as well and has in the main been confined to coercive diplomacy (Taiwan, Kashmir), and to noncritical arenas (at sea, for example, in the Korean case). There is a strong restraint on crossing the nuclear threshold, moreover, and growing acceptance in the region that political disputes must be resolved peacefully. Despite occasional military clashes, for example, no country seeks to resolve the numerous territorial disputes on land and at sea through war. Nor is force relevant to the achievement of national economic goals. Indeed the political, diplomatic, economic, and military cost of employing force has increased significantly in Asia. The point is not that force has become obsolescent but that instrumental and normative considerations are limiting the role of force in Asian international politics.

The fifth and final proposition is that the present security order is likely to persist at least for another decade or two and possibly longer. Change, when it occurs, is likely to be gradual. The relative power of China and, to a lesser degree, that of India are likely to increase, Japan may break out of its decade-long economic malaise, and Russia may become stronger. However, a dramatic shift in the distribution of power, as anticipated in the 1980s and early 1990s, appears rather unlikely in the foreseeable future. Considering that there are and will continue to be several major players in Asia, a genuine region-wide bipolar order for all of Asia also appears unlikely.[6] A hegemonic clash and genuine multipolarity appear unlikely as well in the next decade or two. However, there may be spheres

---

[6]Robert Ross (1999) contends that China is not a rising power but an established power, and that bipolarity already exists in East Asia. Several of the assumptions and claims he makes are questionable.

of influence in which pivotal countries like China, Russia, and India play a central management role in their respective subregions with, and at times without, the blessing and support of the United States. Although unipolarity, especially at the global level, is likely to persist, the translation of preponderant American power into authority hinges on overcoming a number of challenges: accommodation of the interests of the other major players; the adjustment of differences and disputes among the major Asian powers; gaining acceptance of American values of democracy, human rights, and private economic activity; and translating shared understandings into effective institutions, including the creation of inclusive multilateral security arrangements. If these challenges are met, then the security order in Asia could become hegemonic in a Gramscian sense. Diplomacy and law would be the primary instruments of order; force would recede into the background. Settlement of the three key conflicts could provide a boost to the major powers' understanding of each other and to the development of a framework for governing their interaction. However, these are challenges that cannot be resolved quickly. In fact, there is no certainty that they can or will be settled.

There is the further issue of American power and resolve. A severe downturn in the American economy would alter calculations and affect American security commitment and behavior in Asia. A United States in serious economic trouble not only will be less willing to provide public goods but, as illustrated in the 1980s and early 1990s, may also seek to leverage them for its own benefit. Hegemony could become coercive and tension-prone. Much also hinges on the continued economic growth and consolidation of the Asian countries. If the major Asian economies were to falter, as has been the case in Japan over the last decade, or if they were to suffer disruptive political change, as is possible in China, then American dominance would not only be sustained but may even be reinforced.

In terms of the values that will inform order, it appears that private economic activity and participation in the global economy have gained acceptance in Asia, although in time the pendulum may have to be adjusted to address the negative consequences of globalization. Despite resistance in certain countries like China, Vietnam, Burma, Pakistan, and North Korea, there is also growing acknowledgement in Asia that sovereignty resides in the people and not the state, and that public participation in a competitive political process and checks and balances are a must. Democracy has gained increasing acceptance in the last two decades. This trend is likely to continue, although the path will not be smooth. Regression in certain countries is a distinct possibility. Likewise, the imperatives to protect minorities and individual rights are gaining recognition although their translation into policy and enforcement measures is likely to be protracted and tension-prone because of the difficulties of accommodation and the limited capacities of certain states. Nevertheless, the scope of regional political and security order in Asia is likely to increasingly encompass the domestic domain and modify the norm of noninterference in internal affairs. We will return to these propositions in the final chapter.

Definitions

Investigation of security order must begin with a clear understanding of the meaning of order and the challenges confronting the management of security affairs in a region. The concept of order is the subject of Chapter 1. Drawing on that discussion, this study defines security order as rule-governed interaction among states in their pursuit of private and public security goals. Rule-governed interaction makes for predictability, stability, and nonviolent change in international interaction. States can coexist and collaborate in the pursuit of their individual and common goals, differences and disputes can be adjusted peacefully, and change can occur without recourse to war. Rule-governed interaction does not rule out force and war, although their roles and utility will be circumscribed. Rule-governed interaction requires that rules of the game (formal and informal) exist and are acknowledged by key actors who individually and collectively take on the responsibility for enforcing them, and that much of the regional interaction is conducted without violation of these rules and without recourse to the threat and use of force. Five key challenges inform and constrain the development of the Asian security order: disagreement among the major powers on an acceptable status quo, including contention over certain features of the normative structure; problems relating to political survival; the internal conflicts and human insecurity arising from the contested nature of certain nation-states; the persistence of acute international conflicts over identity that involve the major powers; and the spread of weapons of mass destruction and their delivery systems. These challenges are elaborated in Chapter 2. The rest of this section discusses and defines two critical concepts: security and Asia.

Security

A broad conception of security has become the norm throughout much of Asia (Alagappa 1988, 1998b). The concern is not only with international security but also with internal security, and the values to be protected go beyond the traditional concern with political independence and territorial integrity of the state to include political-ideational, economic, sociocultural, and other dimensions. Likewise threats to security are deemed to emanate from internal and international sources and to extend beyond the traditional military threats. In line with this norm, security is defined here to include internal and international concerns. But to keep the study manageable, the scope of security is limited to the concern of political survival broadly defined. In addition to autonomy and territorial integrity, political survival includes the ideational basis of nation and state, the system for political domination, the preservation of internal order and stability, and the promotion of an international context, both normative and material, that is conducive to the attainment of these values. These political values may be threatened not only by military force but also by competing political, economic, and sociocultural values. And such threats may emanate not only from other states but from within the state as well.

The primary concern in the study is with national security and the management of international security affairs. But because the nation, the state, and the system for political domination are problematic in several Asian countries, it is important to distinguish between security of the nation, the state, and the regime. Often threats to the regime and a certain segment of the community are depicted by incumbent rulers as threats to national security. Moreover, the security of individuals and groups is at times violated in the name of national security. Because the concern with regime security and, more broadly, internal security often affects the content of regional security order, this study also focuses on the issues of internal conflict and human security.

Asia

There are three issues to consider here. First: Which is the more appropriate region for this study—Asia or the Asia Pacific? Second: How is Asia to be defined? And third: Should the United States be conceptualized as part of the Asian region or as an outside power?

"Asia Pacific" is a label that subsumes Asia in discussions of security and economics. Intergovernmental and nongovernmental institutions frequently carry the Asia Pacific appellation as a prefix or suffix. The Asia-Pacific Economic Cooperation (APEC) forum and the Council for Security Cooperation in the Asia Pacific (CSCAP) are two such examples. But is Asia Pacific the appropriate region for security matters?

Regions do not exist "out there." They are constructed on the basis of two key criteria: one is interdependence; the other is internal and international recognition. On the basis of these two criteria, the Asia Pacific is the proper region for the study of economic matters because of the large transpacific flows in trade, investment, and services. The term is less apt in the security arena. Most of the security concerns considered in the so-called Asia Pacific security forums are in essence security concerns grounded in Asia and are of greatest concern to Asian states. Security in North America, South America, and the South Pacific are not matters of concern in these forums. Thus the footprint for the ASEAN Regional Forum has been limited to Northeast Asia and Southeast Asia. This, of course, does not imply that non-Asian states have no interest in or are not involved in Asian security. They are—and this is reflected in the membership of the ARF. The security concerns do not arise from the disputes relating to these states, however, and they do not affect them in the same way they affect the geographically proximate Asian states. With few exceptions, the security interdependence among Asian states is much denser than that with non-Asian states.

Thus Asia, like Europe, appears to be the more apt region for the study of security in the post–Cold War era. The North Atlantic was meaningful in the context of the Soviet-American confrontation centered on Europe during the Cold War. In the post–Cold War era, Europe and European security have become the more meaningful terms. This is the case with post–Cold War Asia as well. Should the security dynamics develop a much greater focus on transpacific tensions and dynamics, Asia Pacific may become the more apt region. For the present, then, Asia is the appropriate security region for our study.

The next issue is how to define Asia. Geographically Asia stretches from Afghanistan to the Russian Far East and comprises the subregions usually referred to as Northeast, Southeast, South, and Central Asia. The political conceptualization of Asia has not always followed the geographic definition, however. Although the two did coincide in the 1950s and 1960s in the context of decolonization, recently "Asia" has been deployed to denote Northeast and Southeast Asia. The term "Asia" in the Asia-Europe Meeting (ASEM), for example, excludes South Asia, as does the footprint of the ARF. Membership in the ASEAN Plus Three (APT) forum is also limited to the Northeast and Southeast Asian states.

On the basis of security interdependence, Asia in this study is defined to include Northeast, Southeast, South, and Central Asia. The hub of Asian security is China. Concern with China and Chinese interests in all four subregions of Asia provides the connecting thread for the Asian security region (Alagappa 1998a: 3–4). Indeed there is sufficient security interdependence between China, India, the United States, and Russia to warrant the inclusion of South and Central Asia in the Asian security region. Certainly their inclusion here would present a more holistic picture of regional security. Sino-Indian security interdependence, already quite strong though not quite symmetric, can only grow along with the impact of India on the broader region. Although there are no indigenous major powers in Central Asia, this region is of great concern to Russia and China—as demonstrated by the development of the Shanghai Cooperation Organization. In the wake of the September 11 attack, Southwest and Central Asia have become the concern of the United States as well. The sixteen-nation Conference on Interaction and Confidence Building Measures in Asia (which convened in June 2002 in Almaty, Kazakhstan), attended among others by the heads of government from Russia, China, and India, with the United States participating as an observer, is a testimony to our comprehensive conception of the Asian security region. The Asian security region comprises five subregional complexes and one macrocomplex. The subregional complexes include Northeast Asia (in many ways the core of the security region), South Asia, continental Southeast Asia, maritime Southeast Asia, and Central Asia.[7] These security complexes are linked by a macrocomplex arising from the dynamics of interaction among five key states: China, the United States, Japan, Russia, and India.

Next we turn to the question of the relationship of the United States to the Asian security region. Should the United States be conceptualized as an in-region power or as a global power with deep geopolitical interest in the region? In the former case, the footprint of the security region has to be the Asia Pacific, and transpacific dynamics is an integral part of the security region. In the second conceptualization, the footprint is Asia, the United States is an external but important actor acting on Asia, and transpacific dynamics is not the central focus. In some ways the issue is similar to the U.S.-Europe relationship. The United States is a North Atlantic power but not a European power. In the discussion of European security, the United States is an external actor with deep interests in Europe. The same should apply to Asia: the focus would be on Asian security, not Asia Pacific security. This is the approach taken in the ARF, although its footprint is limited to Northeast and Southeast Asia. In line with this reasoning and our earlier determination of Asia as the security region, the United States is treated here as a global power with deep geopolitical interests in Asian security. The United States is not an Asian power, but it is an integral part of the Asian security system—at least for now and in the foreseeable future.

About This Book

The book is structured in four parts. Part I sets forth the purpose of the study, advances the key propositions, explicates the key concepts, and sets the context for the book. Chapter 1 defines order and develops an analytical framework for the study of security order in Asia. The problem of security order in Asia with a particular focus on the competing conceptions and issues is the subject of Chapter 2. Chapter 3 investigates the practice of sovereignty in Asia and its implications for regional security order. Part II, comprising six chapters, investigates the significance of selected pathways (hegemony, balance of power, regional multilateral institutions, the UN system, nongovernmental institutions, and economic cooperation and interdependence) in the management of Asian security affairs. The six chapters in Part III investigate the management of the three acute con-

[7]Although Asia has been conceptualized to include Central Asia, only a few chapters in the book discuss this subregion. This is simply due to the lack of expertise on the part of the authors.

flicts in Asia (Taiwan, Korea, and Kashmir), the territorial disputes on land and at sea, the spread of nuclear weapons and their delivery systems, internal conflicts, and human security. Drawing on the findings of all these investigations, Part IV explores and further develops the propositions advanced in the Introduction and offers observations on the present and future security order in Asia.

Works Cited

Acharya, Amitav. 2001. *Constructing a Security Community in Asia: ASEAN and the Problem of Regional Order*. London: Routledge.

Alagappa, Muthiah. 1988. "Comprehensive Security: Interpretations in ASEAN Countries." In Robert A. Scalapino, Seizaburo Sato, Jusuf Wanandi, and Sung-joo Han, eds., *Asian Security Issues: Regional and Global*. University of California, Berkeley: Institute of East Asian Studies Research Papers and Policy Studies No. 26.

———. 1991. "Regional Arrangements and International Security in Southeast Asia." *Contemporary Southeast Asia* 12(4): 269–305.

———. 1995a. "Seeking a More Durable Basis for Authority." In Muthiah Alagappa, ed., *Political Legitimacy in Southeast Asia: The Quest for Moral Authority*. Stanford: Stanford University Press.

———. 1995b. "Regionalism and Conflict Management: A Framework for Analysis?" *Review of International Studies* 21(4): 359–87.

———. 1998a. "Introduction." In Muthiah Alagappa, ed., *Asian Security Practice: Material and Ideational Influences*. Stanford: Stanford University Press.

———. 1998b. "Asian Practice of Security: Key Features and Explanations." In Muthiah Alagappa, ed., *Asian Security Practice: Material and Ideational Influences*. Stanford: Stanford University Press.

Allison, Graham, Karl Kaiser, and Sergei Karaganov. 2001. "The World Needs a Global Alliance for Security," *International Herald Tribune* (Paris), Nov. 21.

Baker, James A., III. 1991. "America in Asia: Emerging Architecture for a Pacific Community." *Foreign Affairs* 70(5): 1–18.

Ball, Desmond. 1996. "Arms and Affluence: Military Acquisitions in the Asia-Pacific Region." In Michael E. Brown, Sean M. Lynn-Jones, and Steven E. Miller, eds., *East Asian Security*. Cambridge, Mass.: MIT Press.

Bull, Hedley. 1995. *The Anarchical Society: A Study of Order in World Politics*. New York: Columbia University Press.

Bush, George. 1990. "The U.N.: World Parliament of Peace." Address to UN General Assembly, New York, Oct. 1.

Bush, George W. 2001. Address to a Joint Session of the Congress and the American People. Sept. 20, http://www.whitehouse.gov/news/release/2001/09/20010920-8.html

Buzan, Barry, and Gerald Segal. 1994. "Rethinking East Asian Security." *Survival* 36(2): 3–21.

Cheesman, Graham. 1999. "Asian-Pacific Security Discourse in the Wake of the Asian Economic Crisis." *Pacific Review* 12(3): 333–56.

Christensen, Thomas J. 1999. "China, the U.S.-Japan Alliance, and the Security Dilemma in East Asia." *International Security* 23(4): 49–80.

————. 2000. "Spirals, Security, and Stability in East Asia." *International Security* 24(4): 195–200.

Dibb, Paul, David D. Hale, and Peter Prince. 1999. "Asia's Insecurity." *Survival* 41(3): 5–20.

Dixit, J. N. 1998. *Across Borders: Fifty Years of India's Foreign Policy*. New Delhi: Picus Books.

DOD (Department of Defense), United States Office of International Security Affairs. 1995. *United States Security Strategy for the East Asian-Pacific Region*. Washington, D.C.: DOD.

Friedburg, Aaron L. 1993–94. "Ripe for Rivalry: Prospects for Peace in a Multipolar Asia." *International Security* 18(3): 5–33.

Gilpin, Robert G. 1981. *War and Change in World Politics*. Cambridge: Cambridge University Press.

————. 1997. "APEC in a New International Order." In Donald C. Hellmann and Kenneth B. Pyle, eds., *From APEC to Xanadu: Creating a Viable Community in the Post–Cold War Pacific*. Armonk, N.Y.: M. E. Sharpe.

Goldstein, Avery, 2001. "September 11, the Shanghai Summit, and the Shift in U.S.-China Policy." Foreign Policy Research Institute Wire, Nov. 9.

Ikenberry, John G. 2001. *After Victory: Institutions, Strategic Restraint, and the Rebuilding of Order After Major Wars*. Princeton: Princeton University Press.

Jackson, Robert, and Carl G. Rosberg. 1982. "Why Africa's Weak States Persist: The Empirical and Juridical in Statehood." *World Politics* 35(1): 1–24.

Katzenstein, Peter J., and Takashi Shiraishi, eds. 1996. *Network Power: Japan and Asia*. Ithaca: Cornell University Press.

Kelly, James A., Assistant Secretary of State for East Asian and Pacific Affairs. 2001. *United States Policy in East Asia: Challenges and Priorities*. Testimony before the Subcommittee on East Asia and the Pacific, House Committee on International Relations, June 12.

Keohane, Robert O., and Joseph S. Nye. 1977. *Power and Interdependence: World Politics in Transition*. Boston: Little, Brown.

Kupchan, Charles A. 1998. "After Pax Americana: Benign Power, Regional Integration, and the Sources of a Stable Multipolarity." *International Security* 23(2): 40–79.

Layne, Christopher. 1993. "The Unipolar Illusion: Why New Great Powers Will Rise." *International Security* 17(4): 5–51.

Lugar, Richard, and Joseph R. Biden. 2001. "Out of Area: How to Revitalize NATO." *Wall Street Journal Europe*, Nov. 8.

Lynn-Jones, Sean M. 2001. "Does Offense-Defense Theory Have a Future?" McGill University Research Group on International Security Working Paper No. 12.

Manning, Robert A., and James J. Przystup. 1999. "Asia's Transition Diplomacy: Hedging Against Futureshock." *Survival* 41(3): 43–67.

McDougall, Walter A. 2001. "Cold War II." Editorial in *Orbis*, Winter.

Mearsheimer, John J. 1990. "Back to the Future: Instability in Europe After the Cold War." *International Security* 15(1): 5–56.

Nye, Joseph S., Jr. 1995. "East Asian Security: The Case for Deep Engagement." *Foreign Affairs* 74(4): 90–102.

Rosecrance, Richard. N. 1992. "A New Concert of Power." *Foreign Affairs* 71(2): 64–82.

Ross, Robert S. 1999. "The Geography of Peace: East Asia in the Twentieth Century." *International Security* 23(4): 81–118.

————. 2000. "The 1995–96 Taiwan Strait Confrontation: Coercion, Credibility, and the Use of Force." *International Security* 25(2): 87–123.

Roy, Denny. 1994. "Hegemon on the Horizon? China's Threat to East Asian Security." *International Security* 19(1): 149–68.

————. 2000. "Tensions in the Taiwan Strait." *Survival* 42(1): 76–96.

Waltz, Kenneth N. 1993. "The Emerging Structure of International Politics." *International Security* 18(2): 45–73.

Zagoria, Donald S. 1993. "The Changing U.S. Role in Asian Security in the 1990s." In Sheldon W. Simon, ed., *East Asian Security in the Post–Cold War Era*. Armonk, N.Y.: M. E. Sharpe.

PART I

Conceptual Perspective

CHAPTER ONE

The Study of International Order

An Analytical Framework

MUTHIAH ALAGAPPA

We have before us the opportunity to forge for ourselves and for future generations a new world order, a world where the rule of law, not the law of the jungle, governs the conduct of nations.
—George H. W. Bush, 1991

Order is a term used frequently by policymakers and academics. And the goals of order (such as survival, limitation of violence, peaceful change), as well as the different pathways (like hegemony, balance of power, international regimes) and instruments of order (war, international law, diplomacy), have long been subjects of study in the field of international relations. Yet the concept of order itself has not been central to the study of international politics. Few studies focus expressly on international order; still fewer employ an order-based analytical framework. International order figures prominently only in the English School, and even here the focus is the concept of international society and its role in understanding international politics. Order in the English School is invariably used as a synonym for international society.

Though dated and burdened by several shortcomings, Hedley Bull's (1995) discussion of order is still the most extensive and useful. Recent studies of international order like those of John Hall (1996) and T. V. Paul and John Hall (1999) draw their inspiration from Bull but do not really advance the concept's rigor and utility. Still others—David Lake and Patrick Morgan (1997), for example, and Etel Solingen (1998)—use the term "order" in their titles but do not define or develop the concept in any substantive way.

The reasons for the underdeveloped state of the concept are many: the elusive nature of the concept; the belief in some circles (especially among scholars of the realist persuasion) that order is virtually impossible in a situation of (international) anarchy; the contention in some quarters that because of its alleged conservative bias (emphasis on stability and the status quo) an order-informed study would overshadow concerns such as justice and change; and the fact that many aspects of international order have been studied under other labels (international society, security community, regime theory, and liberal institutionalism). The underdeveloped state of the concept may itself be a reason for scholars to engage in the study of order-related issues through other research programs of international politics.

This chapter defines and develops the concept of order to make it more pertinent to the study of international politics with particular reference to security affairs. Specifically it addresses four questions: What is international order? How does it vary across different conceptions of international social life? How is international order maintained? What explains not only the construction of order but changes in the type of order? We begin with the first question.

Order: Its Meanings and Elements

With more than fifty meanings, order is a slippery concept. Within the international relations community, order is used in multiple ways. Yet policymakers and academics use the term as though its meaning were self-evident. Very few define the concept or even clarify how it is used. And the few who do so invariably hark back to Bull's definition. Let me begin, then, with Bull's definition of order and critique its shortcomings before advancing my own definition and framework for the study of order.

Bull's Articulation of Order

Hedley Bull posits order as a "situation or state of affairs" that may or may not obtain, or be present to a greater or lesser degree, in international politics at a given time and place. He contends that order has always existed in international politics, and he seeks to substantiate this claim by demonstrating the presence of the idea and practice of international society in Europe during the Christian and European eras. For Bull, order exists when international society exists. He views international society as the means "through which such order as exists in world politics is now maintained" (1995: xv). By international society Bull means the existence of "a group of states, conscious of certain common interests and common values, [that] form a society in the sense that they conceive themselves to be bound by a common set of rules in their relations with one another, and share in the working of common institutions" (1966: 13). Based on this understanding he defines international order as "a pattern of activity that sustains the elementary or primary goals of the society of states, or international society" (1995: 8, 16).

Bull's definition of order comprises two elements: goals and methodical arrangement. He is not concerned with all patterns or arrangements, but only those that lead to certain results or promote certain goals. Bull cites six goals as elementary, primary, or universal: preservation of the state system and the society of states that is essential to protect the prevailing form of political organization; maintenance of the external sovereignty of individual states; international peace (which he says is subordinate to concerns of security); limitation of violence in international interaction; keeping of promises (honoring of agreements); and stabilization of possession by rules of property (mutual recognition of jurisdiction over specified territory and people). These goals—which he contends arise from the common desire to avoid insecurity, unrestricted violence, and instability of agreements—are termed primary because their attainment is critical to the pursuit of higher-order goals of the society of states.

The second element in Bull's definition is the pattern of international activity or disposition to sustain these goals. Although he is not entirely clear on this point, it is possible to infer from his discussion of how order is maintained in world politics that by the pattern of international activity he means the rules that govern interstate interaction and the institutions that give effect to the rules. Common interests are important in determining elementary goals, but they do not provide "precise guidance as to what behavior is consistent with these goals" (1995: 64). This is the function of rules, which may have the status of "international law, of moral rules, of custom or established practice, or they may be purely operational rules or rules of the game worked out without formal agreement or even without communication." Bull cites three complexes of rules that are relevant, he says, to the maintenance of international order. One is the fundamental or constitutional normative principles that define the political representation and organization of national community (such as the sovereign nation-state) and the organization of international social life and determine the membership of the resulting international system or society. The second complex comprises rules that set out the minimum conditions for coexistence and prescribe the behavior appropriate for honoring international agreements and respecting property rights. The final set of rules seeks to regulate cooperation in the pursuit of advanced goals in societies where consensus has been reached on a range of objectives beyond mere coexistence.

In the absence of a supranational government, members of international society themselves are responsible for making, communicating, interpreting, enforcing, adapting, and protecting the rules. Self-help is important in carrying out these functions. States also cooperate with one another in varying degrees through the "institutions of international society," by which Bull means "a set of habits and practices shaped toward realization of common goals." Bull cites five such institutions: the balance of power, international law, the diplomatic mechanism, the managerial system of the great powers, and war.

Shortcomings: Conflation of International Order and International Society

Bull's definition of order as a purposive arrangement to sustain the goals of international society is certainly useful and a good starting point. It also suffers from several weaknesses, however, two of which are relevant to this study.[1] A major shortcoming is the conflation of international order and international society. Although Bull defines order generically as "the sustenance of the elementary goals of social life," at the international level he narrows the definition to the sustenance of the goals of a particular form of international social life, namely, the international society. Is international order present only in international society? Bull acknowledges that order can exist in the Hobbesian and Kantian worlds as well. But he excludes order in the Hobbesian world from his definition on the ground that such an order would rest on contingent common interests among states that constitute the international system and their interaction would be governed by rules of expediency and prudence. Order in international society, by contrast, would rest on common interests, values, rules, and institutions. In addition to the rules of prudence and expediency, interaction in an international society would be governed by the imperatives of morality and law. Because of the shared consciousness of its members, order in international society would be substantive and more durable than in the Hobbesian world. Bull also excludes Kantian order from his definition because morality and law in this order do not have the purpose of fostering coexistence and cooperation among states. Their purpose is revolutionary in that they seek "to replace the system of states with a universal community of mankind" (1995: 25–26). The key marker of order for Bull is not substantive consensus on goals and values but the presence of procedural consensus among sovereign states, which he sees as more likely to prevail in a society of states.

Although the presence of procedural consensus and the salience of moral rules and law are useful in distinguishing one type of order from another, they cannot be the reason for defining order exclusively in terms of international society. The articulation of international order must recognize that order can exist in different worlds or forms of social life, although its degree and quality may vary. Building on the proposition that order varies across different conceptions of international

---

[1]On the weaknesses in Bull's conception of international society, see Hurrell (1998) and Buzan (1993).

social life, a spectrum of order may be constructed to facilitate inquiry into how and why the degree and quality of order have changed in a region or vary from region to region at a specific point in time. Concerned with distinguishing order from disorder, Bull's articulation does not permit investigation of change in the quality and type of order. Because of the limitation arising from the straitjacketing of order with society, scholars in the English School tradition have sought to articulate multiple conceptions of international society.

Andrew Hurrell (1998) develops a threefold concept of international society. At the bottom rung is a *minimalist* conception in which order is sustained by contingent common interests and rules that are vague and inchoate. Considerations of power play a major role in the maintenance of order. In fact this is a conception of order in the Hobbesian world that Bull tends to equate with a system. Next is a *pluralist* conception of society that builds on "coexistence and the ethic of difference." Order in this society is sustained not only by common interests and rules that are clearly defined by dialogue and consent but also by shared institutions that enforce the rules. This is Bull's international society. The final rung is the *solidarist* or Grotian conception in which the broad "consensus and solidarity" among states permits the pursuit of higher goals. The interests of the collective rather than those of the individual states inform behavior and interaction in this conception of society, which Hurrell says became more pronounced in Bull's later works.

This threefold conception of international society is similar in some respects to Buzan's (1993) attempt to differentiate societies (system of states, functional or contractual society, and civilizational society) and to develop markers to indicate the transition from a system of states to a society of states, as well as to distinguish a civilizational society from a functional or contractual society. Mutual recognition of sovereignty is his benchmark for the transition from a system to a functional society; a common cultural bond is the criterion that sets a civilizational society apart from a functional one. Buzan says such differentiation is necessary to develop a clear analytical framework to explain the development of international society in the contemporary era.

Another shortcoming in Bull's definition of order arises from his use of international order and international society as synonyms, his definition of the former in terms of the latter, and the distinction of system from international society. Bull and Buzan use the term "system" in two ways, one of which is misleading. In one usage the term is deployed to indicate its meaning and when it comes into existence. According to Bull (1995: 9), a system forms when "two or more states have sufficient contact between them, and have sufficient impact on one another's decision, to cause them to behave—at least in some measure—as part of a whole." This, in our view, is the proper meaning and use of the term. In the second usage, Bull equates system with disorder, whereas Buzan characterizes the international relations in a system without society as analogous to a "madhouse" (1993: 341). For both, the presence of order distinguishes a society from a system. Buzan characterizes society as system plus order or society. The characterization of a system as a condition of disorder is misleading. A system may be orderly or disorderly, and it may be characterized by different degrees and types of order. It should not be conflated with a certain condition of international affairs. Further, the use of order and society as synonyms is confusing. If system + order = society, as Bull implies, then order and society cannot be synonymous. If they were, then the equation could be written: system + society = society (or system + order = order)—which does not make much sense. The definition of order in terms of society can also give rise to the problem of circularity. To avoid the terminology confusion, the logical inconsistencies, and the circularity problem—and, more important, to acknowledge that order may exist in different forms of international social life—it is essential to separate the definition of international order from the notion of international society. Such delinking will also enable the construction of a spectrum of order and facilitate the inquiry into changes in the management of the international affairs of states.

Another shortcoming relates to Bull's articulation of rules and institutions, which together constitute his pattern of activity or arrangement for the maintenance of order. His rules and institutions conflate several distinct elements and levels. His rules, for example, include the organizing principle of the international system and its structure (anarchy/hierarchy), the principles and norms that constitute the metaregime of the system, and the rules and procedures that specify behavior and regulate the interaction of states. Bull also conflates rules and the purposes they may serve like coexistence and collaboration. Here the criticism is focused, not on the shorthand use of the term in a collective sense, but on the failure to disaggregate and specify the roles of the different components that make up the rules. And his use of the term "institution" conflates methods—the balance of power, for instance, and the managerial system of the great powers—with the instruments of order such as war, diplomacy, and international law. The method (termed "pathway to order" in this study) is the way of ordering and regulating relations among states. Each method, such as hegemony and balance of power, has its own distinct way of ordering international interaction. The instruments of order, by contrast, are simply tools that figure in each pathway, and their purpose, role, and importance will vary by pathway. They do not prescribe a specific system of order in their own right. Further, Bull's distinction between balance of power and great-power management is not really useful. Great-power management invariably includes the balance-of-power method. Moreover, great-power management can take several forms including hegemony, concert, and collective security. Because each of these pathways is distinct, each is better treated separately in its own right. To make them analytically useful, then, it is necessary to reconstruct Bull's rules and institutions.

Defining International Order

Building on Bull's articulation of order as purposive arrangement but not equating it with international society, international order in this study is defined as a formal or informal arrangement that sustains rule-governed interaction among sovereign states in their pursuit of individual and collective goals. Rule-governed interaction makes for a predictable and stable environment in which states can coexist and collaborate in the pursuit of their national, regional, and global goals, differences and disputes can be adjusted in a peaceful manner, and change can occur without resort to violence. Order does not proscribe force and war but circumscribes and regulates their utility and roles. Two points need be stressed here. First, order is not an either/or condition. Order is also not an ideal or ultimate condition but a matter of degree. Spanning a spectrum, it ranges from total disorder that is associated with the law of the jungle to the rule of law associated with a cohesive political community in which most people obey the law and in which force is managed on behalf of the community to deal with individual transgressors. Though it is an integral part of order in a community, and it is necessary to make for clear outcomes and ensure the security of expectations, force is not the primary means for regulating interaction in a community. Second, order does not emerge from nowhere. It is a construction by agents over a period of time. The construction of order is a historical process in which intersubjective understandings and their translations into institutions are reached through struggle, conflict, accommodation, and cooperation. Order is dynamic, although certain features may be pronounced in certain periods. The type of order will vary with the organizing principle of the international system, the distribution of power, and the dynamics of international politics that is influenced by ideational and material factors.

In contrast to Bull's definition, which emphasizes "sustaining the elementary goals of international society," the core of our definition is rule-governed interaction. Although goals are certainly important, especially in influencing the content of rules, the key criterion of order is whether interstate interactions conform to accepted rules, not whether they sustain particular goals—which is in any case difficult to ascertain. Thus order is used here as a shorthand term for rule-governed interaction.[2] It implies that interaction among states is not arbitrary but conducted in a systematic manner on the basis of certain rules. Such rules may

[2]Sustaining order, for example, means sustaining rule-governed interaction.

be explicit and codified as international principles, norms, and rules, including law, or they may be expedient and have to be inferred from practice. As Bull observes, rules often emerge from practice. They may simply be "rules of the game worked out without formal agreement or even communication," but in time they may acquire the status "of international law, of moral rules, of custom, or established practice" (1995: 64).

The term "rule" has been used thus far in a collective sense to refer to principles, norms, rules, procedures, and laws. As observed earlier, for analytical purposes it is important to separate the term into its component parts and define their roles. Here we can draw on the work that has been done on international regimes—with the recognition that an international regime deals with governance in a specific issue or issue-area and that an international regime is just one way of sustaining international order. Though there are many definitions, those advanced by Stephen Krasner (1983a: 2) are relatively common. "Principles are beliefs of fact, causation, and rectitude. Norms are standards of behavior defined in terms of rights and obligations." Together the principles and norms constitute the underlying normative belief and framework of the society in question. The principles and norms—at times referred to as the metaregime (Aggarwal 1985) or superstructure—are given effect through specific rules and procedures. International law is a form of specific rule that has legal standing, the violation of which carries a penalty. The elements of rules identified here should be distinguished from the type of rules (constitutive, regulatory) and the functions they perform (coexistence, coordination, and collaboration).

Having defined order as rule-governed interaction and having detailed the elements that comprise rules and their roles, we next discuss the conditions that should be satisfied to assert that international interaction is rule-governed. First, rules must exist and they should be clear to the relevant parties. Though obvious, this condition may not always be the case—especially when rules are in the process of formation or change. In these situations rival principles and norms may be competing to define the normative framework, or specific rules to implement agreed-upon principles and norms may not yet be in place. There may even be contradictions between a changing metaregime and the specific rules in place. Second, the rules in place must be acknowledged, especially by the key actors. States must accept the rules based on considerations of expediency, or on grounds of legitimacy—they believe in the rules and think they have an obligation to obey them. The basis for acknowledgment of rules may vary, but acceptance by those affected by the rules is crucial. This acceptance may be conveyed in several ways—by formal accession to treaties or declarations, for example, and by practice. Third, the behavior of most states should be consistent with the rules.

Deviations are acceptable so long as they are within tolerable limits, not too frequent, and not prolonged. Practice reinforces rules. Constant and egregious violations undermine rules and may invalidate them.

Finally, there must be a cost to violation. In addition to a common understanding of what constitutes rule violation and how it should be dealt with, those with managerial responsibility (individual states, a group of states, or an international organization) must have the commitment and means to punish violators. And other states should support such action. These four conditions may be satisfied to a greater or lesser degree, but their acceptance is crucial for the determination of rule-governed interaction among states. Moreover, most of the crucial interactions among the group of states must be governed by rules. Rule-governed behavior does not exclude the threat and use of organized force in the international relations of states—indeed force may be an integral part of order—but rule-governed interaction requires that the purpose of force and its actual deployment conform to accepted principles, norms, rules, and procedures.

Rules do not appear from thin air; nor do they function in a vacuum. Their content and power derive to a considerable extent from the history of the social interaction of a group of states, their contemporary social life, the degree of cohesion among them, and the goals and values they seek to promote both individually and collectively. The basic rules of coexistence and coordination among a group of states accumulate over time. The rules that govern substantive interaction, however, may vary considerably according to the condition of international social life and the individual and collective purposes of social interaction. These and the accompanying international order can vary widely with many gradations and combinations across time and space.

Typology of Order

For analytical purposes, we can identify three types of order: instrumental, normative-contractual, and solidarist. These three types of order differ in terms of purpose, identity of the participating states, their social cohesion and interests, and the function of rules. The *instrumental* order is oriented toward the realization of private ends. National identity, power, and interests are the dominant considerations. There is virtually no social cohesion among the interacting units. The primary function of rules is to facilitate coexistence and avoid undesirable outcomes. The *normative-contractual* order is oriented toward the realization of private and common goals through rules of collaboration. Although it is underpinned by a shared normative framework and states may identify with an incipient association, national identity is still predominant. Apart from certain sensitive areas, international interaction is governed largely by agreed upon norms

TABLE 1.1

Typology of International Order

Instrumental order	Normative-contractual order	Solidarist order
Nature of Order		
Basic, expedient, tentative; high politics not subject to rule of law; force relevant in wide range of issues	More complex and stable; international interaction mostly informed by norms, rules, and sense of obligation to others; few issues in which force plays central role	Stable and inherently peaceful relations among states based on trust and general obligation; all interaction subject to rule of law
Domain of Order		
Limited to international level. All authority vested in state. Domestic affairs are state's preserve, but domestic conflicts with international security implications are fair game for other states, especially the major powers. Collective international action may be taken on rare occasions to uphold minimum standards of humanity	Limited to international level, but states are not the only actors. Strong commitment to principles of equal sovereignty and noninterference in domestic affairs. Less external interference in domestic conflicts, but humanitarian intervention is more acceptable with consent of affected state	No strict separation between domestic and international affairs. International community may intervene in domestic affairs for just cause. Individual citizen has recourse to international institutions to obtain redress
Identity		
National identity, power, and interests dominant. Common interest limited to developing institutions to enable basic coexistence. No collective identity or interests	National interest still dominant but defined broadly and shaped by common interest and mutual gain. Common interests are more substantive. Collective identity and interests begin to emerge	National interest and goals shaped and often subsumed by collective identity and interests
Goals		
Primary goals: —Survival —Maximization of national power and influence —Preservation of the states system Secondary goals: —Stabilization of possessions —Honoring of agreements —Limitation of violence —Peace	National goals (no strict hierarchy): —Survival (if problematic) —Enhancement of national power —Economic growth and development Group goals: —Peace, prevention of war, stable environment —Limitation of violence —Group survival and well-being —Stable economic system	Community goals: —Permanent elimination of war —Promotion of solidarity and integration objectives —Promotion of economic welfare —Protection and enhancement of individual rights —Defense of community —Propagation of community values and expansion of community

TABLE 1.1, *cont.*

Instrumental order	Normative-contractual order	Solidarist order
	Type and Function of Rules	
Rules of the game, custom, treaty. No moral content. Primary functions: facilitate coexistence and avoid undesirable outcomes	More explicit, formal, thicker, and covering wider area. Some moral content. Primary functions: promote collaboration, facilitate coexistence, avoid undesirable outcomes	Rules grounded in common moral, normative, and legal framework. Rules promote collaboration, integration, and community development
	Pathways to Order	
Rooted in distribution of power. Principal pathways: —Hegemony —Balance of power —Concert of powers Secondary pathways: —International regimes (arms control, conflict avoidance, etc.)	Emphasizes principles, norms, and rules, including law and collective management of power. Principal pathways: —Economic cooperation —International regimes —Collective security —Gramscian hegemony —Concert of powers —Contrived balance of power	Trust and obligation are foundations of order. Principal pathways: —Consolidation and expansion of democratic community —Economic and political integration —International regimes
	Instruments of Order	
—War: legitimate instrument of policy; few limitations on reasons for war; rules for actual conduct of war —Diplomacy: key instrument for peaceful adjustment of differences and disputes —International law: important in facilitating routine interaction but not in resolving political differences	—War: limited reasons for engaging in war; force less salient in intragroup interaction —Diplomacy: key role in negotiating and implementing rules —International law: much greater emphasis on principles, norms, and rules, including law in regulation of international interaction	—War: not relevant in intragroup relations; still an instrument of policy in relations with noncommunity states —Diplomacy: key role in negotiating and implementing agreements —International law: all activities of community governed by rules

and rules. The *solidarist* order is based on trust among the interacting units, their obligation to the community, and the rule of law. Its purpose is to consolidate the community and promote its welfare. In this type of order, national identity and national interests are shaped and often subsumed by the community's common goals and collective identity. These three types of order are detailed in Table 1.1.

The three types of order correspond closely to the main traditions in the study of international politics. The instrumental order, for example, is essentially order in the realist tradition that posits international social life as a constant struggle for security and power. The normative-contractual order corresponds closely to the rational-liberal conception which posits that international politics is character-ized by both competition and cooperation and that common interests can make for cooperation among states. The solidarist order is rooted in the community conception of international social life (republican liberalism, for example, and socialism), which posits an inherently peaceful universal or regional community of nations can be constructed on the basis of certain identities and values.

The conceptions of international social life from which the three types of or-der are drawn are usually presented as fundamentally incompatible and mutually exclusive. However, in this study we take the view that anarchy permits self-help as well as other-help systems (Wendt 1992, 1995), that security orders are essen-tially social constructions, and that it is possible to shift from one type of order to another. Thus it is possible to view the different types of order as occupying dif-ferent positions on a continuum of order. The two hypothetical ends of such a spectrum are a "state of war" where no order exists and "world government" where order at the international level replicates that at the domestic level. In be-tween lie the three constructs presented here: instrumental, normative-contract-ual, and solidarist orders.

Before amplifying the three types of order, it is necessary to observe that our typology of order in some respects builds on the categories developed by Bull (system, international society, Grotian society), Buzan (system, functional soci-ety, civilization society), and Hurrell (minimalist, plural, and solidarist societies). Several qualifications are needed, however. First, as noted earlier, our analytical concept is order (rule-governed interaction), not international society. The con-cept of order focuses the study on our concern, which is the management of in-ternational security affairs. International society, on the other hand, was posited by Bull as evidence for the existence of international order and has been deployed in the ongoing effort of the English School to develop an alternative way of un-derstanding international politics. Second, the dichotomy posited by Bull be-tween system (disorder or primitive order) and society (order) is of limited util-ity in investigating change within and across different types of order. As Buzan observes (1993: 332): "If international society is a synonym for order, the idea potentially stretches across an enormous spectrum of possibilities from early, underdeveloped, and minimal at one end . . . to late, well developed, and maxi-mal on the other." Buzan does not develop categories to investigate the different types of order in the international system, however. He limits himself to specifying a boundary between a system and "system plus society" and investigating how a system becomes a society. Nevertheless his contribution is useful in explaining change and we will draw on it later. Hurrell's threefold conception of international society is similar to ours, but the basis for his typology and the contents of the categories differ.

Instrumental Order

The key elements (domain, identity, goals, nature and function of rules, relevant pathways, and the salience of the different instruments) of all three types of order are set out in Table 1.1. Rather than repeat them, the discussion that follows in this and the ensuing sections focuses on the relationship between the relevant conception of international social life and the various elements of order. In addition to highlighting the nature of each type of order, such discussion will be helpful in investigating change from one type of order to another.

As observed earlier, the instrumental order is rooted in the realist paradigm. Although this paradigm comprises several strands (political realism, structural realism, and mercantilism, among others), they share a common worldview that posits international politics as a constant struggle, with the threat of war ever present (Morgenthau 1978; Waltz 1979). Because survival is not guaranteed in a condition of anarchy, the highest goal of a state is its own security and maximization of power to increase its freedom of action. National interests (defined in terms of security and power) and self-help, including alliances (posited as the only reliable means to security), are the driving force of interstate interaction, which is characterized as competitive and zero-sum. Considerations of cheating and relative gain circumscribe cooperation severely (Grieco 1993). Interstate cooperation, when it exists, is interest-driven, shallow, and temporary. Viewed basically as reflecting the underlying calculations of national interest and the distribution of power, cooperative institutions and strategies are deemed not to have any independent effect (Strange 1983). In any case, they are not viewed as significant in matters of war and peace, which rank high on the agenda of the realist state (Mearsheimer 1995).

War is perceived as a legitimate instrument of state policy. There is no effort to limit the reasons why states may engage in war, although the conduct of war itself may be governed by rules. International law is observed by most states, but it may be overridden by political considerations. International law in the realist world derives from consent among states through practice, custom, and treaty. There is no place for natural law. States—not subnational communities, nongovernmental organizations, transnational groups, or human beings—are the subject of international law. Hence only states have rights and obligations under international law. Individuals have no rights under international law, and matters pertaining to domestic governance, including internal conflicts, remain matters of state jurisdiction. In exceptional cases, international intervention to uphold minimum standards of humanity may be required. Although domestic affairs are the preserve of the state, noninterference in the internal affairs of other states is much more a consequence of self-interest and mutual interest than of principle—at least initially. If national interest demands, states often intervene in the domestic affairs of other states. In time the principle of noninterference could become sanctified with an independent effect.

In this conception the state is vested with all power and authority and is the sole site of decision making on domestic and international affairs. National interest reigns supreme. There are no competing interests or centers of power. Although states sometimes share common interests, they relate primarily to coexistence and the avoidance of undesirable outcomes. There is no notion of collective identity or shared destiny. States may share common cultural values, but there is no bond of solidarity.

Except in the extreme case of the "state of war," order is not absent in the realist world. Such order is basic, expedient, and tentative, however. The goals of order derive almost exclusively from the state's interest in self-preservation. The primary goal is to ensure the state's survival and facilitate its basic interaction with like states. This goal may give rise, in turn, to other goals including the stabilization of possessions, honoring of agreements, and limitation of violence. The goal of survival may also result in a commitment to preserve the state's system, but this is not the same as a commitment to the survival of all states. Bull calls these goals elementary and universal. Rules in the realist world may simply have to be inferred from contemporary practice—or they may have the status of custom or treaty law—but they lack moral content and obligation. The primary function of rules is to enable coexistence—through recognition of property rights and spheres of influence, through honoring agreements that are primarily directed toward avoiding undesirable outcomes like accidental wars, arms races, and unintended escalation of conflict, and through the regulation of commerce. Order in the realist world includes much of Bull's postulation of international society, which Hurrell (1998) divides into minimalist and pluralist societies.

Normative-Contractual Order

The three main strands in the contemporary rational-liberal conception of international social life—commercial liberalism, liberal institutionalism, and neo-Grotianism—in which the normative-contractual order is rooted are in large measure a reaction to the realist conception (Doyle 1997). This worldview is not as well developed as the realist, and is less unified. It accepts several tenets of realism but contests others. International politics in this conception is not always an incessant, war-prone, zero-sum struggle for security and power. It might resemble complex interdependence in which survival need not be precarious and maximizing power is not the only, or even the primary, driving force of international politics. Further: States are not the only actors; there is no necessary hierarchy in issues; and the role of military force is more salient in relations with states outside the complex interdependence group than within it (Keohane and Nye 1977). In the rational-liberal conception, the concerns of security and power do not exhaust the goals of states. Economic well-being is a primary goal whose pursuit may take priority over security concerns in certain situations.

The pacifying effect of economic interaction is the thrust of *commercial liberalism*, which, with its roots in the works of Adam Smith and Joseph Schumpeter, makes three assertions.[3] First, international trade and economic interaction in the capitalist mode are becoming the dominant concern of contemporary international interaction. Second, the mutual benefits of international trade and other forms of economic interaction outweigh the gains of military competition and aggrandizement. And third, war is not in the interest of trading nations and industrial societies. The very high cost of modern war makes it an irrational instrument of policy. Recognition of the cost of war and the fruits of economic cooperation, it is claimed, has led to the rise of a new trading world in the post-1945 period, one that Rosencrance (1986: ix) posits as offering the "possibility of escaping [the] vicious cycle [of recurrent major conflicts] and finding new patterns of cooperation among states."

Although the military-security component continues to be important, commercial liberalism holds that the growing and inextricable connection between national economic well-being and the global economy will reduce the importance of political independence and territorial integrity. Although individual states may still try to improve their relative position, they will do so through commerce and in the context of interdependence. The international behavior of states will be influenced more by considerations of interdependence than by insecurity born of anarchy. Diplomacy and international law, informed by principles and norms, will be the primary instruments in the negotiation and implementation of trade and other international economic regimes. With economic interdependence offering an alternative, force will become less relevant as an instrument of order, although it is conceded that a "tolerable balance in world military politics is necessary to permit a trading system to function" (Rosencrance 1986: ix). In addition to the basic rules of coexistence and coordination, order in this conception entails rules of collaboration as well.

[3]On the commercial pacifism articulated by Smith and Schumpeter, see Doyle (1997).

This is also the case with *liberal institutionalism*, the second major strand in the rational-liberal conception, which posits international politics as a mixed- and variable-sum game. The anarchic structure makes for competitive as well as co-operative relations. Both competitive and cooperative patterns of interaction have been present throughout history (Bull 1981). Which pattern dominates is not predetermined by structure but is contingent on agency and circumstances. A higher degree of cooperation than allowed for in realism is possible in international politics. When it is possible to enhance mutual gain by coordination and collaboration, states will cooperate (Stein 1983, 1990). By reducing uncertainty and stabilizing expectations, in the long run cooperation helps redefine identity and interest and facilitates peaceful change (Keohane 1984, 1989, 1993). Growing political and economic interaction increases the demand for cooperation. The problem of cheating can be overcome, and relative gain is important only in certain situations (Keohane 1993). Because of the often severe consequences of failure, cooperation in the security domain is more difficult (Jervis 1983). But international cooperation, even when the security dilemma is full-blown, can enhance the quality of survival, lead to peaceful adjustment of certain disputes, limit the use, role, quality, and quantity of violence, prevent the accidental outbreak of wars, limit unintended horizontal and vertical escalation of conflict, and promote peace and stability.

The third strand—*neo-Grotianism*—straddles the rational-liberal and solidarity conceptions of social life. Although it is less influential in the contemporary era, it is relevant with respect to the emerging norm of "justified intervention" that legitimates international intervention in the domestic affairs of sovereign states. Opposing Thomas Hobbes's "state of war" world in which states have no binding international obligation, the neo-Grotian strand posits an order in which interaction is governed by the rule of law, and a society that enjoys solidarity to enforce international law (Bull 1966).[4] It does not proscribe war but limits the reasons for which states may engage in this activity. Wars must be confined to just causes (defense, recovery of property, infliction of punishment) determined by law and they can only be waged in the service of the international society as a whole. When individual states engage in war, they should see themselves as acting in the service of society and according to law. On the source of international law, the neo-Grotian view privileges natural law (which applies to humanity as a whole). It is viewed as superior to positive law (which is arrived at by explicit or tacit agreement among states), and also as a source of law in its own right when positive law is silent. Thus the domain of the neo-Grotian international order may be broader in substance than that agreed upon by states. It is also potentially

[4]The discussion in this section draws extensively on Bull (1966).

universal because it is not inherently limited by cultural or geographic boundaries. Ultimately the members of the neo-Grotian international society are individuals, not states. In fact the neo-Grotian society of states derives its legitimacy from the commitment to a universal community of humankind. The rights of individuals may therefore be the subject of transaction between states, and such rights provide the basis for international intervention in domestic affairs. States may intervene in the civil conflicts of other states if there is just cause. The line between domestic and international affairs becomes blurred in the normative-contractual order.

The neo-Grotian tradition was particularly influential after World War I, when there was a widespread revulsion against power politics. The League of Nations Covenant sought the "firm establishment of the understanding of international law as the actual rule of conduct among governments" (League of Nations 1919). Seeking to limit war as an instrument of national policy, the League permitted it only after the channels provided for in the Covenant were exhausted and then only after a three-month cooling period. War was to be waged primarily in the service of the international community against violators of the Covenant, which sought to guarantee the security of all member states. The 1928 Kellogg-Briand Pact went even further by seeking to abolish war as an instrument of national policy and to require all states to resolve their disputes by pacific means.

The rule of law and the proscription of war as an instrument of national policy were downgraded in the UN Charter, which simply calls on member states to refrain from the threat and use of force in their international relations and urges them to settle their disputes through peaceful means. But the neo-Grotian view that individuals can be subjects of international law and action—and that the international community has the right to intervene in domestic conflicts in support of a just cause (such as preventing gross violation of human rights)—is becoming more salient in the post–Cold War era. Although the UN is an intergovernmental organization, its Charter speaks on behalf of people and "reaffirm[s] faith in fundamental human rights [and] in the dignity and worth of the human person." It has adopted several treaties and declarations on the civil, political, and socioeconomic rights of individuals. Gross violation of such rights is viewed by a growing segment of the international community as legitimate justification for it to override the principles of sovereignty and noninterference in domestic affairs (Trachtenberg 1993; Lyons and Mastanduno 1995). In fact, some view international intervention in civil conflicts in order to protect democracy and human rights as strengthening rather than weakening sovereignty, which is claimed to reside in the people and not the state (Flynn and Farrell 1999). The emerging norm of justified intervention blurs the traditional domestic/international divide.

Although it does not ignore the competitive pursuit of power in international politics, the normative-contractual order emphasizes norms and law, limits the role of war, and seeks to attain peace and security by promoting economic inter-dependence and cooperation. International norms, law, and organization figure prominently in rule making, adjudication, and enforcement. Rules in the ra-tional-liberal world are informed by moral content and obligation. Self-help and force are not precluded, but they are circumscribed in the context of the com-mon interest of society. The rational-liberal notion of international social life posits greater solidarity, common interests, and opportunity for cooperation among states. It is presumed that states, as rational egoists, will seek to promote their security and well-being through international law (neo-Grotian), through international regimes (liberal institutionalism), and through economic coopera-tion (commercial liberalism). None of these conceptions, however, envisages the development of a supranational community.

Solidarist Order

The solidarist conception of order posits a world that is inherently peaceful. Survival of states is not problematic. National governments devote their efforts to promote the economic, political, and social rights and well-being of their people through international cooperation and integration. Rule of law grounded in a common moral, normative, and legal framework prevails in their interaction. Force and war cease to be instruments of statecraft and of international order among states. Diffuse rather than specific reciprocity is the norm in the interna-tional interaction of such a group of states. National goals and interests are not absent in the solidarist order, but they are shaped by considerations of collective identity and shared destiny. In this conception the primary goal of order is to eliminate the conditions of war permanently and create the conditions for a sta-ble peace that will endure despite changes in the distribution of military power (Doyle 1997). The peace envisaged is not a consequence of deterrence or the ab-sence of opportunity for war; it is the result of a solidarity or bond among states that makes force an irrational instrument of policy and hence irrelevant. Such a community may be rooted in a common political ideology, like socialism or de-mocracy, or in common cultural values and the adoption of a shared economic and political destiny, like that which began in Western Europe and is now ex-panding to include certain Central and Eastern European states.

With the victory of the West in the Cold War and the collapse of the socialist model, democracy and the capitalist free-market economy have emerged trium-phant. Positing these as universal values, the United States and the West advocate a world community of democratic states in the belief that relations among such states are inherently peaceful. Relations among democratic states are based on trust and a general obligation that goes beyond international law. Differences and disputes are resolved by peaceful means (diplomatic negotiation, mediation, arbitration, legal settlement). Realist strategies (including balance of power) are rejected and force is not an instrument of policy against other democratic states. Also rejected is the strict separation of domestic and international affairs. Indeed democracies have an obligation to intervene in the internal affairs of other countries in order to protect a democratic government or prevent the gross abuse of people's political and civil rights. As a subject of international law, the individual has recourse to redress that goes beyond the nation-state. Democracies are natural allies and have an obligation to defend other democracies and discriminate in their favor in the context of their relations with nondemocracies. These obligations, as well as the methods of sustaining order among democracies, do not apply to their interaction with nondemocracies.

A community may also be built through economic and political integration. This community is similar to the community of democratic states in several respects. In fact the only successful community of this type has been among Western European democracies with free-market economies. And democracy and a free-market economy are the two key conditions for the admission of new members to the European Union. But such a community differs from a community of democratic states in an important way. The latter is a plural community of sovereign nation-states. The European community, by contrast, is an integrated community that goes beyond the nation-state. In this conception the nation-state is viewed as the principal problem to be overcome because of its tendency to war and its inadequacy in meeting people's political, economic, and social aspirations in a postindustrial state. The remedy is to forge an integrated regional community that diminishes national sovereignty and creates new centers of authority and identity above and below the national level. This community has supranational institutions but is not a "world government."

Avoiding war and preserving peace, promoting economic welfare, coping with the challenges of modernity, increasing bloc strength—these are among the goals of the solidarist order. The first three goals are associated with the mitigation and elimination of the security dilemma. The last—increasing bloc strength—would merely transfer the security dilemma to a different level and possibly intensify it at that level. The end product of integration is a community in which the strategic and patterned interaction among a group of states is informed by a new cultural-institutional context, identity, and interests that are more collective than particularistic (Adler and Barnett 1998). In this community, as in the community of democratic states, there is "real assurance that members . . . will not fight each other physically, but will settle their differences in some other [peaceful] way"

(Deutsch 1957: 5) Karl Deutsch calls this a security community.[5] The types of order discussed above differ not only in the goals of order and the rules of interaction but also in the pathways to order.

Pathways and Instruments of Order

The term "arrangement" in our definition of order refers to the architecture for sustaining order (rule-governed interaction) among states. It specifies the methods for sustaining order, the formal and informal rules of the game, how they will be enforced, and the state or organization that has managerial responsibility. These may be negotiated or imposed by a group of sovereign states (or arise spontaneously among them). Although there are numerous arrangements for the management of international security affairs, basically they take three forms. One is the competitive approach, rooted in considerations of relative power, which I refer to as order through power and competition. The second is the cooperative approach, rooted in considerations of mutual interest with norms and rules playing the central role, which I refer to as order through cooperation. And the third approach, which seeks to redefine the state and transform the international normative structure in order to eliminate the security dilemma altogether, I refer to as order through transformation.

Before elaborating these three basic approaches, it is important to distinguish between arrangement, pathway, and instruments of order. An *arrangement*, as noted earlier, is the overall framework for sustaining international order. It comprises one or more pathways. A *pathway* is a distinct method for organizing and sustaining rule-governed interaction. Hegemony, for example, is a pathway that relies on domination by one great power. It is different from the balance-of-power and concert methods, which rely on different distributions of power, principles, and rules to sustain international order. All three, however, belong to the arrangement that emphasizes power and competition. Often, an order is labeled after the dominant pathway in an arrangement (hegemonic order, balance-of-power order, and so forth). *Instruments of order* are the means by which rules are negotiated and enforced. The three key instruments of order are diplomacy, international law, and war. With the possible exception of international law, these do not prescribe a specific method of sustaining order. They are an integral part of each pathway and their salience and role depend on the pathway. The following sections examine the principal pathways and their key features in each of the three basic approaches to order. Because each pathway is complex and has several

---

[5]Several analysts have noted that security communities can form among illiberal states as well if there is agreement on certain norms and goals like economic development, for example. See Acharya (2001).

strands, it is impossible to cover all the strands in detail here. The chapters in Part II of this book discuss the pathways in much greater depth.

Order Through Competition and Power

This approach is grounded in the realist conception of international politics. The distribution of power and its management hold the key and are the mainstay of the instrumental order. Domination by a single power (hegemony), power balancing (balance of power), and concerted action by great powers (concert of powers) are the three principal pathways to order in the realist tradition. Military force and war are key instruments of statecraft and for the maintenance of order. Diplomacy (communication, negotiation, and information) is the key instrument in the peaceful accommodation of differences, adjustment of disputes, and prevention of conflict. Moral and legal rules are deemed to suffer severe limitations in regulating the political interaction (struggle) among sovereign states. International law and institutions are considered epiphenomena with no effect beyond the distribution of power that undergirds them. The key features associated with the three principal pathways—hegemony, balance of power, and concert of powers—are elaborated here.

Pathway 1: Hegemony. Order in this pathway is maintained by a single state that has superior economic and military resources. This state dominates the system, defines the collective goals and rules, and enforces them (Gilpin 1981; Keohane 1984). Order constructed in this mode is based on the interests and values of the dominant power and its vision of the world. The problem of collective action is minimal because the dominant power takes the lead in providing security and economic public goods. Order in this pathway is contingent on the establishment of a clear and unchallenged hierarchy. Successful hegemony promotes stability, cooperation, and the development of international institutions under the leadership of the dominant power. The salience and role of war, diplomacy, and international law are contingent on the legitimacy of hegemony. In a coercive hegemony like that in the Soviet bloc during the Cold War, force figures prominently. In a benign and legitimate hegemony, the role of coercion is limited to dealing with challengers and rogue states. Diplomacy and international law are the primary instruments of order.

Successful hegemony hinges on two sets of factors. First: The hegemon must have superior resources and be willing to provide leadership. The translation of power into leadership depends not only on the political executive of the dominant state but also on its domestic politics and public support, particularly in open societies. Second: The leadership of the dominant state must be accepted by the lesser states. Provision of public goods may lead lesser states to accept the dominant state, form alliances with it, and follow its leadership. Instrumental considerations alone do not ensure durable legitimacy, however. Legitimacy entails not only coincidence of interest but also ideological unity and a common worldview. As Antonio Gramsci (Mouffe 1979) insists, leadership must rest on intellectual and moral foundations. And for this to occur, the goals and values of the system, while reflecting those of the dominant power, must also accommodate the other key states, giving it "the appearance of a universal natural order of things" (Cox with Sinclair 1996: 243). Successful hegemony derives not just from preponderant power but from social acceptance of ways of thinking and doing by the dominant strata in both the dominant and lesser states.

Change in this pathway arises from the decline of the hegemon and the rise of challengers. The preponderant power will seek to preserve its position and prevent the rise of new ones. But there are limits. Eventually disequilibrium between costs and benefits in maintaining the system and differential rates of growth lead to the decline of the hegemon and the emergence of a new one. Such decline is due not only to disequilibrium in power but also to internal conflict over ideas, values, and interests within the dominant state that may be transmitted to the wider world (Cox with Sinclair 1996: 246–47). Hegemonic succession in the prenuclear era is said to have been characterized by struggle and war (Gilpin 1981). Thus while stability characterizes periods when the hierarchy is unchallenged, periods of transition are characterized by conflict and instability. If the transition is between liberal democratic states, however, as between the United Kingdom and the United States in the early twentieth century, then succession, it is claimed, is peaceful (Doyle 1999). Instability arises only if the challenger is an undemocratic state. Further, it is argued that in the nuclear era, "although there are powerful forces that could lead to hegemonic war . . . the potentially destabilizing developments are balanced by the restraint imposed by the existence of nuclear weapons, the plurality of the system, and the mutual benefits of economic cooperation" (Gilpin 1981: 244).

Pathway 2: Balance of Power. Power balancing is the second method by which order is maintained in the realist tradition. For this method to operate, no state must possess preponderant power. Two or more great powers with similar capabilities must exist. In this situation states will balance against each other. Such balancing may be internal (building up one's own military capability) or external (augmenting one's capability through alignment and alliance). Subject to the distribution of power, the resulting order may be bipolar or multipolar. Unlike hegemony, which is consciously constructed, the balance of power may arise spontaneously or may be contrived by states through formal or informal agreement. Only minimal rules of coexistence are likely in a balance-of-power system that arises spontaneously. Formal rules are likely in a contrived system in order to maintain a certain distribution of power—like the classical balance of power in eighteenth century Europe.

Power balancing may serve several purposes: preservation of the independence of participating states; preservation of the multiple-state system; prevention of hegemony; prevention of war; and preservation of peace and stability (Guilick 1955; Wight 1995: 169; Sheehan 1996: 127; Bull 1995: 103–4; Morgenthau 1978: 180). There is no certainty, however, that the balance-of-power method can attain these goals. Indeed some goals may have to be compromised in order to preserve a certain distribution of power among the major powers, especially if the balance of power is contrived. The independence of smaller states, for example, may have to be compromised in order to preserve the distribution of power among the major powers. And the goal of preservation of peace may be compromised in the event that a war has to be fought to prevent domination by a single power. Further, it is difficult to judge when a balance prevails, whether it has been upset, and whether equilibrium has been restored. Nor is it clear which distribution of power (bipolarity, tripolarity, or multipolarity) is conducive to stability.[6] Realists concede that the stability provided by the balance-of-power method is tenuous (Morgenthau 1978: 209–30). Nevertheless, they view power balancing as the most viable method for the management of international security affairs in an anarchic system. They have little faith in collective and cooperative pathways.

War and diplomacy are the key instruments of order in this pathway. War may be necessary to ensure the security of individual states and maintain the power balance. Force is more prominent and less regulated in a spontaneous balance-of-power system. Diplomacy is the key instrument—in both the contrived and the spontaneous types—for peaceful accommodation of differences at the lowest level. International law is limited to codifying the rules of coexistence and the rules of war.

Pathway 3: Concert of Powers. Joint management of international affairs by great powers on the basis of certain common goals, values, and interests is the third realist method for sustaining international order. The concert method combines elements of power balancing and elements of collective security. Historically concerts emerged after major wars to contain and defeat an aspiring he-

[6]There is much discussion in the literature about which distribution of power is more stable. Waltz (1979) contends that having a small number of great powers ensures a more stable system because its principal members can better manage international affairs. Such powers, he claims, understand each other's behavior and are better at making and policing agreements (p. 136). Deutsch and Singer (1964), among others, contend that stability (prevention of war and state survival) is better served by a large number of major powers. A tripolar system is generally considered to be unstable.

gemon. Often the concert is a continuation of wartime collaboration to prevent recurrence of war and enforce the peace settlement (Jervis 1983; Sheehan 1996). The origins of this concept can be traced to the series of treaties and congresses that followed the Napoleonic wars. The idea of a concert of great powers underscored the Holy Alliance (1815–28) and the Concert of Europe (1828–58). It was a key component of the collective security system of the League of Nations (1919–39) and is even more pronounced in the UN system (initiated in 1945).

By preventing hegemony, a concert maintains the multiple-state system and the preferred distribution of power. It can prescribe and enforce political and economic ideologies, as well as the principles and norms for international interaction. A concert does not proscribe war but may limit its scope and function. International law can develop in a concert system but will be subservient to the interests of the great powers that form the core of the system. A concert-based order is essentially a two-tiered arrangement with one set of rules for the great powers and another for lesser powers. A concert maintains order among great powers through the accommodation of their competing interests. It maintains order at large by sitting in judgment of the affairs of the other states and taking enforcement action as necessary.

Inclusion of all great powers, their acceptance of the status quo (distribution of territory, wealth, power, status), absence of exclusive alliances within the ranks of the great powers, shared interests and values among them—such elements are crucial to the successful operation of the concert at the level of great powers. Unlike collective security, where national interests are subordinated to the collective interest, in a concert the national interests of great powers are not substantially restrained. When in conflict they frequently override the common good. Accommodation of the competing interests of great powers requires "brilliant diplomatists and statesmen who know how to make peace, how to preserve peace, and how to keep wars short and limited in scope" (Morgenthau 1978: 457). As in the hegemonic pathway, successful operation of a concert hinges on acceptance of the directorate and associated principles by lesser states—and their willingness to comply with joint decisions of the great powers even when these run counter to their interests. Without such acknowledgment and compliance, a concert-based order will lack legitimacy, and the directorate can enforce its decisions only through force.

Order Through Cooperation

The emphasis on cooperation to sustain rule-governed interstate interaction is rooted in the rational-liberal conceptions of international social life and is the mainstay of the normative-contractual order. While not ignoring the competitive pursuit of power in international politics, the principal pathways in this arrangement emphasize the collective management of power, the regulation of interstate interaction through international institutions, and the pursuit of security through economic interdependence and cooperation. International norms and law figure prominently in sustaining order. Rules in this arrangement have moral content and entail obligation. Self-help and force are circumscribed in the context of the common interest of the society. Collective security, international regimes, and economic cooperation are the three principal pathways in this arrangement.

Pathway 4: Collective Security. Collective security is designed to prevent aggression against any member state through a credible threat of effective collective measures that range from diplomatic and economic sanctions to the threat and use of overwhelming force (Claude 1971). Unlike an alliance, collective security is directed, not against a predetermined state or threat, but against any potential violator of agreed-upon principles and norms for international interaction, including the use of force. It is collective management by all states, not just the great powers as in the concert system. The idea of collective security emerged after World War I and was meant to replace the widely discredited balance-of-power method. Collective security was the centerpiece of the League of Nations system. In a much more diluted form, it is also a critical component of the UN system.

In collective security, the common interests and principles of society take priority over national power and interests. International organizations rather than individual states are assigned responsibility for maintaining international peace and security. Their general organs play a major role in rule making, whereas adjudication and enforcement are vested in the executive of the international organization, the core of which is constituted by the great powers. The charters of these organizations stipulate the principles that should govern relations among sovereign states, the mechanisms and rules for peaceful adjustment of disputes and for judging which actions constitute a threat to international peace and security, the enforcement actions that can be taken, and the obligation of member states to implement the decisions of the executive organ. International law and moral rules are prominent in this pathway. Self-help is circumscribed. National military capacity is pooled and managed on behalf of the international society. In rare cases, a joint military force may be created.

In addition to preserving the survival of individual states and the system of sovereign states, collective security promotes peace and stability by limiting the role of force in international interaction. Collective security has several key requirements: indivisibility of peace (threat against one is seen as threat against all); renunciation of force as an instrument of state policy except in prescribed situations; diffusion of power; monopolization of force by the community through the inclusion of all major powers in the arrangement; and firm commitment by

all states to abide by the joint decisions of the community. It entails clear definition of aggression as well as the rules and procedures for determining its occurrence and appropriate response. Collective security requires strong organizations
for surveillance, decision making, and enforcement. These are stringent requirements. Great powers and other states seldom accept such constraints on their
autonomy.

Pathway 5: International Regimes. Unlike the pathways discussed thus far,
which rely on the management of power, the international regime pathway relies
on principles, norms, and rules as the primary basis to sustain order. Even when
the regime involves military force—as in collective security—the management
and application of force are based on accepted principles and norms. This section
focuses on regimes that promote order through coordination, collaboration, and
assurance—regimes in which the threat and use of force are less central to compliance and enforcement. An international regime has been defined as "principles, norms, rules and decision-making procedures around which actor expectations converge in a given issue-area" (Krasner 1983a: 1). State interests (primarily
but not exclusively economic) and state power are the two fundamental variables
in the development of regimes. Incentives for coordination and collaboration
arise when unconstrained individual choice leads to Pareto-suboptimal and undesirable outcomes (Stein 1983, 1990). Incentives for cooperation may also stem
from two power orientations: one emphasizes the cosmopolitan instrumental
purpose of providing public good for the system as a whole (as in the collective
security pathway); the other stresses the interests of a certain state or group of
states in legitimating their domination of the international system and constructing it in their image to serve their ideational and material interests (as in the
hegemonic and concert pathways).

Although national interest and the distribution of power may figure prominently in their creation, regimes are not "temporary arrangements that change
with every shift in power and/or interest" (Krasner 1983a: 2). Regime-governed
behavior is influenced by principles, norms, and a sense of general obligation, not
just short-term calculation of national interest. It is this "infusion of behavior
with principles and norms that distinguishes regime-governed activity . . . from
more conventional activity" (Krasner 1983a: 3). In time, "lags" and "feedback"
provide regimes with a certain measure of autonomy. By affecting a state's power
and interest, regimes may have an independent impact on its behavior and outcomes (Krasner 1983b: 359–67). Diplomacy and international law are the primary
instruments in rule making, adjudication, and enforcement. Rule-enforcement
sanctions are often legal measures designed to limit or deny the benefits of the
regime to the violator. Sanctions may also involve broad political, diplomatic,
and military measures.

Much of the work on the role and effectiveness of international regimes has been done in the field of international political economy. Few studies have investigated security regimes. In large part this is due to the belief that regimes have little relevance for the zero-sum situation deemed to characterize security interaction. Jervis (1983) asserts that security regimes form only when states have accepted the status quo, when the cost of war is high, and when there is substantial danger of spillover into other areas. Despite the stringent conditions for their formation, security regimes are not absent in contemporary international politics. Such regimes can affect international security interactions in several ways. First, the constitutive function of regimes constrains state behavior. General constitutive principles such as sovereignty and sovereign equality of states, along with the accompanying norm of nonintervention in internal affairs, safeguard the survival of weak states by naturalizing the sovereign state and outlawing imperial, colonial, and other forms of domination. They also provide the basis for taking counteraction against behavior that contravenes such principles and norms. Second, arms control regimes like those that limit the proliferation of weapons of mass destruction help to avoid undesirable outcomes and promote stability. Third, the principles, norms, and mechanisms for peaceful adjustment of disputes present motivated parties with an alternative path to resolve differences and disputes. Finally, given the appropriate conditions, security regimes can facilitate the management of power for cosmopolitan purposes (as in the concert and collective security pathways).

Pathway 6: Economic Interdependence and Cooperation. Unlike the other pathways discussed thus far, the economic interdependence pathway does not seek to alter or regulate security interactions directly. It is an indirect approach that seeks to mitigate the negative consequences of anarchy and eventually eliminate the source of international conflict by transforming the orientation of the political unit and the nature of international politics.[7] The general hypothesis here is that interdependence decreases international conflict or at least reduces the incentives for international conflict (McMillan 1997). One key sub-hypothesis of this argument is that the increasing salience of capital as a factor of production and its increasing mobility decreases the incentive for conquest of territory (which reduces in salience as a source of wealth) and increases the interest in peace and good government (such conditions are necessary to attract investment) (Hirschman 1977). A second sub-thesis is that a high level of commercial interaction produces peace because it is in the self-enlightened interest of affected states. With a mutual interest in each other's wealth and prosperity, disruption would be costly for

[7]For a good review of the main arguments of the connection between interdependence and conflict, see McMillan (1997).

both. Such cost-benefit calculus would lead to a reduction in conflict (Rosen-crance 1986). A third key argument is the effect of international economic inter-action on domestic politics. International trade would bring about a redistribu-tion of domestic political power in favor of those who benefit from international commercial interaction (thus preferring peace) and against those who rely on conquest to increase their power and wealth. It would also increase the power of the individual and nonstate actors and make the political system more demo-cratic. Here the economic interdependence pathway merges with the republican liberalism pathway. At the international level, it connects with the liberal institu-tional and sociological liberal (communication and transaction) pathways.

The primary goals of the economic interdependence pathway are national and common prosperity, peace, and security. The principles, norms, rules, proce-dures, and organizations generated to facilitate smooth international economic interaction also foster rule-governed interaction among states and among non-state actors. The potential for economic interdependence to reduce conflict is contested by the realist school. One strand of the counterargument is that in-creased international interaction may in fact increase rather than decrease the opportunities for conflict as it can create inequality and dependency (the relative gain argument) and create uncertainty in the supply of strategic goods. A second strand is that there is no linkage between commercial activity, which is primarily conducted by individuals and corporations, and matters of war and peace, which are the preserve of the state. Even high levels of economic specialization and inte-gration have not prevented international and domestic wars. Considerations of politics and power trump commercial matters when the two come into conflict.

The economic cooperation and international regime pathways overlap with and may be seen as a prelude to an international order based on a transformed state identity or an integrated regional community.

Order Through Transformation

The competitive and cooperative approaches seek to sustain order by manag-ing the dynamics of international politics. Their emphasis is on reducing uncer-tainty, sustaining peaceful coexistence, promoting collaboration where possible, and diminishing the risks of war—essentially on the basis of the rational calcula-tion of self-interest and reciprocity by participating states. The transformation approach, by contrast, seeks to promote order by altering the cultural-institutional context in which nation-states operate, as well as the political iden-tity of states, and is the mainstay of the solidarist order. The primary goal of this arrangement is to eliminate the conditions for war and create the conditions for a stable peace through the adoption of a common political and economic ideology or the construction of a regional community on the basis of common cultural values and a shared economic and political destiny. The first method, which entails domestic transformation (change in the type of political regime), is an inside-out process. International integration, on the other hand, entails transformation leading to a supranational community and a form of order that is not strictly international. In both cases there is a substantive reconstitution of the normative framework.

Pathway 7: Democratic Peace. Peace through a common ideology and values is an old idea. It figured prominently in communist analysis of international order. With the collapse of the communist world and the worldwide resurgence of democracy, the democratic peace theory has captured the limelight. With its roots in Immanuel Kant's republican liberalism, the democratic peace pathway rests on two contentions—that regime type and not international material structure is the determining factor in matters of war and peace and that democracies do not go to war with each other, or at least that their relations are more peaceful than those among nondemocracies or between democracies and nondemocracies (Doyle 1989; Owen 1994; Russett 1993).[8] Belief in institutional constraints (the weight of public opinion and the checks and balances of the democratic system) and the transferability of democratic norms (compromise and peaceful resolution of conflicts) from the domestic to the international realm underlie this logic. The key concerns of this method are consolidating the community of democratic states, promoting its welfare, defending it against nondemocratic states, propagating democratic values, and enlarging the democratic community.

A key question for this pathway is how to enlarge the community of democracies. War and imposition constitute one method. The current democratic systems in Japan and Germany are the result of the victory of the Allied Forces in World War II and the postwar occupation of these two countries by democratic states.[9] In an earlier era, crusades to promote the Christian and Islamic faiths were common, and force figured prominently in the Soviet attempt to create a socialist community during the Cold War. Proponents of the expansion of democracy, however, shy away from advocating war as a key means to promote democracy, although it is seen as a crucial instrument in defending democracy against aggressive nondemocratic states. The contemporary emphasis has been on constructing a world order that privileges the norms associated with democracy and capitalism and on deploying the enormous power of the United States and the other Western democracies to encourage and pressure nondemocracies to become democratic. The strategies have been classed as follows by Michael

[8]For a good survey and review of the democratic peace literature, see Chan (1997).

[9]Only West Germany was occupied by democratic states. East Germany, occupied by the Soviet Union, was a socialist state until its unification with West Germany in 1989.

Doyle (1999): inspiration (demonstration by example); instigation (indirect support to create the necessary economic and political conditions); and, in select cases, intervention to defend democracy or prevent gross abuse of human rights. The enlargement through conditionality-based absorption that is occurring in Europe is another strategy. While peace may prevail among democratic states, expanding the community of democracy may create disorder within nondemocratic states and in the relations of democracies with nondemocratic states. The promotion of democracy by the West, for example, has been viewed by the Asian communist and authoritarian states as political imperialism and a threat to their national security.

Pathway 8: International Integration. In contrast to the preceding seven pathways that accept the sovereign state as the basic political unit, the integration pathway looks beyond the nation-state. Its fundamental assumption is that functional and economic imperatives and cooperation can triumph over political differences. Since the sovereign nation-state is viewed as the principal problem to be overcome, the different strands of this pathway—functionalism, transactionalism, and neofunctionalism—aim to diminish national sovereignty and create new centers of loyalty and authority in regional and international communities.

By creating a web of transnational and international communities, functional cooperation, it is claimed, will erode loyalty to the nation-state and its sovereignty—viewed as the root cause of international conflict (Mitrany 1966). The functional method avoids politics and situations of conflict. Instead it concentrates on such issues as health, labor, drug control, refugees, and telecommunications that are deemed to be more amenable to cooperation. David Mitrany, the principal postwar exponent of functionalism, thinks an international society is "more likely to grow through doing things together in workshop and marketplace than by signing pacts in chancelleries" (1966: 25). The approach is practical and nonpolitical. It is also utilitarian in that it is grounded in the belief that self-interest is the ultimate determinant of behavior (Harrison 1974).

Communication is the core of the transactionalist method. As communication enables "a group to think together, to see together, and to act together," it is claimed that it has the power to create shared identities and build the fabric of social and political communities (Deutsch 1957). The "we-feeling," trust, and mutual sympathy and loyalty created by transactions in trade, tourism, migration, cultural and educational exchanges, and the like, it is claimed, create a sense of community in which differences are resolved peacefully and war ceases to be an instrument of policy. Although the transactionalist approach to integration is almost dead, the idea of a security community still has currency and is analytically useful (Adler and Barnett 1998).

The expansive logic of economic integration and the belief that economic imperatives can alter political identity and security dynamics are two key features of the neofunctionalist strand of the integration pathway. The expansive logic holds that the benefits of the initial agreements raise expectations and alter values that call for higher levels of economic cooperation which will spill over into new sectors—leading to integration and the formation of an economic community (Haas 1964, 1968; Harrison 1974). Recognizing the benefits of this process and constructing new centers of authority to facilitate it, it is argued, will alter political identities and loyalties and create a more congenial relationship among the affected states.

The integration pathway draws heavily on the postwar experience of the North Atlantic countries and Western Europe. Thus far economic integration has been successful only in Western Europe. And even here the process, which is still ongoing, has been difficult and drawn out. Contrary to the expectations of the theories cited earlier, strong political commitment has been necessary to launch the ostensibly economic initiatives. Preventing war between France and Germany, constraining Germany, and strengthening the Western Alliance in the context of the Soviet threat were important considerations in launching the ECSC and EC initiatives. The aims of meeting the challenges of modernity, limiting American dominance, and enhancing economic welfare subsequently have driven Western European integration, which now has the goal of European union. Although economic considerations have been influential, political commitment has been the key force in moving the European integration process forward. Following the termination of the Cold War, there is an ongoing effort to broaden EU membership to include Central and Eastern European states. Among other requirements, prospective members must demonstrate a commitment to democracy and the free-market economy—features believed to be conducive to peace, security, and prosperity. Here the integration method overlaps and fuses with the democratic peace and commercial-liberal methods.

Although we have discussed the three approaches (competition, cooperation, and transformation) separately—and the conceptions of social life in which they are rooted are usually presented as fundamentally different and competing—no approach is sufficient by itself to sustain order. Features of the different approaches usually coexist and overlap. The post–Cold War security order in Europe, for example, is a combination of traditional alliances, great-power concerts, collective security, and transformation through economic and political community building. Quite possibly one type of arrangement may dominate. In this situation, the elements of the other arrangements are likely to be tempered by the dominant mode. Cooperation in a competitive arrangement, for example, tempers and regulates competition but does not eliminate it. Its primary purpose is to promote strategic stability and avoid undesirable outcomes like accidental war. This was the purpose of Soviet-American cooperation during the Cold War. Similarly a cooperative arrangement does not preclude competitive elements, although such elements would operate in a framework that values cooperation as being in the common interest of all participating states.

Further, pathways often incorporate features of other pathways. Moreover, two or more pathways may coexist with a division of labor between them by issue, level, and so forth. For example: the practice of collective security often incorporates the idea of concert; the balance-of-power and concert pathways often operate simultaneously; hegemony at the global level may be accompanied by power balancing at the regional and local levels or vice versa. These realist pathways frequently include arms control and other regimes as well as economic cooperation. In practice, therefore, elements of the different approaches and pathways coexist and combine in a variety of ways. Their salience, and how they combine, depend on the situation.

Investigating and Explaining Change

Conceptualizing Change

Change may be conceptualized in two ways: change within an order and change of the type of order itself. Change within an order occurs when the basic principles continue to apply but their manifestation alters. A change in the distribution of power from hegemony to bipolarity or multipolarity and vice versa, for example, constitutes a change within an order because the order is still power-based and instrumental. Similarly a change in the principles and norms of a regime or in the composition of its laws constitutes a change within the normative-contractual order. Such change does not alter the fact that order is sustained on the basis of a shared normative and legal framework.

Change in the type of order, by contrast, requires a fundamental shift in the key elements of order: goals, pathways, and the instruments of order. A shift from the instrumental to the normative-contractual order, for example, should be accompanied by a substantial change in goals, from private ends and mere coexistence to common goals that benefit the collective as a whole. Pathways that emphasize the collective management of power on behalf of the community and those that stress principles, norms, and rules like international regime and economic cooperation would become more central, while power-based pathways would recede to a supporting or indirect role. In line with this, force becomes less important as an instrument of order, while diplomacy and international law become more crucial. A shift from the instrumental to the normative-contractual order may also transpire through a change in a specific pathway like hegemony. Hegemony in the instrumental order rests heavily on considerations of power.

When such hegemony develops ideological unity and a common worldview in the Gramscian sense, and is viewed by the lesser states as the natural order of things, the ideational dimension becomes much more significant in sustaining order—signifying a shift in the type of order. Similarly a substantial increase in the normative content of the balance-of-power and concert pathways may also signify a shift in the type of order. Although labeled as realist, naturalization transforms the hegemonic, balance-of-power, and concert pathways. The normative-contractual features and instruments become the mainstay of order, while force recedes to the background.

A shift from a normative-contractual to a solidarist order should be accompanied by substantive changes in goals, pathways, and instruments, as indicated in Table 1.1. At base, it would involve a change in the organizing ideology of participating states, as well as their commitment to move toward a common economic and political destiny. The key in movement from one type of order to another is the relational identity among states and their social cohesion. Relational identity becomes positive and social cohesion becomes stronger as the type of order shifts from instrumental through normative-contractual to solidarist order. This is akin to moving from an indifferent pluralist group to an association of nations with a common purpose (gesellschaft), to a community of nations based on shared values and a common destiny (gemeinschaft). Change—both within an order and in the type of order—may not always be immediately discernible. Firm benchmarks may be established in the abstract, but it will not always be clear that they have been satisfied. Often the determination of change will be a judgment call that may be subject to different interpretations.

Explaining Change

Alteration in the distribution of power and in the interests of the major states—the grist of rational choice explanations—is useful in explaining change within an order and at times also change in the type of order.[10] Change in the distribution of power, for example, is crucial in explaining the transformation from the bipolar order of the Cold War era to the unipolar post–Cold War order. But change in the distribution of power does not determine the content of order. To a degree, the content of order can be explained by the material interests of the major powers that play the managerial role. However, such interests are embedded in and derive from a certain set of values that define the political and economic identities of these major powers. Such values also inform their worldviews and visions of order. The material interests of the United States, for example, de-

---

[10]Though John Hall's (1993) study is not cited directly, the writing of this section was influenced by it.

rive from a set of values—individual rights, democratic governance, free-market capitalist economy—that define the identity of that country. In conjunction with strategic concerns—like preserving primacy and preventing the domination of critical regions by rival powers—these values inform Washington's vision for the post–Cold War order. Ideas also play a crucial role in the legitimation of a specific order, which hinges on social acceptance. Power plays a key role in working out differences among competing interests, but an order that rests only on such accommodation is tension-prone and not durable. To be durable and to work smoothly, it must be based on ideological unity and a common worldview among the managers of order and between them and the lesser states. The dominant power(s) must develop and gain acceptance of a set of values and institutions.

The relationship among ideas, power, and interests is a complex one that does not admit of neat causal connections. Ideas become salient only when they are espoused by the powerful and then only at critical junctures. Also, to matter, ideas must be coherent and have the potential to be translated into distinct interests that can be deployed in the construction of order. It is not uncommon for ideas to be deployed as hooks in the service of the material interests of the dominant players (Krasner 1993). Over time, however, as the ideas become accepted and institutionalized, they develop a force in their own right and cannot be manipulated at will. Sovereignty, a defining principle of international relations, was initially deployed "as just hooks to justify actions that were motivated by considerations of wealth and power, not by visions of justice and truth" (Krasner 1993: 257). Over time, as it became embedded in institutional structures, sovereignty became a key principle that even the weak states could deploy to their advantage. However, ideas do change over time, and such change is not unrelated to the distribution of power, as witnessed by the ongoing struggles over the principle of noninterference in domestic affairs and the new norm of justified intervention.

Alteration in power and interests is often important in explaining change within an order which itself is rooted in a certain ideational framework. Ideas play a larger role in explaining the legitimation of an order and change in the type of order. But even here, it is not a competition of ideas that brings about change. Ideational change is often incremental and evolutionary. More radical change is wrought by alteration in the distribution of power and the interests of the dominant powers in a new environment. The content of the new order, however, is influenced to a considerable extent by the values of the new dominant power(s).

Having defined order and developed a framework to study it in the abstract, we now proceed to investigate the problem of security order and the competing conceptions that have been deployed in the construction of the post–Cold War order in Asia.

Works Cited

Acharya, Amitav. 2001. *Constructing a Security Community in Southeast Asia: ASEAN and the Problem of Regional Order*. London: Routledge.

Adler, Emanuel, and Michael Barnett. 1998. "Introduction and Theoretical Overview." In Emanuel Adler and Michael Barnett, eds., *Security Communities*. Cambridge: Cambridge University Press.

Aggarwal, Vinod. 1985. *Liberal Protectionism*. Berkeley: University of California Press.

Bull, Hedley. 1966. "The Grotian Conception of International Society." Compiled in Kai Alderson and Andrew Hurrell (2000), eds., *Hedley Bull on International Society*. London: Macmillan.

———. 1981. "Hobbes and International Anarchy." Compiled in Kai Alderson and Andrew Hurrell (2000), eds., *Hedley Bull on International Society*. London: Macmillan.

———. 1995. *The Anarchical Society: A Study of Order in World Politics*. New York: Columbia University Press.

Buzan, Barry. 1993. "From International System to International Society: Structural Realism and Regime Theory Meet the English School." *International Organization* 47(3) (Summer): 327–52.

Chan, Steven. 1997. "In Search of Democratic Peace: Problems and Promise." *Mershon International Studies Review* 41(1): 59–91.

Claude, Inis. 1971. *Swords into Ploughshares: The Problems and Progress of International Organizations*. New York: Random House.

Cox, Robert W., with Timothy J. Sinclair. 1996. *Approaches to World Order*. New York: Cambridge University Press.

Deutsch, Karl. 1957. *Political Community and the North Atlantic Area*. Westport, Conn.: Greenwood.

———, and J. David Singer. 1964. "Multipolar Power Systems and International Stability." *World Politics* 16(3): 390–406.

Doyle, Michael W. 1989. "Kant, Liberal Legacies, and Foreign Affairs." *Philosophy and Public Affairs* 12(3): 3–35.

———. 1997. *Ways of War and Peace: Realism, Liberalism, and Socialism*. New York: Norton.

———. 1999. "A Liberal View: Preserving and Expanding Liberal Pacific Union." In T. V. Paul and John A. Hall, eds., *International Order and the Future of World Politics*. Cambridge: Cambridge University Press.

Flynn, Gregory, and Henry Farrell. 1999. "Piecing Together the Democratic Peace: The CSCE, Norms, and the 'Construction' of Security in Post–Cold War Europe." *International Organization* 53(3): 505–35.

Gilpin, Robert. 1981. *War and Change in World Politics*. Cambridge: Cambridge University Press.

Grieco, Joseph M. 1993. "Understanding the Problem of International Cooperation: The Limits of Neoliberal Institutionalism and the Future of Realist Theory." In David A. Baldwin, ed., *Neorealism and Neoliberalism: The Contemporary Debate*. New York: Columbia University Press.

Guilick, Edward Vose. 1955. *Europe's Classical Balance of Power*. New York: Norton.

Haas, E. B. 1964. *Beyond the Nation-State*. Stanford: Stanford University Press.

————. 1968. *The Uniting of Europe*. Stanford: Stanford University Press.

Hall, John A. 1993. "Ideas and the Social Sciences." In Judith Goldstein and Robert O. Keohane, eds., *Ideas and Foreign Policy: Beliefs, Institutions, and Political Change*. Ithaca: Cornell University Press.

————. 1996. *International Orders*. Cambridge, U.K.: Polity Press.

Harrison, Reginald J. 1974. *Europe in Question: Theories of Regional International Integration*. London: Allen & Unwin.

Hirschman, Albert O. 1977. *The Passions and the Interests*. Princeton: Princeton University Press.

Hurrell, Andrew. 1998. "Society and Anarchy in the 1990s." In B. A. Roberson, ed., *International Society and the Development of International Relations*. London: Pinter.

Jervis, Robert. 1983. "Security Regimes." In Stephen D. Krasner, ed., *International Regimes*. Ithaca: Cornell University Press.

Keohane, Robert O. 1984. *After Hegemony: Cooperation and Discord in the World Political Economy*. Princeton: Princeton University Press.

————. 1989. *International Institutions and State Power: Essays in International Relations Theory*. Boulder, Col.: Westview.

————. 1993. "Institutional Theory and the Realist Challenge After the Cold War." In David A. Baldwin, ed., *Neorealism and Neoliberalism: The Contemporary Debate*. New York: Columbia University Press.

————, and Joseph S. Nye. 1977. *Power and Interdependence: World Politics in Transition*. Boston: Little, Brown.

Krasner, Stephen D. 1983a. "Structural Causes and Regime Consequences: Regimes as Intervening Variables." In Stephen D. Krasner, ed., *International Regimes*. Ithaca: Cornell University Press.

————. 1983b. "Regimes and the Limits of Realism: Regimes as Autonomous Variables." In Stephen D. Krasner, ed., *International Regimes*. Ithaca: Cornell University Press.

————. 1993. "Westphalia and All That." In Judith Goldstein and Robert O. Keohane, eds., *Ideas and Foreign Policy: Beliefs, Institutions, and Political Change*. Ithaca: Cornell University Press.

Lake, David A., and Patrick M. Morgan. 1997. *Regional Orders: Building Security in a New World*. University Park: Pennsylvania State University Press.

League of Nations. 1919. "The Covenant of the League of Nations." Reproduced in Louis L. Snyder (1955), *Fifty Major Documents of the Twentieth Century*. New York: D. Van Nostrand.

Lyons, Gene M., and Michael Mastanduno. 1995. "State Sovereignty and International Intervention: Reflections." In Gene M. Lyons and Michael Mastanduno, eds., *Beyond Westphalia: State Sovereignty and International Intervention*. Baltimore: Johns Hopkins University Press.

McMillan, Susan M. 1997. "Interdependence and Conflict." *Mershon International Studies Review* 41(1): 33–58.

Mearsheimer, John. 1995. "The False Promise of International Institutions." *International Security* 19(3): 5–49.

Mitrany, David. 1966. *A Working Peace System*. Chicago: Quadrangle Books.

Morgenthau, Hans J. 1978. *Politics Among Nations: The Struggle for Power and Peace*. New York: Knopf.

Mouffe, Chantal. 1979. "Hegemony and Ideology in Gramsci." In Chantal Mouffe, ed., *Gramsci and Marxist Theory*. London: Routledge.

Owen, John M. 1994. "How Liberalism Produces Democratic Peace." *International Security* 19(2): 87–125.

Paul, T. V., and John A. Hall. 1999. *International Order and the Future of World Politics*. Cambridge: Cambridge University Press.

Rosencrance, Richard. 1986. *The Rise of the Trading State: Commerce and Conquest in the Modern World*. New York: Basic Books.

Russett, Bruce. 1993. *Grasping the Democratic Peace*. Princeton: Princeton University Press.

Sheehan, Michael. 1996. *The Balance of Power: History and Theory*. London: Routledge.

Solingen, Etel. 1998. *Regional Orders at Century's Dawn: Global and Domestic Influences on Grand Strategy*. Princeton: Princeton University Press.

Stein, Arthur A. 1983. "Coordination and Collaboration: Regimes in an Anarchic World." In Stephen D. Krasner, ed., *International Regimes*. Ithaca: Cornell University Press.

———. 1990. *Why Nations Cooperate: Circumstances and Choice in International Relations*. Ithaca: Cornell University Press.

Strange, Susan. 1983. "Cave! Hic dragones: A Critique of Regime Analysis." In Stephen D. Krasner, ed., *International Regimes*. Ithaca: Cornell University Press.

Trachtenberg, Marc. 1993. "Intervention in Historical Perspective." In Laura W. Reed and Carl Kaysen, eds., *Emerging Norms of Justified Intervention*. Cambridge, Mass.: American Academy of Arts and Sciences.

Waltz, Kenneth N. 1979. *Theory of International Politics*. New York: Random House.

Wendt, Alexander. 1992. "Anarchy Is What States Make of It: The Social Construction of Power Politics." *International Organization* 46(2): 391–425.

———. 1995. "Constructing International Politics." *International Security* 20(1): 71–81.

Wight, Martin. 1995. *Power Politics*. London: Leicester University Press.

CHAPTER TWO

Constructing Security Order in Asia

Conceptions and Issues

MUTHIAH ALAGAPPA

In a new era of peril and opportunity, our overriding purpose must be to expand and strengthen the world's community of market-based democracies. During the Cold War, we sought to contain a threat to the survival of free institutions. Now we seek to enlarge the circle of nations that live under those free institutions, for our dream is of a day when the opinions and energies of every person in the world will be given full expression in a world of thriving democracies that cooperate with each other to live in peace.

—William Clinton, 1993

The U.S. recognizes and reaffirms the critical role that our alliances play in security, peace, and stability in Asia. . . . U.S. alliances in the region have long served as the cornerstone of regional security. . . . The United States views the reaffirmation and enhancement of these alliances over the past three years, and the concurrent and complementary development of constructive ties with nonallied states, as evidence of our continued confidence that an integrated network of security relations is in the interest of all Asia Pacific nations.

—Report on U.S. Strategy in the Asia Pacific, 1998

After the end of the Cold War, the world is going in the direction of multipolarization. . . . [However] the United States continues to pursue hegemony and power politics and interfere recklessly in the internal affairs of other countries. . . . All the countries that love peace and justice should unite to oppose hegemony and power politics and promote the establishment of a new, fair, and equitable international order.

—Jiang Zemin, May 13, 1999

Multipolarity is better than unipolarity and political multipolarization is of great significance to world peace, stability, and development. . . . The Five Principles of Peaceful Coexistence, the purposes and principles of the UN Charter, and other universally recognized norms governing international relations, far from being outdated, should constitute the basis of the new international political and economic order.

—Jiang Zemin, Apr. 13, 2000

For regional peace and stability it is important to ensure continued
U.S. presence in this region through Japan-U.S. security arrangements, as well as to promote confidence building through such processes as the ASEAN Regional Forum. It is also important that cooperative relations and mutual trust be enhanced between China and
other countries in the region. We do appreciate the positive role that
ASEAN is playing. Japan intends to continue to play an active role in
cooperation with other Asia-Pacific countries . . . to lay the foundation for peace through promoting democracy and development.
                                             —Keizo Obuchi, May 4, 1998

Asia is the crucible in which a new security order will be fashioned. . .
. existing models like OSCE or OAS do not adequately address the diversity of the requirement of the Asian nations. Clearly the traditional
balance of power approach will not work; neither, by corollary, will
containment. . . . What is needed therefore is a cooperative security
order, rooted in pluralism. Such an order has to be inclusive, but inclusive in a flexible manner for all countries cannot contribute
equally or . . . be equally ready to participate in such an exercise.
                                             —Brajesh Mishra, 2000

More than a decade has passed since the termination of the Cold War, and some
progress has been made in constructing certain features of a new security order in
Asia, but—as highlighted by the epigraphs to this chapter—there are also fundamental differences over the goals and values of the new order, as well as the
pathways to sustain that order. Initially the differences were rooted in competing
value systems (Asian political and economic models versus Western ones that
were claimed to be universal), the belief that a strategic power shift was under
way from the United States and Western Europe to Asia, and the ensuing anticipation that American dominance would be short-lived and the world would soon
become multipolar. The decade-long economic stagnation in Japan and the 1997
financial crisis tarred the Asian economic miracle and the Asian values deemed to
underpin it. The collapse of authoritarian rule, most strikingly in Indonesia in
1998, and the democratic transitions that have been under way in Asia since the
mid-1980s, combined with the search for alternative models in China and Vietnam, also undercut the so-called Asian political model. The 1997 crisis and the
slow growth of the Asian economies since then (with the exception of the People's Republic of China) also altered the perception that a dramatic power shift
was under way. The decade-long robust growth of the U.S. economy and America's unchallenged technological and military might consolidated the initially
fortuitous status of the United States as the sole superpower. Though the American economy has slowed, the depiction of the United States in the 1980s as a

country in irreversible decline and the anticipation that it would soon be overtaken by the Asian juggernauts have disappeared. It is in a context of America's preponderant power that is expected to last at least for a couple more decades that the new security order in Asia is being forged.

Although America's preponderant power is widely acknowledged, its strategic dominance and its vision for global and regional order evoke a mixed response in Asia. Japan, a close ally of the United States and with the world's second largest but stagnating economy, is most supportive. China, which has the fastest growing economy in Asia and seeks a central place in the management of Asian security affairs and its "rightful" position in the world, has serious misgivings. Other countries—Russia, India, and several ASEAN countries (which are by no means unified in their stance)—are ambivalent about American strategic dominance, and are critical or have reservations about specific features of the American vision. Although the values debate is virtually dead, the liberal political values of the American vision still create apprehension and resentment in a number of Asian countries. However, the differences do not all stem from Asian apprehensions and reactions to the strategic dominance of the United States and its vision for global and regional order. They also arise from apprehensions among the Asian states and their competing aspirations in the management of regional order. The dissatisfaction of the Asian powers with the present status quo is a major challenge to the construction of the post–Cold War security order in Asia. Other challenges include contestation of certain features of the normative structure; the persistence of acute international conflicts (Taiwan, Korea, and Kashmir) involving the major powers; the vulnerability of Asian states to internal conflicts that have transnational and regional consequences, including international terrorism; and the proliferation of weapons of mass destruction and their delivery systems. This chapter traces the convergent and competing features of the still-evolving Asian security order through an investigation of the different conceptions of order and the underlying issues.

Three Conceptions of Order

Although ideas and nuances vary from country to country and invariably there are competing visions and strategies within each country, essentially there are three conceptions—hegemony with liberal features, strategic condominium/balance of power, and institutionalism—that have been deployed explicitly or implicitly to shape the post–Cold War order in Asia. The first two conceptions belong to the category of instrumental order discussed in Chapter 1. They have certain features of the normative-contractual order, which if strengthened over time may transform the type of order itself. For now, instrumental features dominate both conceptions. The third conception has instrumental features as well, but the normative-contractual features are more prominent, at least in aspiration. The three conceptions closely approximate the articulations of the United States, China, and ASEAN, although they may not fully capture the complexity and nuances of their visions of order. In addition to China, a balance-of-power order based on a common understanding among the major powers also appeals to Russia and India if it includes them. Japan's "vision" falls in between the hegemonic and balance-of-power conceptions and also has certain institutional features. The major powers' visions of order tend to emphasize intersubjective understanding among them and power-based pathways—hegemony, balance of power, and concert—while the middle and smaller powers in Southeast Asia place greater emphasis on principles and norms and on the multilateral political and economic cooperation pathways to order, at least in the abstract. Used as a heuristic device, the three conceptions and the underlying issues highlight the challenges confronting the construction of a post–Cold War security order in Asia.

Hegemony with Liberal Features

As the sole global power, the United States has articulated a vision of the post–Cold War world that preserves its primacy and embodies its values. President George Bush (1990) envisioned a world of "open borders, open trade, and open minds." His successor President William Clinton (1993a) envisioned a community of market-based democracies. Both assigned Washington the lead role in constructing the post–Cold War order. Primacy is also the goal of George W. Bush's administration, which came to power in 2001. It emphasizes geopolitical competition and downplays the idealist elements that were prominent in the Clinton administration's vision. With a preference for unilateralism over multilateralism and cooperative security, it initially sought to disengage the United States from the roles of regional conflict mediation and nation building. The September 11, 2001, attack on the United States has modified certain aspects, but the policy of primacy and unilateralism does not appear to have fundamentally altered.

The American vision for the Asian region is a derivative of its global vision. Along with Europe and the Western Hemisphere, Asia, particularly Northeast Asia, is viewed as vital to American economic and security interests. A closed and hostile Asia is deemed to be inimical to American security. The only conventional attack on the United States since 1812 came from an Asian country; the only terrorist attack on the United States since 1916 came from a terrorist group harbored by a country in Southwest Asia; the only war the United States lost was in Asia; the potential challengers to American dominance are in Asia. Asia, which accounted for 23 percent of the world's GDP in 1999 in dollar terms and 31 percent based on purchasing power parity (PPP) adjusted exchange rates, is crucial for America's economic health. Washington seeks to expand the international order rooted in Western values to make it a truly global order under its leadership. In a series of addresses, President Clinton and his Asia staff articulated the vision for a Pacific Community and its elements (Clinton 1993b, 1993c, 1993d; Lord 1995; Office of International Security Affairs 1995, 1998).

Although the emphasis on specific elements has fluctuated, the key features of this vision are American predominance and leadership, the development of market-based national economies that are integrated into a global capitalist economy, promotion of human rights and democracy, and a regional security system anchored in the network of American alliances (The White House 1996). Since the early 1940s, a key goal of Washington has been to prevent any power from dominating East Asia. This was reaffirmed in the leaked classified Pentagon policy document prepared immediately after the termination of the Cold War (Mastanduno 1997). The 2001 Quadrennial Defense Review Report (DOD 2001) prepared by the Bush administration emphasizes the enduring national interest in precluding "hostile domination of critical areas." It extends the area of critical importance in Asia to include the littoral between Japan and India, and Southwest Asia. In addition to preserving and enhancing its own capabilities, Washington seeks to lead a dominant coalition in the region by binding key states like Japan and managing the rise of nonallied states like China. The U.S.-Japan Security Treaty was reaffirmed under the Clinton administration, which also revised the guidelines for U.S.-Japan defense cooperation to enable Japan to make a more significant contribution to regional security. Stressing the importance of allies and friends, the Bush administration seeks to elevate the relationship with Japan and to accord it higher priority vis-à-vis China. On China, in place of the Clinton concepts of engagement and strategic partnership, the Bush administration has articulated the notion of strategic competition. This may be undergoing revision in the context of Chinese support for the American-led war on international terrorism, but it is unclear how much of a shift has occurred or will take place and whether the shift is strategic or tactical (Goldstein 2001). The Clinton administration in its final years and the Bush administration appear to have elevated the political, strategic, and economic importance of India and have instituted steps to develop strategic relations with that country. Some analysts view this development as connected to a U.S. policy to contain China (Ross 2001).

Washington's vision of order in Asia is based on liberal values. It fosters free-market systems, regional trade, and investment regimes that are compatible with global regimes, while opposing initiatives like the East Asian Economic Caucus (EAEC) and Asian Monetary Fund (AMF) that would be exclusively Asian or have the potential to undermine global institutions like the IMF in which the

United States has virtual veto power. Washington rejects the notion of Asian values and the accompanying claim that democracy and human rights are unsuited to Asia. Claiming that the democratic aspiration and achievements of the Asian peoples undermine the relativist claims of certain Asian elites, it has expressed determination to promote human rights and democratic governance in China, Burma, Indonesia, Cambodia, and other countries.

In the management of security affairs, Washington views its network of bilateral alliances and forward military presence as the core pillars of regional security and stability. In addition to adapting and strengthening its alliance network in the region, Washington has sought to acquire new staging and basing facilities and to develop military cooperation with a wide range of Asian countries (DOD 2001). Washington supports cooperative security through participation in subregional and regional multilateral institutions like the ARF, but only as a supplement to its alliance system. It opposes exclusive Asian regional bodies—the EAEC, for example—that are deemed to be hostile to the United States. And although it has not opposed the new ASEAN Plus Three forum, it has urged the inclusion of Australia and New Zealand. The key seems to be that Asian forums should include U.S. allies and friends so that such bodies will not be hostile to American interests.

Strategic Condominium/Balance of Power

America's hegemony with liberal values as a prescription for regional order has been contested by China, especially in the context of the deterioration in U.S.-China relations that began in 1998.[1] For a number of reasons—including the lack of capability to seriously challenge American dominance, the lack of trust by fellow Asian states, Beijing's concern not to draw attention to its rising power and to downplay perceptions of the "China threat," and its low capacity to provide economic and security public goods—China has not articulated a specific vision for the Asian region. For the most part it has reacted to American ideas and developments at the global and regional level that it perceives as having the potential to endanger Chinese national interests.

Beginning in 1998, Beijing articulated a "new security concept" for "establishing a more just and equitable international order," which it argues is a better alternative to an order dominated by the United States (Information Office of the State Council 1998, 2000; Finkelstein and McDevitt 1999; Finkelstein 2000). Though couched in normative terms, Chinese thinking about the regional security order has been largely instrumental and pragmatic with strong realist characteristics. The new security concept was given formal standing in China's

---

[1]On the deterioration of Sino-American relations, see Finkelstein (2000), Ross (2001), and Roy (2000).

1998 Defense White Paper, which followed the reaffirmation of the U.S.-Japan security treaty in 1996 and the proclamation of the revised guidelines for U.S.-Japan defense cooperation in 1997. The Chinese conception emphasizes order among sovereign states, and the goal of international order should be to protect state sovereignty and territorial integrity, prevent external interference in domestic affairs, and promote national prosperity and strength. In this conception each country would be free to determine its political system without interference from outside. In addition to the Five Principles of Peaceful Coexistence (mutual respect for sovereignty and territorial integrity; mutual nonaggression; noninterference in each other's internal affairs; equality and mutual benefit; and peaceful coexistence), the new security concept emphasizes multilateral dialogue to build trust and understanding and favors peaceful settlement of disputes. It also advocates bilateral dialogue and partnerships among major powers that are not aimed at third parties. Along with the UN Charter, the Five Principles of Peaceful Coexistence, and other universally recognized principles, the new security concept, Beijing posits, should serve as the basis for constructing the new world and regional orders.

The emphasis on Westphalian principles is accompanied by the Chinese claim that a multipolar world would be more peaceful and stable than a unipolar one under U.S. domination. Although the rhetoric emphasizes multipolarity, the real preference is for a strategic partnership or condominium with the United States in which it is one of two co-managers of Asian security. Failing this, it seeks to balance American power through the construction of a multipolar world and the development of a counterhegemonic coalition. Beijing views the United States, Europe, Russia, China, and ASEAN as the key poles and is silent on Japan and India. The Chinese conception assigns a key role to global multilateral institutions like the UN and its Security Council (where it has veto power) and has become more positively disposed toward regional multilateral institutions like the ARF. Beijing projects the Shanghai Cooperation Organization as the model for the organization and management of regional security affairs in the post–Cold War era. However, bilateralism, which facilitates the deployment of its power and influence to protect its national interests, is the preferred approach in the management of disputes.

Normative-Contractual Conception

The ASEAN conception shares several goals and principles with the Chinese conception. Sovereignty, equality of states, and nonintervention in internal affairs are key pillars of the ASEAN conception of regional security order, which emphasizes peaceful adjustment of disputes and nonuse of force in the international interaction of Asian states. The ASEAN emphasis on principles and norms, as well as its conceptions of comprehensive security and national resilience, stem from the weakness of ASEAN states in power endowment and their weakness as modern states. The difference between the ASEAN and Chinese conceptions lies in the pathway to order. Despite the emphasis on principles, the Chinese conception relies heavily on power balancing and understanding among the major powers. The ASEAN approach emphasizes principles, norms, and rules as the key to regulate international interaction, and places special emphasis on multilateral institutions at the subregional, regional, and global levels. The stress on multilateral institutions is designed to reduce the role of power (in which the ASEAN countries are disadvantaged) and to increase the salience of norms (where the differentiation in power matters less). It is also a strategy to enable the Southeast Asian countries to be players in constructing the post–Cold War regional order. Several ASEAN countries—Singapore, Thailand, the Philippines—have also hedged their bets by engaging in close relations with major powers, especially the United States. The ASEAN conception, especially the emphasis on multilateral institutions, accords with the expected behavior of small and medium powers, but the reluctance to follow through with the construction of formal institutions with the necessary authority does not. The three conceptions of order reflect the state of national consolidation, the history, ideas, and values that inform the constitution and aspiration of nations, the national and group endowment of power, the satisfaction or dissatisfaction with the status quo, and the preferred international identities and roles.

Although the United States has preponderant power and plays a crucial role in the management of security affairs, especially in Northeast Asia, it has not been able to impose its notion of order on the region. The three conceptions coexist uneasily with only minimum integration and no clear division of labor. The competing features of the three concepts generate tension and frustrate the development of a comprehensive and legitimate security order in Asia, making it difficult to decide which features are stabilizing and which are destabilizing. Washington, for example, views the reinvigoration of its alliance network and close coordination among allies as enhancing security and stability, while these same measures are viewed by China as destabilizing.[2] The United States and China disagree fundamentally about the need for—and consequences of—the U.S. alliance network in the region. Increasingly the ASEAN countries and China assign greater salience to regional multilateral institutions, whereas the United

---

[2]Beijing reacted sharply to a proposal unveiled after the Australia–United States Ministerial Consultations in August 2001 for a four-power forum to forge closer defense ties among the United States, Japan, South Korea, and Australia. The Chinese government-controlled *People's Daily* posited the proposal as part of an American strategy to contain China, while another Chinese newspaper dubbed the proposed forum as an "Asia-Pacific NATO" (Symonds 2001).

States supports them only as a supplement to its alliance network. Although China supports multilateral institutions, it has been reluctant to endorse a conflict prevention role for the ASEAN Regional Forum (ARF) and has sought to keep the management of the Taiwan and South China Sea disputes out of the multilateral setting. The competing conceptions also account for the ad hoc manner in which security affairs in the region (like the 1993 nuclear crisis on the Korean peninsula) are managed.

Despite the differences, the three conceptions of order are not mutually exclusive and not always antagonistic. There are areas of overlap and convergence as well. The rest of this chapter highlights the convergent and contested features of the still-evolving post–Cold War order in Asia by examining the goals of order, the clash of values, the dissatisfaction with the status quo arising from the competing aspirations of the major powers, and the implication of the still-unresolved conflicts over Taiwan, Korea, and Kashmir that are rooted in considerations of identity and sovereignty.

Goals: Private Ends Prevail

A perusal of the key documents relating to regional order—the founding declaration of the ARF, the statements of the ARF chair, and the defense white papers and reports of the Asian countries and the United States—indicates three primary goals that should be sustained by an Asian regional security order: national survival, national prosperity, and regional peace and stability. An unstated goal often subsumed in national survival is the legitimacy and security of the incumbent government, especially in authoritarian and communist states. National survival and prosperity are essentially private ends of the participating states. They may generate a common interest in mutual survival and prosperity, but this is not the same as commitment to the survival and prosperity of every state. In fact as the developmental and wealth gap narrows, the concern to maximize national power may work against cooperation that might enhance the prosperity of likely competitors. The attainment of national survival and prosperity through participation in the global capitalist economy requires a stable and peaceful environment. Peace and stability are often a subsidiary goal of Asian states that may be compromised if the demands of national survival require it. In the abstract these three goals—survival, prosperity, and regional peace and stability—appear uncontroversial. But as we shall see, certain aspects of these goals are highly problematic in practice—not only making their realization difficult but also posing substantial challenges to the construction of regional security order in Asia.

All three goals belong to Hedley Bull's primary category and to the instrumental type of order outlined in Chapter 1. Although there are tentative signs of higher-order goals, especially in the economic arena—the ASEAN Free Trade Area, for example, and the APEC plan to liberalize trade by the years 2010 and 2020—in light of the region's poor track record on such matters, it is uncertain whether these goals will be realized. In the political arena, too, there are inchoate references to notions of common identity and a shared future (ASEAN identity, East Asian identity, Pacific Community), but they are still straws in the wind. There is no firm commitment to move toward any form of economic integration and certainly no desire to move toward political integration. And even if a regional economic or political community is envisaged, the new identity at the regional level is unlikely to supersede that at the national level. The primary purpose of the state-centered regional security order in Asia is to consolidate the nation-state, enhance its international power and influence, and create a safe and predictable environment—not to create a new regional community or emancipate the individual and minority communities. Thus the emerging security order in Asia has primarily the features of the instrumental type of order as well as certain features of the normative-contractual order.

Political Survival

Political survival is the most basic goal of Asian states. This concern has four distinct but related aspects: sheer existence as an independent state, territorial integrity, ideational survival, including the preservation of national identity and political organizing ideology, and preservation of sovereignty. Although sheer existence is a concern for very few states (Taiwan, South Korea, North Korea), several others (Singapore, Brunei, Cambodia, East Timor) do not take their survival for granted. For all the others, continued existence as a separate state is not an issue. Since the dramatic adjustment with the onset of decolonization, the political map of Asia has been relatively stable compared to other regions of the world. There has been no sudden burst of new nations as in Eastern Europe, the Balkans, and Central Asia following the collapse of the Soviet Union, the disintegration of Yugoslavia, and the splitting of Czechoslovakia. Only three new states have been created in postcolonial Asia (Singapore in 1965, Bangladesh in 1971, and East Timor in 2002), and only one state (South Vietnam in 1975) has disappeared from the political map. As the current international norms and political consensus in Asia do not support the creation of new states, the political map of Asia is unlikely to change dramatically, although, as we shall see, there are severe internal pressures in some countries.

For the present, sheer survival is a concern for only three states: North Korea, South Korea, and Taiwan. In regard to North and South Korea—with cross-recognition and membership of both Koreas in the UN as well as the altered interests and distribution of power affecting the Korean conflict—the immediate issue is not the disappearance of one state through forceful absorption by the other, but building confidence, preventing the outbreak of accidental war, controlling nuclear and missile proliferation, fostering the normalization of relations between North and South, integrating North Korea into the world community, and preventing turmoil and collapse in North Korea. The Taiwan conflict relates more directly to survival. If Beijing has its way, Taiwan will cease to exist as a separate state. For Taipei the issue is one of survival; for Beijing it is one of national unity, integrity, and legitimacy; for Washington it is a matter of credibility and reputation; for the other regional states it is a problem of regional peace and stability (Alagappa 2001). Of all the conflicts in Asia, it is Taiwan that has the potential to lead to a major regional war involving the PRC, the United States, and Japan. It also raises certain key questions: Is the Taiwan dispute an internal matter as claimed by the PRC or is it an international concern? Should democratic Taiwan be denied the right to self-determination? How should the regional community relate to Taiwan in normal times and in a crisis situation? Certainly the conflict over Taiwan's identity and its existence as a separate political entity are not likely to be settled any time soon. And as two major states (China and the United States) are parties to the conflict, the issues associated with the dispute will continue to challenge and inhibit the construction of a new security order in Asia.

Although sheer existence is not an issue for the other states, many do confront challenges to their territorial integrity, which is a key concern of Asian states. For most countries the internal challenges to territorial integrity are more severe than the external threats. The domestic challenges relate to the issue of national unity and identity. Most Asian states are postcolonial entities with boundaries drawn by the metropolitan powers. Viewing these boundaries as sacrosanct, the postindependence Asian elites seek to build nations out of the multiethnic populations that inhabit their countries. While considerable progress has been made over the last five decades, the basis for the nation-state is still contested in several countries—especially by minority groups, some of whom seek autonomy or secession from the state. Minorities in China (Tibet, Xinjiang), the Philippines (Moro Muslims), Thailand (Malay Muslims), Indonesia (Aceh, West Papua), Burma (several minority groups), India (Muslim Kashmiris, minorities in the northeastern states), and Sri Lanka (Tamils) seek either autonomy or secession. Outsiders support certain of these domestic challenges covertly or overtly. The West supports the Tibetan cause; Pakistan supports the cause of the Muslim Kashmiris; until recently India supported the cause of the Sri Lankan Tamils. The internal challenge to territorial integrity can become even more acute for the individual Asian states and the regional community if the principle of self-determination gains ground in Asia as it appears to have done in Eastern Europe and the Balkans.

Some of the domestic challenges to territorial integrity intersect with interstate conflict. Pakistan supports the cause of the militant Muslim Kashmiri movements that seek to secede from India, for example, while India views such support as a threat to its political identity (secularism) and territorial integrity. Indeed the two countries have gone to war over the conflict twice, and serious breaches erupted in 1999 (the Kargil conflict) and in 2001–2. Apart from these domestic and international challenges to territorial integrity, there are numerous ongoing border disputes in Asia on land and at sea. The more prominent ones include the dispute between Russia and Japan over the Northern Territories, between China and India over their boundary, and the multiple conflicting claims in the East and South China Seas. Most of these conflicts, however, have a colonial or postcolonial origin and are tied to the construction of nation-states and their system of government as well as boundary demarcation. There is no imperial drive in contemporary Asia to conquer territory in order to increase wealth or security as in the earlier colonial era. The contemporary political map, except for the disputes just cited, is accepted by most if not all the Asian states.

Ideational survival, the third aspect of national survival, is a crucial concern of several Asian states. There are two parts to ideational survival. The first relates to the identity of the nation-state, and this has been discussed. The second relates to the system of political governance. Internal opposition to military and authoritarian governments led to contestation and regime change in the Philippines, South Korea, Taiwan, Thailand, Bangladesh, and Indonesia. The democratic systems in several of these countries have not been consolidated. The danger of backsliding and further conflict still exists. Although Burma and China have crushed the democratic challenges, the incumbent political systems lack legitimacy. Along with those in Vietnam and North Korea, the political systems in Burma and China are likely to be targets of internal and international contestation for years to come. The United States and Western Europe are committed to promoting democracy and human rights. They have isolated and sanctioned Burma, condemned human rights violations in China and other countries, oppose authoritarian tendencies, and support democratic forces and development in nondemocratic states. These actions have been perceived by target governments as threatening the legitimacy of their rule and, by extension, the security of their respective states. Several key issues must be addressed in connection with ideational survival: Does the international community have an obligation to promote a specific system of governance? Or should it steer clear of domestic issues and conflicts? If it does have an obligation, what is its responsibility? And how should the principles and norms (such as sovereignty and noninterference in internal affairs) be reconciled with competing principles (such as the right to self-determination and the protection of individual and minority rights)?

Such questions are closely connected to sovereignty—the final aspect of survival. As Asian states have been liberated from colonial or semicolonial rule only in the last five decades and many are still engaged in the process of nation and state building, they zealously guard their right to supreme jurisdiction in domestic affairs and their autonomy in decision making on international affairs. Supremacy in internal jurisdiction is linked to the principle of noninterference in internal affairs. Most Asian states are firmly wedded to this principle that is now being challenged by the norm of justified intervention advocated by the West. One notes that although the United States is a strong advocate for modifying the principle of non-interference in internal affairs to protect minorities and individual rights, it zealously guards its own sovereignty in the political, economic, and strategic domains. Washington has not been reluctant to act unilaterally when its rights and interests are endangered and has been loath to put American troops under foreign national or multilateral command. This is not a case, as frequently depicted, of double standards. It is the luxury of a preponderant power that can choose when and where to act. Moreover the clash over norms is not just between the West and Asia but also an issue of contention among some Asian states. The flexible engagement principle advanced by the Philippines and Thailand, for instance, is opposed by other ASEAN states, China, and India. A key challenge in the construction of Asian regional security is the forging of a common understanding of the meaning and limits of sovereignty and associated norms.

Prosperity

National prosperity—equated with economic growth and modernization—ranks high in the hierarchy of national goals in almost all the Asian countries. China, for example, has identified economic growth as the highest priority in its modernization program. In 1979 the CCP leadership articulated the goal of doubling the per capita income in twenty years. China's tenth five-year plan has the goal of doubling the 2000 per capita income by 2010. Beginning in 1991, India has enacted several measures to liberalize its economy and grow at a target rate of about 7 percent a year. Overall, East Asia and Southeast Asia have made remarkable progress in economic modernization and enhancing national prosperity. Economic growth is viewed as vital for political legitimation, for managing domestic and international tensions, and for enhancing national power and influence in the international arena. Some view economic interdependence and integration as ways of ameliorating the security dilemma and resolving certain political disputes.

With the failure of rival models in the region and the world at large, there is a growing consensus in Asia that the free-market system and participation in the global economy—through membership in global and regional regimes and accessing international capital, technology, and markets—are the best route to prosperity. Consequently, this goal is less contentious but not entirely devoid of domestic and international challenges. The internal challenges relate to the pace of reform, the distribution of benefits and costs, dealing with corruption and the socioeconomic inequality that may arise from the implementation of reform programs, and addressing the demands for increased political participation that arise from sustained economic growth. Often regime and government legitimacy is a factor. Failure to distribute the fruits of development evenly throughout society, failure to undertake political reform, a severe downturn in economic fortunes—all can lead to political unrest and, in the worst case, serious internal turmoil as in Indonesia.

The internationalization and globalization of national economies have also exposed the Asian states to the vagaries of the international marketplace—where most of them are takers rather than makers of rules. The huge domestic and international debts (private and public) of the Asian countries, the massive outflow of capital that precipitated the 1997 financial crisis, combined with the stringent IMF conditions for relief packages and Asian inability to influence the international rules, have sensitized the Asian countries to the negative side of internationalization. The crisis also impressed upon the Asian states not only the urgent need for reform in the domestic and international financial sector, but also the need to develop regional mechanisms to better cope with future crisis situations and exercise greater control. Certain elements in Asia (and the West) also oppose globalization because a disproportionate share of the adjustment cost falls on the poor and the weak, because they fear the cultural imperialism of the West, or simply out of xenophobia. Although growing apprehension of economic and cultural imperialism and curtailment of autonomy in the wake of the recent financial crisis have forced a rethinking of the strategies of liberalization and globalization, Asian states, recognizing the positive side as well, have not turned away from these strategies.

Other international challenges relate to the question of relative gain. This was a key issue in U.S.-Japan economic relations in the 1980s and could well become an issue in U.S.-China relations. Washington's slow and limited response to the financial crisis, as well as the harsh terms imposed by the IMF at the behest of the West, have been perceived in conspiratorial terms in some quarters in Asia. Political considerations still weigh heavily in the economic interaction of certain countries—between the PRC and Taiwan, India and Pakistan, North and South Korea—and in the various growth triangles and quadrangles in Southeast Asia. An initial political commitment is a must to set economic interaction in motion. Once in motion, economic interaction may develop its own momentum, but the political cost-benefit analysis continues to bear upon the economic interaction among states with unresolved tensions and disputes. At the same time, however, the goal of economic development and modernization has restrained the behavior of certain states even when major political issues are at stake—as, for example, in cross-strait relations. The pursuit of national survival and especially national prosperity through participation in the global economy creates a common interest in a peaceful and stable environment.

Regional Peace and Stability

The third goal in Asia is regional peace and stability. Peace is a desirable goal in the abstract and is supported by all states. But the attainment of peace necessitates certain measures that do not always have the support of the region's states. The goal of peace translates into two related objectives: constraints on the quantity and quality of national force and its use (including the collective management of force in the interest of the regional community as a whole) and pacific settlement of disputes.

Asian states seek to develop their individual military capabilities and retain the right to use force and threats of force in managing their international relations. National force plays a key role in the management of the conflicts in the Korean peninsula, across the Taiwan Strait, and over Kashmir. Force is an option, as well, in the management of the numerous territorial conflicts. And coercion is routinely and massively deployed in coping with domestic conflicts over identity and legitimacy. Although the Asian countries and the United States do not accept constraints on their own military capabilities, they do seek to limit the capabilities of others. Positing its alliance system and forward military presence as enhancing stability, for example, the United States seeks to maintain and strengthen its military capabilities in the region while portraying the development of similar capabilities by others as destabilizing. Intent on modernizing and strengthening its military capability, China, for its part, depicts the strengthening of the U.S.-Japan alliance and the development of the NMD and TMD systems as destabilizing and undermining its security, and seeks to limit if not prohibit India's development of missile and nuclear capabilities. It is also critical of Japan's becoming a normal country. The ASEAN states embarked on force modernization when their economies were doing well. While today there is no arms race as such, the continuing importance of force in Asian international politics and the desire to acquire modern military capabilities make the control and regulation of force virtually impossible.

Collective management of force does not appear to be an option at this point. Although the United States presents its alliance network as essential for regional peace and security, the primary purpose of that system is to serve American national interests and those of its allies. As demonstrated on so many occasions, the United States, as the sole global power, accepts no constraints on its autonomy.

Although they may derive certain benefits, the other states, including China, Russia, and India, do not view the U.S. Asia Pacific alliance network as specifically serving their national interest. They have no control over it. China, Russia, and India also reject any collective management of force that constrains them or threatens their interests. Ad hoc concerts may form from time to time to address specific issues, but they do not constitute collective management of force. And although states may support the notion of pacific settlement in principle, they reserve the right to use force on issues of importance to them on the basis that the issues are domestic matters or their national security is threatened. Provisions for pacific settlement mechanisms—as in the ASEAN Treaty of Amity and Concord—have seldom been activated or used. Of late, however, there has been some movement in this direction: Malaysia, Singapore, and Indonesia have agreed to submit their disputes over certain islands to the International Court of Justice; and ASEAN at the informal summit in 1999 approved a Troika comprising the past, present, and next chairmen of the ASEAN Ministerial Meeting as an ad hoc body to more effectively address issues of peace and security in the region.

Although force is still a key instrument of national policy, the cost of using force—and consequently the role of force in Asian international politics—have undergone significant change over the last couple of decades. Despite the many conflicts in the region and the upgrading of national military capabilities, there has not been a full-scale international war since 1979. The actual use of force has been limited to border clashes, to support for militant insurgencies, and to occasional clashes at sea where the danger of escalation is low. Force has also been used in a limited fashion to influence the behavior of states—as in the PRC's attempt to influence the outcome of Taiwan's presidential elections in 1996, for example, and Pakistan's attempt to force India to accept the Kashmir conflict as the core issue in Indo-Pakistani negotiations. Such use of force has had only limited success.

Over the years, it is the deterrent role of force that has become more prominent. The primary function of military force in the Korean peninsula and across the Taiwan Strait is deterrence—preventing aggressive behavior by North Korea, preventing the spillover of internal collapse in North Korea into South Korea, preventing unilateral declaration of independence by Taipei, and preventing the forceful absorption of Taiwan by the PRC. Although the outbreak of war cannot be ruled out in these conflicts, all parties recognize the high human, diplomatic, and economic costs of resorting to the force option. Likewise the primary function of the Indian and Pakistani nuclear capabilities is deterrence. Contrary to the doom and gloom predictions that accompanied the 1998 tests, and the rhetoric of Pakistan and India, the two countries have been careful to limit their military clashes. Conceivably the restraint that issues from the danger of crossing the nuclear threshold and Pakistan's relative weakness in conventional capabilities have emboldened Islamabad to actively support the militant Kashmiri movements in the belief that India will not dare escalate both horizontally and vertically. The dangers of such behavior, however, may be beginning to dawn on Islamabad. In the face of massive Indian military mobilization and American political pressure, it has pledged to take action against all forms of terrorism and to ban militant Islamic movements engaging in cross-border terrorism. However, it is unclear whether Islamabad can and will implement this pledge. Overall, then, the cost of using force is becoming high in Asia, though not prohibitive yet, and the role of force is undergoing substantial change as its utility becomes more circumscribed.

Stability, like peace, is a desirable goal, but countries differ on what constitutes stability. Is it to be viewed in a static or dynamic fashion? Who decides which development is stabilizing or destabilizing? How is change to be managed? By whom? Such questions are particularly germane to Asia, which is home to several large powers that have the potential and aspire to be great powers. Although there is no revolutionary state in Asia, the larger Asian states are not satisfied with the status quo. China, Russia, India, Japan—all seek change. China would like a stable environment in which to pursue its economic modernization program. But stability from China's perspective means a situation that increases its status and capabilities and supports the legitimacy of the CCP while keeping the other Asian powers down and narrowing the gap between it and the United States. Such a definition is not in the interest of Japan, India, or the United States. Japan and India seek to increase their power, influence, and status in the region and in the global community. The United States, by contrast, prefers the status quo, which privileges it. Issues of status and capability are at stake. A key issue is the management of competition among major powers—above all, preventing war among them. The convergence and divergence in the goals of order discussed above affect the regional normative structure and the management of relations among the major powers.

The Normative Structure: Liberal vs. Westphalian Norms

Sovereignty and the accompanying principles of juridical equality and noninterference in domestic affairs became the defining principles of international relations throughout the world in the post–World War II era. These principles that privilege the state have been enshrined in the charter of the United Nations, the most inclusive institution in the world. Though European in origin, these principles that protect the political independence and territorial integrity of states are highly valued by the Asian states for several reasons: their recent liberation from colonial or quasi-colonial rule; their relatively weak position in an international system still dominated by the West; the many internal and international challenges to their ongoing nation- and state-building projects; and the fact that among the countries in the world it is the Asian states that most closely approximate the Westphalian state. The Asian countries occupy a middle ground between the weak and failed states of Africa, the Middle East, and Eastern Europe, on the one hand, and the postindustrialized states of Western Europe on the other. The aspiration of the Asian political elite is to build strong, sovereign nation-states. They view international cooperation—including that in the economic arena—as a means to strengthen sovereignty, not undermine it. The strong attachment to Westphalian principles and norms does not mean that Asian governments do not intervene in each other's internal affairs. They do. But they do not subscribe to a norm that would formally subject them to international scrutiny and legitimize intervention in their domestic affairs by the international community.

The principle of noninterference in domestic affairs has been challenged by the rise of liberal norms from within (by segments of the growing civil society in Asian countries) and from without (largely by the West). The liberal norms emphasize the rights of the individual, the community of humankind, and democratic governance. In the aftermath of the Cold War, the protection of human rights, the prevention of discrimination and of persecution of minorities, prevention of genocide, and promotion of liberal-democratic governance and market-based economies assumed greater prominence in the international policy of the Western states. Indeed the associated norms have been projected by the West as having universal application. For much of the 1990s an intense debate was waged between the proponents of Western and Asian values—each advancing rival models for political development (multiparty democracy versus a single-party-dominant system) and economic development (free market versus the developmental state). Japan's decade-long economic stagnation and the economic slowdown in several Asian countries after the 1997 financial crisis—combined with democratic transitions in the Philippines, South Korea, Taiwan, Bangladesh, and Indonesia—ended this debate, at least for the time being, with the proponents of Asian values and models on the defensive.

Some Asian governments (China, Vietnam, Burma) are still concerned with Western support for democratic change, which they call the "threat of peaceful evolution." This threat is connected to the emerging tension in these countries between an open economy and a closed political system, as well as the challenge of initiating political reform to address demands for participation and accountability but without losing control of political power. Although the governments in these countries reject democracy, they are exploring alternative models (like that of Singapore) that permit elections and limited opposition. Human rights are still an important issue, but a certain degree of accommodation has been reached. Most Asian countries accept the UN Declaration on Political and Civil Rights; the Western countries have accepted a broader notion of human rights that includes the socioeconomic dimension. International attention has now shifted to the implementation of the various UN treaties on human rights. The current issue of contention is the principle of noninterference in domestic affairs—more explicitly, the norm of justified international intervention in domestic affairs to prevent gross violation of human rights and minority rights by the state or in a context where a failed state is unable to maintain domestic order.

Sovereignty, Noninterference, and Intervention

The provision of domestic order and the protection of citizens' rights are the responsibilities of the national government and have been treated by the international community as internal matters that are the exclusive preserve of the state. The primary concern of the international community has been to mitigate the dangers of the external aspect of sovereignty. The internal dimension of sovereignty—the relationship between ruler and ruled—was of concern only when it threatened international peace and security. This is the approach taken in the UN Charter. Although the charter does make the right and exercise of sovereignty contingent upon the state's fulfilling the obligations arising from membership in the organization, Article 2(7) explicitly states: "Nothing contained in the present Charter shall authorize UN intervention in matters which are essentially within the domestic jurisdiction of states." The only exception is when the Security Council determines that a situation constitutes a threat to international peace and security under Chapter 7. Intervention under Chapter 6 (peaceful settlement of disputes) and under the so-called Chapter 6.5 (Uniting for Peace Resolution) requires the consent of the host state.

With the termination of the Cold War, however, the relationship between ruler and ruled became a focus of the international community for several reasons. First was the euphoria in the West about the triumph of its values and the idea that they were universal in nature and should be promoted worldwide. Although the promotion of democracy and human rights had long been a goal of American foreign policy, it gained renewed vigor in the aftermath of the Cold War. Second, in the absence of an overriding geopolitical threat, domestic conflict and human tragedies attracted greater public attention in the West—especially when these tragedies occurred close to home in the Balkans, which in earlier times was of strategic importance to several European powers and indeed triggered World War I. Gradually the notion that the international community had a responsibility to intervene in domestic affairs on humanitarian grounds gained currency in the West and in UN circles (Lyons and Mastanduno 1995). In his Millennium Summit address to the UN Security Council in September 2000,

UN Secretary-General Kofi Annan stated that "the Security Council has a moral duty to act on behalf of the international community" in situations of crimes against humanity and warned that member states should brace themselves for a new era of UN interventionism (UN Press Release 2000; Annan 2000). International intervention raises key questions about the relationship between sovereignty—which in many ways is still the defining principle of international relations—and the responsibility of the international community, as well as about the legitimacy, the modality for decision making, and the means of intervention. Does the international community have a responsibility to intervene on humanitarian grounds? Under what conditions does the international community assume such a responsibility? Who has the authority to decide that a violation of serious proportions has occurred? On what basis is that decision to be made? What is the venue for making that decision? Under what rules and procedures? What should be the appropriate response?

The tension between international responsibility and state autonomy featured rather prominently in Asia, especially in the interaction of Western and Asian countries, but in a more diluted form also among the Asian countries. Most Asian states have not been receptive to the norm of humanitarian intervention. They oppose all forms of external interference in domestic matters. They do not support the Western policy of isolating Burma, and ASEAN has refused to concede to EU pressure to exclude Burma from the bilateral dialogue. Instead it engages in a policy of constructive engagement. Similarly, most Asian countries did not follow the West's lead in sanctioning China after the Tiananmen incident. Even Japan, which acted in concert with the West, decided to resume relations with China long before the others. Apart from the concern that they themselves could be a future target, certain Asian governments think the new norm is just another guise for "neocolonialism, power plays, and the pursuit of selfish national interest" by the new hegemon and the former imperial powers (SIIA 2001). Further, they believe that the norm will be applied selectively and with double standards.

Asian governments still hold firmly to the principles of sovereignty and non-interference in internal affairs. They support the limitation of these principles only in a situation of the most heinous crime, such as genocide, and then only if the intervention is authorized by the UN Security Council under Chapter 7. If UN intervention is to be undertaken under Chapter 6, they argue, the host state's consent is vital. The Asian states supported intervention in East Timor only after Indonesia had consented and the operation had been authorized by the UN Security Council. They strongly oppose intervention outside the UN framework, as in Kosovo. NATO's intervention in Kosovo deeply affected Asian sensibilities. Apart from reinforcing perceptions of the United States as a hegemonic power bent on unilateral action in the pursuit of its own interests, the technological and military prowess demonstrated by the United States in Kosovo created much apprehension even among the more advanced Asian militaries. China most strongly opposed the Kosovo intervention because it bypassed the UN, where it has veto power, and because of its possible implications for the Taiwan conflict.

The principle of noninterference in internal affairs is not only an issue between the Western and Asian countries; it is also an issue between certain Asian countries that advocate a more flexible interpretation of the Westphalian principles versus those who hold to an absolutist interpretation (Hernandez 1998). The difference within ASEAN became public in 1998 when the Philippines and Thailand argued that member states should be able to cross the line of noninterference when developments in neighboring states threaten them. The proposed limitation on sovereignty falls far short of the new norm of international intervention on humanitarian grounds, however, and is in fact not new. It can be inferred from the provisions of the UN Charter that make the exercise of sovereignty contingent upon states' fulfilling their international obligations, which include not posing a threat to other countries. Yet even this minimal change was controversial within ASEAN. After a heated debate, the foreign ministers agreed to disagree and called upon member states whose problems affected neighboring countries to set their house in order. The differences were papered over by the endorsement of a milder policy of "enhanced interaction" to resolve bilateral problems. With a change of government in Thailand, this issue is no longer on the ASEAN agenda. The ASEAN debate and its resolution demonstrate the strength of Asia's attachment to the Westphalian principles and norms. At the same time, however, there is growing recognition that the relationship between ruler and ruled cannot be shielded from international scrutiny and, moreover, that these principles and norms must be modified to accommodate domestic pressures and international demands.

Minority Rights and Self-Determination

Another concern is the relationship of minority groups to the state. Here the issues are the rights of minorities, the protection of these rights, the question whether minority groups have a right to self-determination and political independence, and the role of the international community in protecting minority rights. This concern has not figured as prominently as the protection of human rights and intervention in the international politics of Asia.

Tolerance and protection of minorities have been important components of various European peace treaties and conventions since the sixteenth century (Krasner 1999: 73–74). They also form part of several UN declarations and covenants. Apart from the humanitarian dimension considered earlier, the international concern with protection of minorities is rooted in the belief that such tolerance is necessary for democratic governance and for international stability. The NATO interventions in the former Yugoslavia in the 1990s were considered essential to preserve stability in the Balkans and prevent the spread of ethnic conflict to other countries in the region and beyond.

Most Asian governments have not been inclined to afford special protection for minorities, especially not options like federalism and autonomy. The preference has been for strong unitary states and domination by majority communities. Proposals for federal states and autonomous regions have been rejected because of their association with the divide-and-rule policies of the imperial powers. Until recently, for example, Indonesia firmly rejected the idea of a federal state and autonomy for certain minority groups because of the belief that the Dutch had deployed such proposals to weaken and truncate Indonesia in negotiating that country's independence. Even in countries where a federal state was instituted, as in India, the tendency until recently has been to centralize power and authority. And while China recognizes Tibet and Xinjiang as autonomous regions, in practice it has increased central control over these regions and attempted to alter the political balance by populating them with Han people. Confronted with severe instability and the great cost of fighting secessionist movements, several Asian countries (the Philippines, Indonesia, Sri Lanka) have now become more willing to consider devolving power to minorities that are seeking to secede from the state through the option of autonomy.

Despite this change in attitude, most Asian countries do not accept that the international community has responsibility for protecting minorities. China, for example, labels Western support for Tibet as neocolonialism. International support for minority groups, especially those that seek to secede from the state, are viewed by Asian governments as not only interfering in internal affairs but also threatening their national unity, territorial integrity, and political stability. Asian countries, especially those in Southeast Asia, have by and large stayed out of conflicts between minority groups and the state in neighboring countries. When compelled to, they have supported the state rather than the minority groups, even though they may share religious and ethnic affiliations with them. This has been less the case in South Asia, however, where Pakistan continues to support Kashmiri secessionist movements and India at one point was sympathetic to the cause of the Tamil Tigers fighting for an independent state in Sri Lanka.

Although most Asian countries do not accept a blanket mediation role for the international community in minority conflicts, several have accepted outside involvement when they think it supports their cause and is politically useful. The Philippines accepted interlocutors from the Middle East, Indonesia, and Malaysia. Sri Lanka has accepted Norwegian mediators. India, China, and Burma, by contrast, have refused to accept any international involvement. Except in a case like East Timor, where the Indonesian annexation was not recognized by the international community, international intervention is almost universally rejected in Asia. NATO's intervention in the former Yugoslavia and the creation of several new states are viewed as dangerous precedents. Although certain Asian governments are now more willing to consider the autonomy option, nearly all deny any right to further national self-determination and independence. That right is deemed to have been exhausted by decolonization. Although India is sympathetic to the plight of the Sri Lankan Tamils, it has not supported the demand for a separate Tamil state.

There is a common understanding that acceding to secessionist demands would unravel the political map of Asia, make for acute internal turmoil, and set back the Asian states several years or even decades, as in Indonesia. Because of the grave concern that Indonesia may splinter further and undermine regional stability, there is no support in Asia or in the West for self-determination in Aceh or West Papua. Apart from this, there is still no common understanding of the rights of minority communities and the role of the international community in protecting such rights.

The clash of norms is rooted in large part in the different stages of nation and state consolidation and in the development of viable political systems. As these are long-drawn-out processes and most Asian countries are still in an early stage with distinct possibilities of reversal in certain cases, the issues of human rights, minority rights, self-determination, the responsibility of the international community, and the consequent tension over the principle of noninterference in domestic affairs will linger for some time to come. Certainly the clash over the principle of noninterference is an important issue that has generated tension, yet it has not unduly disrupted relations among the region's states. Its significance, therefore, should not be exaggerated. The tension over principles and norms is also rooted in the international distribution of power that favors the United States and more generally the West.

Major Power Relations: Tension Between Dominant, Rising, and Declining Powers

Nearly every major power—China, Japan, Russia, and India—except the United States is dissatisfied with the present distribution of power, and its status and role in the Asian international system. As observed earlier, the United States has emerged as the lone superpower and the dominant power in Asia. Initial anticipation by certain policymakers and academics (Waltz 1993; Layne 1993) that the world would soon (in one or two decades) become multipolar has not been borne out. Instead the military and technological might of the United States and the decade-long growth of the American economy, combined with the continuing stagnation in Japan and the slow growth of the Asian economies in the wake of the 1997 crisis, highlight the comprehensiveness of American dominance and suggest its persistence. The conventional wisdom now is that the American dominance is likely to endure for another two or three decades (Mastanduno 1997, 1999; Ikenberry 1999). According to Lee Kuan Yew, Singapore's former prime minister and now senior minister, American dominance is likely to last for another fifty years.[3]

Though America's preponderant power is widely acknowledged and the United States plays a critical role in almost every major Asian conflict (Taiwan, Korea, Kashmir), such preponderance and role have not translated into authority. The acknowledgment from key players in the system that is necessary to translate power into authority and legitimate American hegemony has not been forthcoming, at least not without reservation. Washington has yet to forge a collective will that harmonizes American national interest with the still-elusive larger public interest. Although the United States provides invaluable public goods, American actions like those over Taiwan in 1996 and the financial crisis in 1997, and more recently in the global war against terrorism, are frequently perceived as serving narrow American interests. Further, although the U.S. security role is indispensable, Washington cannot manage Asian security affairs without the cooperation of the other Asian powers. The United States has not been able to gain acknowledgment of the rules of the game it advocates, for example in the resolution of the Taiwan and Korean disputes, and of its alliance system as the primary pillar of regional security. A legitimacy deficit exists that is difficult to bridge. American dominance in Asia is thus largely instrumental with a coercive edge.

Dissatisfaction with American dominance is most profound in China, the fast-rising Asian power, which anticipated that the world would soon become multipolar. Growing at an average of 8 percent since 1979, the Chinese economy, though still far behind the United States and Japan and confronting major challenges, has performed well. In 2000 it accounted for 3 percent of the world economy when measured in American dollars and 11 percent on the basis of purchasing power parity. Though defense modernization was listed as the last of the four modernizations in 1979, the Chinese defense buildup accelerated after 1989. Beijing has been steadily developing its nuclear, missile, and conventional military capabilities.[4] The PRC appears to have the greatest potential to rival American

---

[3]Although the United States has many strengths, including the capacity to rebound quickly, such long-term projections should be taken cautiously. It is useful here to recall the projections in the 1980s that the United States was in irreversible decline and would be overtaken by Japan in the early twenty-first century.

[4]On China's defense modernization, see Godwin (2001).

supremacy in Asia,[5] but it is still far from being able to mount a serious challenge. Nevertheless, the PRC opposes American hegemony because of the perceived negative consequences for its security, and its "rightful" status and role in Asia and the world.

The rise of China, in turn, is of concern to the United States, which is keen to preserve its primacy in the region, and also to the other Asian powers— particularly Japan and India, both of which tend to have a more benign view of American dominance than Chinese ascendance. Beijing too suffers a legitimacy deficit that flows from its past behavior especially in the early phase of the Cold War, and its readiness to use force in resolving disputes with other Asian states, as well as from the widespread apprehension in Asia as to how a rising China will use its power. Japan, India, and Russia all aspire to greater status and roles than are currently available, and each also suffers a legitimacy deficit. Japan is distrusted by the victims of its past wars of imperial ambition; the regional ambitions of preponderant India are a cause of apprehension among several of its immediate neighbors; and Russia lacks credibility in the region. The apprehensions among the major powers, their competing aspirations, and their inability to translate power into authority underscore the lack of agreement over an acceptable status quo in Asia, which in turn constrains the development of the rules for the management of Asian security affairs.

The United States: Preserving Primacy

Though it is not a publicly stated policy, it is evident from leaked documents and from practice that Washington's post–Cold War goal is to preserve American primacy and "prevent the rise of a new rival." According to a leaked Pentagon document, which has since been disavowed by the establishment, the preservation of American primacy entails preventing "any hostile power from dominating a region whose resources would, under consolidated control, be sufficient to generate global power. . . . [The American] strategy must now refocus on precluding the emergence of any potential global competitor" (quoted in Posen and Ross 1996–97, and Mastanduno 1997). In practice this goal has been pursued in several ways: maintaining a strong economy and technological lead with due regard to the relative gains of likely competitors; widening the gap in military capabilities with emphasis on high-technology systems, including the development of national and theater missile defense capabilities; widening the power differential by binding key states (Germany, Japan) in a U.S.-centered alliance network; reassuring and accommodating the interests of the other second-tier powers to neu-

---

[5]Here again it is not certain that China will realize its full potential. Serious internal turmoil— like the Cultural Revolution—could set China back several years, if not decades.

tralize their need for the development of sophisticated capabilities and socializing them into the U.S.-centered order; legitimating American dominance by providing security and economic public goods; and exercising power, when feasible, through friendly multilateral institutions. Although nearly every Asian power seeks cordial relations with the United States, the reaction to American dominance and the status quo varies from country to country: stagnating Japan is the most supportive; ascending China has serious misgivings; a weak Russia is vacillating; an uncertain India is warming to but still cautious of the United States.

Japan: U.S. Ally in Identity Crisis

Despite bilateral economic frictions (especially in the 1980s) and a brief exploration of alternatives to increase its policy autonomy in the early 1990s, Japan continues to view the security treaty with the United States as the cornerstone of its security policy. The growing concern with a rising China that is increasingly perceived negatively in Japan—as well as North Korea's nuclear and missile development—has renewed emphasis on the U.S.-Japan security treaty (*Japan Defense White Paper* 2001). Tokyo is eager to ensure continued American engagement in Asia. Thus it reaffirmed the security treaty with the United States in 1996 and revised the guidelines for defense cooperation in 1997 so that Japan could make a more significant contribution to regional peace and security in the surrounding seas. Tokyo's military role expansion in the context of the U.S.-Japan security treaty is also related to Japan's growing desire to become a normal country.

Post–World War II pacifism still runs strong in Japanese society, but the associated inhibitions are gradually dissipating, especially among the political leaders (Berger 2000; Yamaguchi 2000). The leadership would not only like Japan to become a normal country; it also seeks an international status befitting the world's second-largest economy. There is considerable frustration in Japan that Tokyo is not getting the international recognition and respect it deserves. Such frustration comes at a time when Japan is no longer the rising star that "can be number one" and amidst rising concern that it may have to play second fiddle to China. The international lack of respect is due in part to the self-imposed limitation that prevents Japan from playing a more active security role and the historical animosities (arising from its past imperial behavior, especially in Northeast Asia but also in Southeast Asia) that still dog Japan. Equally important is the perception in the region that Japan is a junior partner of the United States and cannot play an independent role. Despite slogans like global partnership and civilian power, and despite its massive ODA disbursement, Japan has not been able to overcome this image. There is an implicit tension between pacifism, a subordinate relationship with the United States, a stagnating economy, and the desire for major-power status. Thus certain Americans who now hold key positions in the Bush administration have projected the U.S.-U.K. relationship as a possible model for the evolution of the U.S.-Japan relationship (Armitage and Nye 2000). Giving substance to Japan's move to become a normal country and its aspiration for a befitting international status are major challenges for both Japan and the international community.

China: Rejection of American Hegemony

The Chinese reaction to American dominance has undergone change. Initially Beijing sought to develop a common understanding and framework with the United States in the anticipation that American dominance would be short-lived and its own power and influence would increase. But as the realization that the world would not soon become multipolar sank in and China began to appreciate the negative consequences of American dominance for its interests, Beijing, which views itself as the principal Asian pole, became critical of American hegemony. Its concerns are twofold. One is the perceived threat to its goals of preserving internal stability, unifying Taiwan with the PRC, and maintaining an independent strategic capability that allows it to deter the United States, Russia, and other Asian powers. In the Chinese view, all these goals are undermined by American interference in Chinese domestic affairs (in the guise of protecting human and minority rights and fostering democratic political change), its support for Taiwan, and its development of the national and theater missile defense systems that have the potential to diminish the value of Beijing's relatively small strategic asset.

The second concern relates to the impact of American hegemony on China's assuming its "rightful" position in Asia and the world. This concern has several strands. First, American dominance and its alliance network, it is argued, create two groups of states—allied states and nonallied states. As China is a nonallied state and desires to maintain its political and strategic independence, it will remain an outsider in a U.S.-dominated framework. It may also become a target of containment of the American alliance network. Second, the U.S. network of alliances, especially the U.S.-Japan alliance, dramatically increases the power differential and widens the gap, making it even more difficult for China to catch up with the United States. Third, the dominant position of the United States reduces the impact of China's growing power and limits its strategic flexibility while enhancing that of the lesser Asian powers. And fourth, to counterbalance the United States, China must gain the support of Russia and the other Asian powers (Japan, India) and in the process enhance their own international status and role—which does not accord with China's desire to be the premier Asian power.

An ascending China resents American dominance. Its initial efforts to cooperate with the United States were designed to address its security concerns and economic interests, as well as to gain prestige and influence by cooperating with the world's premier power. Beijing sought to forge a strategic partnership with the United States and become a comanager of Asian security. Although the United States still is interested in cooperating with China, it will not give way on key issues like Taiwan and missile defense. And Washington, especially the new Bush administration, does not accept a pecking order in Asia that puts China ahead of Japan. The clash of normative and security interests and conflict of status aspirations make the U.S.-China relationship prone to frequent tension.

Beijing still seeks cordial relations with Washington. The United States is a key market and primary source of capital and technology, and can most directly affect Beijing's security concerns as well as it aspirations for status and influence. Beijing's effort to improve relations with Washington was evident after the September 11 terrorist attack on the United States. Concurrent with the effort to forge cordial relations with the United States, Beijing has stepped up its effort to balance American influence through the development of its own strategic capabilities, a strategic partnership with Russia, and cordial political relations and strong economic relations with France, ASEAN, the European Union, the United Kingdom, Japan, and the Republic of Korea.

In strategic terms, the "cooperative strategic partnership" with Russia is the most significant. Russia has become a principal source of military technology and equipment. And, through a series of agreements beginning in 1996, China and Russia seek to coordinate their action on certain issues like missile defense, the expansion and reinvigoration of the American alliance system in Europe and Asia, and preventing external interference in domestic conflicts. This effort has since been codified in the Treaty of Good Neighborliness, Friendship, and Cooperation signed in July 2000. Beijing has also emphasized multilateral institutions at the subregional, regional, and global levels—especially those in which it has a decisive say, like the UN Security Council—as a means to restrain American unilateralism and enhance its own influence. For the same reasons it has become supportive of the ASEAN Regional Forum, although it is reluctant to grant much authority to that Forum in the conflict prevention role.

China is also improving its relations with Japan and India. Though China's perception of Japan is complex and with a strong historical dimension, it appears that Beijing may be changing its take on Japan, with a view to distancing that country from the United States and diminishing American predominance in Asia. This change may be premised on two perceptions—that a strategically independent Japan is not necessarily a threat to China and that Japan will inevitably become a normal country. Hence it is in China's interest to facilitate these developments rather than push Japan further into the embrace of the United States. Sino-Indian relations are complex as well, with many twists and turns. Though strategic perceptions have not significantly altered, the two countries appear to be turning toward dialogue in managing their bilateral relations. In its interaction with Asian states, ascending China has sought to overcome its legitimacy deficit by trying to allay the fears of fellow Asian states, emphasizing that it is a responsible major power that makes positive contributions to regional economic and security well-being. The "China threat," it claims, is a bogey constructed by the United States to tar its image. The reaction in Asia has been mixed. In the economic arena China is viewed both as an opportunity and a competitor. In the security arena, it is no longer viewed as a revolutionary state or an unmitigated threat. But apprehensions still abound.

Russia: In Search of a New Relationship and Position

Russia's concerns stem from its loss of superpower status and its weakness as a state and power. Though its immediate security interests are not affected by American hegemony, NATO's eastward expansion is considered by Russia to be a political affront. Like Beijing, Moscow claims the American alliance network makes Russia an outsider, compelling it to be a taker rather than a maker of rules. The United States and the Western European countries did take a series of measures (partnership for peace, invitation to the G7 meeting, and economic assistance, among others) to assuage Russian security concerns and provide opportunities for Moscow to partly recover lost prestige. Over time, with its descent into political and economic chaos, Russia ceased to be a major factor in the calculus of the NATO countries. The continued expansion of NATO under the Clinton administration and the Bush administration's plan to press ahead with the development of the national missile defense system, even if it requires the abrogation of the ABM Treaty, were indications that Washington did not view Moscow as a key player even in the strategic arena where Russia still had substantial capability.

Under President Vladimir Putin, who succeeded Boris Yeltsin, Russia has regained some stability and international prestige. Keen to stake out a respectable place for itself, Moscow is attempting to forge closer relationships with all major powers, including and especially the United States. In the immediate aftermath of the September 2001 terrorist attack, Putin was the first foreign leader to express sympathy and support for the United States. Substantial differences still remain over the ABM Treaty and other issues like Chechnya, but the two countries appear to be moving toward forging a new relationship although the basis for that relationship remains unclear. However, it is clear that although Russia will differ with the United States on certain issues and may cooperate with countries like China on issues of common concern, it is unlikely to become party to any anti-American coalition. With its Eurocentric focus in the immediate post–Cold War era, a weak Russia hardly figured in the post–Cold War security order in Asia. Now, spurned by Europe, Moscow is reemphasizing its identity as a Eurasian power with interests in Europe and Asia. Preferring a multipolar world, Russia is seeking to cooperate with China, reinvigorate its relations with India, and reach an understanding with Japan; it emphasizes multilateral institutions like the UN, the ARF, and the SCO in the management of security affairs; and it seeks to become involved in the management of regional conflicts like that in the Korean peninsula and in South Asia.

India: Warming to the United States?

India's reaction to American dominance, like China's, is driven by security and economic considerations and status aspiration. The United States is not perceived as a security threat by New Delhi. Its concerns relate to Washington's attempt through international regimes and unilateral sanctions to deny India the opportunity to develop the capabilities necessary to defend its security interests; the concerns also relate to the features of U.S. cooperation with China and Pakistan during the Cold War and with China in the post–Cold War era that are perceived as having a detrimental effect on India's security. In the context of major-power relations, New Delhi's security concerns relate more directly to China because of the border conflict with that country, Beijing's burgeoning strategic capabilities, and its military-technological support for Islamabad, especially in the development of nuclear and missile capability. Chinese intention, it is believed, is to keep India down and prevent it from playing a larger regional role. At this level India's primary concern is to develop the capacity to secure its interests and maintain strategic autonomy.

In the interstice between the ranks of middle and great powers, India with its large size and population, relatively advanced scientific and technological know-how, a stable political system, and an economy that has been growing at an average of 5 to 6 percent since 1991 aspires to be counted in the rank of powers just below the United States. As the United States did not support its concerns and aspirations during much of the Cold War and has emphasized cooperation with China at the expense of India in the post–Cold War era, New Delhi continues to be wary of Washington. The joint Clinton-Jiang condemnation of Indian nuclear tests was particularly galling to New Delhi. Like China, India appears determined to secure its "rightful" place in the region and the world. In this connection, China is the stimulus and model for India (Nayar 1999). The 1998 nuclear tests and the determination not to give up the nuclear and missile option, despite heavy costs, are illustrative of this quest.

Despite the wariness, with its limited economic and strategic alternatives India has become more positively disposed toward the United States and has engaged in selective cooperation with Washington. Beginning in the final years of the Clinton administration, Washington too has begun to view India—a country that has similar political values, does not pose a threat to the United States, and is gradually becoming an important market and a source of skilled personnel—more positively. The new Bush administration appears to want to broaden cooperation with India to include the strategic arena. As there are still certain fundamental issues to be overcome (including India's sensitivity to its independence and the degree to which the United States will accommodate India's concerns and aspirations), the depth and durability of the U.S.-India engagement remain to be seen. The ongoing American war on international terrorism has the potential to create tension in the bilateral relationship. While New Delhi was quick to sign on to the American-led international coalition, it is ambivalent and in some ways disenchanted with the emerging close U.S.-Pakistan relationship. While Washington views Pakistan as a crucial frontline state in the war on terrorism, New Delhi views that country as the promoter of terrorism in India. Thus far this has not led to a serious breach in bilateral relations, with Washington and New Delhi trying their utmost to harmonize the tension between immediate security concerns and long-term strategic considerations. After a short period of uncertainty and apprehension, U.S.-India political and security ties have expanded considerably to include regular cabinet-level dialogue, high level military exchanges, sale of military equipment, joint military exercises, and task sharing in the Indian Ocean and in combating nuclear and missile proliferation. As with the other major powers, there are multiple dynamics at work in India's relations with the United States. In all likelihood this relationship will grow stonger, but with some areas of differences. In the long run, India, like China, would like to see a multipolar world in which order is managed by more than one power and in which it is a key player. New Delhi and Beijing have resumed their dialogue to manage their bilateral problems. New Delhi's relations with Moscow are still good—although they pale in comparison with the earlier Soviet-Indian strategic relationship—and there also appears to be growing (though still limited) convergence in Indian and Japanese strategic perceptions (Seki 2000).

Managing Competing Identities and Role Quests

From the foregoing discussion it is evident that a key problem in the still-evolving post–Cold War security order in Asia is the dissatisfaction over the current status quo and the management of competing identity and role quests. For Washington, the challenge is how to forge a collective will that accommodates the ideas and interests of the Asian powers while maintaining its own dominance and constructing an order underpinned by its values. For the Asian powers, the challenge is how to maintain amicable relations with the world's premier power while seeking to revise the status quo in their favor. The problem is not just between the United States and the Asian powers but also among Asian countries themselves.

China, Japan, and India compete for a higher standing in the pecking order, each trying to frustrate the aspirations of the others. The challenge for all countries is how to arrive at a status quo that is tolerable, if not fully acceptable, and how to manage transitions of power that will still transpire in the region (although more gradually than anticipated in the heyday of the Asian miracle economies). Meanwhile the competing aspirations are likely to result in the acquisition of sophisticated military capabilities to protect their security interests and strategic autonomy.

The Persistence of Acute Conflicts

A final challenge to the construction of regional security order is the persistence of the acute identity conflicts across the Taiwan Strait, in the Korean peninsula, and over Kashmir, all of which involve major powers directly or indirectly. As the issues relating to these conflicts have been discussed earlier in the Introduction and in the other sections of this chapter, discussion here will be limited to highlighting the challenges they pose for the development of regional security order, and the progress that can be made if they are settled. Because they affect the vital interests of the parties to the conflicts and because of the central role of force in their management, these three conflicts are a major obstacle to the development of understanding among the major powers and to the limitation and control of force in Asia. The centrality of the Taiwan conflict to China and its belief that the United States is the primary hurdle to a settlement on its terms underscores, in substantial measure, Beijing's negative reaction to American hegemony, the U.S. alliance system, and Washington's development of the TMD system. Beijing's threat of force and use of coercion to intimidate Taipei and influence political developments in Taiwan are viewed negatively by Washington. The conflict is a key issue in U.S.-China relations. The Korean conflict is much less significant as an issue in major power relations, although even here a settlement could boost major power understanding. The Indo-Pakistani conflict and Chinese strategic support for Pakistan are a major stumbling block in Sino-Indian relations. By removing the major contention between India and Pakistan, a settlement of the Kashmir issue will reduce Pakistan's dependence on China and Chinese influence in South Asia. This may pave the way for more cordial Sino-Indian relations. In fact China has begun to separate its relations with Pakistan from those with India, and an effort is being made by both countries to base their bilateral relations on a more stable understanding. The settlement of the Kashmir conflict will give a boost to this effort and also increase stability in South Asia. Although not comparable to the three acute conflicts, settlement of the Northern territories dispute will give a major boost to Russo-Japanese understanding. The point here is not that the settlement of these conflicts will end geo-

political rivalry among the powers, only that it will remove key issues of contention, facilitate more orderly interaction, and reduce the salience of force.

The threat of force is a key instrument of Chinese and American policy on
Taiwan, of North Korean, South Korean, and American policy in the stand-off in
the Korean peninsula, and of the Pakistani and Indian policy on the Kashmir
conflict. The centrality of force in these conflicts has contributed to the spread of
nuclear and missile capabilities in Asia and has made the control and regulation
of force virtually impossible. The settlement of these conflicts will go a long way
toward reducing the salience of force in the international politics of Asia. Combined with the increased cost of using force, settlement will make it more possible to limit and regulate the role of national force and also make collective management of force more possible. Although a final settlement of these conflicts appear unlikely in the immediate to medium term, there are tentative signs that a
measure of understanding is developing between and among the affected parties
on the rules of the game to manage these three conflicts and reduce the prospects
for war. Such understanding on the Taiwan conflict is due in part to the lessons
of the 1996 crisis, the clear signaling and articulation of American resolve to defend Taiwan against aggression, and Washington's firm communication to Taipei
that it will not support an independent Taiwan. The urgency displayed by the
PRC in the 1990s to unify Taiwan with the mainland has dissipated though not
disappeared. Although still apprehensive of Taiwan President Chen Shui-bian
and his Democratic People's Party, Beijing, with limited options, appears to have
concluded that for now Taipei will not declare independence and that closer economic relations will pave the way for political reconciliation on its terms.

On the Korean peninsula, the Sunshine policy of Kim Dae Jung gave a boost
to North-South relations and improved the prospects for settlement of the Korean conflict. Slow and grudging reciprocity on the part of Kim Jong Il, the decision of the new Bush administration to halt the dialogue begun by the Clinton
administration and subsequently to alter the terms of dialogue, the weakening of
the political position of lame-duck president Kim Dae Jung, and the growing opposition to the Sunshine policy in South Korea have all negated the earlier optimism. Nevertheless, all parties to the conflict now implicitly accept that the conflict cannot be settled by force. Although it may be premature to draw a similar
conclusion, it appears that an understanding may be in the making in the case of
the Kashmir conflict as well. The acquisition of nuclear capability by India and
Pakistan and the fear of escalation to the nuclear level have raised the threshold
for conventional war between the two countries. Nevertheless, assuming that India would be deterred from engaging in a conventional war, Pakistan actively
supported cross-border terrorism by the Islamic militant movement, and Pakistan's regular troops infiltrated into Indian Kashmir, leading to the Kargil conflict

in 1999. The massive Indian mobilization in response to the December 13, 2001, terrorist attack and New Delhi's readiness to engage in a limited war revealed the shortcomings of this strategy. The negative reaction of the international community to the October and December 2001 terrorist attacks on India, Pakistan's many internal problems, and the heavy cost it has incurred from the military struggle with the much larger India may be convincing Islamabad that the solution to the Kashmir problem does not lie in supporting militant movements or in the battlefield. Though it is far too early to arrive at this conclusion, if the conclusion turns out to be correct, then a major turn may be in the offing, with India demonstrating a greater willingness to discuss the Kashmir issue.

Discussion in this chapter has highlighted the major challenges confronting the construction of security order in Asia. However, as observed in the Introduction, Asia is not devoid of security order. Much of the international political interaction in Asia is rule-governed. Despite periodic crisis, there has been no full-scale war. Stability and predictability have characterized Asia for over two decades. International trade, investment, and production have flourished; and Asian countries have prospered. At the same time the dissatisfaction with the present status quo arising from competing identities and aspirations of the major powers, the clash of norms, the lack of agreement over the specific content of the elementary goals of order, and the persistence of acute conflicts inhibit further development of an integrated security order. They account for the existence of multiple pathways and the tensions among them. A central issue here is the tension between the alliance system that enhances American dominance in Asia, the balance-of-power and concert pathways that would increase the influence of the second-tier powers and require the dismantling or at least weakening of the American alliances in the region, and the multilateral pathways that would require a reduction in the salience of brute power and a corresponding increase in the importance of principles and norms. Although it is possible to accommodate the differences on the margins, their integration in a substantive way would require far-reaching changes that are not yet on the horizon. The chapters in Part II of this volume investigate the salience of the different pathways in managing security affairs in Asia and how they complement or compete with each other. Before that, the next chapter investigates the practice of sovereignty in Asia and its implications for regional security order.

Works Cited

Alagappa, Muthiah. 2001. "Introduction: Presidential Election, Democratization, and Cross-Strait Relations." In Muthiah Alagappa, ed., *Taiwan's Presidential Politics: Democratization and Cross-Strait Relations in the Twenty-first Century.* Armonk, N.Y.: M. E. Sharpe.

Annan, Kofi. 2000. "Secretary-General Statement to General Assembly" on the Millennium Report. United Nations website, April 3. http://www.un.org/millennium/sg/report/state.htm.

Armitage, Richard, and Joseph S. Nye. 2000. *The United States and Japan: Advancing Toward a Mature Partnership*. INSS Special Report. Washington, D.C.: National Defense University.

Berger, Thomas U. 2000. "The Death of Japanese Pacifism? What Has Changed (and Not Changed) in the Post–Cold War Era." In *Changing Japanese Attitudes Towards National Security: The End of Pacifism?* Washington, D.C.: Special Report of the Woodrow Wilson Center Asia Program.

Bush, George. 1990. "The U.N.: World Parliament of Peace." Address to UN General Assembly, New York, Oct. 1.

Clinton, William Jefferson. 1993a. "Confronting the Challenge of a Broader World." Address to UN General Assembly, New York, Sept. 27.

———. 1993b. "Building a New Pacific Community." Address to students and faculty at Waseda University, Tokyo, July 7.

———. 1993c. "The APEC Role in Creating Jobs, Opportunities, and Security." Address to the APEC Host Committee, Seattle, Nov. 19.

———. 1993d. "The First APEC Leaders Meeting." Address to APEC leaders in Blake Island, Washington, Nov. 20.

Department of Defense. 2001. *Quadrennial Defense Review Report*. Washington, D.C.: Pentagon.

Finkelstein, David M. 2000. *China Reconsiders Its National Security: The Great Peace and Development Debate of 1999*. Alexandria, Va.: CNA Corporation.

———, and Michael McDevitt. 1999. "Competition and Consensus: China's 'New Security Concept' and the United States Security Strategy for the East Asia-Pacific Region." Honolulu: Pacific Forum CSIS, PacNet 1.

Godwin, Paul H. B. 2001. *China's Defense Modernization: Aspirations and Capabilities*. Alexandria, Va.: Project Asia Monograph.

Goldstein, Avery. 2001. "September 11, the Shanghai Summit, and the Shift in U.S. China Policy," Nov. 9. Foreign Policy Research Institute: E Notes.

Hernandez, Carolina G. 1998. "Toward Re-Examining the Non-Intervention Principle in ASEAN Political Cooperation." *Indonesian Quarterly* 26(3): 164–70.

Ikenberry, John G. 1999. "Liberal Hegemony and the Future of American Postwar Order." In T. V. Paul and John A. Hall, eds., *International Order and the Future of World Politics*. Cambridge: Cambridge University Press.

Information Office of the State Council of the PRC. 1998. *China's National Defense in 1998*. Beijing.

———. 2000. *China's National Defense in 2000*. Beijing.

Japan Defense White Paper. 2001.

Krasner, Stephen D. 1999. *Sovereignty: Organized Hypocrisy*. Princeton: Princeton University Press.

Layne, Christopher. 1993. "The Unipolar Illusion: Why New Great Powers Will Rise." *International Security* 17(4): 5–51.

Lord, Winston. 1995. "Building a Pacific Community." Statement before the Commonwealth Club, San Francisco, Jan. 12.

Lyons, Gene M., and Michael Mastanduno. 1995. "State Sovereignty and International Intervention: Reflections on the Present and Prospects for the Future." In Gene M. Lyons and Michael Mastanduno, eds., *Beyond Westphalia: State Sovereignty and International Intervention*. Baltimore: Johns Hopkins University Press.

Mastanduno, Michael. 1997. "Preserving the Unipolar Moment: Realist Theories and the U.S. Grand Strategy After the Cold War." *International Security* 21(4): 49–88.

———. 1999. "A Realist View: Three Images of the Coming International Order." In T. V. Paul and John A. Hall, eds., *International Order and the Future of World Politics*. Cambridge: Cambridge University Press.

Nayar, Baldev Raj. 1999. "India as a Limited Challenger." In T. V. Paul and John A. Hall, eds., *International Order and the Future of World Politics*. Cambridge: Cambridge University Press.

Office of International Security Affairs. 1995. *East Asia Strategy Report*. Washington, D.C.: Department of Defense.

———. 1998. *The United States Security Strategy for the East Asia-Pacific Region*. Washington, D.C.: Department of Defense.

Posen, Barry, and Robert Ross. 1996–97. "Competing Visions for US Grand Strategy." *International Security* 21(3): 5–53.

Ross, Robert. 2001. "The Stability of Deterrence in the Taiwan Strait." *The National Interest* (Fall). Washington, D.C.

Roy, Denny. 2000. "Tension in the Taiwan Strait." *Survival* 42(1): 76–96.

Seki, Tomoda. 2000. "A Japan-India Front," *Far Eastern Economic Review*, May 25.

SIIA (Singapore Institute of International Affairs). 2001. *Sovereignty and Intervention*. Special Report. Singapore: SIIA.

Symonds, Peter. 2001. "China Reacts Sharply Against US Proposal for Asia Security Forum." *World Socialist Web Site*. Aug. 3. http://www.org/articles/2001/aug2001/paci-a03.shtml.

UN Press Release. 2000. *Secretary-General, Addressing Council Summit on International Peace, Security, Stresses Council Responsibility for Adequate Support of Peacekeepers*. Press Release SG/SM/7535, United Nations website, September 7. http://www.un.org/News/Press/docs/2000/20000907.sgsm7535.doc.html.

Waltz, Kenneth N. 1993. "The Emerging Structure of International Politics." *International Security* 18(2): 45–73.

The White House. 1996. *A National Security Strategy of Engagement and Enlargement*. Washington D.C.

Yamaguchi, Noboru. 2000. "How and Why Are Japanese Attitudes Toward National Security Changing?" In *Changing Japanese Attitudes Towards National Security: The End of Pacifism?* Washington, D.C.: Special Report of the Woodrow Wilson Center Asia Program.

CHAPTER THREE

Sovereignty

Dominance of the Westphalian Concept and Implications for Regional Security

CHUNG-IN MOON

CHAESUNG CHUN

Two major trends have characterized a profound transformation in Asia since the late 1980s, portending a new horizon of peace and security. The first trend has been associated with the overall reconfiguration of the Asian regional system from the Cold War's bipolar confrontation to unipolar American dominance in the post–Cold War era. Sole American leadership, it was hoped, would bring about peace and stability by reducing strategic uncertainty in the region (Kapstein and Mastanduno 1999). The second trend is the liberal anticipation that growing interdependence in the region and dense economic, social, and cultural networks will eventually demolish artificial walls of national borders, bringing countries in the region closer and ultimately leading to a community of security through multilateral security cooperation. Such hopes have become all the more plausible because countries in the region have increasingly embraced the liberal market system and democratic political values (Russet 1993; Adler and Barnett 1998). The logic of commercial liberalism and democratic peace has bred public anticipation of a liberal transition.

In reality, however, neither hegemonic stability under U.S. leadership nor a liberal transition have materialized. Sources of strategic instability abound throughout the region. The "China threat" thesis is no longer fictional. China's economic dynamism, technological progress, and expanding military potential now pose a new challenge to the United States and Japan. Catching up with the United States has become all the more realistic and appealing to China. The Korean peninsula is another trouble spot. Despite the end of the Cold War, the Korean conflict does not show any signs of termination. And Japan's transformation into a normal state through the amendment of the peace constitution could also complicate the region's strategic outlook. Moreover, the Asian region is beset by local and limited conflicts ranging from the protracted friction in Kashmir and Sri Lanka to territorial skirmishes and ethnic disputes in Southeast Asia. Proliferation of weapons of mass destruction further clouds the future of the region's strategic stability (Friedberg 1993–94; Bracken 1999).

The end of the Cold War has not therefore greatly improved the prospects for peace and security in the region. While old conflicts still remain intact, lifting off the Cold War overlay has unveiled new strategic uncertainty. Indeed, stable peace in Asia might well prove elusive as long as the traditional concept of sovereignty remains the basic organizing principle of international and regional politics. Sovereignty has been traditionally defined in terms of internal supreme authority and immunity from external influence. Central to these elements of the Westphalian notion of sovereignty is the preservation of territorial and political integrity. Countries strive to achieve these goals of sovereignty through the traditional means of coercive power, military deterrence, and alliance. Such efforts, however, have often undercut regional security by heightening the potential for major conflict. Proliferation of interstate conflicts can in turn spur the formation of an instrumental regional order in which national power and interests become the primary movers, whereas international regimes and law serve merely as secondary instruments for ensuring peace and stability. Realizing a durable and stable peace under this type of regional order seems especially difficult, however, because of its inherent structural features such as the primacy of the state, anarchic interactions among regional actors, and perpetual uncertainty. Naked pursuit of Westphalian sovereignty, persistent and pervasive interstate conflict potential, an instrumental regional security order—all epitomize the essence of Asian security today.

Against this backdrop, here we investigate the links between sovereignty and security order in Asia. Our findings show that waves of globalization and the rise of the post–Cold War order have not yet eroded practices of the traditional notion of Westphalian sovereignty in Asia. It is still alive and well, shaping and reshaping the terrain of regional peace and security. The traditional notion of sovereignty and the instrumental regional security order associated with it might be effective in ensuring an unstable peace through temporary strategic stability based on power, deterrence, and alliance. But it cannot guarantee permanent, durable, and stable peace in the region. In order to win a stable peace, two major prerequisites must be satisfied. First, the Westphalian concept of sovereignty must be replaced by a notion of sovereignty in which liberal norms, principles, and rules prevail. Second, predominance of an instrumental regional security order must be reconsidered in light of the growing relevance of a normative-contractual and solidarity order that seeks the resolution of conflict through mutual trust, obligation, and multilateral security cooperation. Likewise, the conception of sovereignty can profoundly influence the evolutionary path of security order by affecting patterns of conflict and cooperation in the region.

Some Analytical Considerations

What is sovereignty? In a generic sense, sovereignty can be defined as "supremacy and absolute authority" (Schrijver 2000: 70). The specific meaning of sovereignty depends on the context. Nevertheless, three dimensions (domestic, external, and domestic/external linkage) constitute the core domain. First is the internal dimension. Internally, sovereignty can be defined as "an ultimate right of command in society" (De Jouvenel 1993: 29). In other words: "The government of a state is considered the ultimate authority within its borders and jurisdiction" (Schrijver 2000: 70). The authority and effective control of a government within a state are the essence of domestic sovereignty (Krasner 1999: 11–12). Exercise of public authority, enactment of legislature, a monopoly over legitimate use of force, collecting taxes, and maintenance of law and order and other functions of the state constitute critical elements of domestic sovereignty. These functions become enforceable so long as a state remains independent and autonomous. Thus independence and ultimate authority in a territory and jurisdiction are the defining features of domestic sovereignty.

Second is the external dimension based on the principle of sovereign equality—the equivalent of "juridical sovereignty" (Jackson 1993) or "international legal sovereignty" (Krasner 1999: 14–20). External sovereignty can then be defined as follows: "A State is not subject to the legal power of another state or of any higher authority, and stands in principle on an equal footing with other states" (Schrijver 2000: 71). It is under this notion of international legal sovereignty that states have enjoyed the full legal benefits associated with statehood such as juridical equality, diplomatic privileges, and membership in international organizations (Krasner 1999: 14–20). According to the international legal tradition, countries are not supposed to surrender elements of their sovereignty without their explicit prior consent. Article 2 of the UN Charter further strengthens the position of international legal sovereignty by stipulating the principle of sovereign equality as one of the most important norms in conducting international affairs. In today's world where the logic of power politics and the dynamics of growing interdependence shape terms of interstate engagement, however, the principle of external sovereignty has become increasingly questionable.

Finally, the issue of sovereignty can be approached from the domestic/external linkage perspective. Despite various claims regarding the inviolability of the principle of independence and absolute authority embedded in domestic sovereignty—as well as the inviolability of the principle of juridical equality constituting external sovereignty—they are more often than not violated in practice. The notion of Westphalian sovereignty as immunity from external interference that a state enjoys in its domestic structure of authority (Krasner 1999: 20–23) may be more fictional than real for most countries. All countries are not equal before international law. Some countries are more equal than others, depending on power and influence. Thus the traditional principle of noninterference may be legally binding but is less likely to be honored in the world of real politics. This realist account of sovereignty constitutes the third important dimension of sovereignty, which might also be labeled "empirical sovereignty" (Jackson 1993).

On the basis of internal supreme authority, external juridical equality, and immunity from external influence, sovereignty is justified in order to realize its distinct objectives. The most critical goal must be the preservation of territorial integrity simply because sovereignty cannot exist without securing its own territorial boundary (Zacher 2001). Controlling borders is as crucial as preserving territory since failure to control transfer of people, goods, and services across the border can severely undermine the integrity of a sovereign entity. Preservation of political integrity and legitimacy are equally important since they not only guarantee autonomy against external influence but also allow monopoly over the legitimate use of force internally. From the perspective of juridical sovereignty, international recognition constitutes another significant goal. Countries without international recognition are deformed quasi-states left with nothing more than domestic sovereignty. But domestic sovereignty alone cannot satisfy the conditions of a sovereign entity (Litfin 1997; Krasner 1999; Caporaso 2000; Jackson 2000; Inoguchi and Bacon 2001). These goals of sovereignty dovetail with the universally accepted notion of national interests, which are often defined in terms of territorial and political survival, economic well-being and prosperity, and prestige and identity.

The meanings of sovereignty and ways to achieve its goals are not uniform but vary by epistemological position. International legalists, British liberals, and constructivists alike believe that sovereignty based on the principles of juridical equality and immunity is still intact and viable. Such sovereignty—whether it is "the one and only organizing principle" (James 1986: 34), an institutional component of world society based on shared interests and rules (Bull 1977; Bull and Watson 1984), or a social construct formed through mutual understanding (Wendt 1994, 1999)—is regarded as the most basic institution of international society. And sovereign states are expected to behave in accordance with a set of shared norms, principles, and rules. Refraining from the threat or use of force, respecting the inviolability of frontiers, nonintervention in international affairs, peaceful settlement of disputes, and fulfillment in good faith of obligations under international law are typical of international norms, principles, and rules underlying international society (Jackson 2000). In this line of reasoning, the goals of sovereignty lie in ensuring collective peace and security through international cooperation, international law, and international organization. Such an orientation may mitigate the potential for interstate conflict by contributing to the formation of a normative-contractual regional order. (See Alagappa, Chap. 1 in this volume.)

Realists, however, cast quite a contrasting portrait of sovereignty (Krasner 1999; Kissinger 1957; Jervis 1992; Sofka 1998). The notions of Westphalian and international legal sovereignty are by and large artificial constructs. Both juridical equality and immunity from external interference have been profoundly compromised by power differentials throughout human history. As Philpott (2001: 297–98) succinctly points out: "State sovereignty has been revisable and revised, violable and violated . . . constantly and continuously, for diverse causes and purposes." While the strong states have been able to enjoy full sovereignty in the Westphalian sense, the weak have been constantly subject to external harassment and intervention through such diverse means as conventions, contracts, coercion, and even imposition (Krasner 1999). In fact, history is filled with failed states that did not enjoy their own sovereignty (Jackson 2000). According to this view, too much emphasis on international legal sovereignty and Westphalian sovereignty can distort objective reality. Survival, maximization of national power, and preservation of the state system become the ultimate goals of sovereignty—and in the process of achieving these goals, countries often make partial concession of their sovereignty. In a similar vein, peace and security are shaped by the dynamic interplay of formal and empirical reality as dictated by the power and interests of the countries involved. For realists, conflict is real whereas peace is elusive and regional order is nothing but an instrument for maximizing national interests.

A dissenting view has emerged, however. Proponents of the postmodern sovereignty perspective argue that neither liberal nor realist views offer a satisfactory account of contemporary sovereignty (Rosenau and Czempiel 1992; Deudney 1995). As the metaphors "sovereignty at bay" (Vernon 1971), "cobweb model" (Burton 1972), and "borderless world" (Ohmae 1991) suggest, the structural parameters of the international system have been radically altered. Nation-states are no longer the dominant actors, and the traditional concept of sovereignty has become increasingly obsolete. Growing interdependence through multiple channels of contact and communication over multiple issues, growing decentralization through globalization and localization, and most important, empowerment of global nongovernmental organizations (NGOs) have made the Philadelphian system all the more plausible (Deudney 1995). Along with this, proliferation of transnational activities such as organized crime, drug trafficking, international terrorism, and computer hacking have posed new challenges to sovereign authorities. Despite these new transnational threats, according to this view the rise of postmodern sovereignty is conducive to peace and security because it can improve the chances for a regional order based on solidarity or a security community that can subjugate individual national interests and goals to collective identity and interests. (See Alagappa, Chap. 1 in this volume.)

How can we apply these contending views to the understanding of sovereignty, conflict, and security order in Asia today? None of these perspectives offers a satisfactory account, precisely because the three types of sovereignty and their underlying norms, principles, and rules are in reality intertwined. Nevertheless, it seems plausible to explore the evolutionary dynamics of sovereignty in the region and its ramifications for regional conflict and security order. We argue that there are three distinct trends in Asia.

Preoccupation with Westphalian Sovereignty

The most obvious trend is the preservation of Westphalian sovereignty in a broad sense, comprising territoriality, domestic sovereignty and its inviolability, and external juridical representation and equality. Several factors account for Asia's preoccupation with Westphalian sovereignty. Collective memory of the colonial past, experiences of major wars, and strong nationalist sentiments embedded in most Asian countries have heightened the importance of territorial and political integrity, making it a cherished national asset. Equally critical is the failure to institutionalize a regional security order or cooperative mechanism that can mitigate interstate conflict while fostering a feeling of mutual interdependence among countries in the region.

Preoccupation with the Westphalian notion of sovereignty would not lead to conflict if its intrinsic norms of territoriality and nonviolability were preserved through the enforcement of international law. In reality, however, obsession with Westphalian sovereignty, be it offensive or defensive, often triggers interstate conflicts over territory, resources, and political integrity because neither party is willing to compromise. In other words, excessive exercise of Westphalian sovereignty through power and influence is likely to undermine regional peace and security. The trend of contested sovereignty becomes especially troublesome because it involves the classic pattern of interstate conflict. Contestation over political and territorial sovereignty can easily provoke diplomatic disputes and, in the worst case, escalate into major interstate and even regional conflict. The Korean case, cross-straits relations, and a range of territorial disputes in the South China Sea and Southeast Asia all illustrate that negative amplifying feedback of contested sovereignty can produce major interstate conflicts that destabilize regional order. The impact on regional order depends on the conflict management mechanism that conflicting parties employ. But most parties involved in interstate conflict arising from contested sovereignty tend to resort to the conventional realist prescriptions: maximization of physical power stocks, military deterrence, and alliance politics. Peaceful settlement through international legal mediation or multilateral security cooperation tends to be the secondary choice.

The Gap Between Rhetoric and Reality

Although most countries in Asia attempt to preserve the notion of Westphalian sovereignty, its component parts such as domestic sovereignty, international legal sovereignty, and immunity from external influence are often violated and compromised in reality. An increasing gap between rhetoric and reality represents a second major trend in the exercise of state sovereignty. Westphalian sovereignty can be violated in two significant ways. One is through voluntary compromise; the other is through external intervention.

When countries voluntarily compromise part of their domestic or external sovereignty for the sake of practical national interests, such an exercise might be called "compromised sovereignty." Compromised sovereignty represents an institutional innovation to manage the mismatch between Westphalian sovereignty and empirical sovereignty. It can build peace and security in two significant ways. One way is to mitigate conflict potential by loosening the Westphalian concept of sovereignty—by conceding part of domestic and external sovereignty, for example, while retaining territorial sovereignty (China vis-à-vis Hong Kong). The other way is to make partial concessions of domestic sovereignty for the purpose of maximizing national interests (as in Japan's peace constitution and South Korea's transfer of wartime operational control to the United States). Some countries are willing to compromise their domestic sovereignty in order to ensure their national survival from external threats. Both cases of compromised sovereignty are useful in maintaining peace and security. While the former reduces the potential for intrastate conflict through an explicit adoption of organized hypocrisy, the latter can avoid overt conflicts through alliance formation, balance of power, and military deterrence.

Sometimes a country's domestic and international legal sovereignty may be revised and violated by outsiders. This type of sovereign exercise might be called "intervened sovereignty." There are two types of intervened sovereignty. One is intervention by imposition; the other is intervention by invitation (Krasner 1999). While the former denotes the forced violation of domestic and external sovereignty by the stronger, the latter involves the voluntary abandonment of sovereignty through mutual consent. Both compromised and intervened sovereignty are examples of organized hypocrisy whereby the principle of international legal and Westphalian sovereignty is violated by empirical sovereignty (Krasner 1999).

Here the implications for regional conflict depend on the type. Intervention by imposition against the will of a sovereign entity (Vietnamese in Cambodia, for example, or Indonesians in East Timor) entails military conflict that destabilizes regional order since it is tantamount to committing an outright invasion. But intervention by invitation (UN intervention in East Timor and Cambodia, for example) can be seen as a benign interference designed to promote a stable peace in troubled spots. Thus imposed intervention may disrupt regional order whereas intervention by invitation and involvement of organizations such as the United Nations may help to sustain a stable regional order through multilateral security cooperation.

New Transnational Challenges

Finally, there is a new trend in which state sovereignty is increasingly subject to internal and external challenges. Two types of challenges can be envisaged here. One is internal challenges to (or denial of) domestic sovereignty such as secessionist movements and a subsequent crisis of governance that results in fragmented state sovereignty. The other is external challenges by international organizations or transnational actors that erode state sovereignty. Although both types of challenge are nongovernmental in their origins, they impose enormous burdens on the exercise of state sovereignty.

The issue of fragmented sovereignty arises when a country marginalizes communal groups within its territorial boundary and thus fails to ensure full social and political integration. Countries beset by secessionist movements are prone to experience fragmented sovereignty. Separatist movements, ethnic conflicts, fragmented sovereignty—all are by and large a product of the colonial legacy because forced integration of diverse communal groups within a specific sovereign territory during the colonial period is their root cause. At the same time, postcolonial mismanagement in terms of structural inequality among competing communal groups can exacerbate the problem of fragmented sovereignty.

Fragmented sovereignty is usually predicated on the negation of domestic sovereignty by competing communal groups seeking their own state sovereignty. Although fragmented sovereignty touches mainly on the issue of domestic sovereignty, associated conflicts such as communal friction or secessionist movements are closely intertwined with regional dynamics. Conflicts over fragmented sovereignty are characterized, not only by protracted duration and fluctuation in intensity and frequency, but also by blurred demarcation between internal and external actors (Azar 1990: chap. 1). As the cases of Sri Lanka, Kashmir, and Afghanistan demonstrate, disputes over sovereign identity bear wide ramifications, eventually threatening regional peace and security. Third-party intervention has been less effective in resolving conflicts deriving from fragmented sovereignty. The ultimate solution to this type of conflict rests in the domestic domain: recognition of communal identity, amelioration of structural inequality, and power sharing among communal groups. If domestic settlement becomes implausible, continuing outside pressure through multilateral security cooperation might present a viable solution to the conflict. One caveat, however, is in order here. Compared with Africa, the Middle East, and the Balkans, the case of fragmented sovereignty is less salient in Asia—especially East Asia.

Apart from the internal challenges, state sovereignty in Asia has been subjected to growing outside pressures from transnational players. As the postmodern view of sovereignty implies, we are living in a world where nongovernmental players are competing with sovereign states. Growing interdependence and waves of globalization have increased the power and influence of transnational issues. These new actors constitute another dimension of sovereignty that we might term "transnational sovereignty" (Krasner 1999: 12–14). Transnational sovereignty becomes salient, not only because of the proliferation of nongovernmental actors, but also because of the diverse and formidable threats they pose to sovereign states.

Transnational sovereignty becomes the source of national concern because transnational players and issues can significantly erode the autonomy and independence of sovereign states. They can also threaten the very goals of state sovereignty such as survival, economic prosperity, and social integrity. The sequence of economic crisis, IMF bailout, and economic trusteeship through the imposition of conditions vividly illustrates how an international organization may intervene and undermine a state's autonomy in economic management. At the same time, international drug trafficking, transnational organized crime, transborder movements of pollutants, transnational spread of communicable diseases such as AIDS, and global computer hacking can threaten critical national values such as organic survival, social integrity, and even economic well-being. Although these transnational threats do not provoke overt conflict, they can undercut the other domains of state sovereignty. It is, however, noteworthy that such transnational threats have been instrumental in fostering regional cooperation and collective action. In fact, Asian governments have been willing to pool sovereignty at the global and regional levels in dealing with these challenges.

Beyond the Westphalian Template

The Westphalian practice of sovereignty, therefore, prevails throughout Asia. Indeed, Asian governments have shown an extraordinary preoccupation with state sovereignty in the political and security arenas. Nevertheless, its dominance has become increasingly less real than the rhetoric might suggest. Power politics and the salience of national gains have undercut and violated state sovereignty in one way or another. And while the failure of social and political integration has heightened domestic challenges, the process of globalization and the subsequent proliferation of transnational players and issues have imposed formidable external constraints on state sovereignty. In sum, then, the Westphalian template of state sovereignty is gradually losing its privileged position. What, then, are the implications of this development for regional conflict and security order? Before we get into specific discussion of these issues, it seems worthwhile to explore the historical evolution of sovereignty in Asia. Current debates on sovereignty and the implications for regional conflict and security order cannot be meaningfully appreciated without first unraveling the evolutionary dynamics of sovereignty in Asia.

Evolutionary Dynamics of Sovereignty in Asia

The Westphalian concept of state sovereignty was foreign to Asia before the nineteenth century. Roughly before the mid-fourteenth century, Asia was rather anarchic. Although China was the most powerful state in the region, it constantly engaged in border conflicts with neighboring countries. Because China was the only civilized entity—all the peripheral states were considered barbaric—there were no commonly accepted norms, rules, and procedures governing interstate relations, especially between China and its neighbors, and territorial conquest and annexation became the principal rule of the game. The Shu dynasty, the Tang dynasty, and the Mongolian empire had all attempted to expand their territorial boundary into peripheral countries by dispatching numerous military expeditions. Meanwhile Southeast Asia was composed of three distinctive state groups—Tai states (Shan, Chiang Mai, Laos, Siam), Duiran states (Rakhine, Ava, Taungoo), and Muslim sultanates (Aceh, Samudra, Aru, Malacca)—where Chinese influence was rather limited (McEvedy 1998: 28–29).

With the founding of the Ming dynasty in 1368, however, Asia's political geography began to reveal a new look. China's boundaries were extended all the way to Inner Mongolia in the north and to Dai Viet in the south. Moreover, the Ming dynasty was able to impose quite extensive tributary networks in East and Southeast Asia. While Korea and part of Japan paid tribute to China, an increasing number of Southeast Asian states either paid tribute or acknowledged Chinese suzerainty (Malacca, for instance). This China-centered tributary system was not universally accepted, of course. As the Japanese invasion of the Korean peninsula in the late sixteenth century illustrates, Japan occasionally challenged the Chinese hegemony. The Thais also attempted to consolidate their imperial base by challenging China. More important, colonial expansion of Western powers by the

TABLE 3.1
Historical Evolution of Sovereignty in Asia

Evolution of domestic sovereignty	Period	Domestic political order	Evolution of external sovereignty	Regional security order
Monarchic sovereignty	Before the late 19th century	Confucian–hierarchic order	Hierarchic, compromised sovereignty	Sino-centric hierarchic order/tributary system
State sovereignty	Late 19th century to 1945	Absolute monarchy/constitutional regimes	Westphalian sovereignty introduced/juridical equality compromised	Imperial order by Western powers and Japan
Popular sovereignty	1945–90	Democratic order/authoritarian regimes	Continuing Westphalian sovereignty/sovereignty compromised and intervened	Instrumental order/weak normative-contractual order/weak solidarity order
Sovereignty in transition	Post–Cold War	Democratized, globalized political order	Westphalian sovereignty but increasing challenges from communal and transnational sovereignty	Dialectics of instrumental, normative-contractual, and solidarity order

Dutch (East Indies), the Spanish (Philippines), and the Portuguese (Macao) began to alter the political and territorial landscape of Asia (McEvedy 1998).

As Table 3.1 illustrates, nevertheless, the spread of the Sino-centric tributary system contributed to refining the concept of sovereignty in Asia (Hamashita 1997). Chinese hegemony before the nineteenth century was founded on two factors: a material foundation and a moral foundation. China was the only regional state that could project hegemonic power, and no one was readily able to challenge it. At the same time, the moral hegemony of Confucianism increased China's status in the region. According to Confucianism, based on hierarchic social relationships, China was the center of moral gravity whereas other states were simply barbarians to be enlightened through Confucian teachings. China's Confucian superstructure and moral hegemony, coupled with its material power infrastructure, were instrumental in universalizing the regional order of *shidazishao* ("respecting the great, namely China, while the great takes care of the small"). The China-centered hegemonic order eventually shaped the nature of domestic and external sovereignty in Asia where neither supremacy and absolute authority nor external independence were fully recognized. The principle of *shidazishao* rejected a regional order framed by power hierarchy, however, while advocating a regional order based on Confucian norms and rules. In a sense, the new regional order under the Confucian aegis was instrumental for the birth of a solidarity security order. Thus East Asia during this period can be characterized as a rule-driven international society (Bull 1977; Alagappa, Chap. 1 in this volume)—rather than a power-driven anarchic international system—which was in turn responsible for shaping the contour of the Confucian peace.

The China-centered hegemonic order bore profound implications for domestic sovereignty. Domestic sovereignty in Asia, especially East Asia, was monarchic, but it was fundamentally delimited. Although the local potentates exercised absolute authority over the subjects within their own territorial boundaries, political suzerainty belonged to the imperial court of China. Launching a new dynasty, as well as questions of monarchic succession, required prior investiture by the Mandarin court. Failure to win Chinese imperial approval often led to political crises at the local level over the issue of legitimacy. Economic and social activities were also heavily influenced by tributary relationships. Under the principle of suzerainty and the tributary system, external sovereignty was profoundly limited. Juridical equals were not allowed, and external sovereignty was by and large compromised by the hierarchic order, which was in turn tied to geographic and cultural proximity to China (Fairbank 1968). Countries close to China in terms of geography and culture were more equal than those that were not. In East Asia, for example, China was considered the big brother, Korea a middle brother, and Japan a younger brother (Kim and Moon 1997: chap. 14). China used to intervene whenever this hierarchic order was jeopardized. Ming's intervention in Korea during the Japanese invasion in 1592 offers a good example in this regard.

Although the Sino-centric hierarchic order was instrumental in maintaining a fairly long peace in Asia, a major change took place in the wake of the Opium Wars in 1839–42 and 1856–60. Departing from the old tributary system, China began to transform itself from the hegemonic center of the universe into a modern sovereign state by establishing treaty relations with Western powers such as Great Britain. Forced interactions with Western powers, application of the modern international public law system, port openings—all brought about revolutionary changes in state sovereignty. China's demotion to an ordinary, sovereign state through forced port openings produced profound impacts on the concept of sovereignty in Asia (Krasner 2001). It is during this period that state sovereignty in the Westphalian sense was introduced for the first time in Asian history. But countries in the region traveled diverse paths to domestic sovereignty. Japan was the first to reform its domestic political order from a feudal system to an absolute monarchy through the Meiji Restoration. Meanwhile China was transformed from absolute monarchic sovereignty to popular sovereignty through the 1911 revolution. After enjoying a brief period of state sovereignty, most countries in the region fell prey to colonial domination.

External sovereignty was equally complicated. As the Sino-centric tributary system came to an end because of the imperial expansion of Japan and Western powers, empirical sovereignty emerged as the basic rule of regional politics. Ja-

pan's annexation of Korea and Taiwan, its invasion of China, the American takeover of the Philippines, and Anglo-Franco rivalry over Indochina—all underscore
the prevalence of empirical sovereignty during this period. Inspired by Woodrow
Wilson's advocacy of self-determination for sovereign states, some weak states
called for juridical equality based on international legal sovereignty, but their call
was rarely honored. Compromised sovereignty was commonly practiced. As
Krasner (2001) argues, the logic of interactions between China and the Western
powers was guided by organized hypocrisy. Indeed, international legal sovereignty and empirical sovereignty were compromised in such a way as to maximize the practical interests of parties concerned, including the avoidance of major conflicts. China's territorial concessions to Japan and the Western powers
while retaining its own domestic and external sovereignty were important testimonials to this compromise (Krasner 2001). The process of the Tokugawa's collapse through the Meiji Restoration also reveals how Japan's international legal
sovereignty and empirical sovereignty were compromised (Kohno 2001). It
should be kept in mind, however, that empirical sovereignty prevailed over juridical sovereignty during this period. The unconstrained empirical sovereignty
exercised by Japan and the Western powers eventually led to the outbreak of the
Pacific War.

It was only after the end of the Pacific War that Asia began to shape the current pattern of sovereignty and regional order. The Allied victory in the war and
new international legal norms led to the proliferation of newly independent states
that recovered their lost state sovereignty and wrapped it with popular sovereignty. Constitutionally speaking—regardless of the regime type, democratic or
authoritarian—popular sovereignty constituted the core of domestic sovereignty
where supremacy and absolute control resided in the people. And the establishment of the United Nations and its codification of juridical equality, nonviolability of domestic sovereignty, and the principle of immunity from external interference contributed to strengthening the Westphalian notion of sovereignty as
the guiding principle of external sovereignty. Asian governments have been by
and large obsessed with Westphalian sovereignty—not only because of their historical experiences of "lost sovereignty" but also because of nascent nationalism
and domestic fervor associated with the primacy of state sovereignty.

Nevertheless, the Westphalian notion of sovereignty was constantly altered,
compromised, and violated. Certainly the Cold War bipolar structure and subsequent hegemonic competition between the United States and the Soviet Union
did not allow its smooth operation. Most countries in the region were divided
between the two blocs, and their exercise of domestic and external sovereignty
was by and large constrained by the logic of bipolar politics. Although most Asian
countries were able to avoid becoming satellite states like those in Eastern

Europe, some of them made partial concessions of their sovereignty either through a process of mutual consensus or through imposition or coercion. South Korea, for example, exercised limited domestic sovereignty by conceding its military sovereignty to the United States. Japan too conceded its military sovereignty through the adoption of its peace constitution. American intervention in Vietnam and Soviet intervention in Afghanistan reveal another dimension of deformed sovereignty by external forces within the framework of the Cold War order. But the bloc politics of alliance formation reduced the chance of conflict over sovereignty since it constrained autonomous actions by individual actors. Individual actions over contested sovereignty could easily have escalated into major conflicts. Fragmented sovereignty also posed less of a problem because ethnic aspirations and secessionist movements were suppressed by the Cold War template.

Since the late 1980s, however, Asia has undergone profound changes. The demise of the Soviet Union terminated the Cold War bipolar confrontation, and the advent of the post–Cold War era began to reveal signs of strategic change in the region. First, following the collapse of the Soviet Union, Asia encountered the unipolar moment of American hegemony, though it is not clear whether the United States has the will and intention to play the role of hegemonic leader in the region by capitalizing on the unique momentum in human history (Kapstein and Mastanduno 1999). Second, the unipolar moment notwithstanding, the inertia of the Cold War structure continues, and bilateral alliance management remains the dominant mode of strategic interaction. American pursuit of bilateral or trilateral alliance management (United States–Japan–South Korea, for example) could bring about a countervailing alliance involving China, Russia, and North Korea.

Third, U.S. preponderance cannot be taken for granted. Backed up by its recent economic growth, industrialization, and technological upgrading, China seems to be catching up with the United States—presenting a threat, perhaps, of power transition and major conflicts. Along with this, there has been increasing domestic pressure for Japan's remilitarization. So long as the United States remains in the region, China's hegemonic ascension and Japan's remilitarization may be delayed. But U.S. disengagement from the region could revive and intensify the old Westphalian conflicts in the region by pitting regional actors against each other. Finally, the spread of globalization and increasing interdependence among countries in the region tend to create countervailing forces to the Westphalian trend by increasing the opportunities for multilateral cooperation through shared norms and values. Furthermore, the third wave of democratization in Asia has been instrumental in consolidating popular sovereignty. Thus two sets of trends are likely to affect the evolving nature of sovereignty and regional order. While democratization and globalization shape domestic sovereignty, the dynamic interplay of bilateralism and multilateralism will determine the contour of external sovereignty.

These new trends present both opportunities and constraints. Forces of democratization and globalization are likely to limit the scope of traditional domestic sovereignty in a significant manner. While democratization brings the proliferation of nongovernment organizations that affect the conduct of foreign policy through the exercise of popular sovereignty, globalization will not only foster multiple channels of communication with the outside world but also allow greater space for outsiders' penetration and maneuvers. Weakening of domestic sovereignty and strengthening of interdependent sovereignty may fundamentally erode the traditional pattern of state sovereignty.

External sovereignty will likewise be subject to change. The end of the bipolar structure is likely to sustain and even intensify the notion of Westphalian sovereignty, especially over territorial and political integrity. Consequently, contested sovereignty might emerge as the key issue in regional politics. But an increasing number of countries will have to wrestle with the question of fragmented sovereignty through communal aspirations and secessionist movements. A well-structured power hierarchy in the region and weak enforceability of international legal sovereignty will also continue to encourage organized hypocrisy through compromised sovereignty. Cases of external intervention—either through imposition or invitation—will remain controversial. Although forced intervention might be less plausible because it is too costly and morally unacceptable, humanitarian interventions and third-party intervention in dispute settlements will be increasingly universalized even in Asia. The rise of transnational sovereignty will also profoundly influence the conduct of Westphalian sovereignty in a broad sense.

Sovereignty and Regional Conflict: Asian Perspectives

The foregoing examination reveals that the concept of sovereignty and its exercise in Asia have evolved in accord with changing internal and external circumstances. How have these changes in the exercise of sovereignty affected the patterns of conflict in Asia? We explore this question by looking into three distinct trends of sovereign exercise: a preoccupation with the Westphalian notion of sovereignty, its relaxation through compromise and intervention, and new post-Westphalian challenges.

Westphalian Sovereignty and Interstate Conflict

Most Asian governments are still preoccupied with Westphalian sovereignty as broadly defined. Naked pursuit of state sovereignty often results in contestation over territory, over political integrity, and even over international recognition. Contested sovereignty has been the source of interstate conflict on two occasions in Asia: one is the classic disputes over national boundaries or territories dictated by the sovereign goal of territorial preservation; the other is the much more complex contest over political and territorial integrity as well as international recognition that we observe in divided nations. In this case, two entities claim legitimacy over domestic sovereignty (political integrity), international legal sovereignty (representation in international organizations), and narrowly defined Westphalian sovereignty (territorial integrity as well as autonomy and independence).

Disputes over territorial sovereignty abound across Asia (Segal 1991: 203–33; Smith 1997: 60–61; Zacher 2001). One of the most notable cases is the unresolved dispute between Japan and the Soviet Union over four islands off the northeastern tip of Hokkaido: Etorofu, Kunashiri, Habomai, and Shikotan. These four islands, part of the Kuril chain, used to belong to Japan's northern territories until 1945. But after the Pacific War, citing wartime agreements at Yalta, the Soviet Union took over these islands as war spoils. Japan disputes this Soviet claim, however, arguing that the Yalta agreement does not include any provisions on the four islands. Such disputes over Japan's northern territories might not trigger any major conflicts between Japan and Russia immediately, but the accumulation of grievances and underlying nationalist sentiments could escalate minor quarrels such as those involving fishery rights over the four islands into major conflicts.

Indeed the Asian region is filled with disputes over territorial sovereignty. The South China Sea has become the hotbed of these territorial quarrels. Since the early 1980s, the islands have become a hot spot not only because of their strategic location in sea-lanes of communication but also because of their oil reserves. At present six countries—Brunei, China, Malaysia, the Philippines, Taiwan, and Vietnam—claim territorial sovereignty over some or all of the islands. While China has been increasing its naval power projection capability over this area, Vietnam, the Philippines, and Taiwan have been alert in guarding their interests. The second case is a dispute over the Paracel (Xisha) Islands. Vietnam, namely South Vietnam, exercised its sovereignty over the Paracels by giving oil concessions to Western oil companies in 1973. Protesting this concession, China seized the islands by force in January 1974. Vietnam has not given up its sovereign claims over the islands, however, leaving room for future conflicts. And third, the Senkaku (Tiaoyu) Islands, located 320 km west of Okinawa and 160 km northeast of Taiwan, are another source of territorial disputes in the area. According to the 1951 San Francisco Peace Treaty, the Senkakus belong to the Ryukyu Islands. When the Ryukyu Islands reverted to Japan with the conclusion of the Japan-U.S. security treaty in 1971, territorial sovereignty over the Senkakus reverted to Japan as well. Thus Japan has de facto and de jure control of the islands, but neither

China nor Taiwan recognizes Japanese control. Sporadic skirmishes still continue among the three countries. China's projection of power over the Paracels and the Spratlys and Russia's refusal to return four northern islands to Japan exemplify the primacy of empirical sovereignty over international legal sovereignty. Failure to resolve these territorial issues in a peaceful manner may well undermine regional stability. Thus these disputes over territorial sovereignty can be considered flash points of regional conflict in Asia.

A more critical case involves contestation over political, territorial, and even international legal sovereignty between two sovereign entities. There have been three salient cases in Asia: North-South Vietnam, North-South Korea, and China-Taiwan. The Vietnamese case was resolved with the triumph of North Vietnam over the South in 1974. But the other two cases, still unresolved, affect peace and security in the region. Indeed, cross-straits relations and inter-Korean relations are the two most serious conflict zones in Asia. For both conflicts can easily escalate into major wars by implicating four major powers in the region.

Relaxation of State Sovereignty

As we have seen, contested sovereignty increases the chances of interstate conflicts that can destabilize regional order. But intentional compromising of state sovereignty could prevent conflict or mitigate its potential.

Compromised Sovereignty and Conflict Mitigation. Compromised sovereignty takes place when a sovereign state concedes part of its domestic or external sovereignty to external actors in return for some practical benefits. It might make such concessions, for example, when there are trade-offs between empirical and international legal sovereignty (Jackson 2000; Krasner 1999). To achieve national goals of survival, prosperity, or integration, countries may give up elements of their domestic or external sovereign claims. This is what Krasner calls "organized hypocrisy"—where normative commitments such as sovereign equality are compromised for the maximization of practical interests (Krasner 2001). Most compromised sovereignty involves voluntary, contractual concessions; no elements of imposition or coercion are implied. Three salient cases of compromised sovereignty can be cited.

The first example is South Korea's partial concession of military sovereignty to the United States (Rhee 1986; Moon and McLaurin 1989: 142–43). Article 74 of the South Korean constitution stipulates that the president is commander-in-chief of the armed forces, but South Korea's military sovereignty has been seriously compromised. With the Taejon agreement in 1954, the ROK transferred operational control of its major combat forces to the U.S. Forces Command in South Korea during peacetime and wartime. With the formation of the U.S.-ROK Combined Forces Command (CFC) in 1978, the commander-in-chief—who is a U.S. general officer concurrently serving as commander of the U.S. Eighth Army, the United Nations Command, and U.S. Forces Korea—took over the exercise of operational control over major combat units of ROK forces. Thus the minister of national defense and the chief of staff of each armed service do not exercise operational control over major combat units that are assigned to the CFC (Rhee 1986: 37–39). Since the early 1990s, operational control over major combat units during peacetime has reverted to the ROK. Nevertheless, operational control over major ROK combat units during wartime still belongs to the American commander.

The South Korean case clearly shows the compromise of both domestic and Westphalian sovereignty. As a sovereign state, the ROK wishes to maintain its autonomy and independence. But by allowing U.S. operational control over major ROK combat units, South Korea has violated the principle of supremacy and absolute authority over internal matters as well as the principle of immunity from external interference. South Korea made these concessions with a view to its national survival by fostering alliance ties with the United States as well as improving the organizational efficiency of joint operations during wartime. In essence, then, South Korea violated the major normative nature of sovereignty for the sake of two practical national interests: survival and security. South Korea's compromised sovereignty has indeed promoted its national security posture by mitigating conflict potential through improved alliance ties, balance of power, and military deterrence.

Another example of compromised sovereignty can be found in Japan. After its defeat in the Pacific War, Japan was under American occupation and its new constitution was heavily influenced by the United States, especially General MacArthur's Supreme Command for the Allied Powers. One of the most striking aspects of the new constitution is Article 9. As a way of renouncing war, Article 9 of the Japanese constitution states: "Aspiring sincerely to an international peace based on justice and order, the Japanese people forever renounce war as a sovereign right of the nation and the threat or use of force as a means of settling international disputes." It further states: "In order to accomplish the aim of the preceding paragraph, land, sea, and air forces, as well as other war potential, will never be maintained. The right of belligerency of the state will not be recognized." (See Auer 1993: 69–86.) It is for this provision that the Japanese constitution has been labeled a peace constitution.

The pacifism embodied in the Japanese constitution can be regarded as another form of compromised sovereignty. No matter how consensual the adoption of the peace constitution, the deprivation of regular armed forces is tantamount to violating one of the most essential norms of domestic and Westphalian sovereignty. Possessing regular armed forces, engaging in offensive defense, and exercising normal international activities such as peacekeeping operations are an integral part of domestic and external sovereign rights. Yet the empirical sovereignty exercised by U.S. occupation forces compelled Japan to compromise these rights for its practical interests. Japan, given its economic power and democratic maturity, could have revoked the peace provision. But practical benefits arising from the U.S. security umbrella, justified in part by the peace constitution, have kept Japan from seeking the full exercise of military sovereignty. Recent domestic debates on Japan's return to a normal state might induce the amendment of Article 9, but it will take a long time. Japan's compromised sovereignty, like South Korea's, has been conducive to furthering peace and security while suppressing the potential for conflict. Since amendment of Article 9 of the peace constitution is predicated on Japan's remilitarization, such a development could trigger a fierce arms race with such regional actors as China, Russia, the United States, and Korea, severely undermining strategic stability in the region. Certainly Japan has the capability to project power in the region, but the peace constitution has deterred it from doing so. Thus the organized hypocrisy of compromised sovereignty ends up producing positive peace dividends.

China's handling of Hong Kong represents the third interesting case of compromised sovereignty. After one hundred years of colonial rule, Great Britain returned Hong Kong to China in 1998. But China's way of reincorporating Hong Kong into its own territory has involved a subtle form of organized hypocrisy. China's incorporation of Hong Kong went beyond the simple formula of "one state, two systems" that could only have compromised elements of domestic sovereignty. In the case of Hong Kong, China compromised not only its domestic sovereignty but also its external sovereignty in a significant way. The compromise of domestic sovereignty has involved special administrative and judicial arrangements such as a high degree of local autonomy and the continuation of a legal system based on English common law. More remarkable is China's compromise of external sovereignty. From the perspective of international legal sovereignty, Hong Kong is not juridically independent. Yet China has allowed it to participate in international organizations such as the World Trade Organization, the Asian Development Bank, and the World Health Organization as a full member (full membership in eight organizations, associate membership in six organizations, as part of the Chinese delegation in nineteen organizations). More important, Hong Kong was allowed to issue passports, enforce its own customs procedures, and conclude visa agreements. China did not create this unique set of institutional arrangements because it was weak (empirical sovereignty) or because of binding international legal obligations. China did it simply because such arrangements could further its practical interests by minimizing disruptive effects of the return, maintaining Hong Kong's economic vitality, and fostering an incremental integration.

Intervened Sovereignty and Transitional Conflicts. The core of the Westphalian notion of sovereignty lies in the principle of nonintervention. But in the real world, sovereignty is more often than not violated. Intervention can take place in two different forms: one by imposition, the other by invitation. Imposition means forced intervention against the will of the government and people of the intervened. It is the equivalent of invasion. Intervention by invitation, however, is different. Warring factions in a conflict zone may invite third-party intervention in order to stabilize the situation. In this case intervention becomes consensual, and international organizations usually play the role of third-party intermediary or peacekeeper. In Asia, Cambodia and East Timor offer the classic examples of intervention by imposition as well as invitation. Here we examine the case of Cambodia.

Cambodia, in spite of its independence in 1953, has undergone serious difficulties in consolidating its sovereignty. Competing political sections in Cambodia have resulted in severe domestic strife leading to the intervention of foreign powers—that is, Vietnam and the United Nations. Only after the UN's intervention could Cambodia hold an election and begin to establish sovereign control over its territory and people. The process of consolidating its sovereignty, however, was not an easy one. In 1955, Sihanouk organized his own political movement, the Popular Socialist Community, which won all the seats in the national assembly in the 1955 election and dominated the political scene until the late 1960s. Sihanouk's highly personal ruling style made him immensely popular with the people, especially in rural villages. In foreign relations, Sihanouk pursued a policy of neutrality and nonalignment. He accepted U.S. economic and military aid, but he also promoted close relations with China and attempted to keep on good terms with the Democratic Republic of Vietnam (North Vietnam). As the domestic and international situations had deteriorated by the late 1960s, Cambodia's increasingly powerful right wing challenged Sihanouk's control of the political system. After a violent revolt in 1967 in the northwestern province of Batdambang (Battambang) and the spillover of the Second Indochina War (or Vietnam War) into the Cambodian border areas, Sihanouk was overthrown in March 1970 by General Lon Nol and other right-wing leaders who seven months later abolished the monarchy and established the Khmer Republic. After the March 1970 coup d'état, the Khmer Rouge formed a united front with the ousted leader. In January 1975, communist forces laid siege to Phnom Penh. On April 1, 1975, President Lon Nol left the country. Sixteen days later Khmer Rouge troops entered the city.

The forty-four months the Khmer Rouge were in power was a period of unmitigated suffering for the Khmer people. In 1977, Pol Pot launched a bloody purge within the communist ranks that accounted for many deaths. The slaugh-

ter of the Vietnamese minority living in Cambodia and the Khmer Rouge's aggressive incursions into Vietnam led to fighting with Vietnam in 1977 and 1978.
On December 25, 1978, Vietnam launched a full-scale invasion of Cambodia.
Phnom Penh fell, after minimal resistance, on January 7, 1979, and on the following day an anti–Khmer Rouge faction announced the formation of the Kampuchean People's Revolutionary Council (KPRC) with Heng Samrin as president
of the new ruling body. On January 10, the KPRC proclaimed that the new official
name of Cambodia was the People's Republic of Kampuchea (PRK).

Throughout the 1980s, a host of domestic factions competed for respect and
legitimacy. Relying on foreign powers, the state of fragmented sovereignty was resolved by international intervention in the form of UN supervision of democratic
elections. Cambodia's democratization process began with the signing of the
Paris Accords in 1991 and the subsequent UN-organized elections in 1993. With
this intervention, former warring parties transferred their struggle from the battlefield to the political sphere. Under the guidance of Hun Sen, the Cambodian
People's Party continued to use its military connections as its strategy for defeating its rival FUNCINPEC led by Prince Norodom Ranariddh. Yet the political
process came to be based on sovereign authority coming from the first democratic election in Cambodia (Hughes 2000).

The two types of intervention in Cambodia—one by imposition and the other
by invitation—clearly indicate the fragility of international legal sovereignty.
When a country is weak and fragile, it can secure neither Westphalian sovereignty
nor compromised sovereignty. Empirical sovereignty prevails where naked power
dictates the fate of a country. Nevertheless, third-party intervention through the
United Nations proved to be useful in restoring domestic and external sovereignty. Thus external intervention, despite the Westphalian notion of sovereignty, may not always be negative. The same can be said of East Timor: forced
intervention by Indonesia triggered massive transitional conflicts; UN intervention by the invitation of East Timor and with the consent of Indonesia, however,
contributed to pacifying the situation.

Post-Westphalian Challenges

Despite conscious efforts by Asian governments, the Westphalian notion of
sovereignty can no longer be considered invincible in either the narrow sense
(territorial and political immunity) or the broad sense (domestic sovereignty,
international legal sovereignty, and territorial and political immunity). There are
two major challenges. One is the internal challenge to state sovereignty and the
other is external.

The Internal Challenge. The internal challenge involves fragmentation or paralysis of domestic sovereignty through competing claims over domestic or in ternational legal sovereignty along ethnic or communal lines within a territorial boundary. A sovereign state may fall prey to internal fragmentation because of its failure in nation-state building. The state's failure to recognize other communal groups within the framework of social and political integration often leads to fragmented sovereignty through internal conflict. In this sense, communal identity becomes the most pronounced cause of fragmented sovereignty. In contrast with Africa, the Middle East, and Eastern Europe, the Asian region has been less plagued by communal conflict and fragmented sovereignty. Nevertheless, it is littered with examples of fragmented sovereignty such as Tibet in China, Kashmir in India, Aceh in Indonesia, and Tamil in Sri Lanka. Here we examine the salient case of Sri Lanka.

Protracted communal strife between Tamil and Sinhalese ethnic groups in Sri Lanka represents a painful case of fragmented sovereignty (Rupesinghe and Mumtaz 1996; Singh 1997). Historically Ceylon had been ruled by both Tamil and Sinhalese kings—the Tamil kingdom comprising the north and eastern parts and the Sinhalese kingdoms the western and southern parts of Ceylon. After the island's independence from British colonial rule in February 1948, the first parliamentary election was held under the Soulbury constitution. D. S. Senanayake, leader of the United National Party (formerly the Ceylon National Congress), formed the government as the first prime minister of an independent Ceylon. Independence did not lead to internal cohesion, however. The Ceylon Citizenship Act of 1948 deprived a million Tamils of Indian origin of their citizenship. This measure was followed by the Ceylon (Parliamentary Elections) Amendment Act of 1949, which deprived the Tamils of their franchise as well. Depriving a million Tamils of their citizenship was the result of actions of the Sinhala-Buddhist majority that regarded the island as the exclusive home of Sinhala Buddhism and looked upon the Tamils as invaders from Tamil Nadu in South India.

The strife continued when the Sri Lanka Freedom Party government of Prime Minister S. W. R. D. Bandaranayake established Sinhala as the only official language in June 1956. The enactment of this measure, quite contrary to the prevailing policy of recognizing both Sinhalese and Tamil as official languages, made Tamils second-class citizens. Politically it was a master stroke by the majority Sinhalese to protect jobs in the government and state corporations. The riots that took place in 1956 marked the beginning of a series of racially motivated Tamil pogroms by Sinhalese covertly encouraged by successive governments and overtly supported by the security forces.

In July 1957, Bandaranayake signed a pact with S. J. V. Chelvanayagam of the Tamil Federal Party—popularly called the Bandaranayake-Chelvanayagam pact—giving a measure of regional autonomy in the spheres of land, language, and education. But the pact was nullified by Bandaranayake under pressure from

Sinhalese-Buddhist nationalists. A similar pact signed by Chelvanayagam and Senanayake in 1965 failed as well. The constitution adopted in 1970 incorporated the Sinhala Only Act as part of the constitution and enthroned Buddhism as the foremost religion to be fostered by the state. Amendments moved by the Tamil Federal Party to the draft constitution, demanding a federal constitution and parity of status for Tamils along with Sinhalese, were defeated by the government. Confronted with steadily mounting national oppression and frustrated with the failure of the democratic political struggles, in 1975 the Tamil national parties converged into a single movement. In 1978, yet another constitution was enacted that constrained the Tamils further. In 1979, the Sri Lankan government enacted the Prevention of Terrorism Act to cope with the growing militancy, notably that of the Liberation Tigers.

Because of the Sinhalese army occupation of Jaffna and the state terrorism let loose on the people, hostility began to grow and the emotional division between Sinhalese and Tamils became more acute. A group of highly organized young Tamil militants, first calling themselves the New Tamil Tigers and later the Liberation Tigers of Tamil Eelam, emerged in 1976 to confront the government terrorism by bearing arms. In July 1983, the Tamil Tigers attacked the Sinhalese army in the north and killed thirteen soldiers. This strike ignited yet another Tamil pogrom, surpassing all the previous ones in its intensity and destruction of life and property. In the 1990s, despite the government's proposal to permit Tamil political autonomy, the violence continued to afflict politics in Sri Lanka. The many battles and the recent fighting show that there are not only two separate nations but two separate armies as well, fragmenting domestic sovereignty.

The Sri Lankan case represents a classic example of fragmented sovereignty driven by communal division. Failure to recognize pluralistic communal identity and subsequent communal aspirations has created enormous threats to state sovereignty from within. The Sri Lankan case also suggests how artificial and fragile the notion of state (or Westphalian) sovereignty can be. Several factors account for the Sri Lankan tragedy: British colonial rule; the forced merger of two separate domestic sovereignties into one supreme domestic authority without due legitimizing efforts; and delinquency in nation-state building. An interesting observation can be made here: an unresolved historical legacy may impose formidable post-Westphalian challenges to state sovereignty. And this implication can be extended to other examples of fragmented sovereignty throughout the Asian region.

The External Challenge. The advent of transnational sovereignty has entailed enormous external challenges to the notion of Westphalian sovereignty. International organizations, multinational corporations, and nongovernmental organizations have emerged as new actors competing with state sovereignty on several issues. As the 1997 Asian financial crisis exemplified, nongovernmental players influenced national actors in two significant ways. While speculative international capitalists were by and large responsible for the genesis of the crisis, the International Monetary Fund fundamentally limited the scope of economic sovereignty by imposing its conditions and then monitoring and amending the subsequent policy changes. Moreover, institutionalization of multilateral and regional economic arrangements has begun to undercut the economic autonomy and independence of Asian governments. For many Asian countries, ratification of the Uruguay Round and admission to the World Trade Organization, as well as the admission of increasing numbers of Asian countries to the Organization for Economic Co-operation and Development and, most recently, the launching of the ASEAN Free Trade Area, have all contributed to constraining a country's pursuit of mercantile economic policy. Likewise, forces of spontaneous and managerial globalization have fundamentally constrained the autonomy and independence of a state's economic sovereignty.

In a similar vein, new issues have influenced the exercise of sovereignty. The proliferation of transnational organized crime, international drug and human trafficking, terrorism, and computer hacking, among others, has been significantly threatening the sanctity of state sovereignty (Cusimano 2000; Stares 1998). Most of these threats with transnational origins might not impose any immediate and explicit military danger to sovereign states. But as the September 11, 2001, terrorist attack in the United States, organized crime in the Russian Far East, drug trafficking throughout Asia, and increasingly rampant computer hacking have illustrated, the autonomy and independence of state sovereignty have become sharply curtailed. The supremacy of domestic authority, as well as the inviolability of autonomy and independence, have been significantly eroded by the penetration of transnational actors and issues.

Elucidating Some Correlates

As we have seen, the correlates of sovereignty and conflict in Asia reveal several interesting patterns. First, Westphalian sovereignty as broadly defined is still well entrenched throughout Asia, but its preservation has not necessarily contributed to removing conflict in the region. On the contrary, a blind pursuit of the Westphalian notion of sovereignty has heightened military tension and the potential for conflict. Pervasive disputes over territorial and political integrity, resources, and international recognition throughout the region are testimonials to this trend. As noted earlier, preoccupation with the traditional notion of state sovereignty can be ascribed to several sources: to the historical memory of colonial domination and subjugation, to nationalist zeal and conscious political efforts to avoid failed states, and to the absence of regional cooperative security regimes to prevent, mitigate, and resolve interstate disputes. It is paradoxical that the principle of nonviolability of state sovereignty has been reinforced by realist norms and rules such as the perception of anarchy, the use of force and diplomacy in dispute settlement, and balance of power and alliance.

Second, the Westphalian notion of sovereignty is not absolute but variable. Empirical sovereignty often prevails over Westphalian sovereignty. Thus state sovereignty is a fluid concept. Some countries voluntarily compromise state sovereignty for the sake of national interests or broadly defined sovereignty. Japan's commitment to the peace constitution and suspension of its full military sovereignty as well as South Korea's alliance with the United States and abrogation of its operational command during wartime—both of which are inviolable and integral parts of state sovereignty—illustrate that countries may sacrifice the narrow definition of the Westphalian sovereign (the principle of noninterference) for the sake of other goals of sovereignty such as national defense and survival. China, by contrast, has compromised the principle of domestic sovereignty by granting special status to Hong Kong in order to ensure domestic tranquillity and economic prosperity. As the Cambodian case exemplifies, in the worst case some countries may fall prey to outright intervention by a stronger state. Or they may be saved through benign intervention by international organizations such as the United Nations. These cases clearly show that the Westphalian notion of sovereignty may be violated in reality, but its violation does not necessarily lead to overt conflict. And it should be kept in mind that cases of compromised or intervened sovereignty are the exception rather than the rule. In general, even though its norms and principles are occasionally violated and compromised, the Westphalian notion of sovereignty remains the basic organizing unit of regional interaction.

Third, both the preservation and the violation of state sovereignty imply that national interests and power politics are driving forces of state behavior in Asia. Asian governments are less prone to rule-governed behavior in matters of security and politics. Liberal norms—such as refraining from the use of force, inviolability of frontiers, peaceful settlement of disputes, and recourse to (and compliance with) international law—are rarely observed in countries that are involved in disputes over territorial and political sovereignty. In other words, sovereignty in Asia has by and large created an instrumental order in which national identity, power, and interests prevail over collective identity, international cooperation, and community building. But an interesting contrast can be observed in the Asian context. Whereas Asian governments have inclined toward the exercise of Westphalian sovereignty in political and security matters, they have shown much greater willingness to pool sovereignty on economic and social issues—thus transcending the narrow confines of state sovereignty. This discrepancy points to the bifurcated conduct of foreign policy and national security policy in Asia.

Finally, it is interesting to observe the overlapping layers of contending sovereign exercises. While the notions of Westphalian sovereignty and empirical sovereignty through compromise and intervention constitute the bottom layer, parallel concepts such as communal and transnational sovereignty form the top layer. This multiple-layer structure is a reflection of the empirical reality of international politics in the region. Lifting the Cold War overlay did not lead to the termination of state centrism and power politics. They still represent the main facets of regional and international politics. Furthermore, the forces of globalization have yet to demolish the fortified wall of state sovereignty, especially in the area of peace and security. It is this twilight zone of overlapping layers of sovereign exercise that makes regional security and peace all the more precarious by structuring uncertainty in regional interactions.

What regional security order is needed to cope with the overlapping layers of sovereign exercises and subsequent internal and external conflicts? It seems essential to deliberate on the concept of regional security order itself before suggesting an ideal order. According to Alagappa (Chap. 1 in this volume), regional order is defined as a formal or informal arrangement that sustains rule-governed interaction among sovereign states in their pursuit of individual and collective goals. The core of this definition is rule-governed interaction. While goals are certainly important—especially in influencing the content of rules—the key criterion is whether interstate interaction is based on accepted rules. It implies that interaction among states is not arbitrary but conducted in a systematic manner. Such rules may be explicit and codified as international principles, norms, and regulations, including law, or they may have to be inferred from practice.

Alagappa delineates three types of regional order: instrumental, normative-contractual, and solidarist. The *instrumental* order is oriented toward the realization of private ends. National identity, power, and interests are the dominant considerations. There is little social cohesion among the interacting units. The *normative-contractual* order is oriented toward the realization of private and common goals through rules of collaboration. Although it is underpinned by a shared normative framework and states may identify with an incipient association or group, national identity is still predominant. The purpose of the *solidarist* order, which is based on trust among the interacting units, their obligation to the community, and the rule of law, is to consolidate the community and promote its welfare. In this type of order, the national identity and interests of units are shaped and often subsumed by the collective identity and goals of the community.

Judged on the theoretical and empirical discussions presented here, Asia still seems to be governed by the logic of Westphalian sovereignty. Nation-states are alive and well, and their pursuit of territorial and political integrity primarily defines the landscape of regional politics. Ideally speaking, compliance with the norms, principles, and rules of Westphalian sovereignty could minimize conflict since they are predicated on the immunity and nonviolability of state sovereignty. In reality, however, such norms and rules are rarely observed because of nebulous historical legacies and contested territorial and political sovereignty. Defying liberal gospels of globalization and cascading interdependence, countries are willing to fight each other in order to preserve goals of state sovereignty such as public authority, territory, recognition, and legitimacy. Despite the prevalence of Westphalian sovereignty, pockets of organized hypocrisy have surfaced. Both compromised sovereignty and intervened sovereignty reflect a deviation from the traditional Western paradigm of sovereignty based on domestic supremacy and absolute authority, external juridical equality and recognition, and immunity from external interference. As we have seen, Japan and South Korea have compromised their domestic sovereignty in order to maximize their national interests. And cases of intervened sovereignty, whether by imposition or by invitation, reveal the compromise of international legal sovereignty with empirical sovereignty.

Whether countries abide by the notion of Westphalian or empirical sovereignty, their sovereign goals have been anchored in an instrumental security order. Survival, maximization of national power and influence, preservation of the states' system—these are the primary goals of sovereign states. The realist portrait prevails where public authority is vested in the state, and the Hobbsian *Weltanschauung* dictates the dynamics of regional politics. Under the instrumental order, what the states can do is secure an unstable peace through military deterrence, balance of power, and alliance politics. Pathways to order are determined by the distribution of power among actors in the region rather than compliance with international or regional regimes. While war and diplomacy become the dominant instruments of achieving and maintaining regional order, international law and morality are treated as residual. A realist conception of sovereignty and a pervasive instrumental order make the Asian region all the more uncertain and precarious.

Creating and sustaining a stable peace under the realist instrumental order is quite inconceivable. There should be a gradual shift, therefore, to the normative-contractual order and solidarity order. A stable peace can only be achieved when countries in the region are able to attain a normative-contractual order. Such a liberal transition will materialize when three conditions are met: capitalist peace, democratic peace, and community of security. First, capitalist peace becomes plausible as the spread of free-market mechanisms eliminates the potential for interstate conflict. As commercial liberals argue, deepening market interdependence within a region can reduce the likelihood of war while improving the chances for peace (Morse 1976; Keohane 1989: 165–94). This is because the expansion of markets creates vested commercial interests across borders who would oppose an outbreak of war that might undermine their wealth. The second condition has been suggested by republican liberals (Doyle 1997: chap. 8) who say the republican (democratic) polity can prevent war because it assures openness, transparency, and domestic checks and balances in the management of foreign and defense policy. As Bruce Russet observes, democracies (OECD members, for example) do not fight each other (Russet 1993). Hence enlarging democracy becomes an essential precondition for stable peace. And third, as an extension of capitalist peace and democratic peace, forming a community of security is another prerequisite for building a stable peace. A market economy and democratic polity can foster the formation of such a community through shared norms and values, common domestic institutions, and high levels of interdependence (Adler and Barnett 1998).

When these three conditions are met, conflicts arising from contested sovereignty might be resolved through domestic restraint, international mediation, or multilateral security regimes. The spread of free-market mechanisms, democratic governance, and a community of security is likely to persuade China, North Korea, and other troublesome countries to comply with the normative-contractual order through the emphasis on common interests and mutual gain over particular interests and individual gain. Such a development can also prevent conflicts resulting from intervened sovereignty since the normative-contractual order deters intervention by imposition while encouraging intervention by invitation. Comprehensive and cooperative security, intrinsic to the normative-contractual order, can also forge collective action to cope with various nongovernmental threats emerging from transnational sovereignty.

But a liberal transition alone cannot eliminate the conflict dilemmas. The diffusion of liberal democracy and a market economy cannot resolve the entangled mindsets of people involved in conflict. The dilemma of fragmented sovereignty cannot be solved without remedying the issue of fractured identity through understanding and recognition. Some interstate conflicts arising from contested sovereignty have become protracted precisely because of unresolved issues of identity and recognition—as evidenced by the friction between China and Taiwan, South and North Korea, and India and Pakistan (Kang, Chap. 10 in this volume). Territorial disputes in Asia have often been amplified by historical memories of domination and subjugation that have created an exclusive (and even combatant) collective identity wrapped around nationalism. Cognitive dissonance over the reversed Confucian order is seen as a primary source of Asian instability. Such notions of collective identity have made the structure of finite deterrence an integral part of the conflict system in Asia. When the overlay of the Cold War is completely lifted, new patterns of bilateral suspicion and rivalry are likely to ensue, complicating the process of peace building. Identity, not power and interests, will be the key predictor for strategic interactions among countries in the region—and such identity-driven politics will make Asia more unstable. It is for this reason that there must be a progression from the normative-contractual order to a solidarity order based on mutual understanding, trust, and obligation. A true community of security, where a permanent peace can be realized, can come only through the solidarity order.

The solidarity order, however, cannot come easily. A precondition must be met. The liberal conception of sovereignty should be socialized among policymakers and citizens alike. Liberal norms, principles, and rules should replace realist ones. A feeling of collaboration should be fostered through shared values and interests. Regional security cooperation should be more actively sought by transforming loose institutional arrangements such as the ASEAN Regional Forum into tight arrangements involving collective security. A regional order based on solidarity, trust, and obligation, however, will come only when there is a fundamental realignment of the notion of state sovereignty.

Patterns of Sovereignty and Conflict

Sovereignty in Asia has undergone evolutionary changes from monarchic sovereignty to Sino-centric hierarchic sovereignty. It was only after the late nineteenth century that countries in Asia were exposed to the Westphalian notion of sovereignty by Western powers. Although the Cold War bipolarity undercut some of its elements in the name of bloc politics, the foundation of Westphalian sovereignty remains intact. Yet it is not the only mode of Asian sovereignty: some countries have voluntarily compromised it for practical interests; others have experienced external intervention. Empirical sovereignty has prevailed over Westphalian sovereignty. Some sovereign states have encountered the dilemma of fragmented sovereignty through protracted communal conflicts and secessionist movements. Challenges to political and territorial integrity from within have been as painful as those from without. Moreover, the transnational sovereignty that has emerged along with waves of globalization has become a new source of threats to state sovereignty. The overlapping structure of multiple sovereignties underscores the contour of Asia's political geography today.

Nor have the goals of sovereignty changed. Physical and organic survival, maximization of national power and influence, preservation of territorial and political integrity, promotion of economic well-being and prosperity, international recognition and prestige—these are still the core values of national sovereignty. And preoccupation with these traditional values heightens the chances of interstate as well as domestic conflicts. While contested sovereignty breeds interstate conflict, those countries inflicted with fragmented sovereignty suffer from protracted domestic conflicts with enormous negative spillover to the regional system. Compromised sovereignty, as we have seen, can reduce the probability of regional conflict through alliance politics and credible military deterrence. Intervention by invitation poses a lesser problem to regional stability as well. Intervention by imposition, however, presupposes military conflict between the intervened and the intervener, thus destabilizing the regional system.

Current patterns of sovereignty and regional conflict imply that Asia is still governed by a realist instrumental order in which hegemony, balance of power, alliance politics, and military deterrence constitute the basic rules of the game. But the region is unlikely to achieve a stable peace through this instrumental order. There must be dedicated efforts to transform the instrumental order to the normative-contractual order and, ultimately, the solidarity order. Collective recognition of mutual identity, collective trust and obligation through shared norms and dense networks, collective cooperation on common security problems— these are the critical prerequisites for a stable peace in the region.

Works Cited

Adler, Emanuel, and Michael Barnett, eds. 1998. *Security Communities*. Cambridge: Cambridge University Press.

Auer, James E. 1993. "Article Nine: Renunciation of War." In Percy R. Luney and K. Takahashi, eds., *Japanese Constitutional Law*. Tokyo: University of Tokyo Press.

Azar, Edward. 1990. *The Management of Protracted Social Conflict*. Aldershot, U.K.: Dartmouth.

Bracken, Paul. 1999. *Fire in the East*. New York: HarperCollins.

Bull, Hedley. 1977. *The Anarchical Society*. New York: Columbia University Press.

———, and Adam Watson, eds. 1984. *The Expansion of International Society*. Oxford: Clarendon Press.

Burton, John. 1972. *World Society*. Cambridge: Cambridge University Press.

Caporaso, James. 2000. "Changes in the Westphalian Order: Territory, Public Authority, and Sovereignty." *International Studies Review* (special issue), pp. 1–28.

Cusimano, Maryann K., ed. 2000. *Beyond Sovereignty*. Boston/New York: Bedford/St. Martin.

De Jouvenel, Bertrand. 1993. *On Power*. Indianapolis: Liberty Fund.

Deudney, Daniel H. 1995. "The Philadelphian System: Sovereignty, Arms Control, and Balance of Power in the American States-Union, circa 1787–1861." *International Organization* 49(2): 191–228.

Doyle, Michael. 1997. *Ways of Peace and Ways of War*. New York: Norton.

Fairbank, John K., ed. 1968. *The Chinese World Order*. Cambridge, Mass.: Harvard University Press.

Friedberg, Aaron L. 1993–94. "Ripe for Rivalry: Prospects for Peace in a Multipolar Asia." *International Security* 18(3) (Winter): 34–77.

Hamashita, Takeshi. 1997. "The Intra-Regional Systems in East Asia in Modern Times." In Peter Katzenstein and Takashi Shiraishi, eds., *Network Power*. Ithaca: Cornell University Press.

Hughes, Caroline. 2000. "Dare to Say, Dare to Do: The Strongman in Business in 1990s Cambodia." *Asian Perspective* 24(2): 121–52.

Inoguchi, Takeshi, and Paul Bacon. 2001. "Sovereignty: Westphalian, Philadelphian, and Anti-utopian Paradigms." *International Relations of Asia Pacific* 1(2) (Summer): 169–72.

Jackson, Robert. 1993. *Quasi-states: Sovereignty, International Relations, and the Third World*. Cambridge: Cambridge University Press.

———. 2000. *The Global Covenant: Human Conduct in a World of States*. Oxford: Oxford University Press.

James, Alan. 1986. *Sovereign Statehood*. London: Allen & Unwin.

Jervis, Robert. 1992. "A Political Science Perspective on the Balance of Power and the Concert." *American Historical Review* 97(3): 716–24.

Kapstein, Ethan, and Michael Mastanduno, eds. 1999. *Unipolar Politics*. New York: Columbia University Press.

Keohane, Robert O. 1989. *International Institutions and State Power*. Boulder, Colo.: Westview.

Kim, Dal-choong, and Chung-in Moon, eds. 1997. *History, Cognition, and Peace*. Seoul: Yonsei University Press.

Kissinger, Henry A. 1957. *A World Restored: Metternich, Castlereagh, and the Problems of Peace, 1812–1822*. Boston: Houghton Mifflin.

Kohno, Masaru. 2001. "On Meiji Restoration–Japan's Search for Sovereignty?" *International Relations of Asia Pacific* 1(2) (Summer): 265–83.

Krasner, Stephen. 1999. *Sovereignty: Organized Hypocrisy*. Princeton: Princeton University Press.

———. 2001. "Organized Hypocrisy in 19th Century East Asia." *International Relations of Asia Pacific* 1(2) (Summer): 173–97.

Litfin, Karen. 1997. "Sovereignty in World Eco-politics." *Mershon International Studies Review* 41 (supplement 2): 167–204.

McEvedy, Colin. 1998. *The Penguin Historical Atlas of the Pacific*. New York: Penguin Books.

Moon, Chung-in, and Ronald McLaurin. 1989. *The United States and the Defense of the Pacific*. Boulder, Colo.: Westview.

Morse, Edward. 1976. *Modernization and the Transformation of International Relations*. New York: Basic Books.

Ohmae, Kenichi. 1991. *Borderless World*. New York: Basic Books.

Philpott, Daniel. 2001. "Usurping the Sovereignty of Sovereignty?" *World Politics* 53(2): 297–324.

Rhee, Taek-hyung. 1986. *U.S.-ROK Combined Operations: A Korean Perspective*. Washington, D.C.: National Defense University.

Rosenau, James N., and Ernst-Otto Czempiel. 1992. *Governance Without Government: Order and Change in World Politics*. Cambridge: Cambridge University Press.

Rupesinghe, Kumar, and Khawar Mumtaz, eds. 1996. *Internal Conflicts in South Asia*. London: Sage.

Russet, Bruce. 1993. *Grasping the Democratic Peace*. Princeton: Princeton University Press.

Schrijver, Nico. 2000. "The Changing Nature of State Sovereignty." In the *British Yearbook of International Law*. Oxford: Clarendon Press.

Segal, Jerald. 1991. *Rethinking the Pacific*. Oxford: Clarendon Press.

Singh, Daljit. 1997. *Southeast Asian Affairs*. Singapore: Institute of Southeast Asian Studies.

Smith, Dan. 1997. *The State of War and Peace Atlas*. New York: Penguin Books.

Sofka, James R. 1998. "Metternich's Theory of European Order: A Political Agenda for 'Perpetual Peace.'" *Review of Politics* 60(1): 115–49.

Stares, Paul, ed. 1998. *The New Security Agenda: A Global Survey*. Washington, D.C.: Brookings Institution.

Vernon, Raymond. 1971. *Sovereignty at Bay*. New York: Basic Books.

Wendt, Alexander. 1994. "Collective Identity Formation and the International State." *American Political Science Review* 88(2): 384–95.

———. 1999. *Social Theory of International Politics*. Cambridge: Cambridge University Press.

Zacher, Mark W. 2001. "The Territorial Integrity Norm: International Boundaries and the Use of Force." *International Organization* (Spring): 215–50.

PART II

Pathways to Order

CHAPTER FOUR

Incomplete Hegemony

The United States and Security Order in Asia

MICHAEL MASTANDUNO

What will Asia look like in the years ahead? Will it prove to be a zone of peace, characterized by economic interdependence and cooperative political and security institutions, or a zone of turmoil facing strategic contests, nationalist upheavals, and the threat of military conflict? This pressing question of contemporary world politics will continue to be widely debated by scholars and policy analysts. The Asian region is distinguished by economic dynamism, a diverse set of political systems and regimes, overlapping cultural traditions, and fluid power relationships. There are several key actors: China, a rising state simultaneously testing its regional influence and transforming its domestic politics; Japan, a major commercial and technological power that has experienced a decade of economic uncertainty and stagnation; and India, a waking giant determined to assert itself as a legitimate great power. The United States maintains a formidable presence in the region as well, although some question the durability of its commitment in the absence of a Soviet threat or an equivalent global challenge.

Suspicions and resentments embedded in the history of the region linger some fifty years after the end of World War II.[1] The experience of Japanese imperialism prior to and during the war continues to shape political sentiment in China, Korea, and parts of Southeast Asia.[2] Both the growth of Chinese power and the un-

[1]One recent example is the controversy sparked by a conference intended to play down Japan's record of atrocities during its prewar occupation of China. The conference was sharply criticized by the Chinese government and by historians and others in Japan. See French (2000).

[2]Ralph Cossa (1999: 195) notes in a recent analysis of Korean-Japanese relations that "unfortunately, one of the few things that the people of the South and North have in common is a mutual distrust of Japan."

predictability of North Korea concern Japan. Numerous flashpoints could lead to bilateral or regional military conflict: the troubled relationship between China and Taiwan, instability and ethnic conflict in Indonesia, the continued division of the Korean peninsula, and the Kashmir dispute between India and Pakistan.[3] One does not need to be unduly pessimistic to recognize the potential for instability and conflict in this critical area of world politics.

How is order to be maintained in this region? No definition of security "order" has been universally accepted by political scientists. Hedley Bull has defined international order broadly as the "pattern of international activity that sustains those goals of the society of states that are elementary, primary, or universal" (Bull 1977: 16). Building on Bull, Muthiah Alagappa (Chap. 1 in this volume) defines order as "rule-governed interaction among sovereign states in their pursuit of individual and collective goals" that makes for "predictability, stability, and nonviolent change." He asserts that "order does not proscribe force and war but circumscribes and regulates their utility and roles." The goals and rules to sustain order could be contentious because an international order inevitably benefits certain actors and privileges certain values at the expense of others. Nevertheless, most political scientists would probably concur that a successful regional order involves the absence of a major war among the states in the region. It also involves the management—and ideally the successful resolution—of regional disputes short of major war. Finally, order necessitates the peaceful accommodation of international change. As T. V. Paul and John Hall put it recently: "The success of an international order is predicated on the extent to which it can accommodate change without violence" (Paul and Hall 1999: 2).

My purpose here is to examine the contribution of hegemony to the creation and maintenance of security order in Asia. The hegemonic pathway to order should be distinguished from other paths. Order might be maintained, for example, by a balance of power, whether bipolar or multipolar. It might result from the functioning of a diplomatic concert among the major powers in the region or from the emergence of a pluralistic security community. Order might also result from the development of international institutions—institutions sufficiently legitimate and powerful to constrain the potentially destabilizing behavior of member states. In contrast to these pathways, hegemony refers to the creation and maintenance of security order due to the capabilities and behavior of a dominant state. The hegemonic pathway is directly relevant to contemporary Asia because the United States possesses a preponderance of material resources and has been eager to take on responsibility as a manager of the regional security order.

[3]Prior to his visit in March 2000, President Clinton referred publicly to the Indian subcontinent as "the most dangerous place in the world today." See Perlez (2000).

This chapter advances a set of related arguments. First: Hegemony has material and nonmaterial components. A unipolar distribution of power, by itself, is not sufficient to establish hegemony. There must also be some meaningful degree of acquiescence by other major states in the region. In a hegemonic order, the leader must have followers. And the more these followers are willing to recognize the hegemonic order as legitimate and share its values and purposes, the more durable the order will be.

Second: A partial hegemonic order does exist in the Asia Pacific. The United States has constructed this order over the course of the postwar era and has continued to advance it since the end of the Cold War. Hegemony has contributed in significant ways to the maintenance of regional security. American power and presence have helped to keep traditional power rivals in the region from engaging in significant conflict and have reassured smaller states that traditionally have been vulnerable to major regional powers. The United States has played a key role in managing and defusing regional crises. And by promoting economic liberalization in the region, U.S. officials have curbed the nationalist economic competition that historically has been associated with political conflict. There are limits, however, to what hegemony has contributed to regional order. Although U.S. officials have helped to defuse regional crises, they have failed to foster any fundamental resolution of these crises or their underlying causes. Similarly, the United States has discouraged conflict among major regional powers, but has not made it a priority to promote a significant improvement in their relations. Hegemony has contributed to security order but has been, in effect, a holding operation: it has kept the security environment from deteriorating yet has failed to create enduring solutions to regional security problems.

Third: The U.S. hegemonic order is incomplete. One regional power, Japan, has embraced the U.S-centered order and found its security in the maintenance of this order. A second regional power, China, is considerably more ambivalent—even though the United States has made it a foreign policy priority to integrate China into the present order. A third major player, India, is similarly ambivalent about U.S. hegemony, and the United States has only recently begun serious efforts to integrate India.

Fourth: The United States faces a set of significant challenges in its effort to sustain and complete a hegemonic order in the region. It has the daunting task of successfully engaging China and India. It must maintain domestic support for its hegemonic role. And it must manage the political resentments that inevitably arise when there are gross asymmetries in the distribution of international power and prestige. These challenges, and the ability of the United States to address them, take on renewed significance after the terrorist attacks of September 11, 2001. Because the terrorist threat is a global one, those events provided all the more incentive for U.S. officials to pursue a hegemonic order in Asia. The attacks and the U.S. response also facilitated U.S. efforts to create regional order by opening new opportunities for cooperation with major powers in the region.

Finally, I argue that the pathway of U.S. hegemony, despite its obvious short-comings, has significant advantages over other paths in the contemporary Asia Pacific. There are pathways that are more desirable, but not feasible in the near term. There are pathways that are feasible, but less desirable as a means to secure order. Clearly the hegemonic order will not endure indefinitely. The challenge for the United States and other regional powers will ultimately be to transform the present hegemonic order into one that is more rather than less desirable.

Hegemony and Order

It is ironic that during the time period most political scientists consider the high point of U.S. hegemony—the 1950s and 1960s—the term "hegemony" hardly appeared in the international relations literature. The term came into use during the 1970s, when many U.S. political scientists addressed the issue of "declining hegemony." Hegemony and hegemonic stability became central themes in international relations scholarship during the 1980s (Gilpin 1981, 1987; Keohane 1980, 1984; Lake 1988; Russett 1985; Strange 1987; Katzenstein et al. 1998). Like many core concepts, hegemony has multiple meanings, and different analysts stress different ones. The central point here is to recognize both the material and the nonmaterial aspects of hegemony.

One common understanding equates hegemony with a certain distribution of material resources—one in which there exists an unambiguously dominant state (Krasner 1976). Hegemony, in this view, is essentially equivalent to unipolarity. Some scholars focus exclusively on the international economic structure (Lake 1988); others suggest that a state must be dominant in the distribution of military as well as economic power to qualify as hegemonic.

Others contend that hegemony connotes more than the asymmetric distribution of resources, whether economic or military. Hegemony, they say, should be understood in terms of the ability to control important international outcomes; it is associated not just with material power but with social purpose. Charles Kindleberger (1973) popularized this idea with his well-known argument that one leading state needed to undertake a series of tasks to assure one critical outcome—the robust functioning of a liberal economic order. Robert Keohane argues that hegemonic states possess the capacity to "maintain the regimes they favor" (1980: 136). During the 1980s and 1990s, Bruce Russett, Susan Strange, and Henry Nau challenged the conventional wisdom of the United States as a hegemonic power in decline by pointing to the continued U.S. ability to produce the international outcomes it prefers, such as liberal trade, democratization, and nuclear peace (Russett 1985; Strange 1987; Nau 1990). A hegemonic state has the power to shape the rules of the international game in accord with its own values and interests. A hegemonic distribution of power does not always produce the same international outcomes, however. Outcomes depend on the priorities and purposes of whatever state happens to be dominant.

A third meaning of hegemony is embedded in the question of whether international outcomes benefit other states as well as the hegemonic state. Does the hegemonic state promote the common good? Or does it merely exploit others for its particularistic gain? Scholars distinguish benign from malign hegemony, leaders from dominators, and collective goods producers from predators. Although it makes sense to identify different styles of hegemonic behavior, the key point is that hegemony is unlikely to endure if it is primarily coercive, predatory, or beneficial only to the dominant state. In other words, leaders must have followers. Hegemony requires some degree of consent by other major actors in order to sustain itself. The most durable hegemonic order is one in which there exists a meaningful consensus on the right of the hegemonic state to lead, as well as the social purposes it projects. Gramsci's depiction of hegemony as a power relationship that is internalized, or reproduced and sustained through ideological acceptance, is relevant here (Cox 1983; Keohane 1984). One might say that hegemony works best when it is least noticed or is accepted by others as a routine state of affairs.[4] As Bruce Cumings put it recently: "Hegemony is most effective when it is indirect, inclusive, plural, heterogeneous, and consensual—less a form of domination than a form of legitimate global leadership" (1999: 484).

Hegemony, then, requires a preponderance of material resources, a sense of social purpose, the ability to control international outcomes of importance to the dominant state, and some degree of consent and acceptance from other states in the system. Two qualifications are in order. First, the ability to control outcomes should not be taken to imply that the hegemonic state controls *all* international outcomes or that it wins all the time.[5] No state enjoys such luxury. To establish this as the threshold for hegemony is simply to create a straw man. But in a hegemonic system we should be able to identify, as Russett does, a set of key inter-

[4]A recent *Foreign Affairs* essay by Richard N. Haass is instructive in this regard. Haass argues that the United States should strive, not for hegemony, but for a concert of great powers. His idea of a concert, however, is a system in which other major powers are persuaded to accept conceptions of order that reflect the particular interests and values of the United States. As "common" values he points to economic openness, humanitarian intervention (because people, not just states, enjoy rights), the control and reduction of nuclear weapons, and limits on the use of force. See Haass (1999).

[5]Even early in the postwar era, when the United States was so dominant and other countries so devastated, the United States did not win every battle. See Ikenberry (2002).

national outcomes that are consistent with the preferences and purposes of the dominant state. The hegemonic state should be pivotal in setting the rules of the game, even if it does not prevail in every conflict.

Second, the presence of some degree of consent from other states does not imply that we should expect public displays of affection for the hegemonic order. In a system of sovereign states in which prestige matters domestically and internationally, it is natural to expect government officials to protest the accumulation of power in the hands of a single state. But for French or Chinese officials to complain in a public setting that the United States is a "hyperpower," or to assert that a unipolar world is a dangerous one, is not the same as forming a balancing coalition against U.S. preponderance.[6] Although public criticism may be a precursor to serious opposition, the main issues to consider are whether other states are actively resisting the hegemonic order and to what extent they accept the purposes of the hegemonic state as legitimate and even internalize them as their own.

Emergence of the U.S. Hegemonic Order

The United States emerged as a great power during the late nineteenth and early twentieth centuries (Zakaria 1999). It came out of World War I as the world's leading source of manufactured output, financial credit, and foreign direct investment (Frieden 1988; Kennedy 1987). The dramatic growth in America's economic power, juxtaposed to the relatively modest role the United States played in interwar economic diplomacy, prompted Kindleberger's often cited observation that the United States was able but not willing to lead the world economy during the depression years. The country's relative economic power increased further during World War II, and following that conflict the United States assumed a more prominent global role both militarily and economically.

Washington consistently envisioned international order and its global role in ideological as well as material terms. World War II was fought not simply to adjust the balance of power among leading states; it was also a struggle against fascism, an ideological competitor to democracy and liberalism as organizing principles for political life. The commitment of U.S. officials to a fundamental transformation of the domestic political economies of the defeated powers reflected the deep conviction that fascism was evil and had to be eliminated as an alternative path to political order. A similar sentiment informed the U.S. crusade against communism. America's hegemony during the Cold War was never complete in

[6]Those who anticipate the early demise of U.S. hegemony and the unipolar structure often cite expressions of resentment or anxiety as evidence of mobilization against the hegemonic order. See, for example, Layne (1993).

that the Soviet Union posed a geopolitical challenge and represented a viable ideological alternative. It is tempting, in light of the contemporary political context, to underestimate the appeal that communist ideology held, particularly in the Third World, during the 1950s and 1960s. Until the 1980s, U.S. officials felt the best they could do was to "contain" communism so that it did not penetrate and undermine the capitalist and (sometimes) democratic order under construction in various parts of the world. The end of the Cold War in 1989 represented not just the demise of the Soviet Union as a superpower challenger to the United States but also the demise of the ideological alternative it presented for domestic and international political order.

Another, more limited challenge to U.S. hegemony emerged as the Cold War ended. Japan and the United States, close military allies during the Cold War, by the 1980s had become significant economic competitors in possession of the world's two largest economies. Japan's economic challenge was multifaceted. The ability of Japanese firms to outcompete their U.S. counterparts in merchandise trade was only the most visible manifestation. Japan also challenged the United States for control at the frontier of advanced technologies with military as well as commercial applications. And during the 1980s, the two countries traded places as Japan became the world's largest creditor and the United States the world's biggest debtor (Prestowitz 1990). The Japanese challenge was, in a more modest sense, ideological as well. The widespread view in academic and policy circles was that Japan's economic success was based on "developmental capitalism"—an alternative, Asian way to organize a capitalist political economy (Johnson 1982). In contrast to the laissez-faire model offered by the United States, the Japanese model emphasized tight alliances and long-term relationships among manufacturing firms, close collaboration between industry and government, a commitment to state-led industrial policy and export promotion, the selective protection of home markets, and reliance on banks rather than equity markets for corporate funding. This model seemed to be working during the 1980s—so well, in fact, that a debate emerged within U.S. policy circles over whether the United States should emulate Japan by adopting an industrial policy of its own. As Japan's success mounted, its usually reticent foreign policy officials became more assertive in touting the advantages of their economic model. They urged the World Bank, for example, to stress the key role of government intervention in its 1993 study of the origins and lessons of the Asian economic miracle (World Bank 1993).

The challenge of developmental capitalism was accentuated by the economic accomplishments of the Asian countries. The East Asia and Southeast Asian countries grew at an average annual rate of roughly 6 percent for almost two decades—well above the global annual average of about 2 percent (Oksenberg 2000:

8–9). Sustained high rates of growth enabled the region to take on greater significance in the world economy. Asia was no longer on the periphery; in fact, prominent political economists such as Robert Gilpin foresaw a fundamental shift in the center of global economic activity—and, by implication, geopolitical influence—from Europe to Asia (Gilpin 1987; Ellings and Friedberg 2001). The Asia Pacific began to assume a regional identity symbolized by the emergence of APEC and the initiation in 1993 of annual meetings of the region's leaders. This dawning of the "Pacific Century" and Asia's distinctive approach to political economy went hand in hand. A common metaphor depicted Asia's thriving economies as geese flying in formation behind the leadership of Japan.

The picture that emerged at the end of the 1990s was strikingly different. Over the past decade Japan has experienced economic stagnation. Japan's "bubble economy" burst in the early 1990s, and subsequent efforts at recovery have been hampered by some of the very features of the Japanese model that accounted for Japan's postwar success (Mastanduno 2000; Foot and Walter 1999). Lifetime employment commitments and long-term relationships among firms left the Japanese economy far less flexible than that of the United States in responding to economic downturns and taking advantage of economic disruptions (Christensen et al. 2001). The same close links between banks, firms, and government that helped allocate capital effectively during the high-growth years have proved to be a constraint at a time when many banks are insolvent. Industrial policy was an effective instrument for the mobilization of an economy to catch up in the production of commodities such as automobiles and memory chips. As Japanese officials recognize, industrial policy has turned out to be far less effective as an instrument for innovation at the frontier of technology (Callon 1995). The tendency of Japanese politicians to defer to the professional expertise of the bureaucracy, viewed as a great asset in the consistent implementation of the postwar growth strategy, has proved a liability in an era in which Japan lacks an overall strategy and requires political leadership and vision to change direction.

The Asian financial crisis of 1997–98 further accentuated the weakness of developmental capitalism. The pressure of volatile international capital movements exposed a host of domestic economic vulnerabilities in some of the most promising young tigers of East Asia and Southeast Asia. These problems included the overextension of credit to inefficient enterprises and real estate developers, inadequate supervision of domestic financial systems, a lack of transparency in current and capital account activity, excessive short-term borrowing to cover current account deficits, and the use of reserves to defend rigid exchange rates (Goldstein 1998; Cooper 2000). In the course of a few years, the common characterization of the region by academics and policy analysts has swung from "Asian miracle" to "crony capitalism." The latter depiction overplays Asian weaknesses, no doubt, just as the former overplayed Asian strengths. In the years ahead, the Asian model of political economy is more likely to be modified than abandoned outright. Japan's stagnation and the financial crisis should not be taken to imply either Asia's economic collapse or the triumph of the American form of capitalism. These seminal events of the 1990s do suggest, however, that the Asian model no longer carries the ideological appeal it once enjoyed as a superior form of capitalist development.

The geopolitical position of the United States is also strikingly different at the beginning of this new century. At the end of the Cold War, the U.S. position in global terms appeared to be one of military dominance and relative economic decline. Ten years later, the military superiority of the United States has arguably increased. Even though the Cold War has ended, U.S. defense spending has remained at the average levels of the Cold War and continues to dwarf that of any other state, allied or not. U.S. defense spending will likely increase even further in response to the 2001 terrorist attacks. The U.S.-led interventions in the Persian Gulf at the beginning of the 1990s and then in Kosovo and Afghanistan more recently serve as uncomfortable reminders, even to America's closest allies, of the sizable disparity in intelligence-gathering capacity, military technologies, and power projection capabilities.

Simultaneously the United States has recovered a position of relative economic superiority. Its economy thrived through the 1990s as those of its major competitors struggled. American-based firms and the economy as a whole have taken greater advantage of the revolution in information technology than have the economies of other states (Nye and Owens 1996). What appeared at the end of the 1980s to be a struggle for technological supremacy between Japan and the United States appears, a decade later, to have been resolved in favor of the latter. The Asian crisis accentuated the U.S. relative advantage; the U.S. economy proved less vulnerable than many had expected to the contagion effect of the Asian downturn. And whereas American markets are recognized as crucial by countries seeking to export their way out of decline, Japan has taken criticism from within the region and beyond for its reluctance to stimulate regional recovery by opening its markets and maintaining the strength of its currency.

Some fifty years after the end of World War II, the United States finds itself atop a unipolar distribution of material capabilities. As William Wohlforth recently emphasized, U.S. preeminence is unprecedented: "Never in modern international history has the leading state been so dominant economically and militarily" (1999: 13). Among today's major states, only the United States retains the full array of great power attributes—military, economic, and what some have termed the "soft" power attributes of ideological or cultural appeal (Nye 1990; Nau 1990). The idea of an international structure dominated by the United States may be reassuring to some and repugnant to others (Kagan 1998; Maynes 1998). But the U.S. preponderance in material capabilities should not be taken to imply U.S. control over all or even most international outcomes. Even a cursory glance at international events since the 1990s suggests the limits to U.S. power: Saddam Hussein remains in place in Iraq; other Western nations undermine U.S. economic sanctions; adversaries in the Middle East and the Balkans continue to defy U.S.-crafted initiatives to resolve their differences; and, most dramatically, state-supported terrorists attacked the core symbols of U.S. military and economic dominance. Yet crucial outcomes in world politics, for better or worse, are increasingly consistent with U.S. core values (Russett 1985; Strange 1987; Cumings 1999). As a status quo power, the United States prefers, and currently enjoys, peace defined as the absence of serious conflict among major global powers. The general trend in favor of liberalized trade and financial markets reflects U.S. preferences. The extreme statism of command economies, along with the moderate statism associated with developmental capitalism and import-substitution industrialization, has fallen out of favor. The attributes of political governance favored by the United States—democracy and liberalism—are not universally practiced but have a far greater appeal today than in the past.

During the 1990s, U.S. officials adopted a geopolitical strategy designed to preserve and extend preponderance. This strategy included efforts to discourage the rise of great-power challengers, the selective use of international institutions (WTO, IMF) to reflect and spread U.S. core values, and engagement in key regions where economic power and potential geopolitical influence are concentrated (Mastanduno 1997). Two of the most important regions are Europe and Asia. In Europe, U.S. strategy has centered on the maintenance and expansion of NATO to promote regional stability and discourage great-power challengers. Washington supported German unification on the condition that Germany remain in NATO and has encouraged European defense initiatives only to the extent that they remain subordinate to NATO. In Asia, the U.S. hegemonic strategy takes a different institutional form but reflects similar grand strategic objectives.

Incomplete Hegemony in Asia

The end of the Cold War presented Washington with several options for pursuing order in Asia. The United States could have adopted the role of "offshore balancer" by withdrawing its forward presence from the region and encouraging a multipolar balance of power (Layne 1993). Alternatively, U.S. officials could have focused on building regional security and economic institutions as the principal pathway to order. A third possibility might have been to organize a coalition of states to contain whatever state appeared prepared to mount a challenge to regional order. In light of its size and ambition, China would be the most likely prospect for such a role.[7]

The U.S. Hegemonic Strategy for Asia

Washington has given priority to none of these options. Instead it has pursued a hegemonic strategy—one that reserves a special role for the United States as the principal guarantor of regional order.

The central institutional feature of the U.S. hegemonic strategy is the cultivation of a set of special relationships with key states in the region. Bilateralism, rather than multilateralism, is the key to the U.S. approach. The principal bilateral relationship is with Japan—reflecting the continuity between America's Cold War and post–Cold War regional strategy. Washington similarly has maintained its bilateral alliance structure and commitment to South Korea. And it has reaffirmed its "unique partnership" with Australia.[8] Instead of using these alliances to balance China, however, the core U.S. strategy during the Clinton administration was to develop a special relationship with China as well. Clinton officials termed their approach to China "comprehensive engagement"—a partnership that was less than an alliance but more cooperative than competitive. The Bush administration, while more cautious than that of Clinton, nevertheless has sought to manage China relations more through cooperation than confrontation. The overall U.S. approach to the region might be thought of in terms of a "hub-and-spoke" arrangement: U.S. officials seek to craft a series of special relationships designed to assure key regional players that their relationship with Washington is both crucial and indispensable.[9]

The manner in which the United States has treated multilateral security institutions in Asia clarifies further its hegemonic strategy. Washington tended to view multilateral initiatives skeptically during the Cold War, particularly after the failures of SEATO and CENTO. During the 1990s, it was more supportive of multilateralism as a complement to bilateral security relationships. In a 1993 speech in South Korea, for example, President Clinton focused attention on the crucial role of bilateral alliances and also called for the promotion of new multilateral dialogues in the region on the full range of common security challenges (Cossa 2000).

For U.S. officials, multilateral initiatives afford a useful way to engage the participation of various Asian states in regional security affairs without undermining the hegemonic strategy. Asian security institutions can play a positive role in

[7]Ross (1999) believes the region is already bipolar.

[8]Australian Prime Minister John Howard characterized the relationship this way. See Richardson (2000).

[9]Joffe (1995) analyzes hub-and-spoke strategies for hegemonic powers.

fostering communication and confidence-building measures, but they are not sufficiently developed to take on a central role in the management and resolution of regional security problems. Thus it is not surprising that U.S. officials have supported the Asian Regional Forum (ARF) as a vehicle for ASEAN members to voice their security concerns and explore the potential for preventive diplomacy and maritime cooperation. Washington similarly has supported the Northeast Asia Cooperation Dialogue (NEACD) among China, Japan, Russia, the United States, and the two Koreas. NEACD offers the United States a safe way to involve Japan and Russia in regional security dialogue, as well as an opportunity to explain U.S. bilateral alliances with Japan and South Korea to suspicious Chinese and Russian officials (Cossa 2000).

Washington clearly views multilateral initiatives as supplements to, not substitutes for, its bilateral security relationships. In times of crisis, U.S. officials turn not to these regional institutions, but to U.S.-led diplomatic efforts and institutional structures that the United States can control. In the North Korean nuclear crisis of 1994, the United States relied on ad hoc diplomacy and established a new entity, the Korean Peninsula Energy Development Organization (KEDO), to implement its agreement. During the Asian financial crisis, U.S. officials rebuffed Japan's proposal for a regional financing facility and instead concentrated management of the crisis on the more familiar terrain of the IMF.

Washington's intent to serve as the principal source of regional order is symbolized and reinforced by its forward military presence. Early in the 1990s, the United States scaled back its troop commitments in East Asia and about the same time relinquished its naval facilities in the Philippines at the request of that government. These moves were read in the region and elsewhere as the beginnings of U.S. withdrawal. By 1995, however, U.S. officials had clarified that this was not the case. In fact, their intent was the opposite. The United States planned, in the words of the Pentagon's East Asia strategy document, to maintain a forward political and military commitment to East Asia of "indefinite duration." This policy included the stabilization of the U.S. troop presence in the region at about 100,000 (U.S. Department of Defense 1995; Nye 1995). The United States also intended to maintain its dominant position in maritime East Asia. Washington's alliances with Japan and South Korea provided secure access in Northeast Asia. In Southeast Asia, the U.S. Navy would rely on "places, not bases." By the end of the 1990s, U.S. officials had concluded access agreements for naval facilities in Indonesia, Malaysia, Singapore, and Brunei, along with a status-of-forces agreement with the Philippines (Ross 1999: 85–86).

A final component of the U.S. hegemonic strategy might be called a commitment to a forward economic presence in Asia. Washington has consistently and aggressively promoted the spread of liberal international economic policies in Asian states inclined to be more comfortable with the practices of developmental capitalism. Economic openness plays to U.S. economic interests—particularly given U.S. competitiveness in the export of services, agriculture, and advanced technology. It plays to U.S. security interests, as well, since U.S. officials have consistently held that liberalism and economic interdependence promote peaceful political relations. It is not surprising that U.S. officials have reacted negatively and decisively to initiatives that seemed to suggest closed regionalism or managed trade. In the early 1990s, the United States opposed—and worked hard to assure that Japan would oppose—Malaysia's proposal for an East Asian Economic Group that would exclude the United States. Washington expressed concern at the highest levels and hinted that exclusionary economic arrangements in East Asia might force the United States to reevaluate security commitments (Grieco 1999: 328–29). The role of the United States in APEC has been to push member states more decisively in the direction of liberalization. Washington has promoted trade liberalization bilaterally in negotiations with Japan, China, and South Korea and multilaterally through the WTO. It has pushed financial liberalization in Asia under the auspices of the "Washington Consensus" developed and implemented by the IMF and World Bank (Wade 1998–99).

Hegemony and Regional Order: Contributions and Limits

The United States has crafted a hegemonic strategy for Asia to serve its own geopolitical and economic interests. In the process, U.S. hegemony is also contributing to regional order—though it is important to recognize the limits of U.S. hegemony as the principal mechanism for regional order.

One important contribution of the U.S. position in Asia has been to keep potential power rivals at bay. Japan and China are major powers, each with the capacity to become a great military power. They share geographic proximity and an unfortunate history of conflict and mutual recrimination. Events such as the recent conference in Japan reconsidering the 1937 massacre at Nanking, ongoing disputes over the veracity of Japanese textbooks, and recent remarks by Tokyo Governor Shintaro Ishihara to the effect that Japan must be prepared to put down Korean or Chinese "uprisings" reopen old wounds and keep hostilities alive.[10] The Japanese-Chinese relationship has the makings of a classic security dilemma, one reinforced by bad memories and ethnic conflict. As Tom Christensen noted recently: "Although Chinese analysts presently fear U.S. power

[10]On the first incident, see note 1. On the second, see "Mr. No Blames the Victim" (2000). Ishihara used a racial slur in referring to the potential for ethnic Korean or Chinese uprisings within Japan.

much more than Japanese power, in terms of national intentions, Chinese analysts view Japan with much less trust and, in many cases, with a loathing rarely found in their attitudes about the United States" (1999: 52). Chinese attitudes and suspicions obviously factor into Japan's own anxieties about the rising power and intentions of its large neighbor. In this circumstance, U.S. hegemony plays a critical role in keeping the negative aspects of the relationship from spiraling in a dangerous direction. Through its alliance and commitment to defend Japan, the United States makes it possible for Japan to avoid confronting China directly. A direct Japanese approach to China would only confirm Chinese fears of a revanchist Japan. Although Chinese officials are reluctant to admit it, they recognize that the U.S.-Japan alliance constrains as well as protects Japan. This alliance, combined with the U.S. cooperative approach to China, helps to reassure China that it need not confront Japan directly. The diplomatic game U.S. officials must play is a delicate one: too strong an alliance with Japan arouses Chinese fears of containment; too strong a partnership with China arouses Japanese fears of abandonment. The difficulty of the diplomatic task reinforces the likelihood that in the absence of a U.S. hegemonic role, Japanese-Chinese geopolitical competition would increase substantially.

U.S. hegemony also helps to mitigate the security concerns of smaller states in the region. In many circumstances, hegemonic power can reasonably be feared by smaller states as a threat to their security and territorial integrity. In the Asian context, this is less likely to be the case. For most states, the U.S. presence is more reassurance than threat. One reason is that the smaller powers of Northeast and Southeast Asia live in dangerous neighborhoods. They coexist with larger powers that have varying geopolitical ambitions and conflicts among themselves.[11] And there is an array of unresolved territorial disputes that might become flashpoints for larger conflicts. The United States, in this setting, can manage conflicts with greater credibility than other major powers in the region. The United States has geopolitical interests of its own, but not territorial ambitions. It also possesses power projection capabilities that other major powers in the region lack, granting it credibility as the potential enforcer of regional order. In Northeast Asia, the U.S. presence in both Japan and South Korea helps to reassure the latter in the presence of more powerful neighbors. The U.S. maritime presence in Southeast Asia similarly helps the smaller ASEAN states to deal more easily with China. Although most Southeast Asian states (Singapore is an exception) are reluctant to grant the United States access to their bases to preposition military equipment,

[11]Although China claims the entire South China Sea as its territorial waters, India recently announced it would hold unilateral and bilateral naval exercises there. See "India Challenges China in South China Sea," *STRATFOR.COM Global Intelligence Update*, Apr. 26, 2000.

they welcome the role that U.S. forward-deployed forces play in maintaining regional stability.[12]

A third contribution of U.S. hegemony to order involves the management of security crises that might escalate to local war and even regional conflict. The United States has assumed for itself a significant role in defusing regional crises. Recent conflicts between India and Pakistan over Kashmir offer apt examples. Late in 2001, President Bush intervened personally to discourage the two states from going to war following a terrorist attack on the Indian Parliament that Indian officials traced to Pakistan. In 1999, an Indian-Pakistan conflict came closer to a general war than was publicly acknowledged at the time. When Pakistan established positions in Indian-controlled Kashmir during the spring of 1999, India responded with a general military mobilization that eventually led Pakistan to preparations of its own. Although neither side expected a full-scale war, the potential for these two nuclear powers to stumble into one was not insignificant. President Clinton intervened personally and kept regular phone contact with the leaders of both sides, urging them to show restraint and respect the sanctity of the line of control. Most analysts credit Clinton with a significant (if short-term) success in persuading Pakistan Prime Minister Sharif to withdraw his forces (Lancaster 1999).

Washington similarly has taken the lead role in seeking to discourage North Korea's nuclear ambitions. It fears that a nuclear North Korea would damage nonproliferation norms, especially in the Asia Pacific region. A central concern is that a nuclear North Korea, in the context of Russia and China's possession of nuclear weapons, would create incentives for Japan eventually to reconsider its nonnuclear status. Washington crafted the 1994 arrangement whereby North Korea agreed to a nuclear moratorium in exchange for economic assistance provided by the United States, South Korea, and Japan through KEDO. Asian states did not respond in a decisive manner to North Korea until the United States took the lead. In 1999, Washington again promised economic concessions, this time to induce North Korea not to conduct tests of its long-range missiles. The North Korean test program was especially alarming to Japan—in August 1998, North Korea sent a missile directly over Japanese airspace. Washington recognizes that the North Korean threat is immediate for its Asian allies and remote with regard to the U.S. homeland.[13] Nonetheless it took the initiative to develop a concerted response among Washington, Seoul, and Tokyo, and urged Moscow and Beijing

---

[12]Oksenberg (2000: 10) notes that even China quietly acknowledges the constructive role of U.S. forces, though not publicly, out of concern these forces might be used to defend Taiwan.

[13]Assistant Secretary of State J. Stapleton Roy testified in early 2000 that North Korea's missiles "are unlikely to be used against U.S. territory, but they are a growing threat to U.S. allies and U.S. forces around the world." See Donnelly (2000).

to use whatever influence they could to restrain North Korea (Abramowitz and Laney 1999: 10–11; Shenon 1999).

The United States has also intervened in the increasingly tense standoff between China and Taiwan. The U.S. goal has been to deter China from seeking a military solution (the Taiwan Relations Act of 1974 calls for the United States to come to Taiwan's aid if it is attacked) and, in addition, to dissuade Taiwan from provocative acts of independence. In March 1996, China fired missiles close to Taiwan in anticipation of Taiwanese elections. This action was meant to intimidate Taiwan and had the temporary effect of stalling shipping in the Taiwan Straits. The United States responded by dispatching two aircraft carriers and some fourteen other warships to the area. Through its strategy of "calculated ambiguity" Washington meant to deter possible Chinese aggression and simultaneously to signal its willingness to maintain a cooperative relationship with China. Washington prepared to take similar steps early in 2000 as China once again escalated its rhetoric (this time without launching missiles) in anticipation of another Taiwanese election (Kaiser and Mufson 2000a).

Fourth, U.S. hegemony has contributed to regional order by helping to stave off in Asia the kind of nationalist economic competition (and attendant political friction) that plagued the world economy during the 1930s. The potential for beggar-thy-neighbor policies certainly emerged during the late 1990s. The Asian financial crisis was a profound shock that might well have led to closed markets, competitive devaluations, and a downward spiral of trade and growth. The management of this crisis was found in Washington rather than Tokyo or elsewhere in the region. During the crisis, the U.S. Federal Reserve lowered interest rates to assure global liquidity and maintain high growth in the United States. As the crisis eased, the United States spurred recovery by taking in the huge flood of exports from emerging economies as well as from China and Japan.[14] Washington's response to the crisis reflected its regional economic strategy of seeking to liberalize the developmental capitalist markets of Japan and Southeast Asia while at the same time integrating China into the liberal world economy.

It is important to recognize the limits of hegemony as a means to promote regional order. In essence, the U.S. hegemonic project in the Asia Pacific is more a holding action than a progressive strategy for resolving security problems. It is an effort to stabilize a status quo that reflects U.S. dominance. Although Washington has worked hard to keep relations among major powers in the region from

[14]The United States, in the words of the *Financial Times*, was "an anchor of stability" during the crisis. See the editorial in *Financial Times*, Apr. 15, 2000. But different Asian countries did view the U.S. role more or less critically, depending on their circumstances. Thailand, for example, felt that the United States reacted too slowly and did not come effectively to Bangkok's aid. See Bob (2001: 8).

deteriorating, it does not seem to have a plan for resolving the long-standing tensions in these relationships. In fact, since the United States does not want to encourage a balancing coalition against its dominant position, it is not clear that it has a strategic interest in the full resolution of differences between, say, Japan and China or Russia and China. Some tension among these states reinforces their need for a special relationship with the United States.

Similarly, Washington has defused regional crises in Asia without any fundamental resolution of the underlying disputes. The series of U.S.-initiated economic concessions to North Korea, for example, reflects more an effort to buy time than a plan to transform the politics of the Korean peninsula. Korean unification, in fact, would be a mixed blessing for the United States in light of its hegemonic strategy. Unification, after all, would diminish the need for a U.S. military presence in Korea—a presence U.S. officials believe is important not only to defend South Korea but also to stabilize relations elsewhere in East Asia. Not surprisingly, Washington sought to keep the issue of U.S. forward-deployed forces off the table as the two Koreas began their détente process in 2000 (Harrison 2001).

Washington's diplomacy toward the China-Taiwan dispute proceeds in a similar spirit. Decisive steps by Taiwan toward independence would provoke China and raise the potential for military conflict. An aggressive attempt by China to incorporate Taiwan would force the United States either to defend Taiwan or to appease China—both of which are costly options. For the United States, an uneasy stalemate is preferable in current circumstances to any dramatic attempt at resolution. Washington has managed the conflict by trying to protect Taiwan without emboldening it and trying to deter China without isolating or provoking it.

There are limits, as well, to what hegemony can accomplish in regional economic relations. The United States played a vital role as market of last resort during the Asian crisis—a role that no other state inside or outside the region was prepared to play. But the United States alone cannot engineer lasting prosperity in the region. First and foremost, the United States needs the active cooperation of Japan (Armacost 2000). Japan's inability or unwillingness to pull out of its stagnation or open its economy further will be a continuing source of pressure on the regional economy whatever initiatives the United States takes. The economic collapse of Japan, or China, within the context of the Asian crisis would have posed a stabilization challenge beyond the capacity of any single state, even with the support of international institutions, to manage effectively.

Why U.S. Hegemony Is Incomplete

The limits of U.S. hegemony as a pathway to order must be recognized in a different sense as well. A complete hegemonic order, as argued earlier, requires not just preponderant capabilities but also a degree of acquiescence by other states, especially major ones, in the maintenance of that order. At the outset of the second post–Cold War decade, the United States finds that it has forestalled any serious challenges, individual or collective, to its hegemonic position. It also has earned the strong support of one major power in the region. But it has some distance to cover to obtain the acquiescence of two others.

The strong Cold War alliance between Japan and the United States has persisted. This was not a foregone conclusion. Many analysts, neorealists in particular, anticipated that Japan would distance itself from the United States at the end of the Cold War and adopt a more independent and perhaps assertive foreign policy. Kenneth Waltz argued that Japan was on the verge of transformation; all that remained was for it to "reach for the great power mantle" (Waltz 1993: 55). But Japan has not done so, at least not in the sense anticipated by Waltz. Its willingness to continue to define its national security priorities in terms of its special relationship with the United States not only reflects changes in Japan's national identity that have evolved over the postwar era but attests to the effectiveness of a U.S. strategy designed to assure Japan that its interests would be best served by remaining, in effect, a junior partner in a U.S.-centered regional and global order.

This is not to suggest that Japan's continued acquiescence can be taken for granted. On the contrary, the uncertainty inherent in any alliance is pronounced in the post–Cold War strategic context, since there is no longer any central strategic threat to justify the alliance. Washington appreciated the need, by the mid-1990s, to play down bilateral economic conflicts and focus instead on repairing and expanding its bilateral security relationship with Japan. The 1996 Joint Security Declaration was a step toward revitalizing the bilateral partnership. But by 2000, concern had reemerged on both sides of the Pacific that sustained high-level attention was lacking—leading to a sense of drift in U.S.-Japan relations. The concerns of Japanese officials were reinforced by what they perceived as the Clinton administration's tendency to pay more attention to China than to Japan. A bipartisan U.S. study group produced an important statement late in 2000— the Armitage Report—that called on leaders in both countries to improve, reinvigorate, and refocus the alliance (INSS 2000: 3).

Japan and the United States took an important step in that direction in the aftermath of September 11. The Japanese government responded very quickly with antiterrorist legislation that enabled Japan's naval forces to provide on-site support to U.S. forces in the Arabian Sea. U.S. and Japanese officials were determined to avoid a replay of their conflict during the Persian Gulf War ten years earlier. In that case U.S. officials resented the fact that Japan's offer of financial support came very late and with reluctance. Japan resented what it perceived as

Washington's lack of gratitude. The new Bush administration, which signaled upon taking office that a revived relationship with Japan would be the cornerstone of its Asian security strategy, was clearly pleased by Japan's rapid effort to "show the flag" in contributing more than financial support to the United States in its time of need (Ennis and Tashikawa 2001).

The U.S. relationship with China poses a different set of problems. On the one hand, it is by no means certain that China intends to mount a revisionist challenge to U.S. hegemony. China's interest in economic modernization—especially its inclination to integrate more fully into the institutions of the capitalist world economy such as the WTO—suggests otherwise. On the other hand, it is equally clear that China remains uncomfortable playing a subordinate role in a U.S.-centered order. Chinese rhetoric—in particular its stated commitment to foster a transformation from U.S. hegemony to a multipolar world—is designed to reinforce this point. A key problem for U.S. officials is that China defines its geopolitical interests partly in material terms and partly in terms of status. U.S. officials since the end of the Cold War have sought to convince Beijing that it can be secure and prosperous in a U.S.-centered order. In this effort Washington has achieved limited success. U.S. officials have made progress in satisfying China's economic interests by opening U.S. markets and supporting China's successful bid to join the WTO. They have been less effective in convincing Beijing that the current regional and global order provides it sufficient respect and recognition as a legitimate great power. The Taiwan issue only compounds the challenge: it is difficult for Beijing to accept that a U.S.-centered regional order is a benign one as long as Washington is providing support and protection to what mainland China perceives as a renegade province.

By the beginning of 2001, U.S.-China relations appeared headed into a downward spiral. The two countries squared off when China delayed the return of a U.S. reconnaissance aircraft forced to land on Chinese territory, and when the United States offered a significant arms package to Taiwan. As in the case of Japan, however, September 11 offered U.S. officials the opportunity to renew cooperation. China contributed quietly but significantly by delivering its ally Pakistan to the U.S. war effort. The U.S. assured China it would compensate Pakistan financially and diplomatically. U.S.-Chinese cooperation in antiterrorism has emerged as a bright spot in an otherwise challenged relationship (Hutzler 2001).

U.S. efforts to integrate India into the preferred regional order proved fairly minimal during the first post–Cold War decade. India, like China, perceives itself as a rising power with legitimate security concerns and a claim to major power status —and eventually great power status . International prestige is as important to India as it is to China. And from India's perspective, the United States has tended to treat it more as an underdeveloped country than as an emerging great power. Washington has lectured India on its nuclear proliferation and reluctance to sign the Comprehensive Test Ban Treaty, even as the U.S. Senate itself has rejected that same treaty. India also perceives that the United States favors China excessively and unfairly in terms of economic and diplomatic attention. This perception is especially irritating because India, like the United States, is a large multicultural democracy. India and the United States also share an emerging economic interest: both are at the forefront of developing the Internet and other information technology.

The United States, despite its overall commitment to regional stability and the evolution of its hub-and-spoke security strategy in Asia, has been slow to seize the initiative and improve bilateral relations with this key regional power. President Clinton's visit to India in March 2000—remarkably the first by a U.S. president since 1978—was an important step in the right direction (Perlez 2000). The war in Afghanistan provided additional impetus—it prompted the Indian leadership to enter a defense cooperation relationship with the United States. Although U.S. officials seemed intent on moving in this direction gradually, September 11 and its aftermath accelerated the process, in part to allay Indian concerns over U.S. cooperation with its rival Pakistan (Slater and Hiebert 2001). In the now familiar pattern, U.S. officials have pursued "special relationships" with both India and Pakistan simultaneously.

Can U.S. Hegemony Endure?

Washington speaks of an engagement with the Asian region of indefinite duration and implies that hegemony is sustainable over the long term. Many observers are skeptical. They point to the growing discomfort and discontent about U.S. dominance in a unipolar setting expressed in the region. (See, for example, Marshall and Mann 2000 and Layne 1999.) Clearly U.S. hegemony cannot last forever. But it did endure through the first post–Cold War decade. Can it be sustained for another decade, perhaps two? No one can say with certainty. But one thing at least is clear: There is a set of challenges that U.S. officials must address if the hegemonic pathway to order in Asia is to be sustained and strengthened. Even those most confident in the durability of unipolarity suggest that the United States must play its cards right to sustain it (Wohlforth 1999: 8).

The first challenge is to complete the hegemonic order. This is no easy task. It involves integrating China and India while simultaneously maintaining the support of Japan. The United States does enjoy certain advantages. It can count on the fact that all three powers have an interest in a regional stability that allows prosperity to grow. None would welcome a nuclear arms race or war on the Korean peninsula or Indian subcontinent. None has a strategic interest in Japan's economic collapse or in political chaos and fragmentation in China with its attendant refugee flows and environmental problems (Nye 2000: 162). Washington also holds strong cards in the effort to integrate China and India economically. The fact that China's economy has been increasingly dependent on the world economy in general and U.S. markets, investment, and technology in particular is an important source of leverage for the United States (Papayounou and Kastner 1999; Long 1996). In India's case, there is considerable room to overcome constraints on bilateral trade and investment in labor-intensive sectors (such as textiles) and high technology and to integrate India into international economic institutions such as the WTO and APEC. One difficulty, of course, is that increased wealth and prosperity are necessary but probably not sufficient means to integrate these two powers. Their status demands are equally important and even harder to accommodate. Symbolic political gestures (similar to including Russia in the G8 industrial democracies) are useful to pursue. But U.S. officials will be forced to address the need to share decision-making authority substantively as well as symbolically.

The second challenge is to maintain domestic support for the political and economic strategies to sustain hegemony. Although U.S. officials succeeded during the 1990s, one could argue that they had it easy. They managed to defuse security crises without being drawn into a major military role. Sustained economic prosperity in the United States helped to mitigate any lingering concerns over burden sharing and unfair trade practices—concerns that decisively shaped domestic political debate over Asia policy at the beginning of the decade. Opinion polls suggest that the American public supports U.S. engagement in Asia— but is not deeply informed and, moreover, is sensitive to the costs of engagement (Reilly 1999). In this domestic political context, U.S. officials proved effective at pursuing hegemony quietly and cheaply during the 1990s.

The next decade may prove less accommodating. A major military crisis in the Taiwan Strait or Korean peninsula would strain and possibly undermine domestic support for the hegemonic strategy in Asia. The domestic test would prove most severe if the United States found itself intervening and taking casualties while its closest ally in the region, Japan, begged off a direct role for political or constitutional reasons. For this reason, U.S.-Japan military cooperation in the war against Afghanistan may prove critical in providing the political opening for the two countries to work "side by side" in some future regional crisis.

A sustained economic downturn in the United States would similarly complicate U.S. strategy. The incentives for Asian trading states to embrace a U.S.-centered security order are increased to the extent that Washington is willing to tolerate sizable trade deficits.[15] Slower growth in the United States, however, could rekindle both protectionist pressures and resentment directed at Asian trading partners perceived to benefit unfairly from the asymmetric openness of the U.S. market. In relations with Japan and South Korea, the politically charged issue of whether the United States should be defending states with prosperous economies—states perfectly capable of defending themselves—would be raised anew. A strategic partnership with China—a potential adversary perceived to be taking advantage of the United States economically—would similarly come under serious strain.

Washington also faces the domestic challenge of maintaining support for comprehensive engagement of China, which is necessarily a long-term strategy. An alternative approach to China began to crystallize by the end of the 1990s. Members of the so-called Blue Team—a loose collection of academics, members of Congress and their staffers, and some intelligence and military officials— promote the view that China is a rising and already hostile power destined to threaten vital U.S. interests (Kaiser and Mufson 2000b). Blue Team advocates call for the United States to take a harder line on China's human rights and unfair trade practices, restrict technology transfers, and provide more vigorous support for Taiwan. They have the potential in U.S. politics to mobilize human rights activists, the Taiwan lobby, opponents of religious persecution, and foreign policy conservatives. Although the powerful U.S. business community is arrayed against this coalition, its ability to prevail is not a foregone conclusion. It cannot control China's behavior—a key factor in the domestic debate—and it cannot count on the new Bush administration to be as sympathetic as was the Clinton team to an accommodating strategy toward China. The domestic debate over China moved to the background because of the war in Afghanistan. But China's growing economic and military power assures that the debate will not be forestalled for long.

The third challenge is for Washington to resist the temptations of arrogance, triumphalism, and unilateralism. These are perennial temptations for a dominant state, whatever the international order. The United States, perhaps because its preponderant power is coupled with a domestic political tradition that strongly imbues foreign policy with the values of society, seems especially inclined to preach its virtues, impose its values, and dictate rather than consult. But this behavior inevitably creates political resentment and backlash. Indeed it may provoke the very kind of balancing behavior that the U.S. hegemonic strategy has been designed to forestall.

[15]The U.S. merchandise trade deficit in 1999 was a record $271 billion, much of it with Japan and China. In 1989, at the height of U.S. economic conflict with Japan, the overall deficit was only $92 billion. See Burgess (2000).

By the end of the 1990s, U.S. officials found themselves confronting these re-actions directly. Several U.S. initiatives—NATO expansion, the bombing of Ko-sovo, and the announced intention to modify the ABM Treaty in pursuit of a na-tional missile defense system (NMD)—combined to strain the U.S.-Russia rela-tionship and prompt Russia to explore "antihegemonic" options. The NMD ini-tiative alarmed virtually every major power and enhanced the U.S. reputation for unilateralism. Chinese officials reacted negatively to what they viewed as U.S. ar-rogance in the May 1999 bombing of the Chinese embassy in Belgrade, scandals over Chinese nuclear espionage, renewed public criticism from the United States over China's human rights practices, and the spy plane confrontation of April 2001. India resented U.S. demands for nuclear restraint as the United States de-fied the international community by rejecting ratification of the Comprehensive Test Ban Treaty (CTBT). States in Southeast Asia chafed at the triumphalism that seemed to accompany the U.S. response to the Asian financial crisis. Even Amer-ica's closest ally, Japan, voiced serious complaints over U.S. unilateralism in the handling of North Korea.[16] The accidental sinking of a Japanese fishing vessel by a U.S. submarine early in 2001 brought to the forefront Japanese complaints that the U.S. military is insensitive to the concerns of the Japanese public.

How much damage these events will ultimately inflict on the U.S. hegemonic position remains to be seen. But at the very least U.S. behavior has prompted major states in the region to contemplate their alternatives. In 1999, the Russian prime minister suggested that India, China, and Russia form a partnership to counter the global power of the United States. The presidents of China and France spent time during a recent summit to ponder common responses to the United States as a "hyperpower." Former National Security Adviser Brent Scow-croft observed recently that the United States does not consult effectively and does not think much about the effects of its actions on others: "We behave to much of the world like a latter-day colonial power." State Department officials recognize all of this as the essence of what they have come to call their "hegemony problem," but they have yet to figure out how to solve it.[17] However, they have used the war in Afghanistan to their advantage. For example, a new and improved U.S.-Russia relationship has grown out of the antiterrorist effort, and that relationship has frustrated, at least for now, the likelihood of a Russian-Chinese antihegemony coalition.

[16]Japanese officials were reportedly furious that Washington unilaterally declared in 1998 that funding for North Korean nuclear reactors—most of it coming from Japan—could go ahead de-spite North Korea's missile firing over Japan. See Marshall and Mann (2000).

[17]Scowcroft is quoted in Marshall and Mann (2000). See also STRATFOR.COM (1999), Hack-ett (2000), and Marshall (1999).

U.S. Hegemony vs. Other Pathways

American hegemony is by no means an ideal solution to the security problems of contemporary Asia. It is incomplete, there are limits to what it can achieve, it makes other states uneasy, and at least at some levels it makes the United States uneasy as well. Nevertheless, in the near term it may remain the best pathway to regional order. It is easy to find fault with hegemony. But in the particular circumstances of Asia, it is difficult to find an alternative path that combines desirability and feasibility in a more satisfactory way.[18]

Although there are plausible candidates, it is hard to imagine another actor playing a regional hegemonic role more effectively in the near term. Japanese hegemony would require a more open economy and society than Japan has been prepared to contemplate even in the face of severe economic crisis. Beyond the economic sphere, Japan would confront the constraints imposed on a more prominent regional presence by the legacy of Japanese colonialism. There is also the intriguing question, raised recently by Masaru Tamamoto, whether hegemony in any form is fundamentally unthinkable for Japan in political and cultural terms considering the postwar transformation of Japanese political identity (Tamamoto 2002).

Few would contend that Chinese hegemony is unthinkable in that same sense. On the contrary, a recent essay by David Kang (2002) points to the long tradition of Chinese hegemony in the Asian past. Whether or not contemporary China holds hegemonic ambitions, Chinese hegemony today is constrained by capabilities. One must rely on a series of highly optimistic projections to anticipate a smooth Chinese transformation from developing economy to regional hegemon. The need for continued economic reform, the fragility of the banking system, technological backwardness, the uncertainty of political transition, the challenge of maintaining political and social stability as economic growth proceeds—all point to the difficulty of a Chinese path to regional hegemony. There is, moreover, the fundamental issue of how others in the region—Japan, India, Korea, other ASEAN states—would react to a serious Chinese bid to replace the United States.

Hegemony is not the only pathway to order, of course. Some analysts anticipate a return to a more traditional multipolar balance of power in the Asia Pacific (Friedberg 1993–94; Betts 1993–94). Multipolarity is plausible if one assumes the relative decline of the United States and the emergence of Japan, China, India, and perhaps Russia and Indonesia as roughly equivalent great powers. As a

---

[18]There may be multiple or combined pathways to order that are preferable to hegemony. For a discussion, see the Introduction to this volume.

mechanism for order, a multipolar balance in contemporary Asia would face significant challenges: the uneven spread of military and especially nuclear capabilities among the major contenders; the existence of numerous flashpoints increasing the potential that conflicts would begin and escalate; and the potential inflexibility of alliance commitments due to long-standing friendships (United States and Japan) and rivalries (Japan and China). It would be a mistake to assume that a new multipolarity in Asia would operate similarly and provide the kind of relative stability enjoyed by European powers during the nineteenth century. It is not surprising, therefore, that analysts who foresee multipolarity generally expect Asia to be "ripe for rivalry."

A bipolar balance of power could plausibly emerge as a result of an action and reaction process by China and the United States. A precondition would be the sustained development of China's economic, technological, and military capabilities. One could imagine, to the detriment of the regional and global economy, a political division with states in the region lining up behind one or the other power. The order created in this scenario would depend on the staying power of the two—and only the two—rivals. If China can develop sufficient capacity to challenge U.S. hegemony, then Japan, with a more powerful and sophisticated economy, is certainly capable of challenging China. Russia and India, major land powers with sizable populations, share many, if not all, of the potential great-power attributes of China. A future bipolarity could end with one pole standing or with several emerging. The two major powers also would need to manage the risks that made the Cold War so predictably dangerous. Bipolarity encourages intense ideological conflict and the tests of resolve associated with brinksmanship. The United States and the Soviet Union managed these tests well—or were they simply lucky? China and the United States would face additional challenges so long as their nuclear capabilities remained asymmetric and so long as the United States claimed as an ally a political entity that China considers part of its own territory.

Finally, the creation of security order through the identity transformation and integration of Asian states would be a more desirable pathway to order than hegemony, bipolarity, or multipolarity. The result of integration and identity transformation would be a pluralistic security community—a group of states that share interests and values with sufficient commonality that the use of force to settle conflicts among them becomes essentially unthinkable (Adler and Barnett 1998; Cronin 1999). This regional future would entail, in effect, the Europeanization of the Asia Pacific—a coherent and self-conscious political community organized around shared values, interconnected societies, and effective regional institutions. As the core organizing principle of regional order, political community would offer to member states the value of joint membership and a sense of identity beyond their borders. The community would possess institutions and mechanisms to foster integration and to resolve political conflict.

Because the circumstances required for the emergence of a pluralistic security community are difficult to attain, this regional order may be the least likely outcome. A profound sense of political community among peoples across the borders of sovereign states is an elusive condition that cannot easily be engineered by state leaders. History and geography make this a special challenge in the Asia Pacific. Would shared political identity be trans-Pacific, East Asian, or Asian? What are its core values? On what common cultural, religious, or other foundation does it rest? The absence of political community has been an enduring feature of the Asia Pacific region. Pluralistic security communities also rely on the robust presence of democratic government; the Asia Pacific is marked instead by a significant diversity of regime types, and many of the democracies are still in the early phases of political development.

American hegemony, then, may be the least problematic of a problematic set of alternative pathways to order. Since hegemony often carries the seeds of its own demise, for the United States the challenge is to preserve and build upon the progress already made. From the broad perspective of the region as a whole, the challenge is to transform hegemony into a more, rather than less, desirable pathway to order.

Works Cited

Abramowitz, Morton I., and James T. Laney. 1999. *U.S. Policy Toward North Korea: Next Steps*. Task Force Report. New York: Council on Foreign Relations.

Adler, Emmanuel, and Michael Barnett, eds. 1998. *Security Communities*. Cambridge: Cambridge University Press.

Armacost, Michael H. 2000. "Japan: Policy Paralysis and Economic Stagnation." In Robert B. Zoellick and Philip D. Zelikow, eds., *America and the East Asian Crisis: Memos to a President*. New York: Norton.

Betts, Richard K. 1993–94. "Wealth, Power, and Instability: East Asia and the United States After the Cold War." *International Security* 18(3) (Winter): 34–77.

Bob, Daniel. 2001. *The 107th Congress: Asia Pacific Policy Outlook*. NBR Briefing, Feb. Seattle: National Bureau of Asian Research.

Bull, Hedley. 1977. *The Anarchical Society: A Study of Order in World Politics*. New York: Columbia University Press.

Burgess, John. 2000. "It's a Record: A $271 Billion Deficit." *Washington Post National Weekly Edition*, Feb. 28.

Callon, Scott. 1995. *Divided Sun: MITI and the Breakdown of Japanese High Technology Industrial Policy, 1975–1993*. Stanford: Stanford University Press.

Christensen, Clayton, Thomas Craig, and Stuart Hart. 2001. "The Great Disruption." *Foreign Affairs* 80(2) (Mar./Apr.): 80–95.

Christensen, Thomas J. 1999. "China, the U.S.-Japan Alliance, and the Security Dilemma in East Asia." *International Security* 23(4) (Spring): 49–80.

Cooper, Richard N. 2000. "Asian Financial Crisis: Future Outlook and Next Steps." In Robert B. Zoellick and Philip D. Zelikow, eds., *America and the East Asian Crisis: Memos to a President*. New York: Norton.

Cossa, Ralph A., ed. 1999. *U.S.–Korea–Japan Relations: Building Toward a "Virtual Alliance."* Washington, D.C.: CSIS.

———. 2000. "U.S. Approaches to Multilateral Security and Economic Institutions in Asia." Pacific Forum CSIS. Unpublished manuscript.

Cox, Robert W. 1983. "Gramsci, Hegemony, and International Relations: An Essay in Method." *Millennium* 12(2) (Summer): 162–75.

Cronin, Bruce. 1999. *Community Under Anarchy: Transnational Identity and the Evolution of International Cooperation*. New York: Columbia University Press.

Cumings, Bruce. 1999. "The United States: Hegemonic Still?" In Michael Cox, Ken Booth, and Tim Dunne, eds., *The Interregnum: Controversies in World Politics, 1989–1999*. Cambridge: Cambridge University Press.

Donnelly, John. 2000. "Intelligence Officials: Missile Attack on U.S. Unlikely." *Defense Week*, Feb. 14.

Ellings, Richard J., and Aaron L. Friedberg. 2001. *Strategic Asia: Power and Purpose, 2001–02*. Seattle: National Bureau of Asian Research.

Ennis, Peter, and Takao Tashikawa. 2001. "Normal Country? Japan Embarks on a New Security Policy." *Oriental Economist* 69(11) (Nov.): 1–2.

Foot, Rosemary, and Andrew Walter. 1999. "Whatever Happened to the Pacific Century?" In Michael Cox, Ken Booth, and Tim Dunne, eds., *The Interregnum: Controversies in World Politics, 1989–1999*. Cambridge: Cambridge University Press.

French, Howard. 2000. "Japanese Call '37 Massacre a War Myth, Stirring Storm." *New York Times*, Jan. 23.

Friedberg, Aaron L. 1993–94. "Ripe for Rivalry: Prospects for Peace in a Multipolar Asia." *International Security* 18(3) (Winter): 5–33.

Frieden, Jeffry. 1988. "Sectoral Conflict and U.S. Foreign Economic Policy, 1914–1940." *International Organization* 42(1) (Winter): 59–90.

Gilpin, Robert G. 1981. *War and Change in World Politics*. Cambridge: Cambridge University Press.

———. 1987. *The Political Economy of International Relations*. Princeton: Princeton University Press.

Goldstein, Morris. 1998. *The Asian Financial Crisis: Causes, Cures, and Systemic Implications*. Washington, D.C.: Institute for International Economics.

Grieco, Joseph M. 1999. "Realism and Regionalism: American Power and German and Japanese Institutional Strategies During and After the Cold War." In Ethan Kapstein and Michael Mastanduno, eds., *Unipolar Politics: Realism and State Strategies After the Cold War*. New York: Columbia University Press.

Haass, Richard N. 1999. "What to Do with American Primacy." *Foreign Affairs* 78(5) (Sept./Oct.): 37–49.

Hackett, James. 2000. "A New Anti-American Axis?" *Washington Times*, Feb. 24.

Harrison, Selig. 2001. "Time to Leave Korea?" *Foreign Affairs* 80(2) (Mar./Apr.): 62–79.

Hutzler, Charles. 2001. "China's Quiet, Crucial Role in the War." *Wall Street Journal*, Dec. 18.

Ikenberry, G. John. 2002. "Rethinking the Origins of American Hegemony." In G. John Ikenberry, ed. *American Foreign Policy: Theoretical Essays*. 4th ed. New York: Longman.

"India Challenges China in South China Sea," *STRATFOR.COM Global Intelligence Update*, Apr. 26, 2000.

Institute for National Strategic Studies (INSS). 2000. *The United States and Japan: Advancing Toward a Mature Partnership*. INSS Special Report. Washington, D.C.: INSS.

Joffe, Josef. 1995. "Bismarck or Britain? Toward an American Grand Strategy After Bipolarity." *International Security* 19(4) (Spring): 94–117.

Johnson, Chalmers. 1982. *MITI and the Japanese Miracle: The Growth of Japanese Industrial Policy, 1920–1975*. Stanford: Stanford University Press.

Kagan, Robert. 1998. "The Benevolent Empire." *Foreign Policy* 111 (Summer): 24–35.

Kaiser, Robert G., and Steven Mufson. 2000a. "Analysts Differ on Whether China Crisis Looms." *Washington Post*, Mar. 16.

———. 2000b. "Blue Team Draws a Hard Line on Beijing." *Washington Post*, Feb. 22.

Kang, David. 2002, forthcoming. "Culture and Hierarchy: The Chinese System and Stability in Asia." In G. John Ikenberry and Michael Mastanduno, eds., *International Relations Theory and the Asia-Pacific*. New York: Columbia University Press.

Katzenstein, Peter J., Robert O. Keohane, and Stephen D. Krasner. 1998. "International Organization and the Study of World Politics." *International Organization* 53(4) (Autumn): 645–86.

Kennedy, Paul. 1987. *The Rise and Fall of the Great Powers: Economic Change and Military Conflict from 1500 to 2000*. New York: Random House.

Keohane, Robert O. 1980. "The Theory of Hegemonic Stability and Changes in International Economic Regimes, 1967–1977." In Ole Holsti, Randolph M. Siverson, and Alexander L. George, eds., *Change in the International System*. Boulder, Colo.: Westview.

———. 1984. *After Hegemony: Cooperation and Discord in the World Political Economy*. Princeton: Princeton University Press.

Kindleberger, Charles P. 1973. *The World in Depression, 1929–1939*. Berkeley: University of California Press.

Krasner, Stephen D. 1976. "State Power and the Structure of International Trade." *World Politics* 28: 317–47.

Lake, David A. 1988. *Power, Protection, and Free Trade: International Sources of U.S. Commercial Policy, 1887–1939*. Ithaca: Cornell University Press.

Lancaster, John. 1999. "War Was Narrowly Averted; Kashmir Conflict Flared Dangerously." *Washington Post*, July 26.

Layne, Christopher. 1993. "The Unipolar Illusion: Why New Great Powers Will Rise." *International Security* 17(4) (Spring): 5–51.

———. 1999. "What's Built Up Must Come Down." *Washington Post*, Nov. 14.

Long, William J. 1996. "Trade and Technology Incentives and Bilateral Cooperation." *International Studies Quarterly* 40(1) (Mar.): 77–106.

Marshall, Tyler. 1999. "Anti-NATO Axis Could Pose Threat." *Los Angeles Times*, Sept. 27.

———, and Jim Mann. 2000. "Goodwill Toward U.S. Is Dwindling Globally." *Los Angeles Times*, Mar. 26.

Mastanduno, Michael. 1997. "Preserving the Unipolar Moment: Realist Theories and U.S. Grand Strategy After the Cold War." *International Security* 21(4) (Spring): 49–88.

———. 2000. "Models, Markets, and Power: Political Economy and the Asia-Pacific, 1989–1999." *Review of International Studies* 26 (4) (Fall): 493–507.

Maynes, Charles William. 1998. "The Perils of (and for) an Imperial America." *Foreign Policy* 111 (Summer): 36–49.

"Mr. No Blames the Victim." 2000. *Asian Wall Street Journal*, Apr. 12.

Nau, Henry R. 1990. *The Myth of America's Decline: Leading the World Economy into the 1990s.* Oxford: Oxford University Press.

Nye, Joseph S., Jr. 1990. *Bound to Lead: The Changing Nature of U.S. Power.* New York: Basic Books.

———. 1995. "The Case for Deep Engagement." *Foreign Affairs* 74(4) (July/Aug.): 90–102.

———. 2000. "Implications for U.S. Policy of Power Shifts Between China and Japan." In Robert B. Zoellick and Philip D. Zelikow, eds., *America and the East Asian Crisis: Memos to a President.* New York: Norton.

———, and William Owens. 1996. "America's Information Edge." *Foreign Affairs* 75(2) (Mar./Apr.): 20–36.

Oksenberg, Michel. 2000. "The Asian Strategic Context." In Robert B. Zoellick and Philip D. Zelikow, eds., *America and the East Asian Crisis: Memos to a President.* New York: Norton.

Papayounou, Paul, and Scott Kastner. 1999. "Sleeping with the Potential Enemy: Assessing the U.S. Policy of Engagement with China." *Security Studies* 9(1) (Fall): 164–95.

Paul, T. V., and John Hall. 1999. *International Order and the Future of World Politics.* Cambridge: Cambridge University Press.

Perlez, Jane. 2000. "U.S. and India, Trying to Reconcile, Hit Bump." *New York Times,* Mar. 22.

Prestowitz, Clyde V., Jr. 1990. *Trading Places: How We Are Giving Our Future to Japan and How to Reclaim It.* 2nd ed. New York: Basic Books.

Reilly, John E., ed. 1999. *American Public Opinion and U.S. Foreign Policy 1999.* Chicago Council on Foreign Relations.

Ross, Robert S. 1999. "The Geography of the Peace: East Asia in the Twenty-First Century." *International Security* 23(4) (Spring): 81–117.

Russett, Bruce M. 1985. "The Mysterious Case of Vanishing Hegemony: Or, Is Mark Twain Really Dead?" *International Organization* 39(2) (Spring): 207–31.

Shenon, Philip. 1999. "North Korea Agrees to End Missile Testing in Exchange for Economic Aid." *New York Times,* Sept. 13.

Slater, Joanna, and Murray Hiebert. 2001. "U.S. and India Stage Quiet Rapprochement." *Wall Street Journal,* Dec. 18.

Strange, Susan. 1987. "The Persistent Myth of Lost Hegemony." *International Organization* 41(4) (Autumn): 551–74.

STRATFOR.COM. 1999. "Asian Alliance on the Horizon." Global Intelligence Update, Oct. 14.

Tamamoto, Masaru. 2002, forthcoming. "Ambiguous Japan: Japanese National Identity at Century's End." In G. John Ikenberry and Michael Mastanduno, eds., *International Relations Theory and the Asia-Pacific.* New York: Columbia University Press.

U.S. Department of Defense. 1995. *United States Security Strategy for the East Asia-Pacific Region.* Office of International Security Affairs report. Washington, D.C.: Government Printing Office.

Wade, Robert. 1998–99. "The Coming Fight over Capital Flows." *Foreign Policy* 113 (Winter): 41–54.

Waltz, Kenneth N. 1993. "The Emerging Structure of International Politics." *International Security* 18(2) (Fall): 45–73.

Wohlforth, William C. 1999. "The Stability of a Unipolar World." *International Security* 24(1) (Summer): 5–41.

World Bank. 1993. *The East Asian Miracle: Economic Growth and Public Policy*. New York: Oxford University Press.

Zakaria, Fareed. 1999. *From Wealth to Power: The Unusual Origins of America's World Role.* Princeton: Princeton University Press.

CHAPTER FIVE

Balance-of-Power Politics

Consequences for Asian Security Order

AVERY GOLDSTEIN

Understanding the significance of balance-of-power politics for Asia's security order requires more than a straightforward inventory and comparison of national capabilities. In this chapter I indicate that its nature and dynamics reflect an interplay between the region's and the international system's structure, links between current realities and expectations about the future, the effects of technological change, and the geographic circumstances in which states find themselves.

At its most basic level, power balancing in Asia, as elsewhere, arises from the efforts of states to enhance their security. Security remains a minimal requirement for any regional order that sovereign states will deem acceptable. Indeed power balancing may represent the most fundamental pattern defining Asia's security order. In this book, however, regional security order is defined not just as an observed pattern of state behavior, even one that may serve the limited goal of state survival. It is also defined as an arrangement that serves the ambitious goals of regional peace and prosperity.[1] In addition to exploring the nature and dynamics of balance-of-power politics in Asia, therefore, this chapter also considers its effects on regional security order in this broad sense. I conclude by suggesting that although power balancing will persist because it reflects enduring international causes and the strong survival motives of states, its consequences for peace and prosperity are inherently indeterminate and may be managed more or less wisely.

[1]The first understanding of order corresponds to the type labeled "instrumental" in Chapter 1 in this volume. The second and third correspond to the types of order Chapter 1 labeled "normative-contractual" and "solidarist."

Although my focus is on the order emerging at the start of the twenty-first century, I begin with a highly stylized depiction of the region's balance-of-power dynamics during the Cold War. Such a review not only provides a point of contrast to illuminate the change that has taken place in recent years but also indicates that, simply in terms of relative power, continuity is more noteworthy than change. Both during and after the Cold War, the Asian region has been characterized by a great *imbalance* of power, with the United States in a position of preponderance economically and militarily. Despite this enduring feature in the regional distribution of power over the past half century, the end of the Cold War did mark a change in the global distribution of power with important implications for Asia. Asia remains a subsystem in which the United States is the predominant power, but it is now embedded in a unipolar rather than a bipolar world. Moreover, during the Cold War regional dynamics were shaped by the expectation that the system's bipolar structure would endure and eventually be replicated in Asia. After the Cold War, the expectation is that neither the system's nor the region's unipolar structure will endure. The Cold War prediction of lasting and pervasive bipolarity proved incorrect. Whether the post–Cold War expectation of ephemeral unipolarity is similarly misguided remains to be seen.

The Shadow of Bipolarity

Although no claim goes unchallenged in academic circles, few took issue with the assertion that the international system during the Cold War was bipolar. This definition of the system's structure indicated that there were two states whose capabilities set them apart from all the rest and, moreover, that these capabilities constrained each duopolist to forge its foreign policy with an eye to the potentially decisive reaction of the other. Bipolarity referred neither to equality in the superpowers' capabilities nor to the solidarity of their alliance networks. It simply meant that each possessed an array of capabilities that made their decision making strategically interdependent on issues of major importance. Each was not merely sensitive to the other's position; each also understood that the other had the ability to block actions it deemed unacceptable. One consequence of bipolarity for balance-of-power politics, at least according to Kenneth Waltz, the theory's leading exponent during the Cold War, was that its dynamics were less likely to result in a great-power war than had been the case in multipolar systems of the past (Waltz 1979: 161–93). This assertion rested in part on the observation that the strategic calculations of the great powers in a bipolar world were simplified. For the two superpowers, bipolarity clarified the consequences of acting in ways that might provoke one's principal adversary. With a clear understanding of what great-power war would mean, Waltz's argument suggested that few issues could arise over which even modestly sensible leaders in Moscow or Washington would choose war rather than compromise.

But if bipolarity made war between the system's great powers unlikely, it also ensured intense competition between them short of war because it clarified the risks of inattentiveness that might tempt one's adversary to score decisive gains and the infeasibility of waiting for others to do the dirty and dangerous work of counterbalancing a superpower. Vigilance, even hypervigilance, about the prospects for potentially significant shifts in the balance of power between the two superpowers provided incentives for intervention and even limited fighting on the periphery. Although the relatively meager stakes of such competition in a bipolar world would not be sufficiently high for either superpower to allow the rivalry to escalate to general war, neither could be indifferent to what might be deemed tests of resolve. And during the Cold War, the ideological aspect of competition between the United States and the Soviet Union provided an additional incentive for superpower intervention—the fear that a failure to respond to political challenges from adherents to their rival's camp, even in far-flung places of little intrinsic military value, might cast doubt on the credibility of their international commitments in general.

Bipolarity's conflicting imperatives—to engage in intensive and extensive superpower competition but within tight constraints on escalation to general war and conceivably nuclear catastrophe—resulted in the superpowers diverting their competition to local wars in clearly peripheral regions, often relying on proxy forces so that confrontation could be managed safely.[2] Nowhere was this dynamic more evident than in Asia, where global bipolarity was not a force for peace. Instead the bipolar system's balance-of-power politics exacerbated local conflicts. Moreover, bipolarity had this effect even though the regional distribution of capabilities was not genuinely bipolar. Only one superpower, the United States, deployed the full array of power-projection assets in Asia. Considered in isolation from its overall capabilities, the Soviet Union's assets in the region did not put it in the same league as the United States. Moscow did make a serious effort after 1970 to augment its air, naval, and rocket forces in the western Pacific and to cultivate friends and allies in an arc stretching from South Asia (India) to Southeast Asia (Vietnam) to Northeast Asia (Korea). Yet unlike Moscow's impressive military disposition on its western front—which led some to conclude that the Warsaw Pact held an advantage in Europe checked only by NATO's threats of nuclear escalation—along the Soviets' eastern front the Red Army had its hands full sim-

---

[2]The belief that fear of general war reduces escalation risks and makes limited wars more likely has been termed the "stability/instability paradox." See Freedman (1981: 98–102) and Jervis (1985b: 19–22).

ply coping with the obsolete forces of China. To be sure, Moscow deployed forces in the Far East that sufficed to pose a threat of escalation if the United States directly challenged Soviet vital interests. But it never succeeded in establishing a presence and power-projection capability in the region comparable to that of the United States (Bracken 1999: 17). Though analysts could debate the East-West balance of power in Europe, no comparable debate raged over Asia: the American superiority in capabilities was obvious.

Yet U.S. primacy in Asia did not have the consequences one might expect. Preponderance in the region did not facilitate a Pax Americana enforced by the unfettered might of the U.S. military. Instead regional actors were able to exploit Soviet-American attentiveness to the overall balance of power in order to advance their own interests, including those that might entail the use of force. Smaller states secured superpower support for their local causes by suggesting opportunities for gains in the bipolar competition or, conversely, by raising superpower concerns about potentially dangerous (or at least reputation-besmirching) losses if they failed to respond to a challenge from those politically linked to their rival.[3] During the early decades of the Cold War (in Korea, the Taiwan Strait, and Vietnam), regional rivals succeeded in tapping a superpower patron by portraying local conflicts as a crucial theater for the larger struggle between the two superpower camps. Such efforts were facilitated by the zero-sum perceptions of the superpowers, which were eager to make gains and forestall losses in their global rivalry. For the United States in particular, the fear of falling dominoes primed American leaders to respond to pleas for assistance and intervention against what was understood to be a monolithic communist threat. Over the final two decades of the Cold War, the Sino-Soviet split shattered the notion that ideology defined international strategic alignments. Even when the ideological simplicity of the 1950s and 1960s ended, however, the region's balance-of-power politics continued to unfold in the shadow of bipolarity.

The reality of enduring U.S. preponderance notwithstanding, the region's international relations during the Cold War were driven by echoes of the global bipolar rivalry and by the expectation that the sort of close balance-of-power competition that was most clearly manifest in Europe and in the strategic-nuclear dimension of Soviet-American relations would be replicated in Asia. During the 1970s, increasing Soviet military power in the region (especially Soviet strengthening of its positions along the frontier with China, additions to the Soviet fleet in the Far East, alliance with Vietnam, acquisition of basing rights there, and the major military deployment on the region's southwest flank in Afghanistan) led

---

[3]Schelling (1966) presents a classic account of the importance of reputation in great-power competition. Mercer (1996) questions whether these concerns are warranted.

some to conclude that the expected era of genuine bipolarity in Asia might finally be in the offing. Yet in the end the Soviets failed to muster capabilities that would make them a peer competitor of the United States within the region. In sum, then, bipolarity had shaped power balancing in Asia—but it was the bipolarity of the global system and in particular the concerns it induced about the larger stakes of local conflict.

Balance-of-Power Politics in Post–Cold War Asia

International relations in Asia today are still conditioned by the structure of the international system. But bipolarity has given way to unipolarity, a condition that reinforces long-standing American preponderance in the region. At the same time, however, balance-of-power politics in the era of unipolarity has been shaped by the expectation that this unusual global distribution of power will change as one or more competitors emerge to rival the United States. Beliefs about the transitional nature of unipolarity have reflected underlying, often theoretically grounded doubts about the durability of American material superiority, as well as the durability of American willingness to shoulder the burden that unipolarity imposes on a lone superpower. (See Organski and Kugler 1980; Gilpin 1981; Kennedy 1987; Layne 1993; Waltz 1993.) Although unipolarity has already proved more robust than many expected at the dawn of the post–Cold War era, this fact has simply prompted some to revise their views about the timing of the transition away from unipolarity. Few have altered their fundamental belief in the inevitability of this transition.[4]

Unipolarity and After

Some states fear the anticipated end of unipolarity because they worry about the threat of regional rivals. Those that have benefited from the U.S. provision of security as a collective good have little to gain from a decline in the American ability or willingness to continue to fill the role of supplier. Such states, therefore, encourage the United States to soldier on—even as they complain about American unilateralism. Some (Japan and South Korea) have tapped into U.S. fears about the threatening potential of rogue states (North Korea). Others (Taiwan, the Philippines) have tapped into U.S. concerns about potentially dangerous ri-

---

[4]Chinese analysts, for example, had initially expected a relatively swift transition to a multipolar post–Cold War world. Repeated demonstrations of U.S. military technological prowess in the Persian Gulf and especially the Balkans, the resurgent American economy, the stagnation of Japan, and Russia's continued disarray led many Chinese by 1999 reluctantly to concede that U.S. primacy may last several decades, while emphasizing the importance of working to hasten the advent of multipolarity. Author's interviews, Beijing, Mar.–Apr. 2000 and Oct. 2000.

vals to American power (China). Still others (ASEAN states) have tapped into a general U.S. anxiety that its retrenchment could trigger unpredictable responses by regional states (perhaps China and Japan vying to fill a power vacuum) that might lead to dangerous instability. (U.S. Department of Defense 1998.)

Not all states worry about a diminution of U.S. power in Asia. On the contrary, some eagerly anticipate the end of unipolarity because they view unchecked American primacy as a constraint on their ability to realize international goals (political and economic as well as military) or as a threat to their security. Such states (China, India) hopefully await the end of American hegemony even though they harbor fears about the uncertainty that may follow (China's worries about a more assertive Japan, for instance, and India's worries about a less constrained China). Those resentful or fearful of U.S. dominance in the unipolar era strive to hasten the change, not only by cultivating their own capabilities but also by diplomacy that encourages local actors and the United States to believe that the transition will be a smooth process that does not jeopardize their vital interests. At times, especially during the late 1990s, China has made concerted efforts of this sort—trying to reassure others that it is not a growing power against which others need to balance by relying on an awesome American counterweight (see "Gouzhu Xin Shiji de Xinxing Guojia Guanxi" 1997).

Technology

The connection between the regional and global balance of power and the divergence between expectations about the future distribution of capabilities and its present reality are only two ways in which a grasp of balance-of-power dynamics in Asia requires more than a simple inventory of national assets. A third consideration is military technology. The significance of military technology for balance-of-power politics reflects the logic of the theory that gives balancing arguments their meaning. Balance-of-power theory explains why states coexisting in an anarchic realm face incentives to counter the accumulation of unchecked power. The theory emphasizes the uncertainty about present and future intentions in a realm where commitments are not reliably enforceable—and, therefore, the reasons why states are likely to hedge their bets against the threats others may pose. To the extent possible, they also hedge against the risk of depending on others (allies or international organizations) to cope with such threats. (Dependence on others exposes one to the twin risks of entrapment and abandonment; see Snyder 1984, Christensen and Snyder 1990, and Goldstein 1995.) Therefore, the focus of balance-of-power theory is not on capabilities per se but on the reasons why imbalances in capabilities will concern states and shape their behavior in characteristic ways. It explains, for example, why all states coexisting in an anarchic realm worry about each other's capabilities—but does not explain which shifts in capabilities particular states are likely to find most provocative. For a thorough understanding of state behavior, the analyst must introduce variables that are customarily set aside in constructing a balance-of-power theory that focuses on broad systemic causes and outcomes (Alagappa 1998). Understanding a state's response to changes in capabilities requires the inclusion of factors that determine their threatening character.[5] In Asia, for example, China's growing power may worry some of its neighbors and encourage them to explore ways to cope with the risks it poses. But the most serious efforts at countering China have followed rhetoric and action by Beijing that others view as disturbingly assertive.

Apart from judgments about assertiveness, geography too plays a role in shaping responses to shifting capabilities, as will be discussed below. In the contemporary era, however, military technology has an increasingly profound impact. Balancing behavior during and after the Cold War has reflected a mix of concerns about traditional comparisons of relative capabilities and the new, distinctive capabilities that modern military technologies represent. As balance-of-power theory, though not a crude balance-of-power metaphor, would suggest, states are most responsive to emerging capabilities that pose the most serious threats— even if a prospective adversary is otherwise weak. This divergence between aggregate capabilities and the ability to exploit selected technologies to seriously hurt others is one of the distinctive strategic features of the postwar era. Its importance, moreover, has grown in recent years. Ballistic missiles married to weapons of mass destruction, especially nuclear warheads, constitute the sort of serious threat that renders straightforward assessments of relative capabilities much less informative than before.[6] The development of even limited capabilities of the terrifying sorts that are possible through modern technology triggers a vigorous balancing response by states constrained to live with the uncertainties inherent in an anarchic realm.[7]

Modern technology affects balancing behavior in the contemporary period, not only because it enables the weak to coerce the strong by threatening to inflict

[5]The importance of threats, rather than power per se, is underscored in Stephen Walt's "balance-of-threat" theory. By incorporating variables that explain why states will view capabilities as more or less threatening, Walt identifies incentives for states to respond to imbalances of power (Walt 1988). On the larger debate about the usefulness of various balancing theories, see the exchanges in *American Political Science Review* 91: 4 (Dec. 1997).

[6]Nuclear weapons are singled out because of the speed and certainty with which they inflict devastating punishment. For convenience—but also because I assume states that believe they require the strategic benefits of weapons of mass destruction and have the ability to develop nuclear weapons will choose this most potent alternative—the term weapons of mass destruction refers to the nuclear variety (cf. Bracken 1999: 38–50, 125–48).

[7]The terrorist attacks of September 11, 2001, serve as a reminder that weapons of mass destruction and ballistic missiles are not the only fruits of modern technology that enable the weak to inflict horrifying damage on the strong.

great pain on a militarily superior adversary, but also because it is dramatically altering the requirements for states contemplating the direct application of military force to realize their international goals. While technology may be making it easier to devise coercive strategies, it is making it harder to meet the requirements of strategies that require successful offensive and defensive military operations. Though experts disagree about the true significance of what is usually labeled the revolution in military affairs (RMA), it is generally understood that technology is transforming the employment of force in ways that transcend traditional order-of-battle considerations. (Cohen 1996; Biddle 1996; O'Hanlon 1998a.) Advanced technologies (electronics, precision guidance, computers, sophisticated sensors, high-speed communications) increase the lethality of the implements of destruction and put a premium on logistics and information processing that challenge old-fashioned notions of military power. To reap the strategic benefits of the RMA, states must not only acquire increasingly expensive equipment but also recruit and train officers and soldiers of a new type and recast their military organizations. Although many Asian states have begun to articulate the importance of adjusting to the new realities created by the RMA, economic, political, and cultural constraints on making the adjustment are tight. (See Huxley and Willet 1999: chap. 4; Dibb 1997–98; Joshi 1999.) The extent to which these states will choose to balance against potential security threats by investing in simple, if blunt, weapons of pain—or opt for the arduous and expensive investment in overhauling their military in the fashion necessary to exploit the RMA—will depend in each case on national resources as well as the contingencies (both the purposes and the likely adversary) for which the state deploys its forces (Dibb 1997–98: 106–11).

Those most likely to invest in RMA capabilities in Asia are the region's advanced industrial powers (Singapore, Japan, Taiwan, South Korea)—those that face technologically or economically lagging adversaries, can afford the costly changes, and may be able to benefit from access to the best equipment available on the international market or from a supportive United States (Hsu 2000). Although China and India have developed a keen interest in the implications of the RMA for regional security since witnessing the U.S. performance in the 1991 Gulf War and later in the Balkans and Afghanistan, their resources have prevented them from translating interest into capability. Generally those facing steep opportunity costs (because of sharply limited national resources, the unpalatability or infeasibility of overcoming entrenched organizational interests, the lack of easy access to the best equipment)—or those facing an adversary against whom competition in RMA capabilities seems futile—may well see the wisest course as giving top, though not exclusive, priority to investment in the affordable counterbalance that weapons of mass destruction continue to represent. For countries like China, India, Pakistan, and North Korea this may well be the military burden they choose to shoulder as they strive to cope with the threats they believe they face.

Geography

During the second half of the twentieth century, the role of technology as an influence on balancing behavior grew in importance. In some respects technology now surpasses geography as a determinant of the degree to which another state's power is a threat that requires a response. Weak states with horrifying weapons can trigger a response from distant actors who in the past might have remained indifferent but now must worry. American concerns about nuclear proliferation (as well as the U.S. decision to go to war against the Taliban regime hosting Al Qaeda terrorist cells in Afghanistan) reflect this new reality. Technology not only increases sensitivity to distant threats but also increases the feasibility of responding to them; strong states are now able to project power with a range and effectiveness that partially override geographic considerations. Yet geography continues to be relevant for balance-of-power politics in Asia in at least three respects: the relative size of potential adversaries, the difference between maritime and continental interstate rivalry, and the distinctive position of the region's most powerful state.

First, size still matters. Small states facing large adversaries must devise ways to compensate for a lack of strategic depth. Several options are available either alone or in combination. One is to develop weapons of mass destruction and rely on a deterrent strategy to discourage potential aggressors. Pakistan's decision to develop nuclear weapons—as well as claims about the suitability of nuclear weapons for North or South Korea, Taiwan, Japan, and Singapore—is often associated with such considerations. Another option is to develop a highly sophisticated conventional arsenal (even without fully exploiting the RMA) and rely on a defensive strategy that discourages a larger but poorly equipped rival. The paths that Taiwan, Japan, and especially Singapore have followed are consistent with this approach (Huxley and Willet 1999; Tan 1999). Yet another option for dissuading a larger rival is to seek the backing of a powerful benefactor with the ability to punish or thwart the adversary. In Pacific Asia, the United States has been the benefactor of choice. States worried about bigger adversaries in the region have sought the counterbalance of American backing through formal alliances (Japan, South Korea, the Philippines, Thailand, and Taiwan prior to 1979), as well as through patterns of military cooperation with the United States (joint training and exercises, for example, and visitation agreements such as those with a varying cast of ASEAN states) and tacit, if sometimes tangibly demonstrated, assurances (Taiwan after 1979).

Second, geography affects balancing in Asia insofar as there is a distinction between continental and maritime rivalry. One difference between these arenas for conflict is the relative difficulty of projecting power in maritime disputes. Though distance and terrain may make overland power projection difficult, the air and naval capabilities necessary to support claims at any significant distance across the sea are generally more daunting to deploy. There are, for example, possibilities for overtly deploying (or covertly infiltrating and then supporting) forces against a rival on the Korean peninsula or the South Asian subcontinent that are not available to rivals separated by the Taiwan Strait or the vast stretches of the South China Sea. In short, the logistical problems for projecting power in maritime disputes tend to be greater, especially as the distance increases. The result in some cases is a muted sensitivity to shifts in maritime military capabilities that trigger balancing behavior.

Thus analysts have acknowledged, but discounted, the significance of the large number and improving quality of China's ships and aircraft for the balance of power in the Taiwan Strait and in the South China Sea because Beijing has failed to invest in the necessary logistical systems (not just purchasing hardware but extensively training combined forces with airborne refueling and sea-based replenishment capabilities) that would make its growing power-projection forces militarily useful. In the Taiwan theater, the maritime buffer poses daunting challenges to Beijing that encourage it to emphasize instead the threat of the indirect use of force via a coercive strategy of strategic bombardment (using missiles or aircraft) or efforts to disrupt maritime traffic through mining rather than the direct use of force for invasion or blockade. Taipei's emphasis on upgrading its fighter aircraft and missile defenses—while also cultivating U.S. support that may provide extended deterrent benefits—reflects the priority assigned to balancing against its most plausible military threat.

In the South China Sea, the difficulty of projecting power across the great distances that separate claimants from disputed territories has so far limited balancing behavior to small-scale grabs for tactical military advantage (Mischief Reef, Scarborough Shoal) rather than seriously competitive balancing. Balancing in this theater may also be muted because, unlike the Taiwan theater, the geography of the territory in dispute makes coercive alternatives less viable. (Sensible targets for bombardment are not so obvious; disruption of the sea-lanes risks rapid escalation entangling multiple actors including nonclaimants, most important, the United States.)

Asia's land-based hot spots, by contrast, give rise to more vigorous balancing behavior in response to changing capabilities because there are cheaper and easier alternatives for moving forces across land into contested territory (operating on interior lines). North Korea's prospects for successfully attacking the South may not be bright, but sustaining an attack with its obsolete forces is possible even relying on unsophisticated logistic capabilities. Thus in addition to worrying about the North's ability to coerce (as do even the North's adversaries who enjoy a maritime buffer), the South has faced strong incentives to respond to Pyongyang's deployments that enhance its ability to mount an invasion. Similarly, India and Pakistan have had strong incentives to respond to each other's forces because they may be used directly to threaten vital interests. Aside from the obvious lessons of three Indo-Pakistani wars, the Kargil experience in 1999 suggests that while undeniably costly, it takes less sophistication and expense to mount a challenge across even difficult land routes than across far-flung sea-lanes. In such a strategic context, India and Pakistan remain sensitive to changes at all rungs on the potential ladder of escalation and, within economic constraints that are especially severe for Pakistan, actively balance one another's improving capabilities. (See Gupta 1995; Goldenberg and Norton-Taylor 1998; Kasturi 1999; Ahmed 1999; Anand 1999; Ahmedullah 2000; "Sinha" 1999; Raghavan 2000; "India: Govt. to Purchase Tanker Planes Soon" 2000.)

Third—and perhaps of greatest importance—geography matters for Asia's balance of power because of its significance with respect to the region's most powerful state, the United States. American capabilities deployed in the region, however impressive (or threatening), are there by choice. Such is not the case for the other key states in Asia. As a Pacific Rim state, the United States may be more nearly linked to Asia geographically than were the old European imperialist powers, but it is in a position fundamentally different from states whose homelands are actually situated in the region. For the United States and others, this geographic distinctiveness matters, even if its significance is mitigated by advances in technology that reduce the importance of sheer distance. Most important, the United States has not been a direct party to territorial disputes in the region. Whether and when it weighs in on such conflicts, and plays an active balancing role, is a matter of choice. America's interests in the region are derivative or indirect—involving its international reputation rather than the intrinsic value of territory and resources for its vital security interests. America's decisions about involvement in disputes on the Korean peninsula, in the Taiwan Strait, and potentially in the Spratly Islands are driven much more by the lessons that adversaries and allies will draw from U.S. action or inaction than by the military or economic assets at stake for the United States. Moreover, changes in the capabilities of countries like Russia, Japan, China, India, or Vietnam are more immediately relevant to neighbors than to the distant United States. As we shall see, America's geographic distinctiveness affects the balancing choices of states in the region whether they view the United States as ally or adversary.

Balancing and Alliances in the Nuclear Era

Modern military technology and geography together have been conditioning balance-of-power politics in Asia for nearly half a century. Above all, they have enhanced the attractiveness of the option presented by nuclear weapons technology. Diffusing technology has made it possible for a growing number of states to deploy this capability to inflict great harm quickly on even the mightiest adversary. This threat allows states to dissuade foes whose overall material superiority (based on sheer size, economic wealth, or technological sophistication) would otherwise give them an insuperable advantage (Goldstein 2000). Moreover, these weapons of mass destruction facilitate more self-reliant balancing by the weak against the strong. Thus they are an attractive strategic option for those who lack the backing of a powerful ally as well as for those who worry about the ultimate uncertainty of an ally's pledges of support in an anarchic international system where agreements are self-enforcing. During the Cold War decades, China's determined efforts to develop its own deterrent—even while hoping to benefit from the nuclear umbrella provided by strategic alignment with first the Soviets and later the Americans—offered the most vivid example of the nuclear logic that has appealed to others in Asia.

In the post–Cold War era, the strategic effects of the nuclear revolution not only endure but alter what one might otherwise expect to be two consequences of unipolarity for balancing by the sole superpower's allies and potential adversaries. First, without weapons of mass destruction unipolarity would seem to render attempts to balance overwhelming U.S. material superiority pointless or, if it triggers a strong response, counterproductive. Inasmuch as the logic of balance-of-power theory originates in its assumptions about survival-conscious states coexisting in a condition of anarchy, state behavior that is provocative or self-defeating would hardly be consistent with its expectations.[8] Even the combined capabilities of several states could not suffice to counterbalance the United States. (This would seem to follow directly from what most mean by unipolarity; see Wohlforth 1999; Kapstein and Mastanduno 1999.) The prospects for individual states are, naturally, bleaker still. Consequently, those worried about potential

---

[8]Warming Sino-Russian ties during the 1990s reflected not only the predictable interest in balancing unchecked U.S. power but also the undesirability of making these relations strictly adversarial. The American hegemon's bag of carrots is too attractive and its bundle of sticks too large. Sino-Russian antihegemony rhetoric about balancing and multipolarity, even the seemingly more impressive trial balloon (quickly floated and deflated) about a Chinese-Russian-Indian entente, is thin cover for the pragmatic measures that potential American rivals actually adopt as they seek to maximize their benefits and minimize the costs of living in a unipolar world in which the United States has no economic or military peer. See Marshall (1999: 11); "Delhi-Moscow-Beijing Bloc" 1999; "Russia, India Reject" 1999; author's interviews, Mar.–Apr. 2000 and Oct. 2000.

conflicts with the superpower (or the allies it stands behind) would seem to have little choice but to yield to its demands—in the familiar refrain, the weak would truly be condemned to "suffer what they must." Moreover, unlike the situation that prevailed in the bipolar Cold War world, in the unipolar world lesser powers cannot leverage global rivalry between competing superpowers to their advantage. But nuclear weapons transform this logic. Because they permit weaker states to dissuade others by creating the risk of devastating punishment, they represent an increasingly attractive offset against power that cannot be matched. (See Goldstein 1997–98: 53–54, 70–71; Goldstein 2000; Hagerty 1998; Bracken 1999: 115–19.)

Second, were it not for the advent of nuclear weapons, states whose interests parallel those of the United States, especially its allies, would face weaker incentives to cultivate their own power under unipolarity. Because the overwhelmingly powerful patron's capabilities deployed or pledged on their behalf would more than suffice to deal with regional contingencies, its allies' independent efforts to balance against prospective adversaries would be much less important, perhaps superfluous. States aligned with the superpower would continue to invest in their own military forces—both as a hedge against the uncertainty of commitments under anarchy and to prevent charges of free-riding from undermining the alliance's solidarity. But taken in isolation, the logical implication of unipolarity for balancing behavior is that it weakens the incentives for the superpower's allies to make the sacrifices associated with allocating more for guns and less for butter.[9]

The nuclear revolution, then, alters expectations about balancing behavior under unipolarity, much as it did under bipolarity. Deliverable nuclear (or biological and chemical) weapons do not make the weak strong. Instead they render even the strongest vulnerable in ways that, first, constrain a superpower's ability to coerce still weak but now terrifying adversaries (that is, they offer the weak a feasible approach to balancing against the strong) and, second, erode the credibility of a superpower's promise to support its allies should they become involved in disputes with adversaries possessing the implements of mass destruction (that is, they increase doubts about the wisdom of relying on external balancing). As a way of leveraging technology to balance against capabilities weaker states cannot match—or as a way of hedging against the possibility that a powerful but frightened ally will balk at offering promised support—deploying weapons of mass destruction is a step that has at times appealed to a wide variety of states in Asia under both bipolarity and unipolarity. Balancing logic has not, however, inevitably resulted in all states that could deploy such weapons choosing to do so. Several of

---

[9]This, of course, is the logic behind the argument that smaller allies may free-ride on powerful patrons. For the classic argument, see Olson and Zeckhauser (1966). For a skeptical view that includes references to the debate, see Goldstein (1995).

the region's advanced industrial countries allied with the United States (Japan, Australia, South Korea, Taiwan) have considered or pursued (and then forsaken) the nuclear option. There are at least three important reasons for their abstinence: first, confidence that the quantity or quality of their conventional military capabilities suffices to balance the most plausible threats a prospective adversary's power represents; second, confidence that even a less than ironclad guarantee of support from a heavily armed superpower ally is sufficiently dependable that they do not need to augment their security through a self-reliant capability (updating security treaties between the United States and its Pacific allies, as well as the related assertions of U.S. plans to maintain its forward presence in the region have reassured those worried about future uncertainty or a rising China); and third, fear of easily anticipated domestic or international political and economic costs (perhaps jeopardizing solidarity with the United States) if they decide to pursue a more self-reliant course that would entail the deployment of weapons of mass destruction.

The experiences of Japan, South Korea, Taiwan, and Australia illustrate the interplay of these considerations that affect the ways states choose to balance against what they recognize as a threatening power. Each was at times tempted by the logic of a national nuclear deterrent—in part as a hedge against the ineffectiveness or unreliability of support from a regionally dominant United States. Nevertheless, each judged that worries about the extended U.S. deterrent did not warrant incurring the cost of pursuing an independent nuclear capability. For Japan, the easily anticipated adverse political reaction at home and abroad to any decision to develop nuclear weapons has thus far been sufficient to offset the deterrent benefit such a capability might offer a country that lacks strategic depth and has a close concentration of highly vulnerable population centers.[10] South Korea's interest in nuclear weapons to counter the once-vaunted conventional superiority of the North resulted in a serious development program that was abandoned only under strong pressure from the United States (Oberdorfer 1997; Sigal 1998: 20–21). For Seoul the benefits of the ultimate military guarantee of sovereignty apparently did not outweigh the costs of jeopardizing a highly advantageous alliance with the

---

[10]Japan's interest in acquiring nuclear weapons has been intermittent since the mid-1960s. See "Comments" 1964; "Japan in 1969" 1994. Although the technical hurdles for Japan are low, the domestic political hurdles are high. In addition to an antimilitary, antinuclear, domestic political culture, legal obstacles stand in the way of Japan's production and possession of nuclear weapons—though some argue that if the laws were revised, nuclear weapons would be constitutional so long as they were deployed to fulfill a deterrent role. See Mochizuki (1983–84). Thus while the process of deciding to develop a nuclear capability would almost certainly be divisive and protracted, once a decision was made production reportedly could bear fruit in perhaps a matter of weeks. (See "Japan Ponders" 1995.) For the notion that Japan may already possess a "virtual" rather than an "opaque" deterrent, see Hanami (1995: 127–41).

powerful United States—especially as the conventional balance on the peninsula shifted in the South's favor (O'Hanlon 1998b). Taiwan, too, explored the nuclear option to counterbalance its rival, the PRC. It aborted the effort, however, under strong pressure from the United States—whose anomalous (following the Sino-American entente of 1972 and the normalization of diplomatic relations in 1979) but seemingly effective guarantee of Taiwan's security contributed to the apparent wisdom of nuclear abstinence (Weiner 1997: A7).[11]

In contrast to these abstemious American allies in Asia, China, India, Pakistan, and allegedly North Korea decided that the capabilities of powerful adversaries require the counterbalance that nuclear weapons provide. In each case the perceived need for greater self-reliance (that is, doubts about the availability or dependability of strategic allies) and the seeming infeasibility of the alternatives for military independence (that is, the inability to match the quantity or quality of an adversary's forces) fostered a determination to deploy a punitive capability that would frighten even the most powerful foe. This interest has endured in the shift from bipolarity to unipolarity.

For China the nuclear deterrent—developed during the Cold War with an eye to dissuading threats from each of the superpowers—now serves as its ace in the hole that confronts the otherwise dominant United States with the risk of horrifying escalation should it threaten vital Chinese interests. Since 1996 Beijing has intermittently reminded observers that one of the key differences between the PRC and Iraq or Serbia (or the PRC of the 1950s) is that it now possesses a deliverable nuclear capability. For India, without an ally that might offer sufficient reassurance, concern about the difficulty of balancing against China's conventional military forces, as well as the coercive capability represented by Beijing's nuclear weapons, has spurred a nuclear weapons program that dates to the mid-1960s. China's rapid economic modernization in the 1990s intensified India's concern and contributed to its decision to move from an opaque, recessed deterrent to a declared and fully developed one (Ganguly 1999).[12] To the extent that the China

[11]Declassified documents now reveal a similar picture in the case of Australia. Australia's nuclear determination was strongest during the period (1964–72) when it seemed that a self-reliant means to counter a more potent China threat might be necessary: China had demonstrated its nuclear capability, Britain had decided to terminate its military obligations in Asia, and the United States seemed poised to undertake a major retrenchment of overseas obligations in the Pacific (Walsh 1997). After 1972, as the perceived need to prepare to counter China ebbed and the norms of the nonproliferation regime took root, the benefits of a national nuclear deterrent no longer justified the economic and political costs of moving ahead.

[12]Rejecting the position that India might need to hedge its bets against the potential threat posed by a powerful China, Beijing insists that New Delhi's "China threat" justification for fielding a nuclear force is simply a pretense to mask its lust for greater status. See Zhang (1998); Maxwell (1999); Farooq (1999); cf. "Indian Army Chief" (1999).

factor motivated India's decision, it should be noted, the concern was about balancing power, not threat, since Sino-Indian relations had in fact been improving during the 1990s (Frazier 2000: 8–9). Pakistan's perceived need for nuclear weapons paralleled India's: India filled the role of a mighty adversary against whom internal balancing through conventional military preparations was deemed impractical and external balancing through cultivating strategic patrons was deemed insufficiently reliable. (See Lodhi 1999; Ahmed 1999; Bukhari 2000.)

North Korea's highly opaque weapons development program reflected similar considerations. Given its severe economic and military disadvantage relative to the states it views as threats to its security—and in the absence of even the uncertain external backing that was available during the Cold War (from the Soviet Union or China)—Pyongyang apparently pursued the most effective counter within reach: confronting adversaries with the threat of ballistic missiles tipped with weapons of mass destruction.[13] Indeed North Korea may offer the clearest example of the approach to balancing that is possible in the context of unipolarity for states whose strategic thinking focuses on the dangers that U.S. capabilities may represent. The demonstrated extent of the U.S. conventional military advantage in the Persian Gulf, Balkan, and Afghanistan operations has underscored the infeasibility of traditional self-reliant balancing alternatives. In addition to imbalanced resources, as noted above, the difficulty some states face in exploiting the technologies of the RMA that privilege American forces may tempt them to embrace not only nuclear weapons but other relatively low-tech but terrifying weapons as an alternative (Qiao and Wang 1999).

Will balancing considerations lead others in the region to follow in the footsteps of the existing nuclear Asian states? Other states in Pacific Asia, especially those with whom the United States has reaffirmed its Cold War alliances, do not now face threats that provide a strong security motive to do so. Moreover, international counterproliferation measures (focused on nuclear weapons, missile technology, and fissile materials) and national limitations (economic, scientific, and technological) establish significant obstacles that even motivated small states would need to surmount. But the similarity of response throughout the region by states that have viewed weapons of mass destruction as essential for their security suggests that they will remain an attractive option when states perceive severe

---

[13]In addition to the strategic payoff from developing an opaque deterrent, North Korea has garnered economic and political benefits by reaching agreements to curtail its weapons and missile development program. Given the inevitable imperfections associated with even the most intrusive verification schemes, Pyongyang may be able to have its nuclear cake and eat it too. Uncertainty about the status of the weapons program may induce adversaries to exercise great caution in escalating confrontations with North Korea—and concessions regarding observable activities may induce adversaries to reward the North for its ostensible self-restraint.

asymmetries in size and power that favor their prospective adversary or begin to have doubts about a powerful ally's pledge of support.

The distinctive role of nuclear weapons in the region's balance-of-power politics seems likely to continue. This role has already spanned the divide between the bipolar and unipolar eras; it would not be fundamentally altered by the end of unipolarity. Expectations about the end of unipolarity, however, do have consequences for power balancing in the region even as the influence of nuclear military technology endures. What is expected to follow unipolarity? And how does this expectation affect contemporary balance-of-power politics in Asia?

Balancing and the End of Unipolarity

Although many observers have referred to the likelihood of a multipolar world emerging in the twenty-first century, in Asia the operating assumption (neither publicly articulated nor necessarily correct) now seems to be that within the region, China's economic and military growth is more likely to first give rise to bipolarity.[14] The perception—with only loose links to assessments of China's actual capabilities—is that other candidate great powers will play lesser roles in Asia in the short term or will face stiff challenges likely to delay their ability to do much more. Even if the European Union succeeds in coalescing as a true great power and Russia is able to rebuild its much-diminished capacity, in a multipolar world their principal interests would lead both initially to focus their attention outside Pacific Asia. While concerned mainly about events in Europe, around the Mediterranean, and across Central Asia, Europe and Russia are expected to play a role in the Asia Pacific region—hence China's courting of Russia and the European states, Japan's interest in improved ties with Russia, and the regionwide effort to lend weight to the Asia-Europe Meeting—but one that is less direct than that played by others. Japan, seemingly on the threshold of great-power status as the Cold War ended, could become a third power in the region. But during the 1990s an unexpectedly prolonged economic crisis sharply eroded what had been the country's chief strength and cast doubt on its future trajectory. India might fit the bill, but its new status as a nuclear state will not alone suffice to make it a great power. Instead the likelihood of India playing a regionwide role on a par with the United States and China in the future will depend mainly on the development of its economy and secondly on its growing ability to project conventional, especially naval, power north and east of the subcontinent (Carino 1998). At present, therefore, balancing behavior is shaped by the anticipation that Sino-American

[14]Realists began predicting the advent of multipolarity almost as soon as the Cold War ended. See Waltz (1993); Mearsheimer (1990); Krauthammer (1991); Layne (1993). For an analysis that thinks bipolarity is already taking root, see Ross (1999).

bipolarity in the region is the most plausible immediate successor to what has become an unexpectedly long period of U.S. preponderance, even as many believe
and others hope that Asia will one day be multipolar.[15]

States concerned about the implications of China emerging as at least a regional rival to the United States seek to ensure continued U.S. engagement as a
counterweight but also hedge their bets against the possibility that American
support may become less certain or less effective as China grows stronger. Concern about China's power intensified during the 1990s as many took note of the
PRC's rapid economic growth rates, its determined efforts to modernize its military, and its more self-assured, often bluntly assertive, regional behavior. (Nathan
and Ross 1997; Bernstein and Munro 1997; Goldstein 1997–98.) Although not all
drew worst-case conclusions about a nascent "China threat," uncertainty about
the ways a more capable China would employ its power encouraged some to prepare to balance against the possible dangers. In varying ways, nervousness about
China's growing power has shaped the post–Cold War foreign policies of Japan,
Australia, the Philippines, Vietnam, Taiwan, South Korea, and India.

Japan has been in the distinctive position of being able to piggyback its balancing efforts geared toward the anticipation of increased Chinese power on its
short-term effort to counter the dangerous capabilities North Korea may be deploying. Revising the guidelines for U.S.-Japan military cooperation, embracing
joint research and development on theater missile defenses, strengthening Japan-
ROK military coordination, planning for a more autonomous satellite reconnaissance capability, and initiating a more open debate about Japan's military-
security needs and international role—all were directly linked to the troubling
actions of the North Koreans during the 1990s. (See "DPRK" 1999; Barr 1998a,
1998b; "Japan Says" 1998.) But these efforts simultaneously prepare Japan for an
Asian future in which its most worrisome military planning contingency may be
China. Because of historically rooted sensitivity about Japan's international role,
anticipatory balancing against yet-to-materialize Chinese capabilities is not publicly touted as such (Japan's 1995 Defense White Paper merely raised questions
about China's future) and is sometimes even publicly denied. (Japan insists that
theater missile defense [TMD] is not intended to neutralize China's one area of
real military strength and repeatedly denies that the revised U.S.-Japan security
guidelines necessarily foreshadow support for the United States against China in
future Taiwan Strait showdowns.) Beijing, however, understandably discounts re-
assurances that these various measures are merely aimed at coping with the

---

[15]Whether this structural change within the region would coincide with the emergence of
multipolarity at the global level—and perhaps be affected by extraregional considerations (as Soviet-American bipolarity influenced East Asia during the Cold War despite U.S. preponderance)—
is unclear.

North Korean threat. Instead Beijing argues that they are part and parcel of an incipient strategy of preventive containment directed at China (Zhang Guocheng 1997).[16]

In the mid-1990s, Australia, like Japan, revised its Cold War–vintage security arrangements with the United States—explicitly to ensure that the United States remained engaged in the region and implicitly as a ready counter to growing Chinese power. Proximity and a history of strategic interdependence explain Japan's concern about the implications of an increasingly powerful China. Without the geographic and historical concerns that inform Japanese thinking, Australia's post–Cold War concern is fed instead by the recent activation of multistate disputes involving China, among others, over claims to the vast, allegedly resource-rich, strategically situated islands in the South China Sea. The dangers for Australia are not only the risks of escalating military action in nearby areas but also a future order in which China may deploy much-improved power–projection capabilities to support its diplomatic position. Although the rhetoric of reinvigorated U.S.-Australia security cooperation after the end of the Cold War, as in the case of U.S.-Japan ties, avoided mentioning China by name, the contingency was unmistakable, certainly to the Chinese. Australia is the "southern anchor" of a U.S.-led arc of allies that can be used to counter China—especially as a site for radar installations that would become part of a comprehensive ballistic missile defense system in Asia. (See "Australia, Japan" 1997; Tang 1996; "Australia" 1996; Zhang Dezhen 1997.)

Among the ASEAN states, two—Vietnam and the Philippines—have concerns about China's power that are fed not just by worries about its future growth but also by current disagreements that raise the specter of even greater dangers down the road. Although Vietnam and the Philippines are not the only parties to the many territorial disputes with the PRC in the South China Sea, they have been the two states with which Beijing has had its sharpest differences. In the 1990s,

---

[16]When the *Yomiuri Shimbun* reported that the peripheral region to be covered under the revised guidelines "would be 'the Far East and its vicinity,' including the Taiwan Strait and the Spratly Islands, the Government immediately denied that it would decide in advance which areas should be covered by the guidelines. Instead, said Kanezo Muranoka, the Government's chief Cabinet Secretary, a decision will be deferred until an emergency arises" (WuDunn 1998: A6; see also "Japan Rejects" 1998). If inter-Korean rapprochement continues and Japan still bolsters its defenses and strengthens its ties with the United States, it will become more difficult to portray its policies as a response limited to the threat of North Korean weapons of mass destruction. Analysts at some conservative think tanks in Tokyo acknowledge that Japan's recent interest in fortified military capabilities is driven by a long-term concern about China but is publicly sold as merely a necessary response to the short-term danger of North Korea. Chinese analysts routinely dismiss as absurd the idea that the United States would incur the costs associated with missile defenses (both TMD and NMD) simply to deal with an unlikely North Korean contingency (author's interviews, Tokyo, Mar. 1999; Beijing, Mar.–Apr. 2000).

none of the confrontations escalated beyond accusations, claims, counterclaims, and minor displays of military force. But China's insistence on handling negotiations to resolve these disputes on a bilateral basis—rather than in a multilateral setting such as the ASEAN Regional Forum—has underscored the difficult position these smaller regional actors may find themselves in if they must continue to deal separately with the PRC, especially if its air and naval power-projection capabilities increase as expected in coming years. Even as the PRC has softened its opposition to multilateral forums to discuss South China Sea issues and has indicated a willingness to work toward a maritime code of conduct, it adheres to its preference for bilateral dispute resolution (Acharya 2000: chap. 5).

If ASEAN fails to provide united backing for them, how can these two states respond to their concern about the possible future uses of China's growing power? In limited ways, Vietnam and the Philippines seek to upgrade their military forces (internal balancing) and exploit the counter to China that international partners (external balancing) may offer if needed. In the post–Cold War era, Hanoi, having lost its Soviet ally, has sought to reduce the risk that Vietnam might be diplomatically isolated in the event of conflict with China. In classic balancing fashion, erstwhile allies and adversaries are realigning. Vietnam has joined ASEAN, whose members were once united by a fear of Indochinese communists, and has normalized relations with the United States. Though a far cry from the security dividend actual alliances would offer, these steps, especially the difficult process of reconciliation with the United States, carry the hope of improving Vietnam's prospects for economic growth that will enable Hanoi to augment its own military capabilities more vigorously (Balfour 1999; Burns 2000).

The Philippines' situation differs from Vietnam's insofar as it has long been a formal U.S. ally. But the closeness of the bilateral security relationship has varied with the region's shifting balance of power. After the 1970s, security ties with the United States became strained. Two major reasons account for the near collapse of this once-close relationship. First, during the latter years of the Cold War the communist threat in Asia that China had represented was transformed. As the United States disengaged from the war in Indochina and initiated its strategic entente with China, the Filipino-American alliance lost its unifying adversary. Second, with the external security rationale for the alliance undermined, domestic critics were better positioned to challenge the need for, as well as the desirability of, its continuation. In the mid-1980s, as the Aquino-led reform movement pressed for an end to authoritarian rule, military cooperation with the United States became a victim of nationalist resentment of Washington's longstanding close association with the discredited and despised Marcos regime. When the post-Marcos government confronted a more benign regional security environment, the purchase of U.S. arms diminished and in 1991 the Philippine senate voted to end the American presence at Subic Bay naval base and Clark air force base, key U.S. military installations in the western Pacific. During the 1990s, however, as China assertively laid claim to maritime territories over which the Philippines insisted it had sovereignty (most notably Mischief Reef and Scarborough Shoal), Manila began to look again to Washington—both for assistance in beefing up the Philippines' languishing military capabilities and for the diplomatic muscle that a resuscitation of the seemingly dormant security treaty might provide. (See Simon 2000: 20–22; Morada and Collier 1998: 567–68, 572–75; Lamb 1998; Baguioro 1999; Ghosh 1999.) As for Vietnam, the trend is toward improved Filipino-American relations, though in both cases the process is complicated by the political legacy of the recent past. (See Satchell 2000; "GIs Come Back?" 1999; Ghosh 1999; "The GIs Return" 2000; "Philippines" 1999; Baguioro 1999.)

In short, the uncertain but worrisome implications of the PRC's growing capabilities have encouraged both Vietnam and the Philippines to set aside past differences with the United States and take steps that may enable them to exploit the most effective external means to offset China's power. It should be noted, however, that—like other ASEAN states—neither has embraced a simple-minded strategy that treats China as an implacable foe to be balanced at all costs. Instead, both simultaneously engage China (attempting to reduce the threat by discovering diplomatic solutions to their outstanding disputes) while hedging their bets against worst-case scenarios by improving their options for countering the threat that China could one day pose to their national security.[17]

Taiwan's balancing against the dangers it sees in the PRC's growing power is much less equivocal. Taipei's policy has included determined efforts at augmenting its own military strength (through domestic production as well as the purchase of equipment from the United States and France) and a distinctive diplomacy designed to nurture a quasi-alliance with the United States. (The formal alliance was abrogated when the Carter administration recognized Beijing as the sole government of China in 1979.) Unlike Vietnam and the Philippines, however, Taiwan's world-class economy has provided ample resources for modernizing a military that is now able to pose a daunting defense against any PRC offensive designed to take over the island by force.[18] What Taiwan lacks is the ability

[17]China and Vietnam in 1999 negotiated a demarcation of their land border and began talking about their maritime disputes. Negotiations between China and the Philippines about their disputes in the South China Sea have been difficult, but high-level political exchanges aimed at reducing the persistent tensions about Chinese structures on Mischief Reef and incidents between military craft and fishing vessels in the region continue.

[18]On the cross-strait balance of power, see Goldstein (1997–98: 52–53); O'Hanlon (2000). For up-to-date coverage of assessments, see *Taiwan Security Research* at http://www.taiwansecurity.org/.

to cope with attempts by the PRC to use force indirectly—attempts to coerce Taipei by threatening to inflict punishment rather than military defeat if it does not comply with Beijing's demands. China's ballistic missiles and its growing naval and air power give Beijing the option to punish Taiwan through strategic bombing strikes against the island or, more likely, by creating military hazards along the air and sea routes that are the vital lifelines for Taiwan's trade-dependent economy. Against these threats Taiwan's defenses are already inadequate. How does Taiwan balance against this most plausible danger posed by China's growing capabilities? Where internal balancing fails, external balancing is pursued. The counter to China's coercive capability against which Taiwan cannot defend itself is the risk of escalation created by U.S. support. Taipei's success in nurturing a clear (if under international law unrecognized) commitment from the United States to respond to threats to the island's security helps dissuade Beijing.[19] The shared expectation that there will be an American response to unprovoked military pressure against Taiwan increases China's doubts about the sustainability of coercive military operations (U.S. naval and air power might negate attempts at blockade; imperfect TMD might reduce the punishment inflicted by conventionally tipped ballistic missiles) but, most important, increases fears of possibly uncontrollable escalation in a showdown with the United States. Indeed it is mainly the risk of escalation—especially when the prospective adversaries have nuclear weapons—rather than a comparison of deployed capabilities, that fulfills Taiwan's desire for a counterbalance to China.[20]

Like Taiwan and Japan, South Korea has invested substantial economic resources in its military and has maintained close security ties with the United States (in the case of the ROK a formal treaty). And to an even greater degree than in the Japanese case, the threat from the North Korean regime serves as the

[19]The U.S.-Taiwan relationship is now based on four elements: first, long-standing political ties between the regime on Taiwan and the United States that increase the loss of reputation the United States would suffer if it failed to offer support; second, strong congressional support for Taiwan, manifest most clearly in the Taiwan Relations Act that Congress passed into law in April 1979, giving official expression to the U.S. commitment to the security of the people of Taiwan, even after diplomatic recognition ended; third, Taiwan's status as a prosperous market economy and liberal democracy in an era when U.S. foreign policy explicitly aims to preserve and expand the community of such states; and fourth, the U.S. decision in winter 1996 to move naval forces to the vicinity of the Taiwan Strait—signaling that although much had changed since the previous confrontations of the 1950s, the United States would not simply stand aside if the PRC used military force against the island. See Freeman (1998).

[20]This, of course, is a two-way street. The risk of escalation makes it hard for Beijing to decide to coerce a Taiwan backed by the United States. It also, however, makes the United States wary about intervening. If the two parties are locked in a relationship of mutual deterrence, a crisis in the strait that engaged both sides might well be decided less on the balance of power and more on the balance of resolve. (Who would run the greater risk of triggering uncontrollable escalation and thereby induce the other to back down?)

rationale for balancing behavior in the short term that may pay dividends in the long run should other threats become a central concern for a Korea unified under Seoul's leadership. As long as the threat from the North remains the main military contingency, it is possible for Seoul to defer difficult questions about whether it might be China's or Japan's capabilities that pose the more significant long-term threat to Korean interests.[21] But in either case, an important result of the peninsula's armed confrontation during the Cold War will be a substantial ability for a future unified Korea to rely on both internal and external balancing to cope with any threats it may face. The legacy of Seoul's heavy investment in its own military will be Korea's enhanced ability to counter prospective adversaries independently; the legacy of U.S. sacrifice on the Korean peninsula is a reduced likelihood of American indifference about the country's fate and an increased likelihood that prospective adversaries would have to anticipate U.S. intervention, whether or not American forces continue to be stationed on Korean soil.

Like other Asian states, India anticipates the difficulties a more powerful China could pose in the future. Unlike many other Asian states, India has not had much hope of balancing against China by a strategy that includes direct support from the United States. Many Asian states could carry forward their strategic links with the United States from the Cold War. India could not. Its political determination to stand aloof from the Manichean ideological struggle of the bipolar era may have diminished the extent to which New Delhi had to worry about superpower threats during the Cold War. But it also left India without a strong ally afterward. India's Cold War inheritance was instead an economic hangover from its partial affiliation with bankrupt Soviet-style socialism and strained relations with both countries that emerged in the 1990s as the key players in Asia: China and the United States (both of which were linked in a strategic entente that sided with India's subcontinental adversary, Pakistan, during the last two decades of the Cold War). Despite a legacy of politically tense relations and despite the chill that followed the nuclear tests of May 1998, as U.S.-China relations deteriorated in 1999, U.S.-India relations began to warm. Though the lack of close ties for more than three decades and remaining policy differences (especially about nuclear weapons and America's "new interventionism") promise to make for a still diffi-

---

[21]So long as the peninsula remains divided and the North remains hostile and heavily armed, strategic interests draw Korea and Japan together in ways that do not apply to relations with China. Military cooperation between Seoul and Tokyo has been on the rise, and many view the October 1998 Kim-Obuchi summit as marking a major diplomatic breakthrough in once-chilly Korean-Japanese relations. See "ROK, Japanese Navy Officials" 1999; "ROK, Japan Launch" 1999; "ROK, Japanese Navies to Conduct" 1999; "ROK, Japan Agree" 1999. Whether—in light of deep historical animosities between Korea and Japan—the warming of this side of the Korea-Japan-China triangle would survive the evaporation of the North Korean threat is an open question. See "Football Diplomacy" 1996; "South Korean War Memories" 2000; "Offensive" 1995.

cult relationship, as balance-of-power theory predicts, parallel concerns in Washington and New Delhi about China (and, to some extent, Islamic fundamentalism) drive the process of reconciliation forward (Saleem 1999; Behn 2000; Hussain 2000).[22]

Because of geographic proximity, competing aspirations for recognition as great powers, and a history of territorial disputes and armed conflict along the Sino-Indian border, Beijing's growing power represents a serious concern for New Delhi. Part of India's response entails efforts to reduce tensions with China—though repeated efforts to resolve their border dispute that triggered the 1962 war have proved remarkably difficult. (See "Chronology" 2000; Katyal 2000.) Doubts about the prospects for support from a powerful ally and a lack of confidence in the deterrent power of the conventional military forces it can sustain have predictably led India to hedge against the dangers inherent in China's great power by opting for the self-reliant counterbalance of a nuclear deterrent. Although it is conceivable that India might one day be able (and willing) to exploit an intensifying Sino-American rivalry in an emerging bipolar world in order to establish a strategic entente with the United States, such an opportunity does not yet exist. (See "Will Indo-U.S. Ties" 1999.) And even if this were possible, the unavoidable uncertainty of security commitments under anarchy suggests that such a partnership would not lead New Delhi to abandon the self-reliant nuclear capability that is now a key component of its hedging strategy for balancing against Chinese power.

Balancing in Southeast Asia: A Different Dynamic?

So far I have emphasized balance-of-power dynamics that are driven mainly by the involvement of the most capable regional powers and their links to the role played by global great powers. This focus is reasonable when analyzing sensitive areas of Asia that attract strong interest from far-flung actors. But some of the balancing that goes on in subregions, while unavoidably linked to broad regional and global patterns, is shaped also by its own distinctive dynamics. In post–Cold War Asia, this dynamic is best exemplified in Southeast Asia. This subregion merits additional attention also because it has recently underscored the continued importance of balance-of-power politics despite trends expected to diminish its relevance—specifically, increasing economic interdependence and emerging multilateral institutions.

In the post–Cold War era, especially as the fear of Indochina as a communist threat receded, Southeast Asia finally seemed poised to enjoy a period of peace

[22]In 2001, new strategic thinking in the George W. Bush administration and especially parallel interests in the war against terrorism seemed likely to accelerate this process.

and prosperity in which economic interests would override military concerns and in which interstate disputes might be managed by a strengthened and expanding ASEAN. While some noted that increased affluence in the region was feeding increased military expenditures—a position outlined most clearly in the early post–Cold War vision of Desmond Ball (1993–94; see also Betts 1993–94)—through the mid-1990s affluence also gave Southeast Asia's states a strong vested interest in not disrupting the remarkable economic success that characterized the region. And with Cold War-vintage ASEAN supplemented by an ASEAN Regional Forum (ARF) that included extraregional Asia Pacific powers that might otherwise play a locally disruptive role, a trend toward growing institutionalism seemed to confound the predictions of those realists who had been generally skeptical about the significance of international organizations and especially about their significance in a region allegedly bereft of the historical, cultural, and political traditions that accounted for their effectiveness in the West (Friedberg 1993–94; Goldstein 1997–98: 68–69). Although the dialogues that grew up within and around ASEAN and its ARF were failing to resolve outstanding interstate disputes in Southeast Asia, the importance participants attached to the increasingly frequent meetings sponsored by these organizations was resulting in a degree of institutionalization few had expected at the beginning of the 1990s.

Yet even as such new features of Southeast Asia emerged, states simultaneously hedged their bets by responding in the old familiar ways to dangers that linked the subregion to broad concerns in Asia. Specifically these states saw the continued presence of a dominant United States as an essential counterbalance to a rising and nearby China. Though ASEAN states sometimes displayed unity in the context of discussions with China about the South China Sea disputes (especially in criticizing China's 1995 seizure of Mischief Reef), they showed little interest in balancing against China themselves. For Southeast Asians, balancing had the twin disadvantages of being extremely costly and highly provocative. The United States could afford to shoulder the burden. If it was unwilling to do so, it made sense for ASEAN states to keep open the option of adjusting to Chinese hegemony should that appear inevitable. More revealing than the ASEAN states' muted realpolitik in dealing with the rise of China was the way they responded to the economic reversal of 1997. Events in the late 1990s strongly suggested that the optimism of the mid-1990s about the pacifying consequences of economic interests and evolving subregional multilateral institutions was at least premature.

As Amitav Acharya notes, the economic downturn resulted in increased tensions among Southeast Asian countries and a renewed focus on the important role that powerful states (the United States, China, Japan) outside the subregion should play to help steer them through the crisis (Acharya 2000: chaps. 5 and 9). The reversion to realism was highlighted by the setback in what had been a promising trend toward improved relations and even military cooperation among sometime rivals Singapore, Malaysia, and Indonesia. Singapore's relations with Indonesia in the Suharto era had been put on a solid footing as the sensitive issue of Indonesia's economically successful Chinese minority was muted during the years of improving standards of living prior to 1998. Relations between Singapore and Malaysia, though punctuated by conflict, had also stabilized. Common interests—especially in ensuring the security of the peninsula against external threats as well as underlying concerns about the implications of sharing the neighborhood with a much larger and potentially more powerful Indonesia—had tangible results, including an agreement to permit Singapore's military to fly over Malaysian airspace without prior authorization and establishment of the Singapore-Malaysia Defense Forum in 1996 (Tan 1999).

Yet when tested by the strains of the economic crisis that emerged in 1997, conflicting interests again came to the fore and drove each to behave in ways that underscored their perceived need to hedge against the threat each might pose to the other. Malaysia temporarily withdrew from planned joint military exercises under the Five Power Defense Arrangements, rescinded Singapore's overflight rights, and used sometimes incendiary rhetoric that focused on the two countries' conflicting rather than common interests (Leifer 1998: 54; Acharya 2000: chap. 9). Singapore refocused on the need for military preparedness, reflecting the special sensitivity of a small state that believes it cannot afford to wait to mobilize its resources until after a serious threat develops. Malaysia and especially harder-hit Indonesia were particularly resentful that their more affluent neighbor, less affected by the economic downturn, had proved insufficiently generous in their time of need. Instead prosperous Singapore, already possessing the region's premier military forces, continued to devote its ample resources to a sustained modernization program that has long been geared toward putative threats from Malaysia and Indonesia (Tan 1999).

Also deflating the optimism about the "new security concepts" popular in Southeast Asia was the tarnishing of what some had hoped might be the silver lining to the dark cloud of economic crisis—hard-hit states scaling back ambitious plans for military modernization (Acharya 2000: chap. 9). At the first signs of economic recovery, Southeast Asian states, now more suspicious, quickly rediscovered their appetite for military procurement ("The Arming of Asia" 2000; Rustam 2000).[23] The point is not that this experience proves that realists rather than institutionalists are right about the Asian security order. Such a sterile de-

---

[23]Competitive security concerns are only one reason for increasing arms spending. Corruption, bureaucratic interest, interservice rivalry, prestige concerns, and beliefs in potential technology spinoffs benefiting the civilian economy play varying roles. See Huxley and Willet (1999).

bate obscures the complexity that prevails in this region as elsewhere. These recent events are cited only to suggest that even as states recognize their interest in pursuing mutual economic benefits and become more aware of the opportunity for addressing disputes in regional multilateral institutions, they also understand that such changes modify rather than transform the risky and uncertain international arena in which they must operate.

Consequences

In ways that reflect their different circumstances, states respond to the potential threat posed by other states' capabilities in an anarchic realm. Balance-of-power theory explains why, but not just how, they are likely to respond. National resources and useful allies are important, but they are not the sole influences shaping such decisions. Though balancing continues to be a defining feature of regional order in Asia, relative capabilities alone do not determine the intensity and mix of internal and external balancing. Grasping the nature of balance-of-power politics, as ever, requires looking beyond system-level causes to the attributes of the states and their distinctive circumstances. Military technology, geographic circumstances, beliefs about the intentions of rivals, domestic politics—these are just some of what neorealists label "unit-level" variables that affect the nature and intensity of power balancing. Moreover, balance-of-power considerations, though important, are not the only factors shaping regional security order (Alagappa 1998). What, then, can be said about the implications of power balancing for peace and prosperity in Asia? To put it simply, the consequences of power balancing for the regional security order are indeterminate.

Power Balancing and Peace

Balance-of-power theory establishes no definitive link between the balance of power and peace. Whether states resolve their disputes peacefully depends on whether the parties believe their interests are better served through fighting or negotiating. Neither an imbalance that some states may seek to rectify nor a more even balance among rivals is alone decisive. Although some international relations scholars contend that either great imbalance or rough parity is conducive to peace, neither assertion follows directly from the logic of balance-of-power theory. The theory suggests why one expects to observe balancing behavior—not whether balancing will be conducive to peace. To borrow from Clausewitz: War may well be the continuation of balancing by other means. Balancing behavior will affect the negotiating strength of states that have conflicting interests (both the capabilities they themselves amass and the commitments they gather from allies). And trends in balancing may condition the extent to which states discount the future. Such considerations must be included in any explanation of the causes of war. But power balancing is at best one among a number of independent variables that shape a state's war/peace decision. (See Fearon 1995; Powell 1999; Van Evera 1999.)

Thus decisions about whether or not to resort to force, while certainly shaped by relative capabilities, are affected by many other factors: the goals of states, the character of their leaders, military technology, domestic political interests and culture. Depending on the influence of such considerations, as states balance against what they perceive to be potentially threatening rivals, they may feel more or less secure and their behavior may become more cautious or more adventurous. Some states (perhaps South Korea and Japan), reassured by their efforts to cope with external threats through increasing armaments or firming up alliances, may decide that their greater sense of security makes it safe to resolve disputes through diplomatic compromise or to explore various confidence-building measures. But effective balancing against a powerful adversary may also embolden leaders to adopt a harder line that increases the risk of war. Whether U.S. arms sales and external security assurances to Taiwan or the Philippines make armed conflict or constructive diplomacy with China more likely is an open question that balance-of-power theory cannot answer. Moreover, the theory readily explains Pakistan's deployment of nuclear weapons as a counter to India's hard-to-match conventional capability but does not indicate whether Islamabad's increased sense of security will incline it to compromise or dig in its heels. Similarly unclear are the implications of India's nuclear counter to China and its warming ties to the United States for the peacefulness of Sino-Indian relations.

On the narrower matter of arms racing, too, balance-of-power theory explains the interactive dynamic but not its costs, intensity, or effects on the likelihood of war. Economic constraints and domestic political interests obviously play important roles in shaping decisions about the pace of military procurement—sometimes reinforcing, sometimes offsetting, the balancing incentives rooted in anarchy (as in South Asia and Southeast Asia). So, too, do prevailing technology and strategic beliefs that affect the severity of the security dilemma which underpins arms racing (Jervis 1978).

Balancing and Prosperity

With regard to regional prosperity, the implications of power balancing are not straightforward either. Although states face incentives to respond to the capabilities of others they view as threatening, their response may be more or less demanding of resources. As we have seen, for example, some Asian states (North Korea and perhaps China and India for the near future) that are unable or unwilling to incur the high costs of deploying RMA technology may choose to rely on the bluntly coercive effects of weapons of mass destruction. Such weapons offer a robust and relatively affordable option for states whose goals are limited to dissuading threats to vital interests from more powerful actors. They are less useful for states interested in altering the status quo. For such purposes, more fungible (and increasingly expensive) modern conventional technologies are needed.

States worried about the weapons of mass destruction (especially nuclear) that others possess, and inevitably unsure about their intentions, also face more or less burdensome choices for responding to the dangers they represent. However appealing the concept, constructing a defense against such weapons (highly effective active and passive defenses) promises to be expensive compared with the alternative of relying on the dissuasive effect of threatening retaliatory punishment. A state against which such defenses are deployed will in turn face a choice. It can adopt relatively cheap countermeasures that undermine the adversary's confidence in his defenses and thereby maintain the rival's sense of vulnerability to horrifying punishment (China's advertised response to U.S. deployment of missile defenses). But if it has goals beyond simply dissuading aggression or if it believes that emerging technology could render countermeasures ineffective, it may have to incur the expense of competing in the deployment of sophisticated defenses. Within such a strategic setting, then, a pattern of balancing is predictable and readily explained. But its implications for prosperity depend on the methods chosen. And these methods reflect both the goals of states and their beliefs about the feasibility and acceptability of available alternatives, matters about which balance-of-power theory provides insufficient information.

In short, the implications of balance-of-power theory for regional security order are unclear. But indeterminacy also suggests that although the underlying incentives that lead to balancing may not easily be altered, the role of human agency is far from irrelevant. To modify Alex Wendt's (1992) claim: the consequences of anarchy are partly what we make of them. Standard diplomatic efforts—especially bilateral negotiations about territorial claims, arms control, and military-to-military exchanges—are a few prominent ways in which states may attempt to mitigate the dangers and expense of vigorous balancing. After the Cold War, however, some advocated a more ambitious response: a concert of great powers. Such a diplomatic arrangement accepts balancing as unavoidable but seeks to regulate its dynamics—and is expected to do so more effectively than larger, more inclusive international organizations.

Coping with the Consequences of Power Balancing

The new arguments for a concert approach that arose when the Cold War ended were mainly normative. Rather than focusing on its feasibility, the emphasis was on its desirability as a way to avoid the alleged dangers of unfettered international competition according to the traditional practices associated with bal-ance-of-power politics. Thus, for example, a global concert was needed because history demonstrated that balancing was not a reliable way to prevent war (Rosencrance 1992: 64–69); a European concert was needed because it would be the most practical way to promote collective security arrangements that foster cooperation (Kupchan and Kupchan 1991: 118, 138); and an Asian concert was needed because multipolarity and historical experience suggested that "relying on power balances managed by the United States does not seem a safe bet" (Shirk 1997: 253, 256–57, 259). But even if it might be desirable, or at least preferable to the alternatives, how feasible is a concert approach—specifically in post–Cold War Asia? Answering this question requires a brief assessment of the conditions conducive to forming a concert.

Concerts are best understood as a type of international regime that emerges under very special circumstances in which a handful of great powers have strong incentives to regulate their competitive behavior. Rather than terminating bal-ance-of-power politics, an international concert amounts to an effort to agree to rules of the game by which balance-of-power politics among the great powers will proceed (Jervis 1983: 185; Jervis 1985: 59). Why might self-regarding states, free to choose for themselves in an anarchic realm, do this? Robert Jervis's analysis at-taches great importance to heightened self-interest in reducing the chances that balance-of-power politics will result in armed conflict—a concern that prevails just after the conclusion of a major counterhegemonic war. Such an experience alters the strategic environment in five ways that facilitate the construction of a concert. First, joint opposition to the defeated enemy, seen as an abnormal state, establishes especially close ties among the great powers that are less likely to rea-lign into opposing coalitions. Second, the belief that warfare is too costly a rem-edy for the dangers of imbalanced power reduces the likelihood that military force will be viewed as a practical alternative to diplomacy. Third, the conviction that anarchy and unrestrained rivalry paved the way for horrific war increases the interest in devising effective measures to mute their effects. Fourth, concern about the possibility of the defeated hegemon's resurgence provides incentives for devising methods to maintain unity among the victorious powers. And fifth, satisfied with the peace terms, the victors are more likely to be receptive to ar-rangements that favor the status quo and less motivated to play the balance-of-power game as hard as they might if dissatisfied (Jervis 1985: 60–61, 65, 67, 71). Unlike other assessments of the concert approach to managing security relations, Jervis's does not emphasize the importance of ideological, cultural, or moral con-sensus among the major powers. (Compare Rosencrance 1992: 75; Kupchan and Kupchan 1991: 124; Shirk 1997: 267–68; Acharya 1999: 86–87.) For the Asian region this is the good news, since diversity on this score is most noteworthy no matter which states one counts as essential powers. The bad news is that the other conditions conducive to forming a concert are lacking.

Because the Cold War was not a counterhegemonic war—indeed not a war at all—most of the consequences of such a struggle that facilitate a concert did not emerge after 1990.[24] Although some might have viewed the Soviet Union as a highly motivated imperialist power, by the latter decades of the Cold War it did not appear to be the sort of abnormal state whose single-minded lust for dominance would foster a lasting sense of community among its adversaries. Indeed the Soviet Union appeared to be a rather normal imperialist power against which others cooperated for self-interested reasons. Thus when Soviet power declined and then evaporated, the once-close but purely instrumental bonds between two of the most important actors in Asia, China and the United States, quickly dissolved. Nor was there much concern about the possibility of resurgent Soviet hegemony to foster continued cooperation among other Asian states. Rather than pursuing a concert to hedge against a Soviet/Russian revival, countries in Asia revised their security arrangements and acquired military capabilities based on their separate perceptions of other threats. And if it is important for the principals in a concert to be satisfied with the status quo that follows the preceding war, then the resolution of the Cold War did little to engender optimism about the prospects for an Asian concert. Aside from Asia's many lingering territorial disputes that reflect disagreement about just what constitutes the status quo in the region, one of the two great powers in the region, China, is clearly not ready to accept as the status quo a post–Cold War Asian order in which the collapse of the Soviet Union has reinforced American primacy.

Perhaps most decisively, however, "waging" the Cold War did not change beliefs about the costs of military force as an alternative to diplomacy or the need to devise more effective institutions, such as a concert, to avert another disaster. Consequently there is little reason to believe that the experience has dramatically altered beliefs about the use of force in ways that are necessary to encourage concert building. Though nerve-racking and burdensome, the Cold War was relatively bloodless by historic standards. The enemy, per Sun Zi, was subdued without fighting. Current beliefs about the horror of great-power war reflect a recognition that it might involve the use of nuclear weapons—rather than an aversion rooted in recent warfare. And unlike the fear of repeated hegemonic struggle, to the extent that actors believe the nuclear revolution has made the terrifying prospect of great-power military conflict a sufficiently reliable deterrent, the incentives to devise institutional arrangements to prevent war may in fact have declined. In this strategic context, even the combat that did occur during the Cold War may

[24]In Gaddis's (1986) famous phrase, the Cold War is more aptly termed the Long Peace.

not be much of an incentive for concert building. Aware of the strong inhibitions on general war, the great powers proved quite adept at waging and managing limited wars from which they disengaged when the costs became excessive. Though undeniably tragic for the participants, these limited wars did not provide the sort of trauma that has historically encouraged efforts at dramatic institutional innovations (such as the Concert of Europe, League of Nations, United Nations).

The military legacy of the Cold War, then, may not have yielded strong incentives for a concert—however attractive the idea may be in principle—because it suggested that major war was nearly unthinkable anyway and limited war was tolerable. Nor has the early post–Cold War experience with military force presented compelling new incentives. On the contrary, while the memory of bloody limited wars in Cold War Asia fades, experience with the use of military force since 1990 in Iraq, the Balkans, and Afghanistan may be engendering confidence that war in the new era is very dangerous only for the small and undeveloped countries. If great powers come to believe, not only that general war remains unthinkable because of nuclear weapons, but also that the costs (military and human, not economic) of limited war are in fact diminishing because of the marriage of high technology and military force, the incentives to devise a concert to forestall conflict diminish even further.

In sum, then, worried about the potential risks of unrestrained balancing and skeptical about the effectiveness of large and inclusive international organizations, some have recommended adapting the concert approach to security order employed in nineteenth-century Europe to the circumstances of the twenty-first century. In Asia, however, the conditions favorable to constructing a genuine concert are sorely lacking (Acharya 1999). Even so, realistically embracing some of its allegedly beneficial practices as part of the loose institutional framework for international relations in Asia may mitigate some of the risks associated with balance-of-power politics.

By encouraging multilateral discussion among a handful of states that can make a difference, an Asian great-power forum can play a constructive role even if it falls short of a true concert. If multipolarity ultimately emerges, for example, such a regional forum for regular consultation among the great powers could serve as a hedge against what even realists concede are two of the key risks of balancing under multipolarity that may make war more likely: inattentiveness to shifting capabilities and buck-passing. Limiting the number of participants within a great-power forum, one of the selling points for a concert, increases the chance that the most serious dangers will be noted and that the consequences of buck-passing will be clear—especially if membership is restricted to those with a strong vested interest in regional outcomes. Small size and regional membership would distinguish this sort of arrangement from larger (ARF) or genuinely global (UN) organizations. Arrangements such as the "four-party" talks on Korea reflect the sort of precedent on which it may be possible to build other concert-like structures tailored to particular subregions if not the region as a whole. (See Shirk 1997: 254; also Scalapino 1999.)

But if the goal is to devise ways to mute the threats to peace and prosperity that may arise from balance-of-power politics, it makes little sense to privilege the concert form. By the standards of a concert, the ARF falls short: it is too large (and continues to grow), includes too many states with varying levels of interest in the region, and in principle cedes leadership to a group of small powers (ASEAN). That such an arrangement is ill-suited to the sort of conflict management and resolution one would expect of a concert is hardly surprising. Yet such a multilateral institution has its own virtues as a complementary venue for articulating positions and exploring solutions that may subsequently be taken up by the relevant parties. Whatever the defects of the "ASEAN Way," its premium on protracted discussion and on a search for consensus (defects if one is hoping for a supranational mechanism for dispute resolution) offers a relatively safe setting in which to raise and debate ideas (Leifer 1996). Whether or not the ARF becomes an effective constraint on the behavior of states—perhaps by cultivating sensitivity to "social backpatting and the fear of social opprobrium" (Johnston and Evans 1999: 237, 251–53)—it already serves a useful purpose as the principal international institution within which interested parties regularly address the distinctive regional security problems of Pacific Asia.

In short, formally established and informally developed international institutions, of whatever variety, are neither irrelevant (an extreme position some attribute to realists) nor the antidote for anarchy (an extreme position some attribute to liberals and constructivists). Properly understood, they offer additional opportunities to cope with the consequences of anarchy—one of which is the tendency for states to worry about powerful rivals and take steps to counter the potential danger they represent. Such balancing through patterns of armament and alliance will shape, but alone will not determine, the peacefulness of Asia and the prosperity of the region's member states.

Works Cited

Acharya, Amitav. 1999. "A Concert of Asia?" *Survival* 41(3): 84–101.

———. 2000. *Constructing a Security Community: ASEAN and the Problem of Regional Order*. London: Routledge.

Ahmed, Ishtiaq. 1999. "Pakistan Urged to Recast Defense Doctrine." *Islamabad, the News*, Aug. 14. From Foreign Broadcast Information Service.

Ahmedullah, Mohammed. 2000. "India to Develop Powerful New Imaging Satellites." *Defense Week*, Feb. 14.

Alagappa, Muthiah. 1998. "Asian Practice of Security: Key Features and Explanation." In Muthiah Alagappa, ed., *Asian Security Practice: Material and Ideational Influences.* Stanford: Stanford University Press.

Anand, Vinod. 1999. "Delhi's Conventional Deterrence Discussed." *Pioneer*, July 13. From Foreign Broadcast Information Service.

"The Arming of Asia." 2000. *Foreign Report: Jane's Information Group Limited*, Mar. 16. From LEXIS-NEXIS.

"Australia, Japan: Hashimoto, Howard Discuss Security Issues, Environment." 1997. Tokyo Kyodo, Apr. 29. From Foreign Broadcast Information Service.

"Australia: PRC Criticism over Security Pact with U.S. Noted." 1996. *Melbourne Radio Australia*, Aug. 7. From Foreign Broadcast Information Service.

Baguioro, Luz. 1999. "Manila Senate Ratifies Pact with US." *Straits Times* (Singapore), May 28, p. 47. From LEXIS-NEXIS.

Balfour, Frederik. 1999. "Vietnam Shies from US Trade Accord, Cuddles Up to China." *Agence France-Presse*, Oct. 17. From clari.world.asia.china, ClariNet Communications Corp.

Ball, Desmond. 1993–94. "Arms and Affluence: Military Acquisitions in the Asia-Pacific Region." *International Security* 18(3): 78–112.

Barr, Cameron W. 1998a. "North Korea's Missile Show Tests Japan's Tolerance." *Christian Science Monitor*, Sept. 4. From clari.world.asia.koreas, ClariNet Communications Corp.

———. 1998b. "Weak by Design, Japan Ponders Its Missile Gap." *Christian Science Monitor*, Sept. 2. From clari.world.asia.koreas, ClariNet Communications Corp.

Behn, Sharon. 2000. "Future of US-India Relations Depends on Nuclear Issue: Albright." *Agence France-Presse*, Mar. 14. From clari.tw.nuclear, ClariNet Communications Corp.

Bernstein, Richard, and Ross H. Munro. 1997. *The Coming Conflict with China.* New York: Knopf.

Betts, Richard K. 1993–94. "Wealth, Power, and Instability: East Asia and the United States After the Cold War." *International Security* 18(3): 34–77.

Biddle, Stephen. 1996. "Victory Misunderstood: What the Gulf War Tells Us About the Future of Conflict." *International Security* 21(2): 139–79.

Bracken, Paul. 1999. *Fire in the East: The Rise of Asian Military Power and the Second Nuclear Age.* New York: HarperCollins.

Bukhari, Eas. 2000. "Pak Navy Stronger with New Submarine." *Islamabad, the Nation*, Mar. 16. From Foreign Broadcast Information Service.

Burns, Robert. 2000. "Cohen Urges Asians to Work on China." AP, Mar. 14. From clari.world.asia.china, ClariNet Communications Corp.

Carino, Conrad M. 1998. "Philippines: Indian Warships Visit Manila, to Hold 'Passage' Exercise." *Manila Business World*, Oct. 26. From Foreign Broadcast Information Service.

Christensen, Thomas J., and Jack Snyder. 1990. "Chain Gangs and Passed Bucks: Predicting Alliance Patterns in Multipolarity." *International Organization* 44(2): 137–68.

"Chronology of Major Events in Sino-Indian Ties." 2000. *Xinhua*, Apr. 1.

Cohen, Eliot. 1996. "A Revolution in Warfare." *Foreign Affairs* 5(3): 37–54.

"Comments on Non-Proliferation Background Papers of December 12, 1964." 1964. Memorandum from Robert S. Rochlin to Raymond L. Garthoff, Dec. 31, pp. 3–4. U.S. Arms Control and Disarmament Agency, Department of State Case 9200777, declassified Sept. 5, 1996. Available at National Security Archives, Washington, D.C., Gilpatric Committee File.

"Delhi–Moscow–Beijing Bloc Out of Question—Indian Ambassador." 1999. *Interfax Russian News*, Aug. 13. From LEXIS-NEXIS.

Dibb, Paul. 1997–98. "The Revolution in Military Affairs and Asian Security." *Survival* 39(4): 93–116.

"DPRK Missile Test Prompts Japan to Improve Defense Power." 1999. *Korea Times*, Aug. 29. From Foreign Broadcast Information Service.

Farooq, Umer. 1999. "India's N-Doctrine, China Threat Discussed." *Islamabad, the Nation*, Aug. 21. From Foreign Broadcast Information Service.

Fearon, James. 1995. "Rationalist Explanations for War." *International Organization* 49(3): 379–414.

"Football Diplomacy: Korea and Japan." 1996. *Economist* (US), June 29, p. 43.

Frazier, Mark W. 2000."China-India Relations Since Pokhran II: Assessing Sources of Conflict and Cooperation." *Access Asia Review* 3(2): 5–36.

Freedman, Lawrence. 1981. *The Evolution of Nuclear Strategy*. New York: St. Martin's Press.

Freeman, Charles W., Jr. 1998. "Preventing War in the Taiwan Strait: Restraining Taiwan—and Beijing." *Foreign Affairs* 77(4): 6–11.

Friedberg, Aaron L. 1993–94. "Ripe for Rivalry: Prospects for Peace in a Multipolar Asia." *International Security* 18(3): 5–33.

Gaddis, John Lewis. 1986. "The Long Peace: Elements of Stability in the Postwar International System." *International Security* 10(4): 99–142.

Ganguly, Sumit. 1999. "India's Pathway to Pokhran II: The Prospects and Sources of New Delhi's Nuclear Weapons Program." *International Security* 23(4): 148–77.

Ghosh, Nirmal. 1999. "Philippines Courts US Again to Keep China at Bay." *Straits Times* (Singapore), Mar. 1, p. 34. From LEXIS-NEXIS.

Gilpin, Robert. 1981. *War and Change in World Politics*. New York: Cambridge University Press.

"GIs Come Back? (US Military May Return to Aid Ailing Philippine Armed Forces)." 1999. *Economist* (US), Apr. 24, p. 39.

"The GIs Return." 2000. *Economist* (US), Feb. 19, p. 44.

Goldenberg, Suzanne, and Richard Norton-Taylor. 1998. "Nuclear Crisis: Whose Finger Is on the Red Button?" *Guardian*, May 30, p. 17. From LEXIS-NEXIS.

Goldstein, Avery. 1995. "Discounting the Free Ride: Alliances and Security in the Postwar World." *International Organization* 49(1): 39–73.

———. 1997–98. "Great Expectations: Interpreting China's Arrival." *International Security* 22(3): 36–73.

———. 2000. *Deterrence and Security in the 21st Century: China, Britain, France, and the Enduring Legacy of the Nuclear Revolution*. Stanford: Stanford University Press.

"Gouzhu Xin Shiji de Xinxing Guojia Guanxi" (Building a new type of international relations for a new century). 1997. *Renmin Ribao*, Dec. 8, p. 6.

Gupta, Amit. 1995. "Determining India's Force Structure and Military Doctrine: I Want My Mig." *Asian Survey* 35(5): 441–58.

Hagerty, Devin T. 1998. *The Consequences of Nuclear Proliferation: Lessons from South Asia*. Cambridge, Mass.: MIT Press.

Hanami, Andrew. 1995. *The Military Might of Modern Japan*. Dubuque, Iowa: Kendall/Hunt.

Hsu, Brian. 2000. "Military Sets Aside NT$3bn for E-Warfare." *Taipei Times*, Oct. 15, http://www.taiwansecurity.org/TT/TT-101500.htm.

Hussain, Riffat. 2000. "US 'Inexorable Tilt' Toward Delhi Viewed." *Islamabad, the News*, Jan. 30. From Foreign Broadcast Information Service.

Huxley, Tim, and Susan Willet. 1999. *Arming East Asia*. Adelphi Paper 329. New York: Oxford University Press.

"India: Govt. to Purchase Tanker Planes Soon." 2000. *Hindu*, Apr. 26. From LEXIS-NEXIS.

"Indian Army Chief on Threat Perceptions." 1999. *Pioneer*, Feb. 13, p. 9. From Foreign Broadcast Information Service.

"Japan in 1969 Ensured Nuclear Arms Potential—Daily." 1994. *Reuters*, Aug. 1. From clari.tw.nuclear, ClariNet Communications Corp.

"Japan Ponders Building Nuclear Weapons." 1995. *Associated Press*, May 4. From clari.tw.nuclear, ClariNet Communications Corp.

"Japan Rejects Any Chinese Pressure over Taiwan." 1998. *Agence France-Presse*, Oct. 28. From clari.world.asia.china, ClariNet Communications Corp.

"Japan Says It Can Attack Nkorean Launch Site If Hit by Missile." 1998. *Agence France-Presse*, Sept. 4. From clari.tw.defense, ClariNet Communications Corp.

Jervis, Robert. 1978. "Cooperation Under the Security Dilemma." *World Politics* 30(2): 167–214.

———. 1983. "Security Regimes." In Stephen D. Krasner, ed., *International Regimes*. Ithaca: Cornell University Press.

———. 1985a. "From Balance to Concert: A Study of International Security Cooperation." *World Politics* 38(1): 58–79.

———. 1985b. *The Meaning of the Nuclear Revolution*. Ithaca: Cornell University Press.

Johnston, Alastair Iain, and Paul Evans. 1999. "China's Engagement with Multilateral Security Institutions." In Alastair Iain Johnston and Robert S. Ross, eds., *Engaging China*. London: Routledge.

Joshi, Manoj. 1999. "Army: Now Hyper War." *India Today*, May 10, p. 39. From LEXIS-NEXIS.

Kapstein, Ethan B., and Michael Mastanduno, eds. 1999. *Unipolar Politics: Realism and State Strategies After the Cold War*. New York: Columbia University Press.

Kasturi, Bhashyam. 1999. "India: Daily Analyzes Indian Decision to Buy Russian T-90 Tanks." *Bangalore Deccan Herald*, Jan. 17. From Foreign Broadcast Information Service.

Katyal, K. K. 2000. "India-China Ties." *Hindu*, June 19, p. 12. From Foreign Broadcast Information Service.

Kennedy, Paul. 1987. *The Rise and Fall of the Great Powers*. New York: Vintage.

Krauthammer, Charles. 1991. "The Unipolar Moment." *Foreign Affairs* 70(1): 23–33.

Kupchan, Charles A., and Clifford A. Kupchan. 1991. "Concerts, Collective Security, and the Future of Europe." *International Security* 16(1): 114–61.

Lamb, David. 1998. "Spratly Spat Heats Up Over Chinese 'Bullying'; Asia: Philippines Steps Up Patrols in Response to Increased Activity in the Strategic Island Chain." *Los Angeles Times*, Dec. 15, p. 4. From LEXIS-NEXIS.

Layne, Christopher. 1993. "The Unipolar Illusion: Why New Great Powers Will Rise." *International Security* 17(4): 5–49.

Leifer, Michael. 1996. *The ASEAN Regional Forum.* Adelphi Paper 302. London: Oxford University Press.

———. 1998. "Different Mind-sets Cause Strain in Relations." *Straits Times,* Sept. 25. From LEXIS-NEXIS.

Lodhi, Maleeha. 1999. "Strategic Volatility of South Asia Viewed." *Islamabad, the News,* Mar. 11. From Foreign Broadcast Information Service.

Marshall, Tyler. 1999. "A China-India-Russia Axis: Within the Realm of Possibility." *Los Angeles Times,* Sept. 22, p. 11. From LEXIS-NEXIS.

Maxwell, Neville. 1999. "China's 'Aggression in 1962' and the 'Hindu Bomb.'" *World Policy Journal* 16(2): 111–17.

Mearsheimer, John J. 1990. "Back to the Future: Instability in Europe After the Cold War." *International Security* 15(1): 5–56.

Mercer, Jonathan. 1996. *Reputation and International Politics.* Ithaca: Cornell University Press.

Mochizuki, Mike M. 1983–84. "Japan's Search for Strategy." *International Security* 8(3): 152–79.

Morada, Noel M., and Christopher Collier. 1998. "The Philippines: State Versus Society?" In Muthiah Alagappa, ed., *Asian Security Practice: Material and Ideational Influence.* Stanford: Stanford University Press.

Nathan, Andrew J., and Robert S. Ross. 1997. *The Great Wall and the Empty Fortress: China's Search for Security.* New York: Norton.

Oberdorfer, Don. 1997. *The Two Koreas: A Contemporary History.* Reading, Mass.: Addison-Wesley.

"Offensive." 1995. *Economist* (US), Nov. 18, p. 6.

O'Hanlon, Michael. 1998a. "Can High Technology Bring U.S. Troops Home?" *Foreign Policy* 113: 72–86.

———. 1998b. "Stopping a North Korean Invasion: Why Defending South Korea Is Easier Than the Pentagon Thinks." *International Security* 22(4): 135–70.

———. 2000. "Why China Cannot Conquer Taiwan." *International Security* 25(2): 51–86.

Olson, Mancur, and Richard Zeckhauser. 1966. "An Economic Theory of Alliances." *Review of Economics and Statistics* 48(3): 266–79.

Organski, A. F. K., and Jacek Kugler. 1980. *The War Ledger.* Chicago: University of Chicago Press.

"Philippines to Boost Spratly Presence." 1999. UPI, Oct. 11, 1999. From clari.world.military, ClariNet Communications Corp.

Powell, Robert. 1999. *In the Shadow of Power: States and Strategies in International Politics.* Princeton: Princeton University Press.

Qiao Liang, and Wang Xiangsui. 1999. *Unrestricted Warfare: Assumptions on War and Tactics in the Age of Globalization.* Beijing: PLA Literature Arts Publishing House. Available from Foreign Broadcast Information Service.

Raghavan, V. R. 2000. "The Defence Budget," *Hindu,* Mar. 21, p. 12. From Foreign Broadcast Information Service.

"ROK, Japan Agree on Closer Security Cooperation." 1999. *Seoul Yonhap,* July 14. From Foreign Broadcast Information Service.

"ROK, Japan Launch Emergency Hotline Links." 1999. *Seoul Yonhap,* May 4. From Foreign Broadcast Information Service.

"ROK, Japanese Navies to Conduct Search, Rescue Drill." 1999. *Seoul Yonhap*, July 27. From Foreign Broadcast Information Service.

"ROK, Japanese Navy Officials Agree to Hold Joint Exercise." 1999. *Korea Times*, Feb. 13. From Foreign Broadcast Information Service.

Rosencrance, Richard. 1992. "A New Concert of Powers." *Foreign Affairs* 71(2): 64–82.

Ross, Robert S. 1999. "The Geography of Peace: East Asia in the Twenty-first Century." *International Security* 23(4): 81–118.

"Russia, India Reject Three-way Strategic Axis with China." 1999. *Agence France-Presse*, May 25. From LEXIS-NEXIS.

Rustam, Azrani. 2000. "Industry Firmly Set for Rebound," *Business Aviation*, Feb. 29. From LEXIS-NEXIS.

Saleem, Farrukh. 1999. "Daily Views Growing India-US Partnership." Islamabad, *the News*, Oct. 10. From Foreign Broadcast Information Service.

Satchell, Michael. 2000. "Back to the Philippines (US and Philippines Agree to Military Cooperation)." *U.S. News & World Report*, Jan. 24, p. 30.

Scalapino, Robert A. 1999. "The United States and Asia in 1998: Summitry Amid Crisis." *Asian Survey* 39(1): 1–11.

Schelling, Thomas C. 1966. *Arms and Influence*. New Haven: Yale University Press.

Shirk, Susan. 1997. "Asia-Pacific Regional Security: Balance of Power or Concert of Powers?" In David Lake and Patrick Morgan, eds., *Regional Orders: Building Security in a New World*. University Park: Penn State University Press.

Sigal, Leon V. 1998. *Disarming Strangers: Nuclear Diplomacy with North Korea*. Princeton: Princeton University Press.

Simon, Sheldon W. 2000. "Asian Armed Forces: Internal and External Tasks and Capabilities." *NBR Analysis* 11, no. 1. Seattle: National Bureau of Asian Research.

"Sinha: New Government to Check Fiscal Deficit." 1999. *Bangalore Deccan Herald*, Oct. 11. From Foreign Broadcast Information Service.

Snyder, Glenn H. 1984. "The Security Dilemma in Alliance Politics." *World Politics* 36(4): 461–95.

"South Korean War Memories." 2000. *Economist* (US), Mar. 4, p. 44.

Tan, Andrew T. H. 1999. "Singapore's Defence: Capabilities, Trends, and Implications." *Contemporary Southeast Asia* 21(3): 451–74.

Tang Guanghui. 1996. "Behind the Warming of Australian-US Relations." *Beijing Shijie Zhishi*, Oct. 16, pp. 19–21. From Foreign Broadcast Information Service.

U.S. Department of Defense. 1998. *The United States Security Strategy for the East Asia-Pacific Region*. Washington, D.C.: Office of International Security Affairs.

Van Evera, Stephen. 1999. *Causes of War: Power and the Roots of Conflict*. Ithaca: Cornell University Press.

Walsh, Jim. 1997. "Surprise Down Under: The Secret History of Australia's Nuclear Ambitions." *Nonproliferation Review* 5(1): 1–20.

Walt, Stephen M. 1988. *The Origins of Alliances*. Ithaca: Cornell University Press.

Waltz, Kenneth N. 1979. *Theory of International Politics*. Menlo Park, Calif.: Addison-Wesley.

———. 1993. "The Emerging Structure of International Politics." *International Security* 18(2): 44–79.

Weiner, Tim. 1997. "How a Spy Left Taiwan in the Cold." *New York Times*, Dec. 20, p. A7. From LEXIS-NEXIS.

Wendt, Alexander. 1992. "Anarchy Is What States Make of It: The Social Construction of State Politics." *International Organization* 46(2): 391–425.

"Will Indo-U.S. Ties Scale New Peaks?" 1999. *The Hindu*, Aug. 1, p. HNDU6475636, from InfoTrac OneFile, Gale Group.

Wohlforth, William C. 1999. "The Stability of a Unipolar World." *International Security* 24(1): 5–41.

WuDunn Sheryl. 1998. "Japanese Move to Broaden Military Links to the U.S." *New York Times*, Apr. 29, p. A6. From LEXIS-NEXIS.

Zhang Dezhen. 1997. "Qianghua Junshi Tongmeng Buhe Shidai Chaoliu" (Strengthening alliances is not in keeping with the times). *Renmin Ribao*, Jan. 31, p. 6.

Zhang Guocheng. 1997. "Riben de Daguo Waijiao" (Japan's Great Power Diplomacy) *Renmin Ribao*, Dec. 19, online edition.

Zhang Wenmu. 1998. "China: PRC Expert on India's Hegemonic Behavior." *Ta Kung Pao*, Oct. 20. From Foreign Broadcast Information Service.

CHAPTER SIX

Regional Institutions and Asian Security Order

Norms, Power, and Prospects for Peaceful Change

AMITAV ACHARYA

At the dawn of the twenty-first century, the contribution of regional institutions to security order in Asia evokes little enthusiasm. Critics see the institutions' record as proof of the realist claim that institutions matter only on the margins of international life (Mearsheimer 1994–95). The regional economic crisis and its geopolitical ramifications have further dampened the outlook for institutions—chief among them the Association of Southeast Asian Nations (ASEAN) and the ASEAN Regional Forum (ARF)—which had already earned the label "adjuncts" (to borrow Michael Leifer's assessment of the ARF) to the region's balance-of-power dynamics (Leifer 1996).

While realists dismiss the role of institutions generally, institutionalist perspectives such as integration theory (which investigates why and how states willingly concede their sovereignty through regional interactions) and neoliberalism (which views institutions as contractual entities serving utilitarian purposes) have often found the Asian experience too limited or deviant to be meaningfully integrated into theories of international organization. Asia had no regionwide (as opposed to the subregional ASEAN, which itself only had a indirect security role) multilateral security institution until the 1990s, and it has supported only an underinstitutionalized and noncontractual form of regionalism. It does not offer examples that fit established models of security multilateralism, such as collective security, collective defense, or even the "common security" model developed in Europe. While Europe remains the chief source of theoretical generalizations about regional cooperation, Asia poses a daunting challenge for institutionalist scholars (including the recent constructivist tradition) looking for cases that might support their beliefs and expectations about how institutions work and that might help them respond to their realist critics.

But Asia's security multilateralism, the subject of this chapter, is interesting and important precisely because it challenges, rather than conforms to, our understanding of how multilateral institutions emerge and function. Consider two important claims of Asian regionalists today. The first is that in the ARF, Asia shows how, under certain conditions, weaker states can offer normative leadership in building an institution whose membership includes all the great powers of the current international system. Second, Asian leaders have frequently asserted that their nonlegalistic and consensus-oriented "ASEAN Way" is a distinctive and workable alternative to European-style multilateralism (Acharya 1997a). What accounts for Asia's nonhegemonic and nonlegalistic form of regional security cooperation and what kind of contribution it can make to security order are important and controversial questions that deserve attention from any serious student of international cooperation.

For these very reasons, conventional approaches to security multilateralism are of limited help in explaining Asian regionalism. Thanks to their historical context and normative underpinnings, Asian institutions continue to avoid collective security and collective defense, the two traditional forms of security multilateralism, and have engineered significant adaptations to the doctrine of common security.[1] Equally important, parsimonious power- and interest-based explanations of institution building in international relations theory do not enable an adequate investigation into the origins and effectiveness of Asian regional institutions. This is because, as this chapter argues, ideational forces have been central to the evolution and role of Asian regional institutions, whether formally organized or informally pursued. And the major contribution of regionalism to Asian security order has been in the normative domain. Thus, regional norms developed during the early postwar intra-Asian interactions have been crucial in shaping security multilateralism in later years, as in ASEAN and the ARF. The chief impact to date of the latter on regional security order has been in engaging the major powers of the Asia Pacific and persuading them to consider a rule-based alternative to balancing strategies and behavior.

This chapter investigates the ideational underpinnings of Asian security regionalism and assesses its contribution to regional security order. The discussion that follows is divided into three main parts. The first examines competing explanations of the emergence (especially the late emergence) of regional security institutions in Asia, demonstrating the need to go beyond power- and interest-

---

[1]For distinctions between collective security, collective defense, and cooperative security roles in regional institutions, see Kupchan (1999: 220–21).

based explanations and emphasizing the crucial role norms and identity played in the evolution of Asian regionalism. The second part examines the role of norms in shaping the evolution and character of Asian security institutions. A specific aim of this section is to demonstrate how norms shaped institutionalist strategies in Asia by discouraging "power-based" regionalism (such as collective security and collective defense) while encouraging "process-driven" alternatives (those which rely primarily on socialization, and identity building). The third part assesses the contribution of such form of institution building to regional security order, especially in reshaping the normative climate of international politics in post–Cold War Asia.

The three parts of the chapter are underpinned by a belief that how one explains the rise of Asian institutions (by giving due emphasis to norms and identity) has much to do with the assessment of their contribution to security order. In their origin, Asian institutions were normatively predisposed against power-based multilateralism, such as collective security or defense. But the process-driven institution building in Asia has made important inroads into the region's security architecture hitherto dominated by balance-of-power approaches. Over the long term it has a potential to challenge or modify the exclusive reliance of Asian states on bilateral security arrangements. Hence, calling them mere "adjuncts" to balance-of-power geopolitics is neither appropriate nor accurate.

Power, Interest, and Ideational Forces in Asian Institution Building

Power- and Interest-Based Explanations

A major question for any scholar interested in Asian institution building concerns the region's failure to establish a regional political and security institution in the aftermath of World War II, as was the case with other regions of the world. Power-based explanations of this puzzle typically begin with consideration of U.S. power and policy preferences. The most important example of this work is Donald Crone's assertion that America's "extreme hegemony" in postwar East Asia contributed to a preference for bilateralism in dealing with Asian countries, since Washington saw multilateralism as a needless constraint on its preferences and behavior. Its Asian allies did not want multilateralism, because it might have lessened their opportunities for free-riding. Without American interest and leadership, Asia could not develop strong and European-like economic and security institutions. It was the decline of U.S. power in subsequent decades that created incentives for institutionalization in the Asia Pacific as the Cold War neared its end (Crone 1993).

Crone's "modified realist" approach supplements the hegemonic stability theory by suggesting that the decline of the hegemon can be as important as its ascendancy in institution building. But this view is at best a partial explanation. There is evidence that the United States was never fully committed to a primarily bilateral mode of cooperation in Asia in the immediate aftermath of World War II. Instead, it had considered, but decided against, a multilateral Asian security framework because of concerns that it would clash with the prevailing nationalist norms and identities in Asia (Acharya 2000).[2] Second, if the fear of being constrained is what drives a great power to avoid multilateralism (Weber 1993), then why did the United States endorse multilateralism in Europe and Latin America while rejecting it in Asia? After all, in the aftermath of World War II the power gap between the United States and its European allies was smaller than that with respect to its Asian allies. In that case, the United States should have had a greater fear of being constrained in dealing multilaterally with Europe than with Asia. It is doubtful that being involved in a regional multilateral institution in Asia would have really constrained independent decision making in Washington any more than it did in Europe.

Interest-based perspectives explain the origins of Asian institutions in terms of the expected benefits of cooperation pursued through goal-oriented rational action. Such explanations have been concerned specifically with APEC, viewing it as a logical response to rising regional economic interdependence (Drysdale 1988; Drysdale and Garnut 1993).[3] Dobson and Lee (1994) have viewed the emergence of APEC as a response to the "fundamental need" for a "structure of certainty" in managing Asia Pacific economic relations, while Elek (1995) has highlighted APEC's potential in reducing economic transaction costs. Although APEC fits interest-based explanations more than does a security grouping such as the ARF, the rationale for the latter could also be explained in functional and utilitarian terms: as a conscious effort by regional actors to ensure that regional tensions do not undermine common prosperity. By mitigating the security dilemma, co-

---

[2]The U.S. aversion to multilateral security institutions (albeit a softer version of NATO) in Asia was certainly stronger before the outbreak of the Korean War than after it, and then too mainly because of the political costs associated with it in terms of opposition from Asia's nationalist leaders. Moreover, U.S. opposition to Asian multilateralism was hardly uniform insofar as various government agencies were concerned. Examples of official advocacy or support for a multilateral institution in Asia include the endorsement of quiet and behind-the-scenes U.S. backing of proposals for Asian regional association by U.S. allies found in NSC 48/2, itself a compromise document between the Defense Department and CIA on the one hand and the State Department on the other (Schaller 1982: 404–6) and Dean Acheson's (Secretary of State under Harry Truman) Special Assistant John Howard's concept of an "'offshore' Pacific Pact" (U.S. Department of State 1976: 1159).

[3]Drysdale and Garnut (1993) argued that economic liberalism in the region would produce significant benefits, making regional economic interactions something of a "prisoner's delight."

operative security institutions could prevent any disruption in the economic dynamism that had underpinned growth and prosperity while reinforcing the supposedly pacific effects of interdependence.[4]

But like arguments linking U.S. hegemonic decline with institution building, viewing economic interdependence as a cause of the latter offers only a partial explanation. An important limitation of this view is that available evidence suggests that lack of common economic interest or economic interdependence does not necessarily impede initial efforts toward institution building. To be sure, early postwar efforts at regionalism in Asia were stymied by high economic nationalism and weak intraregional economic linkage. But ASEAN did take off without an appreciable level of intraregional trade (around 15 to 20 percent of the total trade of ASEAN members, lower if one excludes entrepôt trade involving Singapore). Even lower levels of intra-SAARC trade (2 percent of total SAARC trade in 1985) did not prevent its emergence (Dash 1996: 202).[5] Another problem with the interdependence-institutionalization linkage is that the Asian experience turns neofunctionalist "spillover" logic (that "low politics" cooperation leads to "high politics" cooperation) on its head. In the case of both SAARC and ASEAN, economic considerations were secondary to political and strategic factors during the early stages of institution building (Ayoob 1985: 444). Political and strategic considerations were far more important as preconditions for economic cooperation. Thus, interdependence-based perspectives do not explain why and how ASEAN and SAARC emerged despite very low levels of subregional economic linkages. Nor do they explain why there has been no subregional institution in Northeast Asia despite a relatively high degree of economic interaction between China, Taiwan, Japan, the United States, and South Korea.

Identity, Norms, and Asian Institution Building

From power- and interest-based perspectives, the emergence of security and economic multilateralism in Asia appears to be a relatively recent phenomenon, made possible by shifts in material circumstances such as declining hegemony and rising global and regional interdependence. This accords little place to the legacy of earlier or recent normative discourses about regionalism and initiatives based on them, partly because such efforts had not yielded successful institutions until the formation of ASEAN in 1967. But this view can be challenged.[6]

---

[4]For a fuller discussion of such liberal and functionalist views on the relationship between economic interdependence and security, see Soesastro (1994) and Scalapino (1994).

[5]Intra-SAARC trade in 1995 was estimated at a mere $3 billion out of total trade of SAARC members of $80 billion, or less than 4 percent (CASAC 1995: 9, 14).

[6]For an earlier focus on Asian identity, see Haas (1989).

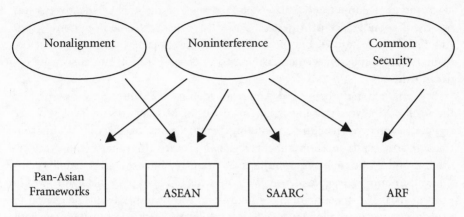

FIG. 6.1. Impact of international norms on Asian institutions

Investigation into the impact of norms and identity on the emergence of regional cooperation has been more popular in Europe than in Asia. Constructivist interpretations of European and transatlantic regionalism recognize the importance of identity and norms in institution building (Risse-Kappen 1996). In Asia, normative explanations of regionalism have been partial and are often focused on the impact of international norms, such as "open regionalism" (Katzenstein 1997) in the case of APEC and the "common security" norm based on the CSCE/OSCE model in the case of the ARF (Dewitt 1994). Other international norms, which have been influential in the past, include nonalignment and noninterference, the two particularly influential norms that were crucial in shaping Asian and Afro-Asian regional efforts in the early postwar period and that later played an important role in the evolution of ASEAN (Fig. 6.1).

Apart from international norms, the identities of external actors have also shaped the fate of Asian regionalism. After reviewing U.S. policy debates concerning Asia during the early postwar period, Hemmer and Katzenstein have argued that "ideas about collective identities" were important in explaining why Washington favored multilateralism in Europe and bilateralism in Asia. American policymakers saw Europe as a more desirable arena for multilateral engagement because they recognized a greater sense of a transatlantic community than a transpacific one. "America's perception of Europe as belonging to the same basic, and in some ways natural, political community as the United States spurred the United States to favor multilateral organizational forms in Europe" while "the absence of this sense of a community in Asia and the belief that the Asian countries belonged to [an] inferior political community led to a U.S. preference for bilateralism there" (Hemmer and Katzenstein 2000: 16). From this perspective, it was not the preponderance of American power (Crone's "extreme hegemony"), but America's conception of Europe as the "self" and Asia as the "other," that explains why Washington seemed disinclined to develop a multilateral security order in Asia.

But *international* norms and American identity constitute only one part of the ideational forces shaping Asian regionalism. Missing from the picture are *regional* normative structures, including regional contextualization of international norms and questions about *regional identity*. In other words, understanding the ideational underpinnings of Asian regionalism must entail an investigation into "collective identities" or "norms of appropriate behavior" *within* postwar Asia. The question of U.S. interest and willingness may not be central in explaining why Asia failed to develop a multilateral institution in the aftermath of World War II. A more relevant story concerns attempts by Asian leaders, especially those who had led the struggle against colonialism, to develop cooperation through a pan-Asian (and its corollary, Afro-Asian) regional framework. These efforts were highlighted in a series of Asian and Afro-Asian conferences held between 1947 and 1955, beginning with the Asian Relations Conference in New Delhi in 1947 and ending with the Afro-Asian Bandung Conference in 1954 (Jansen 1966; Acharya 2000: 43–77).[7] While they did not produce a viable regional institution, they articulated and legitimized norms, including noninterference and avoidance of regional military alliances to serve the particularistic interest of the superpowers, that were to have a long-term impact on Asian approaches to institution building for the coming decades (to be discussed later in this chapter).

These conferences also brought to the fore the importance of regional identity. Identity mattered in preventing the development of a macroregional organization in Asia. Indian Prime Minister Jawaharlal Nehru described the 1947 Asian Relations Conference in New Delhi as an "expression of the deeper urge of the mind and spirit of Asia which has persisted in spite of the isolationism which grew up during the years of European domination" (Nehru 1948: 23). But pan-Asianism found few believers in Asia. Southeast Asian countries in particular preferred to organize around a Southeast Asian identity, which they believed had a stronger

---

[7]The five conferences include: The Asian Relations Conference, New Delhi, 1947; the Second Asian Relations Conference (on Indonesia), New Delhi, 1949; the First Colombo Powers Conference, Colombo, April 1954; the Second Colombo Powers Conference, Bogor, Indonesia, December 1954; and the Afro-Asian Conference, Bandung, Indonesia, 1955. The Colombo Powers were: India, Pakistan, Ceylon, Burma, and Indonesia. (See Jansen 1966; Asian Relations Organization 1948; Fifield 1958; Kahin 1955; Pauker 1955; Appadorai 1955.)

basis in history and culture (Acharya 2000: 46).[8] It is therefore no accident that the creation of ASEAN in 1967 followed the collapse of earlier pan-Asian efforts as well as the crippling of SEATO. But while Southeast Asian in scope, ASEAN also embodied some of the normative underpinnings of the earlier pan-Asian and Afro-Asian gatherings, such as noninterference, nonalignment, soft institutionalism, and "regional solutions to regional problems," the latter reflecting the dangers of entanglement in superpower rivalry that had been articulated in earlier regionalist efforts. And the ASEAN model subsequently influenced SAARC[9] and the ARF (Acharya 1997b).

In Asian subregional contexts, success or failure of institution building has been influenced by attempts at regional definition. ASEAN was clearly influenced by a *quest* for a Southeast Asian identity (Acharya 2000). Through ASEAN, member states saw an opportunity to reaffirm historical linkages among Southeast Asian states that had been disrupted by colonialism. The origins of SAARC, on the other hand, displayed no such effort at identity building.[10]

There has been little mention of "identity" in discussions about institution building in Northeast Asia (Rozman 2000). This is striking, given that Northeast Asia appears to be a more culturally homogeneous universe than Southeast Asia. While Southeast Asian regionalists were united by refuting the older conception of the region as a cultural appendage of China and India, Northeast Asia has been identified positively as the "Chinese culture area" (Fairbank et al. 1989: 1). But Northeast Asia's greater proximity to great-power geopolitics has overwhelmed any regionalist impulses sourced in traditional cultural linkages. Gilbert Rozman (2000) argues that most of the efforts at Northeast Asian regionalism are designed to serve the "national interests" of the actors, such as "helping each country reduce geographic inequality and boost a lagging and sensitive corner of its territory," addressing the North Korean proliferation threat, and reducing Sino-Japanese and Russo-Japanese tensions. Although "influencing the emergence of a

[8]This view was most clearly articulated by Burma's leader Aung San: "While India should be one entity, and China another, South-East Asia should form an entity on its own; and then finally we should come together in a bigger union." But he added, "there was still a long way to go before that [last] stage" (cited in Jansen 1966: 73).

[9]President Ziaur Rahman of Bangladesh, the main inspiration behind SAARC, had been working since 1977 on "the idea of an ASEAN-like organization in South Asia" (Dash 1996: 186), while the organizational structure of SAARC was "largely based on the ASEAN model" (Wickramasinghe 1999: 23).

[10]Wickramasinghe (1999: 6) argues that South Asia's claim to regional identity is tenuous, despite having the Indian Ocean and the Himalayas as boundary markers. The Indian Ocean served more as a highway for the transmission of Indian civilization than to demarcate a regional space, while the Himalayas did not prevent political, linguistic, or religious interactions that underpinned the concept of a "Hindustan" stretching westward from northern India to Afghanistan and beyond.

new, less nationalistic identity in a time of flux" has also been a motivating factor, and there has been some talk about a "Sea of Japan identity," he found "no sign of growing regional identities."

The early institution-building efforts in Asia contains several important lessons. First, proposals for regional security organization that conflicted with the prevailing norm against superpower-led regional alliances failed. The fate of SEATO attests to this. Second, attempts to create macroregional organizations faltered because of differing conceptions of regional identity.[11] Only subregional institutions were possible, especially where actors self-consciously developed a sense of collective identity. ASEAN offers the main example of this. Third, the absence of institutions did not mean the absence of shared norms. They continued to be influential in the absence of formal institutions, as could be seen from the impact of the norm against multilateral security pacts on ASEAN's creation in 1967. Finally, where identity proved divisive, especially at the macroregional level, norms proved unifying. Shared norms have helped bridge the identity gap in regional interactions. Thus, while differing conceptions of regional identity destroyed macroregional institution building, the latter's norms helped create ASEAN, which in turn influenced the development of SAARC and the ARF. This crucial normative link between pan-Asianism and Afro-Asianism, ASEAN, and the current multilateral security framework must be kept in mind in any serious study of Asian institution building.

Collective identity building in international relations does not necessarily presuppose cultural and civilizational affinities. It may take off from socialization processes undertaken self-consciously by actors who, despite social and cultural differences, pursue common objectives. Norms play a crucial role in the emergence and maturing of such socialization processes. Defined as shared beliefs and principles of conduct within a given identity, norms shape the contribution of cooperative institutions to security order.

In the following section, I show how a set of norms originating from the pan-

[11]Further evidence of how identity matters in Asian institution building comes from the experience of APEC. APEC reflected the quest on the part of an epistemic community of scholars, business leaders, and policymakers seeking to capture and legitimize the economic dynamism of East Asia, and the growing interdependence between them and the major Western industrial nations of the Pacific Rim. But this market- and utility-driven construct of "Asia Pacific" was countered by a more intersubjective notion of regional identity which surfaced as the Malaysian-proposed East Asian Economic Grouping (renamed East Asian Economic Caucus) with an exclusively East Asian membership. The fact that Malaysia, despite its domestic economic liberalization programs and declared commitment to open regionalism, championed the EAEC attests to the role of identity in explaining why some institution-building strategies are preferred by states over others (Higgott and Stubbs 1995). Efforts undertaken since the Asian economic crisis to develop an East Asian economic and security forum (called ASEAN Plus Three, or APT) show that identity-driven approaches remain important in Asian institution building.

Asian and Afro-Asian regionalist discourses of the 1940s and 1950s, and continuing through the formation of ASEAN in 1967, influenced institution building in Asia in the 1990s. These norms are (1) rejection of any form of multilateral security and defense cooperation, whether with or without great power sponsorship; (2) general acceptance of Westphalian norms of sovereignty, noninterference, and territorial integrity; and (3) a preference for "soft" or nonlegalistic and formalistic regional cooperation.

Regional Institution Building in Asia: Power vs. Norms

The common forms of multilateral security cooperation in international relations have been collective security and collective defense.[12] Despite apparent differences, collective security and collective defense share three important features. First, both rely primarily on a military instrument, collective security to punish and evict an aggressor which is internal to the system, collective defense to defend against an aggressor from outside the group. Second, implicitly or explicitly, both presuppose, and depend critically on, the leadership role and material resources of strong (great) powers. Third, both rely on formal commitments of reciprocity. In Asia, none of these shared features has found broad acceptance. Indeed, the constitutive principles of Asian regionalism have tended to gravitate in the opposite direction: avoidance of military pacts and multilateral defense mechanisms; the acknowledged leadership role of weaker powers in institution building; and, as noted, a preference for informal and nonbinding cooperation.

In May 1946, while planning the Asian Relations Conference, Nehru had made it known that its agenda "should not only include, but give first place to defense and security problems" (Jansen 1966: 43, 48). This reflected his earlier views concerning the need for regional defense and foreign policy cooperation in the Indian Ocean area. But the issue was dropped from the agenda of the conference, on the ground that "the security of Asia had more than an Asian incidence as it was almost identical with world security" (Asian Relations Organization 1948: 4). It would thus be "unreal" to discuss the defense of Asia without the involvement of the great powers (Jansen 1966: 49). For this and related reasons, ASEAN too has avoided regional defense cooperation. Indonesia did make a vague proposal for intra-ASEAN defense cooperation at the grouping's inaugural summit in Bali in 1976, but it ran into serious opposition and was never revived. At the height of

[12]Ruggie (1993) has described collective security as multilateralism in its "purest" form. While collective defense (as practiced by NATO) was initially seen as a deviation from the UN ideal of collective security, it now shares a place with collective security as a "multilateral" form. Thus NATO is viewed as having many of the "institutional" characteristics of multilateralism (Weber 1993).

TABLE 6.1
Institutionalist Strategies in Asia

	Pan-Asianism and Afro-Asianism	SEATO	ASEAN	SAARC	NEAD	ARF
Collective security	No	No	No	No	No	No
Collective defense	No	Weak	No ("spiderweb" bilateralism)	No	No ("hub-and-spoke" bi-lateralism)	No
Cooperative security (CBMs, PD, dispute settle-ment)	Intended	None	Largely informal and bilateral	Bilateral CBMs only	Bilateral CBMs only	Multilateral CBMs, PD, no dispute settlement yet

the perceived threat from Vietnam in the 1980s, ASEAN consistently rejected any proposal for an ASEAN defense arrangement. The reasons advanced against such proposals were threefold: first, a regional defense pact would unnecessarily provoke potential adversaries (Vietnam in particular); second, a coalition of weak powers would not make a strong one; and third, it would draw the regional actors into the vortex of the great power rivalry since many of them maintained bilateral defense links with outside powers, especially the United States (Acharya 1990). These reasons hold for the region as a whole and explain why no "indigenous" form of multilateral defense has taken root in Asia. Indeed, no one has seriously proposed defense cooperation within the ARF.

Asia has proven inhospitable to collective security proposals. The ill-defined Brezhnev Plan for an Asian Collective Security System was rejected by most regional actors, including many states which were sympathetic to Moscow. Regional collective defense arrangements in Asia involving outside powers have been either weak or short-lived or both, for reasons discussed in the previous section, including the influence of the norm advocated by India and other non-aligned states of Asia against regional defense groupings that linked non-Asian great powers (Jansen 1966: 138). Apart from SEATO, the only other multilateral collective defense in Asia is the Five Power Defense Arrangements (FPDA), established in the wake of the British withdrawal from Southeast Asia. Aimed at helping the transition of Singapore and Malaysia to a self-reliant defense posture with the help of Britain, Australia, and New Zealand, the FPDA has had no real teeth. It has served more as a confidence-building measure between Singapore and Malaysia than as a collective defense instrument. The trilateral ANZUS Pact between Australia, New Zealand, and the United States was partly intended to collectively counter the communist threat in Asia. It was reduced to a bilateral arrangement in the 1980s after the United States cut off defense ties with New Zealand to punish its refusal to accept U.S. nuclear ship visits. ANZUS's relative efficacy speaks to the Asian norm against superpower-led regional pacts, which did not constrain this exclusively non-Asian grouping, while undermining mixed groups like SEATO.

The overwhelming pattern of defense relationships within Asia has been bilateral. There are two main examples of defense bilateralism in Asia; the first represented by the "hub-and-spoke" pattern of U.S. alliances, and the second found in the ASEAN style of "spiderweb" bilateralism.[13] Conceived as Cold War instruments, the U.S. alliances have since had their roles redefined and broadened. The new roles have been variously termed "cooperative defense," "security community," and "enhanced regional cooperation" by U.S. Pacific commanders. Their mission now is less threat-oriented than uncertainty-oriented. ASEAN's spiderweb bilateralism, consisting of intelligence sharing, joint exercises, and training activities, evolved against transborder insurgencies, but it has also served as an important confidence-building measure among the ASEAN members.

Instead of institutionalizing power asymmetries through collective defense or collective security institutions, Asian actors have developed institutions through the leadership role of local actors which seek to reduce power asymmetries through institutional binding. The aim of such institutions has been to engage major powers in ways that increase the cost of their unilateralism and induce them to voluntarily adopt more peaceful strategies to their neighbors.

This strategy is reflected in the leadership pattern of Asian regional institutions. Local leadership and regional self-reliance are common, if rhetorical, slogans of nationalist leaders throughout the Third World, including Asia. Asian leaders have generally avoided regional institutions which were initiated by superpowers or colonial powers. After the collapse of pan-Asian concepts and the decline of SEATO, ASEAN regionalists spoke eloquently, if unrealistically, of "regional solutions to regional problems," as they sought to adjust to the declining credibility and availability of great power protection. ASEAN's first major security initiative, the idea of a Zone of Peace, Freedom and Neutrality in Southeast Asia, reflected this belief in regional self-reliance as a political, if not strategic, objective.

Even within regional institutions with an exclusively Asian membership, the leadership role of strong regional powers has been unpopular. While anticolonialism brought them together, advocates of and participants in pan-Asian gatherings from among the region's smaller powers were significantly inhibited by their

---

[13]On the emergence of ASEAN's "spiderweb" defense bilateralism, see Acharya (1990).

TABLE 6.2
Leadership in Asian Institutions

	Pan-Asianism	SEATO	ASEAN	SAARC	NEAD	ARF
Proposer/ dominant power	India, Burma, Vietnam/ India, China	U.S./U.S.	Thailand/ Indonesia	Bangladesh/ India	S. Korea/ China, U.S.	Australia, Canada, ASEAN/ China, U.S.
Leadership type or pattern	Ideational	Hegemonic/ structural	Consensual	No leader?	Concert-like	Intellectual; entrepreneurial
Degree of self-binding by dominant actors	Low	Limited	High	Low (except Gujral Doctrine)	Absent	No (as yet)

fear of Indian and Chinese domination of any resulting institution.[14] Subsequent efforts at institution building consistently reflect a bottom-up construction. While Indonesia was key to the formation of ASEAN, the initial ideas for a Southeast Asian grouping came from the smaller states, Malaysia and Thailand. The key mover behind SAARC was Bangladesh, while ASEAN occupies the "driver's seat" in the ARF.

This nonhegemonic construction of Asian security regionalism reflects an attempt by weaker states to use institution building to promote what Ikenberry has called "institutional binding" of stronger powers (Ikenberry 2001). Asia offers several illustrations of the importance of institutional binding in explaining the success and failure of regional institutions. Here, institutional binding is a framework initiated by the weaker states whereby the dominant actor agrees to exercise restraint in its dealing with the other members of the grouping while in return gaining support for its objectives and recognition of its leadership.[15] The difference between this strategy and conventional accounts of institution building coming from the hegemonic stability theory can be summarized as follows.

The classic example of successful institutional binding in Asia was Indonesia's role vis-à-vis its smaller neighbors in ASEAN. This has been compared to that of a "golden cage" (Djiwandono 1983: 20). Without this self-binding by Suharto's Indonesia, reversing Sukarno's animosity toward his neighbor Malaysia, the

[14]One Burmese delegate to the Asian Relations Conference in Delhi put it well: "It was terrible to be ruled by a Western power, but it was even more so to be ruled by an Asian power" (Henderson 1955: 466).

[15]Note the important difference between this form of institutional binding and the one proposed by Ikenberry in which the process is initiated by the hegemon, and not the weaker states. My framework, based on generalizations from Asian regionalism, accords the more significant agency role to the weaker states.

TABLE 6.3

TABLE 6.3
Institutional-Binding in Asia

	Hegemonic socialization	Institutional-binding by weaker states
Type of leadership	Structural	Intellectual and entrepreneurial
Platform	Hegemon creates a platform to pursue its interests without having to resort to coercion	Hegemon is offered a platform to pursue its interests that it cannot otherwise realize with or without coercion
Means	Hegemon agrees to voluntary self-restraint	Hegemon is constrained through strategies of engagement
Goals	Hegemon provides the public good of collective defense and free trade	Hegemon is offered the benefits of co-operative security
Socialization	Hegemon seeks to realize its social purpose	Hegemon is socialized

ASEAN dream would have been impossible to attain. The absence of such self-binding by India is a major factor behind the weakness of SAARC. The reasons for this are twofold. Indian policymakers distrusted the motivations behind SAARC as a way of constraining India. Moreover, an active Indian role within SAARC would most likely have killed the organization, in view of the suspicions of India that prevailed within the grouping. India did not volunteer a policy of diffuse reciprocity in dealing with its smaller neighbors, although the Gujral Doctrine of 1997–98 (enunciated by then Prime Minister I. K. Gujral as a willingness on the part of India not to seek strict reciprocity in its bilateral relations with its South Asian neighbors) did indicate a brief but significant departure from this practice, briefly rekindling hope for a more robust South Asian regionalism. The Gujral Doctrine, however, was not applied to Pakistan (Acharya 1999c).

China's role in the ARF begs an important comparison with both SAARC and ASEAN. China's neighbors hope for a relationship with Beijing that is closer to Indonesia's role in ASEAN than to India's in SAARC. But the Chinese response to this quest bears more similarities with India than Indonesia. China has not accepted restraints on matters of sovereignty and territorial claims demanded by its neighbors. Its response resembles the Indian position within SAARC in another respect. India, especially at the beginning of the SAARC process, was worried that "a regional organization might provide an opportunity for the smaller neighbors to regionalize all bilateral issues and to join with each other to 'gang up' against India" (Dash 1996: 187). China has a similar concern about the ARF.

The second set of norms influencing regional institution-building efforts in Asia is derived from Westphalian sovereignty, especially noninterference in the internal affairs of states. Given its contemporary resilience in Asia, it is easy to forget the Western origins of sovereignty and noninterference. As Asian countries

gained independence from colonial rules, regional interactions played an important role in legitimizing these constitutive principles of international society.
With the outbreak of the Cold War, noninterference took on added significance
in Asia. Asia's aligned states, such as Pakistan and the Philippines, invoked this
norm as a guarantee against subversion backed by communist states and as a
means of defending their security ties with great powers (by implying that such
ties did not mean the surrender of their sovereignty). The nonaligned states such
as Sri Lanka also saw this norm as a bulwark against communist subversion of
their own polities and as a means of lessening the dominance of outside powers
in regional affairs through their Cold War allies. Noninterference formed the core
of the "Five Principles of Peaceful Coexistence" originally articulated by India
and China in the 1950s to guide the conduct of their bilateral ties and later applied to regional multilateral conferences such as the Bandung Conference.
ASEAN's own origin and evolution reflected a strong commitment to this norm,
which was seen as a way to enhance regime security and regional order. In 1997,
Singapore's Foreign Minister, S. Jayakumar, reminded the international community that "non interference in the affairs of another country was . . . the key factor
as to why no military conflict has broken out" between members of ASEAN since
1967 (cited Acharya 2001: 57). China and India have vigorously insisted on the
noninterference principle as the defining principle of the ARF.

But as a founding principle of institution building in Asia, noninterference has
become a double-edged sword. On the one hand, continued emphasis on this
norm sustains a principled basis of interaction among Asian states and suggests,
encouragingly, that once institutionalized, fundamental principles would be hard
to do away with. As Muthiah Alagappa notes in Chapter 1 in this volume, sovereignty, the sovereign equality of states, and the nonintervention norm are constitutive functions of international regimes and institutions which "safeguard the
survival of weak states by naturalizing the sovereign state and outlawing imperial,
colonial, and other forms of domination." But in an altered global normative
climate and in the face of new transnational challenges, noninterference is a limiting factor in institutional efficacy and security enhancement. Strict respect for
noninterference (demanded especially by China) explains the reluctance and inability of the ARF to advance its security agenda to areas such as peacekeeping,
preventive diplomacy, and conflict resolution. Strict adherence to this norm has
undermined ASEAN's ability to deal effectively with regional conflicts such as
those in Myanmar, Cambodia, and East Timor. ASEAN's weak response to the
regional economic downturn of 1997–99 has also been blamed on the doctrine of
noninterference, which might have prevented members from warning each other
against corrupt and inefficient policies contributing to the crisis. ASEAN's inac-

tion in the East Timor crisis of 1999 highlighted a growing disjunction between regional and global normative changes.

Regional norms in Asia remain strongly wedded to the protection of West-phalian sovereignty. The Asian case can be contrasted with that of Latin America, where groups like the OAS and MERCOSUR have followed the EU/OSCE prac-tice of asking for a democratic political system as a membership criterion and have provided mechanisms for multilateral mediation and intervention in the event of democratic breakdowns. No regional grouping in Asia has developed such norms concerning the protection of human rights and democracy. There is no Asian regional intergovernmental human rights body similar to those in Europe, or even Latin America.

ASEAN has since the mid-1990s faced increasing demands for modifying its noninterference principle. In 1997, a Thai initiative, called "flexible engagement" sought to allow ASEAN members to comment on each other's domestic devel-opments and policies and develop cooperative approaches to address them if such developments and policies had transnational consequences (Ministry of Foreign Affairs, Bangkok 1998; Acharya 2001: 151–57). This proposal was opposed by Malaysia, Singapore, and Indonesia, which credited noninterference with the maintenance of regional order and warned that any departure now could desta-bilize the region (Funston 1999). Flexible engagement has since been diluted into a far less intrusive approach, labeled "enhanced interaction," and ASEAN's deci-sion to develop a regional economic surveillance process and a diplomatic mechanism for crisis management, called an ASEAN Troika, reflects a modest concession to the principle of sovereignty.

A related Westphalian norm, the sanctity of existing national boundaries, has been more resilient in Southeast Asia than in other parts of the region. In South Asia, Pakistan refuses to accept Kashmir as a part of India, and India's 1971 inter-vention in East Pakistan resulted in the dismemberment of Pakistan. In Southeast Asia, there has been no significant challenge to this norm since the end of Su-karno's war against Malaysia. ASEAN members have generally refused to support secessionist movements in fellow member states, such as Islamic movements in the southern Philippines and southern Thailand. ASEAN members have backed Indonesian territorial integrity in the wake of the separation of East Timor.

Past interstate wars in the Korean Peninsula, Indochina, the Malay archipelago (Indonesia-Malaysia), and South Asia make the international norm concerning the nonuse of force crucial to regional institution-building efforts in Asia. Cre-ated from the ashes of Indonesia's war against Malaysia, ASEAN embraced peaceful settlement of disputes as its leitmotif. It sought to prevent intramural war through a variety of approaches: by developing rules of conduct, serving as a political confidence-building process, and providing avenues, mainly informal, for dispute settlement. With rare exceptions, ASEAN did not, however, directly address bilateral disputes; these were left to bilateral channels. Although SAARC has lacked ASEAN's corporate ethos, its summits have on occasion helped diffuse bilateral tensions.[16] Non-use of force has also been a key rationale for the ARF, which has been especially concerned with avoidance of military confrontation in the South China Sea and the Korean Peninsula. The ARF's agenda is more akin to the OSCE model of confidence building (Adler 1998) than to the collective defense approach of NATO. But China's refusal to rule out forcible assimilation of Taiwan, which it considers to be a breakaway province, and hence a matter of domestic policy, limits the relevance of the ARF in promoting this norm. In terms of its effect on interstate conflicts, nonuse of force is the core norm of pluralistic security communities—groups of states which have developed long-term expectations of peaceful change and ruled out the use of force against each other. Southeast Asia during the Cold War was the only subregion in Asia in which a nascent security community was in the making—thanks to the role of ASEAN (Acharya 1998; Acharya 2001). South Asia and Northeast Asia and the Asian region as a whole are still a long way from developing this attribute.

The third normative pillar of Asian institution-building efforts is "soft" institutionalism (bureaucratic minimalism, preference for consensus over majority voting, and avoidance of legalistic and binding commitments in the initial stages of cooperation). While associated with ASEAN, the groundwork for soft institutionalism in Asia was laid in 1947, when the Asian Relations Conference set up an Asian Relations Organization. This body, operating more as an unofficial think-tank, was short-lived.[17] The vast majority of delegates to the ARC and subsequent regional gatherings had only a "minor and desultory interest" in the idea of a

[16]In November 1986, a meeting between the leaders of India and Pakistan on the sidelines of the 2nd SAARC summit meeting in Bangalore eased tensions over India's troop exercises on the Indo-Pakistan border. In 1987, talks between India and Sri Lanka on the margins of the SAARC Foreign Ministers' Meeting produced an important accord on the Tamil problem (Dash 1996). In January 2002, the SAARC Summit in Kathmandu served to focus international concern over rising Indo-Pakistan tensions and thus might have had a limited constraining impact on them.

[17]Deliberations at the ARC, hosted by India and attended by 28 delegations, were marked by "sharp differences" on the issue of establishing a central permanent organization. Those who argued against a permanent official organization, such as China (nationalist) and the Philippines, insisted that the time was not yet ripe for such a body, because many delegations attending were from countries that had not yet attained independence, and that many delegations were not fully representative of their countries. Another factor against setting up such a body was concern that it would be dominated by India or China; thus "it was better to have nothing than to have an organization dominated by one government" (Jansen 1966: 69–70). The conference finally agreed to set up an unofficial body, to be called the Asian Relations Organization, headquartered in New Delhi. The plan was for members of the ARC to set up national units, but only six would do so.

permanent Asian organization (Jansen 1966: 68–73, 221–22). Debates about process were resolved in favor of the following principles: that regional meetings should be in the nature of "informal talks without commitments"; that "there should be no question of majority or minority votes, but that the consensus of opinion should form the basis of conference decision"; and the "draft communiques should simply give the consensus of opinion on each subject rather than individual resolutions" (Jansen 1966: 148, 149, 193; see also Pauker 1955: 6).

These attributes of early Asian regionalism became deeply embedded in ASEAN, which is known for its preference for consultation and consensus over formalistic and legalistic mechanisms (Jorgensen-Dahl 1982; Askandar 1994; Anh 1996; Acharya 2001). ASEAN's style in turn influenced SAARC and the ARF. The ARF rejected the OSCE's formalistic and legalistic approach to security cooperation and developed a security agenda in which the "design and development [of security measures] have involved evolutionary developments from extant regional structures rather than the importation of Western modalities or the creation of new structures" and in which "decisions are made by 'consensus after careful and extensive consultations' rather than by voting; and the implementation of particular measures eschews legalisms and is left to voluntary compliance" (Ball 1997: 16–17).[18]

The Asian economic crisis has led to calls for more formal, European-style institutions in Asia. ASEAN's aversion to legalization, most evident in its formative years when its founders shared warm interpersonal ties, is under challenge. It is now setting up formal dispute-settlement bodies within the framework of the ASEAN Free Trade Area, the Southeast Asia Nuclear Weapon-Free Zone Treaty, and the provision for an ASEAN Troika to undertake mediation in regional conflicts. Formal instruments of confidence building and preventive diplomacy are also in the offing in the ARF. But we are still a long way from a legalized regional institutional setting of the kind neoliberal scholars have predicted (Kahler 2000).

The foregoing analysis shows the impact of ideational forces (norms) in shaping the emergence and characteristics of Asian regional institutions in fundamental and enduring ways, from the Asian Relations Conference to the ASEAN Regional Forum. Now we turn to a discussion of how this regional metaregime of fundamental principles affects security order in Asia.

[18]Miles Kahler (2000) has made an important distinction between institutionalization and legalization in Asia and has argued that while ASEAN is well institutionalized, it lags considerably in legalizing itself. ASEAN conducts over 300 annual meetings on topics ranging from tourism to forest fires, but has yet to even once activate the High Council provided under the Treaty of Amity and Cooperation to facilitate dispute settlement. The reluctance to legalize is not unrelated to the salience of the noninterference doctrine. It allows member states to keep cooperation flexible and veto proposals and initiatives that are domestically sensitive and unacceptable.

The Effects of Norms and Institutions on Security Order in Asia

Despite decades of intense debate, international relations theory provides no agreed and definitive way of assessing what constitutes "success" and "effectiveness" in regional organizations.[19] Understanding the effects of Asian institutions on state behavior and regional order depends very much on the analytical lens used. Realists, who view institutions as a marginal force in world politics, judge institutional efficacy in terms of the institutions' ability to project power and enforce compliance. To the extent that institutions matter at all, only those such as NATO which have a capacity to use physical force to enforce compliance are worthy of notice. Neoliberal theorists, who see institutions as having a definite potential to moderate anarchy, assess institutions in terms of the institutions' ability to provide mechanisms through which "the conflicting interests of different actors can reach a dynamic, cooperative equilibrium" (Katzenstein 1997). Such theories typically focus on how institutions lower transaction costs, facilitate information exchanges, reduce uncertainty and prevent cheating (Keohane 1984; Keohane and Martin 1995). Important variations of neoliberal theory define institutional efficacy in terms of institutions' impact as "utility modifiers" and "learning facilitators" (Young 1999), and their ability to "improve the contractual environment for cooperation" (Haas et al. 1993).

While neoliberals hold that the power and appeal of institutions derive from the material benefits they offer to their members which cannot be otherwise obtained, sociological theories, including constructivism, take a deeper view of cooperation. Institutions not only constrain state preferences and behavior (a negative view of cooperation) but also provide a much more positive and transformative basis of cooperation by socializing actors and developing a sense of collective interest and purpose. While rationalist theories focus on the regulative effect of norms, constructivism sees norms having a constitutive and transformative function (Finnemore and Sikkink 1999). For neoliberals, the standard institutionalist outcome is a regime in which interests and identities are neither wholly competitive nor wholly compatible. In contrast to such minimalist expectations, constructivists expect norms and institutions to produce not just behavioral shifts but also more fundamental identity changes. Through interaction and socialization, institutions can redefine interests and identities and lead to the development of collective identities.

While rationalist theories like neorealism and neoliberalism judge institutional success by looking at the "product," sociological theories, including con-

---

[19]For further discussion of the problems in assessing the efficacy of regional institutions, see Johnston and Acharya (2001).

structivism, tend to value "process." For rationalists, success is measured in material terms, such as a free-trade area or a collective security organization. Constructivists value these as well, but are prepared to accept the transitional period as important in itself. This is because they expect institutions to produce more fundamental shifts in actor interests and identity than neoliberals. Hence another key difference between the two approaches is the time frame for measuring success. Rationalist theories look for more immediate results, while constructivism is for the long haul.

These debates in institutionalist theory are relevant to assessing the impact of Asian institutions on regional security order. This chapter suggests that the impact of regional institutions could be examined from a somewhat eclectic combination: with a neoliberal-oriented criterion that focuses on their ability to realize goals they had originally set for themselves by constraining state preferences and improving the contractual environment for cooperation; and a sociological criterion that focuses on the quality of interactions the institutions engender and their long-term impact in changing not just preferences but also identities. To this one could add two other important yardsticks: the resort to institutionalist strategies vis-à-vis other competing mechanisms for ensuring security order; and some sense of what would it be like had there been no institutions (counterfactuals).

In Asia, no institution can claim to have achieved all its declared goals. ASEAN, the most successful regional grouping, did not fully accomplish its professed goal of a Zone of Peace, Freedom and Neutrality. The ARF is still far short of developing a "stable and predictable pattern of relations" in the Asia Pacific, its initial declared objective. Nor is it likely, judging by current trends, to see the full realization of its three-step agenda of confidence building, preventive diplomacy, and conflict resolution as outlined in the ARF Concept Paper in the foreseeable future.

Moreover, Asian institutions do not seek to "constrain" national policy in any deliberate way, at least to the extent envisaged by neoliberal theory. ASEAN thrived because, as its founders frequently stressed, it did not impose strict obligations on its members that would have constrained the pursuit of their national interests. Instead, ASEAN's founders called for recognizing and combining a "regional existence" and thinking with national interests, thinking, and identities (Acharya 1998; Levi 1968: 208). The ASEAN Way is thus primarily about socialization, not "constrainment." The latter may result from the former, but it would have to be a voluntary, gradual, and collective change in attitude and behavior. The ARF has adopted a modest set of confidence-building measures that fall mostly in the category of principles and information-sharing measures (important to the neoliberal yardstick), but none of which fall into the category of OSCE-like "constraining measures" (Acharya 1997b). It is facing serious intramural difficulties in developing instruments of preventive diplomacy (even agreeing on a common definition of the term) and conflict resolution.

Asian regional institutions have a mixed record in the prevention of war. Although ASEAN has been able to prevent an intramural war among its original members, no other institution comes close to this. Pan-Asian and Afro-Asian regionalism, while making an important contribution to advancing decolonization, did not prevent war between India and China, the two key Asian states of that period. SAARC has not made war less likely in South Asia, and the ARF needs to make much more headway in addressing hot spots such as the territorial disputes in the South China Sea (here the ASEAN-China talks have been rather more successful) or in keeping tensions in the Korean Peninsula from erupting into outright military confrontation.

Focusing on the *quality* of interactions within regional institutions is more relevant to assessing their long-term effects on regional order. Such an approach requires us to look for evidence of interest redefinition and identity change, and the emergence of new social interests and collective identities. By nature, such transformations take time. ASEAN has had much more time to produce such identity change; SAARC has had some, but fails the test; and the ARF is too new to engender a sense of collective identity.

But there is some evidence that Asian multilateralism of the 1990s (combining APEC, ARF, and the whole range of Second Track dialogues) might already have produced small but significant changes in the attitude of key players toward multilateralism, making them see themselves as regional multilateral players. China's engagement in these processes has induced a certain measure of change in its thinking about its position and role within the region.[20] China is now much less worried that multilateralism would give lesser regional actors an opportunity to "gang up" against it, or that the ARF might develop into a tool in the hands of the Western powers for interfering in its domestic affairs. China now sees itself more as a "constructive" and "reliable" regional partner, and less as an isolated rising power feared by its neighbors. In contrast to the early 1990s, Beijing no longer sees multilateralism as a noose around its neck, but as an opportunity to make itself heard and understood by its neighbors on security and economic matters. In multilateral engagement, Beijing sees a valuable opportunity to ad-

---

[20]These observations are based on extensive interviews with Chinese scholars and with foreign and defense ministry and People's Liberation Army officials in conjunction with the Canada-China Seminar on Multilateralism and Cooperative Security, held annually in either Beijing or Toronto since 1997. See also Johnston and Evans (1999), Johnston (1998), and Foot (1998). Furthermore, as Christensen (1999) has argued, the recent revitalization of the U.S.-Japan alliance could lead China to "consider more positively the benefits of multilateral forums that might reduce mutual mistrust in the region."

dress Asian suspicions about its "hegemonic" ambitions and dampen the talk about a "China threat," while claiming a "leadership" role in the development of regional confidence-building measures and promoting the "economic security" of the region. This change in attitude has already had some impact on its security policy, especially in explaining its stance in dealing with ASEAN on the South China Sea dispute, where the effort to develop a regional "code of conduct" is making slow but meaningful progress.

When the ARF was set up, China's Asian neighbors, as well as other parties such as Canada, the United States, and Australia, viewed institution building as a useful device for reining in China. Now, while China's partners in multilateralism continue to see the ARF as a way of constraining China, China is beginning to recognize the usefulness of the ARF as a means of influencing their thinking about its position and role in the regional security architecture. By encouraging this recognition, the ARF has actively fostered the socialization of China.

The United States too is increasingly viewing itself as a multilateral player in the region. In 1989, the United States, out of fear that multilateral security institutions in Asia would erode the rationale for its bilateral security alliances in the region, rejected multilateralism as a "solution in search of a problem." Although the Clinton administration described multilateralism as being one of the ten pillars of U.S. foreign policy in Asia, American policymakers continue to stress the primacy of bilateral alliances in the U.S. security strategy in the region, while acknowledging the contribution of multilateralism in advancing U.S. interests, and having a long-term potential to engender identity change. The Clinton administration's Assistant Secretary of State for East Asia, Stanley Roth, argued that while the region was "not at the point where the ASEAN Regional Forum is going to solve the South China Sea, or mediate a dispute on the Korean Peninsula . . . that does not mean that the institution should be dismissed for what it is accomplishing now or what it could accomplish in the future" (cited in Cossa 2000: 6).

The U.S. support for Asian multilateralism is due to a number of perceived benefits. The Four-Party Talks involving North Korea, South Korea, China, and the United States were a useful response to North Korea's demands for direct negotiations with the United States which, if accepted, would have severely undermined U.S.–South Korea ties (Cossa 2000: 6–7). The multilateral KEDO, in which Japan played an instrumental role, was a good way for the United States to reassure Tokyo, which had been fearful of losing out to the growing warmth in the Sino-U.S. relationship. Furthermore, both ASEAN and the ARF provide the United States with a useful vehicle for dealing with the South China Sea dispute, especially since the United States has in the past indicated that it did not want to deal with this problem by invoking the U.S.-Philippine Defense Treaty and so provoking China.

While these contributions of institutionalism are still modest, they go some way toward meeting the interest-oriented neoliberal criteria of institutional effi-cacy. Of special importance here is the acknowledgment by the United States of the contribution of the ARF to its professed engagement policy toward China. In 1998, Stanley Roth, Clinton's Assistant Secretary of State for Asia Pacific, argued: "That the Chinese are now on board and actively engaged in the ARF is compel-ling evidence that multilateralism in Asia is coming of age" (Roth 1998: 5). Admi-ral Dennis Blair, as the chief of the U.S. Pacific Command, used the language of "transformation," "confidence," and "community," to describe the objectives of U.S. military strategy in Asia (Blair 1999, 2000a, b). His goal (Blair 2000a) was to "transform the balance of power approach . . . into one that instead aims to pro-duce strategic communities where the *thought of using armed force to resolve dis-putes never arises*" (emphasis in the original). The "strategic community" con-cept, which Blair used interchangeably with the Deutschian vision of a "security community," envisaged a gradual broadening and "multilateralization" of U.S. military exercises in the region hitherto undertaken on a bilateral basis. It called for modifying the existing "hub-and-spoke arrangement," a metaphor that de-scribes the U.S. security posture "with America at the center of bilateral ties among nations who have weak or non-existent military relations with each other," into "a *network* of security relations that build the confidence needed for the formation of strategic communities" (Blair 2000a; emphasis in the original). Although the new Bush administration is less committed to multilateralism in world affairs, American bureaucratic and military officials directly involved in Asia Pacific policy have acknowledged its value. Since the September 11, 2001, ter-rorist attacks, U.S. officials in the Pacific have used multilateral groups such as the Asia-Pacific Economic Cooperation and the ARF to promote a regional con-sensus against terrorism (Asia-Pacific Economic Cooperation 2001; Soh 2001).

As noted above, an evaluation of the impact of Asian institutions on regional security order should look at the extent to which they have induced regional ac-tors to reject or lessen their dependence on competing approaches to regional order, termed by Alagappa in the introduction mechanisms of "order through competition and power." The latter includes hegemony and balance-of-power and concert-of-power approaches. Asian states that accept American hegemony and its balancing strategies against emerging powers such as China as a fact of life are also deeply aware of the pitfalls of basing their security posture entirely or chiefly on them. This has partly to do with the periodic uncertainties about the future of the U.S. military presence in the region (as during the early 1970s and the early 1990s). Moreover, Asian states see certain types of U.S. security ap-proaches in the region as dangerous and counterproductive. For example, America's Asian allies, such as Singapore and Thailand, value U.S. military pre-

ponderance in the region as a counter to the rise of China. But these two countries have also not been in the forefront of an American strategy of "containing"
China. A full-blown American containment strategy is unlikely to command
much support among its allies unless clear indications emerge of Chinese territorial expansion. Even in normal times, the ASEAN countries' support for the
United States in its strategic competition with China is qualified and conditional
(Acharya 1996a, 1999d). It could be undermined, for example, if China were to
offer important concessions to ASEAN on the Spratlys issue (even while maintaining its hard-line stance with respect to Taiwan). In other words, accepting
American hegemony as a general force for stability does not mean acquiescing in
specific American security strategies that flow from American hegemony.

The same can be said of U.S. balancing strategies which rely on its hub-and-
spoke arrangement of bilateral alliances. Many Asian countries support the U.S.-
Japan alliance and continue to value their own bilateral defense links with the
United States. But for them, relying exclusively on the U.S. alliance structure in
the region contains important uncertainties and risks. Apart from possible domestic opposition to close defense links with the United States, Southeast Asian
leaders worry whether the United States would continue to maintain a large military presence in Asia after Korean reunification, however remote that possibility
may seem now (as opposed to in the early 1990s). Even after being "revitalized" by
the U.S.-Japan Defense Guidelines, pockets of domestic reservation in Japan to
the long-term desirability of alliance continues to cloud the future of the alliance.
At the same time, America's allies remain concerned that the guidelines might aggravate the regional security dilemma in view of the strong misgivings expressed
by Japan's neighbors, North Korea and China ("N. Korea Criticizes Japanese Defense Bills" 1999; "Li Peng" 1999; "Russia Expresses Concern" 1999).

Admiral Dennis Blair once argued that "the best argument for multilateralism
[in Asia] comes from looking at some of the alternatives based on a balance of
power approach" ("'Multilateral Pacts'" 1999: 4).[21] Few pro-U.S. governments and
analysts in Asia foresee the ARF and other multilateral processes as a substitute
for the security and reassurance offered by the U.S. military presence and U.S.
bilateral security arrangements in the region. Multilateralism is untested, its gains
too uncertain, while America's hub-and-spoke bilateralism has been around for
some time, with generally good results for ASEAN. But Asian states see multilateral security dialogues and institution-building activities not only as a hedge
against U.S. military retrenchment from the region, but also as a check on po-

---

[21]It should be noted that by "multilateral pacts" the Admiral meant the ARF and subregional
dialogues such as the Four-Party Talks on the Korean peninsula, rather than multilateral defense
alliances.

tential U.S. security strategies (such as containment in the absence of clear indications of Chinese expansionism) that could endanger regional order. Indeed, regional security dialogues in the 1990s might have already served this purpose.

A more "regulated" form of balancing is available from the idea of a "Concert of Powers," which has received adequate attention elsewhere in this volume. Suffice it to say that an Asian concert seems scarcely possible in view of the growing ideological and strategic divide between the United States and China, and the fact that concerts usually emerge in the wake of a major-power war, a condition that does not currently apply to Asia. A limited form of concert diplomacy might have been evident with respect to the Korean peninsula in recent years, but it is highly unlikely that this will develop into an Asia-wide institution that would be politically more appealing than the ARF, which is based on a bottom-up approach (Acharya 1996b, 1999b).

The appeal of, and the case for, security multilateralism in Asia does not rest solely on the dangers of balancing. Even though institution building may begin on the basis of such utilitarian and instrumental reasoning, it could have long-term and sometimes unintended consequences in reshaping how alternative strategies are defined and pursued. Multilateral discourses and socialization in Asia may come to redefine and reshape balance of power as a security approach. In Europe, as Emmanuel Adler has argued, the OSCE's doctrine of common security was instrumental in "teaching" NATO to move away from its deterrence posture and adopt a more cooperative approach toward Russia (reflected in the "Partnership for Peace"). The OSCE also taught the norms of humanitarianism to NATO (Adler 1998). It is unlikely that the doctrine of cooperative security espoused by the ARF and "engagement" policy espoused by ASEAN had no effect on American thinking toward the region in general and China in particular. Although more research is needed to ascertain this with any degree of confidence, it is possible to argue that without the multilateral discourses of the early 1990s, American policy toward China might well have been more antagonistic, with a greater likelihood of impulses toward an outright policy of "containing China."

The last point brings us to look at counterfactuals in assessing the impact of Asian regional institutions in managing security order. While counterfactuals are hard to prove, they should not be, and have not been, ignored in debates about regional order in Southeast Asia. Among ASEAN scholars, Noordin Sopiee (1986), a Malaysian specialist on strategic affairs, should be credited with providing the most effective set of counterfactual arguments about ASEAN's role in regional security. Similar speculation and thinking about whether the discourses about "cooperative security" helped reduce strategic uncertainty, moderated temptations toward aggressive balancing postures in key states, and offered a measure of reassurance to the smaller states in post–Cold War Asia should have their place in debates about the impact of security institution building in Asia.[22]

While the end of the 1990s saw a decline of interest and faith in Asian regional institutions generally, there have as yet been no calls for ending the region's nascent experiment in security multilateralism. Despite a general agreement among Asian states that cooperative approaches to security will not suffice in managing the region's security dilemma in the near term, they have nonetheless found it important to persevere in the tortuous process of institution building. The coming years are likely to see further steps to institutionalize security interactions, especially within the ARF. ASEAN could make a slow departure from its noninterference doctrine, but the nascent ASEAN Plus Three framework (bringing together the ten members of ASEAN and China, Japan, and South Korea) has a potential to take on a more active security role, provided ASEAN and China succeed in concluding a code of conduct agreement on the South China Sea.

Conclusion

This chapter has argued for an analytical lens that looks beyond power- and interest-based understandings of Asian regional institutions. Ideational forces, such as identity and norms, not only facilitate a more complete explanation of emergence and characteristics of Asian institution building, but also open up more fruitful avenues for inquiry into their contribution to regional security order.

They point, first and foremost, to a remarkable degree of consistency and path dependency in Asian institution building despite changing material circumstances from the postwar to the post–Cold War period. Generally, Asian institutions have shunned power-based security multilateralism, such as collective security and collective defense, and embraced even process-oriented approaches. The nationalist aspiration for regional autonomy prevented the emergence of NATO-like hegemonic regionalism in postwar Asia, while contestations over regional identity thwarted early postwar pan-Asian efforts. But the norms then articulated made their impact felt through subsequent experiments in regionalism, including ASEAN, which combined the earlier norms of noninterference, cooperation on the basis of equality, and organizational minimalism with a conscious projection of Southeast Asian identity and processes of socialization. Although these norms were conceived under specific material circumstances (such as decolonization and superpower rivalry), and pursued by regional actors for instrumental rea-

---

[22]The Asian economic crisis during 1997–99 might have had a more adverse impact on Asian interstate relations without the existence of regional multilateral security dialogues and institutions (Acharya 1999a).

sons, they became important and enduring in their own right. They shaped the character and role of most subsequent attempts at regional institution building, even after the initial material circumstances within which they were conceived, changed. As such, the ARF has been led by ASEAN and has followed the norms and practices of "soft institutionalism." There has been no effort to develop collective defense within ASEAN and the ARF. And the noninterference norm in Asian regional institutions has adapted to recent challenges.

Critics might see these characteristics as fundamental weaknesses of Asian regionalism. Yet, as this chapter has shown, institutions so constituted have played, and are now playing, more than just a marginal role in reshaping the attitude and behavior of regional actors. Those who dismiss security institutions in Asia must explain why so many states, including the United States and China, participate in institution-building activities. Being an "adjunct" implies that a particular approach can easily be dispensed with without significant costs to the actors. This can hardly be said to be the case with multilateral security ideas in a region in which no country, including the major powers, believes that balancing strategies are by themselves capable of ensuring long-term stability. The region's weaker states accept that cooperative approaches, even in their underdeveloped form, are important in moderating, if not replacing, the balancing behavior of major powers, and that without multilateral security ideas and dialogues, the security situation of the region could even be more risky and uncertain. To draw an overtly hopeful scenario for institutionalism is not the task of this paper. But Asia's ability to develop an institutionalist approach to manage the security dilemma has come far enough to deserve serious scholarly recognition.

Works Cited

Acharya, Amitav. 1990. *A Survey of Military Cooperation Among the ASEAN States: Bilateralism or Alliance*. Occasional Paper 14. Toronto: Centre for International and Strategic Studies, York University.

————. 1996a. "ASEAN and Conditional Engagement." In James Shinn, ed., *Weaving the Net: Conditional Engagement with China*. New York: Council on Foreign Relations.

————. 1996b. "Making Multilateralism Work: The ARF and Security in the Asia-Pacific." In Michael W. Everett and Mary A. Sommerville, eds., *Multilateral Activities in South East Asia: Pacific Symposium 1995*. Washington, D.C.: National Defense University Press.

————. 1997a. "Ideas, Identity, and Institution-Building: From the 'ASEAN Way' to 'Asia Pacific Way'?" *Pacific Review* 10(2): 319–46.

————. 1997b. *The ASEAN Regional Forum: Confidence-Building*. Ottawa: Department of Foreign Affairs and International Trade Canada.

————. 1998. "Collective Identity and Conflict Management in Southeast Asia." In Emmanuel Adler and Michael Barnett, eds., *Security Communities*. Cambridge: Cambridge University Press.

———. 1999a. "Realism, Institutionalism, and the Asian Economic Crisis." *Contemporary Southeast Asia* 21(1): 1–29.

———. 1999b. "A Concert of Asia?" *Survival* 41(3): 84–101.

———. 1999c. *Engagement or Estrangement: India and the Asia Pacific Region*. Eastern Asia Policy Paper 19. Toronto: Joint Centre for Asia Pacific Studies.

———. 1999d. "Containment, Engagement, or Counter-Dominance? Malaysia's Response to the Rise of Chinese Power." In Robert Ross and Iain Johnston, eds., *Engaging China: The Management of a Rising Power*. London: Routledge.

———. 2000. *The Quest for Identity: International Relations of Southeast Asia*. Singapore: Oxford University Press.

———. 2001. *Constructing a Security Community: ASEAN and the Problem of Regional Order*. London: Routledge.

Adler, Emmanuel. 1998. "Seeds of Peaceful Change: The OSCE's Security Community-Building Model." In Emmanuel Adler and Michael Barnett, eds., *Security Communities*. Cambridge: Cambridge University Press.

Anh Tuan Hoang. 1996. "ASEAN Dispute Management: Implications for Vietnam and an Expanded ASEAN." *Contemporary Southeast Asia* 18(1): 61–80.

Appadorai, A. 1955. *The Bandung Conference*. New Delhi: Indian Council of World Affairs.

Asia-Pacific Economic Cooperation. 2001. "APEC Leaders Statement on Counterterrorism," Shanghai, Oct. 21.

Asian Relations Organization. 1948. *Asian Relations: Being Report of the Proceedings and Documentation of the First Asian Relations Conference, New Delhi, March–April 1947*. New Delhi: Asian Relations Organization.

Askandar, Kamarulzaman. 1994. "ASEAN and Conflict Management: The Formative Years of 1967–1976." *Pacifica Review* 6(2): 57–69.

Ayoob, Mohammed. 1985. "The Primacy of the Political: South Asian Regional Cooperation in Comparative Perspective." *Asian Survey* 25(4): 443–57.

Ball, Desmond. 1997. "A Critical Review of Multilateral Security Cooperation in the Asia-Pacific Region." Paper prepared for the inaugural conference of the Asia-Pacific Security Forum on the Impetus for Change in the Asia-Pacific Security Environment, Taipei, September 1–3.

Blair, Dennis C. 1999. "Collective Responsibilities for Security in the Asia-Pacific Region." Lecture organized by the Institute of Defence and Strategic Studies, Singapore, May 22.

———. 2000a. "Security Communities Are the Way Ahead for Asia." *International Herald Tribune*, Apr. 21.

———. 2000b. "Security Communities the Way Ahead for Asia." *Asia-Pacific Defense Forum* (Special Supplement) 25(1): 6.

CASAC (Coalition for Action on South Asian Cooperation). 1995. *SAARC: Vision for the Second Decade*. Discussion Paper 1. New Delhi: CASAC.

Christensen, Thomas J. 1999. "China, the US-Japan Alliance, and the Security Dilemma in East Asia." *International Security* 23(4): 49–90.

Cossa, Ralph. 2000. "US Approaches to Multilateral Security and Economic Institutions in Asia." Paper prepared for the workshop "The United States and Multilateral Organizations" sponsored by the Dickey Center, Dartmouth College, and Centre for International Studies, Oxford University, Mar. 31–Apr. 1.

Crone, Donald. 1993. "Does Hegemony Matter? The Reorganization of the Pacific Political Economy." *World Politics* 45(4): 501–25.

Dash, Kishore C. 1996. "The Political Economy of Regional Cooperation in South Asia."
Pacific Affairs 69(2): 185–209.

Dewitt, David. 1994. "Common, Comprehensive and Cooperative Security." *Pacific Review* 7(1): 1–15.

Djiwandono, J. Soedjati. 1983. "The Political and Security Aspects of ASEAN: Its Principal
Achievements." *Indonesian Quarterly* 11 (July): 19–26.

Dobson, Wendy, and Lee Tsao Yuan. 1994. "APEC: Cooperation Amidst Diversity."
ASEAN Economic Bulletin 10(3): 231–44.

Drysdale, Peter. 1988. *International Economic Pluralism: Economic Policy in East Asia and
the Pacific.* Sydney: Allen & Unwin.

————, and Ross Garnut. 1993. "The Pacific: An Application of a General Theory of Economic Integration." In C. Fred Bergsten and Marcus Nolan, eds., *Pacific Economic Dynamism and the International Economic System.* Washington, D.C.: Institute for International Economics.

Elek, Andrew. 1995. "APEC Beyond Bogor: An Open Economic Association in the Asian-
Pacific Region." *Asia-Pacific Economic Literature* 9(1): 183–223.

Fairbank, John K., Edwin O. Reischauer, and Albert M. Craig. 1989. *East Asia: Tradition
and Transformation.* Rev. ed. Boston: Houghton Mifflin.

Fifield, Russell. 1958. *The Diplomacy of Southeast Asia: 1945–1958.* New York: Harper and
Brothers.

Finnemore, Martha, and Kathryn Sikkink. 1999. "International Norm Dynamics and Political Change." In Peter J. Katzenstein, Robert O. Keohane, and Stephen D. Krasner,
eds., *Exploration and Contestation in the Study of World Politics.* Cambridge, Mass.: MIT
Press.

Foot, Rosemary. 1998. "China in the ASEAN Regional Forum." *Asian Survey* 38(5): 425–
40.

Funston, John. 1999. "Challenges Facing ASEAN in a More Complex Age." *Contemporary
Southeast Asia* 21(2): 205–19.

Haas, Michael. 1989. *The Asian Way to Peace: A Study of Regional Cooperation.* New York:
Praeger.

Haas, Peter, Robert O. Keohane, and Mark A. Levy, eds. 1993. *Institutions for the Earth:
Sources of Effective International Environmental Protection.* Cambridge, Mass.: MIT
Press.

Hemmer, Christopher, and Peter Katzenstein. 2000. "Collective Identities and the Origins
of Multilateralism in Europe But Not in Asia in the Early Cold War." Paper prepared
for the 2000 annual convention of the International Studies Association, Los Angeles,
Mar. 14–18.

Henderson, William. 1955. "The Development of Regionalism in Southeast Asia." *International Organization* 9(4): 462–76.

Higgott, Richard, and Richard Stubbs. 1995. "Competing Conceptions of Economic Regionalism: APEC Versus EAEC in the Asia Pacific." *Review of International Political
Economy* 2(3): 516–35.

Ikenberry, John G. 2001. *After Victory: Institutions, Strategic Restraint and the Rebuilding of Order After Major Wars*. Princeton: Princeton University Press.

Jansen, George H. 1966. *Afro-Asia and Non-Alignment*. London: Faber and Faber.

Johnston, Alastair Iain, and Amitav Acharya. 2001. "Crafting Cooperation: Regional Institution Design in Comparative Perspective." Unpublished manuscript, Harvard University Asia Center.

Johnston, Alastair Iain. 1998. "Socialization in International Institutions: The ASEAN Regional Forum and IR Theory." Paper presented to the conference "The Emerging International Relations of East Asia," University of Pennsylvania, May.

———, and Paul Evans. 1999. "China's Engagement of Multilateral Institutions." In Alastair Iain Johnston and Robert Ross, eds., *Engaging China: The Management of an Emerging Power*. London: Routledge.

Jorgensen-Dahl, Arnafin. 1982. *Regional Organisation and Order in Southeast Asia*. London: Macmillan.

Kahin, George McT. 1955. *The Asia-African Conference: Bandung, Indonesia*. Ithaca: Cornell University Press.

Kahler, Miles. 2000. "Legalization as Strategy: The Case of Asia Pacific." *International Organization* 54(3): 549–71.

Katzenstein, Peter J. 1997. "Asian Regionalism in Comparative Perspective." In Peter Katzenstein and Takashi Shiraishi, eds., *Network Power: Japan and Asia*. Ithaca: Cornell University Press.

Keohane, Robert O. 1984. *After Hegemony*. Princeton: Princeton University Press.

———, and Lisa Martin. 1995. "The Promise of Institutionalist Theory." *International Security* 20(1): 39–51.

Kupchan, Charles A. 1999. "Regionalizing Europe's Security: The Case for a New Mitteleuropa." In Edward Mansfield and Helen Milner, eds., *The Political Economy of Regionalism*. New York: Columbia University Press.

Leifer, Michael. 1996. *The ASEAN Regional Forum*. Adelphi Paper 302. London: International Institute for Strategic Studies.

Levi, Werner. 1968. *The Challenge of World Politics in South and Southeast Asia*. Englewood Cliffs, N.J.: Prentice-Hall.

"Li Peng Expresses Concern About Guidelines Bill." 1999. *Asahi Shimbun*, Apr. 29.

Mearsheimer, John. 1994–95. "The False Promise of International Institutions." *International Security* 9(3): 5–49.

Ministry of Foreign Affairs, Bangkok. 1998. "Thailand's Non-Paper on the Flexible Engagement Approach." 743/2541, July 27.

"'Multilateral Pacts' Key to Security." 1999. *Sunday Times* (Singapore), May 23, p. 4.

"N. Korea Criticizes Japanese Defense Bills." 1999. Dow Jones Newswires, Apr. 29.

Nehru, Jawaharlal. 1948. "Inaugural Address." In *Asian Relations: Being Report of the Proceedings and Documentation of the First Asian Relations Conference, New Delhi, March–April, 1947*. New Delhi: Asian Relations Organization.

Pauker, Guy J. 1955. *The Bandung Conference*. Cambridge: Center for International Studies, Massachusetts Institute of Technology, Economic Development Program, Indonesia Project.

Risse-Kappen, Thomas. 1996. "Collective Identity in a Democratic Community." In Peter Katzenstein, ed., *The Culture of National Security: Norms and Identity in World Politics*. New York: Columbia University Press.

Roth, Stanley. 1998. "Text: Roth on Multilateral Approaches to Regional Security." Presentation at the Henry L. Stimson Center, Washington, D.C., July 21. http://pdq2.usia.gov/scripts/cqcg.

Rozman, Gilbert. 2000. *Restarting Regionalism in Northeast Asia*. North Pacific Policy Paper 1. Vancouver: Institute of Asian Research, University of British Columbia.

Ruggie, John G., ed. 1993. *Multilateralism Matters*. New York: Columbia University Press.

"Russia Expresses Concern About Passage of Guidelines Bill." 1999. *Asahi Shimbun*, Apr. 28.

Scalapino, Robert A. 1994. "Challenges to the Sovereignty of the Modern State." In Bunn Nagara and K. S. Balakrishnan, eds., *The Making of a Security Community in the Asia-Pacific*. Kuala Lumpur: ISIS Malaysia.

Schaller, Michael. 1982. "Securing the Great Crescent: Occupied Japan and the Origins of Containment in Southeast Asia." *Journal of American History* 69(2): 392–414.

Soesastro, Hadi. 1994. "Economic Integration and Interdependence in the Asia Pacific: Implications for Security." Paper presented at the Eighth Asia Pacific Roundtable, Kuala Lumpur, June 5–8.

Soh, Felix. 2001. "Multilateral War," *Straits Times*, Oct. 27, p. 2.

Sopiee, Noordin. 1986. "ASEAN and Regional Security." In Mohammed Ayoob, ed., *Regional Security in the Third World*. London: Croom Helm.

U.S. Department of State. 1976. *Foreign Relations of the United States, 1950*. Vol. 6: *East Asia and the Pacific*, pt. 2. Washington, D.C.: Government Printing Office.

Weber, Steve. 1993. "Shaping the Postwar Balance of Power: Multilateralism in NATO." In John G. Ruggie, ed., *Multilateralism Matters*. New York: Columbia University Press.

Wickramasinghe, Nira. 1999. "Globalization and Regional Insecurities in South Asia." Paper presented at the Conference on Globalization and Regional Security: Asian Perspectives organized by the Asia-Pacific Center for Security Studies, Honolulu, Feb. 23–25.

Young, Oran R. 1999. *Governance in World Affairs*. Ithaca: Cornell University Press.

CHAPTER SEVEN

Track 2 Diplomacy

Ideational Contribution to the Evolving Asia Security Order

BRIAN L. JOB

This chapter explores an apparent anomaly—namely, the influence of nongovernmental institutions and unofficial processes on the development of the security architecture of an avowedly state-centric regional order. Over the last several decades, a community of intellectuals, academics, and officials, operating transnationally through think tanks, universities, and private and public foundations, has been central to the establishment of economic and security structures in Asia. Their achievements have been instrumental in fostering the formation of such institutions as the APEC forum and the ASEAN Regional Forum, but fundamentally their impact has been ideational. In this regard they have served as agents of change and norm entrepreneurs working to alter perceptions of interests, redefinition of identities (both individual and collective), and acceptance of the key principles of open regionalism and cooperative security. This has been accomplished through methods of diplomacy and dialogue outside the formal governmental system. Scholars, experts, journalists, and politicians have engaged with officials (military and civilian) acting in their private capacities in what has come to be termed Track 2 processes (Capie and Evans 2002: 213–15).[1]

The intriguing questions concerning the impact of Track 2 on the form and function of the Asian security order arise from the complex and symbiotic relationships between the national and transnational, the unofficial and official, and

---

[1]Track 2, or nonofficial diplomacy refers to "unofficial, informal interactions between members of adversary groups or nations which aim to develop strategies, influence public opinion, and organize human and material resources in ways that might help to resolve their conflict" (Montville 1995: 9).

Track 1 and Track 2 processes. Certainly changes in structural conditions have been important. The end of the Cold War in Asia created a climate of fluid power transitions, uncertainty regarding roles, and risk rather than threat in both the economic and the security domain. Governmental and nongovernmental actors alike have maneuvered strategically to utilize Track 2 processes and institutional forms to advance their interests in light of changing power balances and altered national circumstances. But structural factors alone have not dictated the particular direction and content of the transformations that lie at the heart of the regional and subregional security complexes of the contemporary Asian order. Ideas matter. Indeed the development of Asia Pacific economic and security institutions is the story of the norm entrepreneurship and socialization associated with the advance of "open regionalism," "cooperative security," and the "ASEAN Way."

To understand such changes, we must shift from realist and neoliberal perspectives, focused on material interests and instrumental rationalities, to constructivist perspectives focused on the creation of identities (individual and collective), processes of social learning and the formation of communities (epistemic communities and security communities), and the acceptance of norms of conduct governing economic behavior, political decision making, and dispute settlement. Most analysts write from one theoretical perspective or the other regarding the rationale for, and utility of, regional multilateral security institutions in the Asia Pacific. Realists such as Leifer, Dibb, and Buzan have emphasized structural characteristics, power capabilities, deterrence, and alliances and stress the ineffectiveness of regional multilateral institutions, including ASEAN and the ARF, to deal with persistent security issues (Leifer 1996; Buzan and Segal 1994; Dibb 1995). Those attuned to liberal and constructivist notions of interdependence, integration, and the potential for alteration of identities and interests, by contrast, focus on the promise of dialogue, networking, and informal institutions to create a new regional order, skirting questions of their incapacity to resolve current crises and historical animosities (Johnston 1995; Acharya 2000a; Job 1997a; Busse 1999). With few exceptions (such as Acharya 1997 and 2000b), Higgott's complaint about the absence of careful research exploring the relationship of ideas, interests, and identity in the Asia Pacific context remains valid (Higgott 1994).

This chapter takes a few steps to correct this problem. In conceptual terms, it does not hold to a single theoretical perspective, adopting instead what Katzenstein and Okawara (2002) have described as an "analytically eclectic" mode of inquiry. In substantive terms, the chapter focuses upon a subset of the broad spectrum of unofficial, public diplomacy and informal diplomatic processes, namely the development of what has come to be called "Track 2," regional and subregional multilateral security dialogues throughout Asia during the 1990s. Thus it parallels Acharya's treatment of the efforts of the states in the Asian Security System at formal, multilateral institution building (Chap. 6 in this volume). These two regional dynamics of official and unofficial diplomacy cannot be considered separately. In a complex symbiotic relationship, both proceed within the same structural context and operate according to similar norms concerning security, sovereignty, and interstate relations. Both reinforce each other in positive and negative ways and are conducted by cohorts of national elites with many common characteristics. Both face important challenges if their respective agendas are to move forward in the current decade.

Two difficult sets of questions must be confronted. First, reflecting on the past, to what extent have Track 2 processes had an impact on determining the character of the post–Cold War security architecture in Asia? In other words, has the expenditure of time, funding, and human resources in Track 2 security dialogue activities generated results? What evidence can be mustered to bolster any claims of "success"? Second, looking to the future, have the Track 2 processes of the 1980s and 1990s run their course? To what extent are its participants capable of sustaining forward momentum on enhancing the norms and modalities of subregional and regional security cooperation in what many observers believe is a transformed security environment?

The informal nature of Track 2 activities themselves, combined with the lack of agreement about what constitutes criteria for success and the absence of methodologies and institutional mechanisms for data gathering and analysis, frustrate the systematic, empirically based study of the record of and progress of Track 2 (and Track 1) institutional development. A preliminary accounting is attempted in this chapter, leading to several observations. Perhaps somewhat controversially, analysis of the record serves to reinforce a concern that Asia Pacific Track 2 activities may have peaked in the mid-1990s and have been failing to sustain momentum since then. In part this stalling can be attributed to preoccupation on the part of elites with the various political and economic crises that have beset their region since 1997. However, more critical observers point to two other sets of factors. First, the achievements of the 1990s were the product of a particular, positive correlation of structural conditions and actor interests—the combination of post–Cold War climate of economic growth and optimism and the relaxation of political/security tensions, particularly among the major powers on the one hand and, on the other, the concerted action of a cohort of regional elites who successfully advanced both ideational and instrumental goals (an idiosyncratic generational effect). Second, Track 2 security dialogue processes, as currently constituted, have confronted an "autonomy dilemma," an inherent tension between advancing ideas and initiatives and maintaining credibility with governments. In sum, have we reached what Paul Evans (2000a: 3) has described as the "end of the beginning" of a process that will continue to effectuate change, or are we at the "beginning of the end" of Track 2 security dialogue phenomena that have made their mark but will not be sustained, at least in many of their current institutional forms?

The Security Dialogue Process

Much has been written about the impact of the end of the Cold War: the cessation of bipolar strategic and ideological competition, the collapse of the Soviet Union, the ascendance of the United States to global power status, the aspirations of China, India, and Japan to assume major power roles on the regional and world stages, and the dramatic acceleration of economic growth (e.g., Foot 1995). One must remember, however, that significant forces of change had been unleashed in Asia in the decades prior to 1989. With China's modernization begun some ten years before, the tide of economic reform had been set in motion. With ASEAN's founding a full twenty years earlier and the build-up to APEC's establishment in 1989, multilateral institutionalization on economic and security dimensions had taken hold. What the ending of the global Cold War fostered, therefore, was twofold. First, it brought into question the rationale and institutional forms of the existing regional security architecture. Rooted in the structural and ideational context of Northeast Asia, this architecture was based on a pattern of bipolar alliance commitments—grounded in a logic of collective defense and deterrence against the Soviet Union and its client states, organized around a notion of security oriented toward external military threat, and devoted to norms of closed regionalism. Second, it facilitated the realization throughout Asia that to ensure the peace and stability fundamental to sustaining the now-number-one priority of economic growth, a reorientation of regional security institutions (informal and formal) was essential. Such efforts were spearheaded by the states of ASEAN, the peripheral "middle powers" Canada and Australia, and in certain instances by Japan. Their efforts, especially during the early 1990s, coalesced to advance the principle of cooperative security as the ideational foundation for a new security order. Thus, when the United States and China came to modify their resistance to regional multilateral security institutionalization, in part because of the atmosphere created by these norm entrepreneurship activities and in part because of reconsideration of their strategic interests, the path was cleared for the institutional innovations at both Track 1 and Track 2 levels in the Asia Pacific.

Cooperative Security

Again much has been written on the subject of cooperative security.[2] Cooperative security envisages security as a value that cannot be achieved through unilateral action or exclusively defensive behavior. Security is advanced by promoting cooperation rather than confrontation. Inclusion rather than exclusion of non–like-minded actors is to be promoted. Security is conceived in broader terms than the absence of military threats to national security—that is, in terms of alleviation of threats to environmental conditions, social and political stability, economic well-being, and cultural preservation.

As a concept, therefore, cooperative security draws on elements well grounded in Asian (particularly Southeast Asian) thinking: "comprehensive security" in advancing a nonmilitary definition of security that embraced national and regional well-being; "common security" in its inclusion of the non–like-minded and its emphasis on mutual reassurance; and "collective security" in promoting the UN principles of peaceful settlement (Wanandi 1996: 120).

The key champions of cooperative security during the early 1990s were Australia and Canada (Kerr et al. 1995), states which viewed the principles of multilateralism and regionwide institution building as essential both to their self-interest in sustaining a voice in global and regional affairs and to broader goals of sustaining peace and stability over the long term (Job 1997b). Their initial overtures, seen by Asian states as efforts to promote the transference of formal European-style institutional mechanisms to the region, were met with skepticism. Such modalities simply were out of tune with the "security culture" of the Asia Pacific. But once such notions were dispelled, both sides came to realize that efforts to advance cooperative security through gradual, incremental, and unofficial processes were in tune with the norms, ideas, and institutional strategies developed over the years by the ASEAN states—encapsulated in the phrases "ASEAN Way" and "soft regionalism." Thus the principles and practices of the ASEAN Way—soft regionalism, multilateralism, inclusion of the non–like-minded, avoidance of confrontation and arbitration, decision making by consensus, and an aversion to formal institutions and agenda setting—all resonated comfortably with those in ASEAN. Cooperative security thus became the conceptual cornerstone of their collective post–Cold War efforts at developing a multilateral regional security order, one that Acharya has characterized as "a cautious, informal, gradualist and consensus-seeking approach" that emphasized unofficial over governmental channels (1994: 342).

[2]One of the key initial works in this regard was Dewitt (1994).

Track 2 Diplomacy and Security Dialogue

Traditional modes of interstate diplomacy were neither sufficient for nor necessarily sympathetic to multilateral institution building around cooperative security principles. The Asia Pacific region is still a decidedly state-centric environment in which governments guard their monopolies of authority both in domestic contexts (thus the preoccupation with noninterference) and in international relations (thus the strong advocacy of UN principles of sovereignty and equality). This was particularly true of the major regional powers concerning security matters during the Cold War era. Multilateral security institutions and principles of multilateralism held little interest for the major powers. Nor did they appeal to many smaller states suspicious of the prospects of engaging in interstate regional forums in which their voices would be overwhelmed by regional powers.

The dynamic of Southeast Asian institution building arose as a reaction by these nonmajor powers ("small state" is an inappropriate term to apply to Indonesia) to this broad geopolitical dynamic. The initial formation of ASEAN was motivated by their desire to gain a collective voice in regional affairs as well as the coincidence of interests among their national leaders to ensure the security of their respective regimes from internal and external challenges. In time the ASEAN collective, under the leadership of several of its prominent statesmen, took on a greater role in subregional and later regional affairs. This was not, however, accomplished through traditional diplomacy or formal institution building. It was attained through the nurturing of informal, unofficial networks—frequent and sometime regularized meetings of experts, business leaders, officials, and political figures designed to advance functional cooperation and promote mutual trust and confidence, i.e. Track 2 activities.

In the Asia Pacific context, Track 2 has two connotations. At times it refers to the entire complex of informal networking activities, unofficial channels of communication, and people-to-people diplomacy, across national and regional levels, including official and nongovernmental diplomacy, undertaken across social, political, and economic realms of civil society.[3] In this sense, Track 2 characterizes an overall dynamic of changing norms, identities, and institutions.[4] It evokes notions of socialization, community building, nurturing of collective identity, and progress toward establishing a security community. Jusuf Wanandi (1996: 231) makes this clear in the ASEAN context:

Since 1985 activities of NGOs, "second track" networking, and people to people diplomacy have given a new impetus to ASEAN's existence and strengthen ASEAN as an or-

[3]Behera, Evans, and Rivzi (1997: 4–5) list seven unofficial dialogue channels.
[4]Note, for example, the title of Desmond Ball's (1994) article: "A New Era in Confidence-Building: The Second-Track Process in the Asia/Pacific Region."

ganization. It has also added another element to ASEAN, namely the transformation of ASEAN from a *gesellschaft* (or modern social entity that has been founded on rational organizational requisites) into a *gemeinschaft* (an "organic" entity, that has elements of emotional or psychological ties between its members, that brings deeper, wider and stronger relations than in a *gesellschaft*).

But the term Track 2 is used in a narrower context as well, with reference to a particular form of dialogue activity associated, during the 1990s, with the promotion of cooperative security and multilateral security regionalism. Paul Evans refers to this form of Track 2 activity as "blended" dialogues "involving meetings of academics, journalists, and occasionally politicians and also . . . government officials . . . attending in their 'unofficial' or 'private' capacities" (1994c: 125). The key components of Track 2 diplomacy are meetings organized to engage participants from several countries in discussions concerning security issues of mutual concern. These have come to be called multilateral "security dialogues." Here the term "dialogue" is used to distinguish such meetings from the "negotiations" of Track 1 officials. Simultaneously they strive to be inclusive—that is, to engage parties from contending perspectives—and nonconfrontational. Their goal is to achieve a mutual understanding of perceived threats and security goals. Accordingly, they do not tend toward highly technical or scientific treatments of weapons systems and the like but seek to identify new perspectives, develop innovative solutions, and advance confidence and security-building mechanisms (CSBMs).

Advocates of Track 2 security dialogues reject the notion that state officials should monopolize consideration of security matters. They seek to engage participation of leaders from the academic, financial, social, and political sectors of society in order to bring expertise and new ideas to the table and, more important, to foster transnational understanding and confidence building. Officials are not to be excluded, however. Indeed they are regarded as an essential component of the Track 2 dialogue process.

In principle, government officials are supposed to function in their "private capacities," attending and participating without having to represent their governments. This freedom of discussion is meant to facilitate consideration of sensitive subjects and the exploration of ideas too abstract or too creative for the interstate negotiating table. As Sheldon Simon (2001: 3) puts it, the engagement of officials in this mode was to facilitate thinking "outside the box," providing opportunities to "address issues . . . not yet on governmental security agendas as a kind of early warning mechanism, . . . [to] provide fresh approaches to problems, . . . [and to] redefine issues such that policymakers might see new ways of resolution." At the same time, the involvement of officials presumably brings to discussions informed representations of government policy positions and a focusing of attention on the need to advance practical and immediate, rather than abstract or distant, options for action.

In practice, however, the prospect of engaging governments and officials in spontaneous and unrestricted dialogue is inherently problematic, as will be discussed below. A deep tension is created by expecting individuals to function both as uninhibited participants and as informed representatives. Furthermore, governmental interests, political constraints, and societal norms intervene. Some governments have viewed Track 2 diplomacy as another strategic tool for the promotion of their regional security interests. Certainly Australia and Canada have pursued this approach. And if such engagement is benign and facilitative—if their officials and participating citizens are allowed the free rein of discussion desired in Track 2 forums—then an optimal result is achieved. But political and cultural considerations constrain many Track 2 representatives in the Asia Pacific, who cannot or do not wish to stray from their government's official position. Thus many analysts have come to regard the notion of officials acting in a private capacity as a polite fiction at best and discount the promise of Track 2 security dialogues for innovation and path-breaking initiatives (Kerr 1994: 399).

Institutional Forms

Asia Pacific security was a growth industry during the first half of the 1990s. Both official and unofficial dimensions of activity burgeoned as states established bilateral relations with former adversaries, were swept up in the regional and global economic boom, and opened their societies to a greater or lesser degree to information about and participation in regional affairs. The cast of characters involved in security dialogue activities has grown dramatically.[5] Table 7.1 outlines the range of participants. Focused on multilateral entities, it draws a distinction between governmental and nongovernmental institutions and further divides them according to their subregional, regional, or interregional scope.[6]

Table 7.1 draws the reader's attention to several points. First, note the twinning of Track 1 (governmental institutions) with their Track 2 (nongovernmental) counterparts (ASEAN and ASEAN ISIS; ARF and CSCAP; APEC and PECC).[7]

[5]Paul Evans, for instance, estimates that in the short span of 1989 to 1994 the numbers of dialogue mechanisms increased from only three or four to more than fifty—with a corresponding increase in the number of institutions or actors involved in these meetings. See Evans (1994a: 297–318).

[6]This categorization is limited to multilateral entities and does not attempt to classify the diverse set of groups that sponsor regional or subregional meetings. For a running record that includes both official and nongovernmental events, see *Dialogue Monitor* (1995–98). Subsequent updates are posted at http://www.pcaps.iar.ubc.ca/pubs.htm.

[7]Note that there is a third component of institutions such as APEC, CSCAP, ASEAN, and ISIS, namely national-level member committees, think tanks, and secretariats.

TABLE 7.1

Types of Multilateral Institutions Engaged in Asia Pacific Security

Governmental Multilateral Institutions (Track 1)

Subregional[a]
- ASEAN (Association of Southeast Asian Nations)
- SAARC (South Asian Association for Regional Cooperation)[b]
- SCO (Shanghai Cooperation Organization)[c]

Regional[d]
- ARF (ASEAN Regional Forum)
- ASEAN + 3 (ASEAN plus China, Japan, and Korea)

Interregional
- ASEM (Asia Europe Meeting)[e]

Nongovernmental Multilateral Institutions (Track 2)

Subregional institutionalized
- ASEAN ISIS (ASEAN Institutes for Strategic and International Studies)

Regional
- CSCAP (Council for Security Cooperation in the Asia Pacific)

Interregional
- CAEC (Council for Asia Europe Cooperation)[f]

[a]In geographic terms, Asia encompasses four subregions: Southeast Asia, Northeast Asia, South Asia, and Central Asia. The developments of "Asia Pacific" security taken up in this paper have been focused around Southeast Asia and Northeast Asia. Indeed, in order to explicitly note the inclusion of Canada and the United States, the term North Pacific is utilized in certain institutional contexts, as in the CSCAP North Pacific Working Group.

[b]See http://www.saarc-sec.org for descriptive information.

[c]The Shanghai Cooperation Organization is focused around Central Asia. Created in 2001, it is the successor to the "Shanghai Five," i.e., the Five-Power Agreement of 1996. Its membership consists of China, Russia, and the Republics of Kyrgyz, Tajikistan, Uzbekistan, and Kazakstan. See http://www.chinaembassy-org.be/eng/23354.html.

[d]Defining "Asia Pacific" is the subject of much debate. For our purposes, the ARF designation of Asia Pacific will be used—thus including India but excluding the rest of South Asia.

[e]See http://asem2.fco.gov.uk/whatisasem.

[f]See http://www.jcie.or.jp/thinknet/caec.

Second, note the emergence of non–Asia Pacific[8] interregional entities, i.e., institutions involving Asian and European, Latin American, or Central Asian states. Thus one can point, respectively, to ASEM and CAEC set up in 1996; the EALAF,

[8]Membership in "Asia Pacific" institutions is idiosyncratic. North America (Canada, the United States, and Mexico) is a full partner in regional economic institutions (such as APEC) but not in security institutions (such as the ARF and CSCAP), in which only Canada and the United States are members. Indeed, the United States is a member of many so-called Asian institutions. On the other hand, the Pacific Islands have never really been a part of the Asia Pacific, at least not until very recently. Only PNG is in the ARF; and the Pacific Islands Forum only became an observer at CSCAP in December 2001.

established in 1999; and the SCO, reconstituted from the previous Shanghai Five in 2001. Third, note that the Asia Pacific security institutional framework does not encompass all of Asia's geographic subregions. Only India is a member of the ARF, thus effectively precluding the Forum's consideration of South Asian matters. To date, no consideration has been given to inclusion of Central Asia. In Table 7.1 the governmental institution label is reserved for organizations formally constituted with states as members, with officials attending as representatives of their respective governments, and with decisions taken on behalf of governments—that is, Track 1 institutions. There are few such institutions; indeed, their relative paucity has distinguished the security architecture of the Asia Pacific.

The role of governments and the direct linkages of Track 1 to Track 2 institutions vary. In part, these are the issues referred to earlier, i.e., of governments and officials not functioning in their "private capacities." However, there is also a set of cross-over institutions, i.e., institutions in which governments control the agendas and participants for "unofficial" consultations or in which officials in their "private capacities" dominate the meetings. Indeed a separate designation, "Track 1.5," has been coined to refer to such institutions. (See Capie and Evans 2002: 211–12.) Examples of Track 1.5 institutions would include the Northeast Asia Cooperation Dialogue (NEACD)—a security dialogue organized by an American university that directly invites uniformed military and foreign ministry personnel as participants in their *official* capacities—or the so-called "Track 2" workshops officially organized under the auspices of the ARF (rather than through CSCAP).[9]

The number and frequency of meetings of nongovernmental organizations operating transnationally in the Asia Pacific defies precise classification or accurate count.[10] Their degree of institutionalization varies widely. The examples in Table 7.1, such as the ASEAN ISIS and CSCAP, are chartered organizations with a central secretariat, annual budgets, member organizations, and regular meetings. But this leaves out a gamut of semi-institutionalized Track 2 activities, some of which have played very important roles in promoting cooperative security. There is, for instance, the annual Asia Pacific Round Table, sponsored by ASEAN ISIS, that brings together more than two hundred people from countries throughout the region to debate a full range of contemporary security issues. The Round Table has evolved in size and agenda to become the largest regular and most inclusive, regional Track 2 event of the year.[11] Another much-cited example of confidence building through semi-institutionalized Track 2 activity has been the series of workshops organized by Indonesia (and funded by Canada) that have brought

[9]For more on the NEACD, see http://www-igcc.ucsd.edu/regions/northeast_asia/neacd/.

[10]A number of scholars have put forward Track 2 classification schemes. See, for example, Kerr (1994: 397–410) and Kraft (1994: 7–32).

[11]See, for instance, the annual volume of conference proceedings produced by ISIS Malaysia.

together representatives of China and the other claimants in the South China Sea dispute for nonconfrontational technical discussions (Djalal and Townsend-Gault 2000: 109–33).

Efforts to catalog NGOs in the Asia Pacific have been made, including a survey of institutions with mandates for education and policy research (Evans 1994b) and an ambitious effort to account for NGOs with transnational agendas relevant to economic and security issues (broadly conceived).[12] Although no groups representing civil society have been engaged in the Track 2 process, either by choice or by design, their importance is undoubtedly growing.[13]

Leadership and Norm Entrepreneurship

Richard Higgott has noted: "The presence of a big idea is not of itself a sufficient motor for progress. Ideas need articulate intellectual-cum-policy elites to carry them forward onto the political agenda" (1994: 370). Recent scholarship concerning changing norms and the development of institutional identities points to the key role played by so-called norm entrepreneurs in this process— those who take on the advocacy of alternative norms and attempt through creative tactics to promote their adoption.[14]

In the Asia Pacific context, the role of norm entrepreneurs in advancing cooperative security through multilateral institution building in the 1990s has been assumed variously by Australia and Canada, by Japan, and by the ASEAN states acting separately and in tandem. Canada and Australia—experienced internationalist middle powers—both had established track records of norm entrepreneurship, particularly in international trade and in nonproliferation regimes (Cooper and Nossal 1993; Kerr and Mack 1994). As peripheral regional states, both believed that unless the norms and operative principles of the Asia Pacific security order were changed, they could not gain the voice and place in regional affairs to which they aspired and, moreover, the region would remain unstable in

[12]See, for instance, Yamamoto (1995). But given the difficulties inherent in keeping track of the fluid world of nongovernmental bodies, these surveys are capable of capturing trends in numbers and functional distribution rather than precise data records.

[13]It is intriguing to consider whether or not "virtual" networks and on-line dialogues on the Internet should be included in our considerations. With the expansion of Internet connectivity and its use throughout the region, the number, scope, and quality of such instruments is growing rapidly. In my view they represent a significant, possibly transforming, factor in the future development of the Track 2 phenomenon. The most prominent example to date would be the security dialogue networking projects and email news services of the Nautilus Institute (www.nautilus. org). With a regionwide set of corresponding institutes and relatively open access for participation by security experts across the region, the Institute's website and related archives, conference proceedings, and so forth increasingly function as an ongoing, regional, Track 2 dialogue mechanism.

[14]For an overview of recent work on norms, see Finnemore and Sikkink (1998: 887–917).

fundamental ways that threatened their security interests.[15] Thus both championed initiatives for multilateral security institutionalization in Asia, particularly through the skillful advocacy of Track 2 processes. Their reliance on Track 2 reflected a geopolitical reality: Track 1 channels on security were largely closed to them, and both the United States and Asian states were uneasy with schemes to create regional multilateral security institutions. But it also reflected the mobilization in each country of a combined cohort of academics and nongovernmental experts with senior counterparts in their respective foreign ministries (Dewitt and Job 1994). Together their energies were instrumental in advancing initiatives such as CSCAP, encouraging the engagement and inclusion of the non–like-minded, and generally promoting norms of good governance, human rights, and human security—the last particularly by Canada under its activist foreign minister, Lloyd Axworthy, in the late 1990s.

The other agents for regional change were the ASEAN states as a collective, but especially Indonesia, Malaysia, the Philippines, and Thailand. That the ASEAN states should assume a lead role in advancing regional institution building was not a surprise in light of their long experience in nurturing Track 1 and Track 2 collaboration in Southeast Asia. The ASEAN states had a strong common interest in promoting cooperative security in a regional context. (See Acharya 2000a and 2000b.) Thus they acted in concert as entrepreneurs for multilateral institutional initiatives that maintained a key role for ASEAN management and ASEAN norms of inclusion and decision making. For them, too, focusing on Track 2 diplomacy and establishing nongovernmental institutions as precursors or supporters of Track 1 institutional counterparts was critical. Unlike Australia and Canada, the ASEAN states were more comfortable with minimal levels of formal institutionalization oriented toward dialogue rather than dispute arbitration.

Japan, on the other hand, has taken a lower profile and more cautious stance as an institutional innovator, and as a result its role as a norm entrepreneur probably has been underestimated. Although seen as constrained by cultural attitudes, hindered by political and bureaucratic rigidities, and wedded to a bilateral approach to security matters, Japan has adroitly promoted regional multilateralism—particularly on the economic front but also in the political-security dimension, as with the ARF.[16]

But leadership has an important personal dimension as well, which in the Asia Pacific Track 2 realm is seen in two ways. First, the norm entrepreneurial activi-

[15]It is also noteworthy that Mikhail Gorbachev in the late 1980s made some initial efforts at regional norm entrepreneurship concerning the establishment of an Asia Pacific security framework.

[16]Ellis Krauss's recent research yields detailed insight into the Japanese role in this regard, particularly concerning economic institution building. See Krauss (2000).

ties of key states have been associated with the high profile taken by activist national figures, in particular their foreign ministers: for Australia, Gareth Evans; for Canada, Joe Clark and Lloyd Axworthy; for Thailand, Pitsuwan Surin. Each of these figures was willing to challenge the established consensus and norms to provoke debate and action on new initiatives. Indeed the ebb and flow of regional Track 1 and Track 2 innovation over the last several decades can be correlated to a considerable extent with the appearance (and inevitable receding) of such figures from the regional political scene.[17] Second, there is a cohort that can be characterized as the "Asia Pacific Track 2 elite"—a set of individuals whose commitment to regional multilateralism transcends national barriers and who, by virtue of their advantaged positions as directors of think tanks, holders of prominent academic posts, and the like, have been remarkably effective in coordinating their energies to advance institutional innovation. These people come from the upper ranks of the educated urban middle and upper classes. In many instances they will have been "Western-educated," particularly those from Southeast Asia (and Korea in Northeast Asia). Well traveled outside the borders of their own countries, they represent a thoroughly internationalized subset of the population. Many will have served in office as elected representatives, party officials, or senior bureaucrats. Often they will hold multiple roles, serving simultaneously in leadership positions in their countries' PECC and APEC teams, on CSCAP member committees, and in high-profile national institutes. Those within ASEAN especially will have developed close personal relationships. Indeed this tightly knit, cohort of ASEAN think tank leaders, supplemented by select individuals from other countries, including the United States, has been the driving force of economic and security regionalism over the last several decades.[18]

Track 2 Diplomacy in the Asia Pacific

It is worth pausing to note the historical antecedents to the Asia Pacific regional nongovernmental organizations of today. These roots extend back to the

[17]Certainly this is true of Canada. For instance, the North Pacific Cooperative Security Dialogue initiative of the early 1990s was advanced by Foreign Minister Joe Clark but abandoned by his successor. Lloyd Axworthy's activist human security agenda, with its significant Track 2 and NGO components, is likely, too, to be downplayed by future foreign ministers, especially in the aftermath of September 2001.

[18]The author knows of no studies that systematically identify the members of what might be called the ASEAN or Asia Pacific Track 2 elite—that is, network studies that chart their individual backgrounds, career paths, and interactions. Various observers have noted in passing the importance of key figures like Yusuf Wanandi (Indonesia), Noordin Sopie (Malaysia), Carolina Hernandez (Philippines), Paul Evans (Canada), Desmond Ball (Australia), and Joe Jordan and Ralph Cossa (United States)—all, for instance, instrumental in the founding of CSCAP. See, for instance, Kraft (1994, 2000); Evans (1994a); Acharya (2000a, 2000b).

early decades of the last century—to the founding of the Pan-Pacific Union in 1907 and the establishment of the Institute of Pacific Research (IPR) in 1925.[19] The IPR operated with distinction for many years as an agent for mutual under-standing, emphasizing educational activities and cross-cultural programs, until 1960 when it fell victim to McCarthy-era politics in the United States. Woods notes: "In its form, function, and impetus . . . the IPR represents the institutional precursor of the INGOS today" involved in Pacific economic and security coop-eration (1993: 39).

One can draw several lessons from the IPR experience. First, the moments in the wake of major systemic upheaval provide the best opportunity for institu-tional innovation. The IPR was formed at a time when the cosmopolitan busi-ness, social, and education elites from both sides of the Pacific engaged to im-prove relations among their countries and peoples.[20] Second, the institutional format, premiered by the IFR, involving a region-wide council, whose member-ship in turn is composed of representatives from respective national committees, has proved to be the common, and generally successful, pattern for nongovern-mental regional institutions in the Asia Pacific. Third, the apparent asset of hav-ing privileged access to high-level decision makers may prove to be a liability if the political climate changes dramatically—a fate that befell the IPR. Finally, in-stitutions that are basically elite bodies will falter when placed under critical scrutiny or plagued by controversy, unless they have attended to maintaining broad-based public support and identification with the interests of civil society— again the fate of the IPR.[21]

Economic Regionalism

The development of economic regionalism in the Asia Pacific has been studied and chronicled extensively. Clearly the economic dimension sets the context for regional security developments. As Acharya states: "The demand for multilateral institutions in the Asia Pacific is fueled ... [by] a desire to build upon, exploit and maximize the pay-offs of economic liberalization and interdependence" (1997: 323). Security multilateralism, therefore, is regarded as instrumental in ad-vancing the conditions of peace and stability necessary to sustain economic pros-perity. Economic regionalism, having predated the end of the Cold War by al-

[19]The record of Asia Pacific nongovernmental diplomacy through the twentieth century is analyzed perceptively by Lawrence Woods (1993).

[20]The IPR's membership included leaders from all major sectors of public life. Holders of pub-lic office and serving officials, however, were not actively engaged—a contrast to contemporary Track 2 processes. The Institute was privately funded by its national councils. Its mandate was to avoid discussion of contemporary political problems, national and international.

[21]These last two points, along with other "lessons," are developed in Woods (1995).

most two decades, implanted norms and institutional forms that through their success became precedents for Asian states when they took up the reformulation of their regional security architecture.

Indeed one can point to several factors that have influenced the evolution of Track 2 security dialogue processes during the past decade. With the abandonment of ideology and adoption of market economic principles, norms of regional interaction were reoriented to center on principles of market-led integration and open regionalism (Job 1997a). The notion of divorcing economics from political-security matters and issues of governance has eroded as economic interdependence has increased and social issues associated with economic disparities and social safety nets have risen on the regional agenda. Moreover, economic regionalism has firmly established the role of nongovernmental actors in regional institution building. The tripartite engagement of academic experts, private-sector representatives, and government officials has been an accepted principle of regional economic institutions for more than three decades. Select "policy academics" have served as norm entrepreneurs for economic cooperation and played key roles in determining the fundamental choices for domestic economic reform and cooperation among Asia Pacific states. Analysts point to the emergence of an influential community of "neoclassical economists and free trade acolytes" as the norm entrepreneurs for institutional development (Higgot 1994).

In addition, the setting up of semi-institutionalized, nongovernmental institutions as confidence-building instruments and groundbreakers prior to the founding of official multilateral institutions has become an established practice. Thus PAFTAD (established in 1968) and PBEC (begun in 1980) preceded the establishment of APEC by almost a decade. At the same time, formal institutionalization and centralization of capacities for agenda setting, policy research, and regulation have been resisted. Consistent efforts have been made to socialize and positively engage the non–like-minded. Criteria for membership in economic institutions have been formulated creatively to allow for representation of nonstate actors (Taiwan and Hong Kong).

Good economic times during the 1980s and 1990s instilled a false sense of confidence and tended to moot disagreements over principles within regional institutions. With the recent disruption in the economic environment, these disagreements have come to the fore and challenged the capacities of institutions, raising questions as to their representative character and thus their adaptability and long-term viability (Ravenhill 2000).

Track 2 Security Dialogue: Major Trends, Common Characteristics

The beginning of the 1990s was a particularly opportune moment for the advancement of cooperative security and associated strategies of multilateral institution building. Asian economies were booming. Confidence in regional institutions such as ASEAN and the APEC forum was high. No security crises, either domestic or regional, loomed to threaten the region's stability. At the same time, states began to realize that the Cold War security architecture would not suffice. New thinking and new options were required. This set the stage for the surge in Track 2 security dialogue activities, its momentum emanating largely from the institutions and processes already firmly established in Southeast Asia and supported by multilateralists such as Canada and Australia. Although less hospitable ground for such initiatives was found in Northeast Asia, here too there were significant shifts in attitudes toward multilateralism. In South Asia, by contrast, geopolitical conditions and entrenched hostility sustained an atmosphere allowing only tentative efforts at dialogue.

Each subregional environment in the Asia Pacific is itself a unique security complex—a blend of historical experiences of conflict and conquest, cultural affinities and tensions, perceptions of threat, and combinations of regime types. Before contrasting their quite different experiences, however, it is useful to step back and reflect on regionwide similarities of the Asia Pacific Track 2 record of the last decade. These common features may be consolidated around nine points:

1. Track 2 security dialogue multilateralism was motivated by the perceived need to engage both the United States and China in the region's security architecture. The formation of the ARF and CSCAP in the mid-1990s, supported by these two major powers, thus has been the landmark in post–Cold War security-cooperation institution building in the region.

2. The nonmajor powers looked to multilateral forums to voice their individual and collective interests. The states of Southeast Asia, working through ASEAN, sought to foster the formation and management of regional security institutions. In short, ASEAN was the primary engine of the Track 2 process.

3. The "soft multilateralism" of Track 2 processes ensured a minimalist approach to institution building—inhibiting the establishment of bureaucratic capacities, independent secretariats, or monitoring or action capabilities in both Track 1 and Track 2 formations.

4. Membership in Track 2 institutions is confined to states. Security-oriented institutions such as CSCAP have no counterpart to the representation granted Taiwan and Hong Kong in regional economic institutions.

5. The Track 2 enterprise has remained an essentially state-centric process. Individuals—whether from governments, think tanks, universities, businesses, or NGOs—are chosen to participate in Track 2 forums as national representatives. (This does not mean they necessarily advocate national policy positions.)[22]

---

[22]An exception to this rule was created in the agreement negotiated with China, upon its join-

6. The security issues considered in Track 2 forums continue to be defined largely by states. The various elements of comprehensive security beyond traditional military threats have gained a place on the agenda, but internal security matters have been kept off the table.[23]

7. Inclusion of the non–like-minded has been a consistent priority in Track 2 processes and has shown results. Laos, Vietnam, Burma, and North Korea have all been engaged in multilateral forums. Lines of regional membership have been drawn, however. The Asia Pacific of Track 2 includes India but purposely omits the rest of South Asia.

8. Track 2 is process-oriented and process-driven. Dialogue is seen as having intrinsic value as a confidence-building and socializing measure. From this perspective, rather than from a results-oriented outlook, Track 2 security dialogues are regarded as important and successful by most participating Asian states.

9. Economic institutional forms continue to serve as models for the design and operation of both Track 1 and Track 2 institutions.

Southeast Asia

Behera, Evans, and Rivzi (1997: 49) have outlined the key features of the essence and exceptionalism of the Southeast Asian context in this statement:

ASEAN began with a political agreement conceived at the head of state and ministerial level operating well ahead of bureaucratic institutions, policy institutes, the private sector or the general public. In a second phase, bureaucracies and policy institutes have played a major role. Only in the last decade has the private sector been a significant part of the process. The public remains only partially engaged.

Security institution building in Southeast Asia, therefore, began with a path-breaking Track 1 experiment. Chroniclers of ASEAN, notably Leifer (1996, 1999) and Acharya (2000a), point to the special combination of regional and global conditions and idiosyncratic leadership that brought the original member states together. In effect, Indonesia chose to renounce subregional dominance and join a cohort of smaller states to pursue common goals through multilateral collabo-

---

ing CSCAP. Individuals from Taiwan may be invited by the Co-Chairs of CSCAP's Working Groups to participate in these meetings. These individuals, however, must be on a list whose members are agreed upon in advance by CSCAP China and the CSCAP organization. When participating in Working Group meetings, the invited Taiwanese do not sit as a CSCAP member, but rather under a rubric such as "invited" or "other" participants.

[23]But this too is changing in both Track 1 and Track 2 forums. At the ARF, for instance, Burma's domestic situation has been raised by proactive officials. Within CSCAP, the internal economic and political situation of countries such as Indonesia and the Philippines has been openly considered, indeed with the orchestration of these two respective CSCAP members. Of course, APEC finds its annual leaders' meeting increasingly focused on political/security issues of a domestic nature.

ration. Track 2 institutionalization therefore advanced in the wake of the success of official diplomacy and state-to-state cooperation—an exception to the expected sequence of Track 2 laying the groundwork for Track 1 institutions.

ASEAN ISIS was established in 1984, some seventeen years into ASEAN's existence (Stone and Nesadurai 1999). Regarded as the primary Track 2 agent of Southeast Asia, ASEAN ISIS merits special attention. In Herman Kraft's words, "Track 2 in Southeast Asia is largely synonymous with ASEAN ISIS" (2000: 345). It functions as a network of security institutions, one from each state. Its leaders are among the movers and shakers in the political life of their own states, as well as figures in the ASEAN and regional elite, acting as norm entrepreneurs and institution builders in both economic and political-security dimensions. To a substantial degree, ASEAN ISIS became a personalized institution reflecting the close relations among its directors. Its success reflects their ability to maneuver in tricky political waters as well as their abiding commitment to the Track 2 process. With its own governments, ASEAN ISIS has succeeded in gaining a direct voice in ASEAN by holding meetings each year since 1993 with both the ASEAN foreign ministers and senior officials. It therefore exercises influence at the governmental level attained by few other Track 2 institutions in the region.

ASEAN ISIS has served a critical role as an agent of socialization and identity building not only within the Southeast Asian context but even more significantly at the regional level. It has worked to engage, influence, and develop capacity in non-member countries prior to their joining the ASEAN fold. It organizes numerous meetings, including the annual Asia Pacific Round Table. It has been cautiously innovative in broadening the security agenda toward human security and human rights issues. It has also functioned as a gatekeeper, limiting the role for other institutions and restricting invitations and access to meetings (Kraft 2000: 349).

In recent years ASEAN ISIS may be reflecting the symptoms of ASEAN itself. Both have struggled with the entry of new members and the de facto two-tiered organizations that have resulted. Tensions within the network have arisen not only because of the reticence and conservatism of new members but also because of the uncertainty arising from states undergoing dramatic political upheaval (Ortuoste 2000: 5; personal interviews, June 2000). Generational shifts in leadership are also under way, as new figures look to place their own stamp on the organization. Though ASEAN ISIS has not stalled, as ASEAN has (Job 1999), its capacity for action has been slowed—thus demonstrating the vulnerability of Track 2 institutions to shifts in their larger political-security environments.

The ARF and CSCAP

Although the number and variety of regional Track 2 activities grew rapidly in the early 1990s, most of them were ad hoc and not fully inclusive. The feeling grew among the Track 2 elite that an inclusive, regularized, regional institution was needed to ensure a cumulative and lasting impact. ASEAN ISIS played a critical role in orchestrating the ASEAN project to lead the establishment of regional multilateral security institutions. (See Ortuoste 2000; Kraft 1994; Hernandez 1997.) It served as the main organizer of a series of meetings during 1991 and 1992 that brought together a select group of the region's Track 2 elite to design a lobbying strategy for what until this point had remained a vision—namely, an inclusive, regionwide Track 2 institution.[24] These efforts culminated in the Kuala Lumpur statement of 1993 establishing the Council for Security Cooperation in the Asia Pacific (CSCAP). (See Evans 1994c and Ball 1997.)

To its adherents CSCAP is "the most ambitious proposal to date for a regularized, focused, and inclusive non-governmental process on Pacific security matters" (Evans 1994d: 4). CSCAP is organized according to the design and practice of the PECC. Each member state is directed to maintain a broadly representative member committee from which delegates are selected to participate in CSCAP activities. China effectively stalled CSCAP for several years by making its participation contingent on denying direct representation to Taiwan.[25] Five working groups (Maritime Cooperation, CSBMs, Cooperative and Comprehensive Security, Transnational Crime, and North Pacific) were formed for the joint purposes of confidence building, informed debate, and development of policy proposals to be directed to the ARF. Certainly the working groups have been busy. CSCAP has established itself as a viable and valuable organization, although it too is experiencing critical scrutiny from those who want it to be more proactive.[26]

The ARF's formation followed shortly after CSCAP's establishment—the result of effective coordinated action at both official and unofficial levels. Canada, Australia, and Japan joined forces with the ASEAN states to persuade the less multilaterally inclined United States and China not to oppose the forum. The ASEAN ISIS played a key role in the establishment of the ARF (see, for instance, Hernandez 1994), not only in actively promoting its establishment but also in seeking to ensure that ASEAN maintained a central role in the ARF's direction and management. Thus ASEAN ISIS was instrumental in writing the 1995 ARF Concept Paper, a document that cemented the primacy of ASEAN norms of operation and guaranteed roles for ASEAN states in decision making.

Much emphasis has been placed on the need to establish links between CSCAP and its Track 1 counterpart, the ARF. Progress on this front has been limited, however. Although the ARF has made gestures toward CSCAP, most of

---

[24]Besides the directors of ASEAN ISIS, the group included Canadian, Australian, Japanese, Korean, and U.S. institute directors or their representatives.

[25]See note 22 above.

[26]See Ball (2000a), especially chap. 3, "Towards a Critique."

these have not gone beyond rhetorical acknowledgment of the positive support of Track 2 activities. Some promising results have been achieved on issues of maritime cooperation. However, CSCAP's singular success in this regard—what has been hailed as an "exemplary initiative" demonstrating the supportive role that Track 2 diplomacy can play for Track 1 (Ball 2000a: 49)—has been its work to overcome the logjam the ARF encountered in defining "preventive diplomacy." CSCAP ran a "workshop" on preventive diplomacy in Bangkok in 1999 and another in Singapore in 2000.[27] (See Ball and Acharya 1999.) These succeeded in producing a "working definition and statement of principles" that were subsequently taken on by the ARF, with acknowledgment to CSCAP, in 2001.[28]

As Desmond Ball observed just prior to assuming the role of CSCAP co-chair in 2000, CSCAP as a Track 2 organization contains "inherent sources of tension." Proclaiming the achievement of direct utility to the ARF as one of its central goals has diverted attention from the broad value of the confidence and community building achieved through CSCAP's ongoing program of meetings. Furthermore, it has fueled a rather sterile debate within the organization over "the issue of conceptual/policy balance" (Ball 2000a).

Northeast Asia/North Pacific

Nomenclature is important. Thus the distinction between the terms Northeast Asia and North Pacific has taken on significance—especially as it has come to be applied to Track 2 security activities. The most common label, "Northeast Asia," while obviously applying to the countries on the Asian continent, has generally counted the United States as a member of this subregional cohort that involves Japan, the two Koreas, China, Russia, and more recently also Mongolia. The term "North Pacific," by contrast, denotes a subregion with a transpacific dimension, as its members include the states of Northeast Asia, the United States, and Canada. It is the latter phrase, "North Pacific," that has been adopted by CSCAP and Canadian Track 2 activists to describe institutional working groups and initiatives.

There is a striking contrast in the differing levels of receptivity to multilateral cooperative security initiatives and associated Track 2 activities between Northeast and Southeast Asia. Even the most tentative efforts to promote multilateral institutional initiatives, official or unofficial, met strong resistance in the Cold War years. In a security complex dominated by major-power relations centered on the residual Cold War divisions of the Korean peninsula (until 2000) and on

---

[27]Note that CSCAP "workshops" are ad hoc meetings of selected individuals drawn together under the sponsorship of one or more CSCAP member committees. They are not meetings of CSCAP's regular Working Groups.

[28]The author is indebted to Ralph Cossa for clarification on this issue.

conflict over the Taiwan Strait, traditional logics of deterrence and instruments of alliance have prevailed.[29] Nevertheless one can point to two notable developments over the last decade in the Northeast Asia security order. The first concerns the evolving character of major-power relations, particularly those involving China and the United States. Although their bilateral relationship continues to reverberate with the tensions inherent in a situation where a rising regional power encounters a dominant global actor, Washington and Beijing have collaborated to devise solutions. Certainly this has been evident in the management of the various crises instigated by North Korea. One senses as well that a tacit agreement was reached between the two after the 1995–96 crises concerning Taiwan. Some analysts have gone so far as to speak of an informal concert of powers, including Japan and at times Russia, operating in Northeast Asia (Acharya 1999). They point to the establishment of KEDO, the initiative of the Four-Party Talks, and the direct and indirect coordination of humanitarian assistance to North Korea as examples of concert behavior. But as Acharya points out (Chap. 6 in this volume), these efforts, though multilateral, are largely functional arrangements devised as ad hoc responses to crises. The antipathy among the major powers toward establishment of an inclusive, subregional, Track 1 security institution remains. Although a long-term resolution of the Korean peninsula problem undoubtedly will require setting up a major multilateral institutional structure, recent calls for a Track 1 consultative mechanism with up to seven members (including Mongolia) have not received support.

A quite different picture emerges when one turns to the Track 2 dimension of Northeast Asian/North Pacific relations. Here one can point to significant advances in cooperative security, confidence building, and multilateral security institutionalization over the last decade. It was not surprising that Canada has emerged as a vocal norm entrepreneur in Track 2 diplomacy in this subregional context. Seeking a regional voice—but with limited financial and human resources and finding that official, multilateral security institutionalization was firmly resisted—the Canadian government in the early 1990s focused its efforts on opening Track 2 channels. Thus its North Pacific Cooperative Security Dialogue (1991–93) broke new ground (Dewitt and Evans 1993). Though it did not succeed in establishing a subregional dialogue institution—the general feeling was that it was far ahead of its time—it did set in motion networks of contacts that flourished throughout the balance of the decade. It also introduced a set of policy-oriented academics who rapidly became accepted as members of the regional Track 2 elite.

[29]For a sophisticated examination of Northeast Asian economic, political, and security dynamics, see Akaha (1999).

With the removal of Cold War barriers, the opening of official bilateral relations among the states of Northeast Asia (excepting North Korea until very recently) set in motion a corresponding tide of Track 2 bilateral and trilateral consultations among institutes and think tanks that continues to flourish. Government attitudes toward Track 2 multilateral security mechanisms, however, were another matter. Washington, in particular, was vocal in its skepticism about their utility—"solutions in search of a problem," in the words of one senior U.S. official. In Tokyo and Beijing, for different reasons, multilateral forums were rejected as inappropriate for the discussion of bilateral security matters. Gradually, however, these attitudes altered. By 1993, President Clinton was endorsing "the promotion of new multilateral regional dialogues on the full range of common security challenges" (Cossa 1996: 29). Chinese attitudes evolved, too, as Beijing began to realize it could advance its interests and gain regional influence through participation in Track 2 activities.

But in relative terms Northeast Asia/North Pacific still lagged in its support for multilateral security dialogues.[30] CSCAP's establishment of its North Pacific Working Group (NPWG) provided the first inclusive Track 2 vehicle. It remains the subregion's only "full-house" security dialogue, having consistently engaged North Korean and Mongolian participation in its meetings.[31] However, the NPWG realizes both the advantages and disadvantages of this full participation. On the one hand, it has promoted mutual understanding of the threat perceptions and security concerns of all sides. On the other hand, it has had to restrict its agenda to consideration of general and nonsensitive matters and thus has not produced policy papers setting out new initiatives. And because of sensitivity, particularly China's, to the consideration of self-defined "internal" security matters, issues such as the Taiwan Strait cannot be brought to the table.

Note should be made of another prominent security dialogue forum: the Track 1.5 Northeast Asia Cooperation Dialogue (NEACD). Administered through the University of California's Institute on Global Conflict and Cooperation, the NEACD appears in the eyes of some Asian states to remain a U.S.-led activity. It took up the reins following the Canadian NPCSD initiative but has not sustained itself as an inclusive institution: Canada has been excluded from membership; North Korea has not participated beyond attendance at its initial planning session. As a Track 1.5 dialogue mechanism, the NEACD avowedly seeks to advance, if not itself become, a Track 1 forum.

---

[30]Figures calculated from *Multilateralism, Regional Security* (Cossa 1996: 28) indicate that at the 1995 and 1996 peak periods of regional Track 2 activity less than a quarter of the cataloged multilateral initiatives focused on Northeast Asia/North Pacific.

[31]Reports on CSCAP North Pacific Working Group meetings may be accessed through www.iir.ubc.ca.

South Asia

South Asia remains essentially inhospitable to Track 2 diplomacy. By and large, subregional conditions fail to meet the minimal levels of trust and incentives for official and unofficial interaction necessary to support Track 2 security dialogue processes. The geopolitical asymmetry of South Asia, unlike Southeast Asia, has not been overcome. India's dominance of economic, political, and security matters has increased in the post–Cold War period. Hostility between the key actors, India and Pakistan, is sustained by ongoing conflict and inflamed by domestic political actors.[32] Practical barriers to communication, caused by technological problems or imposed by rigid government regulations and influence over the media, inhibit people-to-people interaction across the borders.

There is no regional counterpart at the Track 2 level for the SAARC, the South Asian Track 1 institution. (See Acharya, Chap. 6 in this volume.) Indeed in sharp contrast to the other subregional contexts, the Pakistani and Indian governments do not encourage Track 2 dialogue.[33] Serving government officials have almost always refused to take part—dismissing them as "dove to dove debates [that] lack credibility" (Behera et al. 1997: 41) or as initiatives by outsiders, e.g. the United States, seeking to meddle in subcontinental affairs (Shah 1997: 8). While there have been a number of attempts to orchestrate dialogues between retired or former government officials, these have apparently reverted to "mini-government forums" and rehearsals of standard government lines.

Nor has Track 2 dialogue among nongovernmental experts developed. Over the years, their respective governments have systematically sought to marginalize voices within their own societies that are viewed as dissenting from or challenging government security policies, such as their government's nuclear stances (Nizamani 2000), or their hardline stances on the Kashmir problem. As Shah (1997: 8) states:

In both the countries, track one and track two rarely interact. The bureaucracies on both sides have an interest in maintaining the status quo and are suspicious of nongovernmental dialogue as it poses a threat to their monopoly over bilateral interactions.

---

[32]Acharya, in Chapter 6 of this volume, considers the nature and record of the South Asian Track 1 institution, the SAARC. The discussion of Track 2 activities in this chapter is limited to the India-Pakistan situation, leaving aside Sri Lanka and Bangladesh. Certainly, various attempts, official and unofficial, initiated from South Asia and by outsiders, have been made to end the tragic Sri Lankan civil war. At the time of writing, a ceasefire proposal brokered by the Norwegian Foreign Ministry appeared to hold out some hope.

[33]This discussion draws heavily on Behera, Evans, and Rivzi (1997). Their cataloging of the nonofficial dialogue activities in South Asia is, to the author's knowledge, the only systematic effort of its kind. Their accounting stops with 1996. The *Dialogue Monitor* referred to in note 6 and elsewhere does not take into account subregional South Asia activities. It does, however, monitor the participation of South Asian members in regional dialogues.

Those from both inside and outside the subcontinent who look to the prospect and potential of ultimately establishing a viable Track 2 security dialogue process on the subcontinent, have looked instead to the initiation of "unofficial" dialogue activities as a starting point. Indeed, a substantial number of unofficial dialogues (perhaps forty to fifty) have been organized (usually with the direct or indirect support of outside institutions such as the Ford Foundation) to bring together leading citizens from various walks of life in an effort to establish better understanding and a common ground for reconciliation. Some reach back to the 1950s, but most are recent formations of the 1990s that Behera, Evans, and Rivzi attribute to a changing social and political climate, which evidences some positive prospects for progress. Thus, while state-to-state security relations may remain in stasis (and indeed lurch from crisis to crisis in the post-1998 nuclear environment), the economic engagement and the opening of society to the outside world, particularly by India, move forward quickly. Regional nongovernment elites are becoming more attuned to transnational and unconventional security issues. Behera, Evans, and Rivzi cite the influence of the diaspora of highly educated South Asian students who, from their places of employment abroad or upon their return to the subregion, voice their frustration with what they regard as outmoded security and defense postures. For the generation of the younger, urban, educated, middle-class aspirants, located on or off the subcontinent, increasingly, government elites are regarded as part of the problem—and thus to be sidestepped rather than engaged in dialogue. The hope for change, therefore, is seen to lie in establishing people-to-people dialogue between "younger," engaged professionals[34] and efforts to bring experts together to solve functional problems, such as water distribution or environmental concerns, rather than attempts to tackle directly the conduct of official/nonofficial Track 2 security dialogues as they are found elsewhere in the region. A prime example of the former is the workshops sponsored by the Regional Centre for Strategic Studies (RCSS) in Colombo, which since 1997 have been bringing together selected cohorts of "third generation" professionals from the private sector, academe, NGOs, and the media to "create a network for sustained interaction . . . to [facilitate] the evolution of alternative approaches with a regional perspective, [and] . . . advance the cause of cooperation, conflict resolution and conflict management in the region."[35]

While there has at times been speculation that the heightening of tensions to crisis levels on the subcontinent may crystallize the need for tension reduction

[34]Of course, one must always be cognizant of how the designation of someone as "young" is a subjective determination that varies considerably in the cultures on both sides of the Pacific.
[35]See the www.rcss.org website.

and confidence-building activities, there appears to be little evidence in the aftermath of the 1998 nuclear tests, the Kargil incident of 1999, and the events after September 11, 2001, that any sustained Track 2 security dialogue processes have taken hold.

Finally, South Asia's place in the regional context of multilateral security cooperation is very restricted. India is an invited participant in both Track 1 (the ARF) and Track 2 (CSCAP) institutions. Indeed Behera, Evans, and Rivzi (1997) note the increased participation of South Asians in these and other regional settings. But issues of interstate or intrastate security in South Asia are not on these agendas. India is neither willing to take part in such discussions nor amenable to extending membership in regional institutions to the other South Asian states.[36] Nor are the members of regional institutions, such as the ARF and CSCAP, interested in inviting Pakistan, Bangladesh, or Sri Lanka to join them, presumably seeking to avoid entanglement in the intractable interstate conflicts of South Asia but also to avoid the implications of bringing the tensions arising from political/religious societal conflict more directly into their institutions. In sum, South Asia has been and is likely to remain largely isolated from the broad impact of the evolving norms and confidence-building practices of Asia Pacific security regionalism.

Track 2: Record, Achievements, and Future

Although Track 2 activities, by virtue of their unofficial character, informality, and largely ad hoc nature, are difficult to track in a complete and systematic fashion, an attempt has been made to chart Asia Pacific multilateral security dialogue over the course of the 1990s. The data in the *Dialogue Monitor* yield useful observations regarding general trends and patterns.

Preliminary Data and Patterns

Table 7.2 and Figure 7.1, respectively, provide a tabular and plotted summary of Track 1 and Track 2 dialogue activities from 1993 to 2000. The overall pattern is striking. The peak years of activity were 1994 and 1995.[37] The frequency of Track 2 events rose dramatically prior to 1994, fell off quickly, and then stabilized to about half of the previous high level. Track 1 activity shows a quite different pattern: building quickly in the early 1990s but remaining relatively stable since then.

[36]Indeed, CSCAP India boycotted CSCAP meetings for a period of two years after CSCAP passed a resolution commenting negatively upon its and Pakistan's nuclear testing in 1998.

[37]One should be reluctant to subject these data to extensive interpretation, however, given the extent of nonreporting that may be involved.

TABLE 7.2

*Multilateral Track 1 and Track 2 Meetings on
Asia Pacific Security Issues*

Year	Governmental meetings: Track 1	Nongovernmental meetings: Track 2
1993	3	34
1994	19	93
1995	23 (9)[a]	85 (21)
1996	18 (3)	70 (28)
1997	17 (2)	46 (12)
1998	11 (2)	49 (10)
1999	17 (15)	38 (9)
2000[b]	17	49

NOTE: These figures should be regarded as indicative of trends, not precise data. Information about meetings is provided to the *Dialogue Monitor* on a voluntary basis; there is no "official" registrar of Track 2 meetings.

[a]The figures in parentheses refer to "reserve" meetings that do not fit the normal requirements of the two categories. That is, they may be bilateral rather than multilateral or deal primarily with countries outside the Asia Pacific region. See *Dialogue Monitor*, no. 3, Aug. 1996.

[b]Reserve entries are not included for 2000.

There could be several explanations for this main finding. None is particularly satisfactory, however, or capable of being confirmed on the basis of current data. One conclusion is that Asia was simply the hot topic of think tanks, foundations, and academics during the immediate post–Cold War period. After an initial surge of activity and attention, perhaps other topics or regions captured the spotlight for sponsorship, funding, and attendance. Or instead of representing the rise and fall of a fad, perhaps these numbers reflect a rise in regional confidence levels and a general sense of regional peace and stability. Perhaps observers concerned with the prospect of the Asia Pacific security order unraveling after the Cold War came instead to regard the region by 1995 as having weathered the storm. (This logic would also suggest an upsurge in activity around the storm of the Asian financial crisis, but this is not seen in the data.) Perhaps more intuitively satisfying is the explanation that the establishment of the ARF and CSCAP resulted in the consolidation of Track 2 activities into patterns of regular meetings of the same groups. Thus, for example, the five CSCAP working groups now hold, on average, two Track 2 meetings per year; the ARF schedules its ministerial interssessional and working group meetings on a regular basis.

With regard to national participation rates, Paul Evans, director of the *Dialogue Monitor* project, offers a number of observations. European participation has risen substantially—presumably reflecting the new interest in Asia demonstrated by the formation of ASEM and its Track 2 counterpart, the CAEC. China's

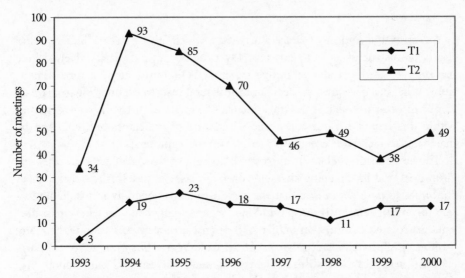

FIG. 7.1. Multilateral Track 1 and Track 2 meetings on Asia Pacific security issues. Note: The data charted are as set out in Table 7.2. Data on "reserve" meetings are not included in the Track 1 data points.

participation had also increased by 1996–97, possibly reflecting a significant change in its attitude toward regional multilateral engagement (as argued by Johnston and Evans 1999; and J. D. Yuan 1998), and signified by its entry into institutions such as CSCAP. Japanese participation appears to have picked up around the same time. North Korea took on greater involvement toward the end of the decade, though at modest levels, given its limited resource base and its apparent continued uncertainty about the pace of its external engagement. In June 2000, South Asians were estimated to be in attendance at about one-quarter of the meetings. But there were few signs of their engagement in the broad regional network of interinstitutional connections.

The thematic tone of the dialogue meetings apparently has changed as well. The connection between economic and security issues became a hot topic in late 1997. Since then the security dialogue agenda has been further broadened. Evans notes that "unconventional security issues such as transnational crime and energy, the new concept of 'human security,' and topics related to sovereignty, humanitarian intervention, and governance questions received greater play."[38]

[38]*Dialogue Monitor*, Jan. 2000–June 2000 issues; available on-line at http://www.pcaps.iar. ubc.ca/pubs.htm.

Assessment

Assessing the impact of Track 2 activities, which are by nature informal and relatively unstructured, is no easy task. Over the last several years, a lively debate has emerged in the academic and policy analysis literature along several dimensions: What has been the "success" of multilateral institution building in the Asia Pacific in general? What is the track record of Track 2 security dialogue activities within this regional framework? And what sorts of indicators and data can be marshaled to facilitate "objective" analyses on these matters?

The first question relates to the overall context of the Asia Pacific security environment and its changing character over the last decade. In this regard, there continues to be a consensus that the region remains generally inhospitable terrain for multilateral institution building, i.e., a strongly state-centric system prevails, articulated around a set of bilateral, defense arrangements, despite the many positive developments since the end of the Cold War. Thus even active supporters of security multilateralism in the region, such as Desmond Ball (2000b: 143) temper their conclusions by acknowledging that "the emerging regional security architecture will be firmly grounded in national self-reliance, with strong and important bilateral connections, and a gradually thickening but still very thin veneer of multilateralism." Admitting this, they go on (as Acharya does in Chap. 6 of this volume) to point out the remarkable changes in the regional institutional landscape. The very formation of the ARF, APEC, and their Track 2 counterparts is an empirical indicator of substantial change.

Skeptics, however, respond by arguing that institutional formation, per se, does not constitute sufficient evidence. Hence as Ellis Kraus argues: "The real test of an institution's influence is its ability to change the preferences of its constituent actors . . . and to substantially affect outcomes in the form of bringing about [state action]" (2000: 490). This, however, is a difficult challenge. While an increase in dialogue meetings and a surge of institutional activity are easily measured, it is hard to demonstrate direct links between such changes and shifts in national policy, particularly, critics demand, for states who "make a difference," i.e., the major powers. In response, advocates point to the United States and China—Washington's change of attitude regarding participation in regional multilateral security institutions (in particular the ARF) and Beijing's recently expanded participation in Track 1 and Track 2 regional security activities. In the latter regard, Alastair Johnston's recent work is notable for its carefully nuanced insights (Johnston and Evans 1999; Johnston 1999)—pointing on the one hand to evidence of socialization toward cooperative security principles and the development of specific communities among Chinese scholars and experts (especially related to arms control), but on the other hand emphasizing the manner in which Chinese participation serves instrumental national interests.[39] Ralph Cossa, among others, has charted the dynamic of post–Cold War U.S. administrations as they came to support regional, multilateral security institutions in the Asia Pacific, "provided that they complement and do not seek to replace America's bilateral alliances" (2000: 46).

An alternative approach is to focus on the issue of ideational change. In other words: Have key states changed their attitude toward cooperative security and the formation of regional and subregional multilateral nongovernmental security institutions? Is there evidence that these institutions and their associated security dialogue processes have altered the manner in which states perceive their security interests and formulate their grand strategies? These are harder questions that have perplexed analysts and policymakers alike.[40] In general, however, there appears to be acceptance that attitudinal shifts have been set in motion (certainly within Southeast Asia and within Northeast Asia, including on the Korean peninsula after the 2000 summit). Specifically, and most importantly, the major powers, over the course of the decade, have altered their stance toward cooperative security and associated regional institutional mechanisms, at both Track 1 and Track 2 levels. As David Capie (2002) argues, the promotion of cooperative security, multilateral institutionalism, and associated Track 2 modalities, served to create a "normative social environment" where the reputational costs and advantages to the United States and China were altered, "especially when weighed against the relatively undemanding institutional form" of multilateral dialogues and soft institutions. He concludes by asserting that "to be a legitimate member of the emerging Asia-Pacific community required a commitment to a certain set of Asia-Pacific norms. Track 2 [processes and institutions] helped to make clear to them what the rules of that alternative regional order [could] be, i.e., non-

---

[39]Shulong Chu (2001) states the Chinese position very succinctly: "The Chinese have accepted the multilateralism forums on regional security dialogue and have become comfortable with the processes. However, they are not ready and do not want to see the ARF and the regional security processes going into any serious discussion on specific security issues related to China, such as the Taiwan Straits and South China Sea disputes."

[40]Alstair Johnston has taken some important first steps toward sorting out the conceptual and empirical issues associated with attempting to distinguish between change in state behavior due to persuasion (i.e., socialization due to factors of identity, culture, and ideology) or social influence (i.e., inducement of behavior conforming to norms caused by the distribution of social rewards and punishments). While his arguments cannot be pursued further here, his central idea is that the design and process of institutions are critical to creating effective environments for socializing actors to redefine their interests. Furthermore, his suggestion that the most effective environments for this purpose would be "informal, weakly institutionalized, [and] consensus-based" has a distinct resonance with the Track 2 logic of the Asia Pacific (2001: 511).

threatening, inclusive, soft-institutionalism," that did not impinge on either their national or bilateral core security interests.[41]

The Benefits and Shortcomings of the Track 2 Process

Track 2 diplomacy cannot be viewed as a self-contained process. Its scope for action and room for innovation are largely determined by the parameters of the overall Asia Pacific security situation: the geopolitical distribution of power, the impact of global economic and political forces on the region, the climate for co-operation among the major powers, and more. Expectations must be tempered by reality and appreciation of the constraints faced by regional Track 2 norm entrepreneurs. But then what criteria should be employed to assess the success of Track 2 within these circumscribed boundaries?

Again, one can point to the formation of institutions themselves as markers. However, this raises a tricky question. How was the process supposed to have proceeded? From unofficial, informal interactions to the formation of Track 2 institutions, which in turn are to set the stage for Track 1 institutions? This certainly is the implicit, if not explicit, assumption found in much of the literature on Track 2. But the Asia Pacific experience has contradicted this model at key junctures, while affirming it at others. Thus, for instance, ASEAN, a Track 1 institution, preceded the formation of ASEAN ISIS. But once established, ASEAN ISIS played a role in the establishment of the ARF and CSCAP. CSCAP, itself, however, was not responsible for the creation of the ARF and really only became functional a couple of years following its formation. The relationship between Track 1 and Track 2 institutionalization, therefore, is symbiotic; but it has not been linear or consistent (as could be expected of processes heavily influenced at times by key personalities or small cohorts and/or by sharp structural changes in domestic or regional economic or security factors).

Another approach could be to assess the results of Track 2 institutions according to the institutional goals they set for themselves. Thus the ARF should be evaluated according to its three-stage progression from confidence building to preventive diplomacy to conflict resolution. (See, for instance, Evans 2000b; Khoo 1999; Ball and Acharya 1999.) CSCAP in turn should be evaluated according to goals of advancing the norms of cooperative security, confidence building, inclusivity, and positive support for the ARF. Both Ball (2000a, 2000b) and Simon (2001) have recently undertaken just this task. Ball focuses much of his attention on the products of CSCAP's Working Groups, pointing out the work of the CSBM Working Group in breaking the logjam on the defining of preventive diplomacy (and later forwarding this to the ARF) and the Maritime Working

---

[41]The quote is from a personal communication with the author, Jan. 2002.

Group's production of several codes of conduct memorandum on naval and ocean matters, as specific achievements in connecting the ARF and CSCAP. But both Ball (2000b) and Evans (2000b: 165) agree that CSCAP's major success has been "in establishing process norms, legitimating multilateral discussion, and the habits of dialogue."

Simon (2001: 5) takes a somewhat different tack, setting out four criteria for CSCAP performance: (1) production of new concepts and proposals, (2) gaining the attention of decision makers, (3) sparking interest in an international, attentive public, and (4) demonstrating "enough shelf-life that some of the principal concepts and proposals remain part of the international dialogue." He, like Ball, focuses attention on the linkage between CSCAP and the ARF. All told, his assessment is mixed: on balance, CSCAP as a Track 2 "epistemic community" has played a significant positive role. However, the report card is not entirely positive. "The most important CSCAP shortcomings echo the ARF's limitations" in its failure to have grappled with the significant security tension spots in the region such as the Taiwan Strait or to have ameliorated the militarization of Northeast Asia (Simon 2001: 28).

In summary, a quick review of the positive features and drawbacks of the Track 2 security dialogue process that has developed through the last decade is in order. Proponents point to six positive features:

1. The norms and modalities of Track 2 activities advance the common interests of all Asia Pacific states in enhancing the stability of the region's security architecture. From the major-power perspective, they supplement and reinforce the bilateral foundations of the regional order. For the other states in both Southeast Asia and the North Pacific/Northeast Asia, the multilateral character of Track 2 processes mitigates the bilateral bias and exclusionary tendencies of the larger players.

2. Virtually all participants and analysts of Track 2 cite its most important role as a socialization mechanism. Track 2 institutions have notably engaged the non–like-minded, shifted the attitudes of the skeptical, and built habits of dialogue. Over the course of a decade there have been changes in the patterns of communication among former adversaries. Though historical legacies and culturally rooted antipathies persist, especially in Northeast Asia and South Asia, their impact at the regional policy debate level has been dampened.

3. The multilateral settings of Track 2 institutions consistently bring together representatives from all countries regardless of the state of their bilateral relations at any particular moment. Thus face-to-face contact is maintained. The opportunity is there, and often used, to open backdoor lines of communication that avoid the spotlight of Track 1 diplomacy.

4. The informality of Track 2 institutions provides another sort of cover as well. Freed from the strictures of having to recite their government's policy, indeed discouraged from doing so, participants have greater latitude to advance new initiatives and vet policy options in an academic fashion.

5. Track 2 institutions have promoted a broad understanding of security and challenged traditional thinking that focuses exclusively on external and military security threats. The Track 2 agenda has become increasingly oriented toward comprehensive security and cooperative security concerns.

6. The ongoing level of Track 2 activities has fostered the engagement of a core group of policy elites. Kraft observes: "This is of great importance in a region where personal bonds underlie positive relations between governments as well as provide the basis for intellectual and policy exchanges" (2000: 346).

Opposition to the conduct of Track 2 diplomacy in the Asia Pacific largely dissipated during the 1990s. The view once held in many foreign ministries—that Track 2 efforts are at best irrelevant and even counterproductive to the management of security affairs—has largely been dispelled. Only in South Asia does one regularly encounter the dismissal of Track 2 activities as those of naive meddlers and amateurs—"well-intentioned people wasting their time and ours" (Behera et al. 1997: 32).

Instead, the criticisms of Track 2 come from those who believe there is an important role for a Track 2 agenda but are concerned with the directions and progress achieved to date. While acknowledging the constraints facing Track 2 initiatives in the Asia Pacific, critics express increasing frustration that the Track 2 agenda has become too narrow, that Track 2 has become too closely aligned with government, that Track 2 institutions are too limited in their capacity to undertake meaningful tasks, and that Track 2 has become too elitist, that is, isolated from broad social movements and security concerns. Closer attention is merited for each of these concerns: agenda, independence, capacity, and detachment.

Agenda. Observers expected Track 2 forums to expand the security agenda beyond its traditional concentration on interstate military matters while at the same time promoting unconstrained debate over contemporary security problems on which governments were deadlocked in their official channels. For different reasons, neither aim has been accomplished. By vigorously protecting what they regard as the bilateral character of their big security problems, states such as China have effectively blocked consideration of matters such as Taiwan and the South China Sea in regional Track 2 settings.[42] As for the first aim—broadening

---

[42]Governments have varied in their rigidity and consistency on this point. Although China supported the Indonesia/Canada workshop series on the South China Sea, it has opposed consideration of South China Sea issues by CSCAP. North Korea has vacillated in its willingness to have

the security agenda—Track 2 has opened this door and brought issues of unconventional security into the spotlight, especially transnational crime and its role in illegal trafficking of drugs, money, and people.[43] But critics do not see the innovative thinking and translation to action that they anticipated. Increasingly Track 2 forums are being faulted for rehearsing the same topics.

Independence. Track 2 institutions, by definition, are engaged in a delicate balancing act. On the one hand, their success depends on maintaining sufficiently close relations with governments to exercise influence. On the other hand, by becoming too closely intertwined with the official side Track 2 runs the risk of being co-opted or directed by Track 1. Kraft characterizes this as Track 2's "autonomy dilemma" (2000: 1). Government influence over Track 2 takes various forms. In some countries, all representatives to Track 2 activities are government employees expected to articulate government policies. In virtually every country, Track 2 institutions and their participants in regional events are dependent on government funding. Even if this funding is provided in a hands-off manner, it places Track 2 entities in a vulnerable position vis-à-vis the priorities of new ministers or governments.[44]

Capacity. Track 2 suffers from an extreme form of the Asia Pacific allergy to formal institutionalization. Reluctant, in the first instance, to create Track 1 institutions with any independent authority or sovereignty-restricting powers, Asian states appear even less willing to give their Track 2 counterparts any decision-making or investigative or monitoring capabilities. The economic and political crises of the late 1990s exposed not only the lack of political will by Asia Pacific states to mobilize their regional institutions but also the abject inability of these institutions to respond before, during, or after the crisis hit. This condition is reinforced by the "institutional tethering" of Track 2 to ASEAN—not only in the literal sense of having ASEAN institutes as secretariats for many Track 2 organizations but also in the figurative sense of imposing ASEAN norms of management style.

KEDO discussed in CSCAP meetings, possibly reflecting its attitude of the moment regarding KEDO-DPRK relations and the broader context of U.S.-DPRK relations.

[43]At time of writing, there are indications that the events of September 11, 2001, and the subsequent war on terrorism against the Taliban and Al Qaeda, coupled with revelations of the latter's activities in Southeast Asia, may have energized Track 2 (and Track 1) institutions. In particular, CSCAP's Crime Working Group has been especially productive. It is too early to tell, however, what lasting results these Track 2 activities may effect.

[44]One very active participant in CSCAP meetings comments that government officials at these meetings "usually make it clear that they are there to hear other views [and] to put forth and defend government positions (despite an occasional trial balloon). Even those who start off with 'this is my personal view' invariably then spout the party line. They are presumed to be doing exactly that. In fact, when one doesn't, it causes some confusion" (personal communication with the author, Jan. 2002).

Detachment. Track 2 institutions have come to be perceived as exclusive clubs (Maull 1994). To many observers, the advantages derived from engagement of elites with privileged access to their respective governments have become over-shadowed in recent years by impressions that Track 2 institutions have become divorced from civil society. To some extent this is a generational phenomenon; in many instances, national Track 2 representatives have held these roles for dec-ades. It is also a reflection of shifting political climates. As the regimes that man-aged postcolonial nation building and economic transformation are being re-placed—usually by overtly populist leaders and more democratic, more transpar-ent, and more domestically preoccupied governments—the established elites of academe, the private sector, and their think tanks run the risk of losing credibility and influence in their societies.

The Future of Track 2 Diplomacy

In sum, then, the movement toward a cooperative security perspective, the surge in multilateral dialogue activities, and the establishment of regional security institutions with the reluctant, then positive, engagement of the major powers in multilateral security institutions during the first half of the 1990s must be appre-ciated as a major turning point in the evolution of the security order of the Asia Pacific. But these achievements must be appreciated as well, as the product of a specific configuration of structural, economic, political, and individual factors. In effect, at this juncture the rising momentum of economic growth and economic regionalism coincided with the abandonment of Cold War ideological antago-nisms and regional security threats.[45] This confluence created a climate receptive to new ideas, to regional institutional experimentation, and to the initiatives of a cohesive and coordinated cohort of elites acting as norm entrepreneurs to ad-vance security multilateralism. The result was a surge in Track 2 diplomacy cul-minating in the formation of the ARF and its Track 2 counterpart CSCAP. These landmark events structured and regularized what until then had been a fairly spontaneous phenomenon.

These opportune conditions, of course, could not be expected to continue. The economic crisis undercut Asian unity concerning economic priorities and regional strategies and exposed the vulnerability of the underpinnings of domes-tic security and stability. By the end of the 1990s, elite consensus was fraying. The effects of generational change and forces of democratization and globalization have brought to the fore issues (such as intervention) and new concepts (such as human security) that do not sit comfortably within the accepted ideational framework. Nor can they be easily taken on by current institutional mechanisms,

---

[45]The exception, of course, remained on the Korean peninsula.

either Track 1 or Track 2. (See Acharya 2000a and 2000b; Job 1999.) We are entering another transitional period. Whether institutions such as ASEAN ISIS and CSCAP can adapt from within to accommodate these new pressures for change remains to be seen.

There is a growing sense that a new mode of security dialogue and transnational activity must emerge—one whose premises may challenge aspects of open economic regionalism and expand notions of security to encompass elements of civil society in what some have already come to call a Track 3 process. Paul Evans (1997: 4) comments:

[Track 3 refers] to dialogues in which (a) representatives of civil society, especially NGO's, play a more prominent role; (b) government domination of the agenda is less pronounced and discussions, while policy relevant, are more frank and academic in character; (c) there is more room for inclusion of participants [e.g.] from Taiwan who are constrained from full participation in Track 2 processes like CSCAP; and (d) there is the ability to deal flexibly and openly with sensitive questions, including cross-Straits relations and specific territorial disputes.[46]

Encompassing the voices and interests of civil society must become a priority for Track 2 if it is to sustain its role in shaping the future of the Asia Pacific security order (Lizee 2000). Tentative steps are being taken to counter the perception that ASEAN and related Track 1 institutions are "government clubs" and that Track 2 processes are monopolized by security considerations largely irrelevant to the concerns of Asian societies. Thus December 2000 saw the inauguration of an ASEAN People's Assembly (Soeryodiningrat 2000).

Track 2 needs to develop more open and supple modalities that allow for the inclusion of Track 3 voices without their being marginalized or co-opted (Lizee 2000: 100). In turn, the NGOs and civil society movements need to adopt a less adversarial relationship to security regionalism. Otherwise their voices will continue to be relegated to protests in the streets rather than seats at the table and positive roles within the institutions of the Asia Pacific of the twenty-first century.

Works Cited

Acharya, Amitav. 1994. *An Arms Race in Post–Cold War Southeast Asia?* Singapore: Institute of Southeast Asian Studies.
———. 1997. "Ideas, Identity, and Institution-Building: From the 'ASEAN Way' to the 'Asia-Pacific' Way?" *Pacific Review* 10(3): 319–46.
———. 1999. "A Concert of Asia?" *Survival* 41(3) (Autumn): 84–101.
———. 2000a. *The Quest for Identity*. Singapore: Oxford University Press.

[46]For a definition of Track 3, see Paul Evans in *Dialogue Monitor* (1997: 4); available on-line at http://www.pcaps.iar.ubc.ca/drm/trendreports.pdf.

————. 2000b. *Constructing a Security Community in Southeast Asia: ASEAN and the Problem of Regional Order*. London: Routledge.

Akaha, Tsuneo. 1999. *Politics and Economics in Northeast Asia: Nationalism and Regionalism in Contention*. New York: St. Martin's Press.

Ball, Desmond. 1994. "A New Era in Confidence-Building: The Second-Track Process in the Asia/Pacific Region." *Security Dialogue* 25(2): 157–76.

————. 1997. *The Council for Security Cooperation in the Asia Pacific: Its Record and Its Prospects*. Canberra Papers on Strategy and Defence, no. 139. Canberra: Strategic and Defence Study Centre, Australian National University.

————. 2000a. *The Council for Security Cooperation in the Asia Pacific (CSCAP): Its Record and Its Prospects*. Canberra: Strategic and Defence Studies Centre, Research School of Pacific and Asian Studies, Australian National University.

————. 2000b. "Multilateral Security Cooperation in the Asia-Pacific Region: Challenges in the Post-Cold War Era." In Hung-mao Tien and Tun-jen Cheng, eds., *The Security Environment in the Asia-Pacific*. Armonk, N.Y.: M. E. Sharpe.

————, and Amitav Acharya, eds. 1999. *The Next Stage: Preventive Diplomacy and Security Cooperation in the Asia-Pacific Region*. Canberra: Strategic and Defence Studies Centre, Australian National University.

Behera, Navnita Chadha, Paul Evans, and Gowher Rivzi. 1997. *Beyond Boundaries: A Report on the State of Non-Official Dialogues on Peace, Security, and Cooperation in South Asia*. Toronto: University of Toronto–York University Joint Centre for Asia Pacific Studies.

Busse, Nikolas. 1999. "Constructivism and Southeast Asian Security." *Pacific Review* 12(1): 39–60.

Buzan, Barry, and Gerald Segal. 1994. "Rethinking East Asian Security." *Survival* 36(2): 3–21.

Capie, David. 2002. "Power, Identity and Multilateralism: The United States and Regional Institutionalization in the Asia-Pacific." Ph.D. dissertation, York University.

————, and Paul Evans. 2002. *The Asia Pacific Security Lexicon*. Singapore: Institute of Southeast Asian Studies.

Chu, Shulong. 2001. "The Chinese Thinking on Asia-Pacific Regional Security Order." Unpublished manuscript, Vancouver, Canada.

Cooper, Andrew Fenton, and Kim Richard Nossal. 1993. *Relocating Middle Powers*. Vancouver: University of British Columbia Press.

Cossa, Ralph. 1996. *Multilateralism, Regional Security, and the Prospects for Track II in East Asia*. Seattle: National Bureau of Asian Research.

————. 2000. "The US Asia-Pacific Security Strategy." In Hung-mao Tien and Tun-jen Cheng, eds., *The Security Environment in the Asia-Pacific*. Armonk, N.Y.: M. E. Sharpe.

Dewitt, David. 1994. "Common, Comprehensive, and Cooperative Security." *Pacific Affairs* 7(1): 1–16.

————, and Paul Evans. 1993. *The Agenda for Cooperative Security in the North Pacific*. Conference report. Vancouver: North Pacific Cooperative Security Dialogue Research Program.

————, and Brian L. Job. 1994. "Asia Pacific Security Studies in Canada." In Paul Evans, ed., *Studying Asia Pacific Security*. Toronto: University of Toronto–York University Joint Centre for Asia Pacific Studies.

Dialogue Monitor: Inventory of Multilateral Meetings on Asia Pacific Security Issues. 1995–98.

University of Toronto–York University Joint Centre for Asia Pacific Studies, nos. 1–5, July 1995–Mar. 1998. http://www.pcaps.iar.ubc.ca/pubs.htm.

Dibb, Paul. 1995. *Towards a New Balance of Power in Asia.* Adelphi Paper 295. London: International Institute for Strategic Studies.

Djalal, Hasjim, and Ian Townsend-Gault. 2000. "Managing Potential Conflicts in the South China Sea: Informal Diplomacy for Conflict Prevention." In Chester A. Crocker, Fen Osler Hampson, and Pamela Aall, eds., *Herding Cats: Multiparty Mediation in a Complex World.* Washington: USIP.

Evans, Paul. 1994a. "The Dialogue Process on Asia Pacific Security Issues: Inventory and Analysis." In Paul Evans, ed., *Studying Asia Pacific Security.* Toronto: University of Toronto–York University Joint Centre for Asia Pacific Studies.

———, ed. 1994b. *Studying Asia Pacific Security.* Toronto: University of Toronto–York University Joint Centre for Asia Pacific Studies.

———. 1994c. "Building Security: The Council for Security Cooperation in the Asia Pacific (CSCAP)." *Pacific Review* 7(2): 125–39.

———. 1994d. "The Council for Security Cooperation in Asia-Pacific: Context and Prospects." CANCAPS Paper 2. Toronto: York University.

———. 1997. *Dialogue Monitor: Inventory of Multilateral Meetings on Asia Pacific Security Issues, Trend Reports.* University of Toronto–York University Joint Centre for Asia Pacific Studies, no. 4. http://www.pcaps.iar.ubc.ca/drm/trendreports.pdf.

———. 2000a. "ASEAN and the ARF: Cooperative Security and Its Discontents." Paper delivered to the conference on "Multilateralism, Bilateralism, and the Search for Security in Asia," Centre for International Studies, St. Anthony's College, University of Oxford.

———. 2000b. "Assessing the ARF and CSCAP." In Hung-mao Tien and Tun-jen Cheng, eds., *The Security Environment in the Asia-Pacific.* Armonk, N.Y.: M. E. Sharpe.

Finnemore, Martha, and Kathryn Sikkink. 1998. "International Norm Dynamics and Political Change." *International Organization* 52(4): 887–917.

Foot, Rosemary. 1995. "Pacific Asia: The Development of Regional Dialogue." In Louise Fawcett and Andrew Hurrell, eds., *Regionalism in World Politics: Regional Organization and International Order.* Oxford: Oxford University Press.

Hernandez, Carolina. 1994. *Track Two Diplomacy, Philippine Foreign Policy and Regional Politics.* Manila: CIDS–University of Philippines Press.

———. 1997. "Governments and NGOs in the Search for Peace: The ASEAN-ISIS and CSCAP Experience." www.focusweb.org/focus/pd/sec/hernandez.html.

Higgott, Richard. 1994. "Introduction: Ideas, Interests, and Identity in the Asia Pacific." *Pacific Review* 7(4): 367–80.

Job, Brian. 1997a. "Norms of Multilateralism in Regional Security: The Evolving Order of the Asia Pacific." Paper presented to the conference "International Norms: Origins, Significance, and Manifestations," Hebrew University, Jerusalem.

———. 1997b. "Multilateralism Matters: The Relevance of the Concept to Regional Conflict Management." In David Laake and Patrick Morgan, eds., *Regional Order: Building Security in a New World.* University Park: Pennsylvania State University Press.

———. 1999. "Is ASEAN Stalled?" Paper delivered to the annual meetings of the American Political Science Association, San Francisco.

Johnston, Alastair I. 1995. *Cultural Realism: Strategic Culture and Grand Strategy in Chinese History.* Princeton: Princeton University Press.

————. 1999. "The Myth of the ASEAN Way? Explaining the Evolution of the ASEAN Regional Forum." In H. Haftendorn, R. Keohane, and C. Wallander, eds., *Imperfect Unions: Security Institutions over Time and Space.* Oxford: Oxford University Press.

————. 2001. "Treating International Institutions as Social Environments." *International Studies Quarterly* 45(4): 487–516.

————, and Paul Evans. 1999. "China's Engagement with Multilateral Security Institutions." In Alastair I. Johnston and Robert R. Ross, eds., *Engaging China: The Management of an Emerging Power.* London: Routledge.

Katzenstein, Peter, and Nobuo Okawara. 2002. "Japan, Asian-Pacific Security, and the Case for Analytic Eclecticism." *International Security* 26(3) 153–85.

Kerr, Pauline. 1994. "The Security Dialogue in the Asia Pacific." *Pacific Review* 7(4): 397–409.

————, and Andrew Mack. 1994. "The Future of Asia-Pacific Security Studies in Australia." In Paul Evans, ed., *Studying Asia Pacific Security.* Toronto: University of Toronto–York University Joint Centre for Asia Pacific Studies.

————, Andrew Mack, and Paul Evans. 1995. "The Evolving Security Discourse in the Asia-Pacific." In Andrew Mack and John Ravenhill, eds., *Pacific Cooperation: Building Economic and Security Regimes in the Asia-Pacific Region.* Boulder, Colo.: Westview.

Khoo, How San. ed. 1999. *The Future of the ARF.* Singapore: Institute of Defence and Strategic Studies, Nanyang Technological University.

Kraft, Herman. 1994. "Security Studies in ASEAN: Trends in the Post–Cold War Era." In Paul Evans, ed., *Studying Asia Pacific Security.* Toronto: University of Toronto–York University Joint Centre for Asia Pacific Studies.

————. 2000. "The Autonomy Dilemma of Track 2 Diplomacy in Southeast Asia." *Security Dialogue* 31(3): 343–56.

Kraus, Ellis. 2000. "Japan, the US, and the Emergence of Multilateralism in Asia." *Pacific Review* 13(3): 473–94.

Leifer, Michael. 1996. *The ASEAN Regional Forum.* Adelphi Paper 302. London: International Institute for Strategic Studies.

————. 1999. "The ASEAN Peace Process: A Category Mistake." *Pacific Review* 12(1): 25–38.

Lizee, Pierre. 2000. "Civil Society and the Construction of Security in Southeast Asia: Setting the Research Agenda." In Anthony C. Mely and Mohamed Jawhar Hassan, eds., *Beyond the Crisis: Challenges and Opportunities,* vol. 2. Kuala Lumpur: ISIS Malaysia.

Maull, Hans. 1994. "Call Girls in the Old World: Of Multilateralism, Think Tanks, Dialogue Programs and Other Promiscuous Activities In and Around Europe." In Paul Evans, ed., *Studying Asia Pacific Security.* Toronto: University of Toronto–York University Joint Centre for Asia Pacific Studies.

Montville, Joseph V. 1995. "The Arrow and the Olive-Branch: A Case for Track Two Diplomacy." In John W. MacDonald and Dian B. Bendahmane, eds. *Conflict Resolution: Track Two Diplomacy.* Washington, D.C.: Institute for Multi-Track Diplomacy.

Nizamani, Haider. 2000. *The Roots of Rhetoric: Politics of Nuclear Weapons in India and Pakistan.* Westport: Praeger.

Ortuoste, Maria Consuelo. 2000. "The Establishment of the ASEAN Regional Forum." Paper presented to the Multilateral Institutions in Asia Seminar. Honolulu: Asia Pacific Center for Security Studies.

Ravenhill, John. 2000. "APEC Adrift: Implications for Economic Regionalism in the Asia Pacific." *Pacific Review* 1(2): 319–33.

Shah, Aqil S. 1997. "Non-Official Dialogue Between India and Pakistan: Prospects and Problems." ACDIS Occasional Paper. Urbana-Champaign: University of Illinois.

Simon, Sheldon W. 2001. *Evaluating Track II Approaches to Security Diplomacy in the Asia Pacific: The CSCAP Experience*. Seattle: National Bureau of Asian Research.

Soeryodiningrat, Meidyatama. 2000. "Reflections of the First APA." *Jakarta Post*, Dec. 5. www.indonesia-ottawa.org/Perspective/December/120500_JP_02.htm.

Stone, Diane, and Helen E. S. Nesadurai. 1999. "Networks, Second Track Diplomacy, and Regional Cooperation: The Experience of Southeast Asian Think Tanks." Paper presented to the Inaugural Conference on Bridging Knowledge and Policy organized by the Global Development Network, Bonn.

Wanandi, Jusuf. 1996. "The Future of ARF and CSCAP in the Regional Security Architecture." In Jusuf Wanandi, ed., *Asia Pacific After the Cold War*. Jakarta: Centre for Strategic and International Studies.

Woods, Lawrence. 1993. *Asia-Pacific Diplomacy: Nongovernmental Organizations and International Relations*. Vancouver: University of British Columbia Press.

———. 1995. "Learning from NGO Proponents of Asia-Pacific Regionalism." *Asian Survey* 35(819) (Sept.): 812–28.

Yamamoto, Tadashi, ed. 1995. *Civil Society in the Asia Pacific Community*. Singapore: Institute of Southeast Asian Studies and Japan Council of International Education.

Yuan, Jing-dong. 1998. *Chinese Perspectives on Multilateralism: Implications for Cooperative Security*. Vancouver: Institute of International Relations, University of British Columbia (typescript ms).

CHAPTER EIGHT

Economic Interdependence and Economic Cooperation

Mitigating Conflict and Transforming Security Order in Asia

MING WAN

Economic interdependence has grown significantly in the Asia Pacific within a capitalist framework since the late 1970s. Today virtually every country in the region has adopted regional and bilateral strategies of economic cooperation. It is only natural, therefore, to ask how this emerging region's economic order affects regional security order (Shirk and Twomey 1996; Harris and Mack 1997; Zoellick 1997–98; Wan 1996). This chapter examines the economic transformation of regional security. I wish to advance two main points. First, I make a commercial-liberal argument that economic interdependence and cooperation have had a stabilizing effect on the regional system. A commercial-liberal pathway is too often dismissed as failing to prevent wars. But this sets the bar too high: no known pathway has prevented war indefinitely. From a more reasonable perspective of conflict reduction, economic cooperation represents a crucial path to a stable security order by encouraging cooperation for mutual gain. Although interdependence and cooperation alone have only a limited capacity to lead countries to resolve conflicts over fundamental issues such as territorial disputes, they have indeed had a mitigating effect.

Second, although Asia-Pacific countries initially engaged in economic cooperation for realist reasons and have often adopted realist measures as principal or fallback options, cooperation and economic interdependence have transformed political configurations and, consequently, definitions and ordering of national goals. Almost all the countries in the region have made economic development a top priority—a collective trend that encourages mutual trust and confidence in economic cooperation as the best way to advance national interests. Moreover, the capitalist nature of interdependence in the region has profound implications for the regional security order. All-consuming revolutionary and counterrevolutionary security agendas have disappeared. Thus the region's economic transformation ensures a normative basis shared by key players for maintaining the present system. In the long run, a liberal economic order will also forge a legitimate security order as it transforms domestic politics in the region.

Regional Economic Interdependence and Cooperation

Economist Richard N. Cooper (1972: 159) sees interdependence as "the *sensitivity* of economic transactions between two or more nations to economic developments within those nations." Political scientists Robert Keohane and Joseph Nye define the concept as "situations characterized by reciprocal effects among countries or among actors in different countries" (Keohane and Nye 1989: 8). Economic interdependence can be measured by cross-border flows of goods, services, and money.

Globalization has replaced interdependence as the buzzword in the 1990s (Lechner and Boli 2000; Held et al. 1999; Friedman 1999). Some scholars argue that globalization is qualitatively different from interdependence. More than simply a nexus of links among distinct national economies, globalization is characterized by diminishing national boundaries (Hirst and Thompson 1999: 7–13; Clark 1999: 103–4). In parallel with globalization, regionalism too has grown since the Cold War ended (Frankel 1998; Mansfield and Milner 1997; Gamble and Payne 1996; Solingen 1998). Here I define globalization as the deepening and widening of global interdependence; regionalization is the deepening and widening of regional interdependence. Rather than dwelling on differences or similarities between interdependence and globalization, I want to focus on the empirical evidence. And because I examine regional rather than global economic integration in this chapter, interdependence offers a more flexible analytical framework.

Interdependence is also an idea about how the world is structured and how states should behave. A state's awareness of changes in international relations affects its strategic choice, which in turn affects the process of interdependence. Thus it is crucial to examine a country's economic cooperation strategies—that is, a government's strategies to realize its partners' economic objectives while advancing its own.[1]

[1]This definition is based on Keohane, who sees cooperation as a process obtaining "when the policies actually followed by one government are regarded by its partners as facilitating realization of their own objectives, as the result of a process of policy coordination" (1984: 51–52).

Regional Economic Interdependence

The Asia-Pacific region has become more interdependent economically since the late 1970s. Intraregional trade as a share of the region's total trade increased from 36 percent in 1980 to 50 percent in 1994 for East Asia and from 59 percent to 74 percent for the Asia Pacific Economic Cooperation (APEC) forum countries (Frankel 1997: 22).[2] A drastic increase in flow of capital from Japan, the United States, Europe, and the newly industrializing economies spurred this trend (Encarnation 1999; Beamish and Safarian 1999; Langhammer 1998; Van Hoesel 1999). Foreign direct investment (FDI) in East Asia increased from around $4.1 billion in 1985 to $65.5 billion in 1996 and $69.9 billion in 1998 (World Bank 2000: 56). Financial integration, measured as increased capital flow and convergence of prices and returns from financial instruments in different countries on a common currency basis, has increased in Asia, and most regional countries have become more open over the past two decades (De Brouwe 1999).[3] Moreover, production networks in Asia built by Japan and other industrial nations have significantly improved economic connections among the nations in the region (Katzenstein and Shiraishi 1997; Hatch and Yamamura 1996; Borrus et al. 2000). Regional interdependence was on full display when the financial crisis that started in Thailand in July 1997 spread like wildfire to the rest of Asia except for China and Taiwan. East Asia went up together and came down together (Pempel 1999).

A high level of intraregional trade does not necessarily mean that the Asia Pacific is becoming a trading bloc. Jeffrey Frankel (1997) has explained how the magnitude of the region's total trade, pace of economic growth, and geography affect levels of intraregional trade. Asia-Pacific trade expansion has been associated with liberalization efforts by countries in the region, especially since the mid-1980s (Drysdale et al. 1998). But as Frankel recognizes (1997: 24), levels of intraregional trade are still useful measures for other issues such as the effects of bilateral trade. This is certainly the case here. This chapter focuses on the impact of close economic ties among the region's countries, with or without regional bias, on the region's security order.

Is the regional interdependence we see today truly unusual from a historical perspective? Peter Petri points out that although East Asian interdependence measured in trade has indeed intensified since 1985, its recent increase has been

[2]Here East Asia includes Brunei, Indonesia, Malaysia, the Philippines, Singapore, Thailand, China, Hong Kong, Japan, South Korea, and Taiwan. APEC includes the eleven economies just mentioned plus the United States, Canada, Mexico, Australia, Chile, New Zealand, and Papua New Guinea.

[3]De Brouwe examined legal restrictions on the capital account, capital flows, interest rate parity, saving-investment correlations, and other measures of Japan, Australia, Hong Kong, Indonesia, South Korea, Malaysia, the Philippines, Singapore, Taiwan, and Thailand.

slight in historical terms. In fact, East Asia was less interdependent in the early 1990s than before World War II (Petri 1993).[4] If it is true that economic integration peaked in 1937, right before the breakout of war, we should not count on present-day interdependence leading to stability and peace. But economic interdependence in the region today is fundamentally different from that before the war. Prewar regional integration resulted from colonialist expansion. Japan colonized Korea and Taiwan, established an informal empire in China's Northeast (Manchuria), and penetrated Chinese treaty ports (Myers and Peattie 1984). While competing with Japan in China, Western powers colonized Southeast Asia and South Asia excepting Thailand. By 1937, France accounted for 97 percent of FDI in Indochina; the Netherlands for 71 percent in what is now Indonesia; Britain for 90 percent in Burma, 70 percent in Malaya, and 76 percent in Thailand; and the United States for 52 percent in the Philippines (Lindblad 1998). India was under Britain's firm control. By sharp contrast, current interdependence is based on willing participation of virtually every regional country.

Asia-Pacific interdependence has grown in a capitalist framework. It is true that Asian capitalist countries differ in important ways from the West concerning the government's role in the economy and that they differ among themselves in business systems (Wade 1990; Safarian and Dobson 1996). It is also true that communist governments still rule in China, Vietnam, and North Korea. But if we compare what we see today with what we observed merely thirty years ago, we must acknowledge that a capitalist economic order is prevailing. Whatever China and Vietnam label their economic reforms, they are undergoing a gradual shift to a market-based economic system—for example, both have legalized private ownership, which has grown at the expense of state ownership. Given recent positive developments in the Korean peninsula, we may also be reasonably optimistic that North Korea will follow the examples of China and Vietnam before long.

Regional and Bilateral Cooperative Strategies

Regional integration results not only from market dynamics but also from political commitments. The region's countries have adopted strategies for regional and bilateral economic cooperation. The term "strategy" is used in a loose sense here to refer mainly to a government's policy measures to achieve broad national objectives or lead the country in a certain direction. To be strategic, a country does not have to have a coherent and well-articulated approach to policy objectives. Countries in the region have created both regional and subregional economic cooperation schemes. In 1967, Indonesia, the Philippines, Malaysia,

[4]By East Asia Petri means China, Hong Kong, Japan, South Korea, Taiwan, Indonesia, Malaysia, the Philippines, Thailand, and Singapore.

Singapore, and Thailand founded the Association of Southeast Asian Nations (ASEAN)—the most successful regional organization in Asia. After admitting Brunei in 1984, Vietnam in 1995, Laos and Myanmar in 1997, and Cambodia in 1999, ASEAN now includes all the Southeast Asian countries. Inspired by ASEAN's success, seven South Asian nations formed the South Asian Association for Regional Cooperation (SAARC) in 1985, although the group has gone nowhere thanks to mutual suspicions and animosities. In 1992, ASEAN established the ASEAN Free Trade Area (AFTA) to be achieved by 2008.

APEC covers roughly the Asia-Pacific region discussed here.[5] The idea of Asian Pacific economic cooperation went through three stages. In the first period, from 1960 to 1967, Japanese thinkers such as Kajima Morinosuke and Okita Saburo advocated the idea of regional economic cooperation. In the second period, from 1968 to 1977, the idea spread to academic and business communities in other countries. In the third period, starting in 1978, regional governments became actively involved and translated ideas into policy. Efforts by Japan, Australia, and others led to the creation of APEC in 1989. China came on board two years later (Soesastro 1994; Funabashi 1999; Aggarwal and Morrison 1998). In 1993, heads of state started attending APEC annual meetings. At the 1994 Bogor meeting, APEC leaders announced a plan to create a free-trade and investment zone by 2020, although they did not specify how to achieve this goal. The Bogor Declaration was reaffirmed at the 1995 Osaka meeting. But the 1998 Kuala Lumpur meeting, the 1999 Auckland meeting, the 2000 Brunei meeting, and the 2001 Shanghai meeting made little progress on account of the Asian financial crisis and a lack of resolve among regional governments.[6]

The creation of APEC has not made subregional arrangements obsolete. In fact, new subregional groups have emerged in the Asia Pacific. In 1990, Malaysian Prime Minister Mahathir bin Mohamad proposed an East Asian Economic Group (subsequently renamed the East Asian Economic Caucus, or EAEC) that would include only East Asian economies. But faced with Washington's strong opposition and Tokyo's unwillingness to challenge the Americans at that time, the Mahathir proposal never materialized. Ironically, while opposing an East Asian trading group, the United States negotiated with Canada and Mexico to form the North American Free Trade Agreement (NAFTA), which came into effect in 1994. Washington's

[5]APEC now has twenty-one members: Australia, Brunei, Canada, Chile, China, Hong Kong, Indonesia, Japan, South Korea, Malaysia, Mexico, New Zealand, Papua New Guinea, Peru, the Philippines, Russia, Singapore, Taiwan, Thailand, the United States, and Vietnam.

[6]But in a significant departure from its traditional practice of avoiding security issues, the participants in the Shanghai APEC meeting issued a joint statement condemning the September 11, 2001, terrorist attacks on the United States and calling for cooperation against international terrorism.

perceived double standard was one reason why East Asian nations continue to explore subregional cooperation. Since 1996 the East Asian group envisioned by Mahathir has quietly taken shape in the framework of ASEAN Plus Three (China, Japan, and South Korea), which has a membership virtually identical with that of the EAEC. (Taiwan is not included in the current structure.)

Unlike Europe's integration, which began in trade, East Asia's started in finance. When financial crisis hit East Asia in 1997, Japan proposed an Asian Monetary Fund (AMF) as an East Asian solution to regional problems. The plan failed when Washington put up strong resistance owing to fears that an AMF would weaken the influence of the International Monetary Fund (IMF). Beijing declined to endorse the plan out of fear that Japan would dominate in the proposed arrangement. At ASEAN's initiation, however, ten ASEAN nations and three Northeast Asian nations (China, Japan, and South Korea) set up a currency swap scheme in Chiang Mai, Thailand, in May 2000 after earlier agreements among financial and banking officials. Although there had been similar agreements to swap and repurchase reserves, the Chiang Mai initiative established a framework for future discussion on regional monetary cooperation. The initiative was formalized during the Asian Development Bank's annual meeting in Hawaii in May 2001. Though small in scale, the currency swap agreements signed in Hawaii indicated East Asia's desire for deeper regional integration.

There have been trade initiatives as well, with more than two dozen potential new subregional trade agreements in the APEC region since the end of 1998 (Scollay and Gilbert 2001). Northeast Asian nations' changing attitudes toward subregional free-trade agreements have been particularly important. They are the only APEC members that do not belong to any subregional bloc (APEC Economic Committee 2000: 29–30). Although Tokyo traditionally saw the General Agreement on Tariffs and Trade (GATT) and its successor the World Trade Organization (WTO) as best serving its economic interests, the Ministry of International Trade and Industry made a dramatic shift in favor of regional free trade in its 1999 White Paper on Trade. As for the Chinese, at the ASEAN Plus China summit in November 2000 Premier Zhu Rongji proposed a China-ASEAN free-trade area. China and ASEAN agreed to create a free-trade area within 10 years at the following ASEAN Plus China summit in early November 2001. Studies are also being conducted in China, Japan, and South Korea for a Northeast Asia free-trade area. As the WTO and APEC have stalled in trade liberalization and as the specter of trade protectionism may rise in America and Europe, East Asians, who are highly dependent on trade, are seeking regional trade as a hedging strategy. Like people elsewhere, East Asians have become convinced of the viability of regional free-trade zones inspired by successful European integration and NAFTA (Castellano 1999; Bergsten 2000).

East Asian economic cooperation is credible because of corresponding political cooperation. In 1996, Singapore initiated the Asia-Europe Meeting (ASEM), a gathering of government and state heads from ASEAN Plus Three and European Union members, which is held every other year. In December 1997, ASEAN held the first annual summit with China, Japan, and South Korea. Since 1999 the ASEAN Plus Three summit has included regular meetings of economic and finance ministers. In 1999, Singapore initiated the East Asia–Latin American Forum (EALAF). These three tracks of political dialogue will facilitate the development of an East Asian political identity in global politics.

Governments' support for regional economic cooperation is consistent with their export-led development strategies. It is no coincidence that Japan, the first export-oriented developmental state in the region, took the lead in regional economic cooperation. In the second wave, resource-poor South Korea, Taiwan, and Singapore turned to export-led strategies in the early 1960s, partly to emulate Japan's success. In the third wave, resource-rich capitalist economies, namely Malaysia, Thailand, the Philippines, and Indonesia, shifted from a development strategy focused on exploitation of natural resources to an export-led strategy as well. In the fourth wave, by the late 1970s, emerging from a disastrous ten-year Cultural Revolution and watching an astonishing economic miracle achieved by its capitalist neighbors, China launched economic reform and opened its doors to the outside world. In the fifth wave, Vietnam followed suit with its strategy of *doi moi* (renovation) in 1986 but moved more cautiously than its northern neighbor China. Indeed Hanoi signed a trade agreement with the United States only in July 2000. India began promoting exports in the 1980s and shifted from a quasi-socialist economic system to closer ties with the global economy in 1991. Even North Korea is now reaching out for foreign trade and investment.

Most countries in the region have also adopted economic cooperative strategies in bilateral relations. What is striking about present Asia-Pacific international relations is that the region's countries see the economic success of their neighbors as crucial to their own economic welfare. The Asian financial crisis is a case in point. Washington was instrumental in IMF bailout packages for East Asia totaling $100 billion. Tokyo claims to have offered more than $80 billion of aid to East Asia. Despite domestic pressure, Beijing kept its promise not to depreciate the yuan, partly to avoid aggravating the economic difficulties of its neighbors. And everyone in the Asia Pacific, including China, wanted Japan to revive its economy quickly and lead the region out of its most serious economic crisis in decades. Realists would have a hard time explaining why countries want their rivals to prosper economically.

Japan has the most developed strategy of economic cooperation in the region (Nishigaki and Shimomura 1997; Koppel and Orr 1993). Tokyo has a broad definition of economic cooperation, which includes not just official aid but also private capital flows. Unlike the United States, which combined military and economic assistance in the early years, Japan has relied almost exclusively on economic cooperation as the instrument of its foreign policy. Japan has been the largest aid donor to East Asia since the 1970s—rising from $502 million in 1975 (59 percent of its total aid) to $3.6 billion in 1998 (42.4 percent)—and it has been the top donor for virtually every Asian nation (see MOFA). Consistent with its notion of economic cooperation, Japan's official development assistance (ODA) has paved the way for massive private capital flows into the region, capital welcomed by recipient countries as facilitating their economic development objectives (Wan 2001a).

Noncommunist countries have often used economic cooperation to engage communist countries, hoping to integrate them into a capitalist economic system and moderate their security behavior. The United States, Japan, and other Asia-Pacific countries have assisted China's modernization drive since the late 1970s and have continued to engage the country even when Beijing became more assertive in the Taiwan Strait and the South China Sea in the 1990s (Johnston and Ross 1999). Similarly, ASEAN nations adopted a strategy to engage Vietnam and succeeded in integrating the country into its organization in 1995. South Korean President Kim Dae Jung has followed a "sunshine policy" toward North Korea since he took office in February 1998, aiming to improve relations with the North through economic cooperation and diplomatic dialogues. Despite strong domestic opposition, Kim's efforts have yielded diplomatic results. The two Koreas held a historic summit meeting in Pyongyang on June 13–15, 2000. Since the summit, relations between North Korea and the West have improved significantly. Thanks in large part to Kim Dae Jung's sunshine policy, the tension in the Korean peninsula has lessened. Kim was awarded the Nobel Peace Prize on October 13, 2000, for his reconciliation efforts with the North as well as his advocacy of human rights.

China, conversely, is developing its own economic statecraft as its economic power grows. China seeks economic cooperation with developed nations like the United States and Japan to facilitate its modernization drive and to smooth relations when tensions arise. Beijing also sees closer economic ties with Taiwan as contributing to modernization and national unification. To increase its economic and political influence and ensure a stable external environment for economic reform, China has actively promoted economic cooperation with its neighbors. In particular, Beijing has encouraged countries like North Korea to conduct economic reform and improve economic ties with other countries.

The regional and bilateral cooperative strategies discussed in this chapter have been surprisingly durable despite changes in other areas, security tensions included. In fact, Asia Pacific economic cooperation has already passed some tough tests. The Asian financial crisis strengthened rather than weakened the region's interest in economic cooperation. As security tensions have risen, key countries in the region are reassessing their security policy and hedging against uncertainty. But regional economic cooperation continues. Although China's policymakers became more concerned about national security after the strengthening of the U.S.-Japan security alliance and NATO's accidental bombing of the Chinese embassy in Belgrade, Beijing worked hard to join the World Trade Organization and did so in November 2001. The April 2001 collision of a U.S. reconnaissance plane and a Chinese jet fighter complicated Sino-U.S. relations but did not change Beijing's basic orientation toward economic opening and cooperation.

An Emerging Trading System

In his book *The Rise of the Trading State*, Richard Rosecrance distinguishes between the "territorial world" and the "trading world." Territorial states are interested in acquiring more land to reduce dependence on others. A trading world, by contrast, "is based on states which recognize that self-sufficiency is an illusion. . . . Assuming trade is relatively free and open, they do not need to conquer new territory to develop their economies and to provide the essentials of a consumer existence" (Rosecrance 1986: 16). While recognizing that trading nations do not abandon military competition and balance of power, Rosecrance observes that since 1945 "a peaceful trading strategy is enjoying much greater efficacy than ever before" (p. ix). Japan, Taiwan, South Korea, and Singapore are among his examples of trading states.

Asia Pacific nations have not abandoned national security and military competition. Territorial disputes and military tensions remain. And regional cooperation has taken place in a shifting strategic environment. Governments do not consider foreign economic policy in isolation but link it to security and other national interests. They pursue active security policy in diverse ways and generally incorporate economic growth and economic security in a comprehensive conception of national security (Alagappa 1998). In a sharp shift from its prewar militarism, Japan chose to strengthen the nation by developing technologies with significance for defense (Samuels 1994). ASEAN nations wanted to reduce internal discord through economic cooperation and to deal with communist Indochina from a position of strength and economic success while reducing the danger of external interference in Southeast Asian affairs (Alagappa 1993). The Chinese government embraced reform and an open-door policy as a better approach to increase the nation's comprehensive strength, which would ultimately improve its defense capabilities. In this respect China emulated Japan and other East Asian nations.[7] A crucial reason for India's decision to open its economy in 1991 was the desire to imitate the successful development strategy adopted by its strategic rival China (Alamgir 2000). The same pressure is being placed on North Korea, whose leadership may finally be recognizing the new regional reality.

When facing threats as well, Asian nations have opted for realist measures. As a rising China poses the greatest security concern for the region, other countries' attitudes toward the Middle Kingdom are indicative of their strategic orientation. Most countries in the region have adopted some sort of engagement strategy with Beijing—varying from enthusiastic South Korea and Singapore to wary Indonesia and Taiwan. But all are hedging against China's uncertain future, and smaller countries in the region, except Malaysia, prefer to balance against China along with the United States and Japan in case their engagement strategy should fail (Johnston and Ross 1999).

Nevertheless, a trading system is emerging in the region in which most states have elevated economic issues from low politics to high politics and are devoting more national energy to economic development relative to national security. Early successes have a demonstration effect on other countries. A shift from a traditional notion of security to a comprehensive notion is itself significant. In a strategic environment, awareness of other countries' shifting national priorities improves one's confidence in the emphasis on economic growth—and mutual confidence increases regional stability. More important, whatever a state's initial intent, this strategic shift creates powerful domestic interests and coalitions pushing to expand international transactions.

Effects of Economic Interdependence and Cooperation

Economics and security can be related in different ways. (See Milner and Baldwin 1990; Kirshner 1998; Mastanduno 1998; Mansfield 1994; Blanchard et al. 2000.) To be sure, security shapes the process of regional interdependence. But interdependence, once created, affects security arrangements. This chapter analyzes how economic interdependence and cooperation affect security order. Their effect depends on how order is defined. Building on Hedley Bull's definition and Muthiah Alagappa's discussion in Chapter 1, I want to examine how economics affects security order defined as a stable pattern of relationships between nations or as a legitimate arrangement accepted by most members in the system.

[7]Deng Xiaoping himself admitted in September 1988 that "although China did not have a large technological gap with Japan in the 1950s, we closed our doors for twenty years and failed to put international market competition on the agenda while Japan became a major economic power in this period" (Deng 1993: 274); the translation is mine.

Commercial-Liberal Pathway to Security Order

Commercial liberalism is central to my analysis. Commercial liberalism has a rich tradition. Ever since the eighteenth century, influential thinkers such as James Mill, John Stuart Mill, Jean-Baptiste Say, Richard Cobden, and Norman Angell have made the powerful argument that close economic contacts contribute to peace by making war irrational and useless. Free trade contributes to peace by allowing the flow of goods across national borders for mutual gains—making war more costly and consequently less likely between trading partners (Howard 1978). Early liberals also saw the emergence of commercial classes in a capitalist system as social forces countering "the passion of power" (Hirschman 1977).[8] Among contemporary scholars, Richard Rosecrance (1986) has energized commercial-liberal research.

My research draws from theories of integration and interdependence. Integration theory, developed in the 1950s and 1960s, offers a research program that emphasizes the formation of common identity facilitated by social mobilization, transformation, and communications (Mitrany 1966; Haas 1958, 1964; Deutsch 1953; Nye 1971). European experience shows that economic integration has positive spillover effects for creating a security community. In the 1970s, scholars argued that interdependence leads to greater welfare gains—thus creating an incentive structure that encourages countries to continue on the path for further gains and avoid actions that may jeopardize expected benefits (Keohane and Nye 1972, 1989). My work also benefits from two other schools of liberal thought: democratic liberalism and sociological liberalism.[9] Democratic liberalism, which suggests that democracies do not fight each other (Doyle 1986), is relevant since I argue that a free-market-based interdependence will lead to more democratic political systems in the long run.[10] Consistent with sociological liberalism (Wendt 1999; Finnemore 1996), I argue that countries change their views and redefine national interests owing to interdependence and transnational connections—a change of mind that contributes to stability and legitimacy of the regional security system.

Economic interdependence and cooperation both stabilize and transform security order. They stabilize the region through facilitating and mitigating effects: they facilitate countries' efforts to cooperate and reduce tensions in security

---

[8]The outbreak of World War I, however, shook liberals' confidence in capitalism. Angell himself began to wonder if capitalism rather than nationalism was connected to war (Angell 1932).

[9]Joseph Nye (1988) notes four major strands in liberal theory: commercial liberalism, democratic liberalism, regulatory liberalism, and sociological liberalism. Of these four strands, the institutionalist arguments are taken up elsewhere in this book and need not be detailed here.

[10]Much has been written on the topic, mostly supporting the notion of democratic peace. For dissent, see Joanne Gowa (1999).

matters by offering economic incentives and creating vested interests in continuous cooperation; they mitigate traditional conflicts by making them more costly. But economic interdependence and cooperation may also transform national purposes through learning. Decision makers may redefine national interests through exchange with their counterparts in other countries. Such a learning process may turn opponents of an international system into constructive participants—thus making the system more legitimate and durable. In the Asia Pacific, a capitalist economic order is emerging. Virtually all the players are moving in the general direction of a market-based economy, which will contribute to a more stable and desirable security order in the region. Moreover, a country's economic development is positively associated with its democratization (Lipset 1959; Diamond et al. 1988; Diamond and Plattner 1998). And democracies rarely fight each other.

Stabilizing and transforming effects are felt in domestic contexts as well. Economic interdependence and cooperation reshape the views of policy elites about international relations and foreign policy. And as recent research on the link between domestic and international politics has shown, internationalization strengthens domestic sectors that gain from international transactions, and domestic political coalitions and institutional context explain variations in policy outcomes in different countries (Solingen 1998; Keohane and Milner 1996). This dynamic applies to the Asia Pacific as well. Economic interdependence and cooperation affect regional security order because they affect preferences of key sectors in a country. Internationalist actors in export-oriented sectors have become more influential in domestic politics because governments have come to depend on these sectors to produce economic growth in a competitive global market. This is particularly important for the developing states in the region, which increasingly link economic performance to political legitimacy. As a result, states hesitate to engage in a military adventure overseas that will endanger their economic performance and consequently their regime's survival.

Trade-Conflict Linkage

A number of empirical studies have demonstrated that trade reduces conflict. Solomon Polachek (1980) found a negative relationship between conflict and trade based on data of dyadic conflict, international trade, and country attributes in the period 1958–1967. Extensive tests conducted since Polachek's work generally support the trade-peace thesis. Surveying dyadic relationships in the period 1950–1985, John Oneal and Bruce Russett demonstrate that economic interdependence, as well as democracy, reduces interstate conflict. Specifically they suggest that economic openness, measured as the total trade/GDP ratio, is inversely related to chance of dyadic conflict. This finding means that while politics may lead to a reduction in trade with a potential adversary, it would be difficult to restrict trade with all countries simultaneously (Oneal and Russett 1997). Polachek, John Robst, and Yuan-Ching Chang have extended the trade-peace model to include foreign aid, tariffs, contiguity, and country size. Using the data from Polachek's 1980 paper, they show that foreign aid and contiguity reduce conflict whereas tariffs increase conflict, that neighboring countries would have greater conflicts but for the mitigating effects of trade, and that trade with large countries reduces conflict more than trade with small ones (Polachek et al. 1999). Covering the years from 1950 to 1992, Havard Hegre has shown that the pacific effect of trade increases with the level of development (Hegre 2000). Besides trade, Erik Gartzke, Quan Li, and Charles Boehmer have demonstrated that capital interdependence also contributes to peace (Gartzke, Li, and Boehmer 2001).

There is dissent, of course. From a study of 270 militarized interstate disputes and fourteen wars in the period 1870–1938, Katherine Barbieri (1996) concludes that "extensive economic interdependence increases the likelihood that dyads will engage in militarized interstate disputes." Adopting some of the procedural corrections made by Barbieri and others, however, Oneal and Russett show that interdependence reduced conflict during the years 1950–1992 among contiguous and major-power pairs. They found no evidence that asymmetric trade increases conflict (Oneal and Russett 1999). Statistical studies give us some confidence, therefore, that interdependence has had a pacifying effect, particularly since the end of World War II.

Not much statistical analysis has been done to test the relationship between economic interdependence and conflict in the Asia Pacific region. But a quick look over the past two decades shows a roughly positive correlation between interdependence and stability. As the region became more interdependent, it also became more stable, despite the presence of serious dangers. Moreover, the subregions with the greatest degree of interdependence have the greatest stability. It is difficult to anticipate any military conflicts among Japan, South Korea, and Taiwan in Northeast Asia, among ASEAN nations in Southeast Asia, between the two subregions, or between the United States and any of these nations.

Statistical analysis, which seeks to generalize the trade-conflict connection, is the first step in this discussion of a commercial-liberal pathway to security order in the Asia Pacific, and a tentative first step at that, judging by the recent controversy over the statistical methods employed in International Relations. (See Green, Kim, and Yoon 2001; Oneal and Russett 2001; Beck and Katz 2001; King 2001.) To understand the role of economic interdependence and cooperation over the past decades, we need to scrutinize how economic forces affect the calculations of policymakers in the region.

Stabilizing Effect of Economic Cooperation

Economic interdependence and cooperation have had a stabilizing impact on security in the Asia Pacific. Before presenting evidence to this effect, I want to dismiss two possible objections to this assessment. First, some thinkers maintain that trade may increase interstate conflict. Lenin's thesis that capitalist expansion leads to major wars is well known (Lenin 1970). Drawing on the notion of "lateral pressure"—a country's reaching out of its territorial boundary to meet demand for resources—Nazli Choucri and Robert North have explained how national growth leads to expansion and conflict (Choucri and North 1975, 1989). Realists argue that conflict arises from global trade expansion and that military force has been used along with trading strategies to create unequal economic relations (Waltz 1979; Cohen 1973). But there is little evidence since the end of World War II to support this line of argument. The research on the regional economics-security nexus has generally demonstrated that economic transactions may lead to friction and vulnerability but that on balance they increase security (Harris and Mack 1997). Despite economic tensions, countries in the region continue to see gains in further economic cooperation and integration.

The second objection is that interdependence may lead to economic and regime collapse, which destabilizes the region. Here Indonesia comes to mind. But again there is little evidence to support this claim. Surveying economic crises in 21 developing countries in Asia and Latin America over the past fifty years, Minxin Pei and Ariel Adesnik have demonstrated that rarely has a regime collapsed because of an economic crisis. Indeed they found that "economic crises in Asia and Latin America have been less likely to produce a regime change over the past two decades than before." There are two nations in which economic crises caused a sudden regime change between 1945 and 1998: Indonesia and Ecuador (Pei and Adesnik 2000). In fact, the Suharto regime had already lost much of its legitimacy before the 1997–98 Asian financial crisis. The crisis was just the last straw, but it had a less destabilizing impact on regional security than initially feared.

Economic cooperation has had a clear facilitating effect and a moderate mitigating effect on security in the region. Such effects are closely related. Economic ordering efforts, which often start out complementing power-based measures, add economic incentives to the realist rationale for security cooperation. Once economic interdependence develops, uncooperative security behavior means loss of welfare. The extent of the mitigating effect from economic interdependence depends on the importance of the issue and the magnitude of welfare loss.

Facilitating Effect. Economic cooperation has facilitated stabilization of regional security by adding economic incentives for security cooperation. After World War II, Washington complemented military alliances with Japan, South

Korea, Taiwan, and certain Southeast Asian nations with economic assistance. The United States wanted to integrate its Asian allies into its hegemonic system (Cumings 1984). When the United States lost interest in Southeast Asia after the Vietnam War, commerce served as a basis for American policy toward the region (McMahon 1999). Close economic ties provide economic incentives for the United States to engage in East Asia, a key element of regional security order.

Japan reentered "free Asia" after the war through reparations. Although driven mainly by economic motives, Tokyo's economic diplomacy also increased its own security and regional security. Through economic cooperation Japan has reduced, if not eliminated, historic animosity in Southeast Asia and has cautiously advanced its political and strategic agenda in the region (Wan 2001a). ASEAN nations have successfully used community building and economic cooperation to reduce tensions in Southeast Asia and manage external interference to the extent that we now see a nascent ASEAN-based Southeast Asian security community (Khong 1997). The woes of Indonesia, the traditional leader of ASEAN, have weakened the regional group, but ASEAN remains a force to be reckoned with in East Asia and continues to play a crucial role in regional integration efforts. In fact, ASEAN is seeking to establish links with Northeast Asian nations as one solution to its difficulties.

Thus we see an emerging zone of peace and prosperity connecting Japan, South Korea, Taiwan, certain ASEAN nations (Indonesia is a notable exception at present), and North America. It is hard to imagine major military conflict among them. Although the United States has provided the security commitment underpinning the regional order, close economic ties have facilitated the emergence of this zone of stability. The discussion would end here if we did not have to look beyond this zone. But the Asia Pacific region also includes the large continental states of Russia, North Korea, China, Vietnam, and India.[11] Tensions along these countries' boundaries in the Korean peninsula, the Taiwan Strait, the South China Sea, and Kashmir, as well as their internal tensions, send seismic waves through the region.

The United States, Japan, and maritime Asian nations have engaged in economic cooperation with Russia, North Korea, China, Vietnam, and India, partly aiming at stabilizing regional security. This is particularly the case with China, a rising power that may well become the biggest security concern for the region in the coming decades. The United States and Japan have cooperated economically with China and vice versa. Indeed, Japan and the United States are now China's top two trading partners. For Washington, economic cooperation complemented its strategic cooperation with China to counter the Soviet Union in the early days

[11] For a study of the post–Cold War East Asian strategic geography, see Ross (1999).

and has become a driver for a bilateral relationship since the end of the Cold War. Without economic cooperation, a strategic imperative to avoid conflict would not provide a strong basis for maintaining a working relationship. For Japan, economic cooperation is crucial for maintaining a stable relationship with China when the two sides remain deeply distrustful of each other because of historical grievances, territorial dispute, and diverging security interests.

Mitigating Effect. The facilitating effect of interdependence does not really counter the realist argument that security is a principal motivation of foreign policy. A harder test for the salience of the commercial-liberal pathway is whether interdependence can mitigate conflict over important issues. I argue that economic cooperation has had a moderate mitigating effect in the Asia Pacific region—even on the acute conflicts in the South China Sea, the Korean peninsula, the Taiwan Strait, and Kashmir.

In the South China Sea, the imperative of economic development and the pacific potential of economic cooperation have factored significantly into decision making in the countries involved. Beijing has alternated between taking unilateral action and seeking dialogue in its effort to maintain a stable environment for its modernization drive.[12] Recognizing China's thinking, Southeast Asian nations have refrained from strong countermeasures because they calculate that Beijing might be enticed to adopt a more moderate policy (Whiting 1997; Wanandi 1996; Storey 1999–2000).[13] In a security dilemma, a strong and collective ASEAN position on the South China Sea would be likely to invite a strong Chinese reaction that would make the region far less stable. Moreover, China's economic growth offers Southeast Asian nations commercial opportunities, thus creating incentives for them to avoid a confrontational approach to Beijing. The November 2001 China-ASEAN agreement to create a free-trade area within 10 years will further political cooperation and confidence building between the two sides.

In the Korean peninsula, attempts at closer economic ties between the two Koreas are reducing tensions in the whole region. South Korean President Kim Dae Jung persisted in his sunshine policy toward the North even after Pyongyang test-fired a rocket over Japan in 1998 and clashed with the South on the sea in 1999. His policy has yielded results. Pyongyang has taken measures to reduce international isolation by establishing diplomatic relations with Australia, Italy, Britain, and Germany. In a historic exchange, Vice Marshal Jo Myong Rok, second only to Kim Jong Il in the military, met with President Clinton in the White House in October 2000. Secretary of State Madeleine Albright paid a return visit

[12]Another reason for China's moderation in the early 1990s was its need to seek Asian allies when it felt isolated by the West after the 1989 Tiananmen Incident.

[13]Two additional reasons are conflicting claims among ASEAN nations—particularly between the Philippines and Malaysia—and the weak position of the group vis-à-vis China.

to Pyongyang later in the month. During her lengthy discussions with Kim, the two sides reportedly made progress in restraining North Korea's missile program in exchange for U.S. diplomatic recognition and economic assistance. Although many countries have participated in the peace process in the Korean peninsula and a variety of policy instruments have been employed, Kim's sunshine policy has contributed to reducing tensions by demonstrating the positive effects of economic engagement and diplomatic dialogue. The Bush administration's initial suspension of missile talks with North Korea and strong domestic criticism in South Korea undercut but did not invalidate Kim's sunshine policy.

Taiwan is the most explosive security issue in East Asia, and a conflict in the Taiwan Strait is the most likely scenario to draw the United States into a shooting war with China. It is thus both surprising and reassuring to see rapidly growing economic ties between the mainland and Taiwan. By Taipei's estimate, Taiwan's trade with mainland China reached $31.25 billion in 2000, accounting for 10.84 percent of its total trade for the year. For mainland China, cross-strait trade accounted for 6.59 percent of its total. The mainland has become Taiwan's number-one FDI destination. By Beijing's calculations, Taiwan has invested a total of $52.13 billion on contract basis, of which $28.12 billion were realized.[14] More significantly, Taiwan's leading high-technology firms have been moving operations to the mainland in recent years. Both sides hope that economic transactions will serve their interests. Taipei wants to moderate Beijing's behavior; Beijing hopes to entice Taiwan into unification with the motherland. Admittedly, Beijing refuses to rule out the use of force, but moderate leaders have recently touted commercial ties as an alternative for achieving unification.[15] Economic interdependence has thus had a mitigating effect in this case. China's and Taiwan's mutual WTO membership will further cross-strait economic integration and is likely to decrease tensions between the two sides as well.

In Kashmir, there is no close economic cooperation between India and Pakistan. India-Pakistan trade represented only 0.4 percent of India's total trade and 2 percent of Pakistan's in 1998 (IMF 2000: 121, 181). India and Pakistan's nuclear tests have shown the limits of the economic rationale and the centrality of geopolitical calculations in their security decisions. The Congress Party government of P. V. Narasimha Rao canceled the planned nuclear tests at the end of 1995

---

[14]Data are from the MAC, DGBASEY, and MOFTEC websites.

[15]For example, Chinese President Jiang Zemin told a group of New York Times journalists in August 2001 that "if with the increase of economic interaction people on both sides have a strong desire for reunification, then why would it be necessary to resort to armed conflict?" But he then added, "China can never renounce the use of force" (Eckholm 2001). Beijing has also learned a hard lesson; its previous efforts to intimidate Taiwan have resulted in electoral gains for the pro-independence forces on the island.

when Washington threatened economic sanctions. The Bharatiya Janata Party, by contrast, conducted nuclear tests because the value of having a nuclear deterrent was judged to be more important than economic costs (Joeck 1999). Facing a changed strategic environment, Pakistan conducted its own tests despite the international community's threat of economic sanctions (and the promise of potential benefits if Pakistan would forgo testing). Economic calculations have had little influence over war and peace in this region. Still, a greater degree of interdependence between India and Pakistan (or between India and China) would reduce tensions by creating mutual interests.

At first glance, these four cases do not give us much confidence in a commercial-liberal pathway to security order. Economic cooperation will not ensure peace in any of these cases. Even so, we should not dismiss the salience of interdependence. First, we do not yet know whether engagement has failed in these ongoing dramas. Second, we should not pretend that interdependence is a sufficient condition for making countries pacifist. Instead we should be asking whether things would have been even worse without interdependence. Third, it is not clear whether the realist options hold any more promise of reducing conflict in these cases. As the region's countries have adopted mixed strategies of power and commerce, any outbreak of major conflict would indicate the failure of realist as well as liberal pathways. And fourth, these acute conflict situations, which are legacies of the past, obviously favor the realist viewpoint. In the scheme of things, however, interdependence has reduced the number of conflicts in the region as certain conflict situations have been transformed into nonconflict situations. In fact, this book shows that Asian security has improved significantly over the past decades. While focusing on ongoing disputes, we should balance them against successful cases of conflict resolution.

Transforming Effect of Economic Cooperation

Economic interdependence transforms security in the region. In fact, we are in the early stage of a fundamental transformation of regional security. We observe transformations of national purposes, of economic systems, and of political systems, all of which stabilize and legitimize a functional regional security order. The competitive nature of international relations and the natural inclination to copy winning strategies are driving this historic process. But historical development does not follow a neat linear trajectory. Governments facing similar structural incentives and constraints do make different choices. And following the logic of path dependence, actions taken at a crucial juncture to reorient a country have huge, often unintended, effects (Jervis 1997). Indeed a country's strategic decisions unleash economic, social, and political forces that condition its future development and have regional security ramifications.

Shifting National Priorities. The countries in the region, one after another, have given economic growth a high priority in their ranking of national purposes. After serious divisions over the revision of the security treaty with the United States, Japan's prime minister, Ikeda Hayato, recognizing economic growth as the only basis for national consensus, announced his "income-doubling plan" in 1960. Abandoning President Syngman Rhee's obsession with national unification in South Korea, Gen. Park Chung Hee projected fast economic growth as the nation's main task in the early 1960s. Around the same time Chiang Kai-shek's son Chiang Ching-kuo decided that the Kuomintang should alter its focus from preparing to reclaim the mainland to promoting economic development in Taiwan. Both South Korea and Taiwan shifted from import-substitution strategies to export-led growth. Facing severe external constraints, Singapore and Hong Kong shifted to export-led development strategies in the 1960s. In Indonesia, after General Suharto seized power in 1966, his military-led New Order government focused attention to domestic political and economic development. In 1979, Deng Xiaoping launched economic reform—giving China's economic growth a higher priority than national defense. After a costly war in Cambodia, Vietnam concentrated on economic development after the mid-1980s. Recovering from a devastating famine that started in 1995, North Korea is cautiously relaxing controls over the economy to promote growth.

Asian countries have not abandoned national security. Realists dominate decision making in all the countries cited here, and all share the realist ambition to enrich the nation and strengthen national security. When they adopt engagement policies toward potential adversaries, they tend to have realist fallback options. Moreover, smaller countries sometimes have little choice but to concentrate on economics since it is unwise for them to make provocative power moves. Nevertheless, a collective shift of national priorities has positive implications for regional security. A collective awareness of changing priorities in other countries fosters mutual trust in the region. Countries in the region do worry about relative gains and future uncertainties. But the shifting national priorities of most countries send a strong signal that they can concentrate on economic growth without undue concern about security at present and can adopt a smart strategy of cooperating (plus hedging moves for insurance) until someone else defects first. As Robert Axelrod (1984) has demonstrated in computer tournaments, a tit-for-tat strategy encourages cooperation. Countries in the region may therefore become collectively more secure. Moreover, changing national purposes have led to a chain of events—often with unintended consequences. Deng did not envision a capitalist China, for example, but the country is irresistibly headed in that direction.

An Emerging Capitalist System. From a historical perspective, the emergence of a capitalist system in the region is striking. This is not the place to generalize the relationship between capitalism and conflict. Instead I want to focus on the security implications of the region's emerging capitalist system.

With its heavy and deliberate government interventions in economic activities, the Asian capitalist system is rather different from market-oriented Western capitalism (Berger and Dore 1996; Albert 1993). One may ponder whether different capitalist systems, such as liberal versus mercantilist, might have different security implications (Buzan 1983: 130–50). But the truth of the matter is that, despite serious trade disputes, a liberal America is allied with neomercantilist Japan and South Korea. The fault line in East Asia is mainly between the capitalist countries and the countries in transition from socialism to capitalism.

Of the three major socialist countries in the region, China has made the boldest move toward a market economy, but state enterprises still play an important part in China's economy after two decades of reform. China's 13-year effort to join the WTO indicates a strong willingness to move even further in the direction of integration with the global economy. Vietnam looked promising after it adopted reforms in 1986. Foreign firms rushed into the country, anticipating another Asian miracle about to take place, but reform has stalled on account of the communist leadership's concern about losing political power. North Korea has yet to make that first significant step. Still, both Vietnam and North Korea are headed, if slowly, in the direction of integration with the regional and global economy.[16]

Interdependence based on a capitalist model has not eliminated conflict. Regional conflicts continue and in some cases may increase. But the transformation of economic systems in the Asia Pacific region has already had a positive impact on regional security. During the Cold War, the United States and the communist camp clashed in two major hot wars in Korea and Vietnam and in numerous conflicts in Asia. Moreover, there were major conflicts fueled to some extent by the Cold War, most notably three wars between India and Pakistan. Thus Asia is different from Europe, where the superpower rivalry created a precarious but stable security order. No country in East Asia still pursues a revolutionary agenda. Consequently, the region has enjoyed an unprecedented period of peace for the past two decades despite dangers lurking around every corner.

The region's economic transformation makes some types of security order more likely than others. The return of a Cold War type of security order is unlikely since countries in the region appear unprepared to engage in a total confrontation. The economic transformation means that countries will cooperate

---

[16]As positive signs, Kim Jong Il praised China's economic reform during his four-day visit to Shanghai in January 2001. At the Vietnamese Communist Party meeting held in April 2001, the Central Committee voted out conservative Le Kha Phieu and selected as the new party chief Nong Duc Manh, who is more receptive to economic reforms.

where they have common interests and clash where they differ—an arrangement that will probably lead to a loose balance of power supplemented by features of hegemonic leadership and a concert of powers, depending on the issues. Furthermore, a market-based interdependence leads to a broader definition of security. By offering greater economic freedom to an ever larger portion of the population, a capitalist transformation has increased people's sense of personal security and their stake in a peaceful system. Cooperation in matters important for security broadly defined—such as the environment and public health—can only reduce tension and suspicion in the traditional security realm. More to the point, capitalist interdependence will have a far greater positive impact when this economic force plays out fully in the future. Rising living standards will lead to a better-educated citizenry and eventually to more open political systems—a decided plus for a legitimate and peaceful security order.

Democratization. Economic growth based on a capitalist model is an important prerequisite for democracy. Countries tend to become more democratic once their living standards have improved. Social change resulting from economic development such as urbanization and rising educational levels leads to shifts in attitudes and beliefs that are conducive to modern democracy—and the emergence of a well-informed middle class has also proved important for democratic success (Lipset 1959). While recognizing that market capitalism might be harmful to democracy, Robert Dahl argues that "democracy has endured only in countries with a predominantly market-capitalist economy" because "certain basic features of market-capitalism make it favorable for democratic institutions" (1998: 166–67). We are in the early phase, then, of a profound political transformation in the Asia Pacific region. As Edward Friedman has pointed out, East Asia has "rich experience with democratization, both successes and failures" (1994: 1). Rapid economic growth in the Asia Pacific has had important political implications for the countries in the region. Although the pace of democratization varies from country to country (Morley 1999), over the past five decades we can detect a halting march toward democracy.

How does all this affect security order? In the early stages, the different paces of democratization have mixed impacts on regional security. On the one hand, it is hard to imagine a major military clash among the fully or almost fully democratic countries in the region. Democratization strengthens other factors conducive to stability—namely military alliance, economic interdependence, and community-building efforts. On the other hand, different paces of democratization may actually lead to greater conflict.[17] The tension across the Taiwan Strait is

---

[17]Democratization may unleash nationalist forces, for example, thus leading to serious conflict (Snyder 2000).

a case in point. Chinese analysts increasingly see differences between political systems as secondary to the central issue of whether China will be unified. But a successful transition to democracy in Taiwan has given voice and power to those supporting a permanent separation from the mainland—a trend furthered by the absence of serious political reform in Beijing. Thus democratization has inadvertently heightened cross-strait tensions. Furthermore, given China's current nationalist sentiment, one may make a reasonable case that in the short run democracy in China may allow pent-up popular nationalism to grow, resulting in a more assertive policy toward disputes with neighboring countries.

But if the major players have all become mature democracies, there are reasons to believe that in the long run we will see a zone of peace in Asia. Certainly China's relations with the United States, Taiwan, and other players in the region are likely to improve if it becomes a mature democracy with its internal development and policymaking transparent to the outside world. Similarly, the emergence of a more democratic Pakistan would make the conflict with India more manageable.

Domestic Politics. Stabilizing and transforming effects work through domestic politics. In the domestic context, interdependence has four security implications: impact on elite perceptions of international relations and diplomacy, impact on society's preferences, impact on political legitimacy, and impact on sectoral preferences.[18]

In the first phase, interdependence affects the elite's perceptions. This is not to say that interdependence has made policy elites in the region liberal thinkers. Indeed Chinese officials and researchers basically hold realist views, though some liberal thinking has also emerged (Deng Yong 1999). And although we hear liberal arguments more often in Japan, the dominant thinking remains neomercantilist (Heginbotham and Samuels 1998). I am simply saying that while they are still committed to national power and national security, Asia's foreign policy elites have increasingly incorporated economic development as a key to accomplishing this objective. Their growing awareness of the incentives and constraints of the global economy has shaped their national strategies (Alagappa 1998). The elite perception that interdependence defines current international relations and that countries can only increase their security and prosperity by integrating into the global economy explains why Asian nations have largely stayed the course despite security and economic crises. Chinese and Japanese policy thinkers have be-

[18]Although domestic institutions are an important intervening variable between sectoral interests and policy outcomes, I do not discuss the institutional context in this chapter owing to space constraints. Moreover, the chapter examines the positive regional trend of economic transformation of security rather than the varying impact of interdependence among regional countries.

come more security-conscious in the past few years, but they have not replaced economics with security as the top priority. While improving defense capabilities, China has pursued WTO membership and Japan continues to cultivate economic cooperation with China. And despite the conclusion drawn by some that premature capital-market liberalization was not a wise policy, the 1997–98 financial crisis did not change the basic outward-looking orientation of Asian countries.

Interdependence and globalization have also affected the preferences of society at large. In his best-selling book *The Lexus and the Olive Tree*, Thomas Friedman (1999) argues that because of the democratization of technology, finance, and information, there is a groundswell for globalization among ordinary people in every country. Certainly this is the case for Asia. Average citizens in most Asian countries are increasingly aware of the world outside their countries and desire the same quality of life as elsewhere. Whether they take to the street, vote with their feet, or simply ignore government policies, their new preferences for modern consumer goods and services put pressure on governments to deliver economically.

And this pressure, in turn, directly affects regime survival. Virtually every government in the region now recognizes that it must perform economically to stay in power—and, moreover, that integration with the international economy is a key condition for economic performance. Although political legitimacy in Asia is a complex issue, economic performance has become a cornerstone of legitimacy for countries in the region (Alagappa 1995). Following Japan's example, most capitalist countries in the region are developmental states that rely heavily on economic performance to legitimize political regimes and governments (Johnson 1982; Deyo 1987; Vogel 1991). For transitional economies such as China and Vietnam, economic performance has become a key to legitimacy for the communist governments. According to an emerging developmentalist consensus in the Chinese government and society, economic growth should be China's primary objective and party dominance is needed to ensure the social stability necessary for economic success. In fact, Chinese believe that China needs to grow by 7 or 8 percent annually to maintain political and social stability (Wan 2001b: chap. 2). Similarly, Vietnam's leaders now see economic growth as vital to the legitimacy of the communist party's political monopoly but remain wary of the consequences of a capitalist development model (Ninh 1998). There are hopeful signs that North Korea will start the same process in the near future.

Interdependence affects domestic sectors differently. In the domestic context there are winners and losers. Export-led developmental strategies and close economic ties with the outside world have strengthened the sectors most competent and exposed to the global economy. Their importance in domestic politics has grown as trade gains importance for the nation as a whole. Governments need internationally competitive sectors to deliver performance and revenues for losing sectors. In democratic and authoritarian countries alike, internationally competitive sectors push governments to further economic ties with foreign countries regardless of potential security threats. Thus the private business community often represents a powerful domestic force opposing those who seek an assertive and confrontational approach—an important domestic reason why economic ties stabilize security relations.

To illustrate how interdependence affects security policy by influencing sectoral interests, let me cite two examples. In the first case, despite growing concerns over China's military capabilities and human rights problems, the U.S. government has maintained an engagement policy with China. The American business community was highly mobilized in its lobbying efforts to persuade Congress to grant China permanent normal trading relations (PNTR), countering the efforts by organized labor and human rights groups to deny China PNTR. In the second case, despite Beijing's repeated threats and military exercises aimed at Taiwan, the Taiwanese business community has lobbied the Taipei government to allow direct linkage in trade, shipping, and post with the mainland. The public generally supports this position in order to create more economic opportunities and decrease cross-strait tensions, but not as a first step toward unification.[19] Given domestic pressure and economic slowdown, Taiwan's president, Chen Shui-bian, has gradually relaxed restrictions on economic ties with China while refusing to negotiate with Beijing under the "One China principle."[20] Conversely, closer economic ties with the outside world explain why moderate Chinese national leaders, trade ministers, and officials from prosperous provinces and cities, who have more to lose economically from military confrontation, take a more cautious approach toward the Taiwan issue than hard-liners in the military and party leadership.[21]

[19]A case in point, in the December 1, 2001, legislative election Chen Shui-bian's pro-independence Democratic Progressive Party (DPP) became the largest party in the parliament (87 seats out of 225, a gain of 15) while the unification-friendly Nationalist Party (68 seats, a loss of 42) lost its position as the majority party for the first time since the Nationalist government moved to Taiwan in 1949.

[20]In April 2000, Chen allowed "mini-three-links," which refers to direct shipping between the offshore islands of Kinmen and Matsu and mainland China. He then ended long-standing restrictions on trade and investment in the mainland on August 26, 2001. Note, however, that Taiwanese businessmen had already evaded the restrictions by investing in the mainland through a third country.

[21]The DPP's victory in the December 1 legislative election has yet to change Beijing's Taiwan policy. Chinese officials continue to express confidence that most Taiwanese want stable relations with the mainland, particularly in the economic area. Such confidence, whether it is founded or not, bodes well for the stability across the Strait.

Prospects

Realists often assert that strong interdependence has not prevented major wars, most noticeably World War I. Looking at Asia, skeptics cite China's missile exercises against Taiwan and its continuous threat to use force against the island as evidence that commercial liberalism has not moderated China's behavior. After all, Taiwanese had invested billions of dollars in the mainland. Furthermore, Beijing's stance on Taiwan increases tension with the United States, which has been China's largest export market for the past few years, reaching around $40 billion a year.

I do not dispute that economic ties alone cannot stop a war if governments are determined to fight. Proponents of globalization readily admit that globalization does not end conflict. Thucydides maintained a long time ago, as Thomas Friedman (1999: 197) reminds us, that nations go to war for "honor, fear, and interest," reasons that remain true to this day. But the fact that realpolitik matters does not mean that interdependence is unimportant. We should not reject the economic pathway for failing to meet an impossible standard. The core argument of commercial liberalism states that wars do not pay—which makes them less likely. After all, realist as well as commercial-liberal pathways existed before World War I. Similarly, virtually all the countries in the region have adopted mixed strategies and different combinations of pathways to security order. Thus if a major conflict did take place, it would be wrong to attribute the cause strictly to commercial liberalism.

No pathway has ever stood the ultimate test of preventing war. With respect to Beijing's policy toward Taiwan, for example, it is not clear which pathway would work better. One can make a reasonable argument that realist measures—containing Beijing, building a balancing coalition against China, arming Taiwan more extensively, integrating the island into the U.S. defense system—would affect the outcome of conflict but not Beijing's decision to start it. In fact, premature realist measures are likely to have a self-fulfilling effect.

A commercial-liberal pathway to security order will continue to be important in the region precisely because the countries engaging in economic cooperation have evinced little faith in economic means alone. Instead, depending on their abilities and preferences, they have combined other means. From a historical perspective the region has done well for the past three decades thanks in large part to these mixed strategies. There are no obvious reasons, therefore, why the region's countries should not stay the course. Although governments must ensure national survival and defense, they also need to meet other national objectives that they now see as directly related to security. Thus economic development and cooperation should be central to any country's strategic outlook. This is particularly the case in the aftermath of September 11, 2001, when economic cooperation has taken on added strategic significance. Moreover, we are still at the threshold of profound transformations of economic and political systems in the region. We must allow these transformations to play out for greater stability. This, of course, is not to deny the importance of being vigilant and strategic. As I have argued elsewhere, strategic and transformative approaches are closely related: "Countries need to play smart to preserve the system before it can be transformed" (Wan 1996: 70).

Works Cited

Aggarwal, Vinod K., and Charles E. Morrison, eds. 1998. *Asia-Pacific Crossroads: Regime Creation and the Future of APEC*. New York: St. Martin's Press.

Alagappa, Muthiah. 1993. "Regionalism and the Quest for Security: ASEAN and the Cambodian Conflict." *Journal of International Affairs* 46(2): 439–67.

——, ed. 1995. *Political Legitimacy in Southeast Asia: The Quest for Moral Authority*. Stanford: Stanford University Press.

——, ed. 1998. *Asian Security Practice: Material and Ideational Influences*. Stanford: Stanford University Press.

Alamgir, Jalal. 2000. "The Strategic Context of Economic Globalization in India." Paper presented at the 41st annual convention of the International Studies Association, Los Angeles, Mar.

Albert, Michel. 1993. *Capitalism vs. Capitalism*. New York: Four Walls Eight Windows.

Angell, Norman. 1932. *The Unseen Assassins*. New York: Harper & Brothers.

APEC Economic Committee. 2000. *APEC Economic Outlook 2000*. Singapore: APEC Secretariat.

Axelrod, Robert. 1984. *The Evolution of Cooperation*. New York: Basic Books.

Barbieri, Katherine. 1996. "Economic Interdependence: A Path to Peace or a Source of Interstate Conflict?" *Journal of Peace Research* 33(1): 29–49.

Beamish, Paul W., and A. E. Safarian, eds. 1999. *North American Firms in East Asia*. Toronto: University of Toronto Press.

Beck, Nathaniel, and Jonathan N. Katz. 2001. "Throwing Out the Baby with the Bath Water: A Comment on Green, Kim, and Yoon." *International Organization* 55(2): 487–96.

Berger, Suzanne, and Ronald Dore, eds. 1996. *National Diversity and Global Capitalism*. Ithaca: Cornell University Press.

Bergsten, C. Fred. 2000. "Towards a Tripartite World." *Economist*, July 15, pp. 23–26.

Blanchard, Jean-Marc F., Edward D. Mansfield, and Norrin M. Ripsman, eds. 2000. *The Power and the Purse: Economic Statecraft, Interdependence, and International Conflict*. Portland, Ore.: Frank Cass.

Borrus, Michael, Dieter Ernst, and Stephan Haggard, eds. 2000. *International Production Networks in Asia: Rivalry or Riches?* London: Routledge.

Buzan, Barry. 1983. *People, States, and Fear: The National Security Problem in International Relations*. Chapel Hill: University of North Carolina Press.

Castellano, Marc. 1999. "Japan, Northeast Asia, and Free Trade: Coming Together at Last?" *JEI Report*, no. 47A, Dec. 17.

Choucri, Nazli, and Robert C. North. 1975. *Nations in Conflict*. San Francisco: Freeman.

———. 1989. "Lateral Pressure in International Relations: Concept and Theory." In Manus I. Midlarsky, ed., *Handbook of War Studies*. Boston: Unwin Hyman.

Clark, Ian. 1999. *Globalization and International Relations Theory*. Oxford: Oxford University Press.

Cohen, Benjamin J. 1973. *The Question of Imperialism*. New York: Basic Books.

Cooper, Richard N. 1972. "Economic Interdependence and Foreign Policy in the Seventies." *World Politics* 24(2): 159–81.

Cumings, Bruce. 1984. "The Origins and Development of the Northeast Asian Political Economy: Industrial Sectors, Product Cycles, and Political Consequences." *International Organization* 38(1): 1–40.

Dahl, Robert A. 1998. *On Democracy*. New Haven: Yale University Press.

De Brouwe, Gordon. 1999. *Financial Integration in East Asia*. Cambridge: Cambridge University Press.

Deng Xiaoping. 1993. *Deng Xiaoping wenxuan* (Deng's selected works). Vol. 3. Beijing: Renmin Chubanshe.

Deng Yong. 1999. "Conception of National Interests: Realpolitik, Liberal Dilemma, and the Possibility of Change." In Yong Deng and Fei-Ling Wang, eds., *In the Eyes of the Dragon: China Views the World*. Lanham, Md.: Rowman & Littlefield.

Deutsch, Karl W. 1953. *Nationalism and Social Communication: An Inquiry into the Foundations of Nationality*. Cambridge, Mass.: MIT Press.

Deyo, Frederic C., ed. 1987. *The Political Economy of the New Asian Industrialism*. Ithaca: Cornell University Press.

Diamond, Larry, and Marc F. Plattner, eds. 1998. *Democracy in East Asia*. Baltimore: Johns Hopkins University Press.

Diamond, Larry, Juan Linz, and Seymour Martin Lipset, eds. 1988. *Democracy in Developing Countries*. Boulder, Colo.: Lynne Rienner.

DGBASEY (Directorate-General of Budget, Accounting of Statistics of Executive Yuan). *Monthly Bulletin of Statistics of Republic of China*, June 21, 2001. Website: www.dgbasey.gov.tw.

Doyle, Michael. 1986. "Liberalism and World Politics." *American Political Science Review* 80(4): 1151–69.

Drysdale, Peter, Andrew Elek, and Hadi Soesastro. 1998. "Open Regionalism: The Nature of Asia Pacific Integration." In Peter Drysdale and David Vines, eds., *Europe, East Asia, and APEC: A Shared Global Agenda?* Cambridge: Cambridge University Press.

Eckholm, Erik. 2001. "Chinese President Is Optimistic about Relations with the U.S." *New York Times*, Aug. 10, p. A8.

Encarnation, Dennis J., ed. 1999. *Japanese Multinationals in Asia: Regional Cooperation in Comparative Perspective*. New York: Oxford University Press.

Finnemore, Martha. 1996. *National Interests in International Society*. Ithaca: Cornell University Press.

Frankel, Jeffrey A. 1997. *Regional Trading Blocs in the World Economic System*. Washington, D.C.: Institute for International Economics.

———, ed. 1998. *The Regionalization of the World Economy*. Chicago: University of Chicago Press.

Friedman, Edward. 1994. *The Politics of Democratization: Generalizing East Asian Experience*. Boulder, Colo.: Westview.

Friedman, Thomas. 1999. *The Lexus and the Olive Tree*. New York: Farrar, Straus & Giroux.

Funabashi, Yoichi. 1999. *Asia Pacific Fusion: Japan's Role in APEC*. Washington, D.C.: Institute of International Economics.

Gamble, Andrew, and Anthony Payne, eds. 1996. *Regionalism and World Order*. New York: St. Martin's Press.

Gartzke, Erik, Quan Li, and Charles Boehmer. 2001. "Investing in the Peace: Economic Interdependence and International Conflict." *International Organization* 55(2): 391–438.

Gowa, Joanne. 1999. *Ballots and Bullets: The Elusive Democratic Peace*. Princeton: Princeton University Press.

Green, Donald P., Soo Yeon Kim, and David H. Yoon. 2001. "Dirty Pool." *International Organization* 55(2): 441–68.

Haas, Ernst B. 1958. *The Uniting of Europe: Political, Social, and Economic Forces, 1950–57*. Stanford: Stanford University Press.

———. 1964. *Beyond the Nation State: Functionalism and International Organization*. Stanford: Stanford University Press.

Harris, Stuart, and Andrew Mack, eds. 1997. *Asia-Pacific Security: The Economics-Politics Nexus*. St. Leonards: Allen & Unwin Australia.

Hatch, Walter, and Kozo Yamamura. 1996. *Asia in Japan's Embrace: Building a Regional Production Alliance*. New York: Cambridge University Press.

Heginbotham, Eric, and Richard J. Samuels. 1998. "Mercantile Realism and Japanese Foreign Policy." *International Security* 22(4): 171–203.

Hegre, Havard. 2000. "Development and the Liberal Peace: What Does It Take to Be a Trading State?" *Journal of Peace Research* 37(1): 5–30.

Held, David, Anthony McGrew, David Goldblatt, and Jonathan Perraton. 1999. *Global Transformations: Politics, Economics, and Culture*. Stanford: Stanford University Press.

Hirschman, Albert. 1977. *The Passions and the Interests: Political Arguments for Capitalism Before Its Triumph*. Princeton: Princeton University Press.

Hirst, Paul Q., and Grahame Thompson. 1999. *Globalization in Question: The International Economy and the Possibilities of Governance*. 2nd ed. Cambridge, U.K.: Polity Press.

Howard, Michael. 1978. *War and the Liberal Conscience*. New Brunswick: Rutgers University Press.

IMF (International Monetary Fund). 2000. *Direction of Trade Statistics Quarterly*. Mar.

Jervis, Robert. 1997. *System Effects: Complexity in Political and Social Life*. Princeton: Princeton University Press.

Joeck, Neil. 1999. "Nuclear Developments in India and Pakistan." *Access Asia Review* 2(2): 5–45.

Johnson, Chalmers. 1982. *MITI and the Japanese Miracle: The Growth of Industrial Policy, 1925–1975*. Stanford: Stanford University Press.

Johnston, Alastair Iain, and Robert S. Ross, eds. 1999. *Engaging China: The Management of an Emerging Power*. London: Routledge.

Katzenstein, Peter J., and Takashi Shiraishi, eds. 1997. *Network Power: Japan and Asia*. Ithaca: Cornell University Press.

Keohane, Robert O. 1984. *After Hegemony: Cooperation and Discord in the World Political Economy*. Princeton: Princeton University Press.

————, and Helen V. Milner, eds. 1996. *Internationalization and Domestic Politics.* Cambridge: Cambridge University Press.

————, and Joseph S. Nye Jr. 1972. *Transnational Relations and World Politics.* Cambridge, Mass.: Harvard University Press.

————. 1989. *Power and Interdependence.* 2nd ed. Glenview, Ill.: Scott, Foresman.

Khong, Yuen Foong. 1997. "ASEAN and the Southeast Asian Security Complex." In David A. Lake and Patrick M. Morgan, eds., *Regional Orders: Building Security in a New World.* University Park: Pennsylvania State University Press.

King, Gary. 2001. "Proper Nouns and Methodological Propriety: Pooling Dyads in International Relations Data." *International Organization* 55(2): 497–507.

Kirshner, Jonathan. 1998. "Political Economy in Security Studies After the Cold War." *Review of International Political Economy* 5(1) (Spring): 64–91.

Koppel, Bruce M., and Robert M. Orr Jr., eds. 1993. *Japan's Foreign Aid: Power and Policy in a New Era.* Boulder, Colo.: Westview.

Langhammer, Rolf J. 1998. "Europe's Trade, Investment, and Strategic Policy Interests in Asia and APEC." In Peter Drysdale and David Vines, eds., *Europe, East Asia, and APEC: A Shared Global Agenda?* Cambridge: Cambridge University Press.

Lechner, Frank J., and John Boli, eds. 2000. *The Globalization Reader.* Oxford: Blackwell.

Lenin, V. I. 1970. *Imperialism, the Highest Stage of Capitalism.* Moscow: Progress Publishers.

Lindblad, J. Thomas. 1998. *Foreign Investment in Southeast Asia in the Twentieth Century.* New York: St. Martin's Press.

Lipset, Seymour Martin. 1959. "Some Social Requisites of Democracy: Economic Development and Political Legitimacy." *American Political Science Review* 53(1): 69–105.

MAC (Mainland Affairs Council). Website: www.mac.gov.tw/english.

Mansfield, Edward D. 1994. *Power, Trade, and War.* Princeton: Princeton University Press.

————, and Helen V. Milner, eds. 1997. *The Political Economy of Regionalism.* New York: Columbia University Press.

Mastanduno, Michael. 1998. "Economics and Security in Statecraft and Scholarship." *International Organization* 52(4): 825–54.

McMahon, Robert J. 1999. *The Limits of Empire: The United States and Southeast Asia Since World War II.* New York: Columbia University Press.

Milner, Helen V., and David A. Baldwin. 1990. *The Political Economy of National Security: An Annotated Bibliography.* Boulder, Colo.: Westview.

Mitrany, David. 1966. *A Working Peace System.* Chicago: Quadrangle Books.

MOFA (Ministry of Foreign Affairs of Japan). *Japan's ODA.* Various years.

MOFTEC (Ministry of Foreign Trade and Economic Cooperation). Website: www.moftec.gov.cn.

Morley, James W., ed. 1999. *Driven by Growth: Political Change in the Asia-Pacific Region.* Rev. ed. Armonk, N.Y.: M. E. Sharpe.

Myers, Ramon H., and Mark R. Peattie, eds. 1984. *The Japanese Colonial Empire, 1895–1945.* Princeton: Princeton University Press.

Ninh, Kim. 1998. "Vietnam: Struggle and Cooperation." In Muthiah Alagappa, ed., *Asian Security Practice: Material and Ideational Influences.* Stanford: Stanford University Press.

Nishigaki Akira and Shimomura Yasutami. 1997. *Kaihatsu enjo no keizaigaku* (Economics of development assistance). 2nd ed. Tokyo: Yuhikaku.

Nye, Joseph S., Jr. 1971. *Peace in Parts: Integration and Conflict in Regional Organization.* Boston: Little, Brown.

———. 1988. "Neorealism and Neoliberalism." *World Politics* 40(2): 235–51.

Oneal, John R., and Bruce M. Russett. 1997. "The Classical Liberals Were Right: Democracy, Interdependence, and Conflict, 1950–1985." *International Studies Quarterly* 41(2): 267–93.

———. 1999. "Assessing the Liberal Peace with Alternative Specifications: Trade Still Reduces Conflict." *Journal of Peace Research* 36(4): 432–42.

———. 2001. "Clear and Clean: The Fixed Effects of the Liberal Peace." *International Organization* 55(2): 469–86.

Pei, Minxin, and Ariel David Adesnik. 2000. "Why Recessions Don't Start Revolutions." *Foreign Policy* 118 (Spring): 138–51.

Pempel, T. J. 1999. "Regional Ups, Regional Downs." In T. J. Pempel, ed., *The Politics of the Asian Economic Crisis.* Ithaca: Cornell University Press.

Petri, Peter. 1993. "The East Asian Trading Bloc: An Analytical History." In Jeffrey Frankel and Miles Kahler, eds., *Regionalism and Rivalry: Japan and the U.S. in Pacific Asia.* Chicago: University of Chicago Press.

Polachek, Solomon W. 1980. "Conflict and Trade." *Journal of Conflict Resolution* 24(1): 55–78.

———, John Robst, and Yuan-Ching Chang. 1999. "Liberalism and Interdependence: Expanding the Trade-Conflict Model." *Journal of Peace Research* 36(4): 405–22.

Rosecrance, Richard. 1986. *The Rise of the Trading State: Commerce and Conquest in the Modern World.* New York: Basic Books.

Ross, Robert S. 1999. "The Geography of the Peace." *International Security* 23(4): 81–118.

Safarian, A. E., and Wendy Dobson, eds. 1996. *East Asian Capitalism: Diversity and Dynamism.* Toronto: Center for International Business, University of Toronto.

Samuels, Richard J. 1994. *"Rich Nation, Strong Army": National Security and the Technological Transformation of Japan.* Ithaca: Cornell University Press.

Scollay, Robert, and John P. Gilbert. 2001. *New Regional Trading Arrangements in the Asia Pacific?* Washington, D.C.: Institute for International Economics.

Shirk, Susan L., and Christopher P. Twomey, eds. 1996. *Power and Prosperity: Economics and Security Linkages in Asia-Pacific.* New Brunswick, N.J.: Transaction Books.

Snyder, Jack. 2000. *From Voting to Violence: Democratization and Nationalist Conflict.* New York: Norton.

Soesastro, Hadi. 1994. "Pacific Economic Cooperation: The History of an Idea." In Ross Garnaut and Peter Drysdale, eds., *Asia Pacific Regionalism: Readings in International Economic Relations.* Pymble, Australia: HarperEducational.

Solingen, Etel. 1998. *Regional Orders at Century's Dawn: Global and Domestic Influences on Grand Strategy.* Princeton: Princeton University Press.

Storey, Ian James. 1999–2000. "Living with Colossus: How Southeast Asian Countries Cope with China." *Parameters* 29(4): 111–25.

Van Hoesel, Roger. 1999. *New Multinational Enterprises from Korea and Taiwan: Beyond Export-Led Growth.* New York: Routledge.

Vogel, Ezra. 1991. *The Four Little Dragons.* Cambridge, Mass.: Harvard University Press.

Wade, Robert. 1990. *Governing the Market: Economic Theory and the Role of Government in East Asian Industrialization.* Princeton: Princeton University Press.

Waltz, Kenneth N. 1979. *Theory of International Politics.* New York: Addison-Wesley.

Wan, Ming. 1996. "Wealth and Power: The Economic Transformation of Security." *Harvard International Review* 18(2): 20–21, 69–70.

———. 2001a. *Japan Between Asia and the West: Economic Power and Strategic Balance.* Armonk, N.Y.: M. E. Sharpe.

———. 2001b. *Human Rights in Chinese Foreign Relations: Defining and Defending National Interests.* Philadelphia: University of Pennsylvania Press.

Wanandi, Jusuf. 1996. "ASEAN's China Strategy: Towards Deeper Engagement." *Survival* 38(3): 117–28.

Wendt, Alexander. 1999. *Social Theory of International Politics.* Cambridge: Cambridge University Press.

Whiting, Allen S. 1997. "ASEAN Eyes China: The Security Dimension." *Asian Survey* 37(4): 299–322.

World Bank. 2000. *East Asia: Recovery and Beyond.* Washington, D.C.: World Bank.

Zoellick, Robert B. 1997–98. "Economics and Security in the Changing Asia-Pacific." *Survival* 39(4): 29–51.

CHAPTER NINE

The UN System as a Pathway to Security in Asia

A Buttress, Not a Pillar

ROSEMARY FOOT

Governmental support for increasing the numbers of formal global institutions, especially since 1945, suggests a widespread recognition that such bodies contribute to international order and security. The definition of order in Chapter 1 relates it to the provision of stability and predictability in relationships and the accommodation of change through nonviolent means—a set of aims that international organizations seem well placed to address, given their origins in the desire to find cooperative solutions to collective problems and their reinforcement of a notion of common interest.

This chapter deals with a select if significant set of the global intergovernmental organizations (IGOs) that have been in operation since 1945—those within the UN system that hold the primary responsibility for the maintenance of a peaceful and secure international order. I draw on Hedley Bull's and Muthiah Alagappa's definitions of a security order (see Chap. 1) and thus relate the concept to state—rather than nonstate—behavior, including state actions within IGOs. I also focus primarily on major conflict, or threats of conflict, in Asia: "Avoidance of armed conflicts must be the primary function of any international order, as without the control of violence many of the other values states and individuals seek can be disrupted" (Paul and Hall 1999: 2).

Bull, in fact, had little to say in his writings about the United Nations. In one of his last lectures in 1985, the year of his death, he contended that it was "hardly possible to argue that the UN is a chief source of international order or of peace and security." In his view, the institutions that best preserve international order are the "older ones, like balance of power, international law, diplomacy, and that operate outside the framework of the UN" (Alderson and Hurrell 2000: 19, n. 40). This chapter takes Bull's position as a point of empirical departure. After outlining the constraints and potential of the UN system in contributing to a regional security order, I present a selective record of the UN's involvement in Asia since 1945 in response to incipient or actual armed conflict and note its contributions along a continuum: as a forum to expose those using force, as third-party mediator to ease the movement toward conflict containment or resolution, and as leader in the search for solutions and the establishment of a stable order.

Overall I conclude that, while the UN has contributed in various ways to providing a security order in this region, it has predominantly been an adjunct rather than a primary player. Bearing in mind the constraints under which this intergovernmental organization has operated since its inception, as well as the problems of measuring its contribution comparatively, it appears that the UN has been less prominent in Asia than elsewhere in the world in the prevention, management, or resolution of some of the most serious sources of tension. Two factors seem especially pertinent. First and foremost are issues relating to state power—that is, the presence of several major states in the region with interests of their own in managing conflict. Second, there is an underlying suspicion of the UN that derives from a widespread perception that the UN system—especially the Security Council and the international financial institutions (IFIs)—are tools of powerful Western states, some of which were once colonial powers in the region. A corollary of this perception of global institutions as hierarchical and inequitable, as well as of the colonial experience, has been a strong attachment to the norms of state sovereignty and noninterference. The Korean War, the China recognition issue, and the IFIs' response to the Asian economic crisis (1997–99) demonstrate some of the causes and consequences of this suspicion. This suspicion also helps to explain some of the regional states' responses to the post–Cold War expansion of the UN's normative agenda. Today the UN is beginning to focus on the conditions that pertain to peace and stability within states rather than strictly between them. The matter of humanitarian intervention—from the perspective of states that still uphold the norm of state sovereignty as traditionally defined—figures prominently here. Finally, the chapter assesses some of the consequences of Asia's experience of the UN system for other pathways to regional order.

The UN system implies the whole set of complex bureaucratic organizations, formally linked to the UN proper, all geared in their different ways to fulfilling the aims of the UN Charter. The UN system includes its principal organs, various subsidiary bodies, specialized agencies, and semiautonomous bodies.[1] The UN

---

[1]Most books on the United Nations include a figure outlining this structure. See, for example,

has also created political opportunities for nonstate actors to operate as advocates of particular causes, though the roles of these groups are not investigated here. Some parts of the UN system—such as the Security Council, the UN Secretary-General, and the International Court of Justice—deal directly with the threat or actual use of force and the peaceful settlement of disputes. It is these bodies that form the primary focus of this chapter. Other organizations, including the United Nations Development Programme (UNDP) and the Bretton Woods institutions, offer institutional means of responding to Article 55 of the Charter and its reference to the need to create the "conditions of stability and well-being which are necessary for peaceful and friendly relations among nations." A third set of institutions—the UN Commission for Human Rights, for example, together with the division of Electoral Assistance in the UN Secretariat—seeks to ease the transition from authoritarian rule to political arrangements that protect individual and minority rights, bolster adherence to the rule of law, and make governments more accountable to their citizens (Russett 1998: 376–83). Especially in the post–Cold War era, each of these various bodies, often in combination, has attempted to move warring societies into a period of stability and order.

Given the comprehensive nature of this structure and the norms it embodies, the UN system has much to contribute to international order. Certainly there has been much for it to do in Asia. Despite the relative peace and economic progress that have been enjoyed across large parts of the region, particularly in the last two decades of the twentieth century, it is hard to deny that it has been home to much social and individual misery. One analyst writing in 1987 recorded 17 million war deaths—civilian and military—since 1945 in East Asia and 2.5 million in South Asia (Segal 1987: 1). A 1999 survey counts 29 major wars in the Asia Pacific between 1945 and 1996—with six still continuing—compared with 27 in Africa, 25 in the Middle East, and 17 in Latin America (Harada and Tanaka 1999: 333). If one measures conflicts in terms of battle-related deaths between 1989 and 1998, then Asia in that decade was on a par with Africa (Wallensteen and Sollenberg 1998).[2] Moreover, the region is the site of numerous unresolved territorial and maritime disputes. Malaysia, for example, has unresolved claims with all of its neighbors except Laos and Cambodia.

Turning to matters of human security, Asia has witnessed two major fam-

---

Karns and Mingst (1995: 22). For an excellent brief description of the UN system, see Roberts and Kingsbury (1993: 5–13).

[2]Levels of intensity are defined as follows: Low intensity is below 1,000 deaths; intermediate represents more than 1,000 deaths during the course of conflict but fewer than 1,000 deaths in any given year; high intensity is defined as more than 1,000 in any one year. In Asia these three headings would include conflicts in Afghanistan, Bangladesh, Cambodia, India, Indonesia, Laos, Myanmar, Nepal, Pakistan, the Philippines, and Sri Lanka.

ines—one in China after the Great Leap Forward and another in North Korea during the 1990s. There has been much ethnic, religious, political, and class-based violence, as well: among Hindus and Muslims; in the course of the various anti-Chinese riots in Indonesia; in Cambodia at the murderous hands of Pol Pot and the Khmer Rouge; in East Timor after the Indonesian invasion in 1975 and especially following a decisive vote in favor of independence in 1999; in Afghanistan before and after the defeat of the Soviet forces that had entered that country in 1979; and against various "rightists" in China in each decade between 1950 and 1980. Other sources of conflict relate directly to the diminishing quality of the environment in a region where "population pressures, ecological degradation and depletion, and the accelerated demand for water, timber, minerals, agricultural land, fisheries, and other natural resources are sending shock waves across remote stretches of the Pacific and upland frontiers of Asia" (Talbott and Brown 1998: 53–60). Notwithstanding the importance of these aspects of security, this chapter primarily explores order among states and its relationship to the danger of major conflict.

The UN System's Limits and Promise

Were the member states of the UN system able to realize many of the aspirations outlined in the UN Charter and those of its agencies, there would be little doubt about the UN's ability to contribute mightily to global and regional order. The collective security function of the UN, however, reflected principally in Chapter VII of its Charter, has long been hobbled by the frequent inability of the five permanent members on the UN Security Council to agree on a joint response to an act of aggression. Even in the post–Cold War era—a time when several operations have been undertaken under Chapter VII provisions and the overt use of the veto is rare—the UN still engages in selective rather than collective action.

The early realization of the difficulties of advancing the notion of collective security prompted the expansion of the "good-offices" role of the UN Secretary-General and the development of UN involvement in peacekeeping operations (PKOs), a function not provided for in the Charter but seen as helpful to the containment of conflict. In the post–Cold War era, such PKOs have vastly increased in number, sometimes to include those where the UN authorizes an internationally constituted force (as with Afghanistan in December 2001) rather than creating and administering the force itself. Peacekeeping has also increased markedly in scope, particularly as a result of involvement in civil wars that have drawn the UN system into managing conflicts requiring three transitions: the shift from war to peace (including the cantonment, disarmament, and demobilization of combatants and the repatriation and reintegration of refugees and internationally displaced persons); the transformation of controlled economies to a free-market system; and movement from authoritarian rule to some form of pluralist democracy (Forman and Patrick 2000: 5). Such operations, however, represent a demanding long-term task and one that has found the UN system inadequate because of its members' well-established reluctance to allow the formation of a standing UN army, their frequent failure to vote for the necessary resources, and their unwillingness to see it increase its capacity to plan multitask operations.

In recognition of these difficulties, in 1992 the UN Secretary-General, Boutros Boutros-Ghali, called on regional organizations to ease the UN's impossibly demanding mandate as originally intended under Chapter VIII of the UN Charter. Sharing the burden, he argued, could help compensate for the UN's financial and material weaknesses, lend special insight on the basis of local knowledge, lead to swifter military responses to conflict, and offer a greater sense of global participation in international conflict management (Boutros-Ghali 1992). His argument has fallen on infertile ground. Few regional organizations have the capacity to take on the complex operations typical of the post–Cold War era. Nor are they accepted as neutral managers of conflict in their own regions.

In the post–Cold War period, therefore, as in earlier decades, the UN remains constrained in its role of ensuring international peace and security. Nevertheless it can contribute to the security order in less tangible ways. This unique organization has "always been a theatre for standard-setting and myth-making—for appealing to higher standards than those which commonly prevail in international relations, and for holding out the promise of a better-ordered world" (Roberts and Kingsbury 1993: 21)—and this alone makes it valuable to international society. Many of its aspirations are set out in the UN Charter and the various conventions and resolutions the organization has adopted since 1945. These norms—such as nonuse of force except in self-defense, restrictions on weapons of mass destruction, the need for protection of human rights and promotion of human dignity, the meaning and methods of preventive diplomacy, ideas of good governance—have had some influence on states' behavior and remain a powerful source of ideas when it comes to composing parallel documents at the state or regional level.

For all its limitations in the matter of conflict mediation, resolution, and management, the UN does have some resources at its disposal, provided the major states acquiesce. For example, it can act as a third-party mediator via the good-offices function of the Secretary-General (or his representative) or adjudicate on issues in dispute via the International Court of Justice; it can use its economic agencies to help with the rehabilitation of war-torn societies or galvanize other actors to promote the conditions that sustain human life at tolerable levels; and it can draw on its special monitoring capacities, such as the International Atomic Energy Agency (IAEA), or its peacekeeping function to ascertain whether agreements are being kept. It can also use coercive means—economic or military—to enforce peace if so directed by the UN Security Council or—in exceptional circumstances—the General Assembly.

One consequence of the UN's universal membership and the member states' subscription to a single set of principles is that there is no higher legal, moral, or political authority in the international system. This gives the UN a special form of influence. Certainly it is a politicized body with a structure that allows member states (especially Security Council members) to select the situations in which the UN can become involved. But once there is a mandate, its actions are presumed to conform to the terms of the mandate, which makes it impartial in this crucial sense. Such impartiality reinforces the legitimacy the UN lends to its operations, a resource that is invaluable in the search for peaceful settlement. It can also deny legitimacy to others—for example, by withholding formal recognition of political bodies of different kinds. This power goes beyond governments to include nongovernmental actors and regional organizations. The UN, then, has both a unique role to play as an intergovernmental organization and a special stature that gives it normative power. It is more than the sum of its parts. At the same time, however, it is essential to remember that the member states, especially the most powerful among them, can withhold their assent and deny the UN a serious role in providing a security order. The UN cannot "take strong action on its own initiative irrespective of the views of states" (Roberts and Kingsbury 1993: 16). Its structure does not allow for this—a point that should be borne in mind when evaluating its activities in Asia.

The UN's Record

Each of these roles—the UN as "teacher of norms" (Finnemore 1993), provider of resources, and legitimator of certain actors and events—has been invoked by states in the Asian region since 1945 in their efforts to establish or maintain a benign environment or to deal with actual conflict. Inevitably, however, these roles have been drawn upon selectively and not necessarily consistently.

Normative Influence

The most influential UN Charter norms, at least as reflected in regional and subregional charters, have been those contained in Article 2, with their reference to the sovereign equality of all states, the pacific settlement of disputes, constraints on the threat or actual use of force, and nonintervention in matters that fall within the domestic jurisdiction of states. Neglected, therefore, have been those Charter provisions—such as sections of Article 55—that dilute an absolutist interpretation of state sovereignty. Wording influenced by Article 2 (or at least general reference to the broad aims of the UN Charter) has appeared in several formal agreements reached in the region—in the five principles of peaceful coexistence (Panch Sheel) first enunciated by India and China in 1954, in ASEAN's founding treaty of 1967, and in its 1976 Treaty of Amity and Cooperation, the terms of which were endorsed by the ASEAN Regional Forum (ARF) in July 1994. The SAARC Charter of 1985 also makes general reference to the principles of the UN Charter in its preamble although, like ASEAN, it was not set up to deal directly with security issues. Such norms have not prevented the outbreak of conflict, but they have set some bounds to states' behavior and "reinforced the idea that there is a strong presumption in most cases against the legitimacy of the uninvited use of force by a state outside its accepted international frontiers." This understanding has helped to legitimize the demands made repeatedly in the UN General Assembly for an end to the Indonesian occupation of East Timor, the withdrawal of Vietnamese forces from Cambodia, and removal of Soviet troops from Afghanistan (Roberts and Kingsbury 1993: 23–25).

The UN has also been closely associated with various arms control treaties such as the Biological and Chemical Weapons conventions (BWC and CWC), the Nuclear NonProliferation Treaty (NPT), and the Comprehensive Test Ban Treaty (CTBT), together with preventive mechanisms such as the UN Conventional Arms Register (UNCAR). These treaties and mechanisms have generated a degree of support in the region. Although the NPT and CTBT have been viewed with suspicion and aversion, especially in South Asia, for reasons explained in Chapter 10, all major Asian states have signed the BWC and CWC, and most have signed the NPT. Furthermore, the ARF states agreed in 1998 that, in the absence of a regional arms register, member states could voluntarily agree to circulate among ARF members the returns they had made to the UNCAR. China's signature by 1996 of 85 to 90 percent of all arms control arrangements that it was eligible to sign (including the NPT and CTBT)—despite Beijing's previous criticism that such agreements were discriminatory—owes at least some part of its explanation to China's recognition that its seat on the UN Security Council imposes certain obligations on it. China's desire to burnish its international image was best achieved, so its leadership thought, through "responsible" behavior in areas sanctioned by this universal international body (Swaine and Johnston 1999: 93, 101, 108–9). Thus international agreements, often negotiated at the UN and designed to maintain international order, have spilled over to individual states of the region and made a contribution at this level too.

The advent of the post–Cold War era has focused attention on regional security organizations. In Asia it has even led to new institutions such as the ARF, a body that has drawn on global security norms in order to advance its cooperative security objective. Ideas of preventive diplomacy, for example, outlined in Article 1 of the UN Charter but elaborated and systematized by Secretary-General Dag Hammarskjold and then introduced anew in 1992 in Boutros Boutros-Ghali's *Agenda for Peace*, led to an expansion of regional interest in this concept. The idea appeared in the concept paper introduced at the ARF's second meeting in 1995. Thus the ARF was led to sponsor three seminars on preventive diplomacy between 1995 and 1997 (Ball and Acharya 1999) and to issue stronger statements in support of the concept at ARF annual meetings. ASEAN has shown interest in the idea too. In July 2000, it formally established a troika made up of past, present, and future ASEAN chairs to respond to incipient emergencies. Japan, constrained for historical and constitutional reasons from working directly to help with the management and resolution of conflicts, has found for itself a role in conflict prevention. For these reasons, Japan's regional diplomacy reflects the approach it has taken as a UN member: offering major economic support for humanitarian aspects of the UN's agenda, supporting disarmament issues, and strengthening the position of the UN Secretary-General under Article 99 of the UN Charter (Ogata 1995). (China, however, remains less enthusiastic about preventive diplomacy. Beijing worries that such a policy might encourage interference in intrastate conflicts and lead to a breach of the principle of state sovereignty as traditionally defined [Shi Chunlai 1999: 184–85].)

Boutros-Ghali's *Agenda for Peace*, moreover, referred to the International Court of Justice (ICJ) as an "under-used resource for the peaceful adjudication of disputes." States such as Malaysia, with its many outstanding territorial disputes, have so far found it impossible to make use of the regional High Council established in the ASEAN Treaty of Amity and Cooperation (1976) to assist with their resolution, fearing that the High Council could never be impartial in an adjudication. This fact, together with the somewhat higher profile given the ICJ in the post–Cold War era, may have added to the essentially economic reasons why Malaysia and Singapore (in 1994) and Malaysia and Indonesia (in October 1996) asked the ICJ to settle their sovereignty disputes over the islands Pulau Batu Putih/Pedra Branca, Pulau Ligitan, and Pulau Sipadan (Kahler 2000: 564). These requests highlighted acceptance of the legitimacy of certain global institutions and acknowledgment that a body like the ICJ could act more impartially than any regional mechanism.

Overall, therefore, the UN has provided valuable benchmarks for determining acceptable rules of behavior, especially in the matter of conflict prevention and containment. The UN's actions have reduced the need for Asian states, only too aware of a regionwide lack of community, to attempt to negotiate treaties, agreements, and mechanisms in a variety of specialist and technical fields. When the UN norms serve national or regional purposes, they have been embraced unilaterally.

Legitimating Functions

As well as representing a source of normative and legal ideas, the UN's unique stature and procedures have made it a place where Asian states can publicize their grievances, receive approval or reprimand for their behavior, and support or undermine particular political groupings. As Indonesians fought for their political independence from Dutch colonial forces in the late 1940s, they favored UN involvement as a means of enlisting sympathy for their cause and boosting their bargaining position despite military weakness (Miller 1967: 38). Far less welcome so far as Jakarta was concerned, East Timor had a prominent place on the UN's agenda after 1960. This attention prompted a series of resolutions calling on Jakarta to allow self-determination for the East Timorese, to withdraw its occupation forces, and to facilitate the role of the Secretary-General in bringing together all concerned parties.[3] Although UN-sanctioned talks between Indonesian and Portuguese ministers did not get off the ground until 1992, the UN's participation had weakened the legitimacy of Indonesia's occupation of the territory by then and kept the issue before the international community. This involvement helped the East Timorese resistance movement to expand the basis of its international support—assistance on which it could draw as the independence issue reached a crisis point in 1999 (Gunn 1997).

The ASEAN states also made use of the UN's arena and legitimation functions to keep the pressure on Vietnam after its intervention in Cambodia in 1978 and installation of the Hun Sen regime; the latter was unable to acquire the UN seat of the ousted government of what was then called Democratic Kampuchea (Berdal and Leifer 1996: 30; Harada and Tanaka 1999: 334–41). ASEAN also involved the UN in hosting an international conference in July 1981 at which the subregional organization proposed a settlement plan—based on one that UN officials Perez de Cuellar and his aide Rafeeuddin Ahmed had persistently advocated—including provisions that Vietnam's military forces be withdrawn, all warring Khmer factions be disarmed, an interim administration be set up, and free elections be held under UN auspices. Although the proposed solution did not bear fruit at the time, all the points raised in 1981 eventually formed the basis of a settlement a decade later.

Two elections organized by the UN and held in the 1990s—in Cambodia and East Timor—have been important steps along the rocky road designed to lead to

[3]Certain Asian states— India, Japan, the Philippines, and Thailand—voted against UN Resolution 3485, which deplored the Indonesian invasion and called for Indonesian troop withdrawal.

a new political order in these two territories. The UN's standing has made it difficult for opposition groups to mount a sustained legal challenge to the outcome of elections conducted in this manner. Whether regional order has been improved overall as a result of these elections, however, is far less certain at this early stage of state building in the two countries. Moreover, the verification function proved important in closing a chapter of the conflict that has long engulfed Afghanistan, when fifty UN observers under the UN's Good Offices Mission in Afghanistan (UNGOMAP) confirmed that more than 100,000 Soviet troops had left the country in 1988. Verification of a different kind—this time undertaken by the newly assertive IAEA in 1992 and with rather mixed results (including North Korea's threat to withdraw from the NPT)—led to the discovery of discrepancies in the amount of plutonium that North Korea claimed it had produced from its nuclear reactors (Oberdorfer 1997: 268–71, 274–80). Although this IAEA discovery represents only one piece in the huge puzzle concerning possible nuclear weapons production in North Korea, it was a step along the road of definition and then containment of this particularly tense phase of the crisis.

First-, Second-, and Third-Generation Operations

Clearly, then, the UN performs a somewhat passive, enabling role in the effort to resolve tensions, deal with conflict, or prevent its outbreak. But beyond this role, as well as its normative influence, the UN has also tried actively to engage in mediation or to employ nonmilitary coercion (that is, sanctions) in response to conflict in Asia. The UN has put a great deal of energy into peacemaking in the region, often using special envoys as in Burma or Afghanistan. It has also involved itself in mediating an end to major wars, most recently in December 2001 helping to broker a pact between four Afghan factions designed to create a broadly based interim government for the post-Taliban era in Afghanistan. Since the end of the Cold War, major states have permitted the UN to play a more prominent role in conflict resolution, as in Cambodia (especially given the 1991 Paris agreement) and between Indonesia and East Timor (from 1999). Even so, this leaves twenty or so major conflicts in Asia since 1945 in which the UN has not been effective to date in bringing the fighting to an end or been prominently involved in mediating termination of the wars.

Asia has certain unique characteristics when it comes to the UN's peacekeeping, peace-building, and peace-enforcement functions. It holds the doubtful distinction of hosting one of the world's longest-running observer-cum-peacekeeping operations: the UN's Military Observer Group in India and Pakistan (UNMOGIP) has been stationed in Jammu and Kashmir since January 1949. The region has also been the site of a UN "second-generation" operation: peacekeeping plus peace building in Cambodia, where it acted on the basis of a mandate exceeding those of all previous UN peacekeeping operations. According to Jarat Chopra (2000: 27), Asia is distinctive again because the UN for the first time in its history had been "exercising sovereign authority within a fledgling nation" in East Timor before East Timorese independence in May 2002. (But note the parallels that could be drawn with the Kosovo operation.) Finally, Asia was the site of the first UN military enforcement operation: the Korean War (1950–53).

The following sections discuss these cases in some detail because their level of violence has been sufficient to disturb the regional security order, because they illustrate the relationship between the major states and the UN in Asia in the conflicts where it has been most extensively involved, and because they show the constraints on UN action. Broadly, they demonstrate that, subsequent to the 1950s Korean operation and only when major states have had little direct interest in the conflict—as in Cambodia and East Timor in the post–Cold War era—do we see the UN making a more central contribution to the security order and conflict resolution.

The Korean War and Military Enforcement

The UN's involvement in the Korean War is pertinent to my argument in several ways. First, the Soviet boycott of the UN Security Council at the time of initial UN deliberations over the North Korean use of force showed that only under exceptionally peculiar circumstances in the Cold War era could the Security Council reach agreement under Chapter VII. Second, the development of UN Command forces demonstrated the organization's total dependence on the armed forces of other states, especially the Western powers, to carry out its mandate. Third, Beijing's experiences during the war heightened its distrust of the UN as a neutral body and its wariness of the concept of collective security. Finally, for all Security Council members it reinforced their attachment to the veto.

The UN first became involved in the Korean reunification issue in 1947. In the next year elections held in the South under UN auspices led to the creation of the Republic of Korea. The UN had created a Temporary Commission on Korea (UNTCOK) to supervise the process and "observe and report any developments which might lead to, or otherwise involve, military conflict in Korea"—essentially a preventive diplomacy function.

This observer function failed to prevent North Korea's attack on the South in June 1950, and in response to the outbreak of fighting the United States led a coalition of South Korean forces and those of fifteen other states—mainly U.S. allies—under a UN flag. Not content with pushing North Korean forces back to the 38th parallel, the U.S.-led UN Command troops, backed by a UN General Assembly resolution passed in October 1950, crossed north of the dividing line and pushed on to the Yalu River border between North Korea and China. North Ko-

rea's losses prompted wholesale Chinese intervention in the fighting, which resulted in a vast expansion in casualties on all sides and the prolongation of the
conflict for almost three more years. Undoubtedly this war would have been a far
less controversial operation had UN forces simply restored the status quo ante.
Even with these more modest aims the UN operation would still have made two
major points: force should not be used for settling issues in dispute, and those
who ignore such norms will be resisted.

The conflict did little to increase the prestige of the UN. Nevertheless, the fact
of a U.S.-led UN response eventually contributed to regional order by convincing
pivotal major states that they needed to take control of threats to the status quo
within the region. Thus it was Beijing, Moscow, and Washington that subsequently placed the necessary constraints on their allies to prevent further outbreaks of serious conflict. After 1953, Chinese and Soviet leaders became more
circumspect in their relations with Kim Il Sung, operating their own version of
containment of any military ambitions the North Korean leader might have continued to nurse for reunifying the peninsula. Over the course of the war U.S. defense expenditures nearly quadrupled, and either during the conflict or shortly
afterward Washington signed bilateral defense treaties with Japan, South Korea,
Taiwan, South Vietnam, the Philippines, and Thailand and set up an ill-starred
multilateral security organization, the South East Asia Treaty Organization. The
U.S. intent was to create local balances of power, thus obviating the need for the
United States to bear the sole burden of ensuring order. During this search for a
U.S.-sanctioned regional order, however, the United States was drawn into another bloody military operation, this time in Indochina. Though the ends America sought took time to develop, in the course of establishing these commitments
it willed the means for its grand strategy of containment to be global in scope, for
it to become and remain the preponderant power in East Asia, and for the UN to
be pushed to the sidelines in the management of the regional security order.

The UN was not to operate again as it did in Korea until the Gulf War in 1990–
91. The UN's experiences in the 1950s reinforced the understanding that during
the Cold War the contemplation of enforcement actions was likely to lead to a use
of the veto by one side or the other. In recognition of this structural constraint,
the UN, under the secretary-generalship of Dag Hammarskjold, took the decision
to give higher priority to the UN's peacekeeping role. These operations were to involve the deployment of lightly armed military personnel, with the consent of the
warring parties, after the cessation of hostilities. Often such operations resulted in
little more than freezing the conflict in the hope that the containment of violence,
and the passage of time, would lead to the cooling of passions, the introduction of
confidence-building measures, and an environment possibly conducive to the
eventual resolution of the dispute.

Kashmir, Indo-Pakistani Conflicts, and Peacekeeping

Asia's unique experience in hosting a UN-backed military operation during the Cold War was matched by its involvement with the longest-running PKO—but with little evidence of the UN's capacity to advance the cause of conflict resolution. The India-Pakistan war over Kashmir quickly drew the UN into its second major peacekeeping action in the form of an observer force. (The first was Palestine.) India introduced the Kashmir issue into the United Nations not only because Nehru's worldview accorded that body—for a time at least—a prominent and authoritative security role (Krishna 1985), but more instrumentally because he expected the UN to declare Pakistan an aggressor (Ganguly 1994). In December 1948, a Security Council resolution, accepted by India and Pakistan, provided for a ceasefire and established a ceasefire line. Between 1950 and 1958, four UN mediators were appointed to find some solution to the conflict, but to no avail—the last of the mediators' reports was not even debated.

Thus containment of violence became the main focus of UN efforts. The United Nations Military Observer Group in India and Pakistan helped the two sides agree to a series of confidence-building measures in the mid-1960s and placed some constraints on the escalation of minor ceasefire infractions that helped maintain reasonable calm between 1949 and 1965. But neither the UN-MOGIP presence nor the confidence-building measures moved the conflict nearer to resolution or prevented its periodic eruption into more deadly phases—as has occurred again since December 2001—once the two governments decided they no longer wished to maintain relative stability. After the 1971 Indo-Pakistani war, India withdrew operational cooperation from UNMOGIP, and since that time it has prevented observers from carrying out their duties on the Indian side of the ceasefire line. Moreover, New Delhi argued that the Simla Accords of 1972 affirmed that the Kashmir issue would be solved bilaterally—an unsuccessful effort on India's part to undercut Pakistan's policy of internationalizing the conflict (Bajpai 1996: 20–21; Dawson 1995: chap. 12). India's perspective on events has led to the constant rebuff of UN efforts to start the bilateral negotiations provided for in the accords. In sum, then, UNMOGIP has become of "political rather than operational value to Pakistan, and a political rather than operational irritant to India" (Dawson 1995: 312).

Cambodia and Peace Building

The post–Cold War era has witnessed a steep increase in global attention to intrastate conflicts. This change, together with normative developments that have come more sharply into focus with the end of the Cold War, has led to certain key changes in the scope of UN actions. The organization has now more clearly

than in the past moved beyond peacekeeping into the area of peace building—
and thus into functions that involve more intrusive shaping of the domestic
structures of states. Especially after 1987, a year that marked the former Soviet
Union's change of attitude toward the UN, the body has taken on a number of
complex, multifunctional operations designed to implement peace agreements
and build the foundations for stable, legitimate government. Two such operations have occurred in the Asia Pacific: in Cambodia after the signature of the
Paris Peace Agreement in October 1991, which led to the UN Transitional
Authority in Cambodia (UNTAC), and in East Timor beginning with an assistance mission (UNAMET) to help with the administration of the election and
then, in October 1999, the establishment of the UN Transitional Administration
in East Timor (UNTAET).[4] The UN is also contributing to a third peace-building
operation in Asia, this time in Afghanistan. It involves similarly exacting tasks of
reconstruction.

The Cambodian operation was based on a complex and precedent-setting
mandate in excess of what the UN had undertaken in Namibia (UNTAG), for example. Set up by a unanimous UN Security Council resolution in February 1992,
the ambitious aim in Cambodia was to produce a "just and durable settlement."
Specifically this envisaged a UN role in guaranteeing a "neutral political environment" during which free and fair elections would be held and a new political
assembly established, with the objective of drafting and approving a liberal
democratic constitution. After a legislative assembly and new government were
created, UNTAC would withdraw—leaving the field to presumed economic sta-
bilizers such as the IMF and World Bank. Other UN agencies involved in the operation included the office of the UN High Commissioner for Refugees to assist
with refugee repatriation routes, resettlement areas, and reception centers. Other
parts of UNTAC's mandate covered areas such as elections, civil administration,
human rights, police, military, repatriation, and rehabilitation. In the matter of
civil administration, it was directed to supervise foreign affairs, defense, finance,
public security, and information. In the human rights area it was to implement
an education program, foster an "environment in which human rights would be
ensured," engage in investigations of alleged violations, and "where appropriate"
take the necessary "corrective action." Its rehabilitation tasks were equally demanding, if somewhat vague: to "benefit all areas of Cambodia, especially the
more disadvantaged, and reach all levels of society" (Doyle 1995; Findlay 1995).
By the time elections were held in May 1993—judged free and fair—some $1.7

---

[4]Another multifunctional peacekeeping operation, UNSF/UNTEA, had a brief existence in
West Irian in 1962 to facilitate the passage of that territory from Dutch to Indonesian sovereignty.
UNTAET finished its mission in May 2002 with East Timor's independence and has been replaced
by UNMISET, UN Mission of Support in East Timor.

billion had been spent, much of the funding provided by Japan, and 22,000 civilian and military personnel had been deployed. The UN operation was the first involving Japanese SDF personnel (8 officers and 600 engineers) (Heinrich et al. 1999: 113) together with about 400 Chinese engineering troops and 47 military observers—a contingent about 20 times larger than any previous Chinese contribution to a PKO (Gill and Reilly 2000: 45).

The major achievements of this operation were the holding of elections, the establishing of a new, if shaky, governing coalition, and the weakening of the Khmer Rouge as a political and military presence—although it must be admitted that this weakening occurred because the Khmer Rouge had lost its big power backers by this time. Peace building, however, has proved more resistant to successful completion. This is not surprising, of course, since it represents a long-term and demanding task made harder still by the weakness of the Cambodian state and economy and its shallow-rooted civil society. The coup of 1997 was almost inevitable given the complex political arrangements adopted by the previously warring factions. To forestall this potential unraveling of its efforts, the UN joined with ASEAN in denying political recognition of the postcoup government until new elections were held. Recently the UN Secretary-General has turned to the matter of accounting for the large-scale slaughter of earlier times, pressing for international involvement in prosecuting those suspected of gross violations of human rights in the Khmer Rouge era. Overall the UN has contributed to the termination of this conflict, and substantial efforts have been made to effect post-conflict reconciliation. Cambodia has taken its place in the subregion via membership in ASEAN and in the wider region via participation in the ARF. But Cambodia's peace is fragile and the prospects for future stability uncertain.

East Timor and State Creation

The UN's East Timor operation had an even more expansive mandate, for UNTAET had full legislative and executive power (Chopra 2000: 29). Its direct and expanded involvement in the territory came in the wake of the ending of the Cold War, which removed a significant layer of U.S. protection from Indonesia, a state that Washington had regarded as being of major strategic importance in the Asia Pacific. The Asian economic crisis further weakened the Suharto regime in Jakarta, already enfeebled by the ailing president's unwillingness to give up power and by corruption in the country that had reached intolerable levels. Suharto's successor, President Habibie, dramatically announced in late January 1999 that, in the absence of international support for Indonesia's position over East Timor (especially his presumption that he had lost the support of the one major Western government—Australia—which had recognized Indonesian sovereignty over the territory), he would offer a vote on autonomy to the East Timorese. At this point the UN stepped in to administer the ballot; security during the election campaign and during the voting itself remained the responsibility of the Indonesian government. As the violence increased throughout East Timor's thirteen districts, the pro-integration militias, aided and abetted by the Indonesian military, extended their attacks even to the personnel of the ICRC and UNAMET. The ballot, twice delayed because of the poor security situation, was finally held on August 30. With some 99 percent of those eligible voting, 78.5 percent rejected autonomy and opted for independence. Those unreconciled to this outcome then went on a murderous rampage, pushing 200,000 East Timorese—among those who survived the onslaught—into West Timor and others into the hills or over to neighboring islands. Of a population of 800,000, some 500,000 were estimated to have been displaced by mid-September. Some 70 percent of the physical infrastructure was destroyed.

President Habibie was finally induced on September 12—the same day that a five-member UN ambassadorial team arrived in Dili and immediately after the IMF postponed a visit to Jakarta—to accept a multinational force to restore order. UN pressure came in two main ways. First, the IMF and World Bank (together with the ADB and Japanese government) held up $1.4 billion in loan disbursements from the $43 billion rescue package negotiated in response to the impact of the Asian financial crisis on the Indonesian economy. Second, the president of the World Bank, James Wolfensohn, made clear to Habibie that further economic costs would be incurred if order were not restored. Human rights abuses attracted UN attention, too. On September 10 the UN Secretary-General, citing the "Nuremberg Principle," announced that senior Indonesian officials risked prosecution for crimes against humanity if they did not allow the deployment of the multinational force that had been assembled. Efforts to contain the human rights violations continued with the holding of a special session of the UN Commission on Human Rights in late September, which passed a resolution calling for the Secretary-General to establish an international commission of inquiry to investigate evidence of abuse, a task entrusted to the UN High Commissioner for Human Rights (*Human Rights Watch World Report 2000*: xiv–xv, 196–201). Crucial, too, was the Australian government's willingness, under domestic pressure, to send in its army to restore order—together with Washington's use of direct diplomatic and economic leverage. The Clinton administration suspended arms sales and ties to the Indonesian military, but of even greater concern to Jakarta were U.S. statements that all international grants and loans would be stopped. As the President stated at a White House conference, if Indonesia did not "end the violence it must invite the international community to assist in restoring security. It would be a pity if the Indonesian recovery were crashed by this, but one way or another it will be crashed . . . if they don't fix it, because there will be overwhelming public sentiment to stop the international economic cooperation" (Taylor 1999: xxxiii; Bell 2000: 172).

Having obtained Habibie's grudging assent, the Security Council determined that the situation in East Timor constituted a threat to peace and security. Thus it adopted Resolution 1264 on September 15 sanctioning the actions of the Australian-led International Force in East Timor (INTERFET) and Resolution 1272 on October 25 establishing UNTAET. UNTAET's mandate consisted of the maintenance of law and order, establishment of an effective administration, assistance in the development of civil and social services, the coordination and delivery of humanitarian assistance, support for "capacity-building for self government," and the "establishment of conditions for sustainable development"—implying strong links between UNTAET and a wide range of UN agencies operating in the social welfare and economic realms. UNTAET operates on the basis of robust rules of engagement somewhere between peacekeeping and peace enforcement.

It is still too early to assess East Timor's future prospects. As in Cambodia, the UN successfully administered elections and beyond that regained control over the violence. UNTAET became involved in the complex task of helping to build a viable state and in May 2002 handed over the reins to a legally constituted independent state of East Timor. But the East Timorese people remain uncertain about their political and economic futures and about the security of their neighborhood. Internal disturbances continue to wrack Indonesia itself. Separatist crises have been acute in Aceh and Irian Jaya, not helped by military and militia violence in the two provinces. One consequence of Indonesian weakness has been a loss of momentum for ASEAN and an increased sense that the subregional security order has become more fragile despite the UN's steering of the East Timor crisis into a more peaceful and stable phase.

A Buttress, Not a Central Pillar

In sum, then, the past fifty years have seen a varied UN operational presence in the Asian region. This presence was at its height in the early years of the Cold War, when the UN began to deal with some of the consequences of Japan's World War II defeat and broad questions of decolonization. It has been prominent again in the post–Cold War era during its engagement in two ambitious and demanding peace-building operations. Less prominently, but frequently, since 1945 the United Nations has provided a forum where major state conflicts can be defused and arguments aired. Its normative influence, too, has been apparent: regional and subregional states in their security charters have drawn upon the norm of the nonuse of force to settle disputes, have signed global arms control agreements, and have taken up the ideas of confidence building, preventive diplomacy, and the like. The UN has also attempted—often unsuccessfully—to mediate an end to conflict and between 1949 and 1988 organized three traditional peacekeeping operations. In these ways it has contributed positively to the security order in the region. But the UN cannot be credited with the role of primary pillar of the security order. This role, denied to it for structural and political reasons, instead has been performed predominantly by major states that sometimes choose to operate in tandem with the UN and sometimes outside it.

Nor has the UN been able to promote its presence in the region through a division of labor with regional organizations. Unlike Africa, the Middle East, Europe, and Latin America, Asia has no institution that falls under Chapter VIII of the UN Charter and hence no organization that can take primary responsibility for the resolution of conflict in its own region.[5] The reasons for the absence of strong, legalized institutions relate to Asia's political, economic, legal, and cultural heterogeneity. Important, too, is the lack of agreement on the source and even the nature of primary threats—together with the presence of several major states that would find it difficult to coexist, let alone come to agreement, within any organization that takes an active role in containing and terminating threats to regional peace and security. This lack of community has not been so severe at the subregional level, of course, and ASEAN has proved its worth as a conflict prevention mechanism among its members. Yet even here we see an inability to resolve interstate conflicts through subregional mechanisms or to respond to serious intrastate violence.

Neither do regional states find it easy to respond institutionally in an era where there is increased global attention to domestic conflict. A number of them share a colonial past, and China was a semicolony. These experiences add weight to their strong attachment to the Westphalian norm of state sovereignty and noninterference—making them especially wary of intervening in domestic conflicts, as shown particularly clearly in ASEAN's behavior toward the East Timor crisis. The advent of UN peace-building operations draws attention, as well, to one other weakness in the region: few nongovernmental organizations in the Asia Pacific have the experience that would make them valuable adjuncts to international organizations and governments when societies seek rehabilitation and reconciliation. These operations are complex and expensive, too, and thus deter states that have no experience in mounting coordinated operations and lack the decision-making procedures that would be required. Thus neither Asian security institutions nor the UN system itself, either in combination or alone, have been

[5]At the seventh meeting of the ASEAN Regional Forum in Bangkok on July 27, 2000, the chairman reported that Thailand, as Chair of the ARF, had initiated informal contact with the United Nations. This may portend the distant prospect of formal UN recognition of the ARF under Chapter VIII arrangements. In the early years of the ARF's existence, UN requests for observer status were rejected.

major architects of the security order in the region. In the next section I examine the reasons why the United Nations has not played more than a buttressing role in this part of the world.

The UN on the Sidelines

Even taking account of the constraints that the UN's structure imposes on its ability to undertake independent initiatives anywhere in the world—the UN has had less of a peacekeeping presence in Asia than is perhaps warranted by the number of conflicts the region has endured (www.UN.org/Depts/DPKO). And despite earlier reference to the use made of the ICJ by Singapore and Malaysia and by Indonesia and Malaysia, few Asian states refer cases to this body (Roberts and Kingsbury 1993; ICJ website). Governments often find it easier to make concessions to a neutral institution than to a political opponent; yet this tendency has not overcome resistance to the ICJ. If the disputes over ownership of islands in the South China Sea were to be passed on to such a body, that would be a turning point indeed.

Cold War Constraints

During the Cold War, superpower rivalries curbed the UN's capacities to contribute to conflict resolution. In Cambodia, for example, UN Security Council resolutions condemning the Vietnamese occupation were stymied by a Soviet veto, and denunciations of the Pol Pot regime were avoided because of Chinese and American support for its anti-Soviet and anti-Vietnamese credentials. Similarly, UN resolutions after Indonesia's annexation of East Timor in 1975 were never acted upon because the Jakarta regime enjoyed the tacit support of the West and the backing of several Asian states generally fearful of destabilizing a country deemed to be of prime strategic importance in Asia. When the UN did begin to play a leadership role in East Timor—for example, in the post–Cold War era—this involvement came about because Moscow lacked interest in Indonesia's fate and Washington was willing to apply pressure on Jakarta, provided an ally with military credibility and political interest—Australia in this case—would supply the muscle. In Cambodia, the end of the Cold War and the cessation of Sino-Soviet rivalry, together with Japan's economic largesse, provided the enabling conditions for a UN role.

The Kashmir issue too has been affected by superpower involvement on opposite sides of the argument. Moscow (India's supporter) and Washington (Pakistan's) were joined in the fray by Beijing (on Pakistan's side) in the wake of the 1962 Sino-Indian border war and the Sino-Soviet dispute. The 1971 Indo-Pakistani war, which resulted in the Pakistani loss of East Pakistan and the establishment of the state of Bangladesh, was also orchestrated and eventually resolved primarily outside the United Nations. The UN did play an important peace-building role in Bangladesh after 1971, and India did feel obliged to prepare a detailed case to present to the United Nations in explanation of its actions. But what most influenced the outcome of that 1971 war—aside from the impact of the fighting—was the signature of the Indo-Soviet Treaty of Peace, Friendship, and Cooperation in August 1971, Pakistan's long-standing links with a weakened Chinese regime, and Islamabad's role in facilitating a prime U.S. goal at the time: Washington's rapprochement with Beijing.

Important too was the threat of a U.S., Soviet, or Chinese veto hovering in the background to these events. Thus between the Bangladesh declaration of independence on March 26, 1971, and the onset of fighting on December 3, neither India nor Pakistan nor any of the major states called for a meeting of the UN Security Council, and when it did meet on December 4 it quickly became deadlocked, only to reconvene on December 12 in conjunction with the surrender of Pakistani troops in East Pakistan. Despite the presence of some 10 million refugees in India, New Delhi first declined a UN request in July to station observers—who were to assist with the voluntary repatriation of refugees—on either side of East Pakistan's border with India and then refused a similar request made by the UN Secretary-General to station UN High Commission for Refugees' representatives instead of the observers (Dawson 1995: 260, 266).

With respect to the Korean War, without the Soviet Union's boycott of the UN Security Council the United States would not have been able to draw the United Nations into the enforcement operation. If the West had not been able to command the majority view in the UN General Assembly in 1950, the "Uniting for Peace" resolution, designed to circumvent the Soviet veto during the course of that conflict, would not have passed. The United States soon lost enthusiasm for operating within the context of the UN in the wake of the loss of its majority support in the General Assembly in the 1960s and strong General Assembly criticisms of Israel after the 1967 Arab-Israeli War. One consequence of Washington's disillusionment was determined U.S. resistance to any UN role in the Vietnam War, despite vigorous efforts by UN Secretary-General U Thant to suggest means of moving the conflict toward resolution. At the height of the Vietnam War in the mid-1960s neither Beijing nor Hanoi was represented at the UN at all.

Thus superpower rivalries during the Cold War form a large part of the explanation for the restraints placed on a UN contribution to the management of conflict in the Asian region. But this is only a partial explanation. Various parties to a number of the major conflicts, even in the post–Cold War era, have resisted a prominent UN role in their management. The explanation is threefold: the type of conflict; the belief among states with a primary interest in the disputed issue that wider international involvement might limit their ability to control its management; and the perception—especially in China, India, and the Southeast Asian countries—that the UN is a Western-dominated organization seeking to encroach on their sovereign exercise of power.

Conflict Type

As one scholar has argued, the Kashmir conflict is central to the self-image of both India and Pakistan—the former because Kashmiri exclusion threatens its identity as a genuinely secular state, the latter because of its desire to complete state formation through incorporation of a Muslim-majority area (Ganguly 1994: 49–50). This essentialist quality to the dispute makes it difficult for either side to compromise. Similar arguments might be made with respect to two other major conflicts in the region—between China and Taiwan and between North and South Korea—for each side, at various stages of the dispute, has believed its legitimacy to be threatened by the separate existence of the other. The qualities inherent in these three bilateral disputes contribute to one or the other party's unwillingness to give up unilateral defense efforts or to renounce, as a consequence, nuclear and missile development despite the existence of UN and other conventions.

Major States and Their Spheres of Influence

In the China-Taiwan, Kashmir, and the Korean peninsula disputes, however, the primary reason for excluding the UN is India, Washington, and Beijing's belief that they are better able to defend their interests outside the UN framework. Indeed, in the case of Kashmir, developments since India's and Pakistan's nuclear tests in 1998 and after the September 11, 2001, terrorist attack on the United States have aroused a far greater U.S. interest in the resolution of this conflict than in the past, which again has the potential to eclipse anything that the UN has been able to do thus far.

In the case of Korea, the United States has played the dominant role for over five decades. It still has 37,000 troops stationed in the South and has maintained its bilateral defense treaty with Seoul. It has shown fidelity as an ally—especially when compared with Beijing and Moscow, the North's partners, both of which have normalized relations with the South. As the conflict over North Korea's putative nuclear status moved toward the prospect of another major war in 1994 and then subsided in intensity, the United States stayed in the driver's seat throughout. The Agreed Framework signed by the United States and North Korea in October 1994 established the Korean Peninsular Energy Development Organization headed by a U.S. executive director and charged with the task of organizing an international consortium to provide the North with light-water reactors in return for Pyongyang's cessation of activity on its existing nuclear reactors. Although

North and South Korea have subsequently taken direct if halting steps to normalize their relationship, the United States remains a major guarantor of the South's
security. The United States also seems to be a major source of legitimation as far
as the North is concerned—shown by Pyongyang's intermittent efforts to obtain
U.S. diplomatic recognition. U.S. support for President Kim Dae Jung's
"Sunshine Policy," especially during the Clinton era, and regular consultations
among Seoul, Tokyo, and Washington were having some effect in convincing the
North that direct links with the South were necessary should it wish to abandon its
political and economic isolation. Should these direct contacts, which started with
President Kim Dae Jung's summit in the North in June 2000, eventually result in
the peaceful unification of the Korean peninsula, the United States will have
played a leading role, alongside its major Asian allies, not only in containing this
conflict but in moving it toward resolution. Washington, therefore, rather than
the United Nations, will have made the major contribution to regional order.

With respect to Taiwanese reunification with the mainland, China, the United
States, and the Taiwanese themselves have been the major influences determining
the level of tension. On the outbreak of the Korean War the United States stationed its Seventh Fleet in the Taiwan Strait to contain the geographic dimensions of the Korean conflict. In 1954, the United States signed a defense treaty
with the Republic of China and came to its assistance in the strait crises of 1954–
55 and 1958.[6] It also reined in any Chinese Nationalist ambitions to reunite with
the mainland by force. As international political support for Taiwan weakened
over the course of the 1960s, Washington—recognizing the legitimacy conferred
by UN membership—continued to work actively to keep Taipei in the United
Nations and Beijing out, a policy maintained until 1971. Not until 1979 did the
United States establish full diplomatic relations with Beijing (while maintaining a
high level of informal representation in Taipei). With this switch in formal recognition came a decade of efforts by both Beijing and Washington to keep the
Taiwan issue contained—an aim that has been more difficult to sustain with the
end of the tacit Sino-American anti-Soviet alliance, the democratization of Taiwan, and the island's growing demands for independence. Nevertheless China has
managed to prevent discussion of the Taiwan issue at meetings of the ARF and—
as a veto-wielding member of the Security Council—has blocked UN debate of
the matter of Taiwan's membership. Although Taiwan itself has attempted to internationalize the dispute and over the last few years has persistently sought UN
recognition in the General Assembly and membership in UN specialized agen-

---

[6]In the first crisis, the United States considered prompting New Zealand to introduce a UN
resolution calling on all parties to stabilize the situation and restore the status quo. This idea, however, fell victim to differences between America and its allies over the terms of this resolution, U.S.
commitments made to Chiang Kai Shek, and U.S. domestic politics (Foot 1990: 151–59).

cies, the Chinese rejection of these attempts stands between it and these goals. Were China to use force against Taiwan, Beijing's Security Council membership ensures that the UN's response would at most be one of censure and attempted mediation. The UN simply does not have the political, economic, or military power to organize collective action against the wishes of a major state such as China.

Thus Taiwan's security still rests heavily on its connection with the United States. It purchases U.S. weaponry in sufficient quantities to create strategic dilemmas for Beijing in its contemplation of a forceful takeover of the island, and it calls when necessary on U.S. protection—as in 1996 when the United States signaled to China, via the dispatch of two aircraft carriers, that Beijing had overstepped the bounds of acceptable behavior in its test-firing of missiles in the Taiwan Strait on the eve of the island's presidential elections. Even with the improvement of U.S.-China relations since September 11, 2001, as a result of Beijing's assistance to U.S. efforts in crushing the Al Qaeda networks, were either China or Taiwan to make destabilizing moves with respect to their bilateral dispute, U.S. preoccupation with the so-called "war against terrorism" would not prevent Washington from exerting heavy pressure on both to regain control of their conflict. Overall, it is America together with China and Taiwan, and not the UN, that contains the tension. The keys to conflict resolution lie in Beijing and Taipei.

Distrust of the UN System

If the presence of the United States and China—and in some instances the conditioning effects of past Sino–Soviet–American rivalries—explain some of the constraints on the UN's role in shaping the regional order, another cause is the skepticism felt in parts of Asia. The sources of this skepticism toward the international body are certainly not peculiar to the region and undoubtedly can be found elsewhere in the developing world. These states have witnessed the Security Council's arbitrary responses to conflict, creating a perception that, if any of them were to be attacked, the UN would rush to their support only if other strategic interests were engaged. Moreover, the postcolonial state, wherever it is located, tends to distrust institutions constructed primarily by the Western powers, and this lack of trust has manifested itself over the decades throughout the UN system. Such suspicion may well be growing in the post–Cold War era as bodies such as the IMF and World Bank impose loan conditions that encroach on areas of domestic governance. For those states that do not enjoy a dominant position within international institutions—unlike the P-5 in the Security Council and the United States, other Western states, and Japan in the Bretton Woods institutions—they risk having their domestic structures challenged by international organizations whose jurisdiction has expanded.

Despite the widespread nature of this wariness of UN institutions expressed in the developing world, two developments connected with the expansion of the UN system's normative agenda have had a decided impact on Asian perceptions, placing in sharp focus questions relating to the legitimacy of various UN activities: first, the policy requirements that emerged in connection with the Asian financial crisis of 1997–99; and second, the issue of humanitarian intervention together with the matter of accountability with respect to human rights abuses—both issues brought to the fore in the course of the East Timor crisis.

The Asian economic crisis was particularly threatening because many in the region adhere to a notion of security that they term "comprehensive," a concept that relates ideas of national economic resilience to state and regime security and a regional security order. Indeed the collapse of the Indonesian economy proved to be the pivotal moment for the authoritarian and increasingly corrupt Suharto regime. With the IMF eventually taking the lead and—spurred by U.S. prompting—quashing earlier Japanese efforts to establish an Asian Monetary Fund, those Asian states most affected by the crisis (excepting Malaysia) found themselves faced with no alternative but to accept the domestic structural adjustment that the IMF demanded before it would help. According to Richard Higgott, "the nature of the IMF reform packages, and especially the overt 'power politics' manner in which they have been imposed, has brought a north-south divide back into the open" in the region. Indeed, Higgott goes on to argue: "Across the most affected states a discourse of 'robbery,' or a 'new imperialism'—not heard since the years of the immediate post colonial era—is strong. This is not only in Malaysia, where Prime Minister Mahathir has gone as far as to argue that western governments and financiers have deliberately punished Asia for its arrogance and refusal to converge more quickly towards Anglo-American, liberal, approaches to democracy, market opening, labour standards and human rights. Similar themes have been, indeed are still, heard in Thailand, the Philippines, South Korea and Indonesia." Nor is there much evidence that this bitterness has weakened as a result of recent signs of economic recovery (Higgott 2000: 19, 27, 33).

These responses to what has been depicted as an intrusive agenda on the part of the IMF—an institution the United States can dominate through the practice of weighted voting—are reflected more broadly in reactions to the expanded normative agenda of global institutions since the end of the Cold War. Many Asian states perceive it as an agenda that affects the weak but does not apply to the strong. As Andrew Hurrell has noted, they perceive that collective action regarding security in this new era is not a manifestation of collective security. Instead it "has depended to an uncomfortable extent on the political interests of the United States and its allies and on the military capabilities built up in the course of the Cold War." (Hurrell 1999: 265). Thus it is the United States that will continue to have a large say in where the UN will get involved in dealing with threats to international security, much as it had done in the past. This understanding, in turn, has led middle-range states, such as China and India,[7] to take a hard line with respect to UN Secretary-General Kofi Annan's articulation of ideas connected with the new sovereignty and humanitarian intervention as outlined in his speech in September 1999 (UN General Assembly 1999), since they think these remarks promote a Western agenda. To some extent their strong opposition relates to their recognition that because of their size and regional power they do have sufficient influence to shape the debate. But obviously they are also concerned about the disputes within their own borders that threaten their territorial integrity—disputes that have led to severe human rights abuses: Kashmir in the case of India, Tibet and Xinjiang in the case of China. In several of the years since the Tiananmen bloodshed of June 1989, Beijing has been the focus of ultimately unsuccessful efforts to pass a condemnatory UN Commission for Human Rights resolution in which problems in Tibet have frequently been highlighted. As an angry and defensive Premier Zhu Rongji retorted in response to a journalist's question linking Kosovo and Tibet: "Do you want to send troops to Tibet? You only listen to the opinions of so-called dissidents and don't listen to the opinions of the Chinese government. Is this fair?" (BBC 1999).[8]

There are long historical roots to this distrust of the UN in both India and China. In New Delhi's case, an initially supportive attitude in Nehru's time eroded over the years as the Indian government came to view the UN as favoring Pakistan's position, not on the merits of its case, but because Pakistan came to be seen in the West as an anticommunist bastion. The Indian takeover of Portuguese Goa in 1962, for example, was effected in twenty-four hours in order to keep the Security Council out of the picture (Krishna 1985: 281–82). In Beijing's case, its reluctance in the 1970s (since reversed) to endorse or pay for UN peacekeeping operations, its abstention in the key vote in 1990 during the Gulf

---

[7]India's position was somewhat different in 1971 during the Indo-Pakistani War. At that time India justified its intervention on the grounds of an urgent need to respond to the suffering East Bengali population and its 10 million refugees fleeing the territory. India was strongly supported in its stance by the former Soviet Union and equally strongly opposed by the United States (Roberts 2000: 9). Other Asian states at the UN in September 1999 that, like China, emphasized the benefits of the principle of state sovereignty and noninterference included Indonesia, Burma, and Vietnam. The Malaysian prime minister gave more emphasis to the inequalities in world power that had led to a Western emphasis on human rights. As Mahathir put it: "For the poor and the weak . . . the twenty-first century does not look very promising. Everything will continue to be cooked in the West" (UN General Assembly 1999). For other statements, see the plenary sessions of the 54th Session of the UN General Assembly, September to December 1999.

[8]Looking to a possible worst-case future, Taiwanese commentators have shown themselves favorably disposed to the concept of humanitarian intervention for reasons that presumably relate mainly to the prospect of future conflict with China (Liu and Wu 2000).

War, and its reactions to the idea of humanitarian intervention are not unrelated
to its Korean War and UN-recognition experiences. Over the course of the Korean conflict and as a consequence of China's overt intervention in the fighting in
November 1950, the United States prompted the UN to label Beijing (and Pyongyang) an "aggressor," to organize an embargo on trade in strategic items, and
to impose a moratorium on debate of China's membership in the United Nations
until 1961—and thereafter to determine the matter of its entry an "important
question" requiring two-thirds approval of UN members. Most Asian states—
whether they feared or admired Beijing—believed it had the right to take up the
China seat (Foot 1995: chaps. 2 and 3).

China's sense of victimhood and its wariness of the UN's expanded normative
agenda has led it to reaffirm the Security Council's primacy in the management
of threats to international peace and security outside its direct sphere of influence
(and hence to sustain the veto-wielding power of its members, which renders
Beijing's position on UN Security Council reform somewhat problematic) and to
hold onto the Westphalian interpretation of state sovereignty and noninterference. These norms, China avers, have been the "basic principles governing international relations" and their absence would lead to a new form of "gunboat diplomacy" that would "wreak havoc."

However, it is not simply India and China that are concerned about UN operations in the post–Cold War era. States throughout Asia have been debating
these arguments over humanitarian intervention and the depth of the challenge
to ideas of state sovereignty and noninterference when internal conflicts spill over
into neighboring countries (Dickens and Wilson-Roberts 2000). This particularly
came to the fore during the crisis involving East Timor and Indonesia. ASEAN's
reactions to what it perceived as an internal Indonesian problem were circumspect, which led in turn to a perception that the organization was helpless in the
face of critical developments affecting one of its member states. To outsiders
ASEAN members appeared to be paralyzed until Indonesia gave its reluctant consent to international help in halting the violence.[9] After Jakarta had given its consent, members of ASEAN then came forward with offers of support for the international effort, first through INTERFET (which had a Thai deputy commander)
and then later through UNTAET, where Thailand provided the force commander. They were united in their firm belief that UN involvement should only
take place with the agreement of the Indonesian state. Significantly, most believed it also essential to explain that the ASEAN countries' commitment of

[9]In fact, heads of seven ASEAN countries present in Auckland at an APEC meeting pressed Indonesia on September 12, 1999, to accept an international force and responded positively to Jakarta's call that ASEAN member states provide sizable contingents for that force, thus diluting the
Australian presence. China, Japan, and the Republic of Korea also put pressure on Jakarta.

forces was not a coordinated ASEAN operation but rested on each state's decision and capacity (Dupont 2000: 167; NIDS 2000: 38, 40–41).

ASEAN's response, while true to the norms on which the organization had long been based, emphasized the constraints that its interpretation of noninterference placed on regional solutions to regional problems and has fueled an internal debate about the merits of "flexible engagement." Similarly restrictive interpretations of sovereignty elsewhere in the region, where the matter of Indonesian consent and noninterference in internal affairs was also deemed crucial, underscored the inability of a regional body such as the ARF to take an active role in controlling regional violence. Beijing, as a member of the UN Security Council, probably would not have voted for the UN operation in East Timor without Jakarta's and the ASEAN states' acquiescence. With that consent and UN endorsement, however, Beijing was willing to provide assistance by offering civilian police for the first time in a UN operation (Gill and Reilly 2000: 48–49). All Asian members of the UNCHR, for reasons that are also related to the noninterference norm, voted against or abstained on a UN resolution, introduced at a specially convened session of that body, which called on the UN Secretary-General to set up an international commission of inquiry into violations of international law in East Timor (*Human Rights Watch World Report 2000*: xxiv).

Consequences

There is, then, considerable tension between the expanded normative agenda under which the UN has been operating and the norms that predominate at the regional level. Although some circumspection has set in, the expanded role of the UN system is unlikely to be fully reversed, especially in this era of numerous domestic conflicts, many of which have cross-border consequences. Thus countries across Asia—perhaps as a consequence of developments in Burma, Cambodia, Indonesia, or Kashmir—are likely to face once more the dilemma of balancing their concerns about noninterference with the perception that regional institutions are fair-weather organizations that cannot contribute to regional order in times of crisis. ASEAN in particular seems destined to face this dilemma, one that has already divided Thailand and the Philippines—the two states most supportive of UN action in East Timor—from other member states. African states, by contrast, seem to have acknowledged the need for UN help to resolve instances of bloody internal strife in the post–Cold War era and thus have modified their view of noninterference. Governments in Central America have accepted UN mediation, given the big powers' unwillingness to continue fueling their internal conflicts. Despite the UN's new activism, the conditions that would prompt a widespread reconsideration of the noninterference norm across Asia are not present.

Three consequences might arise from this dilemma. There could be a heightening of tensions between the UN and regional states, which could result in greater use (or threatened use) of the Chinese veto should there be any attempt to bypass the matter of state consent. There could also be a deepening of the fissures in belief among Asian states or within the subregional organization, ASEAN, about what a UN or regional role should be in the maintenance of order, including the exposure of differences in perception about the circumstances under which the UN should embrace humanitarian intervention or whether such intervention should be contemplated at all.[10] Finally, and more positively for the prospects of the security order, we might witness over the next decade a strengthening of regional capacities to deal with regional crises—a development that could lead to a division of labor, or true complementarity of action, between regional and global institutions. As noted earlier in the context of East Timor, ASEAN was required to face up to a strategic opportunity as well as a political challenge. As the Deputy Foreign Minister of Thailand put it in September 1999: "We [ASEAN members] have always said that we don't want other countries, especially superpowers, to interfere in the region. The time has come to show that we can solve the region's problems ourselves with the cooperation of countries outside the region" (Dupont 2000: 168–69).

It is far too early to pronounce on this question. But there are signs that various subsets of states in the region are attempting to improve regional capacities in both the economic and the security dimensions. Although serious political obstacles remain in the path of such moves, small steps have been taken. In July 2000, ASEAN decided to set up a troika of its past, present, and future chairs to operate in a good-offices role in order to prevent disputes from undermining regional stability. A year later, ASEAN approved procedures to extend its High Council—a mechanism designed to facilitate the peaceful settlement of regional disputes—to non-ASEAN members who wish to accede to its jurisdiction. And although troops of major ASEAN countries were operating under international and not ASEAN command in East Timor, they were for the first time involved in such operations in the territory of another ASEAN state. The ARF, too, has been making a somewhat greater effort to explore the concept of preventive diplomacy.[11]

---

[10]At the 54th UN General Assembly discussion in New York on September 24, 1999, Singapore's foreign minister argued that if the UN were to remain relevant in the twenty-first century, then "rules and objective criteria" for interventions based on humanitarian premises had to be established. He expected the international community to "face many more situations which will pose the dilemma of reconciling state sovereignty with international intervention to redress violations of human rights" (Jayakumar 1999).

[11]At this stage, four overlapping confidence-building/preventive diplomacy proposals have been agreed by the ARF: an enhanced role for the ARF Chair; an ARF register of experts and emi-

In the financial area some regional agreements have also been reached. Many Asia-Pacific governments believe the financial crisis had a detrimental impact on the overall security environment of the region. In the autumn of 1997, the Japanese were unsuccessful in establishing an Asian Monetary Fund—a proposal that attracted the critical attention of the United States, which preferred the IMF to lead the response to the region's economic crisis. Yet this did not prevent ASEAN member states meeting in Manila in December 1997 from agreeing to establish a mutual surveillance mechanism in order to anticipate future crises. They were joined later by Northeast Asian countries to explore a framework that would lead to observance of short-term capital movements. In May 2000, Japan suggested the establishment of an East Asian system of currency swaps, an idea that came to fruition in March 2001 at a meeting in Chiang Mai of the ASEAN Plus Three (APT) grouping. This measure would allow East Asian countries to borrow from each other in the short term by making use of currency reserves—which, among the APT, stood at $800 billion in 2000 (Higgott 2000: 21–22; Webber 2001).

While the final outcome of these economic developments remains uncertain, they could push the IMF and World Bank in the direction of increasing Asian representation, thus undercutting the expressed need for these states to go off on their own. At the same time, the deepening of collective activity at the regional level could improve relations among the involved states, expand their levels of cooperation in the fields of security and economics, and perhaps in the distant future provide the basis for the UN system to work in partnership with a viable regional organization.[12] Perhaps such a future arrangement—and it is only a distant prospect at this point—could help to eliminate the type of criticism that was leveled at the IMF and World Bank in the course of the UN's Cambodian operation, where they were accused of a devastating ignorance of the kind of society they wished to assist (Peou and Yamada 2000: 94). More significantly, such multilateral political and economic developments could mute the role of the major states that are presently so determinative in shaping the region's security order.

Conclusions

The UN has not had a prominent place in mediating, managing, or resolving some of the major conflicts that have wracked the Asian region. The continuing

---

nent persons; provision of annual security outlooks; and voluntary background briefings on regional security issues.

[12]This is only a distant prospect, of course, with respect to the ARF. The Beijing government, for example, wants to "preserve the authority of the Security Council in handling international emergencies." Moreover, Pakistan is not even a member of the ARF. However, the ASEAN Plus Three arrangement is worth watching in this connection.

tension between North and South Korea and between China and Taiwan, the earlier wars between North and South Vietnam, China and India, and India and Pakistan, to name but a few of the most serious instances of violence, have been dealt with largely in the absence of major UN initiatives. During the Cold War, either the superpowers engaged in conflict management or resolution or major regional states such as India and China resisted UN involvement, where the PRC was not even a member until 1971. Moreover, many of the region's internal conflicts could not be tackled through the UN during this period because of the structural constraints the Cold War imposed. Even during the post–Cold War era the United States in particular, but also China and India, continue to manage many of the sources of tension in what they perceive as their spheres of influence. China and the United States, because their positions are well understood, do not have to threaten (or actually use) the Security Council veto to maintain their predominance, though both options remain available to them. The UN has adopted a front-line role, as in Cambodia and East Timor, only when major states have determined the circumstances to be propitious and regional and subregional states have hesitated to get involved in the resolution of local conflicts. Unless these circumstances pertain—and major states insist on direct UN action—its contribution is tightly constrained.

This is not to argue that the UN has played no part in security management in this region. As we have seen, the UN has often provided vital support, acting sometimes as a third-party facilitator or neutral mediator, and sometimes it has operated in important ways behind the scenes. It has also acted as a source of ideas—the provider of normative and legal frameworks that constrain certain forms of state behavior—and as an arena where interests can be exposed, legitimized, or delegitimized. Because regionwide preventive diplomacy mechanisms have proved difficult to formulate, this too has provided opportunities for a UN contribution through regional adoption of UN-negotiated agreements and norms. In more recent years it has bolstered political support for governments through the monitoring of elections and helped in the reconstruction of war-torn societies. In all these ways the organization has contributed positively, if sometimes indirectly, to order at the regional level.

Nevertheless there are clear constraints on the role the UN can play and has played in contributing to a regional security order. And it derives not solely from the actions of the major states but also from the wariness of weak or postcolonial states toward an institution they perceive to be Western-dominated and not attuned to their concerns. In developing countries, such concerns often revolve around securing or enforcing domestic unity rather than interstate conflict per se, which further distances them from many UN activities. The priorities of these states ensure the maintenance of a strong attachment to the norms of nonintervention and sovereign equality, thereby heightening their distrust of a UN that is more active at the beginning of the twenty-first century and more attentive to what goes on within (rather than simply between) states.

It is a wariness that appears magnified in the Asian region. Suspicions of the organization seem greater here than in other parts of the world, even for relatively stable or strong states such as China and India. The distrust of these two states can be traced to their earlier experiences with the United Nations—during the Korean and Kashmir conflicts—that added to their perception of the organization as one that was unsympathetic to their interests. And within their borders, domestic conflicts have invited an unwanted (although not unwarranted) level of external scrutiny. Beyond Beijing and New Delhi, the Asian financial crisis occurred precisely at a time when UN-associated bodies had expanded their areas of surveillance. To those states most deeply affected this brought home especially sharply the humiliation that is associated with having external bodies dictate domestic policies. Moreover, while this huge and diverse region contains many well-established states that play a significant part in managing the security order, it also contains states that are neither strong economically nor successful in resolving internal conflicts of varying levels of intensity. When states such as Afghanistan, Burma, Cambodia, Indonesia, Nepal, Sri Lanka, and Vietnam have contemplated questions concerning humanitarian intervention—or the conditions imposed by various UN bodies when assistance is needed—they undoubtedly respond with these matters of unequal power in mind.

The UN system generally has been more active than in the past in its efforts to promote order in the post–Cold War era, and this is no less true in Asia. The UN's activism in Cambodia and East Timor, together with the financial institutions' responses to the East Asian economic crisis, seem to be prompting parts of the region to reconsider the noninterference norm as well as the need to develop preventive mechanisms at the regional level. The twin crises of East Timor and the financial downturn undoubtedly disturbed the region's security order, especially in Southeast Asia, and led to a period of flux and uncertainty that is only now beginning to abate. If these crises have had the effect of galvanizing regional bodies, eventually a more satisfactory division of labor could emerge between global and regional efforts at maintaining order. It is something of a paradox that a more activist UN, combined with regional suspicion of its motives, may contribute to the development of regional institutions. Of all the pathways to regional order, this global-regional combination seems the most desirable.

This outcome can only be regarded as a long-term, even uncertain, prospect, however, in light of the thin sense of community in Asia. Indeed ASEAN faces several significant challenges: beyond the problems of its expansion and the impact of the economic crisis, its coherence and credibility have been damaged by the deep-seated problems that preoccupy Indonesia, the subregional organization's most important member. At the regional level, bodies such as the ARF and APT have to maneuver skillfully and can evolve only slowly if they wish to retain the commitment of the dominant states in Asia. The behavior of China, India, and the United States thus far, both inside and outside the ARF, suggests that they would oppose any attempt to develop a fully regionwide security organization that carried real clout.

Thus in the context of weak regional institutions and the presence of two veto-wielding states, the United Nations will probably be kept on the sidelines in the three issues that could cause major disruptions to the security order—Kashmir, China/Taiwan, and Korea—but will be saddled with the main burdens should serious intrastate conflict break out in, for example, Burma or Indonesia. In these latter instances, the UN could be called upon to perform a mediatory role; in the former cases it is unlikely to play a primary part in conflict resolution or management. Neither will the UN have regional bodies to work with any time soon. As before, the UN's response to crises will depend on its ability to establish ad hoc coalitions of the willing—in the context, of course, of the great powers' acceptance that it should perform this role.

Even at a time when a large part of Washington's energies and resources are absorbed in the destruction of terrorist networks, the United States will retain its place as the main architect of the security order in Asia, although its patterns of alignments and some of its priorities have undergone certain shifts in emphasis. U.S. prominence in constructing the security order has been illustrated in the positive response of many Asian states to America's policy requests after September 11, 2001, in the economic, intelligence, and military fields. The United States has long been predominant in the region because of its deep and sustained relations with its Asian allies, especially in comparison with the former Soviet Union and its Asian partners. The UN's dependence on collective state agreement ensures the continuation of its role as a buttress to the security order.

Works Cited

Alderson, Kai, and Andrew Hurrell, eds. 2000. *Hedley Bull on International Society*. Basingstoke, U.K.: Macmillan.

Bajpai, Kanti P. 1996. "Conflict, Cooperation, and CSBMs with Pakistan and China: A View from New Delhi." In Sumit Ganguly and Ted Greenwood, eds., *Mending Fences: Confidence- and Security-Building Measures in South Asia*. Boulder, Colo.: Westview.

Ball, Desmond, and Amitav Acharya, eds. 1999. *The Next Stage: Preventive Diplomacy and Security Cooperation in the Asia-Pacific Region*. Canberra: Australian National University.

Bell, Coral. 2000. "East Timor, Canberra, and Washington: A Case Study in Crisis Management." *Australian Journal of International Affairs* 54(2) (July): 172–77.

Berdal, Mats, and Michael Leifer. 1996. "Cambodia." In James Mayall, ed., *The New Inter-ventionism 1991–1994: United Nations Experience in Cambodia, Former Yugoslavia, and Somalia.* Cambridge: Cambridge University Press.

Boutros-Ghali, Boutros. 1992. *An Agenda for Peace: Preventive Diplomacy, Peacemaking, and Peacekeeping.* Report of the Secretary-General pursuant to the statement adopted by the Summit Meeting of the Security Council on Jan. 31.

BBC (British Broadcasting Corporation. 1999). *Summary of World Broadcasts,* Asia-Pacific, FE/3514, G/2, Apr. 21.

Chopra, Jarat. 2000. "The UN's Kingdom of East Timor." *Survival* 42(3) (Autumn): 27–39.

Dawson, Pauline. 1995. *The Peacekeepers of Kashmir: The UN Military Observer Group in India and Pakistan.* Bombay: Popular Prakashan.

Dickens, David, and Guy Wilson-Roberts. 2000. *Non-Intervention and State Sovereignty in the Asia-Pacific.* Wellington, N.Z.: Centre for Strategic Studies.

Doyle, Michael W. 1995. *UN Peacekeeping in Cambodia: UNTAC's Civil Mandate.* Boulder, Colo.: Lynne Rienner.

Dupont, Alan. 2000. "ASEAN's Response to the East Timor Crisis." *Australian Journal of International Affairs* 54(2) (July): 164–71.

Findlay, Trevor. 1995. *Cambodia: The Legacy and Lessons of UNTAC.* SIPRI Research Report no. 9. Oxford: Oxford University Press.

Finnemore, Martha. 1993. "International Organizations as Teachers of Norms: The United Nations Educational, Scientific, and Cultural Organization and Science Policy." *International Organization* 47(4): 565–97.

Foot, Rosemary. 1990. "Search for a Modus Vivendi: Anglo-American Relations and China Policy." In Warren I. Cohen and Akira Iriye, eds., *The Great Powers in East Asia 1953–1960.* New York: Columbia University Press.

———. 1995. *The Practice of Power: US Relations with China Since 1949.* Oxford: Oxford University Press.

Forman, Shepard, and Stewart Patrick, eds. 2000. *Good Intentions: Pledges of Aid for Post Conflict Recovery.* Boulder, Colo.: Lynne Rienner.

Ganguly, Sumit. 1994. *The Origins of War in South Asia: Indo-Pakistani Conflict Since 1947.* 2nd ed. Boulder, Colo.: Westview.

Gill, Bates, and James Reilly. 2000. "Sovereignty, Intervention, and Peacekeeping: The View from Beijing." *Survival* 42(3) (Autumn): 41–59.

Gunn, Geoffrey C. 1997. *East Timor and the United Nations: The Case for Intervention.* Lawrenceville, N.J.: Red Sea Press.

Harada Shiro, and Akihiko Tanaka. 1999. "Regional Arrangements, the United Nations, and Security in Asia." In Muthiah Alagappa and Takashi Inoguchi, eds., *International Security Management and the United Nations.* Tokyo: United Nations University Press.

Heinrich, L. William, Akiho Shibata, and Yoshihide Soeya. 1999. *United Nations Peace-keeping Operations: A Guide to Japanese Policies.* Tokyo: United Nations University Press.

Higgott, Richard. 2000. "ASEM and the Evolving Global Order." Paper prepared for the 2000 Seoul Summit: The Way Ahead for the Asia Europe Partnership, Seoul, July 11–12.

Human Rights Watch World Report 2000. New York: Human Rights Watch.

Hurrell, Andrew. 1999. "Security and Inequality." In Andrew Hurrell and Ngaire Woods, eds., *Inequality, Globalization, and World Politics.* Oxford: Oxford University Press.

ICJ (*International Court of Justice*) Website at http://www.icj-cij.org/

Jayakumar, S. 1999. 54th Session of the UN General Assembly, Sept. 24.

Kahler, Miles. 2000. "Legalization as Strategy: The Asia-Pacific Case." *International Organization* 54(3) (Summer): 549–71.

Karns, Margaret P., and Karen A. Mingst. 1995. *The United Nations in the Post–Cold War Era*. Boulder, Colo.: Westview.

Krishna, Gopal. 1985. "India and the International Order: Retreat from Idealism." In Hedley Bull and Adam Watson, eds., *The Expansion of International Society*. Oxford: Clarendon Press.

Liu, Fu-Kuo, and Linjun Wu. 2000. "The Antiquated Principle of Non-Intervention on the Verge of Transformation? Taiwan's Perspective." In David Dickens and Guy Wilson-Roberts, eds., *Non-Intervention and State Sovereignty in the Asia-Pacific*. Wellington, N.Z.: Centre for Strategic Studies.

Miller, Linda B. 1967. *World Order and Local Disorder: The United Nations and Internal Conflicts*. Princeton: Princeton University Press.

NIDS (National Institute for Defense Studies). 2000. *East Asian Strategic Review 2000*. Tokyo.

Oberdorfer, Don. 1997. *The Two Koreas: A Contemporary History*. Reading, Mass.: Addison-Wesley.

Ogata, Sadako. 1995. "Japan's Policy Towards the United Nations." In Chadwick F. Alger, Gene M. Lyons, and John E. Trent, eds., *The United Nations System: The Politics of Member States*. Tokyo: United Nations University Press.

Paul, T. V., and John A. Hall, eds. 1999. *International Order and the Future of World Politics*. Cambridge: Cambridge University Press.

Peou, Sorpong, with Yamada Kenji. 2000. "Cambodia." In Shepard Forman and Stewart Patrick, eds., *Good Intentions: Pledges of Aid for Post Conflict Recovery*. Boulder, Colo.: Lynne Rienner.

Roberts, Adam. 2000. "The So-Called Right of Humanitarian Intervention." Expanded text of a lecture presented at Trinity College, Melbourne, Nov. 23, 1999.

———, and Benedict Kingsbury, eds. 1993. *United Nations, Divided World: The UN's Roles in International Relations*. 2nd ed. Oxford: Clarendon Press.

Russett, Bruce. 1998. "A Neo-Kantian Perspective: Democracy, Interdependence, and International Organizations in Building Security Communities." In Emanuel Adler and Michael Barnett, eds., *Security Communities*. Cambridge: Cambridge University Press.

Segal, Gerald, ed. 1987. *Arms Control in Asia*. Basingstoke, U.K.: Macmillan.

Shi Chunlai. 1999. "Preventive Diplomacy and the Asia-Pacific Region." In Desmond Ball and Amitav Acharya, eds., *The Next Stage: Preventive Diplomacy and Security Cooperation in the Asia-Pacific Region*. Canberra: Australian National University.

Swaine, Michael D., and Alastair Iain Johnston. 1999. "China and Arms Control Institutions." In Elizabeth Economy and Michel Oksenberg, eds., *China Joins the World: Progress and Prospects*. New York: Council on Foreign Relations.

Talbott, Kirk, and Melissa Brown. 1998. "Forest Plunder in Southeast Asia: An Environmental Security Nexus in Burma and Cambodia." *Environmental Change and Security Project Report* 4 (Spring).

Taylor, John G. 1999. *East Timor: The Price of Freedom*. London: Zed Books.

UN General Assembly. 1999. Opening speeches at the 54th session, 1999, A/54/PV/4, 20/9/99.

UN website: http://www.un.org/Depts/DPKO/p_miss.htm and http://www.un.org/Depts/ DPKO/c_miss.htm.

Wallensteen, Peter, and Margareta Sollenberg. 1998. "Armed Conflict, 1989–1998." In M. Sollenberg, ed., *States in Armed Conflict 1998*. Research Report 54. Uppsala: Uppsala University, Dept. of Peace and Conflict.

Webber, Douglas. 2001. "Two Funerals and a Wedding? The Ups and Downs of Regionalism in East Asia and Asia-Pacific After the Asian Crisis." *Pacific Review* 14(3): 339–72.

PART III

Management of Specific Issues

CHAPTER TEN

Acute Conflicts in Asia After the Cold War

Kashmir, Taiwan, and Korea

DAVID KANG

In Asia three acute conflicts have endured for decades. India and Pakistan, created by the end of British colonial rule, continue to eye each other warily across Kashmir, and intermittent violence has marred that relationship since 1947. Taiwan and China still have not found a stable modus vivendi since 1949, despite China's opening to the West and the economic development of both countries. On the Korean peninsula, recently there has been considerable movement toward rapprochement although true unification or normalization still appears decades away. The range of scholarly perspectives on these three conflicts has been vast—from a focus on domestic politics, ideology, or ethnicity to structure, realism, or superpower conflicts. (See Ganguly 1999; Ahmed 1999; Heisbourg 1998; Tremblay 1996; Groves 1998.)

Scholars have generally studied these disputes in isolation from each other, yet these cases are all part of a larger set of conflicts. Indeed they share a number of traits. All three conflicts began in the period immediately following World War II in areas that to some degree had originally been unified. All three involve a security dilemma due in large part to the geographic proximity of the interested nations; there are no buffer zones. All three conflicts are zero-sum: unlike disputes over trade or human rights, conflicts over territory and identity are harder to reconcile. In all three cases, too, both parties claim sole sovereignty over the disputed idea of nationhood and the territory therein. Although actual violence has occasionally marked these conflicts, in none of them has a war been fought that resolved the situation conclusively. All three, moreover, fall within a somewhat similar security environment: during the Cold War the Soviet Union and the

United States were the dominant extraregional actors; after the collapse of the Soviet Union, the rise of China became the dominant issue. And, finally, in all three cases the United States has accused one side in the conflict of exacerbating regional tensions by exporting missile and nuclear technology (Pakistan, China, and North Korea).

Despite these similarities, the end of the Cold War had a differing impact on the three conflicts. In the 1990s the situation in Korea began to show movement toward reconciliation. In Taiwan, however, the situation has grown more acute. In Kashmir the dispute has flared up again and shows no signs of moving either toward outright conflict or toward resolution. Why has there been more movement on the Korean peninsula than in the other two conflicts? Why has the situation worsened in Taiwan and Kashmir, but not in Korea?

In Korea, as we shall see, systemic forces have pushed movement toward reconciliation; in Taiwan, domestic political change is the major cause of increased conflict with China. The balance of power changed dramatically against North Korea during the 1990s, whereas a U.S. commitment to the defense of Taiwan keeps the situation in rough balance and inhibits major change. The situations in Korea and Taiwan are similar: intense great-power interest focuses on one small point under a glaring spotlight. The end of the Cold War was devastating for North Korea. During the 1990s the North lost its two major allies and fell so far behind South Korea and the United States that it was forced to seek an alternative to continued confrontation on the peninsula. In the case of Taiwan, it was not changes in the strategic balance that increased tension. Rather, the turn to democracy in Taiwan is the real driver behind heightened tension over the Taiwan Strait, as this political shift is accompanied by an increased likelihood of a formal declaration of independence from China. Other factors are also involved in raising tensions, such as the PRC's urgency in unifying. Yet the main cause of heightened tension over the last decade was the rapid change in Taiwanese domestic politics. Kashmir presents an interesting third case. The superpowers were never closely involved in the dispute between India and Pakistan, and the end of the Cold War has affected this conflict the least. Here the conflict has continued for domestic, ideological, and religious reasons, and the regional balance of power in South Asia is more important than the global balance.

However, while material factors and the balance of power are important in all three cases, these cases also involve conflicts over national identity. On the Korean peninsula one nation has existed since the Silla unification of the peninsula in the seventh century A.D., and two rival states currently claim to be representing an indivisible and legitimate Korean nation. China claims that Taiwan is immutably "Chinese," while the Taiwanese claim that the island has been no more than a close neighbor of China. In both these cases issues of national identity are bound in both history and competing claims over which national identity is more legitimate. The conflict over Kashmir also involves issues of national identity, despite—and because of—the relatively recent formation of both India and Pakistan as nation-states. Pakistan sees Kashmir as intrinsic to its identity as a Muslim nation-state in South Asia, while India sees Kashmir as important for its notion of secular democracy that can accommodate different ethnic and religious groups.

In none of the three cases has the issue of national identity been directly addressed by either party. The management of the conflicts has been largely military, with an emphasis on deterrence, alliances, and threats. Correspondingly, proposals for resolution have not touched on the question of identity. In the Korean case, the issue of identity has been put to the side for tactical reasons; the focus is instead on reducing tension before tackling the issue of what exactly is "Korea." In the case of Taiwan, suggestions have been raised by both sides—such as China's "one nation, two systems" approach—but neither side has seriously addressed these issues. In Kashmir proposals have emphasized the difference in identities without attempting to redefine national identity in a way that would allow the reconciliation of the two sides' interests.

Identity matters, but power is also important. Indeed the research presented here reveals that identity may not matter if one party has overwhelming power and the political will to settle the question of identity by force. In none of the three cases has this been the case; but in all three conflicts such an imposed resolution is a distinct option if conditions change sufficiently. In Korea, although the North is growing weaker, the balance of power remains roughly equal. A strong U.S. commitment to the defense of Taiwan has discouraged Beijing from using force to settle the issue of identity. In the case of Kashmir, neither India nor Pakistan has tried to impose a resolution through force, partly because of the rough balance of power in South Asia.

My aim here is most assuredly not to present a comprehensive historical description of each conflict and a wealth of significant ethnographic detail. Instead I want to focus on a few key analytic questions and then generalize and synthesize across the cases. After discussing third-level and second-level analyses of international relations with respect to the cases of Korea, Taiwan, and Kashmir, I conclude by assessing why there has been more movement in Korea than in Taiwan or Kashmir and then by comparing these acute Asian conflicts with three major disputes in Europe.

Theory

One way in which international relations theorists order the world is through levels of analysis. Kenneth Waltz has specified three levels: the individual, domestic politics, and the international system itself (Waltz 1959; Singer 1961; Jervis 1976). The structural, or third, level of analysis emphasizes that the structural forces of the international system shape and constrain the choices of individual states. In general terms, structural analysis focuses on nation-states, the distribution of power, and the goal of survival. Within this perspective the focus is on understanding the effect of larger forces on a state's choices and options. This "third-image" approach does not look at domestic actors but focuses on the nation as a whole.

When examining conflict management, a third-image approach emphasizes (although not exclusively) material resources and tends to look at the various capabilities and alliances that each side brings to the bargaining table. Management ranges from a decisive war at one end of the spectrum to a treaty at the other. Between these two poles is a continuum of potential state behavior such as deterrence, balancing, and the search for allies. Changes in the relative power of the contestants, for example, can have a crucial impact on how conflicts are managed and resolved. (See Morrow 1993; DiCiccio and Levy 2000; Kugler and Lemke 1996; Lemke and Werner 1996.)

A domestic-level (second-image) approach, by contrast, examines the effect of domestic forces on international relations. This view focuses on domestic politics, culture, society, and political institutions. Scholars have studied how revolution affects the likelihood of war, for example, and how democratic and authoritarian states may differ in their approach to international trade (Walt 1992; Lake 1992; Verdier 1994).

Here I want to emphasize identity as a second-level approach. How nations conceive of their collective principles, values, interests, and history has a direct impact on their foreign policy behavior (Cruz 2000; Connor 1994; Smith 1991; Gellner 1983). Identity shapes the "field of imaginable possibilities"—a plausible range of scenarios about "how the world can or cannot be changed and how the future ought to look" (Cruz 2000: 277; Anderson 1991: 50). When a nation is bargaining with other nations or attempting to resolve international conflicts, issues of identity are often the most intractable. Although it may be possible to resolve material issues such as trade barriers and levels of military armament, disputes over what exactly defines a nation and how it should look tend to be less amenable to compromise. When two nations have competing national identities, the solutions either are imposed through force by one side over the other or require a new conception of identity that allows for compromise (Laitin 1998: 22; Swidler 1986: 274). Neither of these alternatives is easy. Thus nations tend to focus on the third-level and material aspects of conflict management such as deterrence and alliances.

My purpose is not to test these two approaches against each other; nor do I wish to argue that one approach takes priority over the other. Indeed this essay points out the essential complementarity of major research paradigms. Focusing on issues of both material and identity—and distinguishing clearly between third- and second-level analysis—will allow a full discussion of the issues involved in the management and resolution of these three acute conflicts.

Korea: A Shifting Distribution of Power

The issue in Korea is perhaps the most easily understood: two superpowers, concentrating intense interest on a tiny focal point, create enormous pressure and tension on the peninsula itself. The collapse of one of the two large tectonic plates has forced change in North Korea. Korea has all the natural elements of the worst-case scenario: a spiral of conflict, no room for a buffer zone, and intense outside interest in the peninsula (Kang 1995). With the end of the Cold War, North Korea is searching for a path that brings accommodation to the outside world without voluntary surrender.

In 1945 the Soviets and the United States divided the Korean peninsula as a way of disarming the Japanese. When the United States and the Soviet Union began the Cold War, however, the temporary division of the peninsula became permanent, and by 1948 both North and South Korea had held elections and begun the process of nation building. After an inconclusive Korean War that left the peninsula in ruins but the borders essentially identical with the status quo ante, North and South faced each other over what has been widely called the most militarized and dangerous border in the world. Both countries relied heavily on their superpower patrons for material and diplomatic support, and both countries armed themselves heavily.

During the Cold War, tensions remained high as Korea was now on the front line. The United States stationed nuclear weapons and up to 100,000 troops in South Korea and poured billions of dollars of aid into the military government to bolster its bulwark against communism (U.S. AID 1981; Sigal 1998). In South Korea, from 1961 to 1987 a military government ruled in draconian fashion and a widely despised "National Security Law" allowing the South Korean government to stifle virtually any opposition voices was still in force in 2000. Widespread anti-Americanism among the South Korean populace did not weaken Seoul's determination to retain U.S. forces deployed in South Korea, nor did it reduce the South's deterrent posture toward the North (Shin 1996). The conflict was prolonged because superpower rivalry sustained and exacerbated the pressure on the peninsula. For its part, North Korea received material and rhetorical support

TABLE 10.1

North and South Korea's GNP and Per Capita GNP, 1953–94

Year	GNP(billion dollars)		Per capita GNP(dollars)	
	North	South	North	South
1953	0.44	1.35	58	76
1960	1.52	1.95	137	94
1965	2.30	4.78	192	165
1970	3.98	7.99	286	248
1975	9.35	20.85	579	591
1980	13.5	60.3	758	1,589
1985	15.14	83.4	765	2,047
1990	23.1	237.9	1,064	5,569
1993	20.5	328.7	904	7,466
1994	21.2	451.7	923	10,076

SOURCE: "North Korea's Economy, 1953–1990" (1995); National Unification Board (1988: 30).

from China and the Soviet Union during the Cold War. Until the collapse of the Soviet Union, even though the North had fallen far behind the South, it might have been possible for the North to sustain a belief that it could survive and compete with the South. After the collapse, however, such a belief was impossible. By the mid-1980s North Korea had fallen far behind the South by almost every measure (Table 10.1).

The end of the Cold War has had a greater impact on the Korean peninsula than on Kashmir or Taiwan. Indeed its abrupt end drastically altered the security environment in the region. The collapse of the Soviet Union and China's opening to the West had a profound effect on North Korea. The new balance of power made the North especially vulnerable, and its actions after 1990 show that it was well aware of the international environment. Yet North Korea's actions also demonstrate that it wishes—however cautiously—to join the U.S.-dominated world community.

A structural view of North Korea leads to the conclusion that the North should be experiencing fear. The intensity of the security dilemma, the loss of allies, the tremendous economic growth in South Korea—all are evidence that North Korea's external situation has severely worsened. China and Russia have reduced the level and intensity of their ties with North Korea significantly over the past decade. Soviet aid to North Korea, for example, fell from $260 million in 1980 to no aid at all in 1990 (Figure 10.1). By 1992, moreover, both China and Russia had officially recognized South Korea and established formal diplomatic relations with Seoul, leaving North Korea with no partisan allies. Already lagging economically, by the late 1990s, North Korea had fallen far behind its neighbors (Figure 10.2).

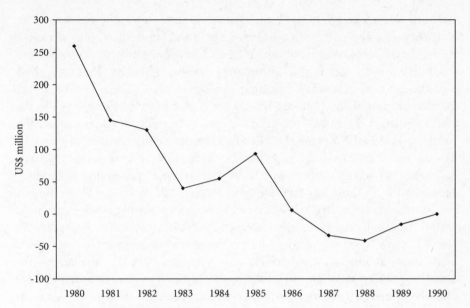

FIG. 10.1. Soviet Aid to North Korea, 1980–90

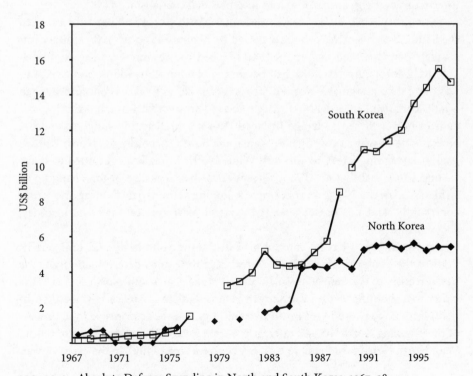

FIG. 10.2. Absolute Defense Spending in North and South Korea, 1967–98

North Korea's response has been twofold: hunker down and open up. The North began to approach both the United States and Japan in an effort to relieve the military and economic problems it faced. Even South Korean observers note that North Korea's doctrine has undergone extensive rethinking (Kim 1995). And North Korean rhetoric today, reflecting a change in North Korea's international position, is profoundly different from what it was thirty years ago. While the North's rhetoric from the 1960s did not preclude military action against the South, by 1988 North Korea's rhetoric was reflecting serious concern over South Korean and U.S. intentions. In September 1988, Kim Il Sung (1989) declared North Korea's foreign policy aims to be "self-reliance, peace, and fraternity." Moreover, North Korea has begun to promote ties with the United States in what has become known as the "triple survival strategy": improving relations with the United States, Japan, and other advanced capitalist countries; strengthening North Korea's "own way of socialism" at home; and opening up to the outside world under a staggered schedule (Ha 1996; Kim 1995). The first strategy has focused on military and diplomatic relations in an effort to normalize ties and reduce the perceived threat that North Korea faces. The third strategy, economic in nature, has emphasized the tentative exploration of how the North might reform its economic system and expose it to international capitalism.

By 1990 and even earlier, it was clear that North Korea had "lost the race" to the South. North Korea's economy lagged far behind the South's. Its military was smaller, poorly armed and trained, and lacked the resources of the combined U.S.-ROK forces. And its allies had begun to abandon it. In addition, the balance was more than marginal—North Korea is twenty times weaker economically than South Korea and its neighbors (Table 10.2). This overwhelmingly negative balance of power forced a change in North Korea's strategy. No longer could the North hope to win a power game against the South. Accordingly, North Korea's goal turned from victory to survival. While North Korea has continued to make sacrifices to signal that it will not surrender easily, it has also begun changing its stripes. Today the North is focusing on joining rather than fighting the world community, and this has engendered a wholesale modification of its ideology, rhetoric, and goals.

Yet North Korea has no intention of disarming voluntarily and unilaterally. Perhaps the best example of North Korea's signaling of its determination was the nuclear crisis of the mid-1990s, when the United States and North Korea came closer to a shooting war on the Korean peninsula than at any time since 1953. In the spring of 1994, a series of misunderstandings and recalcitrance led the process of investigating North Korea's nuclear program inexorably toward confrontation. With North Korea promising to turn Seoul into a "sea of fire" in the event of war,

TABLE 10.2
North Korea and Its Neighbors, 1998

	GDP (billion dollars)	Landmass (km^2)	Population (millions)
North Korea	21.8	120,410	21.3
South Korea	584.7	99,274	45.3
Unified Korea	???	219,684	66.6
Japan	2,903	377,727	125.4
China	4,420	9,560,900	1,231
Russia	697.5	16,995,800	145.4
United States	8,511	9,372,610	269.4

SOURCE: *CIA World Factbook 1999.*

the United States and South Korea began reinforcing their troops in the region and preparing their people for war (Sigal 1998). Although a deus ex machina in the form of Jimmy Carter averted a conflict, it became clear that North Korea would not surrender voluntarily and that U.S. attempts to pressure the North would be met with stubborn recalcitrance.

Another sign of North Korea's seriousness is its missile program. The North's missile program is intended to deter U.S. adventurism. North Korea is not engaging in provocative actions: it could detonate bombs in downtown Seoul or Tokyo (or Washington, D.C.) every week if it wanted to. But the North's goal is not suicide and random destruction but survival (Suro 2000; Cha 1999; "Why Is U.S. So Scared" 2000). As for the notion of "rogue states" and their alleged plans to fire a couple of nuclear warheads at the United States, there are two basic reasons to doubt this threat in North Korea's case. First, any attack on the United States would result in massive American retaliation, and North Korea's efforts over the past decade show that it has an intense desire to survive. Second, why develop an expensive ballistic missile to shoot at the United States when it would be so much easier just to smuggle in a nuclear weapon?

The unrealistic nature of concerns about North Korea have been amply demonstrated by the events and repercussions of the tragic attacks on New York and Washington of September 11, 2001. It was quickly revealed that any nation-state (such as North Korea) is extremely vulnerable to a military response from the United States in the event that it would actually choose to attack the United States. Additionally, it was shown how concerned the Americans are about a true "rogue" operating at the level of individual or small group, rather than that of nation-state. Those identifiable nation-states such as North Korea, Iraq, and other potential rogue nations have even had cautious responses to the events of September and the resulting U.S. military action in Afghanistan.

It is important to distinguish between capabilities and intentions. North Korea already has the capability to blow up bombs in its adversaries' cities; but its intentions are aimed at survival, not increasing tension. And while missiles will not give North Korea any more functional capability than it already possesses or would possess if it were a terrorist nation, missiles do provide a strong military deterrent (Kang 1995). North Korean diplomats have explicitly stated that their missiles are a deterrent against a U.S. campaign of "Yugoslavian-type aggression" against the North. The NATO air war against Yugoslavia made a deep impression on Asian military planners, including Chinese and North Koreans. One North Korean diplomat has noted: "The Agreed Framework made American generals confident that the DPRK had become defenseless; the only way to correct this misperception is to develop a credible deterrent against the United States" (Nautilus Institute 1999). Indeed, North Korean rhetoric in all likelihood is designed to bolster domestic support and ease U.S. aggression against the North. It implies neither that North Korea plans to initiate a war on the peninsula nor that it will engage in random lobbing of missiles across the Pacific. North Korean diplomats point out that "whether we test-fire a satellite or a missile is a legitimate independent right to be exercised by a sovereign state because it in no way runs counter to the DPRK-U.S. Agreed Framework as well as to the recognized international convention" (see "DPRK Warns U.S." 1999).

Given the dire situation in which the North finds itself, one must question whether the North Koreans are serious about their indicated desire to open normal relations with the rest of the world. In practical terms this means examining first and foremost whether North Korea genuinely wishes to repair relations with the United States, as well as with Japan and South Korea. The evidence seems to point to an affirmative answer. While one might examine only the military and conclude that nothing has changed in North Korea, in fact the economic dimension has changed dramatically. The proper question is not how close North Korea has come to effecting a genuine capitalist transformation (not very far), but rather how far it has come from the command economy of 1989 (very far).

A North Korean opening, however, will not be the unconditional embracing of Western values that the United States desires. Observers expecting that reform will include wholesale rhetorical and ideological changes will be disappointed. There is growing evidence that North Korea is serious about opening to the West and desires normal political and economic relations with the rest of the world. Politically North Korea has changed a number of its laws and the constitution itself in order to provide a legal framework for foreign investment. In 1999 the joint production law and the joint venture law were amended to allow for projects outside the Rajin-Sonbong area. Until that time foreign enterprises were al-

lowed to invest money only in the Rajin-Sonbong area.[1] The government continues to create the legal foundations for international investment—for example,
there were eleven constitutional amendments in 1998 alone.

North Korea has also been attempting to join a number of international institutions. Realizing that it can no longer remain autarkic, North Korea will be
subject to the same socializing effect that institutions have on other countries. To
join these institutions, a country must become more open and transparent, as
China is finding out. A country's representatives, even if only elites, will gain
further knowledge of global capitalism, and the nation will come to see the benefits of openness. To date North Korea has tried unsuccessfully to join the Asian
Development Bank (in 1997) and has recently indicated that it may apply to join
the IMF (see Kim 2000). Moreover, Pyongyang has been actively courting mid-
level powers around the region. Australia and Italy have recently normalized ties
with the North; Canada has been approached; Australian National University
trains North Koreans in economics (Smith 2000). In the summer of 2000, the
Philippines became the last ASEAN country to normalize relations with North
Korea.

In economic relations, South Korea has led the way. South Korean conglomerates are rapidly expanding their activities in the North with the blessing of both
governments. Hyundai, the most ambitious South Korean company, has pledged
over $1 billion of investment to North Korea over a period of five years. Samsung
recently began exporting consumer electronics from its industrial complex of
over 1.65 million square meters in the North; LG has been manufacturing televi-
sions in North Korea since 1996. There are more than 700 South Koreans working in North Korea today, and Nampo port has 180 South Korean companies
("Samsung" 2000). While many of these businesses are not yet profitable, their
importance lies in both the beginnings of change in the North Korean system and
the prospects for further opening over the very long run.

Perhaps even more significant than these major shifts in North Korean foreign
policy are the quiet changes. International agreements and government negotiations tell one story, but the changing behavior of the average North Korean is just
as important. In 1995, English replaced Russian as the mandatory foreign language
in high school. Interpreters get daily articles from the *Wall Street Journal* and other
Western newspapers. UN personnel have now visited every county in the North.
Chinese investors have begun to locate in the North. The World Food Program has
foreigners living in every province—previously unheard of. CNN and the BBC are
available in Pyongyang. On a recent visit to Pyongyang, Ken Quinones, director of

[1]For the full text of the current and past DPRK constitutions, see the Japanese-run People's
Korea site (http://www.korea-np.co.jp/pk/).

the Mercy Foundation, was asked by North Koreans to bring videos of *Titanic* and *The Little Mermaid* (Quinones 2000). Some of these changes, of course, are minor. And the overall progress has come nowhere near to creating an open society. The relevant point is how North Korea today compares with the country even five years ago. The changes are obvious and consequential, and they could not possibly have occurred without the explicit consent of the top leadership. Even the North Korean military has been reported to support these recent moves.[2]

For all the movement toward tension reduction on the Korean peninsula, the key intractable issue of identity has not been addressed. In large part this has been a deliberate omission by both sides. Kim Dae Jung's "Sunshine Policy" specifically avoids the larger issue of what exactly "Korea" is; the North has responded as well by putting off these larger issues. By stating openly that he did not intend to promote unification through absorption of the North, Kim Dae Jung reemphasized the initiatives taken in the 1991 "Basic Agreement" between North and South Korea (Hong 2001). For the moment both sides have been content with rapid gains on issues of family reunions, trade, and diplomacy.

On the North Korean side, the opening has required a minor shift in its worldview: from one of implacable conflict with the West to one where dealing with former enemies is possible. North Korea has also begun to examine whether economic reform of some kind might be possible. Two points concern us here. First, although North Korea's leadership has begun tentatively to consider major changes such as reform or a peace treaty with the United States, no major change has yet occurred. Second, the change in worldview is driven by the North's declining power relative to South Korea and the rest of the world. North Korea has responded to its deteriorating position in the local and global balance of power by emphasizing diplomatic and engagement strategies. Although North Korea has certainly not abandoned its military deterrent posture, it realizes that it must seek accommodation with the United States if it wishes to survive. By the 1990s the distribution of power had become so unbalanced that North Korea was forced to respond accordingly. Yet the response has meant an approach to the enemy and, moreover, has begun to engender a change in the way North Korea defines itself. No longer can North Korean leaders claim legitimacy based on an anti-U.S. or anti-South Korean ideology. Thus North Korea is attempting to adjust to the realities of the international system without surrender or collapse.

[2]According to the South Korean newspaper Jungang Ilbo, Jo Myong-rok, First Deputy Chairman of the DPRK National Defense Commission, said on June 15 that the commission appreciates the foundations of unification begun with ROK President Kim Dae Jung's visit to Pyongyang. At the farewell luncheon hosted by DPRK leader Kim Jong Il, Jo said: "Let's practice the joint declaration with all our heart and with loyalty." See Jungang Ilbo, June 15, 2000 (http://www.joins.com/top.html).

The South Korean response has been measured, and it avoids any discussion of the ultimate resolution of the conflict. Kim Dae Jung's Sunshine Policy explicitly avoids any discussion of identity—favoring instead the incremental and immediate steps of drawing North Korea into a series of high-profile but substance-free summit meetings, railroad and transport agreements, and other economic and cultural exchanges (M. Yu 1999). The United States has responded cautiously, too, focusing on North Korea's missile programs and other military aspects of the relationship. For now, both sides continue tentatively to explore ways of easing tension without discussing the grave identity issues between North and South.

Taiwan and China: Democracy and the Second Image

In contrast to the situation in Korea, wholesale changes in China-Taiwan relations have not implied greater conflict in Taiwan. In Taiwan, domestic change is driving the conflict and exacerbating it. At first glance the increased tension across the Taiwan Strait in the recent past might seem puzzling (O'Hanlon 2000). Why would China provoke a war over Taiwan that it cannot win militarily? Why would China, just to retain Taiwan, jeopardize its entry into the WTO, risk frightening its neighbors, and endanger its economic growth if nations impose sanctions? The answer lies in China's view of Taiwan as an essential element of its national identity—and China's willingness to bear the serious costs of such actions.

A system-level view of China and Taiwan, in fact, would point to an increased defensive posture on China's part. During the Cold War, China was able to play a middle position between the United States and the Soviet Union and, with détente in the 1970s, even to become an ally of sorts with the United States against the Soviets. With the collapse of the Soviet Union, the United States emerged as the world's only unquestioned superpower and increasingly turned its attention to a potentially dangerous China (Friedberg 1993; Bernstein and Munro 1997; Kristof 1993). Thus China has come into more direct conflict with the United States than before and, moreover, from a weak position relative to the United States. A structural view would expect to see China declining to take provocative actions against U.S. allies in the region. Yet the opposite has occurred.

Taiwan first became a focal point of the Cold War in Asia when the Kuomintang (KMT) lost mainland China to the Chinese Communist Party (CCP) in 1948–49. The loss of mainland China in 1949, long assumed to be a strong U.S. ally, was a blow to American interests in the region. The Communist victory precipitated both a determination by the United States to halt the spread of communism in Asia and also a shakeout of the foreign policy establishment in Washington (Thomson et al. 1981; Christensen 1997). Taiwan's existence cannot be understood without reference to the United States and other external powers that created the Cold War tensions. But the root cause of tension has been the unresolved issue of Taiwan's status.

The creation of Taiwan as the KMT's stronghold came on the heels of the Chinese Communist victory on the mainland in 1949. The KMT fled to the island of Taiwan, claimed to be the rightful ruler of all China, and swore to retake the mainland. With the CCP initially situating itself as part of a unified communist bloc and allying with the Soviet Union, the capitalist KMT became the bulwark of America's China strategy. Taiwan's indigenous population was not entirely pleased with the arrival of the KMT, however, and a series of bloody confrontations resulted in a schism between power and wealth. Until recently, the "mainland" KMT party controlled the state and political apparatuses, but the indigenous Taiwanese owned most of the businesses (Cheng 1990: 142). Given that the Taiwanese were never very happy with the KMT's arrogation of power on the island, it made political sense for the KMT to fragment business in order to prevent wealth from concentrating in the hands of Taiwanese who might eventually challenge the political structure.

In the 1950s, tensions were high across the Taiwan Strait. In 1954 and again in 1958 there was a possibility of serious escalation of conflict between China and Taiwan (Chang 1988). China was deterred by an explicit U.S. military protection of Taiwan backed with veiled threats of nuclear weapons. By the 1970s the global geopolitical situation had changed. The United States had begun to approach China in an effort to isolate the Soviet Union and in 1979 normalized ties with China at the expense of Taiwan. Taiwan was quickly ousted from a number of international organizations, including the UN. Taiwan's survival has always depended on the United States as an ally that could guarantee safety against the mainland. Although the United States has generally obliged, the Taiwan Relations Act of 1979 made the U.S. military commitment to defend Taiwan more tentative than previously. In 1996, however, the United States did send two aircraft carriers to the Taiwan Strait after China engaged in a series of provocative missile launches. Washington's strategic ambiguity focused on leaving doubt in both Taiwan and China as to whether the United States would intervene—a strategy to forestall either adventurous tactics by the Chinese or unilateral declarations by the Taiwanese (Benson and Niou 2000). Although President Bush's ascendancy marked a tougher line toward China and more favorable statements regarding the U.S. willingness to defend Taiwan, the United States has also made clear that it does not support Taiwanese independence. Figures 10.3 and 10.4 examine the Taiwanese military and its defense spending. Figure 10.3 shows that over the past twenty years the Taiwanese military has reduced its troop levels by 40 percent. Defense spending, however, has increased (Figure 10.4) as Taiwan buys more sophisticated weaponry and upgrades its forces.

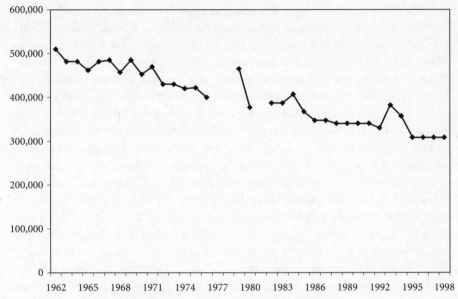

FIG. 10.3. Taiwan's Military Strength (Army and Air Force), 1962–98

FIG. 10.4. Taiwan's
Defense Spending,
1980–97

In the 1980s one might have thought that China's economic opening to capitalism under Deng Xiaoping would portend an easing of tension between China
and Taiwan. Yet the most important change of the 1980s was Taiwan's turn to
democracy. In 1986 Taiwanese president Chiang Ching Kuo, son of KMT founder
Chiang Kai Shek, initiated political reform with the lifting of martial law. Over
the next ten years the political space was incrementally widened—first with the
legalization of the opposition Democratic Progressive Party (DPP), then with the
holding of National Assembly elections, and ultimately with the free presidential
election in 1996 (Wu 1995; Soong 1992). The more Taiwan becomes a mature
democracy, the more it exacerbates tension with the mainland. The Taiwan issue
is also very much a case of competing identities. The traditional KMT and CCP
had similar goals: both parties wanted to rule all of China. Taiwan was a case
where both sides could potentially coexist—both calling for a unified China, neither one willing to upset the status quo, and the stalemate undergirded by the
physical barrier of water and the needs of the two political entities (Hughes 1997).
To this extent the intensity of the issue was muted. And ironically these two political entities have been comfortable dealing with each other precisely because
they agree on so many of the basic assumptions regarding what "China" is. The
conflict exists because of issues of identity, however, and Taiwan's consistently
ambiguous historical relationship with China.

Taiwan has always existed uneasily in the shadow of China. Although nominally independent, Taiwan has also traditionally served as a refuge for the losers of
mainland strife. Taiwan was not a formal province of China, but neither was it a
recognized independent state in the manner of Korea, Japan, and Vietnam. In
1644 the Ming loyalists retreated to Taiwan to harass the triumphant Qing (Spence
1991: 50; Copper 1990). Led by Admiral Koxingga, the Ming loyalists would sally
forth from Taiwan. Although the Qing eventually subdued the Ming loyalists,
Taiwan was not made a formal province of China until 1886. Before that time it
was considered a part of Fukien province, administered by Manchu officials assigned from Beijing. Official Chinese records in the eighteenth century, however,
also refer to Taiwan as a "frontier area" (Copper 1990: 21). Although clearly a
"part" of China, Taiwan was not considered a part of Han China. Thus the issue of
China and Taiwan poses an interesting dilemma for realists. Are China and Taiwan nation-states? If they are not, how do we make sense of them and the conflict?

While the West's answer to the question whether or not Taiwan is a nation-
state is obvious, the Chinese answer is exactly the opposite (Hughes 1997; Yahuda
1996). China may truly view Taiwan as an internal problem. Xu Dunxin, former
Chinese ambassador to Japan, expresses a common Chinese refrain: "The Taiwan
issue is China's business. It is China's internal affair. No country, including the

U.S., has a right to concern itself with this issue" (Lawrence 1999: 19). Although such pronouncements tend to be dismissed in the West, the Chinese have held a consistent policy toward Taiwan. It is perhaps premature to pretend that China is not sincere in expressing this attitude (Christensen 1999).

This Chinese perception has two implications. First, imposing a Western conception of international relations on China may be missing the point. The nations of Asia have made an implicit pact with Taiwan: Exist as a quasi-nation and enjoy the benefits of the international system. Indeed this has been the traditional solution to the Taiwan issue (Oksenberg 2001). So long as Taiwan was willing to abide by these rules and accept its status as a quasi-nation, the benefits of being a nation-state were available to it. Taiwan's leaders could travel the world and play golf and perform quasi-diplomatic functions, Taiwan's firms could trade and invest overseas. Taiwan's status was not threatened, even by China. But while Taiwan could act like a nation-state, it could not officially become a nation-state (Klintworth 1995). The furor over the 1996 and 2000 Taiwanese elections—Lee Teng-hui's 1996 statements in particular—revealed the consequences of breaking the rules. As various Taiwanese leaders became more assertive in their claim to full sovereign nation-state status, the rest of the world became increasingly cautious. And the reaction to Beijing's military maneuvers was especially telling (T. Yu 1999). In good realist fashion, America's fury was directed almost exclusively at China for being provocative. The rest of the Asian states were muted in their response to Chinese military intervention, however, and off the record were extremely upset at Taiwan for provoking China. These states feel that "Taiwan broke the pact" (Rigger 1997).

Second, but more important, it was only as Taiwan began the transition to a genuine modern nation-state with democracy that the issues became intractable with China. Until now China has been content to allow Taiwan to act like a normal nation-state and conduct its affairs with little interference from Beijing (Goldstein 1997). But a formal declaration of independence would cause China to respond, most likely with a punitive expedition. This should not be considered an idle threat. The conflict also reveals China's belief that it has the right to order its relations in its surrounding areas (Wu 1994). Indeed, the conflict itself has been exacerbated as Taiwan has consolidated its democratic institutions. While Taiwan was under the control of the KMT and authoritarian governments during the Cold War, there was little disagreement between China and Taiwan over the rules of the game or the ultimate place that Taiwan occupied in relation to China: Taiwan was clearly part of mainland China. The only dispute was who—the KMT or the CCP—was the legitimate ruler of all China. Events of the past fifteen years, however, have seen Taiwan's identity shifting to that of a modern nation-state.

This shift is most notable in the gradual move to democracy. Taiwan has become a strong, vibrant democracy where people have the right to voice their opinions and elect leaders in contested elections (Cheng 1990). As such, Taiwan, although not recognized formally as a nation-state by the United States, has become in the eyes of much of the world a legitimate political entity.

And therein lies the heart of the issue. While China's conception of itself remains roughly the same, Taiwan's is changing. Hence the clash between a democratic, capitalist, wealthy, and industrialized Taiwan deciding its own fate versus an authoritarian, quasi-capitalist, semitraditional China attempting to control the fate of Taiwan (Tien 1996). Realism has much to say about how the conflict was managed during the Cold War. But without understanding these competing visions of the world, it is impossible to understand why the conflict has endured—or indeed why it has become much more acute in the 1990s.

China's view of international relations, by contrast, is considerably more subtle. Although realist in its practices, this view also incorporates many non-Westphalian elements. For its part China is comfortable with a loose definition of "nation." China has already agreed to a "one-nation, two-systems" approach with respect to Hong Kong. Although it is too early to draw firm conclusions, the first three years of Hong Kong's return to political control by the mainland show that China has in large part respected the two-systems principle by allowing Hong Kong its own currency, legal system, and even military forces. Moreover, the border dispute between India and China has never been formally resolved. Both countries have agreed to leave the border undefined. Beijing's effort to derive an identity that allows for the "one-country, two-systems" principle with Hong Kong is one example of how identities can be reconfigured to allow for accommodation. This policy has met with opposition in Taiwan, however. In September 1997, for example, Lin Chong-pin, Vice-Chairman of the ROC Mainland Affairs Council, said: "We wish to reiterate that the 'one country, two systems' formula is by no means applicable to cross-Strait relations" (Lasater 2000: 135; Gong 2000). So long as Taiwan existed in a traditional, poorly defined, and partial relationship with China, both sides were content. But Taiwan's increasingly democratic political institutions are causing trouble with China.

Despite the increasing conflict over the issue of identity, the balance of power remains salient. Above all, a strong U.S. commitment to defend Taiwan has precluded China from imposing a solution against Taiwan's wishes. Indeed the issue of identity is consequential in large part because of American support, which prevents Beijing from overwhelming Taiwan through coercion or force. So long as this is the case, identity—although at the heart of the conflict's solution—remains less important than power.

India and Pakistan: A Loose Configuration
of External Powers

Kashmir represents an interesting case. The Kashmir issue has never been as tightly coupled to superpower conflict as the cases of Korea and Taiwan. This gives the issue more opportunity to be influenced by regional and domestic politics and by ideology and religion, and it means that the status of Kashmir has come to revolve around issues of identity. Although the management of the conflict has been realist in nature and has included a balance of power between India and Pakistan in which the tensions and level of resources associated with the balance have been slowly escalating, the core issue of identity has never been resolved. Nor have the parties taken seriously the need to craft a solution that explicitly addresses the matter of identity. Who, and what, are Kashmir, Pakistan, and India? This question lies at the core of the conflict.

Whereas Korea and Taiwan were created by disputes that arose between the superpowers at the end of World War II, India and Pakistan came into existence with the British withdrawal in 1947. The major issue became how to define boundaries that had never been historically defined. The process of decolonization required the creation of nation-states in a region that had been under British rule since the eighteenth century and, before that, had been a set of principalities. The British decision to create nation-states of both India and Pakistan, although not explicitly aimed at creating one predominantly Hindu state and one predominantly Muslim state, was fraught with inherent tensions, since the issue became where to draw the boundary between two intermixed populations. The Kashmir region borders both Pakistan and India but has a Muslim majority population. The Kashmiris themselves seemed to prefer neither country. Different proposals for deciding Kashmir's fate were put forward by India, Pakistan, and the UN (Varshney 1991). Unable to agree on a format for deciding the ownership of Kashmir, India and Pakistan clashed in 1947. Since then Kashmir has come to represent the broad range of tensions involved in India-Pakistan relations. Since their founding over fifty years ago, the two countries have not been able to reconcile their relationship. And this unstable situation has resulted in arms races, periodic conflicts, and nuclear proliferation.

The conflict between India and Pakistan has simmered for decades, occasionally flaring into widespread violence. Since independence, Pakistan and India have fought three wars—in 1947, 1965, and 1971—and skirmished intermittently over the status of Kashmir. There were 3,000 fatalities in the 1947 fighting, 20,000 fatalities during the 1965 fighting, and 11,000 in the Pakistan-India War of 1971 (IISS 2001). (By way of comparison, the Korean War from 1950 to 1953 resulted in an estimated 4 million fatalities, both civilian and military.) Since 1989 there have

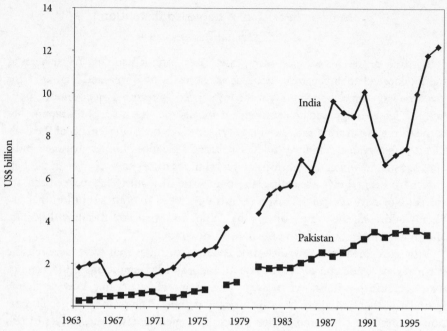

FIG. 10.5.   Absolute Defense Spending in India and Pakistan, 1963–97

been 22,000 deaths in the region as a result of violence, and during the 1990s the estimated cost to both India and Pakistan of the conflict in Kashmir was $22 billion (IISS 2001). The fighting during the summer of 1999 involved some 450 official casualties on the Indian side.

Both India and Pakistan have been highly sensitive to the regional distribution of power. The nuclear weapon programs of both countries are perhaps the most stark example of the attention paid to the balance of power. By the 1970s both Pakistan and India had nascent nuclear weapons programs. In the late 1990s both India and Pakistan were developing intermediate-range ballistic missiles with ranges of up to 1,500 km: the Agni I and II in India and the Ghauri I and II in Pakistan. The most dramatic evidence of their competition in the nuclear arena came in the virtually simultaneous nuclear tests performed in May 1998 (Joeck 1999; Huntley 1999). Both India and Pakistan have devoted large sums to defense spending as well, and their deployment of forces has reflected the changing local balance. Figures 10.5 and 10.6 show that while India outspends Pakistan in absolute terms on defense, Pakistan's expenditures as a percentage of GDP are roughly double those of India.

Moreover, India and Pakistan have been willing to endure severe international costs over their dispute. After the recent nuclear tests on both sides, the world community, in particular the United States and the IMF, imposed sanctions on both countries and reduced aid and loan commitments. Yet both sides have been willing, even eager, to bear the costs. On December 31, 2000, a moratorium on interest payments on Pakistan's $38 billion in foreign debt expired, and without an IMF loan in place, Pakistan was unable to negotiate another loan (Rashid 2000: 28). Although coup leader General Musharaf attempted to negotiate a further loan in 2000, there was little willingness to make major concessions. Such stark economic costs in order to signal military and political resolve are evidence of Pakistan's commitment to balancing India's power. Since then, the events of September 11 and General Musharraf's willingness to support the U.S. anti-Taliban campaign in Afghanistan resulted in a U.S. decision to renew aid payments and some loans.

Why has this conflict remained acute for more than five decades? This conflict has never been central to the global balance of power in the sense of the Taiwan and Korea conflicts. Because South Asia was peripheral to the superpower conflict of the Cold War, both the United States and the Soviet Union paid little attention to the dispute. At the beginning of the Cold War, the United States saw China and the Far East as strategically important to containing communism, and "neither India nor Pakistan met criteria determining American military priori-

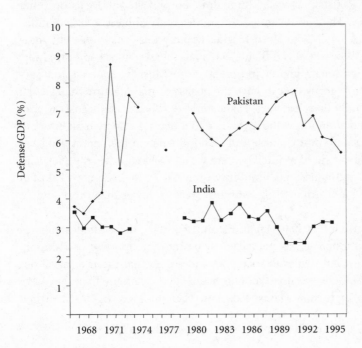

FIG. 10.6.
Defense Spending
as a Percentage of
GDP, India and
Pakistan, 1968–97

ties" (Singh 1986: 209). As the Cold War continued, however, the superpowers were reluctantly drawn into South Asia, if only to balance each other's potential influence. During the 1950s India followed a strong unaligned stance, while Pakistan actively courted U.S. support. During that decade the United States and Pakistan concluded a Mutual Defense Assistance Treaty, and Pakistan joined the Southeast Asia Treaty Organization (SEATO) and the Central Treaty Organization (CENTO). In addition, the Communist victory in China in 1949, the Korean War of 1950, the assassination of Iranian Prime Minister Razmara Ali on March 7, 1951, all caused the United States to feel it was on the defensive in South Asia (Brands 1990). As the United States and the USSR scrambled to create spheres of influence across the globe, India sided with the Russians and the United States with Pakistan. But in contrast to Europe and Northeast Asia, where the spheres of influence were stark and clear, the picture in South Asia was considerably more complex.

Washington attempted to avoid entanglements in South Asia while also balancing the Soviet influence (Husain 1997). The United States remained neutral during the 1965 conflict between India and Pakistan. And despite its perceived leaning toward Pakistan (Singh 1986: 211), in the period 1962–77 the United States gave India twice as much aid as it gave to Pakistan (Table 10.3). Since 1966 China, not the United States, has been Pakistan's main arms supplier. The Soviet Union courted India and Pakistan, as well, although it too preferred to focus on other regions of the globe. The Soviets aimed to counter both Chinese and U.S. influence in the region, and this involved forging friendly relations with both India and Pakistan. This, however, was difficult to manage. Between 1954 and 1975 India received over $1.2 billion in grants and credit from Moscow and was the only country outside the Warsaw Pact to have the license to manufacture the MiG jet (Foot 1986: 192–93). By 1965, however, Pakistani leaders had visited Moscow, too, and Moscow shifted from a pro-Indian stance to a neutral stance in an effort to woo both countries and limit Chinese and U.S. influence in the region. Pakistan agreed to let the Soviets hold a peace conference at Tashkent after the 1965 war, although it proved inconclusive (Choudhury 1974: 11). By the late 1960s Pakistan was receiving Soviet aid, although the amounts were far lower than those offered to India.[3]

During the 1971 conflict between India and Pakistan, the United States remained neutral, although it was perceived to be more supportive of Pakistan. Sumit Ganguly, however, denies this support and argues that the U.S. naval deployments in the region were aimed more at signaling the Chinese than they were at deterring Indian aggression against Pakistan (Ganguly 1994: 111). As it turned

---

[3]In 1966, for example, Pakistan received $84 million in Soviet aid (Foot 1986: 193).

TABLE 10.3

Total U.S. Economic and Military Aid to India and Pakistan, 1946–77
(millions of dollars)

	1946–48	1949–52	1953–61	1962–77
Pakistan	0.1	11.1	1,926.9	3,819.7
India	39.9	248.7	2,407.6	7,187.1
Aid to India as percentage of aid to Pakistan	39,900	2,240	124	188

SOURCE: U.S. AID (1981).

out, the United States did nothing to deter India's offensives and did not prevent the breakup of Pakistan. Moreover, China and the Soviet Union clashed diplomatically over the 1971 war. As the International Institute for Strategic Studies (IISS 1971: 1) noted: "Nothing could have dramatized the new patterns more than the spectacle in December of the Soviet Union and the PRC vilifying one another in the Security Council about the third Indo-Pakistani war while the United States shuffled on and off the sidelines."

The end of the Cold War loosened these alignments even further as India opened its economy, pursuing a path of globalization, and the United States and China became the major external powers in the region. Global powers never pushed as intensely on South Asia as they did in Northeast Asia. The loosening of alignments had two effects. First, it kept the issue from being arrogated by the superpowers for their own ends (Ahmed 1999: 194). Second, the end of the Cold War had less of an impact in South Asia than in other regions: Kashmir is not subject to the same external forces brought to bear on Korea and Taiwan. With superpowers out of the picture and with tensions so high on the subcontinent, what has kept India and Pakistan from fighting a conclusive war? The Kashmir issue might seem the easiest of the three to solve. After all, the existence of neither India nor Pakistan is at stake, and the global powers have little stake in the outcome. The issue over Kashmir is a conflict over national identity, however, and thus has proved both substantively intractable and analytically different from the other two cases studied here.

At its heart, then, the conflict in South Asia is about identity. India and Pakistan's national identities are built on mutually exclusive ideational foundations. India is a secular, multicultural democracy; Pakistan is a sectarian quasi-democracy prone to coups and instability. Indians argue that allowing the Kashmir Valley to become independent or join Pakistan would betray the essence of India's existence as a secular democracy (Kohli 1997). If a Muslim-majority state like Kashmir cannot fit comfortably in India, it would set a precedent for other provinces to demand independence. Pakistan's original raison d'être, by contrast, was as a Muslim-majority state. If Kashmir is allowed to become Indian, then Pakistan's existence itself is called into question: there are over 100 million Muslims in India, and perhaps Pakistan itself has no need of existence. If religion is the defining characteristic of people, then Muslims and Hindus should not live in the same country (Perkovich 1996). For these reasons Pakistan's claim on Kashmir is difficult to relinquish. At the same time, and in precisely the opposite manner, India's claim is central to its identity as a nation.

Pakistan did lose control of its Muslim eastern wing in 1971, with the creation of Bangladesh, without losing its religious basis for a claim on national identity. However, even though the religious rationale is not as strong as it was before the creation of Bangladesh, as Ashutosh Varshney (1991: 1000) writes: "If Pakistan tries to liberate Kashmir, or if Kashmir breaks away with its help, Pakistan runs the risk of endangering the welfare of 100 million Muslims in India. . . . An inevitable [Indian] nationalist cry, however, is: how many times will India be partitioned due to the so-called Muslim Question? Muslims of pre-1947 India already have two homelands, Pakistan and Bangladesh. Would Kashmir be a third? Ultimately, the breakup of nation-states is not a rational question." Table 10.4 shows the ethnic makeup of the three states in the Kashmir region and reveals just how difficult it is to define which religious group should be considered predominant. While the Kashmir Valley is 95 percent Muslim, the Jammu region is 66 percent Hindu and over half the Ladakh region is neither Hindu nor Muslim.

Most solutions proposed since 1947, however, have not addressed the issue of national identity. The 1947 Indian Independence Act allowed individual princes to choose whether or not their state would incorporate with India or Pakistan (or, hypothetically, choose independence).[4] The case of Kashmir quickly became a political quagmire as all sides put forth various proposals. With the issue still not decided by August 15, 1947—the day British rule ended—India and Pakistan both became involved in the dispatch of troops, and hostilities ensued. Although the UN appointed mediators, neither India nor Pakistan could agree on the terms on which a plebiscite would be held (Bajwa 1996; Buzan 1986).

Both India and Pakistan refused to cede the right of decision, and the people of Kashmir became a political football for the two sides to kick around. Article 370 of India's constitution allowed for Kashmiri autonomy within the Indian Union. But despite the Delhi Agreement of 1952 between Kashmir's leader Abdullah and India's leader Nehru, India gradually pulled Kashmir more firmly under its control. Pakistan, meanwhile, held that the part of the Kashmir state which

[4]For an interesting eyewitness account of the initial negotiations between India and Pakistan, see Ali (1967). See also Lamb (1997) and Jha (1996).

TABLE 10.4
Ethnic Makeup of Kashmir

	% Muslim	% Hindu	% Other
Kashmir Valley	94.96	4.59	0.45
Jammu	29.60	66.25	4.15
Ladakh	46.04	2.66	51.30[a]

SOURCE: "India and Pakistan" (1999).
[a]Buddhist.

had fallen to it in 1948 was still part of a single unit and therefore the final conclusion was still to be decided. After a decade of turmoil in the 1960s, the Simla Agreement of 1972 specified that all issues must be resolved bilaterally—which only made the problem more intractable (Raza 1997). At no time did the leaders of either India or Pakistan attempt to reconfigure their conception of national identity in a way that might allow for compromise. Instead, over the decades, the positions of both sides have hardened. This is not the place for a detailed history of the negotiations, but a few general points can be made. Both Pakistan and India see Kashmir as a single entity; thus division of the state into sections is unacceptable. Nor is independence any longer an option, closing off another avenue. Without directly addressing the issue of how India or Pakistan might adjust their national identity to allow for resolution of the conflict, the military option at best provides for an uneasy management of the conflict that sporadically flares into violence and threatens to spread into a wider Indo-Pakistani confrontation (Tremblay 1996).

Thus Kashmir provides an interesting contrast to both Korea and Taiwan. The tightly coupled balance of power in Northeast Asia has undergone change in both cases, though for different reasons. In the case of India and Pakistan, local conditions have far more influence and seem to be sustaining the acute conflict in South Asia. Given that the Cold War was not responsible for the initiation of the conflict and did not exacerbate it to any great degree, the changing global balance of power has had far less impact on the region. The only path to attenuation of conflict in South Asia appears to be a domestic reconfiguration of national identity. Without some reconfiguration of identity in these countries away from diametrically opposed images, the conflict over Kashmir seems certain to endure.

Identity Matters

Why was there progress in the Korea dispute but not in Taiwan and Kashmir? The basic answer is that power has shifted more dramatically on the Korean peninsula than in either Taiwan or Kashmir. South Korea's sustained economic development, as well as the end of Chinese and Soviet support for North Korea, have led to a stark and ever-widening power differential in South Korea's favor. This difficult situation has forced North Korea to begin cautious attempts at reform and at opening to the outside world. In Taiwan, Washington's support of the island prevents Beijing from imposing a solution—if the United States were to withdraw its ambiguous yet palpable commitment to Taiwan, Beijing would most likely increase its pressure on Taipei. In South Asia, both Pakistan and India have engaged in a subdued arms race that keeps the balance of power relatively even. So long as both countries maintain roughly equal military power, the cost of using force as an option for imposing a solution remains prohibitively high. Thus a stalemate exists. The actual management of the conflict—focused on a realist balance of power—has masked any genuine discussion of the issue of identity and has also limited progress in Taiwan and Kashmir.

The next step in this line of research would be to examine these cases more closely to understand why second-level variables matter in some cases and third-level variables matter in others. To this end, a comparison with acute conflicts in other regions of the world might prove enlightening. In Europe, for example, the clash between Turkey and Greece over Cyprus might approximate the Kashmir case; the case of Northern Ireland is similar in intensity and tone to that of Taiwan; the Korean case most closely approximates that of Germany. Discovering the key factors in the European cases might illuminate the Asian cases.

The comparison is not encouraging. In Cyprus the partition between Turkish and Greek ethnicities, though nominally under a federal national system, has in fact hardened into an ethnic partition. Neither Turkey nor Greece nor the ethnic groups on Cyprus have shown willingness to search for workable alternatives, and observers doubt whether membership in the European Union will spur any improvement (Bahcheli 2000; Berwin 2000; Theophanous 2000). The situation in Northern Ireland, while improving marginally over the past few years, remains intractable (Kaufmann 1998; Kumar 1997). The Catholic minority calls for union with Ireland; the Protestant majority wishes to remain a part of the United Kingdom. The 1914 partition did not resolve the issue, nor has any subsequent agreement done so. Germany provides perhaps the most encouraging case from this perspective. As in Korea, the two Germanys were countries artificially divided by the superpowers in 1945. With the end of the Cold War, German unification was preceded by the collapse of one side, and the issue of identity and nation became moot.

In all three cases studied here, the management of the conflicts has emphasized realist aspects of international relations. Conflict was contained through deterrence, the building of alliances, military buildups, and other material means. The issue of national identity—and more important, whether such identities could be reconfigured in a way that allows for compromise—has not been explored seriously by the interested parties. In the case of Korea, the North's response to its decline in power has led to the potential for improving relations on the peninsula. But the progress in tension reduction has been made by sidestepping the larger issue of what a united Korea should be. In Taiwan, the changing identity brought about by democratization has exacerbated the relations between the mainland and the island—forcing into stark contrast the differing notions of what it is to be Chinese and how the issue of sovereignty should be decided. In South Asia, a realist management of the conflict exacerbates tensions, as both sides have engaged in a balance-of-power and slow-motion arms race that after fifty years has resulted in two nuclear-armed nations no closer to resolving the status of Kashmir. Although numerous proposals have been offered by both India and Pakistan, none of them have sought to reconceptualize the issue of identity in order to resolve the conflict.

This study has revealed the complementarity of levels of analysis. By focusing first on a third-level approach and examining the balance of power and other international factors surrounding the conflicts, we have seen that management of the disputes has pursued a realist approach. We have also seen why progress has been made in Korea but not in the other two cases. By examining the second level and focusing on issues of national identity, we have seen how deeply rooted are issues of identity in these disputes—and how little attention policymakers have paid to their effect on the conflicts.

Works Cited

Ahmed, Samina. 1999. "Pakistan's Nuclear Weapons Program." *International Security* 23(4) (Spring): 178–204.

Ali, Chaudhri Muhammad. 1967. *The Emergence of Pakistan.* New York: Columbia University Press.

Anderson, Benedict. 1991. *Imagined Communities: Reflections on the Origin and Spread of Nationalism.* New York: Verso.

Bahcheli, Tozun. 2000. "Searching for a Cyprus Settlement: Considering Options for Creating a Federation, a Confederation, or Two Independent States." *Publius* 30 (Winter/Spring): 203–16.

Bajwa, Farooq Naseem. 1996. *Pakistan and the West: The First Decade 1947–1957.* Karachi: Oxford University Press.

Benson, Brett, and Emerson Niou. 2000. "Comprehending Strategic Ambiguity: US Policy Toward the Taiwan Strait Security Issue." Manuscript. Duke University.

Bernstein, Richard, and Ross H. Munro. 1997. *The Coming Conflict with China.* New York: Knopf.

Berwin, Christopher. 2000. "European Union Perspectives on Cyprus Accession." *Middle Eastern Studies* 36(1) (Jan.): 21–34.

Brands, W. 1990. *India and the United States: The Cold Peace.* Boston: Twayne.

Buzan, Barry, ed. 1986. *South Asian Insecurity and the Great Powers*. London: Macmillan.

Cha, Victor D. 1999. "The Rationale for 'Enhanced' Engagement of North Korea: After the Perry Policy Review." *Asian Survey* 39(6) (Nov./Dec.): 845–66.

Chang, Gordon. 1988. "To the Nuclear Brink: Eisenhower, Dulles, and the Quemoy-Matsu Crisis." *International Security* 12(4) (Spring): 96–123.

Cheng, Tun-Jen. 1990. "Political Regimes and Development Strategies: South Korea and Taiwan." In Gary Gereffi and Donald Wyman, eds., *Manufacturing Miracles: Paths of Industrialization in Latin America and East Asia*. Princeton: Princeton University Press.

Choudhury, G. W. 1974. "Pakistan and the Communist World." *Pacific Community* (Oct.): 3–24.

Christensen, Thomas. 1997. *Useful Adversaries: Grand Strategy, Domestic Mobilization, and Sino-American Conflict, 1947–58*. Princeton: Princeton University Press.

———. 1999. "China, the US-Japan Alliance, and the Security Dilemma in East Asia." *International Security* 23(4) (Spring): 49–80.

CIA World Factbook 1999, http://www.odci.gov/cia/publications/factbook/.

Connor, Walker. 1994. *Ethnonationalism: The Quest for Understanding*. Princeton: Princeton University Press.

Copper, John. 1990. *Taiwan: Nation-State or Province?* Boulder, Colo.: Westview.

Cruz, Consuelo. 2000. "Identity and Persuasion: How Nations Remember Their Pasts and Make Their Futures." *World Politics* 52 (Apr.): 275–312.

DiCiccio, Jonathan, and Jack Levy. 2000. "Power Shifts and Problem Shifts: The Evolution of the Power Transition Research Program." Manuscript. Rutgers University.

"DPRK Warns U.S. of 'Unpredictable Consequences.'" 1999. *People's Korea*, Aug. 7, p. 1.

Foot, Rosemary. 1986. "The Sino-Soviet Complex and South Asia." In Barry Buzan and Gowher Rizvi, eds., *South Asian Insecurity and the Great Powers*. New York: St. Martin's Press.

Friedberg, Aaron. 1993. "Ripe for Rivalry: Prospects for Peace in a Multipolar Asia." *International Security* 18(3) (Winter): 5–33.

Ganguly, Sumit. 1994. *The Origins of War in South Asia*. Boulder: Westview.

———. 1999. "India's Pathway to Pokhran II." *International Security* 23(4) (Spring): 148–77.

Gellner, Ernest. 1983. *Nations and Nationalism*. Oxford: Blackwell.

Goldstein, Avery. 1997. "Great Expectations: Interpreting China's Arrival." *International Security* 22(3) (Winter): 36–73.

Gong, Gerrit, ed. 2000. *Taiwan Strait Dilemmas: China-Taiwan-U.S. Policies in the New Century*. Washington, D.C.: CSIS Press.

Groves, Denise. 1998. "India and Pakistan: A Clash of Civilizations?" *Washington Quarterly* 21(4) (Autumn): 17–20.

Ha, Young-sun. 1996. "View on Korean and Northeast Asian Regional Security Issues." *Sindonga* (Apr.): 198–215.

Heisbourg, François. 1998. "The Prospects for Stability Between India and Pakistan." *Survival* 40(4) (Winter): 77–92.

Hong, Kyu-dok. 2001. "South Korean Policy Toward North Korea." In James Lister, ed., *Korea's Economy 2000*. Washington, D.C.: Korea Economic Institute of America.

Hughes, Christopher. 1997. *Taiwan and Chinese Nationalism: National Identity and Status in International Society*. New York: Routledge.

Huntley, Wade. 1999. "Alternate Futures After the South Asian Nuclear Tests: Pokhran as Prologue." *Asian Survey* 39(3) (May/June): 504–24.

Husain, Ross Masood. 1997. "Threat Perception and Military Planning in Pakistan: The Impact of Technology, Doctrine, and Arms Control." In Eric Arnett, ed., *Military Capacity and the Risk of War: China, India, Pakistan, and Iran*. Oxford: Oxford University Press.

IISS (International Institute for Strategic Studies). 1971. *Strategic Survey*. London: IISS.

———. 2001. *The Military Balance 1999–2000*. London: IISS.

"India and Pakistan." 1999. *Economist*, May 22, p. 10.

Jervis, Robert. 1976. *Perception and Misperception in International Politics*. Princeton: Princeton University Press.

Jha, Prem Shankar. 1996. *Kashmir, 1947: Rival Versions of History*. Delhi: Oxford University Press.

Joeck, Neil. 1999. "Nuclear Developments in India and Pakistan." *Access Asia Review* 2(2) (July): 11–21.

Kang, David C. 1995. "Preventive War and North Korea." *Security Studies* 4(2) (Winter): 330–64.

Kaufmann, Chaim. 1998. "When All Else Fails: Ethnic Population Transfers and Partitions in the Twentieth Century." *International Security* 23(2) (Fall): 120–56.

Kim, Hak-joon. 1995. "North Korea After Kim Il-Song." *Security Dialogue* 26(1) (Mar.): 73–91.

Kim Hyoung-min. 2000. "IMF Indicated Bailout Loan for North Korea." *Korea Times*, Apr. 19.

Kim Il Sung. 1989. "Complete the Great Task of Socialism and Communism to the Utmost by Holding Aloft the Revolutionary Banner of Juche." In *Korea Central Yearbook 1989*. Pyongyang.

Klintworth, Gary. 1995. *New Taiwan, New China: Taiwan's Changing Role in the Asia-Pacific Region*. New York: St. Martin's Press.

Kohli, Atul. 1997. "Can Democracies Accommodate Ethnic Nationalism?" *Journal of Asian Studies* 56 (May): 325–44.

Kristof, Nicholas D. 1993. "The Rise of China." *Foreign Affairs* 72(5) (Nov./Dec.): 59–74.

Kugler, Jacek, and Douglas Lemke, eds. 1996. *Parity and War: Evaluations and Extensions of the War Ledger*. Ann Arbor: University of Michigan Press.

Kumar, Radha. 1997. "The Troubled History of Partition." *Foreign Affairs* 76(1) (Jan./Feb.): 22–34.

Laitin, David. 1998. *Identity in Formation: The Russian-Speaking Populations in the Near Abroad*. Ithaca: Cornell University Press.

Lake, David A. 1992. "Powerful Pacifists: Democratic States and War." *American Political Science Review* 86 (Mar.): 24–37.

Lamb, Alastair. 1997. *Incomplete Partition: The Genesis of the Kashmir Dispute*. Hertingfordbury, U.K.: Roxford.

Lasater, Martin. 2000. *The Taiwan Conundrum in U.S. China Policy*. Boulder: Westview.

Lawrence, Susan. 1999. "Yearning to Lead." *Far Eastern Economic Review*, Sept. 16, p. 19.

Lemke, Douglas, and Suzanne Werner. 1996. "Power Parity, Commitment to Change, and War." *International Studies Quarterly* 40 (June): 235–60.

Morrow, James. 1993. "Arms Versus Allies: Trade-offs in the Search for Security." *International Organization* 47 (Spring): 207–33.

National Unification Board. 1988. *The Economies of South and North Korea*. Seoul: National Unification Board.

Nautilus Institute. 1999. *DPRK Report* 19 (July–Aug.).

"North Korea's Economy, 1953–1990." *Vantage Point* 19(3) (July 1995): 18.

O'Hanlon, Michael. 2000. "Why China Cannot Conquer Taiwan." *International Security* 25(2) (Fall): 51–86.

Oksenberg, Michel. 2001. "The Issue of Sovereignty in the Asian Historical Context." In Stephen Krasner, ed., *Problematic Sovereignty: Contested Rules and Political Possibilities*. New York: Columbia University Press.

Perkovich, George. 1996. "India, Pakistan, and the United States: The Zero-Sum Game." *World Policy Journal* (Summer): 49–55.

Quinones, Kenneth. 2000. Remarks at the conference "The North Korean System at the Dawn of the 21st Century," University of California, Apr. 7.

Rashid, Ahmed. 2000. "Military Facelift." *Far Eastern Economic Review*, Sept. 14, p. 28.

Raza, Rafi. 1997. *Zulfikar Ali Bhutto and Pakistan, 1967–1977*. Karachi: Oxford University Press.

Rigger, Shelley. 1997. "Competing Conceptions of Taiwan's Identity." In Suisheng Zhao, ed., *Across the Taiwan Strait: Mainland China, Taiwan, and the 1995–1996 Crisis*. New York: Routledge.

"Samsung Group Chairman Wants to Visit North Korea." 2000. *Asia Pulse*, May 3.

Shin, Gi-wook. 1996. "South Korean Anti-Americanism: A Comparative Perspective." *Asian Survey* 36(8) (Aug.): 787–803.

Sigal, Leon. 1998. *Disarming Strangers: Nuclear Diplomacy with North Korea*. Princeton: Princeton University Press.

Singer, J. David. 1961. "The Level-of-Analysis Problem in International Relations." In Klaus Knorr and Sidney Verba, eds., *The International System: Theoretical Essays*. Princeton: Princeton University Press.

Singh, Anita Inder. 1986. "The Superpower Global Complex and South Asia." In Barry Buzan and Gowher Rizvi, eds., *South Asian Insecurity and the Great Powers*. New York: St. Martin's Press.

Smith, Anthony. 1991. *National Identity*. London: Penguin.

Smith, Heather. 2000. Remarks at the conference "The North Korean System at the Dawn of the 21st Century," University of California, Apr. 7.

Soong, James Chul-yul. 1992. "Political Development in the Republic of China, 1985–1992: An Insider's View." *World Affairs* 155 (Fall): 62–66.

Spence, Jonathan. 1991. *The Search for Modern China*. New York: Norton.

Suro, Roberto. 2000. "Ex-Defense Officials Decry Missile Plan." *Washington Post*, May 17, p. A02.

Swidler, Ann. 1986. "Culture in Action: Symbols and Strategies." *American Sociological Review* 51 (Apr.): 273–86.

Theophanous, Andreas. 2000. "Prospects for Solving the Cyprus Problem and the Role of the European Union." *Publius* 30 (Winter/Spring): 217–41.

Thomson, James, Peter Stanley, and John Curtis Perry. 1981. *Sentimental Imperialists: The American Experience in East Asia*. New York: Harper & Row.

Tien, Hung-mao. 1996. "Building Democracy in Taiwan." *China Quarterly* 148 (Dec.): 1141–70.

Tremblay, Reeta Chowdhari. 1996. "Nation, Identity, and the Intervening Role of the State: A Study of the Secessionist Movement in Kashmir." *Pacific Affairs* 69 (Winter): 471–97.

U.S. AID (U.S. Agency for International Development). 1981. *U.S. Overseas Loans and Grants and Assistance from International Organizations, July 1, 1945–September 30, 1980.* Washington, D.C.: Government Printing Office.

Varshney, Ashutosh. 1991. "India, Pakistan, and Kashmir: Antinomies of Nationalism." *Asian Survey* 31(11) (Nov.): 999–1001.

Verdier, Daniel. 1994. *Democracy and International Trade.* Princeton: Princeton University Press.

Walt, Stephen. 1992. "Revolution and War." *World Politics* 44 (Apr.): 321–68.

Waltz, Kenneth. 1959. *Man, the State, and War.* New York: Columbia University Press.

"Why Is U.S. So Scared of Those Rogue States?" 2000. *Toronto Star*, May 7, p. 1.

Wu, Hsin-hsing. 1994. *Bridging the Strait: Taiwan, China, and the Prospects for Reunification.* Oxford: Oxford University Press.

Wu, Jaushieh Joseph. 1995. *Taiwan's Democratization.* Oxford: Oxford University Press.

Yahuda, Michael. 1996. "The International Standing of the Republic of China on Taiwan." *China Quarterly* 148 (Dec.): 1319–39.

Yu, Myung-hwan. 1999. "South Korea's Policy of Engagement with North Korea." In *Korea Approaches the Millennium.* Washington, D.C.: Korea Economic Institute of America.

Yu, Taifa. 1999. "Relations Between Taiwan and China After the Missile Crisis: Toward Reconciliation?" *Pacific Affairs* 72(1) (Spring): 39–55.

CHAPTER ELEVEN

Territorial Disputes and Asian Security

Sources, Management, and Prospects

JIANWEI WANG

Territorial disputes among nation-states have been a major source of interstate conflict all over the world. Thus a viable security order at both global and regional levels is not feasible without an effective mechanism for dealing with territorial disputes. In the modern history of international relations, the single most common issue over which states fight wars is territory. One scholar points out: "It is difficult to think of a war that did not have some territorial component to it" (Vasquez 1993: 2). Nations will go far to defend their territorial integrity. Even when the territory has little strategic or economic worth, its symbolic value is often sufficiently powerful to motivate states to go to war.

In Asia, territorial disputes have been pervasive. Almost every country in East, South, and Southeast Asia has bilateral or multilateral territorial quarrels with its neighbors. During the Cold War these territorial disputes led to numerous military and nonmilitary conflicts that made the region the third-ranking in terms of the frequency of armed conflict after Africa and the Middle East (Bercovitch and Jackson 1997: 11). In the post–Cold War period, no full-scale war has been fought for territorial purposes since 1990, but numerous territorial disputes remain unresolved and many flash points with potential for military confrontation are related to competing territorial claims.

In investigating the implications and management of territorial disputes for order, this chapter argues that in the post–Cold War era the bilateral territorial dispute remains a potential source of conflict in Asia but that overall its salience has been declining in the emerging regional security order. That no war has been fought for territory in East Asia since the late 1980s indicates a tendency to seek peaceful settlement of the remaining disputes. The shift to peaceful means can be attributed to many factors: the diminution of the intrinsic value of the land, the relaxation of major-power rivalry in the region, and changes in domestic priorities and foreign policy norms, all related to changes in power structure, national goals, and threat perceptions. Moreover, the emphasis in conflict management is shifting from conflict prevention to conflict resolution/termination. The post–Cold War period has ushered in a wave of new initiatives to settle outstanding bilateral territorial quarrels. China, for example, has taken the lead in this trend and resolved some of its most difficult border disputes with its neighbors. In terms of conflict management, multilateral mechanisms (regional organization, international regime, third-party mediation and arbitration) have been evolving and becoming increasingly important. Even so, bilateral consultation remains the most effective and fruitful pathway to conflict prevention and resolution and hence to the regional security order. Future territorial disputes are likely to remain a function of the external relations and internal transitions of major players in the region.

Several disclaimers are in order regarding the scope of this chapter. First, I focus on land territorial disputes rather than maritime disputes because the latter are considered elsewhere in the book. This is justifiable because maritime territorial disputes are relatively new and involve features quite different from territorial disputes on land.[1] Second, I focus on bilateral rather than multilateral disputes such as the quarrel over the South China Sea because most border quarrels are bilateral rather than multilateral in nature.

Territorial Disputes and International Order

A territorial dispute is defined here as a disagreement between two states over where their common borders should be drawn or over the ownership of territory either within the borders of one country or outside of both countries. Territorial disputes are as old as human history. Although the literature on such disputes has not been overwhelming, most scholars in the field concur that the territorial dispute is the most disruptive threat to international order and the most common cause of international conflict. Indeed, there is a high correlation between territorial disputes and war. John Vasquez argues that territorial issues have persistently caused warfare for almost 350 years of modern history. States that are contiguous or involved in arguments over territorial contiguity tend to go to war with each

---

[1]Paul Huth, for example, excludes offshore disputes over maritime zones or continental shelves (Huth 1996a: 26). Ailleen San Pablo-Baviera also thinks maritime disputes are somewhat different from land disputes—particularly since it is difficult to determine boundaries on water for purposes of enforcing jurisdiction and exercising sovereign rights (1997: 36).

other more frequently than other states (Vasquez 1993: 131–32). K. J. Holsti's review of major wars from 1648 to 1989 found that territory has been the predominant issue in each of the five historical periods. This means that for most of the modern global system, contests over territory have provoked more wars than any other issue (Vasquez 1993: 128). The territorial dispute has also been the main cause of military conflict since the end of World War II. One study indicates that among the 292 international conflicts between 1945 and 1995, 122 involved territorial disputes—by far the largest category (Bercovitch and Jackson 1997: 14). Michael Brecher and Jonathan Wilkenfeld (cited in Huth 1996a) have studied over 280 international crises between 1946 and 1988—and in close to 50 percent of the cases, territorial issues were either a direct cause of the crisis or played a primary role in the deterioration of relations between states and the onset of conflict. By the same token, Paul Huth found that of the 21 wars fought between states since the end of World War II, territorial disputes were a primary cause of armed conflict in 14 cases (1996a: 4–5). Stephen Kocs's study of territorial disputes and interstate war between 1945–87 also concluded that the existence of an official territorial dispute is a key variable in determining whether war occurs (Kocs 1995).

Although territorial disputes are clearly a major source of international conflict, "territoriality and the territorial concerns to which it gives rise make war neither inevitable nor constant" (Vasquez 1993: 151). In other words, a territorial dispute per se is not necessarily a sufficient condition for hostility, conflict, and war. Studies indicate that in the postwar period between 1950 and 1990, of the 129 territorial disputes only 36 (about 28 percent) developed into enduring rivalries (Huth 1996b: 8). In the same period, moreover, less than one-third of all international borders have been disputed. More than half of all territorial disputes did not involve the threat or use of military force. Although most wars involve conflicts over territory, territorial disputes do not always pose a high risk of war (Huth 1996a: 8–10). And although territorial disputes have resulted in more wars historically than any other single issue, the percentage of wars fought over territorial issues has been declining (Mitchell 1999: 171).

In sum, then, scholarly theorizing and empirical evidence both suggest that the territorial dispute is a critical variable in determining the formation and evolution of international order.[2] Compared with other forms of dispute among nation-states, territorial quarrels are more likely to lead to military conflict and war. Most territorial disputes, however, are handled peacefully among states. More often than not, a territorial dispute is used by nation-states as a catalyst for other

---

[2]As Vasquez (1993: 151) put it: "Territoriality issues are so fundamental that the behavior associated with their settlement literally constructs a world order."

political and strategic conflicts. In this regard, the intrinsic value of territory is not as important as broad foreign and domestic policy goals in explaining the conflict. Because the post–Cold War circumstances in Asia present new opportunities and challenges for the management of territorial disputes, their impact on the regional and global international order should be understood from a perspective broader than the traditional nexus between war and territory.

Territorial Disputes in Asia

Territory has been one of the persistent issues characterizing international relations in Asia in the postwar period. Indeed, territory tends to be a salient issue for countries at the early stage of nation building. When the formation of modern nation-states started in Europe in the sixteenth and seventeenth centuries, countries fought numerous bloody wars to define national borders and expand national territory.[3] Most countries in Asia, however, entered the family of modern nation-states only after World War II.[4] Consequently the Westphalian notion of national sovereignty and territorial integrity carries more currency in the region. As in other less developed areas of the world such as Africa, Central and South America, and the Middle East, territorial disputes have been more frequent in Asia than in Europe. As some scholars suggest, Europe's past might be Asia's future (Huntington 1997: 220). This difference between Europe and Asia in terms of territorial disputes is supported by empirical data. Paul Huth in his systematic study of such disputes in the postwar period identified 129 territorial quarrels between 1950 and 1990. Their geographic distribution is as follows: Europe, 14; the Caribbean, Central America, and South America, 18; Middle East, 17; Africa, 31; Central, East, and Southeast Asia, 32. It is no coincidence that Asia had the largest number of territorial disputes while Europe had the smallest (Huth 1996a: 27–29). Another interesting finding is that there were 54 borders still in dispute at the end of 1990. The highest ratio of unresolved disputes relative to total disputed borders was in Central and South America (67 percent) and the Far East and Southeast Asia (78 percent). Fifty-seven borders once in dispute were settled— with the highest ratio of resolved disputes relative to total disputed borders (77 percent) located in Europe (Huth 1996a: 32). Territorial disputes tend to be a more serious issue, it seems, in Asia.

Certainly Asia is where most divided nations are located. During the Cold

---

[3]F. S. Pearson (1974: 441, 453) has pointed out that middle-sized and small countries engage in territorial conflicts more often than major powers because the latter settled most of their territorial disputes in Europe and North America a long time ago.

[4]The frequency of border disputes reached its peak in 1960–62 at the height of the emergence of newly independent states (Mandel 1980: 450).

War, Korea, Vietnam, and China were all divided. Even today, largely as a legacy of the Cold War, both Korea and China remain divided. The rivalry between two states within one nation is always about sovereignty over territory. The dispute over which government has the legitimate right to represent and rule the country often has the highest probability of leading to military conflict and war. Although the issue of divided nations is discussed elsewhere in this volume, it is necessary to point out here the importance of the territorial dimension.[5]

Numerous interstate territorial disputes can be found in the region. As seen in Table 11.1,[6] the first cluster of such disputes is located in Northeast Asia centered on China. China probably harbors the largest number of territorial disputes with its neighbors in the world.[7] Today China still has various border disputes with Russia, India, Tajikistan, Bhutan, and North Korea. Until recently its borders with Kazakhstan, Kyrgyzstan, and Vietnam were contested. China also has a maritime dispute with Vietnam over the Paracel Islands and with Japan over the Diaoyu/Senkaku Islands. Moreover, it is involved in a complex dispute with five other countries over the Spratly Islands in the South China Sea. Besides China, other Northeast Asian countries have their share of territorial quarrels with each other. Russia and Japan have a bitter dispute over the so-called Northern Territories. Japan and South Korea have competing claims over the Liancourt Rocks (Takeshima/Tok-do) in the Sea of Japan.

Another cluster of territorial disputes can be found in Southeast Asia. A complex of border quarrels troubles the Vietnam–Cambodia–Thailand–Laos–Burma (Myanmar) relationship. Sections of the border between Vietnam and Cambodia are in dispute. Cambodia has an undefined border with Thailand. Parts of Thailand's border with Laos have not been settled. Thailand also has a quarrel with Burma over alignment of the border. Moreover, the Philippines have yet to fully revoke their claim to Sabah State in Malaysia. The area is permeated by maritime disputes as well. The Philippines, Malaysia, Vietnam, Brunei, China, Taiwan, and Indonesia are engaged in a multilateral dispute over the Spratly Islands. In addition, Malaysia has two islands in dispute with Indonesia and another two islands in dispute with Singapore. Cambodia's maritime boundary with Thailand is not clearly defined. Finally, Vietnam has a quarrel with Cambodia over some offshore islands.

---

[5]Many studies, such as Paul Huth's, do not differentiate territorial disputes between two nation-states from those within a nation.

[6]I do not include territorial disputes in Central Asia in the table unless they involve countries in Northeast, Southeast, or South Asia.

[7]China has been cited as one of the two most disputatious countries during the period 1950–90. In the late 1950s, China was a party to ten disputes involving India, Pakistan, Burma, Nepal, Afghanistan, Taiwan, USSR, South Vietnam, Japan, and the Philippines (Huth 1996a: 26).

TABLE 11.1
Territorial Disputes in the Asia Pacific

Disputants	Disputes	Current intensity
Northeast Asia		
China–Russia	Border	Low
China–Japan	Marine (Senkaku/Diaoyu)	Mediate
China–North Korea	Border	Low
China–Tajikistan	Border	Low
Japan–Russia	Marine (Northern Territories)	Mediate
Japan–South Korea	Marine (Tok–do/Takeshima)	Mediate
Southeast Asia		
Vietnam–China	Marine (South China Sea)	Mediate
Vietnam–Cambodia	Border and marine (Gulf of Thailand)	Mediate
Vietnam–Philippines	Marine (Spratlys)	Mediate
Thailand–Cambodia	Border and marine	Mediate
Thailand–Myanmar	Border	Mediate
Thailand–Laos	Border	Low
Thailand–Malaysia	Border	Mediate
Indonesia–Malaysia	Border and marine (Ligitan and Sipadan)	Mediate
Malaysia–China	Marine (Spratlys)	Mediate
Philippines–Malaysia	Border (Sabah) and marine	Mediate
Philippines–China	Marine (Spratlys)	High
Singapore–Malaysia	Marine	Low
South Asia		
China–India	Border	Mediate
China–Bhutan	Border	Low
India–Pakistan	Border (Kashmir, Jammu)	High
India–Bangladesh	Border and marine (New Moore/South Talpatty)	Mediate
Afghanistan–Pakistan	Border	Low

SOURCES: CIA (2001); Allcock et al. (1992); Bercovitch and Jackson (1997); Ganesan (1999); Biger (1995).

The third cluster of territorial disputes involves the South Asian subcontinent. The relationship between India and Pakistan has long been troubled by the territorial dispute over the status of Kashmir and Jammu, and there are water-sharing problems over the Indus River (Wular Barrage). Among all bilateral territorial disputes, the India-Pakistan conflict is perhaps the most explosive in the region. A portion of India's border with Bangladesh has not been defined yet. The two countries also have a quarrel over New Moore/South Talpatty Island. Pakistan and Afghanistan have an unresolved dispute over the eastern side of their common border.

Categorizing Intensity

Although territorial disputes are rampant in Northeast, Southeast, and South Asia, their intensity and therefore their impact on the Asian security order may vary. These disputes can be divided into four categories according to their intensity.

The first category comprises the territorial disputes that have triggered full-scale war between the claimants. The India-Pakistan dispute over Kashmir has caused two major wars (in 1947 and 1965) as well as numerous other military conflicts. The Sino-Indian border war in 1962 and the Sino-Vietnamese border war in 1979 fall into this category too. These large-scale military clashes often incurred heavy casualties and disrupted the regional order. The hostility created by these major military conflicts could last for many years. In short, such territorial disputes often create enduring rivalries between disputants.

The second category consists of territorial disputes that also resulted in armed conflict and human fatalities but with lower intensity. Although the duration of these conflicts was relatively short, they could recur. For various reasons they did not escalate into a full-fledged military showdown between the two countries. The brief naval engagements between China and Vietnam in 1974 and 1988, as well as the border clashes between China and Nepal in 1960 and between China and Burma in 1969, belong to this category. Most of the border incidents involving Southeast Asian nations also fall into this category. Although such militarized disputes did not seriously disrupt normal relations between countries, their cumulative effect on the regional order could be considerable.

The third category contains territorial disputes that have remained at the political and diplomatic level and have not evolved into open military clashes—although in some cases military forces were mobilized. While the territory was significant to both sides, it was not sufficiently crucial for both sides to resort to force. Instead the territorial disputes were conducted through diplomatic protests, detention of personnel from the other side, propaganda offensives and the like. The Sino-Japanese dispute over the Diaoyu/Senkaku Islands, the Russo-Japanese quarrel over the Northern Territories, and the Malaysia-Philippine conflict over Sabah fall into this category. The quarrels over these territories seldom lead to military conflict. In fact the bilateral relationship may be fairly good in other respects.

The fourth category of territorial disputes includes quarrels so minor that they do not constitute outstanding issues in bilateral relations—for example, the border disputes between China and Bhutan, between China and Pakistan during the 1950s and 1960s, and between China and North Korea. Although these disagreements may remain unresolved, they seldom become a source of conflict and hence do not need to be managed. In other words, these territorial disputes rarely have serious consequences for security order in the region.

Their intensity, of course, may change. The intensity of territorial disputes between China and the Soviet Union, for example, has experienced a curve of low–high–low. The same can be said of the Sino-Vietnamese border dispute. The intensity of the dispute between Malaysia and the Philippines over Sabah has gone from high to mediate to low. Table 11.1 ranks all territorial disputes at three levels: high, mediate, and low. "High" indicates territorial disputes that have a serious prospect of triggering large-scale military conflict (or have already caused militarized conflict). "Mediate" points to territorial disputes that have a low probability of escalating into military conflict but remain a substantial irritant to bilateral relations. "Low" refers to territorial disputes that either are close to being resolved or remain inconsequential to the regional security order.

Sources of Territorial Disputes and Intensification

The sources of territorial disputes in Asia can be explored from two related perspectives. First, where do these disputes come from in the first place? Second, under what conditions may these disputes escalate into open diplomatic and military conflict? Here C. R. Mitchell's differentiation between conflict situations and conflict behavior and between latent and manifest conflict may illuminate the dynamics of territorial disputes. According to Mitchell, a conflict situation is any situation in which two or more social entities or "parties" believe they possess mutually incompatible goals. Conflict behavior means actions undertaken by one party in any situation of conflict aimed at the opposing party with the intention of making that opponent abandon or modify its goals. Basically the former can be seen as latent conflict and the latter as manifest conflict (Mitchell 1981: 17, 29, 49). By the same token, a latent territorial dispute must become manifest before we can speak of its impact on the regional security order.

General Sources

A conflict situation or latent dispute over territory in Asia originates from various sources. The source may affect the nature of the dispute as well as the degree of difficulty in conflict management. A cursory examination finds several sources of territorial disputes. Quite a few disputes were formed in the process of historical evolution. They are the outcome of long-term interactions between the concerned parties with little outside interference. Often there is no formal treaty or set of historical documents clearly establishing a boundary line. As a result, bordering countries present contrasting versions of the border. Even when there are agreements between the two parties, they may not be precise enough to resolve conflicting claims. Undefined borders in Vietnam, Cambodia, Thailand, Laos, and Burma are often the source of historically shaped territorial disputes between those countries. Thailand and Cambodia, for example, disputed the ownership of Preah Vihear Temple and surrounding land. Both countries claimed that the treaty they signed in 1907 established that the temple was located within their own national territory. Another example is the dispute over the China-Nepal border due to contradictory treaties concluded in the eighteenth and nineteenth centuries. Consequently the border had never been officially demarcated.

Some territorial disputes result, not from political and social interaction between nation-states, but from geological evolution. The dispute between India and Bangladesh over New Moore Island/Talpatty Island, for example, is fairly recent, as this is a new island formed after a cyclone and tidal wave in the Hariabhanga River that separates Bangladesh and India. Both countries claimed sovereignty over the island (Allcock et al. 1992: 426). Another example is the Thai-Burma (Myanmar) border. Unlike conventional territorial disputes, disagreement in this case often results from the changing course of the Moei and Salween rivers separating the two countries. Heavy rains and sedimentation sometimes change the course of these rivers, creating a zero-sum situation in which one country's gain is the other's loss and leading to tension between the two countries (Ganesan 1999: 21).

A number of territorial disputes in Asia are related to colonial rule in the region. Great Britain, France, and the Netherlands as well as Japan played a key role in defining the boundaries of many countries in the region. Most of the boundaries in Southeast Asia, for example, were drawn by the colonial powers (Solomon 1970). The boundaries left by the colonial powers often led to disputes between newly independent nation-states. The most typical example in this regard is the territorial disputes between India, Pakistan, Bangladesh, and Afghanistan. The 1947 partition of the subcontinent when Great Britain withdrew from the region left many unresolved territorial issues, including Kashmir and Jammu. In the late nineteenth century, for example, Britain imposed a boundary between Afghanistan and what was to become Pakistan to include territory inhabited by a major Afghani tribe, the Pushtun (Pathan), in Pakistan. The border between Bangladesh and India too was hastily and arbitrarily drawn in 1947 (Bercovitch and Jackson 1997: 65, 169). The territorial legacy of colonial powers can be found elsewhere in the region as well. The Sino-Indian border dispute was largely a result of the "McMahon Line" drawn by Sir Henry McMahon in his secret negotiation with the Tibetan government in the early twentieth century. Although China has never recognized this line, India has accepted it as the official border between the two countries, leading to serious dispute. The quarrel over Sabah—between Malaysia and the Philippines and between Malaysia and Indonesia—is related to British colonial role in Malaya and the British decision to grant political independence to Brunei, British North Borneo, and Singapore while enlarging the territorial limits of the Federation of Malaya in 1963.

Other territorial disputes in the region originated from unequal treaties signed between weak countries and major powers or from deals made among victorious countries regarding defeated nations. That is, they resulted from an imbalance of national power; consequently one country lost territory to another. A series of treaties concluded between Czarist Russia and the weak Qing dynasty during the nineteenth century, for example, transferred vast tracts of Chinese land to Russia, sowing seeds of territorial dispute for later rulers in both countries. The Northern Territories issue between Russia and Japan may also be seen as a function of the imbalance of power between the victorious United States and Russia and the defeated Japan in World War II. In the secret Yalta agreement signed in 1945, the Soviet Union was awarded southern Sakhalin, the Kuril Islands, and a special Russian interest in Manchuria for its promise to join the Pacific War. Then in the 1951 San Francisco Peace Treaty, Japan was forced to renounce its rights and claims to southern Sakhalin and the Kuril Islands. The term "Kuril Islands," however, was not precisely defined. Japan argued that the phrase did not include the four disputed islands. The Soviets insisted that the four islands are part of the Kurils and thus belong to the Soviet Union.

These general sources of territorial disputes are delineated here for analytic purposes only. In reality, a territorial dispute might have multiple sources. In many cases in Asia, disagreements resulting from the historical interaction between two indigenous populations were often exacerbated by colonial rule and the intervention of outside major powers. In the Sino-Indian border dispute, for instance, the dispute over the western section evolved through the historical interaction between the two countries because the border area was never clearly delimited. The dispute over the eastern section, by contrast, is basically a product of the McMahon Line drawn by an outside colonial power. By the same token, the Japanese-Russian dispute over the Northern Territories has indigenous historical roots, but major-power rivalry at the end of World War II made it much more difficult to resolve.

What are the implications of these general sources of dispute? It is reasonable to argue that the degree of difficulty increases along the following trajectory: from historical interaction to colonial legacy to unequal treaties. Territorial disputes born of historical interaction should be the easiest to settle if they do not involve a sizable loss of territory to either side and require only formal delimitation or better demarcation of the border. Some of them, even those unresolved for a long time, remain nonissues in bilateral relations. Territorial disputes based on the colonial legacy may be more difficult to settle because boundaries drawn by colonial powers could well lose their legitimacy after the colonial powers have left the scene. Such boundaries are easily perceived as favoring one side over another. The persistent conflict between India and Pakistan over Jammu and Kashmir is evidence of such a colonial legacy. Territorial disputes rooted in unequal treaties or deals are even harder to resolve because they often involve an explicit change of territory from one side to the other—thus invoking strong feelings of injustice and humiliation. Territorial irredentism may well develop from such feelings.

Territorial Triggers

Such sources contribute to the formation of a conflict situation over territorial issues in the region. But they are not sufficient conditions for conflict behavior. In most cases territorial disputes do not lead directly to military conflict. Like volcanoes, they only erupt under certain conditions. In other words, specific triggers are needed for a territorial dispute to turn into a territorial conflict. And removing these triggers is likely to pave the way for conflict resolution.

These triggers can be divided into territorial and nonterritorial causes. The former are related to the significance of the territory; the latter point to broad political, security, or even psychological considerations. Gary Goertz and Paul Diehl believe that the salience of territorial disputes depends on the characteristics of the territory itself. Often it is the value of the territory that decides when states will fight and when they will resolve their differences peacefully. Goertz and Diehl differentiate between the intrinsic and relational importance of territory. A territory's intrinsic importance refers to characteristics that can be recognized as valuable no matter whose perspective is considered. A territory's relational importance refers to characteristics that may have a different significance for different states. Intrinsic characteristics include the territory's natural resource base (minerals, energy, water), its market value, and the value of the land (it may be a fertile area that could greatly improve a country's food production or export capacity). Relational characteristics include the territory's geographic location relative to other states, the ethnic composition of its population, and its historical importance (Goertz and Diehl 1992: 14–21).

Paul Huth has tested the significance of factors related to the intrinsic and relational importance of territory. In terms of intrinsic importance, for example, one variable he tested is the natural resources of economic value within the disputed territory and found that economically valuable bordering territory (e.g. rich in natural resources with export potential, providing an outlet to the sea, or containing scarce water resources) had a higher probability of causing a territorial dispute. When a territory is thought to be rich in natural economic resources, nation-states have strong incentives to lay claim to it. This is particularly true for developing countries because their economy is much more dependent on the export of natural resources and raw materials (Huth 1996a: 75). In Asia, previously insignificant territories have become hot spots for competition among nations owing to newly discovered economic values. The race to grab islands in the Spratlys, for example, did not start until the 1970s when reports about the area's oil potential surfaced. One after another, countries bordering the Spratly Islands declared their sovereignty over the islands or neighboring waters and challenged China's historical claim. In February 1996, a dispute between Japan and South Korea over sovereignty of an uninhabited small island group in the Sea of Japan (Takeshima/Tok-do) escalated into active controversy when in the same month both governments declared 200-mile exclusive economic zones encompassing the disputed islands.

In terms of relational importance, Huth found a positive relationship between the strategic location[8] of the territory and the intensity of the dispute. The desire to gain control over strategic territory is a powerful motive behind the territorial claims of challenger states (Huth 1996a: 49–50, 74). Certainly this factor looms large in the territorial disputes of Asia. In the Sino-Indian border dispute, China showed strong determination to secure control over the Aksai Chin because it contains the only year-round passable route from Xingjiang to Tibet. China's dispute with Vietnam over the Paracel and Spratly Islands also has something to do with their close proximity to major shipping lanes in the South China Sea. The dispute between Japan and Russia over the Northern Territories has its strategic dimension, too, as the four islands provide ice-free access from the Sea of Okhotsk to the Pacific Ocean as well as much-needed deepwater harbors for Russia.

Another variable of relational importance is the border area's ethnic composition. Huth's findings indicate that common ties of language and ethnic background increased the likelihood of a territorial dispute between two countries (Huth 1996a: 78). Following the same logic, it is safe to say that the existence of ethnic minority groups across border areas may well stimulate irredentist claims on either side and further complicate the border dispute. In Asia many examples can be found in which ethnic minority groups in the border area serve as a trigger for conflict: the China-Vietnam, China-India, China-Burma, India-Pakistan, and China-Soviet disputes, as well as the many disputes among ASEAN countries. The effort to control tribal groups—the Kachins and the Shans who lived along the China-Burma border and did not intrinsically identify with either China or Burma—led to a major border clash between the two countries (Bercovitch and Jackson 1997: 137–38). Clashes between Thailand and Burma are often caused by the border crossings of Burmese troops dealing with minority insurgencies (Ganesan 1999: 18).

A territory's intrinsic or relational importance is not limited to the material or physical dimensions, of course. Disputed territory also serves a psychological function as a basic source of "sovereignty" and "identity," both for the states and

---

[8]Whether a piece of territory has "strategic" value cannot always be determined in an objective manner.

for the people who live there. Focusing only on the material aspects of territorial disputes misses the point that territory provides the very identity of nation-states (Forsberg 1996: 438). Safeguarding territorial integrity is almost without exception regarded as a vital national interest. Few countries are willing to lose territory, no matter how useless a piece of land may be in material terms. As a senior Chinese leader put it: "The Chinese people have always cherished the enterprise built by our ancestors, particularly the territorial integrity. The concept of 'losing a thousand soldiers but not an inch of land' is deeply rooted in the heart of the Chinese people. The land left by our ancestors should never become smaller in the hands of our generation" (*People's Daily*, Dec. 8, 1995). This mentality—equating territory with the very meaning of a country's existence—often leads to the nationalistic sentiment underlying intensified territorial disputes. As mentioned earlier, this is often the case if the dispute triggers strong feelings of injustice resulting from seemingly unequal treaties or a humiliating defeat in war. Japan, for example, feels strongly about the Northern Territories because of a sense of injustice based on the belief that the Soviet occupation of the islands was illegal. Material concerns such as fish and mineral resources were perceived as less important (Forsberg 1996: 440).

Nonterritorial Triggers

There is another set of variables that may not relate directly to the disputed territory itself but can nevertheless trigger the outbreak of territorial conflict. Here we examine broad political and security factors that may either increase or reduce the probability of conflict resulting from territorial disputes.

Certainly the overall state of bilateral relations may determine whether a territorial dispute remains latent or becomes active. When two countries want to maintain good bilateral relations because of common interests in other areas, territorial quarrels may be put on hold. When bilateral relations sour, however, territorial disputes may come to the forefront. A territorial dispute is often a symptom of more profound problems in bilateral relations. During the Sino-Soviet honeymoon in the 1950s, the border dispute between the two countries did not constitute a serious problem for either side. Even in the 1950s there were border incidents, but the border officials in both countries were able to settle the disputes without interference from the central authorities (Ginsburgs 1993: 268). With bilateral relations deteriorating in the 1960s, however, territorial disputes became a major source of irritation leading to bloody border clashes. A similar pattern applies to the Sino-Vietnamese border dispute. When China and Vietnam fought the United States shoulder to shoulder in the 1960s and early 1970s, they were able to maintain a relatively peaceful border because of their strategic interest in confronting the Americans. After the unification of Vietnam, however, tensions in the border area soon rose to the point of explosion. Whether the two countries in a dispute share a common security adversary therefore makes a big difference. If they do, they are likely to seek compromise in the territorial quarrel. Empirical data show that a military alliance between two countries is associated with a lower probability of a territorial dispute. Even if a dispute does occur, their common security interest may prevent it from escalating into full-fledged conflict (Huth 1996a: 88, 122). In the post–Cold War period, however, sharing a common security adversary is not the only factor that can reduce the severity of territorial disputes. Common interests in economic prosperity and regional stability may serve the same purpose.

Sometimes the intensification of territorial disputes is stimulated by factors beyond the two parties. During the Cold War, strategic rivalry between the two superpowers and other major powers often intensified otherwise localized territorial disputes. In the late 1960s and early 1970s, border skirmishes and conflicts between Vietnam, Cambodia, Thailand, and Laos often had something to do with the U.S. involvement in the Vietnam War. China's cross-border military offensive against Vietnam in 1979 had more to do with punishing Vietnam for its invasion of Cambodia than with the territorial dispute per se. In this case the conflict reflected contention not just between China and Vietnam but also between China and the Soviet Union. In such cases, conflict resolution becomes feasible as soon as nonterritorial strategic and security sources of tension are eliminated.

Similarly, if a country is engaged in political-military disputes with other states, it may lessen its diplomatic and military pressure against the target country over disputed territory. It may also become more reluctant to escalate the conflict (Huth 1996a: 54). Moreover, a country involved in multiple disputes has reason to avoid confrontation with certain states and thereby persuade them to support its claims in a dispute with another adversary. The territorial dispute between China and Pakistan, for example, did not become a serious issue because China wanted Pakistan's support in its quarrel with India. In the 1970s, China pursued an accommodating policy toward Japan over the Senkaku/Diaoyu Islands as Beijing tried to induce Japan to form an anti-Soviet coalition in the region.

Finally, quite a few studies point to the importance of domestic politics in territorial disputes. It is often difficult, however, to pin down a direct link between a country's domestic politics and its policy toward territorial disputes. The impact of domestic politics on territorial disputes has two aspects: the influence of different political systems and the domestic political circumstances under which a country handles its territorial disputes. As a country becomes more democratic, one argument goes, political leaders are less likely to resort to the threat or use of violence to resolve international disagreements, including territorial disputes

(Huth 1996a: 62–63). Huth's data give some support to this argument in terms of the escalation of conflict. Among 41 disputes with a high level of escalation, only one involved a challenger state with a well-established pattern of democratic rule. In about 98 percent of the cases, the challenger was nondemocratic. But Huth's study (pp. 136–37) also shows that in a substantial number of cases the non-democratic state did not apply high levels of diplomatic or military pressure on the target country.

Until recently, however, most countries in the region were nondemocracies. Thus the degree of democratization cannot explain much variation in territorial disputes. While Japan as a democracy has not been involved in militarized disputes over territory, India, also a democracy, has frequently engaged in militarized territorial disputes with other countries. ASEAN countries, by contrast, most of them authoritarian until recently, by and large did not resort to force in settling their territorial disputes. It remains to be seen whether the change of political systems in the region in the post–Cold War period has brought any telling difference in their approach to settling territorial disputes.

As for the second aspect of the domestic factor—the influence of domestic politics on the way a country handles territorial disputes—it can be argued that regardless of the political system, domestic pressures arising from various sources may rigidify and intensify a government's position on territorial issues. Leaders often adopt foreign policies that risk conflict with other states because of domestic political concerns. Once a territorial dispute emerges, it tends to become part of the domestic discourse and therefore self-sustaining because of domestic political dynamics. And when the domestic situation is bad (either economically or politically), political leaders tend to use territorial issues to "compensate for bad domestic outcomes with good foreign policy outcomes" (Heldt 1999: 451–78). Examples of domestic politics serving as a trigger for territorial disputes can be readily found in the Asian region. The bloody border conflict between China and the Soviet Union in 1969 can be partially attributed to the radical domestic politics of the Cultural Revolution in China. The Philippines' increasingly assertive position on the Spratly Islands in the South China Sea in recent years can be traced to the demands of domestic politics. Indeed, the Philippine government's attempt to renounce its claim over the Sabah dispute was thwarted by domestic opposition.

This discussion of the sources of territorial disputes and their intensification is by no means exhaustive. My purpose is simply to highlight the salient ones. The escalation of territorial disputes, like their creation, tends to have multiple causes. By the same token, effective conflict management of territorial disputes must remove obstacles at different levels. The configuration of the sources of territorial disputes has been changing in the Asian region. Certainly the strategic rivalry of major powers has been much dampened, particularly in the early 1990s, thus paving the way for the resolution of territorial disputes of smaller countries in the region. And because of the high-tech revolution, the traditional military value of territory has been decreasing. In the meantime, most countries in the region have undergone a process of economic modernization.[9] Although the conventional strategic value of territory may have declined, its symbolic value may well increase as a new wave of nationalism surges in many countries. Territorial disputes are much more subject to the influence of domestic politics when countries throughout the region are experiencing profound political and economic shifts.

Conflict Management During the Cold War

As we have seen, the impact of territorial disputes on the regional security order is determined not so much by how many disputes exist as how they have been managed. That is, the impact depends on the extent to which countries in the area can prevent latent disputes from becoming manifest disputes. Conflict management can be defined as "processes, methods, devices, techniques and strategies employed to resolve or manage a conflict" (Caballero-Anthony 1998: 41). C. R. Mitchell (1981: 253–79) has delineated four forms of conflict management that can be employed at different stages of the dispute: conflict avoidance, conflict prevention, conflict settlement, and conflict resolution. Conflict avoidance is defined as a method to ensure that situations involving goal incompatibility do not arise. Conflict prevention involves methods to prevent the parties from crossing the threshold between recognition of incompatible goals and destructive behavior in pursuit of those goals. Put simply, conflict prevention ensures that no (latent) conflict situation leads to undesired forms of (manifest) conflict behavior. Conflict settlement and conflict resolution are means of arriving at a solution once a latent conflict becomes a manifest conflict. Conflict settlement aims primarily at altering conflict behavior (stopping the use of violence and coercive strategies or achieving some form of temporary truce); conflict resolution, by contrast, aims at providing a resolution by modifying all three aspects of conflict—situation, behavior, and attitudes. Given that most territorial disputes in Asia have existed for a long time, the first form of conflict management—conflict avoidance—is not very relevant here, since a territorial dispute is by definition a conflict situation. The other three forms of conflict management, however, can be applied to the management of territorial disputes in the region.

The management of territorial disputes in Asia has taken many forms, corre-

[9]However, while economic modernization may reduce certain traditional economic values of territories, some other economic values of territory, particularly maritime resources, may become more critical in territorial disputes.

sponding to the complexity of the quarrels as well as the geopolitical arrangements in the region. It can be explored from two angles. One is conflict management after territorial disputes have turned into open military conflict—namely, conflict control and settlement. The other is conflict management to intervene before territorial disputes escalate into armed conflict or to remove the source of the conflict once and for all—namely, conflict prevention and resolution (termination).[10] Since the end of the Cold War, few territorial disputes in Asia have turned into open military conflict. Most militarized territorial disputes took place during the Cold War. In the following discussion, therefore, the first dimension of conflict management—conflict control and settlement—applies to the situation during the Cold War while the second dimension—conflict prevention and resolution—applies to the post–Cold War period.

During the Cold War, force was frequently used in territorial disputes. After a territorial dispute escalated into a military clash, the conflict management largely took one of three forms. First, one side in the dispute initiated a military offensive to settle the dispute and won a decisive victory through superior military power. This can be called a "hegemonic pattern" of conflict management in the sense that one side imposes a change of territorial status quo on the other. The Chinese-Indian border war in 1962 and the Chinese–South Vietnamese naval clash in 1974 are two examples of this pattern. The Vietnamese all-out invasion of Cambodia in 1978 and the Chinese invasion of Vietnam in 1979 also reflect this hegemonic pattern of conflict settlement, although in these two cases the offensive side did not win a complete victory.

Second, both sides in the dispute did not want to see the conflict escalating into a full-blown war and were able to prevent it through negotiations. This can be called the "de-escalation pattern" of conflict management. After a major border clash in June 1960, for example, China and Nepal agreed to officially demarcate the border. A border pact was signed in October 1961. Since then no border incidents have been reported (Bercovitch and Jackson 1997: 95). The Sino-Soviet border clash in 1969 was followed by high-level political consultations between prime ministers, which prevented the conflict from escalating into a large-scale border war.

Third, because of various domestic and international factors, some bilateral territory conflicts simply attenuated without much conflict management. This may be called the "diversion pattern" of conflict management. In 1969, for example, Burmese forces clashed with Chinese troops across the border several times. About 300 fatalities resulted from these skirmishes. Only one negotiation attempt

[10]Muthiah Alagappa (1995: 369) defines conflict management as having three components: conflict prevention, containment, and termination.

was made, but it did not succeed. Nevertheless the dispute eventually disappeared altogether as Burma turned its attention to a serious guerrilla insurgency at home (Bercovitch and Jackson 1997: 137–38). The Nepal-India border incident in 1962 ended without much conflict management because the dispute was soon overtaken by the Sino-Indian war in the same year.

Most conflict management of militarized territorial disputes during the Cold War was handled at the bilateral level. Third-party involvement in conflict settlement—either by a third country or a multilateral institution—was neither the norm nor always effective. Yet it had not been totally absent from the equation of conflict management. Some bilateral territorial negotiations were conducted under the supervision of third parties. Negotiations between China and India after the border war in 1962, for example, were held in Colombo under the auspices of the prime minister of Ceylon, Sirimao Bandaranaike, and involved representatives from Burma, Ceylon, Ghana, Indonesia, Cambodia, and Egypt (Bercovitch and Jackson 1997: 113). In some cases, outside mediation or arbitration was used or at least recommended. In the Cambodia-Siam (Thailand) border conflict in 1958, for example, Cambodia referred the dispute to the United Nations. UN mediator Baron Johan Beck-Friis managed to ease tensions along the border, secure the release of Siamese prisoners arrested by Cambodia for border violations, and create conditions allowing ambassadors to return to their posts by February 1959. The UN also intervened in the military conflict between Indonesia and the Netherlands over West Irian (Irian Jaya) in 1962 to prevent the spread of the conflict (p. 108). The UN acted as mediator in the second Kashmir war between India and Pakistan in 1965 and was able to secure a cease-fire. It also supervised troop withdrawals (p. 127). In the Cambodia-Thailand border conflict of 1979–80, both the UN and ASEAN were involved in conflict management. ASEAN offered peace proposals, and UN Secretary-General Kurt Waldheim acted as mediator. These efforts brought a partial settlement and cessation of hostilities in early August 1980 (p. 194).

One of the few cases of third-party arbitration involved the Rann of Kutch dispute. This was a southern sector of the India–West Pakistan border. The territorial dispute became acute shortly after India and Pakistan emerged as independent states in 1947. In 1965, Pakistani and Indian forces engaged in battles involving several thousand troops. After the intervention of Britain, both parties agreed to a cease-fire and submitted the dispute to settlement by arbitration. Pakistan and India each nominated a nonnational member of the tribunal. The UN Secretary-General appointed the tribunal's chairman. Ultimately, the tribunal awarded some 90 percent of the Rann to India and 10 percent to Pakistan. Success in this case was possible because the dispute over the Rann did not represent a conflict of major national interest between the two countries. Not only did the territory itself have little economic or strategic value, but there was a serious dispute over Kashmir going on between the two countries—a quarrel much more vital to the interests of both (Copeland 1999).

Post–Cold War Conflict Management

Conflict prevention and resolution/termination have become more salient in post–Cold War Asia. The good news is that since 1988, except for South Asia, no territorial dispute in East and Southeast Asia has evolved into active military conflict although minor incidents have been reported. This, of course, has something to do with the overall relaxation of international tension in the region due to the end of the Cold War—characterized by the elimination of hot spots such as the Cambodia conflict and the development of more cooperative relations among major powers. Such an international environment provides the conditions for conflict prevention in territorial disputes. Countries have made an effort to settle their territorial quarrels by trying not only to prevent conflict but to eliminate its sources. Three main patterns of conflict prevention and termination can be delineated.

Pathway 1: Bilateral Consultation and Negotiation

Bilateral consultation and negotiation are still the preferred approach to resolving territorial disputes by major actors in the region. Here I want to focus on China's efforts to settle its border disputes with neighboring countries. China's record on settling territorial disputes has been mixed since World War II. Once the most territorially disputatious country in the region, China was involved in bloody border wars with India, Vietnam, and the Soviet Union. In the 1950s and 1960s, however, China resolved its border issues with a number of countries, including Burma, Nepal, Mongolia, Afghanistan, and Pakistan. The post–Cold War period witnessed yet another wave of China's campaign in conflict management of territorial disputes. This initiative largely stemmed from the significant adjustment of Beijing's domestic and foreign policy goals: from political purification to economic prosperity; from national survival to regional stability. China has engaged in simultaneous bilateral consultation with its neighbors Russia, Tajikistan, Kazakhstan, Kyrgyzstan, India, Vietnam, Laos, and Bhutan as part of its "good-neighbor" drive. Roughly speaking, these bilateral discussions fall into two categories. The first type is aimed at completely demarcating state boundaries in order to eliminate the source of conflict between the two countries. The second type of consultation does not take the delimitation of borders as its immediate goal. Instead it is aimed at maintaining the status quo and stabilizing the situation in the border area. That is, the former is about conflict termination whereas the latter is about conflict prevention.

The Sino-Russian Dispute. China's border negotiations with Russia and Vietnam belong to the first category—conflict termination. In terms of its origin, the Sino-Russian territorial dispute is a combination of two sources discussed earlier: historical evolution and unequal treaties. Historically the border between China and Russia had never been clearly demarcated. But the disputes resulted mainly from a series of treaties signed between the two countries in the nineteenth century. China regarded these treaties as "unequal" and considered the consequent Russian annexation of Chinese territory (more than 1.5 million km^2 according to the Chinese account) to be illegal. The intensification of the dispute, however, had more to do with the deterioration of overall relations in the 1960s. Since the first border incident in 1960, the border dispute gradually became public and nasty and a primary source of conflict between the two countries.

Although China and the Soviet Union started their negotiations on the border dispute as early as 1964, the talks were soon suspended. With tensions increasing during China's Cultural Revolution, both China and the Soviet Union built up massive military forces along the border. The conflict came to a boiling point in March 1969 when sizable armed clashes occurred on the island of Zhenbao (Damansky) in the Ussuri River. Soon the conflict spread to other sections along the Sino-Soviet border. Both sides suffered heavy casualties, and some 3,000 Soviet and Chinese troops were killed during the fighting (Bercovitch and Jackson 1997: 114). The two countries narrowly escaped a full-scale war thanks to a hasty meeting between Soviet Prime Minister Kosygin and Chinese Premier Zhou Enlai in Beijing in September 1969. The two sides agreed to sign a temporary pact to stop hostilities and maintain the status quo in the border region. As a result, the Sino-Soviet border talks were resumed at the deputy foreign minister level in October 1969. The talks were off and on until 1979 without substantial progress. After the Soviet invasion of Afghanistan, the talks were suspended (Allcock et al. 1992: 446–47).

Entering the 1980s, both sides began to view the border issue as part of the larger process of normalizing their relationship. Soviet President Leonid Brezhnev called for a normalization of Sino-Soviet relations in his famous Tashkent speech in 1982. The Chinese side emphasized three obstacles to normalization: the deployment of large numbers of Soviet troops on the Chinese border and in Mongolia; the Soviet invasion of Afghanistan; and Soviet support for the Vietnamese occupation of Cambodia. From Beijing's global strategic perspective, the latter two obstacles were crucial. Talks at the deputy foreign minister level on normalizing relations started in 1982. During the talks, the Chinese side always raised the Afghanistan and Cambodia issues while the Soviets insisted these issues involved third parties and did not belong in bilateral negotiations (Allcock et al. 1992: 449–50). On the border issue per se, the Chinese side maintained that, first, the "unequal" nature of the treaties signed by the Qing dynasty and the Russian Czarist government should be recognized; second, however, the settlement of the boundary question could be based on these treaties (p. 448). In other words, China did not seek to dramatically change the status quo of the border between the two countries. Clearly the success of the border talks was contingent upon the improvement of overall Sino-Soviet relations. Such a breakthrough, however, could only come from the top leadership of both countries.

When Mikhail Gorbachev became General-Secretary of the Soviet Communist Party in 1985, both sides were ready to seek a thaw in the relationship. On his first day in office, Gorbachev stated that the Soviet Union would seek "serious improvement in relations with China." In a speech made in Vladivostok in 1986, Gorbachev for the first time showed willingness to make concessions on some of the three conditions put forward by China—including troop reductions on the Chinese border and troop withdrawals from Mongolia and Afghanistan. He also raised the possibility of making territorial concessions along the border on the Amur and the Ussuri rivers. Soon the border talks were resumed at the deputy foreign minister level in 1987. Now the normalization process and border talks went hand in hand. With the overall atmosphere between the two countries improving, the border talks began to show progress. Chinese leader Deng Xiaoping stated his readiness to meet Gorbachev personally under only one condition instead of three: the withdrawal of Soviet support for the Vietnamese occupation of Cambodia. In 1988, however, the Soviet Union made progress on all three "major obstacles," thus paving the way for the summit meeting between Gorbachev and Deng Xiaoping in 1989 (Allcock et al. 1992: 450–52).

The long-awaited summit in 1989 formally indicated the normalization of state-to-state relations between China and the Soviet Union. Against this much brighter background, the border talks gained new momentum. The breakthrough came in May 1991 when the foreign ministers of the USSR and PRC signed a historic agreement on the demarcation of the eastern sector of the Sino-Soviet border. Although the Soviet Union collapsed in December of the same year, the Russian Supreme Soviet ratified the treaty in 1992. The disintegration of the Soviet Union, however, did complicate the process of negotiation. China's 7,000-km-long border with the former Soviet Union was now reduced to about 4,300 km. Instead of negotiating solely with the Soviet Union, China now had also to deal with three newly independent Central Asian countries—Khazakhstan, Kyrgyzstan, and Tajikistan. In September 1994, China and Russia signed a boundary agreement on the western sector.

These two historic border agreements largely resolved the border dispute between the two countries. What they left out was basically the ownership of three large islands: Ussuriyskiy and Tarabarova (on the Ussuri River near Khabarovsk) and Bolshoy (on the Argun River). All three are still under Russian jurisdiction. By 1999, China and Russia had completed an exhaustive demarcation of 97 percent of their common border. After seven years of work that resulted in two treaties and 175 detailed maps, the Chinese-Russian border demarcation commission was ready to disband. The commission had put up more than 2,084 signs and markers along the 4,180-km eastern border, from Mongolia to the Tumen River near the Sea of Japan, and the 53-km western border, from Kazakhstan to Mongolia. Some 2,444 islands on rivers along the border had been divided as well, with 1,163 going to Russia and 1,181 going to China ("China-Russia Border Disputes" 1999). China has also made progress in its talks with other former Soviet republics. China and Kazakhstan signed three border treaties in 1994, 1996, and 1998 to resolve their territorial disputes. No differences relating to border issues now exist between the two countries ("Kazakhstan President" 1999). In 1996, China signed a boundary agreement with Kyrgyzstan. Beijing signed a partial border agreement with Tajikistan in August 1999.

The Sino-Vietnamese Dispute. Another country with which China has engaged in intensive border negotiations is Vietnam. China and Vietnam have disputes along their common land border of over 1,200 km, the demarcation of the Gulf of Tonkin (Beibu), and islands in the South China Sea. These disputes are a combination of historical evolution and colonial influence. The land border between the two countries was largely defined by two conventions signed between the French government and the Chinese Qing empire in the late nineteenth century. The Franco-Chinese convention covered the demarcation of the Gulf of Tonkin as well, although both sides had different readings of the text. China did not challenge this borderline and considered it settled; the Vietnamese, however, thought the French had given some Vietnamese territory to China. The disputes over the Paracel Islands and the Spratlys resulted largely from historical relations between the two countries.

In terms of conflict intensification, just like the Sino-Russian border dispute "the Sino-Vietnamese border dispute has historically been more of a barometer of tensions between China and Vietnam, allowing both countries to express disagreements and challenge each other in contained ways, than a dispute in and of itself" (Sutter 1993: 45). China and Vietnam were able to maintain a relatively peaceful border during the years of the Vietnam War as both countries fought the United States. Ironically the relationship soured after the reunification of Vietnam in 1975. A number of factors triggered the China-Vietnam border conflict. Vietnam's security and economic alliances with China's archenemy at that time, the Soviet Union, its hegemonic desire to establish a "federation of Indochina," its campaign to persecute and expel thousands of ethnic Chinese—all contributed to the rise of tension in the border area. The frequency of armed clashes increased significantly in the late 1970s, causing many fatalities on both sides. The Vietnamese invasion of Cambodia in 1978 was for China the last straw. Resolved to punish this junior hegemon in the region, China launched a limited military invasion in 1979 to "teach Vietnam a lesson." The bloody border war was said to have cost China and Vietnam more than 50,000 troops (Bercovitch and Jackson 1997: 189). From the very beginning, China insisted that peace talks between the two countries could take place only after Vietnam withdrew from Cambodia. Because of this precondition, there were no attempts at conflict management.

Tensions along the border, however, gradually diminished in the second half of 1988. Border trade was resumed. Ethnic minorities living on both sides of the border were able to visit each other again after a decade of separation (Amer 1993: 322). By 1989 there were clear signs that Hanoi had begun to take initiatives to ease tensions between the two countries. The first hint of a thaw came in January 1989 with a deputy ministerial meeting between the two governments held in Beijing. In the same year, the newly elected Secretary-General of the Vietnamese Communist Party, Nguyen Van Linh, indirectly expressed his wish to visit China. Again the Chinese leader, Deng Xiaoping, cited the end of Vietnam's occupation of Cambodia as a precondition for normalizing relations (Zhang 2000: 38–39). Vietnam's declaration in September 1989 that it would withdraw all its troops from Cambodia by the end of 1989 removed the main obstacle to improved relations. In September 1990, for the first time since 1977, Vietnam's top three leaders, Nguyen Van Linh, Do Muoi, and Pham Van Dong, met their Chinese counterparts in Chengdu, China, on a secret visit. During the talks the two sides signed a "memorandum of understanding." The Chengdu meeting was the turning point in Sino-Vietnamese relations. In November 1991, Do Muoi, Secretary-General of the Vietnamese Communist Party, and Jiang Zemin, Secretary-General of the Chinese Communist Party, held a summit meeting in Beijing to formally mark the normalization of the relationship, ushering in a new phase in relations between the countries (Kim 1992: 51–53).

It was against this broad background of Sino-Vietnamese relations that the management of territorial disputes became viable. The situation along the border further relaxed in the 1990s. In mid-February 1996, the cross-border rail service between Hanoi and Nanning was resumed after having been suspended for seventeen years (Chang 1997: 140). Border negotiations between China and Vietnam started in 1993. Moreover, the issue became a constant topic on the agenda of the Sino-Vietnamese summits. In 1997, the top leaders of both countries set up a timetable: the two countries would resolve their border dispute by 1999 and finish demarcation of the Gulf of Tonkin by 2000 ("Jiang Notes Headway" 1998). Such a deadline infused a sense of urgency into the border talks, and the new momentum was maintained by frequent high-level exchanges between leaders. In 1999, the target year for resolving the border dispute, the summit diplomacy reached a climax. In February of that year, Jiang Zemin and his Vietnamese counterpart Le Kha Phieu agreed in Beijing on the establishment of a future-oriented relationship of long-term stability and all-round cooperation ("Chinese Premier Calls" 1999). The two leaders further reiterated their commitment to settle their border dispute by the end of 1999 and agreed on the need to do so as soon as possible ("China, Vietnam Agree" 1999). Just before the December deadline, Chinese Premier Zhu Rongji visited Hanoi in early December to give a final push to the talk. His trip concluded serious negotiations between the two countries and left only a few technical problems unresolved ("Vietnam, China OK" 1999). Finally, on December 30, Vietnam Foreign Minister Nguyen Manh Cam and Chinese Foreign Minister Tang Jiaxuan signed a landmark border agreement covering some seventy disputed areas. The two countries then focused on resolving the territorial dispute in the Gulf of Tonkin by 2000 ("Vietnam, China Sign" 1999). Again meeting the deadline, China and Vietnam signed a two-part settlement during Vietnamese President Tran Due Luong's visit to Beijing on December 25, 2000. The Gulf of Tonkin agreements include a demarcation of territorial waters, delineation of the exclusive economic zones of the two sides, and an agreement on fishing ("China and Vietnam Sign" 2000).

The Sino-India Dispute. China's border consultation with India belongs to another category of conflict management: conflict prevention. The objective of these talks is not to delimit the disputed border immediately, but rather to build mutual confidence, maintain the status quo, and prevent conflict. India is another country that China has fought in a bloody border war since the establishment of the communist regime. China and India share a common border of 4,500 km. As for the dispute's origin, colonial rule and historical evolution can be cited as the two main sources. The quarrel focuses on two geographic areas. In the eastern sector of the border extending from Bhutan to Burma, the controversy concerns the validity of the McMahon Line drawn by the British in 1914. In the western sector where Kashmir borders on Tibet and Xinjiang, the dispute is over 24,000 km^2 of territory comprising northeastern Ladakh and the Aksai Chin. India's claim is based on a treaty signed between India, Tibet, and China in 1842; China, however, insists that the treaty did not clearly define the border. China has not accepted either the McMahon Line in the eastern sector or India's claims to the Aksai Chin in the western sector (Huth 1996a: 227; Basu 1991: 105). With regard to the intrinsic value of the territory, the Aksai Chin is strategically more important to China, as it forms the link between Tibet and Xinjiang. Indeed,

China built a road across it to connect the two regions. The intensification of the dispute came in the 1960s. Following numerous border incidents, China launched a counterattack against India along the border in October 1962, and India was forced to retreat. China declared a cease-fire on November 21 and withdrew across the border. The war cost China more than 1,000 troops, and India lost 2,000 (Bercovitch and Jackson 1997: 112–13).

Since then the relationship between the two countries has been bitter to say the least. China and India did not restore full diplomatic relations until 1976 and did not trade with each other until 1977 ("The Border Holds the Key" 1991). Management of the border dispute slowly improved in the late 1980s and early 1990s. Changes in Sino-Indian relations were responsible for the improvement—especially the reduction and eventual end of Cold War strategic rivalry of major powers in the region and the formation of new common interests: promoting economic modernization, fighting separatist and Islamic fundamentalist movements, and preventing Western hegemony in the post–Cold War era (De Castro 1999: 67–70).

From the very beginning, China and India took somewhat different approaches to conflict management. China's initial view was that the border dispute should not be tackled until bilateral relations in the spheres of trade and scientific and cultural exchange had been strengthened—the approach China took in dealing with Russia and Vietnam. India's position was that normalization of relations required the simultaneous consideration of the border dispute. With regard to the border dispute per se, China preferred to maintain the status quo of the line of actual control (LAC), whereas India wanted to change the status quo, as it considered itself to have lost territory to China during the 1962 border war. This difference increases the degree of difficulty in conflict resolution. Border negotiations started in December 1981 after Chinese Foreign Minister Huang Hua's visit to India. During the talks Beijing expressed its desire for a comprehensive agreement involving China's recognition of the McMahon Line in the eastern sector and India's surrender of claims to the Akai Chin in the western sector. New Delhi, however, preferred the Colombo proposals—formulated by six nonaligned Asian and African countries in 1962—which provided for China's withdrawal from the western sector. China rejected the plan. As a result, the talks did not get very far (Basu 1991: 106–8). Eventually the Indian side accepted China's approach by suggesting that, since the settlement of the border dispute would take time, bilateral relations in other fields should be expanded. Indian Prime Minister Rajiv Gandhi's state visit to China in December 1988 marked a breakthrough in bilateral relations. A number of economic, scientific, and cultural agreements were signed to promote overall cooperation. In the meantime, China also agreed to a time frame for reaching a fair and reasonable solution of the border dispute through peaceful and mutually acceptable means (pp. 110–12).

With no immediate settlement of the border in sight, both sides switched the direction of their consultation to build confidence in the border area. Soon after Gandhi's visit in 1988, China and India concluded an agreement to establish a Joint Working Group (JWG) of technical personnel to settle the dispute. During Indian Prime Minister Narasimha Rao's visit to Beijing in 1993, China and India signed an agreement on "Maintenance of Peace and Tranquility Along the Line of Actual Control" that established confidence-building measures. Both sides abjured the use of force and promised to respect the LAC until the border issue is resolved through negotiation. Both sides agreed to maintain minimum forces along the border. An "expert group" was set up within the JWG to facilitate consultations to implement the agreement. This agreement was hailed by India's media as a "vital breakthrough" (Gupta and Chakravarti 1993: 22–24). A second agreement was signed in November 1996 during Chinese President Jiang Zemin's visit to India. This pact called for partial demilitarization of the disputed border and stipulated measures related to troop reduction, troop withdrawal and deployment notification, conflict avoidance, and communication measures ("China, India Sign" 1996). Specifically the agreement prohibited military exercises involving more than 15,000 troops along the LAC and also barred military aircraft from flying within 10 km of the border (De Castro 1999: 95).

Implementing these two historic agreements, however, has been no easy task. Above all, the agreements provide no firm timetable for the implementation of confidence-building measures such as troop withdrawal; nor do they specify the number of troops that would be pulled back from the border. Moreover, since the LAC has never been actually demarcated on the ground, the two sides could not agree on it. India was reluctant to demarcate the LAC because of strong domestic opposition. Some political groups in India argued that demarcation of the LAC would be tantamount to an international boundary and would therefore signal India's willingness to concede the Aksai Chin region to China. Critics regarded the 1996 agreement as "kow-towing to China" without making progress toward the return of land in the Aksai Chin region (Burns 1996). Moreover, the border talks have increasingly been embroiled in other issues not directly related to the territorial dispute—such as China's growing economic and military power, China's military ties with Burma, nuclear tests by both countries, China's strategic relations and arms transfer to Pakistan, China's nonrecognition of Sikkim as a province of India, and India's support of the Tibetan separatist movement. Consequently conflict management of the border dispute became hostage to other issues in the relationship such as security and political interests. Although four summits had been held and two important agreements had been signed between 1988 and 1998, the implementation of these agreements made no significant progress. The two sides failed to divorce the border dispute from other contentious aspects of Sino-Indian relations (De Castro 1999: 73–104).

Management of the border dispute was further thwarted by India's nuclear test in May 1998. India's citation of China to justify its nuclear test offended Beijing. As a result, the sixth round of talks on the border issue in June 1998 ended with no progress whatsoever. The leaders of both countries, however, soon took measures to control the damage. In August 1998, Indian Prime Minister Atal Bihari Vajpayee remarked that India wanted to improve its relations with China ("Vajpayee" 1998). Beijing responded by signaling that China was preparing to recognize the state of Sikkim as an inalienable part of India's territory.[11] In December 1999, the Chinese ambassador to India said that China hoped a security dialogue with India could be started soon. Any issue, he said, could be discussed in the dialogue ("China Hopes" 1999). The first round of broad-based security dialogue was held in Beijing in March 2000—the first of its kind between the two nations ("China, India to Hold" 2000). With bilateral relations once again conciliatory, the border talks were put back on track. Following the security dialogue in March, the JWG meeting was resumed in April 2000 ("India, China Start Talks" 2000). In May, Indian President K. R. Narayanan made an important visit to China—the first by an Indian head of state to China since May 1998—further indicating the warming of relations. Narayanan and Chinese leader Jiang Zemin agreed that both sides should work for an early and reasonable resolution to the border dispute ("Indian President Returns" 2000). The border talks eventually produced substantial progress in demarcating the boundary in November 2000. For the first time, both sides exchanged boundary maps of the less controversial "middle sector" covering 545 km of land ("India Says Makes Progress" 2000). The exchange of maps of the "middle sector" was followed by another exchange of maps of the more controversial western sector in June 2001 ("India and China Talk Borders" 2001). This kind of incremental approach in conflict management indicates that the advance from conflict prevention to conflict resolution may still take a long time to accomplish.

The Japan-Russian Dispute. The dynamics of conflict management of territorial disputes via bilateral consultation is not limited to China, of course. Other countries in the region have made efforts to ease their territorial disagreements with their neighbors. Another outstanding territorial dispute in the area is the Russian-Japanese quarrel over the Northern Territories. The origin of this con-

---

[11]In the past, Beijing was unwilling to recognize Sikkim as part of India and referred to it only as the "protectorate" of India ("China Prepared" 1999).

flict was discussed earlier. It concerns four islands off the northeastern coast of Japan: Shikotan, Kunashiri, Etorofu (or Iturup), and the Habomai group. The former Soviet Union occupied these islands at the end of World War II, and Japan has insisted upon their return ever since. In terms of their intrinsic importance, the four islands, although very tiny, have military and economic value. They have been home to a Russian military base and radar station, for example, and some 20,000 to 30,000 Russian citizens make their living from the area's rich fishery.

The dispute over the Northern Territories has become a long-standing and apparently insurmountable obstacle to the normalization of Russian-Japanese relations. In addition to the incompatible claims of the two countries, strategic confrontation between the United States and the Soviet Union and between the Soviet Union and China has complicated management of the issue. During negotiations on a peace treaty between the two countries in 1956, the Soviet Union promised to return to Japan two islands—Shikotan and Habomai—once the peace treaty had been signed. Japan, however, was unable to accept the deal. Secretary of State John Foster Dulles threatened that if Japan reached a compromise with the Soviet Union over the Northern Territories by agreeing to the return of only two islands, the United States might not return Okinawa to Japan (Kimura 1998: 2). The Soviet Union revoked its offer when Japan renewed its security alliance with the United States in 1960. Moscow wanted all foreign troops to leave Japanese territory before it would keep its promise under the 1956 Joint Declaration.

During the heyday of the Cold War in the 1970s and 1980s, the Soviet Union refused even to recognize that there was a territorial dispute between the two countries. Moscow did not want to give up a strategic asset that protected its nuclear submarines against the United States. The Soviet Union also feared that returning the four islands would spark a chain reaction in Eastern Europe. Occasionally, too, Japan became a victim of the contention between China and the Soviet Union. When Japan and China signed a treaty of peace and friendship in August 1978, for example, the Soviet Union protested by stationing troops in the Northern Territories (Kimura 1998: 2).

The Soviet policy toward Japan started to soften after Mikhail Gorbachev took office in 1985. He acknowledged the existence of the dispute over the four islands. Today, with a growing need for economic and financial aid, Moscow has been more willing to discuss the disputed territory with Tokyo. Various proposals have been put forward by scholars—such as joint rule of the islands or placement of the islands under UN trusteeship (Zhang 1989: 18). So far, however, little substantial progress has been made. The collapse of the Soviet Union and emergence of a democratic Russia did not change the situation. The difficulty in conflict resolution, first and foremost, stems from the territory's symbolic importance, which is rooted in the national psyche of both countries. The dispute touches upon the "ideational survival" dimension for both countries. In Japanese eyes, the Northern Territories represent the perceived injustice Japan suffered, not so much over Japan's defeat in World War II but more over the Soviet Union's abrupt surprise attack on Japan in 1945 and its insistence on taking over some territory in return for its one-week participation in the war against Japan. Such an injustice must be rectified before Japan can trust Russia. The Japanese public strongly supports the return of all four islands as a precondition for the normalization of relations. Every year, the Japanese mark Northern Territories Day nationwide. In Russia, nationalist sentiment has been on the rise ever since the disintegration of the Soviet Union. After losing most of their republics, the Russian public's tolerance for further loss of territory is close to zero. Public opinion surveys show that more than 70 percent of the Russian people oppose returning the islands to Japan.

The strong nationalist sentiment attached to the islands puts tremendous pressure on politicians in both countries not to make concessions. Under enormous political pressure at home, Gorbachev was unable to revive the 1956 Soviet position of returning two islands in his visit to Japan in 1991. Even the most liberal politician in Russia, Grigory Yavlinsky, never went so far as to say he favored returning the islands (Hakamada 1998: 3). Before President Boris Yeltsin's official visit to Japan in 1992, there were signs that he was willing to consider the possibility of returning some islands to Japan. Hard-liners in the Russian government, however, forced Yeltsin to cancel his trip to Japan with only four days' notice (Quillen 1993: 659). The domestic political pressure in Japan similarly made the Japanese leaders much less flexible. From the very beginning Japan insisted that no peace treaty could be signed and no large-scale economic assistance would be provided before Russia agreed to return the four northern islands.[12] Such an approach is quite different from the Sino-Russian, Sino-Vietnamese, or even Sino-Indian cases of conflict management discussed earlier.

During 1997 and 1998, there were signs that leaders in both countries were ready to move forward on the issue. In November 1997, Japanese Prime Minister Ryutaro Hashimoto and Russian President Boris Yeltsin held a summit in Krasnoyarsk in which the two leaders set a goal of concluding some sort of peace agreement by the end of 2000. During Yeltsin's visit to Kawana, Japan, in 1998, Hashimoto put forward an informal proposal to Russia on the territorial issue. According to this proposal, Japan and Russia would demarcate their state bound-

---

[12]As a Japanese commentator put it: "The Japanese have frequently offended Russian sensibility by trying to wrest away the islands [with offers] of money" (Kimura 1998: 5).

ary with the four islands defined as Japanese territory but remaining under Russian administration for the time being. Russia, however, preferred to sign an interim peace treaty without touching upon the territorial issue ("The Prospect" 2000). These two proposals are obviously far apart.

Since 1999, Russian leaders have been in no position to concede the northern islands to Japan. In 1999, with a war in Chechnya going on, any territorial compromise to Japan would have provoked a nationalistic backlash. Former Japanese Prime Minister Hashimoto visited Moscow in November to push for a peace treaty by 2000. The Russian Duma responded by drafting a statement saying: "Any treaty implying the loss or restriction of the sovereignty of the Russian Federation over the South Kuril islands has no prospects of being ratified by the State Duma" (Ferguson 1999). Facing tremendous domestic pressure, Yeltsin once again had to cancel his scheduled visit to Japan in December 1999. In 2000, both countries experienced a leadership change that many hoped would bring new momentum to the effort to conclude a peace treaty by the end of the year. The expectation proved illusory, however, owing to the dynamics of domestic politics in both countries. Although the new Russian president, Vladimir Putin, enjoyed a high degree of popularity at first, he suffered a series of domestic setbacks in "Black August" before his visit to Japan in September: terrorist bombings in Moscow and elsewhere, the sinking of the nuclear attack submarine *Kursk*, and the Ostankino television tower fire. His response to the incidents raised doubts about his leadership skills. In the meantime, Yoshiro Mori, who succeeded Keizo Obuchi as Japan's new prime minister in April, soon became the most unpopular prime minister in postwar Japan and found himself unable to be more flexible on the territorial issue. As a result, the summit between Putin and Mori in September produced no breakthrough. Putin refused to accept the Kawana proposal of 1998 and did not mention the Krasnoyarsk agreement of 1997, in which both countries were committed to signing a peace treaty by the end of 2000 ("Putin Refused" 2000). Before Mori left office, he met again with Putin in March 2001 to discuss the territorial disputes. Apparently they agreed to use the 1956 declaration as a starting point whereby Russia would return two of the islands once a peace treaty had been signed. However, Tokyo once again hardened its position after Junichiro Koizumi took office as the prime minister. In his first letter to Putin in May, he asked for the return of all four islands. One reason for his tough stand was to pacify some of the more conservative elements of his Liberal Democratic Party (Ibison 2001).

In short, Russia and Japan have made little progress in resolving their territorial dispute. A lot of promises and gestures have been made, but few concrete actions resulted. The only significant development from the negotiations is mutual visits between Japanese citizens and the Russian residents of the Northern Territories. The framework for such visits was set by Soviet President Gorbachev's visit to Japan in 1991. During his visit to Japan in 1993, Yeltsin promised to withdraw all Russian military troops other than border troops from the Northern Territories (MOFA 1999). Apparently the process has not been finished.

Summary. In these four cases of managing territorial disputes via bilateral consultations, the Sino-Russian and Sino-Vietnamese examples were more successful than the Sino-Indian and Japanese-Russian. Several observations can be made.

First of all, the feasibility of conflict prevention and termination among these countries can be attributed to the overall relaxation of international tensions in the region following the end of the Cold War, characterized by the easing of superpower rivalry and major-power competition. That is, the progress in territorial conflict management can be seen as peace dividends of the structural change in Asia. China would have found it almost impossible to resolve its border disputes with such bitter adversaries as Russia, Vietnam, and India without this new structural environment. One can conclude, therefore, that effective management of bilateral territorial disputes demands a favorable international environment, which reduces threat perception and facilitates conflict management. One may argue that the problem in the Sino-Indian case is that irrespective of macrostructural changes, both countries still perceive each other as a potential strategic adversary.

Second, these four cases of bilateral conflict management seem to display two different underlying sequences. One approach was to emphasize the importance of improving bilateral relations in the hope that a thaw in trade, security, and scientific and cultural exchange would have a spillover effect to the territorial issue and pave the way to settlement. Essentially China adopted such an approach. The other approach was to regard settlement of territorial disputes as a prerequisite for further improvement of bilateral relations. Japan's attitude toward the Northern Territories issue and India's initial thinking on its border dispute with China represent such an approach. In the case studies examined here, the first approach has been more effective than the second. In the Sino-Russian and Sino-Vietnamese disputes, the two sides did not insist on the solution of territorial quarrels as a precondition for the normalization of relations. Japan, by contrast, has insisted all along on the return of the Northern Territories before it is willing to sign a peace treaty with Russia. Clearly there is a lesson to be learned from the experience: conflict management of territorial disputes is much easier if both sides are able to divorce the territorial dispute from other contentious issues in the relationship. The Sino-Indian border talks, for instance, suffered a lot from the many nonterritorial issues between 1996 and 1998.

Third, the case studies show that the leadership's strong political commitment to the resolution of territorial disputes is critical. Such a commitment, of course, is strongly associated with change in national goals and values and their convergence. In both the Sino-Russian and Sino-Vietnamese cases, in light of other more important objectives and interests, political leaders were determined to put the border dispute behind them. In the Sino-Russian case, the momentum of conflict resolution was maintained by seven summit meetings between Chinese leader Jiang Zemin and Russian leader Boris Yeltsin. The border agreement signed in 1991 was resisted by provincial leaders in the Russian Far East, who charged that the agreement was unfair and infringed upon Russian interests.[13] The provincial leaders launched a fierce campaign, calling for renunciation of the treaty and refusing to transfer any land to China. Once new border controls were in place, moreover, they refused to cooperate with Chinese authorities to strengthen ties along the border (Rozman 1998: 101; Lukin 1998: 827–28). President Yeltsin, however, was resolved to carry out the border agreement. The two border agreements were "sacred and unchangeable," he said, and Russia would stand firmly by them (Akaha 1996: 106). Similarly, Chinese and Vietnamese leaders showed their political courage by setting a target date for settling border and water disputes. The deadlines virtually brought the negotiation process to the point of no return, as failure to meet the deadline would make the leaders look politically bad both at home and abroad. By contrast, one reason the Sino-Indian border talks have not been very fruitful is that the top leaders have not committed themselves to finding a final solution. In the case of the Northern Territories, Russian leaders have never made a political decision to solve the territorial dispute with Japan once and for all.

Finally, the significance of the disputed territory to a country's national identity and psyche is also crucial in determining the outcome of conflict management. If either side nurses strong feelings of injustice, unfairness, or humiliation and therefore demands a significant change of the status quo, the difficulty of conflict management and resolution will increase immeasurably. In the Sino-Russian and Sino-Vietnamese disputes, the solution was based on maintaining rather than changing the status quo. Neither side demanded the unilateral return of considerable land from the other side. Instead territorial adjustments were made in a give-and-take fashion. In the two relatively unsuccessful cases, one side would not accept the status quo. In the Sino-Indian dispute, India did not want to legitimize China's control of the land it took in the 1962 Indian border war, whereas China preferred to maintain the status quo of the LAC. In the Japan-Russia dispute, Japan wants the transfer of four islands that have been under Rus-

---

[13]The agreement did involve a transfer of territory to China that had been occupied by the Soviet Union in the 1930s in violation of the "unequal" treaties concluded in the nineteenth century.

sian jurisdiction since 1945. Thus a territorial dispute involving a unilateral transfer of substantial territory is much more difficult to settle than a dispute involving no significant exchange of land (or involving the exchange of land on a roughly equal basis).

Pathway 2: Multilateral Confidence-Building Regimes

Another indicator of the gradual evolution toward a normative-contractual order in Asia is the emergence of multilateral confidence-building regimes to manage territorial disputes. These regimes involving more than two countries do not require a formal multilateral organization. Such a multilateral framework, however, is not a substitute for bilateral negotiations on territorial disputes. Rather, it is aimed at building confidence and reducing tension in the border area in order to make the overall security environment more conducive to the settlement of territorial disputes. The settlement of disputes is still handled bilaterally, but the confidence-building measures are implemented at the multilateral level. China, Russia, and three former Soviet republics in Central Asia are the main practitioners of this method of conflict prevention. China calls this the "new mode of security cooperation."

One manifestation of this new mode was the agreement on confidence building in border regions signed by China, Russia, Tajikistan, Kazakhstan, and Kyrgyzstan in April 1996. The initial purpose of the agreement was to create a stable and peaceful border of more than 7,000 km—one of the longest common borders in the world. The Chinese media praised the agreement as the first of its kind in the Asian region in terms of multilateral peace and security (*People's Daily*, Apr. 26, 1996). The five countries signed another agreement in Moscow in 1997 to cut their military forces along the border. Under this agreement the five have reduced troop levels, limited military activity, and increased security transparency along their borders. It was in such a favorable security environment that China settled its border disputes with Russia, Kazakhstan, Kyrgyzstan, and Tajikistan. Among other confidence-building measures, China and the four former republics of the Soviet Union agreed on a partial pullout of troops from the 100-km zone along their mutual border. The agreements also envisage the renunciation of any military exercise in the zone involving more than 40,000 troops, as well as the reduction of troop strength to 25,000. A joint monitoring group was established to coordinate inspection activities. To increase the transparency of the implementation, for example, in October 1999 Chinese military inspectors visited the Russian Far East city of Vladivostok to observe a withdrawal of Russian troops outside the 100-km zone from the border with China. Chinese inspectors have paid special attention to the Far East military district, whose units and subdivisions are covered by the agreement ("Chinese Military Inspectors" 1999).

Since 1996, leaders of the five countries have held six summits to discuss various security issues, including border questions. Such multilateral consultations have become a regular mechanism of the "Shanghai Five," with the objective of improving stability along China's lengthy border with Russia and the three former Soviet republics. The agenda has gradually expanded from the border issue to other security issues of common concern. Each summit has resulted in a signed agreement or a statement dealing with major security issues in the region. The fourth summit, for example, was held in Bishkek, Kyrgyzstan, in August 1999. Five countries signed an agreement to cooperate on fighting crime and drug traffic across their borders. This broad policy statement was then implemented by specific agencies in the respective countries. Soon after the fourth summit in Bishkek, officials of the public security and law enforcement agencies met in December 1999 to sign a memorandum agreeing to strengthen mutual cooperation to fight international terrorism, nationalist separatism, religious fundamentalism, and organized crime. The leaders of the five countries emphasized that they would not allow their territory to be used against the sovereignty, security, and social order of any other member of the Shanghai Five ("China, Russia, Kazakhstan" 1999).

The fifth summit was held in Dushanbe, Tajikistan, in July 2000. A joint statement specified that all parties would work to turn the Shanghai Five into a regional mechanism to conduct multilateral cooperation in all areas. Although the statement shied away from declaring a formal regional organization, the move toward institutionalization is clear—as shown in the decision to establish a council of national coordinators nominated by the five countries (Ministry of Foreign Affairs, PRC n.d.). This development parallels ASEAN in its formative stage. The mechanism also displays a top-down function: foreign ministers and defense ministers of the Shanghai Five meet on a regular basis, thus shaping a "multilevel and multiarea consulting mechanism" (Ren 2000). The Shanghai Five has since evolved into a formal regional organization—the Shanghai Cooperation Organization (SCO)—in June 2001 at the Sixth Summit Meeting. Uzbekistan was admitted as a new founding member of the SCO, expanding the Shanghai Five into the Shanghai Six. The focus of the summit, however, was no longer border disputes but rather a wider range of security and economic issues, including a convention against Islamic terrorism and separatism ("China, Russia, 4 Others" 2001).

In short, the Shanghai Five represents an interesting experiment of combining bilateral and multilateral management of territorial disputes—all based on sound political and security relations among members. In such a regime, norms and rules are more important than power in sustaining regional order. The two major players, China and Russia, have played a key role in sustaining the momentum of the organization. China's initiation of a multilateral security organization signals a modest departure from its otherwise bilateral-oriented approach toward conflict management that is deeply embedded in its adherence to the Westphalian order. Although the multilateral consultation began with the border issue, it spilled over into other security questions. Eventually an informal regime evolved into a formal institution. For the time being, at least, this pathway has created a stable security order among the participants.

Pathway 3: Conflict Management by Multilateral Institutions

Because ASEAN was for a long time the only viable security organization in the Asian region, it is worth investigating the organization's efficacy in managing territorial disputes among its members. There are numerous territorial disputes among ASEAN members, and most of them have not been resolved. As to their origin, the two main sources are historical evolution and colonial history. These two causes often interact with each other and in this case have created particularly complex disputes. The boundaries of Southeast Asia—mostly imposed by the European colonial powers—were often ill-defined, not demarcated, or poorly demarcated. Since many of the maps differ, the borderlines drawn during colonial times have not been widely accepted by postcolonial states. Successor states tend to accept boundaries in their favor; otherwise they complain that the lines were drawn arbitrarily by the colonial powers (Djiwandono 1994: 36). In terms of conflict intensity, most disputes in the area are of low and mediate intensity. Except for the Cambodia-Vietnam dispute, territorial quarrels seldom lead to full-scale military conflict in Southeast Asia.

The founding of ASEAN in 1967 was the result of Southeast Asian countries' seeking to create an association that could provide a framework for successful management of disputes among members, including territorial quarrels. During the first half of the 1960s, serious conflicts erupted between Indonesia and Malaysia and between Malaysia and the Philippines. The former dispute was related to Indonesia's opposition to the creation of Malaysia in 1963, the latter to the Philippines' opposition to the inclusion of Sabah in Malaysia.[14] The dispute over Sabah has proved to be one of the most serious and enduring territorial conflicts among ASEAN members. Malaysia and the Philippines severed diplomatic relations twice in the 1960s, and throughout the crisis the Philippines has refused to participate in ASEAN meetings (Tuan 1996: 66). Even after the two countries restored diplomatic ties in 1969, relations remained cool—for more than two dec-

---

[14]Sabah once belonged to the sultan of Sulu. It became a British colony in 1946. In the early 1960s, Filipino President Pacapagal argued that Manila was the heir of the old Sultanate of Sulu and claimed Sabah as Philippine territory.

ades, there was no top-level visit between them. Not until 1993 did the Filipino president, Fidel Ramos, pay the first top-level visit to Kuala Lumpur (Djiwandono 1994: 38). The dispute not only created strains in relations between the two countries but also interfered with ASEAN cooperation.

How has ASEAN fared in handling such territorial disputes among members? The first year of ASEAN did not produce a formal mechanism of conflict resolution. The ASEAN Declaration (Bangkok Declaration) adopted in 1967 did not even refer to conflict management. It was almost ten years later that ASEAN was able to come up with norms and rules for conflict management—in the Declaration of ASEAN Concord (DAC) and the Treaty of Amity and Cooperation (Bali Treaty) signed in 1976. The DAC applies only to ASEAN members; the Bali Treaty is open to nonmembers. The Bali Treaty provides specific guidelines for conflict management, particularly with regard to peaceful settlement of disputes. It stipulates, for example, that signatories should refrain from the threat or use of force to settle disputes. Articles 14 and 15 envisage the creation of a High Council to be composed of a ministerial-level representative from each of the signatories. Its function is to take "cognizance" of existing disputes or situations that could threaten regional "peace and security." The High Council may act as a mediator if no solution to a dispute is reached through "direct negotiation between the parties to the dispute." The council may also recommend appropriate means of settlement to the contending parties (Amer 1998: 36–39).

To what extent has this mechanism of conflict resolution worked? If we judge this issue from the perspective of preventing military conflicts, ASEAN has been successful: no territorial dispute has led to a militarized interstate conflict since 1967. It is difficult, however, to establish a direct link between this outcome and the mechanism of conflict management in ASEAN documents. And while no territorial dispute has burst into a military conflict, most of them remain unresolved. The dispute over Sabah, for example, continues to be an irritation between Malaysia and the Philippines after more than thirty years. The Philippines has yet to formally drop its sovereignty claim over Sabah. Therefore it is reasonable to say that ASEAN has done a better job in conflict prevention than in conflict termination or resolution.

Moreover, ASEAN's function of conflict prevention tends to be indirect. ASEAN provides a framework of interaction for member states in which their behavior is modified by the organization's ground rules and norms. Thus membership in ASEAN seems to be the most effective mechanism of conflict prevention. ASEAN has "acted as a brake which persuaded the members to restrain themselves in their dealings with each other" (Tuan 1996: 64). Malaysia and the Philippines, for example, agreed to normalize their relations in 1969 out of consideration for ASEAN's viability. In order to join ASEAN, Vietnam and Laos also became more constructive in handling their territorial disputes with other countries (Amer 1998: 46).

ASEAN's limitations in conflict settlement can be seen in its difficulty in establishing the High Council stipulated by the Bali Treaty. After more than twenty years, the High Council has yet to be established. In the Indonesia-Malaysia territorial disputes over Ligitan and the Sipadan Islands, Indonesia proposed that the High Council should be formed to settle the dispute. But Malaysia preferred to refer the matter to the International Court of Justice rather than the High Council. Apparently ASEAN members still lack sufficient trust toward each other. Certainly Malaysia was concerned about the High Council for good reason: except for Cambodia and Laos, it has outstanding border or maritime disputes with all the other ASEAN countries. Thus it had no confidence that other council members would be unbiased when making a judgment (Amer 1998: 44; Caballero-Anthony 1998: 50). More profoundly, one can see that ASEAN members are not ready to accept a formal and multilateral decision-making body with considerable power over nation-states. Nor do they want bilateral territorial disputes to be multilateralized (Amer 1998: 48). In short, the Westphalian principle of sovereign equality still prevails.

Without a serious multilateral mechanism of conflict management, most territorial disputes are handled by bilateral consultation and negotiation within ASEAN. The most typical practice is to establish joint commissions to deal with border issues—such as the Malaysia-Thailand and Malaysia-Indonesia General Border Committees and the Cambodia-Vietnam Joint Border Commission. Of the original ASEAN members, Indonesia and Thailand seem to have been the most successful in resolving territorial disputes with other members. They have been more willing than others to strive for conflict resolution/termination rather than just settling for conflict prevention. Moreover their border disputes tend to be easier to resolve than quarrels involving other ASEAN countries (Amer 1998: 43).

Third-party mediation has not been officially adopted by ASEAN as a form of dispute management. But occasionally an informal mediation role has been offered by a third party. In the Malaysia-Philippine dispute over Sabah, for example, President Suharto of Indonesia was instrumental in getting both sides to agree to a cooling-off period and his mediation helped in normalizing relations between the two countries. It was through Indonesia's intervention that the first ASEAN Summit was made possible in 1976 when the Philippines agreed not to raise the issue of Sabah at the meeting (Caballero-Anthony 1998: 54, 61). In recent years, apparently, third-party mediation and arbitration have become more acceptable to ASEAN countries as a way of settling territorial disputes if bilateral consultation fails to yield results. Malaysia and Singapore, for example, and Malaysia and Indonesia agreed to submit their respective territorial disputes to the International Court of Justice for resolution. In both cases, the parties have agreed to abide by the court's decision.

The question is, When will ASEAN establish its own formal mechanism of third-party mediation? At the second informal meeting of ASEAN heads of government in Kuala Lumpur in December 1997, ASEAN leaders put forward a bold vision to eliminate all the causes of conflict in the region and to resolve all territorial disputes and other quarrels in Southeast Asia by peaceful means by the year 2020 (Amer 1998: 48). The goal, in other words, is to move from conflict prevention to conflict resolution. If ASEAN leaders are serious about fulfilling this vision, ASEAN's current mechanism of conflict management is not sufficient to do the job.

Implications

Bilateral territorial disputes used to be the most serious threat to the security order in Asia. In the post–Cold War era, on balance, they have become less acute. Today most of them are latent rather than active sources of conflict in the region for several reasons. First, the new strategic environment eliminated the rationale for ideological and strategic contention among nation-states, thus making their territorial disputes less critical. Indeed, many military conflicts resulting from territorial disputes during the Cold War could be attributed to strategic rivalry among major players in the region. At present virtually no country in the region has an imperial design for systemic territorial aggrandizement. Consequently, most territorial disputes are related to nation states' "ideational survival" rather than "sheer survival." Second, in the post–Cold War context the focus of national strategy and priority has shifted from external expansion to internal economic development. The convergence of national desire to create a peaceful and stable external environment for domestic modernization expedited the pace of conflict management and resolution in territorial disputes. As a result, some of the most explosive territorial quarrels such as the Sino-Russian and Sino-Vietnamese border disputes have been largely put to rest. And third, the intrinsic and relative value of the traditional border has declined in an age of revolutionary development of transport, communication, and military technology. Countries are more willing to make concessions of land if it is not strategically or economically indispensable. In the meantime, given the increasing importance of ocean resources and the globalization of the world economy, countries in the region tend to attach more significance to maritime disputes than to quarrels over land. As we can see from Chapter 12 on maritime disputes, maritime quarrels are indeed more likely to threaten the region's security order.[15]

As these sources of conflict have been eliminated, management of territorial disputes in the region has borne fruit. China, the most active territorial disputant in the region, has made remarkable efforts to settle its territorial quarrels with neighboring countries. In the 1990s, China signed border agreements with Laos, Russia, Vietnam, Kyrgyzstan, Kazakhstan, and Tajikistan. Other countries in the region have also made efforts to resolve their territorial disputes. ASEAN countries have devised mechanisms to reduce tension and build confidence along their borders. By 1997, the Western Pacific had at least fifteen delimited maritime boundaries and three bilateral cooperative agreements over shared petroleum resources (San Pablo-Baviera 1997: 35). Vietnam and Thailand, for example, resolved their maritime boundary in 1997. The number of militarized territorial disputes has declined as well. No border war has been fought in Northeast Asia or Southeast Asia in the post–Cold War period. A cyclical pattern of favorable regional security environment and management of border disputes has been emerging. While the structural change resulting from the end of the Cold War has paved the way for more effective management of bilateral territorial disputes, the resolution of territorial disputes in turn will reinforce a more peaceful and stable regional security order. Studies show that countries that can reach agreements to set boundaries are more likely to live in peace (Vasquez 1995: 287–88). Overall, with some exceptions, the role of power and force has been decreasing whereas the role of norms and rules has been increasing in settling territorial disputes in the region, a sign of transition from an instrumental order to a normative-contractual order.

Echoing the region's political and strategic diversity, there is currently no universal model of managing bilateral territorial disputes. Thus bilateral consultation is likely to remain the principal mode of conflict management. Although multilateralism has been the fashion in discussing security order in Asia, some of the most impressive progress has been accomplished through serious bilateral negotiations. Multilateral institutions such as ASEAN have been more successful in conflict prevention than conflict termination. Even within the multilateral framework of ASEAN, most territorial disputes have been handled bilaterally. However, the importance of multilateral institutionalism as a pathway to a rule-governed management of territorial disputes has been on rise in the region. In the future, ASEAN's role in mediating and arbitrating territorial disputes among

---

[15]Compared with land disputes, it is more difficult to determine boundaries on water for purposes of enforcing jurisdiction and exercising sovereign rights. See San Pablo-Baviera (1997: 36–37).

member states is likely to increase if it seriously wants to become a security community.[16] China, Russia, and three Central Asian states developed a new model of conflict management in dealing with their border disputes: a combination of multilateral consultation and bilateral negotiation. Until June 2001, this approach could be regarded as multilateral security cooperation without a formal organization. It served as a useful interim mechanism for conflict prevention and resolution among the participants. The final institutionalization of the Shanghai Five mechanism (SCO) further points to the promising function of multilaterism in subregional security-order building.

Although the salience of bilateral territorial disputes in the regional security order has declined significantly, they remain a destabilizing factor. These quarrels continue to irritate bilateral and multilateral relations. Some are more flammable than others. The Indo-Pakistan dispute over Kashmir, for example, has been persistently active and potentially explosive. A new conflict could be catastrophic, given that both India and Pakistan are now declared nuclear powers. It is fair to say that a large number of bilateral territory disputes have been managed rather than resolved. When things go wrong, serious conflict may arise from these otherwise latent disputes—not just between ancient enemies such as China and India but between ASEAN members too (San Pablo-Baviera 1997: 38). Even settled territorial disputes may still harbor difficulties.[17] With respect to sources of intensification, the overall strategic environment for dispute settlement has become more favorable in the post–Cold War period. But the weight of domestic politics as an obstacle to conflict resolution seems to be increasing—particularly now that many countries in the region have been experiencing a transition from authoritarian to democratic political systems. The transformation from dictatorship to democracy has yet to show its soothing effect on territorial disputes, however. As the Russo-Japanese dispute over the Northern Territories demonstrates, democratization in Russia may have facilitated its resolution of territorial disputes with China but has not made its conflict management with Japan any eas-

---

[16]Because bilateral tensions are still pervasive among ASEAN members, N. Ganesan (1999: 56) does not think that ASEAN constitutes a security community.

[17]For example, China and Russia have yet to find a solution to the three disputed islands on the Argun and Amur Rivers six years after signing two border agreements. China once proposed trading Bolshoy Island in the Argun River for two is
lands in the Amur River near Khabarovsk, but Moscow refused (Pi 1996: 25). Moreover, it was reported in June 2001 that some members of parliament in Kyrgyzstan demanded the abolition of the boundary treaty signed with China, complaining that Kyrgyzstan had made too many concessions to China ("China-Kyrgyzstan Border Dispute" 2001). Although China settled the border dispute with Vietnam in 1999, clashes still occasionally occurred along the border ("China Official Killed" 2002). It was not until June 2002, six years after the two countries signed the first border agreement, that the Kyrgyz parliament approved the Kyrgyzstan-China border agreement ("President Jiang Zemin" 2002).

ier. And although countries like China and Vietnam remain authoritarian, they have shown flexibility in their management of territorial disputes because of changes in their domestic and international priorities.

Could a bilateral territorial dispute derail the regional security order in Asia? The answer depends on many variables, and three in particular. The first is the state of bilateral relations between the two countries. Territorial disputes and overall bilateral relations may be mutually reinforcing. A dispute may irritate bilateral relations, but a solid bilateral relationship may offset the negative impact of territorial disputes. One of the tactics China used to offset the negative influence of the Mischief Reef incident in 1995, for example, was to cultivate mutually beneficial areas, such as trade and investment, in its relations with the Philippines. When the bilateral relationship is in bad shape, however, any small excuse could trigger a crisis in the border area. As an Indian observer visiting a sensitive border post that recently opened to tourists along the Indian-China border commented: "These changes can go into reverse if relations between India and China deteriorate" ("Politics-India" 1999).

The second variable is the configuration of major power relations in the region. Many territorial disputes in the region escalated during the Cold War against a backdrop of superpower contention. The relative stability of China-Russia-U.S.-Japan-India relations in the 1990s has created a favorable framework for handling bilateral territorial disputes. The improvement in Sino-Russian relations, for example, was instrumental in easing tension along the Sino-Vietnamese border. Probably we will see more territorial disputes becoming active if antagonism returns to major-power relations in Asia. In this regard, the ramifications of the "9/11" terrorist attack on the United States in 2001 and of the subsequent war on terrorism in Afghanistan and elsewhere for major-power relations in the region remain to be seen. If the war leads to further harmonization of such relations, the trend of peaceful management and settlement of territorial disputes may continue. On the other hand, if the war causes new divisive and frictional realignment among major powers, it is not inconceivable that the dying embers of territorial disputes may glow again. The renewed tension in Kashmir between India and Pakistan illustrates such a possibility.

The third variable is the significance of the territory's strategic, economic, and symbolic values. Countries seek territory for both tangible and intangible reasons. Because of the strategic and symbolic value of Taiwan and Tibet, China is unlikely to give them up. Other territorial disputes may seem insignificant in terms of tangible value but nevertheless have great symbolic and ideational power for nation-states. National sovereignty and territorial integrity are still the paramount goals of national policy for most Asian countries—partly because they represent a key source of domestic legitimacy. Domestic politics, therefore, will often inflame territorial disputes with other countries, as we have seen throughout this chapter. The way to pursue conflict resolution and avoid militarization of territorial disputes is to divorce territorial quarrels from other issues, particularly the question of national identity.[18]

Works Cited

Akaha, Tsuneo. 1996. "Russia and Asia in 1995: Bold Objectives and Limited Means." *Asian Survey* 36(1) (Jan.): 100–108.

Alagappa, Muthiah. 1995. "Regionalism and Conflict Management: A Framework for Analysis." *Review of International Studies* 21: 359–87.

Allcock, John, et al. 1992. *Border and Territorial Disputes*, 3rd ed. Harlow: Longman Group.

Amer, Ramses. 1993. "Sino-Vietnamese Relations and Southeast Asia Security." *Contemporary Southeast Asia* 14(4) (Mar.): 314–31.

———. 1998. "Expanding ASEAN's Conflict Management Framework in Southeast Asia: The Border Dispute Dimension." *Asian Journal of Political Science* 6(2) (Dec.): 33–55.

Basu, A. R. 1991. "India's China Policy in Historical Perspective." *Contemporary Southeast Asia* 13(1) (June): 103–15.

Bercovitch, Jacob, and Richard Jackson. 1997. *International Conflict: A Chronological Encyclopedia of Conflicts and Their Management 1945–1995*. Washington, D.C.: Congressional Quarterly.

Biger, Gideon, ed. 1995. *The Encyclopedia of International Boundaries*. New York: Facts on File.

"The Border Holds the Key." 1991. *Business India*, Dec. 9–22, p. 30.

Burns, John. 1996. "China and India Pledge to Withdraw Troops on Disputed Border." *New York Times*, Nov. 30.

Caballero-Anthony, Mely. 1998. "Mechanisms of Dispute Settlement: The ASEAN Experience." *Contemporary Southeast Asia* 20(1) (Apr.): 38–66.

Chang, Pao-Min. 1997. "Vietnam and China: New Opportunities and New Challenges." *Contemporary Southeast Asia* 19(2) (Sept.): 136–51.

"China and Vietnam Sign Accord Settling Gulf of Tonkin Dispute." 2000. Reuters, Dec. 26.

"China Hopes for Security Talks with India Soon—PTI." 1999. Reuters, Dec. 21.

"China, India Sign Agreement to Ease Border Dispute." 1996. CNN, Nov. 29.

"China, India to Hold Security Dialogue." 2000. *LatelineNews*, Mar. 3.

"China-Kyrgyzstan Border Dispute Came Back." 2001. *Chinesenewsnet*, June 6.

"China Official Killed in Vietnam Border Incident." 2002. *LatelineNews*, May 31.

"China Prepared to Recognize Sikkim as Part of India." 1999. *Itar-Tass*, Jan. 29.

"China, Russia Border Disputes Resolved, Russian Official Says." 1999. Associated Press, Apr. 27.

"China, Russia, 4 Others Form Bloc." 2001. *LatelineNews*, June 15.

"China, Russia, Kazakhstan, Kyrgyzstan, Russia, and Tajikistan Signed a Joint Memorandum to Fight International Terrorism." 1999. *Chinesenewsnet*, Dec. 3.

[18]As Vasquez (1995: 290–91) put it, one way to promote peace might be to "de-territorialize" identity issues.

"China, Vietnam Agree to Settle Border, Terr Issues Soon." 1999. *Itar-Tass*, Feb. 26.

"Chinese Military Inspectors to Visit Vladivostok." 1999. *Itar-Tass*, Oct. 13.

"Chinese Premier Calls for Consolidation of Sino-Vietnamese Relations." 1999. *Xinhua*, Dec. 2.

CIA. 2001. *The World Factbook, 2001*. CIA Publications.

Copeland, Carla S. 1999. "The Use of Arbitration to Settle Territorial Disputes." *Fordham Law Review* 67(6) (May): 3073–3108.

De Castro, Renato Cruz. 1999. "Probing the Bounds of the Post-1991 Sino-Indian Rapprochement: A Focus on the Border Talks." *Issues and Studies* 35(3): 61–104.

Djiwandono, J. Soedjati. 1994. "Intra-ASEAN Territorial Disputes: The Sabah Claim." *Indonesian Quarterly* 22(1) (Jan.): 34–43.

Ferguson, Joseph. 1999. "Weathering War, Elections, and Yeltsin's Resignation." *Comparative Connections*. Pacific Forum CSIS, 4th Quarter: Japan-Russian relations, pp. 1–4.

Forsberg, Tuomas. 1996. "Explaining Territorial Disputes: From Power Politics to Normative Reasons." *Journal of Peace Research* 33(4): 433–49.

Ganesan, N. 1999. *Bilateral Tensions in Post-Cold War ASEAN*. Singapore: ISEAS.

Ginsburgs, George. 1993. "The End of the Sino-Russian Territorial Disputes?" *Journal of East Asia Affairs* 7(1) (Winter): 261–320.

Goertz, Gary, and Paul F. Diehl. 1992. *Territorial Changes and International Conflict*. London: Routledge.

Gupta, Shekar, and Sudeep Chakravarti. 1993. "Vital Breakthrough." *India Today*, Sept. 30, pp. 22–26.

Hakamada, Shigeki. 1998. "Yeltsin's Sacking of His Cabinet and Visit to Japan." *Japan Echo* 25(4): 1–6.

Heldt, Birger. 1999. "Domestic Politics, Absolute Deprivation, and the Use of Armed Force in Interstate Territorial Disputes, 1950–1990." *Journal of Conflict Resolution* 43(4) (Aug.): 451–78.

Huntington, Samuel. 1997. *The Clash of Civilization and the Making of a New World Order*. New York: Simon & Schuster.

Huth, Paul. 1996a. *Standing Your Ground: Territorial Disputes and International Conflict*. Ann Arbor: University of Michigan Press.

———. 1996b. "Enduring Revelries and Territorial Disputes, 1950–1990." *Conflict Management and Peace Science* 15(1) (Spring): 7–41.

Ibison, David. 2001. "Japan Takes Tougher Line on Disputed Islands." *Financial Times*, May 15.

"India and China Talk Borders." 2001. CNN, June 28.

"India, China Start Talks on Border Dispute." 2000. *LatelineNews*, Apr. 28.

"Indian President Returns from Landmark Trip to China." 2000. *LatelineNews*, June 4.

"India Says Makes Progress in Border Dispute with China." 2000. *LatelineNews*, Nov. 24.

"Jiang Notes Headway on Sino-Vietnam Territorial Issue." 1998. *Itar-Tass*, Oct. 21.

"Kazakhstan President to Visit China." 1999. *Xinhua*, Oct. 15.

Kim, Poon. 1992. "The New Phase in Sino-Vietnamese Relations Since 1989." *Riad Bulletin* 1 (Mar.): 51–76.

Kimura, Hiroshi. 1998. "Talks with Russia: Learning from the Mistakes of the Past." *Japan Echo* 25(4): 1–6.

Kocs, Stephen. 1995. "Territorial Disputes and Interstate War, 1945–1987." *Journal of Politics* 57(1) (Feb.): 159.

Lukin, Alexander. 1998. "The Image of China in Russian Border Regions." *Asian Survey* 38(9) (Sept.): 821–35.

Mandel, Robert. 1980. "Roots of the Modern Interstate Border Dispute." *Journal of Conflict Resolution* 24(3): 427–54.

Ministry of Foreign Affairs. PRC. n.d. "Dushanbe Statement of the Heads of State of the Republic of Kazakhstan, the People's Republic of China, the Republic of Kyrgyzstan, the Russian Federation, and the Republic of Tajikistan."

Mitchell, C. R. 1981. *The Structure of International Conflict.* New York: St. Martin's Press.

Mitchell, Sara McLaughlin. 1999. "Beyond Territorial Contiguity: Issues at State in Democratic Militarized Interstate Disputes." *International Studies Quarterly* 43(1): 169–83.

MOFA (Ministry of Foreign Affairs of Japan). 1999. "Japan's Northern Territories."

Pearson, F. S. 1974. "Geographical Proximity and Foreign Military Intervention." *Journal of Conflict Resolution* 18(3) (Sept.): 432–60.

Pi, Ying-hsien. 1996. "The Dynamics of Sino-Russian Relations." *Issues and Studies* 32(1) (Jan.): 18–31.

"Politics-India: Sensitive Border Post Turns Tourist Destination." 1999. International Press Service, Nov. 26.

"President Jiang Zemin Met with Presidents of Tajikistan, Kazakhstan, Kyrgyzstan and Uzbekistan." 2002. *People's Daily*, June 8.

"The Prospect for the Japanese-Russian Peace Treaty Is Dim." 2000. *Chinesenewsnet*, Sept. 6.

"Putin Refused to Accept Japanese Proposal on Northern Territories." 2000. *Chinesenewsnet*, Sept. 4.

Quillen, Amy B. 1993. "The 'Kuril Islands' or 'Northern Territories': Who Owns Them?" *North Carolina Journal of International Law* 18(3): 633–61.

Ren Xin. 2000. "Fruitful Dushanbe Summit." *Beijing Review*, July 17–23, pp. 10–11.

Rozman, Gilbert. 1998. "Sino-Russian Relations in the 1990s: A Balance Sheet." *Post-Soviet Affairs* 14(2): 93–113.

San Pablo-Baviera, Ailleen. 1997. "Managing Territorial Disputes." *Asian Studies* 33: 35–41.

Solomon, Robert. 1970. "Boundary Concepts and Practices in Southeast Asia." *World Politics* 23(1) (Oct.): 3–16.

Sutter, Karen. 1993. "China's Vietnam Policy: The Road to Normalization and Prospects for the Sino-Vietnamese Relationship." *Journal of Northeast Asian Studies* 12(2) (Summer): 21–46.

Tuan, Hoang Anh. 1996. "ASEAN Dispute Management: Implications for Vietnam and an Expanded ASEAN." *Contemporary Southeast Asia* 18(1) (June): 61–80.

"Vajpayee: India Wants to Improve Ties with China." 1998. *Xinhua*, Aug. 4.

Vasquez, John A. 1993. *The War Puzzle.* Cambridge: Cambridge University Press.

———. 1995. "Why Do Neighbors Fight? Proximity, Interaction, or Territoriality." *Journal of Peace Research* 32(3): 277–93.

"Vietnam, China OK Land Border Deal." 1999. Associated Press, Dec. 3.

"Vietnam, China Sign Land Border Agreement." 1999. Reuters, Dec. 30.

Xue, Mouhong, et al., eds. 1987. *China Today, Diplomacy.* Beijing: Chinese Social Science Press.

Zhang, Qing. 2000. "The Brotherhood Remains After Twists and Turns." *World Affairs* 2: 38–40.

Zhang, Yaohua. 1989. "Moscow's New Japan Policy." *Beijing Review*, May 1–7, pp. 17–19.

CHAPTER TWELVE

Maritime Issues in Asia

The Problem of Adolescence

JEAN-MARC F. BLANCHARD

To the states that populate Asia the sea is vital.[1] The Sea of Japan, the Java Sea, and the Andaman Sea, for instance, are critical sources of food, supplying an important percentage of the region's nutritional needs. Furthermore, approximately 70 percent of Middle Eastern oil destined for Japan, Taiwan, and South Korea passes via the sea, specifically the South China Sea. Millions of Asians, moreover, derive their livelihood from the sea. Finally, the sea serves as a major transport artery between the countries of the area and the rest of the world. (See Valencia 1991: 1157, 1182; Weeks 1998; Lee 1998; Ji 1999: 162–63; Song 1999: 12; Vitasa and Soeprapto 1999.)

Given the sea's importance, all Asian states have a general interest in preserving the area's maritime security order.[2] Unfortunately, island ownership quarrels, boundary (maritime and continental shelf) controversies, friction over sea lines of communication (SLOCs), and piracy all threaten it in varying degrees (Weeks 1998: 2–4; Kim 2000: 1–17). Indeed, in Northeast Asia maritime disputes have caused serious interstate friction in the past (Buzan 1978: 37). Moreover, the Gulf of Thailand, South China Sea, and Andaman Sea have been the scene of militarized conflict relating to maritime quarrels. (See, respectively, Nguyen-Vo 1992: 78–79; Studeman 1998: 4–5; IBC n.d.) The acquisition of enhanced naval capabilities by many Asian states places additional dark clouds on Asia's maritime setting (Kim 2000: 1). Nevertheless, Asia's maritime scene is relatively stable at pres-

---

[1]Maritime Asia represents the space from the eastern Indian Ocean to the western Pacific.

[2]In this book security order is defined as "a formal or informal arrangement that sustains rule-governed interaction among sovereign states in their pursuit of individual and collective goals" (Alagappa, Chap. 1).

ent. What explains fluctuations in the incidence of maritime conflict in Asia, differences in the conflict potential of particular disputes, and variation in the extent to which particular countries threaten Asia's maritime security order?

We can better understand the past and attain a more accurate assessment of the future if we recognize the effect of adolescence on Asia's maritime security setting. In the 1970s and 1980s, for example, rapid growth and shifting national identities, coupled with various contextual factors, created or intensified many of the region's territorial and maritime problems. Since the early 1990s, by contrast, the maturation of the region's states, which has derived from participation in institutional arrangements and from slowing growth, has brought these problems under control, although it has not eliminated them. Regardless of whether the period is quiescent or tumultuous, Asia's most adolescent states have contributed most to its maritime problems. Ultimately the course of events in the region will depend in large part on the extent to which Asia's states mature (or "mature" states become adolescent). Indeed, Alagappa (Introduction to this volume) hypothesizes that the consolidation of Asia's states is an important factor contributing to the area's current peacefulness and stability. In any event, the existence of multiple pathways to order gives hope over the near term that adolescence, at least where it persists, will not pose a severe problem.

Adolescent States and Asia

Scholars and policymakers often look at the characteristics of states in order to understand their foreign policy behavior. (See, for example, Walt 1996 and Ripsman 2001–2002.) To date, however, they have not considered the implications of a state's maturity level. In particular, they have not considered the implications of adolescent statehood. This seems odd given that they regularly describe countries as becoming full members of the international community, undergoing a soul searching, or breaking from a mother country. Conventionally adolescence is understood as a phase between childhood and adulthood. It is a period of dramatic change where there is rapid and sometimes uneven growth. Moreover, adolescents abandon old identities, partially or completely, while acquiring new ones. During this phase adolescents learn to handle adult tasks and develop economic independence. These changes and the stresses they produce lead adolescents to behave erratically and consume voraciously. They also spur adolescents to act in an uncoordinated fashion and to seek membership in groups that can give them a sense of identity. Finally, they push adolescents to guard their domains zealously and to focus heavily on status. (See Sebald 1977: 4–6, 103, 201–25; Kroger 1989: 1–2; Schave and Schave 1989: 2–11; Atwater 1992: 2–7, 49–56, 223–35, 394–95; Cotterell 1996: chap. 1.)

The Logic of Adolescence

Adolescence can be a useful way of thinking about states, even though states do not go through puberty and need not experience set developmental stages. As a result of population growth, for instance, states go through periods of rapid and uneven growth. Moreover, changes in leaders or domestic political regimes, the collapse of old peer relationships, or the failure of traditional ways of interacting with the world can lead a state to discard old national identities and embrace new ones. China and Japan are classic examples. Furthermore, countries often act in an uncoordinated fashion because they lack control over their entire corpus. In contemporary Russia, for example, subnational actors have acted in a fashion contrary to the foreign policy preferences of the central government and thereby hindered its participation in regional economic institutions (Blanchard 2002).

An adolescent state, then, is one that is growing rapidly and perhaps unevenly, that is unsure of its identity, that has not adopted adult behaviors, and that is excessively concerned with its domain and status. The more of these traits a state possesses, the higher its degree of adolescence. The country that possesses all of these characteristics is a long way indeed from reaching adulthood. Unfortunately adolescence is likely to have adverse consequences for neighboring countries, for the region, and perhaps even for the international community as a whole. These adverse consequences, as we shall see, include an intense quest for resources, a search for new identities and the protection of old ones, a zealous defense of borderlines, and uncoordinated behavior.

The growth requirements of adolescence spur a demand for foodstuffs and other natural resources (oil, iron, minerals), trade and investment opportunities, and employment-generating activities. Adolescent states require resources to satiate the consumption needs of their people and to supply industry and the military with the inputs they require to achieve their objectives. In addition, adolescent states crave trade and investment opportunities to boost living standards and national wealth. Finally, they have a serious need for job-generating activities to promote growth. Such needs give adolescent states powerful incentives to advance and defend claims to resource-rich spaces, to secure areas that facilitate commerce and investment, and to protect territorial and maritime expanses that support employment.

Adolescent states are unsure of their identities. Hence, they reject current identities, put renewed emphasis on traditional identities, or embrace portions of completely new identities. To replace or supplement existing identities, states explore a variety of sources, including history, culture, and the nation. Given that national identities often have a "here feeling" in addition to a "we feeling," one should not be surprised that countries also seek identity in terms of territorial space (Deudney 1996: 129–45; Blanchard 1998: 92). If an adolescent state places great stress on the territorial component of identity, it is likely to vigorously defend areas that it controls, endeavor to acquire noncontrolled spaces that constitute part of its national identity, or lay claim to areas that are integral to its sense of self.

As noted earlier, adolescent states are hypersensitive about their domain. This is a function not only of their great concern to define and protect their identities but also their powerful urge to assert their independence as they grow up and separate from others. Boundaries, whether territorial or maritime, are highly germane to states concerned about their domain as a result of the fact that borderlines constitute the state and specify the range of each state's legal jurisdiction (Blanchard 1998: 90). Hence adolescent states are likely to take serious offense at any intrusion, real or imagined, against their sovereignty. They also are inclined to take action to demonstrate their sovereignty to others.

Finally, adolescence leads to uncoordinated behavior because there is incomplete control over the corpus of the state. For instance, the center of the state may not have complete command over branches of the military or branches of the government such as the interior or security forces. In addition, it may lack control over constituent parts such as provinces or states. Adolescent states that lack full command over their corpus are likely to give favors to some components in order to facilitate control over others. These favors might include a greater role in the construction or implementation of foreign policy, a greater share of the national budget, or reduced and irregular supervision. Lack of control over the military, bureaucracies, or constituent parts also suggests that leaders will strive to build popular support so as to gain resources that can be used in political struggles. One common way of building popular support is to deliver economic goods. Since this delivery depends on access to resources at reasonable prices and employment opportunities, adolescent states have an incentive to claim or defend economically valuable areas.

Consequences for the Region's Maritime Scene

The concept of an adolescent state is relevant for an analysis of Asia's maritime dynamics. First, many states in the region have experienced or will be experiencing rapid growth. Second, a number of countries have identities that are in flux. Third, a number of countries are seriously concerned about protecting their turf and status. Fourth, a number of countries lack full control over their corpus. These facts are significant as they have implications for the area's maritime security order.

From the 1960s through the early 1990s, many states in Asia participated in the so-called Asian Miracle. Among other features, the Asian Miracle was characterized by rapid GDP and per capita income growth, an increasing share of industry in GDP, and a greater share of world exports (Hellmann and Pyle 1997; Tongzon 1998; Choo 2000: 34–38). In 1997, though, the miracle ended for many Asian countries. As a result of the Asian financial crisis, they experienced massive capital flight, increased bankruptcies, slowdowns or declines in GDP growth, dramatic surges in unemployment and poverty, the exhaustion of foreign exchange reserves, and massive declines in stock and other asset values (World Bank 1999: chap. 2).

Today, however, there are abundant signs of recovery: growth declines have stopped or reversed; industrial output is up; per capita consumption has improved somewhat. Moreover, the region's countries have rebuilt their foreign exchange reserves, paid down their international debts, and received new international investment. Countries like India and Vietnam, which did not participate in the initial Asian Miracle, have begun to invigorate their economies through tariff reductions, deregulation, and the embrace of foreign investment and markets. Admittedly there are countries like Indonesia and Japan where serious economic problems persist. Nevertheless, the region as a whole is recovering. (See IMF 1999b: 13–15, 19–21, chap. 2; IMF 1999a: 15–20; U.S. SPPD 2000: chap. 3; World Bank 2000: chaps. 1, 3, app. 1.)

The recovery of many of these economies has resulted in the growth of trade, a greater demand for energy, and higher levels of mineral and foodstuff consumption. The U.S. Department of Energy reports that oil use in developing Asia increased by almost 400,000 barrels per day in 1999, for example, and was expected to increase by a similar amount in 2000 (U.S. EIA 2000). China alone is expected to require 2.3 million barrels of oil a day more over the next decade. India will need 1.5 million barrels more (Song 1999: 7, 10). Undoubtedly these trends will increase the demand for the sea by boosting the value of islands and maritime zones that convey rights to areas that may be energy- and mineral-rich. They also will augment the consumption of fish—which in turn means that maritime areas that harbor rich fisheries will become more valuable. Furthermore, such trends will magnify the worth of SLOCs because they are important for the flow of commerce, natural resources, and foodstuffs. Finally, these trends will raise the importance of the sea because it serves as a source of employment. In combination, these factors will give Asian states a powerful interest in enclosing the sea within fixed and well-specified boundaries. This is not surprising given that boundaries allow countries to specify their resource endowments, to establish the breadth of water over which they can enforce their laws, and to determine their economic transit routes and those of others (Blanchard 1998: 80–86).

Often market mechanisms will suffice to manage the region's increasing demand for foodstuffs, energy, and other raw materials. Producers will supply more goods in response to increased demand, and companies will substitute materials for production inputs that are unavailable. In cases of rapid growth, however, market mechanisms may prove inadequate, infeasible, or intolerable. Substitution and conservation of materials are often nonviable options. And prices—the ultimate market mechanism adjusting demand and supply—may skyrocket beyond the bounds of political acceptability (Blanchard and Ripsman 1996, 2001).

Beyond a possible return to strong rates of growth, a number of Asian states have fluid national identities. Japanese policymaking elites, for instance, contest whether Japan should be an Asian or a Western power, a leader or a follower, a normal power equipped with a traditional military or a civilian superpower (Bessho 1999: chap. 1). Chinese foreign policy decision makers are deciding whether to be a responsible power or a disruptive nation at odds with the international community, whether to be a victimized developing power or a major power (Bessho 1999: chap. 2; Yahuda 1999). Vietnamese leaders are increasingly questioning the value of a national identity based on socialism and anti-Chinese and anti-French sentiments; instead they are turning to a national identity that sees Vietnam as the fatherland and part of the Southeast Asian community (Ninh 1998). According to one scholar, India is seeking a new identity given the increasing meaninglessness of its national identity defined in terms of nonalignment and a state-led mixed economy (Mehta 1998: 404–5).

Changes in leaders and political regimes have largely produced this fluid state of affairs with respect to Asian national identities. In the realm of regime change, South Korea, the Philippines, Thailand, and Taiwan have moved away from their authoritarian pasts to embrace democracy (Ichimura and Morley 1999: 3–34). China too has undergone a regime change, primarily in the economic sphere, though there have been noteworthy political changes such as the development of village elections (Bernstein 1999: 83–119). Certainly Vietnam's Leninist regime has evolved—as reflected in the abolition of central planning and alterations in the relationship between the Vietnamese Communist Party and the government (Vasavakul 1999: 59–82). And in India the Bharatiya Janata Party has taken center stage at the expense of the long-dominant Congress Party (Kapur and Mehta 1999).

There is, moreover, at least one clear case of state change in the region. According to a number of specialists, the Indonesian state that for almost five decades was based on patrimonialism and authoritarianism, a dominant military, and weak social forces and institutions has come to an end. In its place a new state has emerged: an Indonesia with true democratic institutions and new and influential social forces. The geographic configuration of the Indonesian state is in flux as well, with the separation of East Timor and threatening separatist activities in Aceh and Irian Jaya (Mackie 1999: 123–41; Bird 1999).

With respect to the Asian maritime scene, the quest for identity implies that states will claim or defend islands and maritime areas that are linked to sources of their identity. In Asia, states presently are defining these identities in terms of their historical extent during times of perceived national grandeur, boundaries associated with an outward as opposed to an inward orientation, and borderlines that link them to certain regions of the world. Some observers doubt that maritime space can serve as a source of identity in the same manner that territorial space has for the past three hundred years (Buzan 1978: 45). It must be recognized, though, that the 1982 United Nations Convention on the Law of the Sea (UNCLOS) will "ensure that to a greater extent than ever before the sea will be conceived as an extension of the land" (Booth 1985: 37). In other words, the "parcelization" of the sea implies that "greater meaning will be invested in the new boundaries. . . . Nations will feel protective and sensitive—indeed patriotic—about these patches" (p. 45). Moreover, the socialization of Asian elites and people through government propaganda, training, and education, the development of new military doctrines that stress the significance of the sea, institutional efforts—such as ASEAN regional workshops and Council for Security Cooperation in the Asia Pacific (CSCAP) declaratory initiatives—a reduction in the salience of land boundary problems, and new understandings of power all compound the identity effects of UNCLOS.

The history of some states in the region—Malaysia, India, Indonesia, and Vietnam—as colonial dependencies of other states intensifies their concern over the protection of their domains. Furthermore, the exploitation that many of these countries suffered under Western imperialism or the aggressiveness of others such as Japan—China is a good example—magnifies their natural sensitivity to any encroachment on their perceived rights. Although maritime boundaries do not constitute the state in the sense of land borders, UNCLOS makes it abundantly clear that in the contemporary era maritime boundaries do provide a basis for states to claim rights and assert legal jurisdiction. Consequently, states have begun to pay more attention to the need to assert their sovereignty over islands and maritime boundaries (Valencia 1996: 91). It is not surprising, therefore, to see Asian states placing greater stress on flying the flag. They have begun to describe the movement of foreign ships through their territorial waters as invasions and are displaying increased sensitivity to the movement of foreign vessels in their waters even if those ships are simply passing through their exclusive economic zones (EEZs) (Booth 1985: 40–42). Finally, Asian states, across the board, are attempting to modernize and improve their navies to protect islands and maritime areas they regard as theirs. (See, for example, Ji 1999: 162.)

This strong concern over sovereignty has further implications. First, it makes it more difficult to resolve overlapping island and maritime claims (Ninh 1998: 457). Second, it pushes states to take a more restrictive attitude toward navigation rights in territorial seas, archipelagic waters, and international transit straits, which has implications for SLOC security. Third, it encourages each country to send its navy on patrols, survey missions, and the like. Fourth, it makes it harder for states in the region to accept joint development schemes that afford multiple parties an opportunity to exploit maritime resources.

The problem of uncoordinated state behavior is pervasive in Asia. Commentators report that states such as Burma, Indonesia, South Korea, Thailand, and Vietnam do not have full autonomy from their militaries. (See, respectively, Than 1998; Anwar 1998; Moon 1998; Wattanayagorn 1998; Ninh 1998.) Analysts of Indonesian politics report that President Abdurrahman Wahid's vacillating policies toward Irian Jaya and Aceh and his inability to control military elements in these areas demonstrated his government's lack of control over its troops (*Economist* 2000: 50). Observers of the political scene in China point to secession struggles, the absence of formal institutional mechanisms for the allocation of political authority, and battles over economic policy as factors that bolster the already impressive influence of the People's Liberation Army (PLA). This power has allowed it to sell missile equipment to Pakistan—contrary to the wishes of the Ministry of Foreign Affairs—and to press for a more aggressive policy in the South China Sea (Lewis et al. 1991; Lewis and Hua 1992; Garver 1992).

A lack of state control could affect the region's maritime security order in several ways. First, it could empower navies as power brokers which in turn could give navies leverage to press for new or more aggressive island and maritime claims. Alternatively, navies could use their leverage to press for modernization or expansion, which could threaten SLOCs and spur other states to improve their naval capabilities. Second, inadequate control could drive adolescent states to covet or aggressively protect economically valuable maritime spaces to ensure that they can deliver economic goods and secure popular support. Third, it may permit government units to engage in deviant behavior, including piracy.

One might not devote so much attention to Asia's adolescent states except for the fact that so many of them are well armed. China, for instance, has enlarged or modernized its navy by acquiring antisubmarine warfare capabilities, replacing older vessels, purchasing and developing missiles, improving ports, and enhancing naval air capabilities (Till 1996: 337; USNI 1998; IISS 1999; Ji 1999; Kim 2000). Financially strapped states like the Philippines, by contrast, have had to concentrate their modest resources on the acquisition of smaller ships like guided-missile patrol craft and patrol boats. The Asian financial crisis placed additional constraints on such countries and forced some of them to cancel procurement contracts and reduce defense spending (USNI 1998: 596–601; Thayer 2000b: 7–9). Overall, the strong are getting stronger while the weak are getting weaker—and this trend is likely to continue. Only a select group of states will have the eco-

nomic means to buy the technically advanced naval equipment needed to defend
EEZs and SLOCs.

In sum, then, adolescence may have a number of consequential effects on
Asia's maritime setting. First, it may intensify claims to resource-rich maritime
areas. Second, it may create a strong concern for control over SLOCs. Third, it
may produce a higher incidence of piracy. Beyond these effects, adolescence may
make it more difficult to resolve the area's territorial and maritime controversies
and may spur the further militarization of the area's waters. It is true, of course,
that mature states (e.g., Japan) covet resource-rich waters, worry about SLOCs,
or act obstinately about their island and maritime claims. The point of the preceding section, though, is not that adolescent states are the only states that create
challenges for Asia's maritime security order, but rather that they are noteworthy
because they have multiple impulses vis-à-vis boundaries and more intense interests than other states. The next section surveys a mix of Asian island and maritime boundary disputes.[3]

Maritime Disputes

There is an abundance of ongoing territorial and maritime disputes in Asia
such as the South China Sea controversy, the South Korean–Japanese quarrel
over Liancourt Rocks (Tok-do/Takeshima), and the Indian-Bangladeshi dispute
over New Moore Island. (On these disputes see Prescott 1985: 176, 217–30; Valencia 1991, 1995; Ball 1993–94: 88–89; U.S. GAO 1995; Prescott 1995–96; Paik 1996;
Smith and Thomas 1998a: 58–60.) Changes at the international and domestic levels in the 1970s and 1980s provided a permissive context for or spurred many of
these conflicts. First, the end of the cold wars in Asia (between the United States
and the USSR, China and the USSR, and Cambodia/ASEAN and Vietnam) gave
states an opportunity to turn their attention to other issues. Second, technological improvements made it feasible to exploit the ocean to a greater extent than
previously possible. Third, the rapid growth of Asian states in this period increased their need to use the sea as a transport artery, source of resources, and
avenue for economic development. Finally, the emergence of UNCLOS had a
powerful impact because it gave states new rights and a basis for claiming rights
already thought to exist (Buzan 1978: 1, 38; Sohn and Gustafson 1984: iii–v; Koh
1986: 33–37).

I concentrate here on UNCLOS because of its importance to Asia's maritime
security order. UNCLOS not only created or magnified many maritime disputes
in the region but also shapes the legal and normative discourse on the area's

---

[3]The Russo-Japanese dispute over the Kurile Islands/Northern Territories is covered in Chapter 11 in this volume.

maritime affairs. Subsequently we will take a theoretically informed look at the myriad of island and maritime boundary disputes in the area—especially the South China Sea controversy because of its prominence, the number of countries involved, and the fact that this dispute, aside from those involving Cambodia and Vietnam, has resulted in the most militarized conflict among Asian states.

The Law of the Sea and UNCLOS III

UNCLOS, which came into force in 1994, created a number of zones of jurisdiction such as the internal waters, the territorial sea, the contiguous zone, the continental shelf, and the EEZ—all of which extend from a state's baselines.[4] With respect to the territorial sea, UNCLOS allows states to claim a 12-mile territorial sea in which they have full sovereignty over the sea, the airspace over the sea, and the seabed and substratum within the sea. Regarding the contiguous zone, UNCLOS permits states to claim a 24-mile contiguous zone where they can exercise the control necessary to prevent violations of customs, fiscal, and immigration laws, as well as laws established for the territorial sea (Sohn and Gustafson 1984: 113). UNCLOS also endows states with the right to declare a 200-mile EEZ. In this zone states possess sovereign rights to explore, exploit, conserve, and manage all living and nonliving resources of the seabed, its subsoil, and superjacent waters. In addition, they have certain rights to construct, operate, and maintain artificial islands, installations, and structures and to control research (Sohn and Gustafson 1984: 121, 142–46; Forbes 1995: 78–79, 81). With respect to the continental shelf, UNCLOS gives states the right to explore and exploit the seabed and subsoil of the continental shelf in an area beyond that afforded by provisions concerning the EEZ.[5] Guidelines also give states unrestricted control over the natural resources of the continental shelf (Sohn and Gustafson 1984: 158–59; Forbes 1995: 78).

UNCLOS significantly enlarges the amount of water and continental shelf over which states can claim territorial sovereignty, exercise powers to protect their sovereign rights, and control natural resources. Since islands offer countries a basis from which to claim territorial seas, EEZs, and continental shelves, it is not

[4]Baselines represent "the starting point for measuring the breadth of the various jurisdictional zones" (Forbes 1995: 62). In general, they follow the low-water mark or low-tide elevation along the coast, though in cases of coastal indentation states can use straight baselines that connect two appropriate points along the coast. There are, however, special rules for baselines for rivers, bays, islands, harbor structures, and archipelagic states (Sohn and Gustafson 1984: chap. 3).

[5]A continental shelf is defined as the seabed and subsoil of the submarine areas that extend beyond a state's territorial sea throughout the natural prolongation of its land territory to the outer edge of the continental margin, or to a distance of 200 miles from the state's baselines. The continental shelf, however, cannot exceed 350 miles from the state's baselines or 100 miles from the 2,500-m isobath (Sohn and Gustafson 1984: 157).

surprising that Asian states acquired a powerful interest in claiming and exerting control over the region's islands, no matter how small or economically inconsequential.[6] Overall, then, UNCLOS made it more likely that states will quarrel over islands. Moreover, it increased the potential for conflict over maritime boundaries. The right to declare a 200-mile EEZ, for example, put opposite or adjacent coastal states on the road to conflict by empowering them to make overlapping maritime claims. Finally, UNCLOS created new naval missions and hence a basis for the acquisition of destabilizing naval capabilities (Forbes 1995: 79; Kim 2000: 18). Although these consequences are serious, UNCLOS is not responsible for all of the region's maritime problems. Even before UNCLOS, states saw worth in certain islands and waters (Smith and Thomas 1998b: 15–16). Furthermore, UNCLOS helps to maintain Asia's maritime security order, though its value should not be exaggerated.

Island and Maritime Disputes

Table 12.1 demonstrates that many island quarrels and maritime controversies in Asia, whether relating to sea boundaries or to the appropriate extent of continental shelves and EEZs, have a resource or economic dimension.

Material concerns, though, are hardly the sole drivers of these disputes. A number of contested areas involve questions of national identity. Indonesia's national identity, for instance, is grounded in the "idea of *Wawasan Nusantara,* or Archipelagic Outlook . . . [with] all of the [Indonesian] islands and the seas in between . . . regarded as forming one indivisible entity" (Anwar 1998: 486). The Diaoyu/Senkaku Islands dispute between China and Japan is related to China's search for a new national identity—specifically its effort to portray itself as a nation cleansed of all the vestiges of a century of national humiliation. Moreover, the quarrel pertains to China's definition of itself as an entity that is, in part, anti-Japan (Blanchard 2000: 122). The Tok-do/Takeshima controversy between South Korea and Japan is linked to national identity concerns too. On February 1, 1996, for instance, a South Korean foreign ministry official stated: "Tok-to cannot be subject to any diplomatic negotiations or review by the International Court of Justice inasmuch as it is an integral part of Korean territory historically, geographically, and legally" (IBRU n.d.).

---

[6]All islands do not matter equally in terms of the rights they afford a state. Small islands or rocks that cannot sustain human habitation or economic life, for example, have only a territorial sea and contiguous zone. Artificially created islands do not afford a territorial sea, EEZ, or continental shelf (Sohn and Gustafson 1984: 46–47; Charney 1995: 732–34). There is an important political dimension to this issue. Specifically, the "appropriateness" of rights conveyed by ownership of an island depends on its size, its proximity (to both the putative owner and its neighbors), and its political status (is it an independent country?) (Smith and Thomas 1998b: 1, 18–25).

TABLE 12.1
Resource and Economic Dimensions of Select Island and
Maritime Disputes in the Asia Pacific

Resource or Dispute	Disputants	Economic Issue
New Moore Island[a]	India and Bangladesh	Oil
Narcondam Islands[b]	India and Burma (Myanmar)	Energy
Pattani Trough and Gulf of Thailand (sea boundary and continental shelf)[c]	Cambodia and Thailand	Oil and gas
Gulf of Thailand (sea boundaries, continental shelves, EEZs)[d]	Vietnam and Cambodia; Thailand and Malaysia; Thailand and Vietnam; Vietnam, Thailand, Malaysia; Vietnam, Cambodia, Thailand	Oil, gas, fish
Diaoyu/Senkaku Islands[e]	China and Japan	Oil, fish, SLOCs
Tok-do/Takeshima[f]	South Korea and Japan	Oil and fish
Yellow Sea (continental shelf)[g]	China, Japan, South Korea	Oil and fish

[a]Roy-Chaudhury (1999).
[b]Prescott (1985: 176–78).
[c]IBRU (n.d.).
[d]Valencia (1991); Thao (1997); IBRU (n.d.).
[e]Blanchard (2000: 95); Dzurek (2000: 409).
[f]IBRU (n.d.).
[g]Ji (1995).

The desire to guard sovereignty is another factor influencing the dynamics of Asia's maritime setting. The controversy between Singapore and Malaysia over the ownership of Pedra Branca/Pulau Batu Putih, for example, has clear sovereignty overtones. Indeed, a member of Singapore's parliament declared that joint administration of the island by Singapore and Malaysia "would be tantamount to giving part of the country's territory away" (IBRU n.d.). Remarks by both Chinese and Vietnamese officials in April 1998 show that sovereignty considerations affect the dispute over the Paracel Islands (IBRU n.d.). For many, the Diaoyu/Senkaku Islands quarrel is an emotional sovereignty issue whether or not its putative energy resources are ever realized (Till 1996: 332; Blanchard 2000). As shown by Foreign Ministry statements and the rhetoric of members of the South Korean and Japanese parliaments, the Tok-do/Takeshima quarrel too is related to matters of national sovereignty (IBRU n.d.).

Logic and history lead us to expect disputes over islands and the sea when resources are involved, when islands and maritime spaces represent sources of national identity, or when turf is at stake. The preceding survey confirms these expectations. In addition, the details of these disputes show that the most sensitive controversies seem to be those in which all three factors—resources, national identity, and sovereignty—are involved. Among such controversies are the Cambodian-Vietnamese disagreements over island and maritime rights, the Sino-

Vietnamese dispute over the Paracel Islands, and the Sino-Japanese quarrel over the Diaoyu/Senkaku Islands. In line with this chapter's argument, the historical record of Asia's island and maritime disputes indicates that Asia's more adolescent states—China, the Philippines, and Vietnam—are some of the more aggressive claimants to the islands and maritime areas cited here.

Rivalry over the South China Sea

The South China Sea Islands lie in Asia's largest sea and encompass several major island groups, including the Spratlys, Pratas, Paracels, and Macclesfield Bank groups. Very few of the more than 200 features (islands, rocks, and reefs) in the South China Sea are of any notable size, and almost none can sustain human life. At present there are four major trouble spots in the South China Sea. First, China, Indonesia, and Vietnam dispute the northern waters off Indonesia's Natuna Islands. Second, China and Vietnam have yet to definitely settle their quarrel about the Gulf of Tonkin.[7] Third, China, Taiwan, and Vietnam contest the Paracels. And fourth, Brunei, China, Malaysia, the Philippines, Taiwan, and Vietnam challenge each other's claims to the Spratlys: China, Taiwan, and Vietnam claim all the islands in this group; the Philippines and Brunei claim areas adjacent to their mainland territory. To buttress their position against other states, claimants have erected structures and markers, stationed garrisons, and sent military forces into contested areas. (See Prescott 1985: 209–11, 218–21; Gallagher 1994: 172; Valencia 1995: 6, 8–10; Till 1996: 330–34; Catley and Keliat 1997: 1–9, 25–39.)

The contemporary dispute over the South China Sea began in December 1973 when North Vietnam notified China that it would begin prospecting in the Gulf of Tonkin. In mid-January 1974, the Chinese launched an offensive in the Paracels leading to their capture of all South Vietnamese-held islands in the group, as well as producing a number of Vietnamese casualties and prisoners. In April 1975, North Vietnam seized six islands in the Spratlys that South Vietnam had occupied in February 1974. Only one month later, newly united Vietnam revised its maps to incorporate all the Spratlys. In September, Vietnamese Premier Le Duan raised the issue with the Chinese at an official level for the first time (Garver 1992: 1001–6; Blanchard 1998: 416–29).

In April 1987, the dispute in the South China Sea intensified anew after Vietnam occupied one of the largest reefs in the Spratlys: Barque Canada. China demanded that Vietnam immediately withdraw from it, as well as nine other islands in the archipelago. From late 1987 through early 1988, the PLA Navy (PLAN)

---

[7]China and Vietnam have signed an agreement settling their dispute over maritime boundaries in the Gulf of Tonkin, though the agreement has not yet been ratified.

conducted investigations in order to identify areas where it could construct out-posts. It also stepped up its air patrols. The Vietnamese responded by sending aircraft and warships to watch Chinese construction activities and ships. Al-though there were a number of near clashes between China and Vietnam, it was not until March 14, 1988, that Sino-Vietnamese friction exploded into violence. On that date the PLAN sank three Vietnamese vessels in the vicinity of Johnson Reef, resulting in about seventy Vietnamese dead. In April the Chinese took fur-ther steps to consolidate their control by planting flags and occupying six reefs in the area. Two months later, the PLAN established China's first permanent mili-tary post in the Spratlys. (See Gallagher 1994: 172; Till 1996: 331; Catley and Keliat 1997: 82; Studeman 1998: 4–5; Ji 1999: 218–20.)

In 1992, the Chinese took new measures to bolster their position in the Sprat-lys. In the beginning of the year, China sent to the Spratlys a huge inspection group that placed a marker and raised a monument. On February 25, China's National People's Congress (NPC) passed a territorial sea law claiming sover-eignty over the South China Sea and authorizing the use of force to keep out for-eign naval and research vessels. In March, Chinese forces landed on a reef (Da Ba Dau) near a Vietnamese island, which led to a clash on March 19. In July, China sent additional troops to the islands in the Spratlys it had occupied, and it landed troops to erect a sovereignty marker on a Vietnamese-claimed reef. China also contracted with an American firm, Crestone Energy Corporation, to explore in a concession not far from the Vietnamese coast (Valencia 1995: 13–14; Catley and Keliat 1997: 82–83; Studeman 1998: 5–6). China was not the only country on the move in the first half of the 1990s. In July 1994, for example, the Philippines hired an American company to undertake oil exploration in the eastern Spratlys. Two months later, the Philippines captured a number of Chinese fishermen who had tried to set up residence on the islands they claimed. Five months afterward, the Chinese retaliated by arresting 35 Filipino fishermen.

In the beginning of 1995, the tit for tat between China and the Philippines es-calated after China seized Mischief Reef (Meijijiao or Panganiban), an area close to the Philippines. The Chinese seizure caused the Philippines to increase its na-val patrols in disputed areas, arrest yet more Chinese fishermen, remove Chinese structures, destroy Chinese markers, and expand military facilities on its Kalayaan Islands. The Mischief Reef incident was seminal because it represented the first time China took action against an ASEAN member (Hyer 1994: 18; Va-lencia 1995: 44–47; Dzurek 1995; Austin 1998: 87–90). Following the Mischief Reef incident, there were sporadic encounters over the Spratlys but no major violence. In 1996, for example, there was an unexplained clash between the Philippine navy and PRC ships northwest of Manila. In 1997, the Philippines and China clashed over Scarborough Shoal (Huangyan Island) in the Macclesfield Bank group, which the Philippines claimed for the first time. Scarborough is special because it is the only above-water feature in China's claimed Zhongsha Islands. The Philippines forced Chinese ships away, tore down Chinese markers, and placed its flag on contested areas. In late October 1998, the Philippines discovered that China was building fortifications on Mischief Reef using armed military supply ships. Subsequently it detained 20 Chinese fishermen and impounded their boats. In May 1999, the Philippine navy sank a Chinese fishing vessel (Valencia 1999; Zou 1999: 73–76). On a positive note, the Philippines signed several accords with China in May 2000 that were designed to ease tensions in the South China Sea. The two countries pledged to resolve their differences peacefully and in accord with international law, including UNCLOS. They also agreed not to take any action that might complicate or escalate the situation in the South China Sea.

Thus the history of the South China Sea dispute shows that it has been an active and sometimes explosive controversy. Furthermore, it reveals that although almost all Southeast Asian states claim islands and waters in the area, China, the Philippines, and Vietnam are particularly zealous. Finally, it demonstrates that frictions over territorial and sea boundaries in maritime Asia can erupt in violence with potentially deadly consequences. Why are the countries of the region so vigorously contesting the South China Sea islands and waters? And why are China, the Philippines, and Vietnam such aggressive claimants?

Analysts of the South China Sea traditionally direct their attention to its economic value. They observe, for example, that the seabed around the Spratly and Paracel Islands may be rich in oil, gas, and sea-based minerals. (See Till 1996: 332; Catley and Keliat 1997: 11; Kim 2000: 69.) They also highlight that the South China Sea is one of the richest fishing grounds in the world. Hence it can provide not only nutrition to Asian countries but also an exportable good to the region's seafood consumers. Moreover, it is widely acknowledged that the South China Sea is economically important because it straddles critical SLOCs between the Middle East and Northeast Asia. (See Roy 1994: 163–64; Gallagher 1994: 171; Ong and Hamzah 1996: 29; Till 1996: 332–33; Catley and Keliat 1997: 1, 3, 11, 47, 50–60; Kim 2000: xiii.)[8]

The South China Sea's importance as a source of national identity also warrants consideration. Several analysts have pointed out, for instance, that recovery of the South China Sea appears to offer Chinese leaders a means to erase a century of national humiliation by allowing them to establish new borders that are not associated with China's period of dismemberment and exploitation at the hands of foreign powers (Garver 1992: 1020; Valencia 1995: 16). A number of commentators,

[8]In reality, key SLOCs are generally quite distant from the bulk of the features in the South China Sea, though actual distances depend on which features are under consideration. Scarborough Shoal, for instance, is close to important shipping lanes.

moreover, have highlighted the importance of the South China Sea in terms of sovereignty. Focusing on China, Chen Jie (1994: 892) states: "It is embedded in the . . . national psyche that the Spratly archipelago has been part of the motherland's territory since ancient times." Indeed, the PLA tends not to write about the dispute because it is seen as a "domestic issue" (Shambaugh 1999–2000: 74).

In sum, then, a host of Asian states assert ownership of the South China Sea and its islands for a number of reasons: because it is a potentially vast source of living and nonliving resources; because its islands and waters are a source of national identity; and because territory and maritime spaces in the South China Sea have importance for states concerned with protecting their sovereignty. But other issues are in need of clarification. Why is the South China Sea dispute more problematic than other maritime controversies? And why do some countries assert their claims more aggressively, both in word and in deed, than others? The answers to both of these questions lie in the argument about adolescence. Since adolescent states need resources, seek sources of national identity, and are zealous in protecting their sovereignty, we would expect claimant states to be highly reluctant to cede their claims or make concessions. After all, the South China Sea is associated with not just one of these coveted attributes but all of them. Moreover, the most aggressive states seem to be the countries that are most adolescent. To illustrate: China is growing rapidly, working to achieve its national identity, fervent in protecting its sovereignty, and not in full control over itself. Similarly, Vietnam is growing rapidly; its sense of self is evolving; and it is extremely vigorous in defending its sovereignty. The Philippines too has a serious appetite for economic values, a tumultuous national identity, and a lack of complete control over its corpus.

Overall, then, the implications of adolescence for the area's maritime scene are not good. Adolescence suggests there will be disputes over islands and maritime boundaries, a lack of compromise, and disrupted SLOCs. It also suggests a possibility of militarized conflict. Adolescence, however, does not take place in a vacuum. As discussed in a later section on pathways to order, there are several options for maintaining order in maritime Asia. Some pathways can contain the negative spillover that adolescence creates; others have the potential to transform adolescent states by pushing them along the path to mature statehood.

The Struggle over SLOCs

Asia's SLOCs connect the Middle East and the Indian Ocean with Southeast Asia, Southeast Asia with Northeast Asia, and Northeast Asia with North America. Free and open SLOCs, therefore, are vital to the countries of the region. They are vital because many Asian states are trade-oriented and a significant and growing percentage of this trade is carried in ships. In addition, Asian states are major shipping nations in terms of tonnage and volume of trade handled at their ports. Furthermore, Asian states import significant quantities of energy, food-stuffs, and minerals. (See Swinnerton 1994; Weeks 1998; Lee 1998: 3–4; Song 1999: 12; U.S. EIA 2000; Ji 2000: 2–5, 9–11; Kim 2000: 35.) Finally, Asian navies need free and open SLOCs to perform their missions such as securing disputed islands and maritime spaces.

At present a variety of factors can hinder use of the area's SLOCs: territorial and maritime quarrels, the conflict over Taiwan (which could lead to the mining of SLOCs or missile attacks on shipping), piracy, naval rivalries, and domestic insta-bility. The other noteworthy problem for the region's SLOCs is differing interpre-tations of UNCLOS, which, on the one hand, gives foreign ships and aircraft cer-tain rights of passage (innocent, transit, and archipelagic sea-lane passage) through or over territorial seas, straits used for international navigation, and archipelagic waters, and endows vessels with freedom of navigation in the contiguous zone, the EEZ, and on the high seas. On the other hand, UNCLOS allows states to establish certain rules and regulations for foreign vessels. (See Sohn and Gustafson 1984: 121–22; 126–27; Forbes 1995: 72–73; Rothwell 1996: 80–84; Weeks 1998: 3; Amer 1998: 88–93.)[9] Given the competing nature of these rights, their correct interpretation is a source of heated debate. There are disagreements, for example, about whether or not submarines need to surface when in international straits, about the rules that should be applied to ships transiting archipelagic waters, and about notification and authorization requirements for military exercises within another state's EEZ (Buzan 1978: 41; Amer 1998: 93–94; Ji 2000: 7–8). Furthermore, the Philippines does not accept the regime of archipelagic sea-lane passage, contending that its ar-chipelagic waters are internal waters (Amer 1998: 93–94).

Controversies over the interpretation of UNCLOS provisions are more than arcane legal debates; they are emotion-laden political and security issues. To

---

[9]According to UNCLOS, "innocent passage" occurs when a vessel goes through a territorial sea or is transiting to or from internal waters and a territorial sea. Innocent passage must be continu-ous and expeditious and cannot present a threat to peace, order, and security. Moreover, subma-rines are supposed to surface. Although coastal states are not supposed to hamper innocent pas-sage, they can impose laws and regulations on vessels. Furthermore, they have the right to deny noninnocent passage and to suspend the right of innocent passage when national security is at stake. The regime of innocent passage applies not only to territorial waters but also to straits used for international navigation and archipelagic waters. "Transit passage" applies to straits used for international navigation between the high seas or EEZ or another area. There is freedom of navi-gation for continuous and expeditious passage subject to the laws and regulations of the coastal state that do not delay, hamper, or impair transit. Coastal states cannot suspend the right of transit passage, and the transit passage regime imposes no vessel restrictions. (Submarines, for example, do not have to surface.) Finally, the right of "archipelagic sea-lane passage" affords passage through designated lanes or "normally used" routes in archipelagic waters. Coastal states cannot suspend this right, and there are no vessel restrictions (Amer 1998: 89–93).

demonstrate their strong preference for a regime of innocent as opposed to free passage, for example, both Malaysia and Indonesia threatened in 1972 to close the Strait of Malacca to vessels larger than 200,000 tons (Buzan 1978: 41). In 1978 and 1988, Indonesia tried to close the Lombok and Sunda Straits as a way to assert its sovereignty (Till 1996: 330; Ji 2000: 8). Recently China drew archipelagic baselines around the Paracels (Dzurek 1996) that would "remove the enclosed waters from the freedom of navigation regime" and subject foreign warships to an authorization requirement (Valencia 2000).

Because of its dependence on the sea for food, energy, and commerce, Japan is highly concerned about the security of SLOCs. This concern has pushed it in several directions. First, it has sought to develop military capabilities commensurate with its goal of protecting SLOCs up to 1,000 miles from Japan. Second, it recently hosted an international conference on SLOCs. Third, it has assumed a higher diplomatic profile. During the 1995 Mischief Reef controversy between China and the Philippines, for instance, Japan called for restraint and peaceful settlement, while stressing its interest in the safety of sea-lanes in the South China Sea (Dzurek 1995: 69; Kim 2000: 168–77). China too is concerned about threats to SLOCs because of its large foreign trade, need for imported energy, and growing maritime industries. Hence it has signed a number of bilateral maritime transport agreements and issued statements supporting freedom of navigation in the South China Sea (Ji 2000: 11–12).

There is no doubt that Asia's SLOCs are important. It is open to question, however, whether they are at risk to the extent some believe or whether the closure of SLOCs would be as devastating as some assert it would be. With respect to the former, conflicts over the Spratly Islands should not have much of an effect on SLOCs because sailors avoid the area and key shipping routes are distant from the islands; similarly, major sea-lanes are not close to Taiwan (Dzurek 1995: 66; Weeks 1998: 2). With respect to the latter, it is not clear that a rerouting of ships would be impossible or impose crushing burdens. Many ships that normally sail through the Strait of Malacca, for instance, could go through the Lombok or Sunda Straits. In the event of a major crisis in the South China Sea or around Indonesia, ships could travel around Indonesia and even the Philippines (United Kingdom 1987: chaps. 9–10; Ji 2000: 2–3). If a ship opted for Lombok rather than Malacca, it would only have to travel 150 more miles and would take only four more days to make the trip from the Middle East to Shanghai or Yokohama (Swinnerton 1994; Ji 2000: 3). Although operating costs would undoubtedly increase, Swinnerton estimates it would be by only 8.5 to 13.5 percent—noteworthy but hardly disastrous.

Adolescence influences the security of the region's SLOCs both directly and indirectly. First, adolescent states are likely to patrol their SLOCs more aggressively than mature states because of the paramount importance of asserting sovereignty. Second, countries that rely on their naval forces to maintain control are likely to modernize their navies in such a way as to threaten the freedom of SLOCs. Finally, to the extent that adolescence affects either the existence or the intensity of state claims to Asian islands and maritime boundaries, it also affects the security of SLOCs.

Piracy

Although piracy is an increasing global problem, it is especially noteworthy in Southeast Asia and East Asia. Analysts describe the waters of the region as some of the "most dangerous on earth" and one of "two hot-spots of vessel attacks"— the other being Africa. (See Till 1996: 329; Kellerman 1999: 3, 8; U.S. EIA 2000; Gottschalk and Flanagan 2000: 23–27, 63, 86; Kim 2000: 33.) There are regular reports of incidents in the Malacca and Singapore Straits, around Indonesian and Filipino ports, and in the Hong Kong–Luzon–Hainan zone (Weeks 1998: 2; Kellerman 1999; Gottschalk and Flanagan 2000: 73–74).

For the same reasons they are worried about SLOCs, the Japanese are quite alarmed about piracy. In April 2000, at the first Regional Conference on Combating Piracy and Armed Robbery Against Ships, which Japan proposed and hosted, Tetsuma Esaki, Japan's senior state secretary for foreign affairs, made this concern manifest: "Piracy not only poses a threat to the transportation routes of Japan . . . [but] could also have a major impact on the social stability and economic prosperity of the entire region" (MOFA 2000). This concern is not surprising given that a representative of the Japanese Navy reported that sixty Japanese ships had been "chased, inspected, fired upon, or otherwise threatened" in the period between 1991 and 1995 (Kim 2000: 33).

Piracy represents a real threat to mariners, their personal property, and their cargoes. It also may threaten the freedom of SLOCs (Ji 2000: 10). Nevertheless, piracy is more of a nuisance than a serious economic threat. In fact, piracy-related losses in maritime Asia probably run under $40 million annually. Moreover, piracy affects only a trivial amount of overall shipping traffic and cargo volumes (Till 1996: 329; Gottschalk and Flanagan 2000: 86–93). Furthermore, much piracy is directed against ships in ports or internal waters rather than in international shipping lanes (MOFA 2000). Finally, piracy in international waterways seems to be on the decline (Kim 2000: 34). Even so, piracy could become a major political as well as economic problem if it became linked with terrorism or separatist activities. The seizure and destruction, by terrorists or separatists, of a tanker in port carrying liquid natural gas would be a true catastrophe.

Intensified patrolling, joint action by the coast guards of Asian states, and even economic growth have worked in the past to put a dent in the number of piracy incidents, as well as to minimize its consequences—such as the amount of violence directed against ship crews (Weeks 1998: 3; U.S. EIA 2000). But piracy will continue to be a problem worthy of attention so long as there are adolescent states in the region. Adolescent states like China and Indonesia often lack full control over their navies and agencies (customs, coast guard, police), which means that these personnel sometimes get involved in maritime robberies, hijackings, or kidnappings. (See Till 1996: 329; Kellerman 1999: 12; Ji 2000: 13; Kim 2000: 34; Gottschalk and Flanagan 2000: 116.) Moreover, adolescent states frequently have problems with ethnic groups (Muslim separatists in the Philippines, for instance) that attack shipping to finance their activities, gain publicity, or cause trouble for local authorities (Kellerman 1999: 9; Gottschalk and Flanagan 2000: 115–16).

Pathways to Order

There are many conceivable paths to ensuring Asia's maritime security order. These options, many of which are specified in Chapter 1 of this volume or are analyzed by contributors to this volume, include balance of power, multilateral organizations, and nongovernmental organizations. Other devices include multilateral dialogues and international arbitration, as well as defense white papers and military exchanges. (See, for example, Kim 1999: 66–70; Kim 2000: 149–53.) States may even pursue unilateral options to prevent or manage conflict in maritime Asia. In 1977, for instance, when Japan passed a law establishing a 200-mile exclusive fishing zone, it opted not to apply the law to Chinese and South Korean nationals and chose not to extend the zone beyond its territorial sea in the west (UN DOALOS 1994: 71; Valencia 1996: 107). Here we focus on three specific policy options—U.S. hegemony, global regimes, and regional regimes—because countries in the region have used these pathways and observers often highlight these options as some of the most promising ones. Below we examine their positive and negative attributes—especially their ability to contain or transform adolescence, to protect the security of SLOCs, and to eradicate piracy.

American Hegemony

After the end of World War II, the United States emerged as a hegemon in Asia. As noted in Chapter 4, it used its tremendous military, political, and economic resources to contain the Soviet Union and China, to push its preferred liberal economic and political order, and to achieve other objectives in line with its preferences. American hegemony in the region manifested itself in a variety of forms, including a major military presence, a network of bilateral alliances and bases, and strong support for liberal political and economic institutions. The end of the Cold War signaled the continuation rather than a rejection of these elements. The United States plans to maintain a military presence of approximately 100,000 troops in the region. It is also working to strengthen its alliances with Japan, South Korea, and Australia and has signed several access arrangements with Asian countries. Finally, it continues to conduct bilateral and multilateral military exercises on a frequent basis. Despite these continuities, the American strategy in the post–Cold War era has incorporated several new elements: support for multilateral ventures such as the Asia Pacific Economic Cooperation (APEC) forum, ASEAN, the ASEAN Regional Forum (ARF); engagement with China; and backing for transparency and confidence-building measures such as military exchanges. Furthermore, maritime territorial issues have jumped onto the U.S. security agenda. The United States now stresses its commitment to freedom of navigation in the region, as well as to secure SLOCs. (See U.S. DOS 1997; U.S. DOD 1998; Weeks and Meconis 1999: 17–29, chap. 2.)

Alagappa (Introduction), Mastanduno (Chap. 4 in this volume), and Danzig (1997: 6–8) observe that U.S. hegemony has contributed to the maritime security order in Asia. They argue that it has contained the Sino-Japanese rivalry, ensured the security of the region's smaller states, and facilitated the management of crises (between China and Taiwan, for instance) that could spill over into Asia's maritime scene. They also assert that American hegemony has helped to maintain order in the region by reducing the incentives to build powerful navies that could secure SLOCs and counter the modernization activities of other states. Furthermore, they allege that American hegemony has deterred states from aggression since aggression is likely to be counterproductive if challenged by the United States.

In the near term it is reasonable to expect American hegemony to continue to dampen problems created or fueled by the region's adolescent states. Certainly the U.S. Pacific Fleet's unmatched arsenal of nuclear and conventional carriers, guided missile destroyers and frigates, nuclear attack submarines, and fighter bombers (Weeks and Meconis 1999: 134–56) is a powerful guarantee that SLOCs will stay open. Even though the United States is officially neutral on disputes like the Sino-Japanese quarrel over the Diaoyu/Senkaku Islands and the multinational disagreement over the South China Sea, America's hegemonic position helps to ensure that these disputes take place within certain confines. After all, any aggressor has to take into account the fact that American defense treaties with the Philippines and Japan may obligate the United States to assist these countries in the event they are attacked in the disputed islands (IBC 1998). Furthermore, through its unmatched influence in international and regional economic organizations and regimes, the United States has the ability to further, if only indirectly, the resource acquisition and economic development activities of Asian states. Finally, American power ensures that piracy will never become anything more than a minor nuisance in the region.

Although it has value as a containment device, American hegemony does not transform adolescence in any way. It does not directly satiate the desire of the region's states for resources. Nor does it temper their zeal for protecting their sovereignty, give them a valued source of identity, or increase their control over their constituent parts. Indeed, one of the major flaws of this pathway is that it has trouble accommodating the identity demands of countries such as China, India, and Russia that crave status and decision-making responsibilities. Although American hegemony is likely to make a continued contribution to the stability of the region's maritime scene, in the long run American domestic politics may make the hegemon less willing to keep a lid on those forces that threaten Asia's maritime security order. The possible demise of American hegemony greatly elevates the importance of other pathways to order.

Global Regimes

International legal scholars embrace the view that UNCLOS represents a viable path to protecting the region's maritime security order (Rothwell 1996: 8). For instance, Koh (1986: 43–44) contends that UNCLOS contributes "to the promotion of international peace, by replacing a plethora of conflicting claims by coastal states with universally agreed limits for the territorial sea, the contiguous zone, the exclusive economic zone, and the continental shelf." Others assert that UNCLOS represents a path to order because of its conflict resolution provisions and its calls for cooperative action and the peaceful resolution of disputes (Rothwell 1996: 88–89). Specifically UNCLOS declares that opposite or adjacent countries have an obligation to mutually delimit their EEZs and continental shelves or, failing such agreement, to enter into provisional arrangements pending the final settlement of such boundaries. Furthermore, in the absence of objections to dispute settlement provisions for conflicts existing prior to the disputants' entry into UNCLOS, signatories are obliged to pursue third-party settlement (Sohn and Gustafson 1984: 63, 77).

To date, all Asian states with the exception of Cambodia, Thailand, and North Korea have signed and ratified UNCLOS. Hence it would seem to have promise as a device for maintaining order. Furthermore, many countries in the region see it as offering a framework they can use to handle navigational, shipping, and communication issues (Amer 1998: 94–96). With respect to the issue of adolescence, UNCLOS, as a source of norms and rules, can help channel the behavior of the region's adolescent states in the right direction. Hence it has the potential to contribute to the management (as opposed to elimination) of disputes over island and maritime boundaries. Moreover, it can help to ensure the freedom of the region's SLOCs—which, to some degree, improves the chances that the resource needs of the region's states can be met.

Despite these positive aspects, studies prepared by the United Nations and others show that compliance with UNCLOS is spotty. Although most states in the region have proclaimed straight baselines in conformity with the convention, in a number of cases the baselines are vague or based on a loose interpretation of UNCLOS rules (Prescott 1985: 212; Valencia 1991: 1158; Dzurek 1996; Kawasaki-Urabe and Forbes 1996–97: 93). And although no country in the region claims more than a 12-mile territorial sea, many states have "security zones" extending beyond the 24-mile contiguous zone that UNCLOS allows (UN DOALOS 1994: 65–67; Charney 1995: 743; UN General Assembly 1999). If one looks at the archipelagic states of the region (Indonesia and the Philippines), one also sees mixed compliance. On the one hand, Indonesia's baselines and ratio of land to water within the archipelago area are in conformity with UNCLOS. On the other hand, there are questions whether the Philippines is justified in its maritime claims (Prescott 1985: 211; UN DOALOS 1994: 69; Charney 1995: 731–32). Moreover, China has drawn archipelagic baselines around the Paracels although it is not an archipelagic state and its ratio of land to water does not follow UNCLOS guidelines (Charney 1995: 732; Dzurek 1996: 84–85). Finally, states in the region generally ignore UNCLOS restrictions pertaining to the construction, operation, and use of artificial islands, installations, and structures within EEZs (UN DOALOS 1994: 70).

Even if we dismiss these examples of spotty compliance—after all, spotty compliance does not imply the regime's irrelevance—UNCLOS is still quite limited in what it can do. First, its norms and principles are general or vague. Second, it does not supply decisive criteria for evaluating the competing claims of states. Third, the availability of several dispute resolution options in UNCLOS means that states can completely avoid any requirement for third-party intervention and prolong the resolution of disputes. Fourth, the dispute settlement language in UNCLOS does not apply to island disputes. (See Sohn and Gustafson 1984: 241–45; Charney 1995: 725; Ong and Hamzah 1996: 26–27; Thomas and Dzurek 1996: 310; Amer 1998: 94–96.) Finally, UNCLOS encourages and legitimizes claims to the sea and continental shelf that otherwise might not have been made and hence increases the potential for conflict. Beyond these limitations, UNCLOS does not feed the resource hunger of Asian states or give them a source of identity, though it does help them to guard their sovereignty. With respect to the control or elimination of piracy, it cannot contribute anything.

Regional Regimes

Decision makers and analysts have used or proposed a plethora of regional and subregional arrangements to bring order to Asia's maritime scene. (See, for example, Wanandi 1993: 9–15 and Valencia 1995: 63.) To date the best-known multilateral regime for managing the region's maritime security order is the

"ASEAN regime complex."[10] The ASEAN regime complex consists of ASEAN, its norms (peaceful settlement, noninterference, sovereign quality), ASEAN-sponsored institutions such as the ARF, and Track 2 options like the quasi-official workshops on the South China Sea.[11]

In 1992, ASEAN officials took the first steps to give the organization a leading role in regional security issues, including maritime problems, by deciding to initiate dialogues with non-ASEAN states on regional security cooperation and to increase intra-ASEAN dialogues on security cooperation. Thus ASEAN formed the ASEAN-PMC (Post-Ministerial Conference) at which ASEAN members and officials from the European Union, China, Japan, South Korea, the United States, and other countries can discuss economic and security issues. It also established the ARF as a forum for security dialogue among the ASEAN states and their PMC dialogue partners. Furthermore, it formulated principles geared toward stabilizing the maritime security order in the South China Sea. Finally, it has taken steps to increase the military component of interactions among its member states, conceivably to discourage the unilateral acquisition of maritime space. This component includes military exchanges, dialogues, and joint naval exercises.

Drawing upon the work of the 1991 nongovernmental workshop on the South China Sea in Bandung, Indonesia, ASEAN issued the Manila Declaration in 1992. This declaration, which has been periodically reaffirmed by ASEAN, called for the shelving of sovereignty and jurisdictional issues while the relevant states explored opportunities for cooperation in navigation safety, communication, search and rescue, antipiracy operations, marine conservation, and marine scientific research. Moreover, it called for the avoidance of force and the resolution of disputes through dialogue and consultation. In 1995, China's actions in Mischief Reef resulted in the appearance for the first time of the South China Sea dispute on the agenda of the newly formed ARF. Moreover, ASEAN itself challenged China's occupation of Mischief Reef and called for restraint based on the 1992 Manila Declaration.

In 1996, members of ASEAN agreed there should be a regional code of conduct for the South China Sea to permit activities such as scientific research and to

[10]"ASEAN regime complex" is my term. Except as noted, the following discussion is based on Lee (1995: 538–39), Thomas and Dzurek (1996: 311–12), Dosch (1997: 3–6), Denoon and Colbert (1998–99: 512–13), Henderson (1999: 58), AFP (2000a, 2000b, 2000c, 2000d), Thayer (2000c: 65–66), and Thayer (2000a: 70).

[11]Although distinct from ASEAN, CSCAP is another facet of the ASEAN regime complex at the unofficial level. It is linked to the ASEAN regime complex because it has overlapping country membership, its secretariat is in Malaysia, and it aims to maintain close links with the ARF. CSCAP has various working groups that study maritime issues. In 1997, it promulgated "Guidelines for Regional Maritime Cooperation" in order to ease tensions, reduce the risk of conflict, and build an ocean regime consistent with UNCLOS.

facilitate efforts to combat piracy and drug trafficking while putting aside the issue of sovereignty. Over the past five years, ASEAN and Chinese officials have
discussed a code of conduct for the South China Sea. This code of conduct would
cover dispute resolution, confidence-building measures, and cooperation in such
areas as environmental protection. Despite a number of meetings, China and the
ASEAN working group handling the issue have not been able to hammer out a
code of conduct. The various parties have not been able to agree whether the
code would apply to the Paracels. Furthermore, they have not been able to agree
whether China would specifically pledge not to occupy more reefs, shoals, and
islets in the Spratlys.

Indonesia has hosted almost ten "unofficial" workshops and seminars on the
peaceful development of South China Sea resources since 1990, with participation
by academic experts and government officials acting in an informal capacity.
These meetings have led to agreements to conduct technical studies on topics
such as biodiversity in the South China Sea. In addition, they have established the
scientific and technical aspects of a resource management regime, as well as technical working groups on scientific research, resource assessment, and legal matters. They have not, however, spurred any multilateral diplomatic initiatives.
Moreover, it has proved impossible to put conflicting sovereignty claims, except
at the most general level, on the workshop agenda. Finally, it does not appear that
the workshops will be formalized or institutionalized (Valencia 1995: 50–52; Ong
and Hamzah 1996: 35–36; Thomas and Dzurek 1996: 311–13). Ironically, according
to one informed participant in this project, Track 2 is under great pressure and
Indonesia itself has reduced its support for such activities.

As a path to order, the ASEAN regime complex is appealing in a number of
ways. For instance, it has created an institutional identity—the "ASEAN Way"—
based on consultation and dialogue rather than confrontation and unilateralism,
and security is understood to encompass economic and domestic concerns, as well
as traditional external military issues (Dosch 1997: 2–3; Narine 1998: 202; Bessho
1999: chap. 3). This ASEAN identity offers an alternative to states such as Vietnam,
which have traditionally understood their national identity in conventional Westphalian terms. Indeed, by some accounts the ASEAN regime complex has changed
the identities of its members and made friends out of enemies (Simon 1998: 197).
Even if this ASEAN identity is relatively loose, some think the ASEAN regime
complex has the potential to build a sense of community. After all, it encourages
regular government-to-government contacts, as well as the growth of a web of regional links (Narine 1998: 202). The ASEAN regime complex, then, deals head on
with one aspect of adolescence by providing a source of identity.

Moreover, supporters of the ASEAN regime complex note that it has set down
"principles for conflict management in the South China Sea" (Lee 1995: 540). It

helps to identify problems, improve and widen channels of information gathering and dissemination, and facilitate policy coordination. It promotes predictability, empathy, trust, and confidence. It provides these benefits because it establishes norms of behavior, creates transparency, generates confidence-building measures, and provides opportunities for cooperative behavior. (See Valencia 1995: 51; Dosch 1997: 11, 13; Simon 1998: 205; Kim 1999: 70.) In other words, if the ASEAN regime complex fails to transform adolescence, at least it promises to channel it in a more positive direction. If the ASEAN regime complex does indeed produce trust and confidence among its participants, for example, it may reduce the incentives for states to take preemptive action to secure SLOCs or contested islands.

In sum, then, the ASEAN regime complex has many positive attributes, including some that allow it to contain or transform the problem of adolescence. But the activities transpiring under the aegis of the ASEAN regime complex have not led to the resolution of a single boundary controversy in maritime Asia. Furthermore, the ASEAN regime complex has not resulted in an agreement on any concrete measures for dealing with smuggling, piracy, or joint resource development (Simon 1998: 207). Finally, states participating in the ASEAN regime complex continue to take unilateral action despite their pledges to avoid such actions (Valencia 1995: 52). A recent example is the actions of China and the Philippines with respect to Scarborough Shoal (Zou 1999). Nevertheless, there are indications that a concern for the ASEAN regime complex has caused states to tone down their frictions and signs that the ASEAN regime complex has built trust and mutual confidence.

In the long run, the ASEAN regime complex may diminish in value. Many believe, for example, that the Asian financial crisis damaged the ASEAN identity, since ASEAN and its associated institutions proved unable to stop the crisis or buffer it (Denoon and Colbert 1998–99: 505; Ball 1999: 2). Moreover, the ongoing expansion of ASEAN, ASEAN-PMC, and the ARF may dilute the culture of dialogue and consultation—cynics prefer to call it a culture of avoidance—that is integral to the ASEAN identity. The inclination of more democratically minded states like Thailand and the Philippines to put the domestic political affairs of other states on the ASEAN agenda might very well undermine the ASEAN identity (Narine 1998: 209–12; Henderson 1999: chap. 2). Assuming that ASEAN can build a strong sense of identity among its members, it is unclear how this sense of identity would help in cases (India, China) where the states are pursuing identities that are defined in part by great-power status. Finally, the present weakness of Indonesia, which has always played a leadership role in the ASEAN regime complex, is not encouraging.

We have considered a number of pathways to order in the region, including American hegemony and global and regional regimes. Since each of these pathways has certain disadvantages, it may be necessary, in the final analysis, to use a combination of these approaches to stabilize the region's maritime scene. Multiple pathways are preferable because some are more effective at containing adolescence while others have the potential to transform it. In the long run, the potential demise of American hegemony is a serious concern. American hegemony not only imposes powerful constraints on adolescent behavior. It also creates the space in which other mechanisms—such as the ASEAN regime complex—have an opportunity to assist states in becoming mature members of the international community.

Bilateral Arrangements

In lieu of these three pathways, or as a supplement to them, Asian states can deal with the region's maritime issues bilaterally. They can conclude treaties that set sea boundaries, delimit continental shelves, and divide territorial seas. They also can coordinate joint SLOC or antipiracy patrols. Furthermore, they can operate joint fishery or energy development zones. In the late 1960s and through the 1970s, bilateral agreements were indeed a favored instrument. Asian states, particularly India and Indonesia, signed a number of accords that delineated continental shelf and maritime boundaries, regulated fishing, and, in a few cases, created joint exploration and development areas. (See, for example, Prescott 1985; UN DOALOS 1994; Prescott 1995–96; Paik 1996; Valencia 1996; Thao 1997; Roy-Chaudhury 1999; Ball 1999.) Clearly there is a place for bilateral arrangements in the management of the region's maritime security order since states can tailor such arrangements to their specific interests and the specific maritime, continental shelf, or EEZ features at issue. Bilateral arrangements can help by clarifying control over SLOCs and providing for the joint exploration and exploitation of resources. Moreover, such arrangements can satisfy sovereignty concerns by decisively specifying the ownership of islands and maritime boundaries. And they can aid in the fight against piracy: Indonesia and Malaysia, for instance, have conducted joint naval and police exercises, as well as joint patrols along their common borders in the Malacca Strait, and have thereby made a significant dent in the incidence of piracy (Weeks 1998: 7).

Although there are positive aspects to bilateral arrangements, they can be difficult to negotiate. Furthermore, the incentives to conclude such arrangements depend on the global and regional distribution of power, the existence of global and regional regimes, and other contextual factors. Hence the three pathways considered here are hardly moot where bilateral arrangements are concerned. Bilateral arrangements are not well suited, moreover, to the interdependent nature of maritime affairs. In any event, states already know they have such an option. Bilateral arrangements have long been a standard way of handing territorial and maritime issues.

Prospects

Despite Asia's positive maritime milieu at present, many analysts are glum about its future prospects. Though the vast majority do not expect a major war, many believe that island and maritime disputes, SLOC quarrels, and piracy threaten the peace and prosperity of the region. The future course of events in maritime Asia will depend on a multitude of familiar factors such as the distribution of capabilities at the global and regional level, technology, events in the Middle East, and domestic politics in the United States. (See, for example, Friedberg 1993–94: 5–6; Betts 1993–94: 41.) Less obviously, it will depend on the maturity level of states that populate the region. To the extent there is a large percentage of adolescent states in a region, one should expect a chaotic maritime scene. After all, adolescence implies that island and maritime controversies will be more widespread, more intense, and harder to resolve. It also suggests that SLOCs will be insecure. Furthermore, it signifies that the incidence of piracy will be higher than normal. This is particularly troubling because, as we have seen, some of the region's adolescents are armed.

Nevertheless, dark clouds are unlikely to descend on Asia's maritime scene anytime soon because the region has several pathways that help to contain and transform adolescence. So long as they endure, these pathways will limit the adverse effects of adolescence. Moreover, they will help to push the region's states to maturity. These pathways to order may be sorely tested, however, if American hegemony wanes. In this event, the region's leading states may have to assume balancing roles to control the more aggressive states. Alternatively, they may have to develop new institutional arrangements such as a concert system to directly tackle the demands (or consequences) of adolescence.

In the Introduction to this volume, Alagappa writes that "over the last several decades considerable progress has been made in many Asian countries in building nations, constructing viable political systems, and strengthening state capacity." He also observes that consolidation is not complete in several states and that the process of consolidation can be predictive of conflict. Reversals are also possible. Adolescence is unlikely to disappear as a factor in Asia's maritime security setting. First, not all Asian states have matured. Second, changes in developmental status are quite possible. The recent independence of East Timor from Indonesia, for instance, shows how the appearance of a new state can unsettle boundaries and raise maritime issues that others thought had been settled. One can only imagine the regional implications if Aceh and Irian Jaya should achieve independence from Indonesia. Most challenging of all for Asia's maritime security order would be the regression of a mature state such as Japan that, despite a decade of economic malaise, continues to wield tremendous wealth and military power.

Works Cited

AFP (Agence-France Presse). 2000a. "Spratly Agreement with China a Milestone." May 17.

———. 2000b. "ASEAN Wins No Movement from China on Spratlys Code of Conduct." Oct. 11.

———. 2000c. "Code of Conduct on South China Sea Unlikely to Be Signed This Year." Nov. 8.

———. 2000d. "China Pushes Peace But Ignores Spratlys Code." Nov. 25.

Amer, Ramses. 1998. "Towards a Declaration on 'Navigational Rights' in the Sea-Lanes of the Asia-Pacific." *Contemporary Southeast Asia* 20(1) (Apr.): 88–102.

Anwar, Dewi Fortuna. 1998. "Indonesia: Domestic Priorities Define National Security." In Muthiah Alagappa, ed., *Asian Security Practice: Material and Ideational Influences.* Stanford: Stanford University Press.

Atwater, Eastwood. 1992. *Adolescence.* 3rd ed. Englewood Cliffs, N.J.: Prentice-Hall.

Austin, Greg. 1998. *China's Ocean Frontier: International Law, Military Force, and National Development.* St. Leonard's, U.K.: Allen & Unwin.

Ball, Desmond. 1993–94. "Arms and Affluence: Military Acquisition in the Asia-Pacific Region." *International Security* 18(3) (Winter): 78–112.

———. 1999. "Security Developments and Prospects for Cooperation in the Asia-Pacific Region, with Particular Reference to the Mekong River Basin." Working Paper 333. Canberra: Strategic and Defence Studies Centre, Australian National University.

Bernstein, Thomas. 1999. "China: Growth Without Political Liberalization." In James W. Morley, ed., *Driven by Growth: Political Change in the Asia-Pacific Region.* Armonk, N.Y.: M. E. Sharpe.

Bessho, Koro. 1999. *Identities and Security in East Asia.* Adelphi Paper 325. Oxford: Oxford University Press.

Betts, Richard K. 1993–94. "Wealth, Power, and Instability: East Asia and the United States After the Cold War." *International Security* 18(3) (Winter): 34–77.

Bird, Judith. 1999. "Indonesia in 1998: The Pot Boils Over." *Asian Survey* 39(1) (Jan.–Feb.): 27–37.

Blanchard, Jean-Marc F. 1998. "Borders and Borderlands: An Institutional Approach to Territorial Disputes." Ph.D. dissertation, University of Pennsylvania.

———. 2000. "The U.S. Role in the Sino-Japanese Dispute over the Diaoyu (Senkaku) Islands, 1945–1971." *China Quarterly* 161 (Mar.): 95–123.

———. 2002. "Giving the Unrecognized Their Due: Regional Actors, International Organizations, and Multilateral Economic Cooperation in Northeast Asia." In Daniel W. Drezner, ed., *The New Bargaining: International Institutions, Domestic Politics, and Transnational Negotiation.* Ann Arbor: University of Michigan Press.

———, and Norrin M. Ripsman. 1996. "Measuring Economic Interdependence: A Geopolitical Perspective." *Geopolitics* 1(3) (Winter): 225–46.

———. 2001. "Rethinking Sensitivity Interdependence: Assessing the Trade, Financial, and Monetary Links Between States." *International Interactions* 27(2) (June): 95–127.

Booth, Ken. 1985. *Law, Force, and Diplomacy at Sea.* London: Allen & Unwin.

Buzan, Barry. 1978. *A Sea of Troubles? Sources of Dispute in the New Ocean Regime.* Adelphi Paper 143. London: International Institute for Strategic Studies.

Catley, Bob, and Makmur Keliat. 1997. *Spratlys: The Dispute in the South China Sea*. Aldershot, U.K.: Ashgate.

Charney, Jonathan I. 1995. "Central East Asian Maritime Boundaries and the Law of the Sea." *American Journal of International Law* 89(4) (Oct.): 724–49.

Chen Jie. 1994. "China's Spratly Policy: With Special Reference to the Philippines and Malaysia." *Asian Survey* 34(10) (Oct.): 893–903.

Choo, Myung-Gun. 2000. *The New Asia in Global Perspective*. London: Macmillan.

Cotterell, John. 1996. *Social Networks and Social Influences in Adolescence*. London: Routledge.

Danzig, Richard. 1997. "Asian Futures, Naval Futures: How Do They Intersect?" Lecture at Stanford University, Stanford, Calif., Mar. 13.

Denoon, David B. H., and Evelyn Colbert. 1998–99. "Challenges for the Association of Southeast Asian Nations (ASEAN)." *Pacific Affairs* 71(4) (Winter): 505–23.

Deudney, Daniel. 1996. "Ground Identity: Nature, Place, and Space in Nationalism." In Yosef Lapid and Friedrich Kratochwil, eds., *The Return of Culture and Identity in International Relations Theory*. Boulder, Colo.: Lynne Rienner.

Dosch, Jorn. 1997. "PMC, ARF, and CSCAP: Foundations for a Security Architecture in the Asia-Pacific?" Working Paper 307. Canberra: Strategic and Defence Studies Centre, Australian National University.

Dzurek, Daniel J. 1995. "China Occupies Mischief Reef in Latest Spratly Gambit." *Boundary and Security Bulletin* 3(1) (Apr.): 65–71.

———. 1996. "The People's Republic of China Straight Baseline Claim." *Boundary and Security Bulletin* 4(2) (Summer): 77–89.

———. 2000. "Effect of the Diaoyu/Senkaku Islands Dispute on Maritime Delimitation." In Martin A. Pratt and J. A. Brown, eds., *Borderlands Under Stress*. London: Kluwer Law International.

Economist. 2000. "No Flags for Papua." Oct. 14, p. 50.

Forbes, Vivian Louis. 1995. *The Maritime Boundaries of the Indian Ocean Region*. Singapore: Singapore University Press.

Friedberg, Aaron L. 1993–94. "Ripe for Rivalry: Prospects for Peace in a Multipolar Asia." *International Security* 18(3) (Winter): 5–33.

Gallagher, Michael G. 1994. "China's Illusory Threat to the South China Sea." *International Security* 19(1) (Summer): 169–94.

Garver, John W. 1992. "China's Push Through the South China Sea: The Interaction of Bureaucratic and National Interests." *China Quarterly* 132 (Dec.): 999–1028.

Gottschalk, Jack A., and Brian P. Flanagan (with Lawrence J. Kahn and Dennis M. LaRochelle). 2000. *Jolly Roger with an Uzi: The Threat and Rise of Modern Piracy*. Annapolis, Md.: Naval Institute Press.

Hellmann, Donald C., and Kenneth B. Pyle, eds. 1997. *From APEC to Xanadu: Creating a Viable Community in the Post–Cold War Pacific*. Armonk, N.Y.: M. E. Sharpe.

Henderson, Jeannie. 1999. *Reassessing ASEAN*. Adelphi Paper 328. Oxford: Oxford University Press.

Hyer, Eric. 1994. "'Dangerous Shoals': An Introduction to the South China Sea Disputes." *American Asian Review* 12(4) (Winter): 6–22.

IBC (International Boundary Consultants). n.d. "Boundary Bits."

———. 1998. "American Defense Commitments and Asian Island Disputes." Aug. 15.

IBRU (International Boundaries Research Unit). n.d. http://www-ibru.dur.ac.uk/cig-bin/data.pl.

Ichimura, Shinichi, and James W. Morley. 1999. "Introduction: The Varieties of Asia-Pacific Experience." In James W. Morley, ed., *Driven by Growth: Political Change in the Asia-Pacific Region*. Armonk, N.Y.: M. E. Sharpe.

IISS (International Institute for Strategic Studies). 1999. *The Military Balance 1999–2000*. London: Oxford University Press.

IMF (International Monetary Fund). 1999a. *World Economic Outlook, May 1999*. Washington, D.C.: International Monetary Fund.

———. 1999b. *World Economic Outlook, October 1999*. Washington, D.C.: International Monetary Fund.

Ji, Guoxing. 1995. "Maritime Jurisdiction in the Three China Seas: Options for Equitable Settlement." Policy Paper 19. San Diego: U.C. San Diego, Institute on Global Conflict and Cooperation. http://www-igcc.ucsd.edu.

———. 2000. "SLOC Security in the Asia Pacific." Occasional Paper. Honolulu: Asia-Pacific Center for Security Studies.

Ji, You. 1999. *The Armed Forces of China*. London: I. B. Tauris.

Kapur, Devesh, and Pratap Bhanu Mehta. 1999. "India in 1998: The Travails of Political Fragmentation." *Asian Survey* 39(1) (Jan.–Feb.): 163–76.

Kawasaki-Urabe, Yutaka, and Vivian L. Forbes. 1996–97. "Japan's Ratification of UN Law of the Sea Convention and Its New Legislation on the Law of the Sea." *Boundary and Security Bulletin* 4(4) (Winter): 92–100.

Kellerman, David N. 1999. "Report on Worldwide Maritime Piracy." http://www.maritimesecurity.com.

Kim, Duk-Ki. 1999. "Cooperative Maritime Security in Northeast Asia." *Naval War College Review* 52(1) (Winter): 53–77.

———. 2000. *Naval Strategy in Northeast Asia: Geo-Strategic Goals, Policies, and Prospects*. London: Frank Cass.

Koh, T. T. B. 1986. "Negotiating a New World Order for the Sea." In Alan K. Henrikson, ed., *Negotiating World Order: The Artisanship and Architecture of Global Diplomacy*. Wilmington: Scholarly Resources.

Kroger, Jane. 1989. *Identity in Adolescence: The Balance Between Self and Other*. London: Routledge.

Lee, Lai To. 1995. "ASEAN and the South China Sea Conflicts." *Pacific Review* 8(3) (Aug.): 531–43.

Lee, Seo-Hang. 1998. "Security of SLOCs in East Asia." Policy Paper 33: Maritime Shipping in Northeast Asia. San Diego: U.C. San Diego, Institute on Global Conflict and Cooperation. http://www-igcc.ucsd.edu/publications/policy_papers/pp33.html.

Lewis, John, and Hua Di. 1992. "China's Ballistic Missile Programs: Technologies, Strategies, Goals." *International Security* 17(2) (Fall): 5–40.

Lewis, John, Hua Di, and Xue Litai. 1991. "Beijing's Defense Establishment: Solving the Arms-Export Enigma." *International Security* 15(4) (Spring): 87–109.

Mackie, Jamie. 1999. "Indonesia: Economic Growth and Depoliticization." In James W. Morley, ed., *Driven by Growth: Political Change in the Asia-Pacific Region*. Armonk, N.Y.: M. E. Sharpe.

Mehta, Pratap Bhanu. 1998. "India: The Nuclear Politics of Self-Esteem." *Current History* 97(623) (Dec.): 403–6.

MOFA (Ministry of Foreign Affairs of Japan). 2000. "Opening Speech by Mr. Tetsuma Esaki, Senior State Secretary for Foreign Affairs, Regional Conference on Combating Piracy and Armed Robbery Against Ships." Apr. 27.

Moon, Chung-in. 1998. "South Korea: Recasting Security Paradigms." In Muthiah Alagappa, ed., *Asian Security Practice: Material and Ideational Influences*. Stanford: Stanford University Press.

Narine, Shaun. 1998. "ASEAN and the Management of Regional Security." *Pacific Affairs* 71(2) (Summer): 195–214.

Nguyen-Vo, Thu-Huong. 1992. *Khmer-Viet Relations and the Third Indochina Conflict*. Jefferson, N.C.: McFarland.

Ninh, Kim. 1998. "Vietnam: Struggle and Cooperation." In Muthiah Alagappa, ed., *Asian Security Practice: Material and Ideational Influences*. Stanford: Stanford University Press.

Ong, David, and B. A. Hamzah. 1996. "Disputed Maritime Boundaries and Claims to Offshore Territories in the Asia Pacific Region." In Sam Bateman and Stephen Bates, eds., *Calming the Waters: Initiatives for Asia Pacific Maritime Cooperation*. Canberra: Australian National University, Strategic and Defence Studies Centre.

Paik, Jin-Hyun. 1996. "Exploitation of Natural Resources: Potential for Conflicts in Northeast Asia." In Sam Bateman and Stephen Bates, eds., *Calming the Waters: Initiatives for Asia Pacific Maritime Cooperation*. Canberra: Australian National University, Strategic and Defence Studies Centre.

Prescott, J. R. V. 1985. *The Maritime Political Boundaries of the World*. London: Methuen.

———. 1995–96. "Indonesia's Maritime Claims and Outstanding Delimitation Problems." *Boundary and Security Bulletin* 3(4) (Winter): 91–97.

Ripsman, Norrin M. 2001–2002. "The Curious Case of German Rearmament: Democracy and Foreign Security Policy." *Security Studies* 10(2) (Winter): 1–47.

Rothwell, Donald. 1996. "The Law of the Sea as a Maritime Confidence Building Measure." In Sam Bateman and Stephen Bates, eds., *Calming the Waters: Initiatives for Asia Pacific Maritime Cooperation*. Canberra: Australia National University, Strategic and Defence Studies Centre.

Roy, Denny. 1994. "Hegemon on the Horizon? China's Threat to East Asian Security." *International Security* 19(1) (Summer): 149–68.

Roy-Chaudhury, Raul. 1999. "Trends in the Delimitation of India's Maritime Boundaries." *Strategic Analysis* 22(10) (Jan.). http://www.idsa-india.org/an-jan9-5.html.

Schave, Douglas, and Barbara Schave. 1989. *Early Adolescence and the Search for Self: A Developmental Perspective*. New York: Praeger.

Sebald, Hans. 1977. *Adolescence: A Social Psychological Analysis*. 2nd ed. Englewood Cliffs, N.J.: Prentice-Hall.

Shambaugh, David. 1999–2000. "China's Military Views the World: Ambivalent Security." *International Security* 24(3) (Winter): 52–79.

Simon, Sheldon W. 1998. "Security Prospects in Southeast Asia: Collaborative Efforts and the ASEAN Regional Forum." *Pacific Review* 11(2): 195–212.

Smith, Robert W., and Bradford Thomas. 1998a. "Island Disputes and the Law of the Sea: An Examination of Sovereignty and Delimitation Disputes." In Myron H. Nordquist and John Norton Moore, eds., *Security Flashpoints: Oil, Islands, Sea Access, and Military Confrontation*. The Hague: Martinus Nijhoff.

———. 1998b. "Island Disputes and the Law of the Sea: An Examination of Sovereignty and Delimitation Disputes." *Maritime Briefing* 2(4): 1–25.

Sohn, Louis B., and Kristen Gustafson. 1984. *The Law of the Sea.* St. Paul, Minn.: West.

Song, Jin. 1999. "Energy Security in the Asia-Pacific: Competition or Cooperation?" Report on the Energy Security in the Asia-Pacific Seminar, Asia-Pacific Center for Security Studies, Jan. 15. http://www.apcss.org/Report_Energy_Security_99.html.

Studeman, Michael. 1998. "Calculating China's Advances in the South China Sea: Identifying the Triggers of 'Expansionism.'" http://www.nwc.navy.mil/press/Review/1998/spring/art5-sp8.htm.

Swinnerton, Ross. 1994. "A Description of Regional Shipping Routes: Navigational and Operational Considerations." Paper presented at the Malaysian Institute of Maritime Affairs–Centre for Maritime Policy Workshop, Kuala Lumpur, Malaysia, Dec. 7–8. http://www.anu.edu/au/law/pub/icl/mstudies/maritime_studies_87/rsr.html.

Than, Tin Maung Maung. 1998. "Myanmar: Preoccupation with Regime Survival, National Unity, and Security." In Muthiah Alagappa, ed., *Asian Security Practice: Material and Ideational Influences.* Stanford: Stanford University Press.

Thao, Nguyn Hong. 1997. "Vietnam's First Maritime Boundary Agreement." *Boundary and Security Bulletin* 5(3) (Autumn): 74–78.

Thayer, Carlyle A. 2000a. "China-ASEAN Relations: China's 'New Security Concept' and ASEAN." *Comparative Connections* 2(3) (Oct.): 65–75.

———. 2000b. "Regional Military Modernization Strategies and Trends." Paper presented at the Conference on Security and Societal Trends in Southeast Asia, Washington, D.C., Sept. 6–7.

———. 2000c. "China-ASEAN Relations: China Consolidates Its Long-Term Bilateral Relations with Southeast Asia." *Comparative Connections* 2(2) (July): 62–72.

Thomas, Bradford L., and Daniel J. Dzurek. 1996. "The Spratly Islands Dispute." *Geopolitics* 1(3) (Winter): 300–26.

Till, Geoffrey. 1996. "Maritime Disputes in the Western Pacific." *Geopolitics and International Boundaries* 1(3) (Winter): 327–45.

Tongzon, Jose L. 1998. *The Economies of Southeast Asia: The Growth and Development of ASEAN Economies.* Cheltenham, U.K.: Edward Elgar.

United Kingdom. Hydrographer of the Navy. 1987. *Ocean Passages for the World.* 4th ed. Somerset: U.K. Ministry of Defence.

UN General Assembly. 1999. *Oceans and the Law of the Sea: Report of the Secretary-General.* A/54/429 (30 Sept.), http://www.un.org.

UN DOALOS (UN Office of Legal Affairs. Division for Ocean Affairs and the Law of the Sea). 1994. *The Law of the Sea: Practice of States at the Time of Entry into Force of the United Nations Convention on the Law of the Sea.* New York: United Nations.

U.S. DOD (United States Department of Defense). 1998. "The United States Security Strategy for the East Asia-Pacific Region." Nov. 23.

U.S. DOS (United States Department of State). 1997. "Secretary of State Madeleine K. Albright's Statement to the ASEAN Regional Forum." July 27.

U.S. EIA (United States Department of Energy. Energy Information Administration). 2000. *International Energy Outlook* (Mar.). http://www.eia.doe.gov/oiaf/ieo/index.html.

U.S. GAO (United States General Accounting Office). 1995. "Impact of China's Military Modernization in the Pacific Region." Washington, D.C.: U.S. GAO/NSIAD-95-84.

USNI (U.S. Naval Institute). 1998. *The Naval Institute Guide to Combat Fleets of the World 1998–1999: Their Ships, Aircraft, and Systems.* Annapolis: Naval Institute Press.

U.S. SPPD (United States Pacific Command Strategic Planning and Policy Directorate).

2000. *Asia-Pacific Economic Update* (Jan.). http://www.pacom.mil/direct/apeu00/apeu00.htm.

Valencia, Mark J. 1991. "Vietnam's Maritime Disputes: Hydrocarbon Resource Potential and Possible Solutions." *Energy* 16(9): 1157–84.

————. 1995. *China and the South China Sea Disputes*. Adelphi Paper 298. Oxford: Oxford University Press.

————. 1996. *A Maritime Regime for North-East Asia*. Hong Kong: Oxford University Press.

————. 1999. "Tiny Reef a Litmus Test for Chinese Intentions." *Honolulu Advertiser*, Feb. 2, pp. B1, B4.

————. 2000. "Beijing Is Setting the Stage for Trouble in the South China Sea." *International Herald Tribune*, July 3.

Vasavakul, Thaveeporn. 1999. "Vietnam: Sectors, Classes, and the Transformation of a Leninist State." In James W. Morley, ed., *Driven by Growth: Political Change in the Asia-Pacific Region*. Armonk, N.Y.: M. E. Sharpe.

Vitasa, H. R., and Nararya Soeprapto. 1999. "Maritime Sector Developments in ASEAN." Paper presented at the United Nations Conference on Trade and Development Maritime Policy Seminar, Jakarta, Indonesia, Oct. 11–13. http://www.asean.or.id/secgen/articles/msd_ase.htm.

Walt, Stephen. 1996. *Revolution and War*. Ithaca: Cornell University Press.

Wanandi, Jusuf. 1993. "Asia-Pacific Security Forums: Rationale and Options from the ASEAN Perspective." In Desmond Ball, Richard L. Grant, and Jusuf Wanandi, *Security Cooperation in the Asia-Pacific Region*. Washington, D.C.: Center for Strategic and International Studies.

Wattanayagorn, Panitan. 1998. "Thailand: The Elite's Shifting Conceptions of Security." In Muthiah Alagappa, ed., *Asian Security Practice: Material and Ideational Influences*. Stanford: Stanford University Press.

Weeks, Stanley B. 1998. "Sea Lines of Communication (SLOC) Security and Access." Policy Paper 33: Maritime Shipping in Northeast Asia. San Diego: U.C. San Diego, Institute on Global Conflict and Cooperation. http://www-igcc.ucsd.edu/publications/policy_papers/pp33.html.

————, and Charles A. Meconis. 1999. *The Armed Forces of the USA in the Asia-Pacific Region*. London: I. B. Tauris.

World Bank. 1999. *Global Economic Prospects and the Developing Countries, 1998/99: Beyond Financial Crisis*. Washington, D.C.: World Bank.

————. 2000. *Global Economic Prospects and the Developing Countries, 2000*. Washington, D.C.: World Bank.

Yahuda, Michael. 1999. "China's Search for a Global Role." *Current History* 98(629) (Sept.): 266–70.

Zou, Keyuan. 1999. "Scarborough Reef: A New Flashpoint in Sino-Philippine Relations?" *Boundary and Security Bulletin* 7(2) (Summer): 71–81.

CHAPTER THIRTEEN

Nuclear Weapons, Missile Defense, and Stability

A Case for "Sober Optimism"

VICTOR D. CHA

There is probably no place in the world today where nuclear proliferation concerns are more acute than Asia.[1] Actors in the region either possess or clearly desire nuclear weapons and ballistic missile capabilities. These weapons programs are being cultivated in the context of intense rivalries over power and territory and are embedded, in many cases, in a cauldron of unresolved historical hatreds. There are no regional arms control regimes, and participation in global ones is sporadic. The danger with regard to these programs is exacerbated by their lack of transparency, their illiberal political sponsors (in some cases), and their profiles as small, unsafeguarded programs. For "proliferation pessimists," Asia represents the worst of two worlds: small nuclear powers operating under conditions of security scarcity, where fierce animosities and rivalries do not bode well for rational or stable deterrence.

How accurate is this assessment? Is the first use, intentional or accidental, of a nuclear weapon since 1945 fated to be in Asia? More broadly, how should we be thinking about proliferation and the second nuclear age in East Asia and South Asia in the twenty-first century? What are the prospects, if any, for regional arms control? If these prospects are poor, what is to be the ultimate form of order with regard to nuclear and missile proliferation in the region?

Here I wish to make two arguments with regard to the causes and consequences of the second nuclear age in Asia. Regarding causes of proliferation, I argue that these are *overdetermined* in Asia. As in the first nuclear age, proliferation

---

[1] Here Asia includes both Northeast Asia and South Asia. I focus mostly on China, Japan, and the two Koreas in Northeast Asia and on Pakistan and India in South Asia.

derives largely from the intersection of security needs and resource constraints. But in addition to these basic security drivers, there is a plethora of secondary drivers—domestic forces relating to political currency (insurance and bargaining), prestige, and a healthy dose of skepticism regarding First World hypocrisy— that explain the region's proliferation. The combination of these primary and secondary drivers not only ensures that proliferation is overdetermined in Asia; it also means that a rollback of these capabilities, though desirable, is not likely.

I also want to address the consequences of proliferation. Contrary to the pessimistic assessment regarding the causes of proliferation, I make a case for "sober optimism" regarding the prospects for stability. Asian nuclear and missile proliferation is certainly dangerous, but not nearly so disastrous as has been popularly predicted. Swaggering, competitive testing, crises, accidents, and outright conflicts may certainly occur. But there is no reason to expect that the likelihood of this behavior escalating to a nuclear exchange is any greater today than in the first nuclear age. Deterrence (albeit in a different form than the superpower experience) is likely to continue, augmented by an appreciation of the taboo on nuclear first use.

The argument for sober optimism with regard to Asian proliferation as put forth in this chapter refers largely to interaction between nation-states with nuclear capabilities. The terrorist attacks of September 11, 2001, in New York and Washington, although conventional in nature, raise the specter of potential nuclear or other weapons of mass destruction employed by non-state actors. While non-state proliferation goes beyond the scope of this work, the implications of such a trend do not comply with the argument for sober optimism put forth here. As noted below, in many ways it is the attributes of being a nation-state that enable a more soberly optimistic assessment of proliferation. Without such attributes (mutually targetable populations, national concerns about international stigma, etc.), deterrence is much less capable of functioning.

An argument for sober optimism with regard to Asian proliferation is *not* meant as an argument against nonproliferation. Stemming the spread and appeal of nuclear weapons and missile technology to rogue regimes as well as to other potential proliferators remains extremely important. But there is no necessary connection between an enthusiasm for nonproliferation and pessimistic assessments of proliferation consequences for the region. The two have been conjoined in almost stereotypical depictions of the agents of the second nuclear age as irrational, maniacal, and irresponsible. In some cases such a characterization may be true. But there is no reason a priori to assume this as a hard and fast rule for the entire region. In short, one can still be an advocate of nonproliferation and remain soberly optimistic that the consequences of proliferation for the region, should it occur, are not unequivocally disastrous. Moreover, given the understanding of what drives proliferation in the region, a number of specific recommendations emerge for the nonproliferation effort. I open with a brief empirical overview followed by arguments regarding the causes and consequences of proliferation in the region. I conclude with a short discussion of the role that current and new nonproliferation institutions can play in reinforcing and improving the prospects for nonuse outcome in Asia.

The Second Nuclear Age in Asia: Apples and Oranges

The second nuclear age is substantively different from the first. In the first nuclear age, whether this term refers to the United States and the Soviet Union or to the next tier of nuclear powers (Britain, France, China), there were fewer agents and, generally speaking, greater uniformity among them.[2] To compare the second nuclear age with the first, by contrast, is like comparing apples and oranges. Not only are the levels of proliferation greatly varied, but they differ on a whole range of dimensions. China, the South Asian states, the two Koreas, Japan, and Taiwan display a range of extant and recessed nuclear and ballistic missile capabilities that varies in quantity and quality of systems, accuracy, range, infrastructure, and transparency. These capabilities are accompanied by varied degrees of commitment to nonproliferation regimes; moreover, they operate in an international structure no longer defined by bipolarity—a structure in which fears of abandonment, local threats, and uncertainty are brought into sharp relief. A brief empirical survey makes these differences clear.

China possesses the most advanced nuclear weapons and ballistic missile (BM) programs in Asia. Its BM infrastructure offers a wide variety of land and sea-based systems. (See Appendix A for details.)[3] It is in the midst of a wide-ranging modernization program that aims to improve range, payload, and accuracy (through development of solid propellants, improved rocket motors, and targeting technologies) to replace older systems deployed in the 1970s and 1980s. Improvements are also being sought regarding the survivability of its forces, command, control, and communication capabilities, stealth technologies, as well as countermeasures to ballistic missile defense (decoy warheads, multiple-reentry vehicles, electronic and infrared jammers). China's nuclear arsenal consists of

---

[2]This is admittedly less the case for China. On second-tier nuclear powers in the first nuclear age, see Goldstein (2000).

[3]China remains the only power besides Russia with the ICBM capability to reach the United States and until a recent U.S.-China nontargeting agreement (June 1998) was believed to have the majority of its long-range ICBM force of twenty missiles targeted on the United States. (It is believed to keep its missiles unfueled and without warheads.)

approximately 400 to 450 devices. Beijing relies largely on the land-based leg of the triad, reserving nearly 250 of these "strategic" warheads for medium- and long-range strike missions mated with the BM program.[4] Chinese efforts to modernize this arsenal were manifest in a series of tests, completed in 1996, that yielded the information China needed to finalize weapon designs. (China has conducted 45 tests over thirty-three years versus 1,030 by the United States.)[5] China is not currently producing more fissile materials for nuclear weapons but has a stockpile sufficient to increase or improve its weapon inventory.

At the next tier in terms of demonstrated capabilities are India and Pakistan. The South Asian rivals have two of the more advanced BM programs in the developing world. India's program, in particular, is capable of design and production of relatively advanced missiles (solid propellants, multistage, mobile, medium-range distances) with little foreign assistance.[6] Pakistan's missile program, although not as self-sufficient or deep in variety and range of missiles as India's, remains competitive in short-range missiles.[7] The object of much attention since the 1998 tests, India and Pakistan's nuclear programs mirror their missile programs with respect to levels of relative development. India's active nuclear energy program has produced the facilities to support a complete nuclear fuel cycle. Al-

[4]The bomber leg of the triad comprises approximately 120 Hong-6 bombers (range of 3,100 km, each capable of delivering one to three bombs of 10 kT to 3 MT) and 30 Qian-5A attack aircraft (range of 400 km, capable of delivering one nuclear bomb of 10 kT to 3 MT) deployed in 1965 and 1970 respectively. The sea-based leg consists of about twelve JL-1 SLBMs deployed in 1986 on one Xia-class submarine. Experts consider the air and sea legs of the triad less threatening. The bomber force is old, highly vulnerable to air defense, and incapable of reaching the United States. The SLBM program has proved less successful than ICBMs despite the four decades of development invested in it. Moreover, China is believed to possess about 150 tactical weapons made up of low-yield bombs, artillery shells, atomic demolition munitions, and short-range missiles (although it does not officially acknowledge possession of tactical weapons). For a concise overview, see Manning et al. (2000: 15–37).

[5]China conducted its first nuclear test in 1964. It exploded a hydrogen weapon in 1966 and began production of nuclear weapons in 1968 and thermonuclear weapons in 1974.

[6]India's most capable operational missile, the Prithvi-150, has a 1,000-kg payload and a range of 150 km, although India has tested and developed longer-range systems (e.g., Agni). Modernization plans include the acquisition of submarine-launch capabilities. India also possesses an ambitious space-launch vehicle program for which the ready availability of guidance sets and warheads gives it additional recessed BM capabilities.

[7]Pakistan's most capable missile, the Hatf-2, has a 500-kg payload and range of 280 km, although it has test-launched longer-range missiles (e.g., Ghauri). The SRBM industry includes rocket motor production and test facilities. Substantial support for the Hatf series has come in the past from China (M-11 equipment transfers in the early 1990s). Recently Pakistan has concentrated its efforts on testing and developing missiles of the Ghauri and Shaheen series (1,300–3,500 km range) largely based on transfers of the North Korean Nodong missile series (Appendix A). Neither country is a member of the MTCR.

though the majority of Indian nuclear reactors are under IAEA safeguards, the others have been producing weapons-grade plutonium and enriched uranium for weapons use (as at the Bhabha Atomic Research Center). India's nuclear weapons program started in the early 1960s. After its peaceful nuclear explosion in 1974, India remained an undeclared nuclear power, its operational weapons capability limited to oversized bombs deliverable by airplane. From the mid-1980s, India sought to modernize these capabilities in terms of miniaturization and accuracy, which was one of the purposes of the 1998 tests. Pakistan's nuclear weapons program originated in response to the 1971 war and accelerated after India's nuclear explosion in 1974. Like India's, only a portion of Pakistan's nuclear facilities are under IAEA safeguards.[8] But unlike its rival, Pakistan is able to produce plutonium and highly enriched uranium yet still depends on foreign suppliers (China) for sophisticated materials and technologies to expand its program. Though Islamabad has asserted its willingness to sign the NPT should India do so, both remain nonparties to the regime.

Since the early 1980s, North Korea stands in a separate category. Its ballistic missile program has produced a range of missile systems, either deployed or tested, demonstrating progress beyond most expectations (see Appendix A).[9] Mated with the missile program have been dedicated DPRK efforts at acquiring nuclear weapon capabilities. Deriving from atomic energy agreements with the Soviet Union in the 1960s,[10] Pyongyang's nuclear industry was capable of supporting a complete nuclear fuel cycle by the 1980s. Subsequent reactors (an operational 5-MW reactor and construction of 50- and 200-MW reactors) presaged an annual reprocessed plutonium production capacity that could sustain in excess of ten nuclear weapons. Though these activities remain frozen and are subject to dismantlement as a result of the 1994 U.S.-DPRK Agreed Framework, sus-

[8]Three operating reactors are under IAEA safeguards (KANUPP power reactor in Karachi; PARR I and PARR II research reactors near Islamabad). The Chashma nuclear power plant is under IAEA safeguards as well. Pakistan also operates unsafeguarded reactors that are capable of producing weapons-grade plutonium.

[9]Despite its dire material constraints, the North accomplished this largely through reverse engineering of SCUD-B missile technology acquired from the Soviet Union. The North's first indigenous operational missile, the Nodong series, derives from SCUD technology. The August 1998 test flight of the Taepodong 1 over Japan demonstrated an unexpected leap in IRBM technology (despite a failed three-stage payload launch). In defiance of MTCR norms, North Korea has been the most active producer and provider of SCUD missiles and missile technology to Iran, Syria, and Pakistan—often described as the agent that could single-handedly undermine the entire regime. Concerns abound regarding future proliferation of longer-range systems (e.g., Pakistan's Ghauri and Shaheen series are derivative of Nodong technology). For further discussion, see Medeiros (n.d.: 4).

[10]An agreement with the Soviet Union on the peaceful use of atomic energy enabled the North to develop a small nuclear research reactor and a basic understanding of nuclear physics, engineering, and reactor operations.

picions remain regarding the North's plutonium reprocessing history, alleged covert activities outside Yongbyon, and possible crude nuclear devices.[11]

Latent or recessed capabilities are evident in the missile and relatively advanced civilian nuclear energy programs in Japan, South Korea, and Taiwan. Japan's potential ICBM capabilities deriving from its SLV program are well known—as are the normative and constitutional constraints on realizing such a capability. The combination of the DPRK's missile threat and the expiration of a U.S.-ROK 1979 agreement limiting ROK missile ranges has focused more attention on South Korea's missile capabilities and aspirations.[12] Regarding civilian nuclear energy, there are no explicit links between nuclear energy and weapons. But the promotion of civilian power reactors (with safeguards on nuclear materials) encourages latent nuclear weapons capabilities by allowing states to develop the research reactors, industrial infrastructure, technology, and materials that could eventually be converted to bomb-making purposes.[13] In this vein, Northeast Asia is the only region in the world where nuclear energy is viewed increasingly as a substitute for fossil fuel resources.[14] By the mid-1990s, nuclear power was supplying 36 percent of ROK energy, 28.8 percent for Taiwan, and 33.8 percent for Japan (versus 2 percent for China). And by 2010, the U.S. DOE estimates that nearly half of the world's nuclear energy capacity will be in East Asia.[15] The

[11]Many are concerned about possible reprocessing activities in 1989 and May–June 1994 that would have provided the North with enough weapons-grade plutonium for several nuclear weapons.

[12]The South's missile capabilities are modest: a 1979 bilateral agreement with Washington limited ROK missile ranges to 180 km. (The quid pro quo for this voluntary agreement was the transfer of U.S. technology for the South's Nike-Hercules-2 missile.) But with the agreement's expiration in 1999 and with the North's BM program, the South has favored independent development of longer-range missiles. (Pursuant to the North's Taepodong test flight in August 1998, in April 1999 the South tested a surface-to-surface missile, demonstrating Seoul's capabilities and determination to develop a more advanced missile deterrent.) U.S.-ROK bilateral discussions center on upgrading the South's missile capabilities in line with MTCR guidelines, but Seoul's aspirations are for research and development of missile ranges in excess of this. The South Koreans also aspire to gain an SLV program. While the South's BM capabilities are less advanced than Japan's, arguably they are also less "recessed." On the BM and SLV programs, see Cha (2001).

[13]This threat resides in the capacity to produce highly enriched uranium (for reactor use early in the fuel cycle) and to reprocess plutonium or accumulate it from the spent fuel. Uranium formed the core of the atom bomb (used at Hiroshima); plutonium formed the implosion bomb used at Nagasaki. Crude implosion bombs require no more than 10 kg of plutonium—a fraction of what can be extracted from the spent fuel of a civilian nuclear reactor (Sagan 1996–97: 56–57).

[14]For resource-poor countries in Asia, nuclear electricity is price-competitive with coal-based electricity (assuming stable capital costs for plant construction). Some argue that nuclear electricity is actually cheaper than coal-based energy because cost calculations for nuclear power include cautionary expenses related to disposal, safety, and radiation protection, whereas coal does not factor in the cost of pollution and other negative externalities (May 1998: 20).

[15]The United States, by contrast, is projected to reduce its nuclear energy capacity by 10 percent by 2010. South Korea stands out as likely to experience the largest relative increase in nuclear

Tokyo, Taipei, and Seoul governments have all forsworn nuclear weapons and acceded to the NPT regime; nevertheless, the increasing reliance on nuclear energy in combination with the lack of storage space in Asia creates strong incentives for reprocessing spent fuel (Katahara 1997; Harrison 1996; IGCC 1998: 20–21; Calder 1996: 62–74). Moreover, connected with this dynamic is the vision of energy self-sufficiency through the development of fast-breeder reactor technology (as in Japan), which creates additional incentives for reprocessing and stockpiling plutonium. Hence latent nuclear capabilities are present in Asia's nuclear energy activities as are insecurity spirals deriving from the long-term proliferation dangers of plutonium stockpiles.

The Causes of Proliferation

The causes of nuclear and missile proliferation in Asia, as noted, are overdetermined. Three arguments substantiate this claim. First, despite the asymmetry of capabilities within the region, states in Asia proliferate for similar reasons. Second, these causes are generally similar to those that drove proliferation in the first nuclear age. And third, while the causes of proliferation are similar across the first and second nuclear ages, the entire spectrum of domestic and international factors cited by experts as highly potent drivers of a state's need for nuclear weapons and delivery systems is especially salient to Asia. Moreover, these drivers are both abundant and long-lasting.

The Security Rationale

The first cause relevant to all cases of proliferation in Asia operates at the intersection of security needs and material constraints. States seek security against perceived threats and seek to close gaps with rival competitors within tight resource limitations; moreover, the self-help imperatives of anarchy render reliance on allies for security an unattractive proposition (when abandonment fears are high) or an unfeasible one (when there are no allies) (Sagan 1996–97; Deutsch 1992; Goldstein 2000). As Goldstein (2000: 57) argues, nuclear weapons therefore offer the single most efficient means for addressing security needs, abandonment fears, and resource constraints. Internal balancing against an adversary with conventional forces is less useful for these purposes for a number of reasons. The most important reason is gaps too large to overcome. Nuclear weapons are also more "fungible" than conventional forces in that they remain relevant security assets in most cases, regardless of wholesale changes in future adversaries or con-

---

energy capacity in the next decade—more than doubling its current capacity (not including the additional power generation stemming from two 1,000-MW reactors in North Korea as a result of the 1994 Agreed Framework implementation).

tingencies.[16] Goldstein observes: "National nuclear weapons enable states to satisfy basic security requirements self-reliantly and relatively economically. They are not cheap but when married to deterrent doctrines nuclear weapons can dissuade even much more powerful adversaries without incurring the high costs of comparably effective conventional defenses" (2000: 225).

The security/cost calculus of proliferation is common to all cases in Asia. In the case of China, there is general agreement that the Chinese sought nuclear weapons dating back to January 1955 as a direct function of several threats: perceived U.S. nuclear threats against China during the Korean War and offshore islands crises in the mid-1950s; the U.S. security alliance with Taiwan; superior American conventional capabilities; and the turn to a "New Look" and massive retaliation in U.S. strategic doctrine. Loss of confidence in the Soviet security commitment in a potential Sino-American conflict also weighed heavily in Beijing's decision to seek an independent nuclear capability (Manning et al. 2000: 15–16; Lewis and Xue 1988; Goldstein 2000: 62–67, 250–51; Godwin 1999; Lin 1988).

In the case of India, multiple external threats, resource constraints, and alignment uncertainties caused a shift away from its earlier adherence to disarmament norms. The 1962 Sino-Indian border war and 1964 Chinese nuclear test gave the initial impetus to India's nuclear program (Alagappa 1998: 5).[17] The ensuing 1965 Indo-Pakistani conflict over Kashmir—and, in particular, veiled Chinese threats to open a second front on the Himalayan border—forced the Indians to contemplate seriously the inadequacy of their conventional deterrent and rethink the traditional emphasis on disarmament. The absence of external support also mattered in India's decision making. In particular, the reluctance of the British, Americans, and Soviets to answer New Delhi's entreaties for nuclear guarantees informed the Indian decision to test in 1974.[18] Moreover, superpower security dy-

---

[16]For further discussions on the relative advantages of nuclear over conventional deterrents, see Goldstein (2000: 35–40, 54–55).

[17]India was roundly defeated in the 1962 war over territorial disputes that are still unresolved. Devin Hagerty (1999: 20–21) claims: "The national security roots of India's nuclear weapon programme lie in the 1963 defeat, and in China's 1964 nuclear explosive test. The programme's raison d'être is to deter another attack by China, which, while considered highly unlikely, cannot be entirely ruled out by any future leader."

[18]India's requests for such guarantees were raised at the UN Disarmament Conference (and after the 1965 Indo-Pakistan War) as a quid pro quo for British and American efforts to halt further proliferation in the aftermath of the Chinese test. The issue came up again in 1968 when the United States, Britain, and the USSR sought India's accession to the NPT without offering credible guarantees to nonnuclear weapons. To some extent one could attribute the delay between Indian threat perceptions in 1965 and the decision to test in 1974 to Indira Gandhi's August 1971 treaty of peace with the Soviet Union, which Ganguly (1999b: 153–57, 159) argues has been underestimated in terms of the security guarantees provided to India by Moscow.

namics in Central Asia created alignment patterns that heightened India's threat perceptions. The Soviet invasion of Afghanistan in December 1979 led to a consolidation of U.S.-Pakistani relations during the Reagan administration (a $3.2 billion assistance package, F-16 sales, and CIA training of Afghan resistance fighters from Pakistan), which in turn supplemented Indian concerns about Chinese support of Pakistan. These threat perceptions led India to develop (under the Defense Research and Development Organization's Integrated Guided Missile Development Program) and test-fire India's first IRBM (Agni) in 1989 (Ganguly 1999b: 162–64; Alagappa 1998: 7). With regard to the most recent tests, the Chinese threat remains the permissive condition for India's nuclear capability. (One cannot imagine caps on the Indian program without retaining a minimum deterrent against China.) But the specific cause of the 1998 test was related to Pakistan (Alagappa 1998; Gordon 1994: 662–73; Hagerty 1999: 20–21). Certainly Pakistan's test of the IRBM Ghauri in April 1998 demonstrated an increased capability to target Indian cities, to which India had to respond.

As in India and China, a similar mix of threats and resource constraints determined Pakistani nuclear and missile proliferation. From the late 1950s, Islamabad exhibited little interest in a nuclear program. But after the 1965 war with India, the government became more concerned about a growing Indian conventional force superiority. Following the 1965 war, Pakistan's defeat in the 1971 war, India's 1974 test, and the Prithvi missile program (perceived to be designed specifically for targeting Pakistan) set Pakistan firmly on the path of acquiring nuclear weapons as the only equalizer to Indian conventional and nuclear capabilities.[19] Exacerbating the need to proliferate were unsettling variations in the level of aligned support for Pakistan from outside parties. One of Islamabad's justifications for the nuclear program was that it could not rely on the United States for its security. Indeed, U.S. support of Pakistan has varied widely. The low points were the end to arms transfers after 1965, cool relations during the détente years, and the imposition of sanctions during the Carter administration. Relations improved during the Reagan years largely as a function of Soviet actions in Afghanistan. But with the end of the Cold War, Pakistani confidence in the United States plummeted as Islamabad saw a growing American alignment with India as a counterweight to China. This policy was manifest in U.S. unwillingness to provide security guarantees in the face of India's May 1998 tests, ultimately spurring the Pakistani decision to test.[20]

---

[19]As Hagerty (1999: 22) and Yasmeen (1999: 43–44) argue, the 1971 war was for Pakistan what the 1962 war was for India. The core aim of Pakistani nuclearization was to avoid a repetition of the humiliating defeat in 1971 (when India's superior conventional capabilities enabled a successful intervention in the Pakistani civil war). See also Aslam (1989).

[20]Proponents of this view also pointed to Secretary Albright and Undersecretary Pickering's

The security/cost calculus is relevant to the cases of Japan, South Korea, and Taiwan. Even though all are committed non-nuclear weapons states (NNWS) and supporters of the nonproliferation regime, all have latent capabilities and face salient external threats. For the most part, what obviates the perceived need for any of these countries to seek extant capabilities and delivery systems is American security guarantees (explicit in the former two cases and implicit in the third). The likelihood of any of these states proliferating would grow measurably if credibility in the U.S. commitment waned. South Korea's pursuit of an independent nuclear weapons capability in the late 1960s and 1970s was not a function of heightened external threats but a direct function of fears of U.S. abandonment deriving from the Nixon Doctrine and the withdrawal of the Seventh Infantry Division in 1970–71 (Cha 1999).

In this regard, ironically, the success of U.S. alliances in East Asia might contribute to future proliferation. A stabilization of the security situation on the Korean peninsula, for example, would lead to a drawdown of the American forward presence. For the allies, U.S. extended nuclear guarantees in the absence of this presence would not be very credible—prompting greater interest in autonomous capabilities. An even more radical interpretation would question the credibility of the U.S. nuclear umbrella to Asian allies today because the end of the Cold War structurally renders extended nuclear deterrence less credible to allies. During the Cold War bipolar conflict, what rendered credible the notion that the United States would respond to an attack on an ally and risk retaliation at home was the belief that this conflict would be decisive in terms of the wider geostrategic superpower competition. But a similar nuclear exchange scenario (prompted, say, by a DPRK chemical attack on Seoul in which the United States would respond and risk retaliation by the DPRK against Hawaii or San Francisco) would not carry the same stakes and, logically speaking, should be less credible for the ally.

Domestic Political Factors

A contributing factor on the domestic front for proliferation is widespread perceptions of First World hypocrisy. From the perspective of new proliferators, there are fundamental inconsistencies between the statements and the actions of nuclear weapons states (NWS). These states call for global nuclear disarmament,

---

visits to New Delhi in October 1997 and Bill Richardson's April 1998 visit as evidence of America's new embedding of South Asia policy in the larger Sino-American context. The United States offered a variety of incentives to Islamabad not to respond to the Indian test (e.g., a high-level visit to Washington; repeal of the Pressler Amendment and release of the previously suspended purchase of twenty-eight F-16s; and $5 billion in World Bank and IMF loans over five years) but provided no concrete assurances against India's use of nuclear weapons (Yasmeen 1999: 43–44, 46; Ahmed 1999: 180–90; Hagerty 1999: 22).

controls on technology transfer, and a comprehensive test ban and do not officially recognize any new nuclear powers. Yet at the same time they do not consider a rollback of their own capabilities. Indeed, NWS readily acknowledge in their own security doctrines the centrality of the nuclear deterrent.[21] And if smaller nuclear powers like Britain and France, for whom the Cold War was the primary driver of their acquisition of capabilities, do not willingly disarm, why should others not acquire nuclear arms (Goldstein 2000: 228, 234–35)? This "do as we say, not as we do" criticism pertains not only to NWS but also to NNWS states like Japan, Canada, Australia, and Germany whose commitments to nonproliferation regimes ring hollow because of the U.S. nuclear umbrella and their plutonium stockpiles (Katahara 1997).

First World hypocrisy reduces domestic constraints on new proliferators in two ways. It undercuts the legitimacy and emasculates the arguments of domestic constituencies opposed to the weapons programs. And it is easily manipulated by proliferation advocates to press forward with the program on normative grounds (Alagappa 1998: 3). In Pakistan, for example, the government portrayed the international nonproliferation norms as a First World conspiracy aimed at preventing Pakistan from attaining its rightful place in the world. Moreover, U.S. efforts to block Pakistan's acquisition of nuclear technology (Kissinger's threats to Bhutto, for example, and U.S. pressure on France to renege on reprocessing deals with Islamabad in the 1970s) all had the effect of lionizing nuclear weapons in domestic politics as a symbol of national sovereignty (Ahmed 1999: 185).

The hypocrisy arguments were heard most loudly in India, where proliferation advocates could silence the critics and keep the nation's nuclear option open by appealing to moralistic arguments about the inequities practiced by the First World's "nuclear apartheid" (Singh 1998: 41–52). New Delhi condemned the NPT in 1970 as an attempt by the nuclear club to prevent others from going nuclear (after China)—but, at the same time, not granting security guarantees to those NNWS countries left vulnerable (Ganguly 1999b: 158). India denounced the indefinite extension of the NPT on the grounds that a half decade after the end of the Cold War it was a travesty that the NWS could pull off such a feat while still relying on their nuclear deterrent (Hagerty 1999: 27–28; Singh 1998: 41). First World hypocrisy drove proliferation, not only by allowing virtually any regime to legitimize its drive for nuclear weapons in normative/equity terms, but also by counterintuitively raising the incentives to test every time a new nonproliferation milestone had been reached. The NPT extension and the finalization of the CTBT in the mid-1990s, for example, prompted potential proliferators to consider test-

[21]Plesch (2000) presents examples of such contradictions in the U.S. Secretary of Defense Annual Report 2000 and the 1999 NATO Strategic Concept.

ing sooner rather than later as First World–backed nonproliferation regimes were slowly closing the window of opportunity.[22]

Political Currency of Capabilities

Yet another domestic calculation common to all cases of proliferation in Asia relates to the political currency of acquiring these capabilities. Apart from the strategic rationale for proliferating, states perceive various political benefits to follow from becoming nuclear- and BM-capable. This is not to deny that substantial political costs are imposed by the nonproliferation regimes on new proliferators. But these costs are not seen to outweigh the benefits in terms of insurance, prestige, and bargaining position.

The bargaining and insurance motives are interlinked. On the one hand, nuclear and long-range BM capabilities, while sought for security and "equalizer" purposes, can serve as tools of political coercion to gain bargaining advantages. Arguably the DPRK through its fledgling BM capabilities was able to politically coerce international attention to its food problem as well as coerce the engagement efforts by the United States, Japan, and South Korea. No one (except perhaps Pyongyang) intended this to be the case. Yet this has been the net result—and, moreover, one that might not otherwise have happened without the DPRK's missile program (Cha 2000). Similarly, Indian statements in the aftermath of the May 1998 tests hinted at diplomatic coercion based on its new demonstrated capability. Home Minister Lal Krishna Advani stated after the tests that India had a new qualitative edge in solving the Kashmir problem and that Pakistan should "realise the change in the geostrategic situation . . . and roll back its anti-India policy." In a more blatant example, the Indian army chief made a symbolic visit to the Indian part of Kashmir shortly after the tests to "discuss the elements of a 'new strategy' with local commanders."[23]

On the other hand, the flip side of the bargaining motive is the insurance motive. For fear of demonstration effects from cases like the DPRK that might inspire other local adversaries to action, states choose to proliferate precisely to prevent becoming vulnerable to political coercion and nuclear blackmail. While security was certainly a driver of Pakistan's nuclear and missile program, an important motive was to avoid allowing its rival the political leverage to dictate its

[22]Such concerns prompted Prime Minister Rao to begin preparations for an Indian test at the end of 1995 on the grounds that it was "now or never" (Ganguly 1999b: 168). The test was never carried out.

[23]Quotes come from Yasmeen (1999: 54). Similarly, when Pakistan realized that the implicit threat of nuclear action succeeded in deterring India from violating the line of control in the 1990 Kashmir conflict, "the success of the nuclear bluff reinforced the leadership's belief in the value of nuclear weapons both as a deterrent and as a tool of diplomatic bargaining. . . . This became enshrined as an article of faith" (Ahmed 1999: 189–90).

terms on significant political or sovereignty issues in a way unacceptable to Pakistan (Yasmeen 1999: 44).[24] Similarly, after the test at Lop Nor in October 1964, voices in India called for a change in India's policy on nuclear capabilities to counter the political influence that China would gain with the nuclear advantage. Sisir Gupta (1966), an Indian diplomat, said: "Without using its nuclear weapons and without unleashing the kind of war which would be regarded in the West as the crossing of the provocation threshold, China may subject a non-nuclear India to periodic blackmail, weaken its people's spirit of resistance and self-confidence and thus achieve without a war its major political and military objectives in Asia" (Gupta 1966: 62; cited in Ganguly 1999b: 152). India's insurance motive for proliferation was also evident in its behavior after the 1974 test. For nearly a decade thereafter, the country's nuclear program consisted of awkward, oversize, tactically challenged bombs that were not integrated into military operations. They served as a political hedge against Chinese nuclear blackmail, not as strategically relevant assets.

Prestige

The political currency that derives from proliferation in Asia is also related to issues of prestige and status. As Sagan (1996–97) has argued, states acquire nuclear weapons not only to balance against external threats but also as symbols. For many countries in Asia, nuclear weapons and ballistic missiles are the contemporary equivalent of national armies in the postcolonial era (Bracken 1999a: 420). They serve as marks of modernity and power. Many post–Cold War analyses of Asian security (Betts 1993–94; Friedberg 1993–94; Calder 1996; Bracken 1999b) have drawn attention to the region's avid nationalism—a function of history, colonial legacies, and economic growth. Inherent in this nationalism are aspirations to rise in the international prestige hierarchy and to be treated as a "great" or "major" power. Nuclear weapons and ballistic missiles have become a conspicuous badge of this status. In extreme terms, these capabilities are like national airlines. Countries seek to acquire them because of the way they reflect on one's identity and level of development.

In the case of nuclear weapons, this is most certainly a function of their awesome destructive power.[25] But it is also a function of careful observation of precedents and examples of nuclear prestige set in the West. For France, for example,

---

[24]For example, the IRBM Ghauri test in April 1998 was hailed as now enabling Islamabad to negotiate with India from a position of parity and strength.

[25]Jervis (1989: 182) notes that when the weapon is so powerful that the two can destroy each other, power converts to outcomes not through military clashes but by indirect processes and subjective assessments.

after the devastation of World War II and colonial defeats in Southeast Asia, becoming a nuclear weapon state was a symbol of returning to historic great-power status.[26] Some argue that without nuclear weapons (Wheeler 1990: 36; Pullinger 1994: 2) the United Kingdom would have no special reason for claiming a permanent seat today on the UN Security Council. Perhaps most important for Asian eyes were the prestige precedents set by China's nuclearization in the 1960s. China became the last enshrined member of the hallowed nuclear club in 1970 (with the NPT)—after which all others could only be NNWS or illegitimate NWS. Subsequent events such as Nixon's decision to visit China in 1971 (and Sino-American rapprochement), the ousting of Taiwan from the UN, and the bestowing of a permanent Security Council seat to Beijing were all seen as tangible elevations to China's international stature that were directly related to its nuclear status. These lessons were not lost on India.[27] New Delhi's attitude toward nuclear and missile capabilities is strongly influenced, as acknowledged by prominent Indians, by ambitions to achieve "great-power status." As two Indian opinion leaders noted: "The bomb is a currency of self-esteem." Or as K. Subrahmanyam said: "Nuclear weapons are not military weapons. Their logic is that of international politics and it is a logic of global, nuclear order. . . . India wants to be a player in, and not an object of, this global nuclear order" (Talbott 1999: 116). Prestige mattered for Pakistan too—not just in the sense of being perceived as India's equal in South Asia, but also as the first Islamic country capable of such technological feats despite severe resource constraints. *Izzat* (honor) or *sharam* (shame) constituted the terms in which the country pursued its nuclear and Ghauri missile programs (Yasmeen 1999: 44; Ahmed 1999: 179, n. 3; Gordon 1994: 667).

Security or Symbols?

This is not to say that prestige and political currency are the primary drivers of proliferation in Asia. The mix of security needs and resource constraints is still the most compelling reason for states to perceive nuclear weapons as the most robust and efficient means of "equalizing" power disadvantages. At the same time, though, prestige and political currency are not merely peripheral factors. Status concerns are more than just the language with which proliferators embel-

[26]As Sagan (1996–97: 78) notes: "The belief that nuclear power and nuclear weapons were deeply linked to a state's position in the international system was present as early as 1951 when France's first five-year plan saw the links between nuclear weapons and France as a powerful country."

[27]As Hagerty (1999: 21) observes: "Indian leaders noted the symbolic bestowal of great-power status on China and the fact that the membership of the Security Council and the nuclear club were now identical." For concurring arguments, see Scheinman (n.d.).

lish or justify their drive for nuclear and missile programs (Goldstein 2000: 271–72). Prestige concerns are more than just afterthoughts. At times, they are also the forethoughts that inform or cause proliferation decisions.

The significance of these factors derives from the fact that anomalies in certain preeminent cases of proliferation in Asia cannot be explained by basic security arguments. The 1998 South Asian tests, for example, did not make strategic sense, strictly speaking, in that they showed little value added militarily. The Indian tests exhibited some ability to miniaturize and weaponize with missiles, but neither set of tests showed a capability for increased accuracy in weapons and delivery vehicles to the point of being able to demonstrate counterforce targeting capabilities. Hence the South Asian balance still rested on mutual deterrence based on countervalue capabilities—which means that in terms of their payoff the tests were more for symbolic reasons. They represented both countries' declared nuclear status and the shift away from recessed nuclear deterrence (Abraham 1998; Ganguly 1999a: 438–40).

More anomalies appear if one looks at either the India-China or Pakistan-India dyad. If the purpose of testing is deterrence, then you want to make certain you have achieved a threshold deterrent capability *before* testing. In other words, you must have the infrastructure and the ability to rapidly "plus-up" in capabilities (in terms of stockpiles of fissionable material, missiles, warheads, command and control, and the like) prior to taking an act that declares your capability. Otherwise, testing without the capabilities and infrastructure would leave you very vulnerable to preemption. Neither the Indian tests vis-à-vis the Chinese in 1974 nor the 1998 Pakistani tests vis-à-vis India reflect this logic. In the former case, New Delhi was a decade away from weaponizing its capabilities—and therefore by testing was actually putting itself in a more vulnerable position by raising Beijing's incentive to preempt.

An alternative line of argument says that what may have been true in the past is no longer true today. In other words, proliferation did give rise to some benefits in terms of status and bargaining power to countries like China; but since the NPT in 1970 and the ostracism imposed by the nonproliferation community, any benefits from proliferation are fleeting and negated by the costs (Goldstein 2000: 254). While this argument may hold true in the future (and indeed should be a goal of the nonproliferation effort), there is not enough evidence to suggest its validity. In the South Asian cases, for example, the net result of the tests has been far from negative. The United States imposed sanctions on the two countries after May 1998, as mandated by the Nuclear Proliferation Prevention Act (1994), and withdrew support for World Bank and IMF loans. But one month later the United States reinstated agricultural exports because of pressures from the American farm lobby and by early November further eased sanctions (to cover only high technology and military exports) as New Delhi and Islamabad announced testing moratoriums and pledged to sign the CTBT. And although other nonproliferation leaders like Japan followed suit, sanctions were largely ineffective as the Japanese government did not prevent private companies from operating in India. Neither the United Nations, the Group of Eight, nor the European Union took any action beyond a verbal statement condemning the tests (Rauf 1999a: 14–16). For Pakistan, Islamabad understood that responding to the Indian tests in May 1998 would attract economic sanctions. But it calculated that enthusiasm for punitive actions would fade, as the international community could not indefinitely sanction one-fifth of the world's population (Yasmeen 1999: 50; Ahmed 1999: 190).[28] For India, arguably, the benefits of testing were a Clinton-Vajpayee summit in March 2000 that resulted in the Agreed Principles—institutionalizing a regular summit-level dialogue, foreign minister meetings, and finance and commerce minister meetings with the United States. Some argue that the 1998 tests marked a watershed in U.S. attention to the South Asian problem, moving from policies that were poorly conceived, reactive, and ambivalent to an uncharacteristic focus and organization (Rauf 1999a: 2).[29]

The costs of proliferating will be higher for the states that are embedded in the international arena—hence skewing the cost calculations for regimes like Pakistan and North Korea in favor of proliferation. Finding ways to raise these costs is part of the solution to nonproliferation, but this is not to discount prestige and political currency as significant causes of proliferation. Again, they do not outweigh the security factors but operate alongside them and sometimes play a more prominent role. Without these variables, proliferation anomalies cannot be explained.

Ballistic Missile Defense

A key variable for the region's future proliferation prospects is missile defense. America's plans for ballistic missile defense can be seen as a consequence and, arguably, a cause of nuclear and missile proliferation. On the consequence side, the growing numbers of countries acquiring or seeking to acquire MRBM, IRBM, and ICBM capabilities form the primary rationale for U.S. deployment of theater and national missile defenses (TMD and NMD).[30] Such defenses would protect not only against accidental launches but also against attacks or threats by rogue

[28]This assessment was informed by previous U.S. one-time waivers of the Pressler Amendment to sell $360 million in military hardware to Pakistan.

[29]The text of the Agreed Principles is available at http://usinfo.state.gov/regional/nea/mena/ india1.htm.

[30]See Rumsfeld et al. (1998). For a critique of the Rumsfeld report, see Cirincione (2000: 125–32).

states or aggressively intended actors against the U.S. homeland, overseas bases, and U.S. allies.[31] Standing debates on this side of the equation are largely technological—the extent to which the proposed systems of radars, sensors, and hit-to-kill technology will prove capable of effectively tracking, distinguishing (from decoys and other penetration aids and countermeasures), and intercepting incoming missiles.[32]

More controversial and problematic issues arise on the cause side of the BMD/proliferation equation—that is, the extent to which BMD (and in particular NMD), while meant to contend with proliferation, actually contributes to the pace of proliferation as states react to the deployment of an American missile shield. According to this logic, BMD would become an engine for further proliferation in three general ways that are potentially destabilizing to overall security order in the region: it would spur greater production and deployment of missiles by others seeking to overwhelm any defensive shield (and thereby maintain the integrity of the country's missile deterrent force); it would create incentives for countries to renounce current arms control and nonproliferation agreements; and it might spur proliferation among allies as they perceive missile defense to be giving the U.S. "decoupling" options that undermine the credibility of the extended nuclear deterrence umbrella. For an illustration of the first two dynamics, consider China and Russia. First-phase deployment of the midcourse interceptor system (twenty to one hundred interceptors) would undermine a Chinese missile deterrent of twenty ICBMs (DF-5).[33] Beijing's likely response would be to ramp up production and deployment of missiles focused particularly on replacing the DF-5 with more mobile, solid-fuel ICBMs (DF-41). In addition to deploying larger numbers of offensive forces to avoid a loss of deterrent power, Beijing would also develop countermeasures (decoys, chaff, miniaturization, multiple warheads) to penetrate a BMD shield. Some argue that such countermeasures would require testing and development that would undermine Chinese support (if such support had not already degraded as a political response to BMD) for the CTBT, the Fissile Material Cutoff Treaty negotiations, and commitments to abide

[31]A detailed discussion of missile defense systems and potential architectures for Asia is beyond the scope of this chapter. For discussions of the current midcourse interceptor system, lower-tier (Patriot-3 and Navy Area) and upper-tier (THAAD and Navy Theater Wide) proposed theater systems, and alternative technologies (e.g., boost-phase intercept), see Wilkening (2000), BMDO (2000), and Cochran (2000).

[32]Ruina (2001) offers a concise historical look at the technical problems with BMD dating back to the 1960s. O'Hanlon (2000) presents a concise overview of current programs.

[33]The Russian deterrent (approximately a thousand or more warheads) would not be undermined by the current NMD system. Russian concerns center on the U.S. introduction of the radar and satellite infrastructure that later could be upgraded to accommodate a much larger system of interceptors (beyond the currently planned 250).

by MTCR principles.[34] Other responses that would exacerbate proliferation problems include the likely rescinding of China's no-first-use pledge, deployment of antisatellite capabilities, and a higher state of readiness with regard to its nuclear forces (that is, no longer unfueled and disassembled).[35] In terms of the drivers of proliferation laid out earlier, BMD augments the basic security driver of proliferation by raising new sets of vulnerabilities that states will seek to overcome. (See Appendix B.)

Both critics and supporters of missile defense acknowledge that some form of proliferation in response to deployment of such a system is likely. But proliferation alone is not a priori and unconditionally destabilizing. The salient question then becomes, In what ways does BMD deployment undermine security order in the region? The answer lies largely in the secondary and tertiary dynamics set off by states adjusting to BMD deployments that in turn aggravate regional tensions. One could consider these BMD cascade effects in three sets of dynamics.

The first set relates to the tertiary effects of states responding to Chinese reactions to BMD. One clear and highly likely scenario in this regard applies to South Asia. Chinese ramping up of MRBM and IRBMs in response to an American BMD (NMD or TMD) system would be seen as threatening to India in terms of these enhanced capabilities as well as in terms of the benefits that such Chinese capabilities might accrue to Pakistan. Almost certainly this would elicit counter-reactions from India in terms of developing its own MRBM capabilities (such as Agni) as well as nuclear weaponization. This, in turn, would prompt a Pakistani response.[36]

The second set of dynamics relates to the political cascades set off by BMD. In Northeast Asia, for example, deployment of a U.S.-Japan based TMD system (Navy Theater) would not only raise Chinese concerns about a potential Japanese role in Taiwan's defense (if the United States were to respond to Chinese missile threats against Taipei) but also heighten Sino-Japanese tensions considerably— thereby undercutting dialogue between Beijing and Tokyo experts on security issues. These initiatives are small-scale and unofficial but nonetheless promising. On the Chinese side, for instance, these talks give voice to expert groups that understand Japan's need for some form of defense against North Korean missiles. These experts are able to engage those on the Japanese side who understand Bei-

---

[34]The counterargument is that China is undertaking many of these measures as part of its ongoing military modernization. For example, the DF-5 is an old, liquid-fueled missile vulnerable to a first strike and in need of replacement whether or not the United States moves forward with missile defense. On the Chinese missile modernization program, see Lewis and Di (1992).

[35]For studies on Chinese responses to missile defense, see Green and Dalton (2000: 32–43) and Stokes (1999).

[36]For these reasons India has explicitly opposed BMD (Green and Dalton 2000: 53–55).

jing's trepidations regarding Japan's potential entanglement in a Taiwan Strait crisis. (For this reason they have called, for example, for explicit Japanese statements that Japan's cooperation in U.S.-based missile defense should not be construed as part and parcel of the revised U.S.-Japan Defense Guidelines; see Urayama 2000.) Rapid American and Japanese movement toward deployment would undercut this dialogue and reinforce the "shields-to-swords" proponents in Beijing (those who see Japanese participation in U.S. BMD research as aimed at remilitarization) and the "China-threaters" in Tokyo.

The third set of cascades relates to how BMD can affect relations between allies. At one level, the enthusiasm with which the George W. Bush administration is pursuing missile defense has meaning for how the United States defines allies and friends in the region in the future. Whereas in the past such definitions were based on where the United States was allowed by host countries to maintain a forward presence, in the future it may be defined by who consents (and commits to) remaining within the BMD umbrella and who does not. South Korea, for example, has been a stalwart American ally that has explicitly chosen not to participate in initial American discussions about TMD architectures in the region. Japan participates in the research phase but has reserved judgment on the testing and deployment phases. Full-fledged American initiatives on missile defense might redefine the region's security landscape, creating new friends and allies and distancing old ones.

At another level, missile defense may upset security order by creating disputes between American allies in the region. Again the relevant dynamic relates to the tertiary effects of Chinese responses. Many experts agree that the likely Chinese response to a degrading of their missile deterrent by American BMD deployment would be, not to ramp up ICBM development, but to expand greatly their short-range missile arsenals (which are less defensible by Navy Theater Wide and THAAD). The net security effect in this instance for Japan would be negative: the added security of missile defense systems would be outweighed by the proliferation of Chinese SRBM and MRBM deployments. Japan's response to this might not be defense, but deterrence in the form of creating its own missile capability. While such a deterrent might be directed against China, it would undoubtedly raise concerns among American allies, particularly South Korea, about renewed Japanese militarism.

Consequences of Proliferation: Sober Optimism

For reasons of security needs, resource constraints, political currency, and First World hypocrisy, nuclear proliferation is overdetermined in Asia. Two implications follow from this observation. First, proliferation is not likely to decline in the future because of the abundance of these factors; second, the likelihood of getting new proliferators to roll back their capabilities is low.[37] So long as the forces that drive proliferation abound in Asia, the potential for vertical and horizontal proliferation remains serious. What, then, are the consequences?

Proliferation Pessimism

"Proliferation pessimists" (Karl 1996–97) see grave implications to these trends in Asia. Three basic arguments inform this viewpoint. The first focuses on the exceptional nature of the Cold War nuclear deterrence. The U.S.-Soviet nuclear confrontation was based on a unique set of circumstances (territorial separation, no previous history of hostility, status-quo orientations, simplicity of the bipolar rivalry) that created a balance of terror and stable deterrence (Karl 1996–97: 90–93; Dunn 1982, 1991; Kaiser 1989; Miller 1993; Evron 1994). This experience is the obverse of Asia's. In Asia one sees close proximity, high levels of interstate conflict, antagonistic histories, and non-status-quo orientations among many of the regional powers. Contrary to Waltzian arguments (Waltz 1979) for nuclear stability, the exceptionalist school argues that differentiation among the units matters in terms of outcomes and, moreover, that the nonuse experienced in the American-Soviet dyad is not replicable in post–Cold War Asia.

A second school of thought (Feaver 1992; Blair 1993; Sagan 1994; Sagan and Waltz 1995; Bracken 1999b) focuses on the dangers associated with accidents, organizational flaws, judgment errors, and failed fail-safe systems. This school argues that the many problems evident in elaborate systems constructed by the Americans and Soviets would be exponentially worse in the rudimentary systems of Asia. A third set of arguments (Chang 1988, 1990; Karl 1996–97: 96–97; Richelson 2000–2001) derives from preventive/preemptive war logic and draws attention to the asymmetric advantages created by proliferation and how these advantages, particularly when they are either temporary or vulnerable to attack, give rise to windows of opportunity for preemptive or preventive action.

Although proliferation is likely to continue in Asia, this may not warrant such a pessimistic assessment. If states are proliferating for three basic purposes (security, avoiding blackmail, and prestige and political currency), the outcome may not be nearly so dire as the conventional wisdom predicts. This proposition neither assumes nor implies that nonproliferation is a wasted effort. Instead it argues that, aside from individual cases of rogue regime proliferation, there is no intuitively obvious reason to equate Asian proliferation and the pessimist school's predictions of disastrous outcomes as many nonproliferation advocates have done. The reasoning in this vein is far from airtight, in fact, and does a disservice

---

[37]The implications of these findings for nonproliferation regimes are discussed later.

to the nonproliferation school by basing its arguments on weak analogies or inconsistent logic.

Ethnocentrism

Informing all of the pessimistic proliferation views, either explicitly or implicitly, are "First World socialization" presumptions that the dangers of U.S.-Soviet proliferation were mitigated by mutual abhorrence of violence among the public and political leadership, an understanding of the high stakes involved with such destructive weapons, and rational calculations. In the Third World, however, a combustible combination of historical resentment, religious rivalry, and hypernationalism makes nuclear weapons use more likely. One of the key differences between the first and second nuclear ages is that the second generation is dominated by fierce nationalism and fanatic leaders who embrace nuclear and BM technology as the great equalizer against hated enemies: "Asian nationalism harnesses all the immaturity and energy unleashed by the French Revolution and by communism in its expansionist heyday" (Bracken 1999a: 420). This emotionalism is said to contrast with the former world's cool and calm competition of sophisticated thinkers, rational deterrence models, and responsible leaders. As Bracken puts it: "The idea of budding defense intellectuals sitting around computer models and debating strategy in Iran or Pakistan defies credulity" (Bracken 1999b: 112–13; Calder 1996).

There is no denying that Asia has its fair share of conflicts steeped in peer competition, history, race, and religion. Moreover unredeemed resentment characterizes many of the dyads in which proliferation potential exists or has already been realized. But there is no evidence to validate the assumption that the animosities are especially raw and vulgar in Asia.[38] Some have even argued (Kang 1999) that in a broad historical perspective, the level of bloodshed in Asia pales in comparison with that in Europe. There is no reason a priori to assume that animosity in Asia is any less informed by rationality than the emotions that reigned during the first nuclear age.[39]

Moreover, the causal link between hate and nuclear action is spurious. Even if one were to accept that Asian hatreds are inherently more intense and aboriginal than in the West, there is no necessary connection with the propensity to use nu-

---

[38]Again quoting Bracken (1999a: 420): "The sources of instability in Asia are ones that cannot be eliminated through hot lines and high-tech locking devices to prevent the unauthorized launch of weapons. It may be better to have these safety measures in place than not to have them, but they divert attention from the more primitive animosity that lies below the surface and can be inflamed." See also Friedberg (1993–94).

[39]For critiques of ethnocentrism in the proliferation debate, see Waltz's arguments in Sagan and Waltz (1995); see also Feaver (1995) and Hashim (1995).

clear weapons. The decision to wage nuclear destruction on another is not based on how much you loathe your opponent but on how much you value the target of your opponent's retaliation: your own constituency.[40] Hence ethnocentric arguments about nuclear exchanges in Asia should focus, not on hate, but on the willingness to commit suicide as the primary cause.

These arguments also fail to comprehend how much the bipolar superpower experience has prejudiced our thinking on nuclear deterrence and stability. The conventional wisdom demonstrates an insufficient appreciation of the uniqueness rather than the generalizability of the superpower experience. For example, organizational arguments assume that the profile of the Asian programs as small and underdeveloped makes them more prone to accidents, "loose nukes," or inadvertent use. But if the arsenals are small in size and few in number, they are, as a rule, easier to monitor and control. Moreover, many of the organizational pathologies made famous by Sagan require complexity in the nuclear infrastructure and decision-making trees—a precondition that is irrelevant in Asia because the infrastructures are basic and, in many cases, divorced from the military bureaucracy (another pathology often cited) (Goldstein 2000: 276–79). In a similar vein, poor command, control, and communication infrastructures in Asia have not resulted in "use-or-lose" mentalities but have bred more caution (as in the Indo-Pakistan conflicts). Limited overhead and reconnaissance capacities have not encouraged confidence in the ability to hide one's arsenals but have discouraged confidence in carrying out successful first strikes. And many of these fledgling programs, by virtue of resource constraints, remain at an underdeveloped stage (dealerted, detargeted, disassembled weapon systems, warheads separated from delivery vehicles) (Canberra Commission 1996; National Academy of Sciences 1997). The upshot is that until an accident or outcome confirms the organizational school's view in the second nuclear age—and given what is now being unearthed about the near-misses and near-disasters in the first nuclear age—there is no a priori reason to assume a causal connection between small programs and destabilizing outcomes.

Existential Deterrence

Proliferation pessimists fixate on assured second-strike capability as the primary agent of deterrence and underestimate the validity of other forms of deterrence among smaller nuclear powers. The pessimist's assessment rests on faith in the "use-or-lose" logic—when states do not have assured second-strike capabilities, they live in constant fear of being hit by a debilitating first strike. Thus in a crisis between adversaries with small nuclear forces, the incentive to preempt (as

---

[40]Thanks to Avery Goldstein for raising this point.

well as the fear of being preempted) gives rise to a destabilizing "use-or-lose" mentality.[41]

There are two problems with this argument. First, in deductive terms, there is no denying that assured second-strike capabilities can form the backbone of stable deterrence; but this does not mean that the absence of this condition necessarily leads to instability. Second, the empirical record does not bear out the "use-or-lose" argument. As Hagerty (1995–96: 79–114; 1999: 24–26) notes, preemption has not occurred in any of the crises involving smaller nuclear powers (Cuba 1962, Sino-Soviet 1969, Arab-Israeli 1973, Kashmir 1990). What appears to operate instead among small nuclear powers is existential deterrence: "The mere existence of nuclear forces means that, whatever we say or do, there is a certain irreducible risk that an armed conflict might escalate into a nuclear war. The fear of escalation is thus factored into political calculations: faced with this risk, states are more cautious and more prudent than they otherwise would be" (Trachtenberg 1985: 139; see also Bundy 1984: 3–13 and Hagerty 1998: 26).

What prevails in the second nuclear age in Asia, therefore, may not be assured second-strike capability but first-strike uncertainty. Stable deterrence derives from having just enough capacity to raise uncertainty in the mind of opponents that they cannot neutralize you with a first strike. The precedent for this form of deterrence had already been set by the second-tier nuclear powers in the first age. As Goldstein (2000: 44–46) shows, existential deterrent doctrines drove China, Britain, and France's pursuit of an independent but not second-strike-assured nuclear deterrent against their superpower adversaries. In the new nuclear age in Asia, where cost constraints among new proliferators will be acute, smaller arsenals counterintuitively will not incite attack. Moreover, the opaque conditions under which programs in Asia develop increase first-strike uncertainty, as worst-case assessments generally tend to err on the side of caution.

The South Asian case appears thus far to validate existential deterrent claims. Because of resource constraints, neither India nor Pakistan will be able to develop an assured survivable force. Moreover, neither will possess the missile guidance and accuracy capability to move beyond countervalue targeting. Both, however, will have sufficient fissile material for a small number of atomic bombs on aircraft (Mirage, MiG-27, MiG-29, SU-30, and Jaguar for India; the A-5, F-16, and Mirage 3 for Pakistan) as well as the potential for weaponized warheads on some ballistic missiles (Prithvi-150 for India and Hatf-2 for Pakistan), but not to the level of a successful first strike (Hagerty 1999: 23–24; 1995–96). Neither country has attempted preemptive destruction of the other's nuclear facilities, and both signed a nonattack agreement in 1991 based on their de facto nuclear status.

[41]For the classic statement, see Schelling (1960: chap. 9).

The fact that these are now de jure capabilities should not make a difference (Alagappa 1998: 6). India's draft nuclear doctrine makes reference to pursuing a triad, but most experts see this as "grandiose" and contradicting India's more realistic objective of a minimum deterrent (Ganguly 1999a: 440; Yasmeen 1999: 49).[42] Moreover, nuclear weapons have instilled a fear of escalation in bilateral conflicts that tempers action on both sides. In the Indo-Pakistani crises of 1987, and especially 1990, 1999, and 2002, many cite the calming effect of New Delhi's explicit concern about rapid ascent up the ladder of escalation (Ganguly 1996: 76–107).[43]

Nuclear Taboo

Another factor reinforcing the stability of first-strike uncertainty in the second nuclear age is the potential for new nuclear powers to become compliant with the norms against the use of nuclear weapons. As Russett (1989: 185) argues, the first nuclear age recognized that such weapons were in fact unusable across much of the range of military and political interests. Despite the absence of restricting international laws or conventions—and without the explicit threat of symmetric retaliation—nuclear powers refrained from using such weapons in military situations where it might have altered a neutral or losing outcome. The United States did not use them in Korea or Vietnam, the Soviets did not use them in Afghanistan, and the Chinese did not use them in Vietnam (Paul 1995).

Proliferation pessimists do not deny the existence of the nuclear taboo. They do, however, regard it as a notion shared only by First World proliferators. Is this a fair assessment? Tannenwald (1999) argues that a taboo takes effect when the agent realizes the exceptional nature of the weapon (in terms of its destructive power), recognizes the absence of effective defenses (that is, vulnerability), and fears the political and social consequences of taking such an action. All these conditions readily hold as well for new nuclear powers. Moreover, the revulsion

[42]For additional arguments on how crisis stability and strategic stability conditions deriving from first-strike uncertainty are reinforcing for India and Pakistan, see Ganguly (1999b: 177). For the draft nuclear doctrine, see the Embassy of India website at http://www.indianembassy.org/policy/CTBT/nuclear_doctrine_aug_17_1999.html. For reaffirmations of India's minimum credible deterrent arguments, see the Clinton-Vajpayee joint vision statement, March 2000, "US-India Relations: A Vision for the 21st Century," at http://usinfor.state.gov/regional/nea/mena/india1.htm.

[43]This is not to say that everything is rosy. Two problems sit on the horizon. First, if first-strike uncertainty and the fear of escalation stabilize conflict at the nuclear level, then instability at lower levels of violence may eventually result. On the stability/instability paradox, see Jervis (1984: 31) and Snyder (1965). Second, existential deterrence is most problematic in the Sino-Indian dyad. Although Beijing has the capacity to inflict a high level of damage on India, at current levels it could not be assured of a successful first strike. With the growth of Chinese capabilities (and India's inability to develop ballistic missiles to target Chinese assets with confidence), however, first-strike uncertainty could be undermined.

against nuclear weapons use (first use) has become so institutionalized in an array of international agreements and practices that new NWS operate in an environment that severely circumscribes the realm of legitimate nuclear use.

Proliferation pessimists therefore underestimate the transformative effects of nuclear weapons on these new proliferators. They assume that the interests for aspiring nuclear powers remain constant before and after acquisition. They do not consider that once states cross the nuclear threshold, they become acutely aware of the dangers and responsibilities that come with these awesome new capabilities. The likelihood of such a learning process is even higher if nuclear weapons are valued for their political currency. While security needs certainly drive proliferation in Asia, as noted, another predominant factor is the striving for prestige and international recognition as an NWS state. And if the taboo equates the use of nuclear weapons with an "uncivilized" or "barbarian" state (Tannenwald 1999: 437), then states that are status-conscious will be that much more attuned to the taboo. The effects of the taboo on Asian proliferators are therefore both regulative and constitutive. In the regulative sense, as these states further embed themselves in the international community, the costs of breaking any rules regarding nuclear use increase. The taboo's constitutive effects are evident, too, in that any use would undermine one of the primary purposes for which the capabilities were sought (prestige, for instance, or a badge of modernity).

Although it is still early in the game, there is evidence that the acquisition of nuclear capabilities has been accompanied by a change in what is considered acceptable behavior. While India has outright rejected any notions that it might roll back its newfound capability, it has readily admitted that as an incipient NWS, it now has certain responsibilities that include a no-first-use policy and not sharing nuclear weapons technology with irresponsible states (Ganguly 1999a: 440; Alagappa 1998: 6). Similarly, Pakistan previously rejected nonproliferation norms as inhibiting and degrading to the national character.[44] Otherwise Pakistan might have been swayed by the benefits of not responding to the Indian tests as a shining example of a country adhering to nuclear nonproliferation norms. Perhaps it is only after becoming an incipient NWS that such arguments about nonproliferation gain value. Nowhere is this perverse dynamic more evident than in both sides' views of the CTBT. Once perceived as an instrument intended to preempt nuclear spread beyond the first age, the CTBT is now arguably seen by India and Pakistan in less antagonistic terms—and even among some as a responsibility to be borne as a nuclear state.

[44]Domestic groups who counseled against the May 1998 tests held little sway (Yasmeen 1999).

The Role of the Nonproliferation Regime?

This chapter has made two points with regard to proliferation in Asia. First, proliferation is overdetermined; hence rollback, though desirable, is unlikely. And second, while the likelihood of continued Asian proliferation in the future is serious (given the abundance of causes), this does not necessarily presage disastrous consequences for regional stability (contrary to proliferation pessimists).

What, then, are the implications of this argument for the nonproliferation regime? The argument does not connote the futility of nonproliferation. It does, however, imply that nonproliferation arguments based on an inherent equating of new proliferation with irrational or inadvertent nuclear use are spurious (and ultimately do a disservice to the objectives of the nonproliferation community). Moreover, the argument shows that the challenges faced by the nonproliferation advocates are formidable. The abundance of causes means that more states are likely to try to proliferate—and if they are successful, rollback, although ideal, will be very difficult except in certain circumstances.[45] Moreover, the nonproliferation community's focus on rollback may in fact be detrimental to stability because it fails to acknowledge the security factors that drove proliferation in the first place. Without addressing the former, one cannot have a rollback of the latter (Alagappa 1998: 2–3). Rollback should be, not a normative prescription, but a pragmatic decision based on an assessment of the region's proliferation drivers.

And because rollback is problematic, the nonproliferation community's efforts are at a premium in terms of stopping proliferation before it happens and maintaining and reinforcing a robust norm against nuclear nonuse. Indeed, fostering the region's compliance with current global regimes on the control of technology and materials, as well as building upon regional and bilateral institutions, can greatly reinforce the nonuse outcome in Asia. At first glance, the region's record of compliance with global conventions and international treaties

---

[45]Positing the conditions for nuclear rollback is beyond the scope of this chapter. As Sagan (1996–97: 60–62) argues, the likelihood of rollback increases when security threats moderate or when security guarantees are forthcoming from other interested parties. Thus South Africa publicly disposed of its program of six disassembled weapons in 1991 after the Soviet threat in Angola and Namibia ended. Argentina and Brazil abandoned their programs in 1990 because they no longer saw each other as threats. And Ukraine, Kazakhstan, and Belarus all gave up the arsenals they inherited from the Soviet Union because of security assurances from the United States. But as Goldstein (2000: 222) argues, such optimistic predictions from the security model for proliferation have to be tempered by the technological considerations. So long as nuclear weapons remain the dominant technological innovation in military strategy, "the presence of nuclear weapons, regardless of polarity, drives a strategic logic that weakens confidence in security as a collective good supplied through international alliances and encourages the pursuit of an independent deterrent capability as the ultimate guarantee of national security."

appears spotty.[46] (See Appendixes C and D.) Moreover, the absence of leadership among the First World nuclear powers (particularly the United States on failure to ratify the CTBT and its discussions of NMD and abandonment of the ABM treaty) simply reinforces perceptions of First World hypocrisy among the new proliferators (Sands n.d.).

Despite these setbacks, there is still room for optimism. Even though key violators like Pakistan, India, and the DPRK remain outside the NPT regime, the treaty's indefinite extension in 1995 sets an important precedent with regard to universal membership and compliance, a precedent these states cannot simply ignore or dismiss. Moreover, Chinese participation in arms control and nonproliferation regimes over the past fifteen years has increased substantially. In addition to membership in the NPT, CWC, and BWC, China became a Zangger Committee member in 1997. In spite of earlier transfers of nuclear technology and missile parts to the Middle East and South Asia, Beijing has since committed to adhering to the NSG triggers list and to abide by the MTCR principles (in a bilateral agreement with the United States) (see Appendixes B and C). Moreover, it announced a self-imposed testing moratorium in 1996 and has committed to upholding the CTBT despite the U.S. failure to ratify. Beijing also acceded to the Rarotonga protocols in 1997 (Appendix D), and supports FMCT negotiations (Medieros n.d.; Johnston and Evans 1999). This is not a perfect record, but it is still far from hopeless.

At the regional and subregional level, one development that raises confidence in the region's ability to organize support for nonproliferation institutions is the nuclear-weapon-free zones (NWFZ). Of the four that exist today, two are in Asia. (See Appendix E.) These zones generally entail a legal obligation to place all nuclear materials and installations under full-scope IAEA safeguards; clearly demarcate geographic limits of the NWFZ; and specify the obligations, rights, and responsibilities of parties with regard to disavowing nuclear weapons. The South Pacific Nuclear Free Zone (Treaty of Rarotonga) of 1986, for example, forbids the manufacture, acquisition, possession, or control by its member states of any nuclear explosive device inside or outside the treaty zone. It also forbids testing, stationing, dumping, or transfer of nuclear materials or equipment to any state not subject to IAEA safeguards. The regime has been relatively successful in getting the NWS to observe the three protocols of 1996 barring them from similar activity in the region.[47]

[46]China is a member of the NPT and signed the CTBT but has transferred nuclear and missile technology to Pakistan and Iran. India and Pakistan are not members of NPT, CTBT, or MTCR and actively oppose some of these conventions because they see them as making permanent the gaps in capabilities between established powers and themselves (Plesch 2000).

[47]France was dropped as a dialogue partner in 1995 after its tests but was reinstated in 1996.

Because nuclear and missile programs in Asia are not likely to disappear, embedding these programs in global nonproliferation regimes as well as encouraging the creation of new regional institutions can reinforce stability in Asia in two ways that support nonproliferation objectives. First, such institutions ensure that the barriers to entry regarding nuclear and missile capabilities remain high. If nuclear rollback is not a feasible option, the next best option is to make acquisition of these capabilities as difficult and costly as possible. This contributes to the nonuse outcome in Asia by at least slowing the pace of proliferation. It also lowers the danger of accidents: those that undertake the effort to surmount these barriers are also likely to be the more responsible proliferators. And second, such institutions create normative pressures to forgo acquisition as parties deeply enmeshed in the regimes greatly discount the benefits of going nuclear by the reputational costs of violating the regimes. For those that have already proliferated, moreover, the robustness of these regimes further socializes these states to the nuclear taboo.

Two additional possibilities deserve mention here. One is a limited nuclear-weapon-free zone in Northeast Asia centered on the Korean peninsula and Japan (after moderation of the North Korean threat). The foundation for such an institution could be built on a bundling of events in the region that act as permissive factors to such a zone: the 1992 North-South Denuclearization Declaration; KEDO; Japan's nonnuclear principles; the 1994 Agreed Framework; and the 1991 U.S. declaration regarding the removal of nuclear weapons from the region.[48] Track 2 groups have looked at various proposals in this regard.[49] In South Asia there is little likelihood of a nuclear-free zone. The salience of unresolved conflicts renders rollback difficult and heightens the regional players' perceived need for deterrent capabilities. This does not negate the potential for a no-first-use zone, however. This could be bundled around the India-Pakistan Nonattack

---

Parties to the South Pacific zone are Australia, Cook Islands, Federated States of Micronesia, Fiji, Kiribati, Nauru, New Zealand, Niue, Palau, Papua New Guinea, Republic of Marshall Islands, Solomon Islands, Tonga, Tuvalu, Vanuatu, Western Samoa. The dialogue partners are Canada, China, the EU, Japan, ROK, the United Kingdom, the United States, and France. The Southeast Asia Nuclear Weapon Free Zone (SEANWFZ) Treaty is even more stringent than Rarotonga. It requires negative security assurances from the NWS and extends the nuclear-free zone within the seven ASEAN members' continental shelves and exclusive economic zones. (No NWS have signed yet; the United States and France object to the unequivocal nature of the treaty's security assurances.) The 1997 Almaty Declaration called for a Central Asia NWFZ endorsed by Kyrgyzstan, Kazakhstan, Tajikistan, Turkmenistan, and Uzbekistan (CNS 1997; Rauf 1999b: 5–8).

[48]For details of each of these agreements, see CNS (1997: 62–63).

[49]See work by the Center for International Strategy, Technology, and Policy at Georgia Tech's Northeast Asia Cooperative Regional Security Initiative since 1992 at http://www.cistp.gatech.edu/programs/lnwfz-nea.html. This might also garner Chinese support, as Beijing has expressed interest in NWFZs and announced in July 1999 that it would sign the SEANWFZ protocols (which would make China the first NWS to do so).

Agreement of 1988,[50] the South Asian Association for Regional Cooperation (SAARC),[51] and the Clinton-Vajpayee summit joint vision statement (in which India in principle supports forgoing future tests, seeks support of starting talks on FMCT, and favors export controls).[52] Other possibilities include a Northeast Asia fissile material register and a North and South Asia technology control regime.[53]

Thus an assessment of sober optimism with regard to the consequences of proliferation in Asia does not preclude the importance of current or future nonproliferation regimes. These regimes are not only critical to raising the material and reputational costs of proliferating; they also reinforce norms of safety and taboos on nonuse once proliferation has occurred. For nonproliferation advocates, however, to focus on nuclear rollback in Asia without addressing the causes (of which there are many) is fruitless.

The case for sober optimism is not meant to imply that all will be rosy in Asia. Nuclear weapons will not have an inherent pacifying effect on conflict and rivalry in the region. Indeed, such rivalries will continue and may even heighten. There may be more saber rattling and swaggering, more attempts at political coercion, more hostile rhetoric and threats, and even subnuclear conflicts in the new nuclear age in Asia. But there is nothing as yet that can lead one to conclude that, relative to conflicts in the first nuclear world, such conflicts are more likely to escalate and that this second nuclear age is more dangerous than the first. Such conflicts are undoubtedly worrying. But they do not necessarily undermine arguments about a minimum-deterrent Asian nuclear world bounded by taboos on nuclear use.

[50]Parties agree to refrain from direct or indirect actions aimed at undermining any nuclear installation or facility and agree to provide lists and descriptions of nuclear facilities and locations annually and whenever there is a change to the status quo. Both sides claim the other's lists are incomplete. See CNS (1997: 63–64).

[51]Established in 1985 to promote collective self-reliance in South Asia. In the past, proposals for a South Asian nuclear weapons ban and disarmament have been raised in this venue (Pakistan in 1987).

[52]China's behavior indicates that it too might be positively disposed to the zone. Beijing, more so than the United States (because of extended deterrence commitments), has proposed multilateral no-first-use (NFU) and negative security assurance (NSA) agreements among P-5 countries. It has a bilateral NFU with Russia (September 1994) and NSAs with Ukraine (December 1994) and Kazakhstan (February 1995). See Jozef Goldblat, "The State of Nuclear Arms Control and Disarmament: Reversing Negative Trends," Disarmament Diplomacy no. 44, www.acronym.org.uk/44neg.htm.

[53]In the former case, all the countries in the region have in principle supported starting CD negotiations on the banning of further production of weapons-usable fissile material as a barrier to further nuclear proliferation—in conjunction, perhaps, with the development of a comprehensive register of highly enriched uranium and plutonium stockpiles. In the latter case, membership for this new entity would consist of four current groups: Zangger Committee, Nuclear Suppliers Group, Australia Group, and MTCR. Outstanding countries like the two Koreas, India, and Pakistan have committed in principle to these groups.

Appendix A: The Second Nuclear Age

Ballistic missiles	Range/payload	Nuclear capability	Comments
China			
Dong Feng-3/3A (CSS-2)	2,800 km/2,150 kg	nuclear warhead (1–5 MT)	1-stage, liquid propellant; surface-to-surface; 50–120 missiles; deployed 1971
DF-4 (CSS-3)	4,750 km/2,200 kg	nuclear warhead (1–5 MT)	2-stage; 20–30 missiles; deployed 1980
DF-5/5A (CSS-4)	12,000–15,000 km/ 3,200 kg	nuclear warhead (1–5 MT)	2-stage; storable liquid fuel; 7–20+ missiles; deployed 1981; possible MRV
DF-21/21A (CSS-5)	1,800 km/600 kg	nuclear warhead (200–300 kT)	2-stage; solid propellant; replacing DF-3; 10–36+ missiles; deployed 1986
DF-15/M-9 (CSS-6)	600 km/950 kg	nuclear warhead (50–350 kT)	1-stage; solid fuel; dual capable; M-9 version for export; 100+ deployed (1995)
DF-11/M-11/ RDF-11S (CSS-7)	300 km/500 kg	nuclear warhead (50–350 kT)	2-stage; solid fuel; dual capable; M-11 version designed for export; 40+ deployed (1995)
M-7/8610 (CSS-8)	160 km/190 kg	conventional warhead	2-stage; solid fuel
DF-31	8,000 km/700 kg	nuclear warhead (200–300 kT)	tested 1999; under development; 3-stage; solid propellant; to replace DF-4; possibly MIRV/MRV
DF-41	12,000 km/800 kg	nuclear warhead (200–300 kT)	in development; will replace DF-5 in 2010; 3-stage; solid propellant; possibly MIRV
JL-1 (CSS-N-3)	1,700 km/600 kg	nuclear warhead (200–300 kT)	2-stage SLBM; solid fuel; 12–24 missiles; deployed 1986
JL-2 (CSS-NX-4)	8,000 km/700 kg	nuclear warhead (200–300 kT)	3-stage SLBM; solid fuel; same as DF-31; in development
India			
Prithvi-150	150 km/1,000 kg	1974 PNE	operational; from Russian SA-2
Prithvi-250	250 km/200 kg	May 1998 tests	operational; from Russian SA-2
Prithvi-350	350 km/500 kg		in development; from Russian SA-2
Dhanush	250 km/500 kg		in development; from Prithvi
Sagarika	300 km/500 kg		in development; from Prithvi
Agni	1,500 km/1,000 kg		tested Feb. 18, 1994; from Scout
Agni-2	2,000 km/1,000 kg		tested Apr. 11, 1999; from Scout
Surya	1,200 km/? kg		in development; from Polar Satellite Launch Vehicle and Agni-2
Pakistan			
M-11	280 km/800 kg	May 1998 tests	in storage
Hatf-1	80 km/500 kg		operational
Hatf-1A	100 km/500 kg		operational
Hatf-2	300 km/500 kg		in development; M-11 derivative?

Hatf-3	600 km/500 kg		in development; M-9 derivative?
Ghauri	1,300 km/ 500–750 kg		tested Apr. 6, 1998; from Nodong
Ghauri-2	2,000 km/100 kg		tested Apr. 14, 1999; from Nodong
Ghauri-3	3,700 km/3,500 kg		engines tested July 23 and Sept. 29, 1999
Shaheen-2	2,500 km/1,000 kg		mobile; 2-stage; solid fuel; in development; from Nodong-2; unveiled at April 2000 Pakistan Day parade; "to be tested shortly"

North Korea

SCUD-B	300 km/1,000 kg	weapons-grade plutonium reprocessing capabilities	operational; in production
SCUD-C	500 km/700 kg		operational; in production
Nodong-1	1,000 km/ 700–1,000 kg	2 LWRs (1994 Agreed Framework)	in development; tested
Nodong-2	1,500 km/770 kg		in development
Taepodong-1	1,500–2,000 km/ 1,000 kg		tested Aug. 31, 1998; combined Nodong and Scud
Taepodong-2	3,500–6,000 km/ 1,000 kg		in development

South Korea

Nike-Hercules-1	180 km/300 kg	civilian nuclear energy	operational; modified SAM
Nike-Hercules-2	250 km/300 kg	reprocessing capability	in development; modified SAM

Taiwan

Ching Feng	130 km/400 kg	civilian nuclear energy	operational; from Lance; from Green Bee
Tien Ma	950 km/500 kg		in development; from Sky Horse
Tien Chi	300 km/500 kg		in development; modified SAM

Japan

M-3 (SLV)	4,000 km/500 kg	civilian nuclear energy	capability
H-1 (SLV)	12,000 km/500+ kg	reprocessing capability	capability
H-2 (SLV)	15,000 km/4,000 kg		capability

SOURCES: Compiled from Center for Nonproliferation Studies at http://ns.miis.edu/cns/projects/eanp/pubs/chinanuc/bmsl.htm; http://cns.miis.edu/cns/projects/eanp/pubs/chinanuc/nstock.htm; Cirincione (2000); Carpenter and Wiencek (1996: 67); *Jane's Defense Weekly*; and Manning et al. (2000: 22–23).

Appendix B: Regional Reactions to U.S. BMD

TMD	NMD
Japan	
Supports U.S. deployment; engaged in joint research with United States on NTW but has reserved judgment beyond this stage	Strict neutrality; but June 2001 statements by Koizumi that Japan must "carefully consider" its position suggest slight departure from previous position
South Korea	
Supports U.S. deployment of ground-based PAC3 (considering PAC3 purchase for SAM-X program); in 1999 decided not to participate in upper-tier TMD	Seoul has reserved judgment on U.S. NMD plans; President Kim has said it is "too early" to have a policy; resisted Russian pressure for an anti-NMD statement during 2001 summit
Taiwan	
Supports U.S. deployment; desires PAC3	No declared policy
Australia	
Supports U.S. deployment	Supports U.S. NMD arguments; cooperating in areas relevant to Australia (e.g., early warning radar stations)
China	
Opposes U.S.-Japan cooperation on TMD research; strongly opposes U.S. deployment in Taiwan or Taiwanese possession	Strongly opposes NMD
North Korea	
Opposed; has threatened missile test resumption and abandoning of Agreed Framework	Opposed
Russia	
Opposed but also interested in sharing TMD technology	Opposed
India	
Opposed, but in May 2001 scaled back criticism at Armitage-Vajpayee meetings	Opposed

SOURCE: Adapted from Green and Dalton (2000); "Press Release issued by Ministry of External Affairs on visit of U.S. Deputy Secretary of State Richard Armitage to New Delhi," May 11, 2001, available at http://www.indianembassy.org/press_release/2001/may/may_11.htm.

Appendix C: Global Regimes

Country	IAEA	CD	NSG	ZAC	MTCR	AG	WAAS	Comments
United States	Yes	Yes	Yes	Yes	Yes	Yes	Yes	
Russia	Yes	Yes	Yes	Yes	Yes	Yes	Yes	
China	Yes	Yes	No—invited to join; adheres in principle to NSG trigger lists	(97)	Bilateral with United States	No—declined U.S. offer to join in 1997	No—urged to join by United States but decline to do so	ZAC member 1997; bilateral with United States on MTCR 1992
Japan	Yes	Yes	Yes	Yes	Yes—original member	Yes	Yes—original member	AG original member
DPRK	Yes	Yes	No	No	No	No	No	
ROK	Yes	Yes	Yes	Yes	No	Yes	Yes	AG member 1996
ROC		N/A	No	No	No	No	No	
India	Yes	Yes	No	No	No	No	No	
Pakistan	Yes	Yes	No	No	No	No	No	
Australia	Yes	Yes	Yes	Yes	Yes	Yes	Yes	
NZ	Yes	Yes	Yes	No	Yes	Yes	Yes	

SOURCES: Compiled from CNS (1997); "Northeast Asian Participation in Arms Control/Nonproliferation Regimes" available on the CNS website at cns.miis.edu/cns/projects/eanp/fact/nearegms.htm; "Japanese Participation and Positions Regarding Various Arms Control and Nonproliferation Agreements, Organizations, and Regimes, July 1999" cns.miis.edu/cns/projects/eanp/fact/japan.htm.

GLOBAL REGIMES:

AG: Australia Group (est. 1985)—informal association aimed at limiting the spread of CBW through control of chemical precursors, equipment, and BW agents and organisms (dual-use chemicals).

CD: Conference on Disarmament (est. 1979)—primary multilateral disarmament negotiating forum for the international community.

IAEA: International Atomic Energy Agency (est. 1957)—aimed at encouraging atomic energy usage for peaceful purposes and administering safeguards to ensure nonmilitary use of nuclear facilities.

MTCR: Missile Tech Control Regime (est. 1987)—informal nontreaty association of governments with common interests in restricting the proliferation of missiles, unmanned aerial vehicles (UAVs), and related technologies for systems larger than 300 km and 500-kg payload.

NSG: Nuclear Suppliers Group (est. 1975)—also known as the "London Club," requires IAEA safeguards as condition of supply of nuclear materials and restricts supply to countries with proliferation potential.

WAAS: Wassenaar Arrangement on Export Controls for Conventional Arms and Dual-Use Goods and Technologies (est. 1995)—successor to COCOM.

ZAC: Zangger Committee (est. 1971)—trigger list of materials and equipment for processing, use, or production of fissionable materials; status is informal; not legally binding on members.

Appendix D: International Treaties

Country	NPT	CTBT	PTBT	BWC/ CWC	OST/ SBT	Geneva/ OPCW	IWC	Nuclear material	Comments
United States	Yes	Signed/ not ratified	Yes	Yes/Yes	Yes/Yes	Yes/Yes			
Russia	Yes	Signed/ not ratified	Yes	Yes/Yes	Yes/Yes	Yes/No	Yes	Yes	
China	Yes	Signed/ not ratified	No	Yes/Yes	Yes/Yes	Yes/Yes	Yes	Yes	Unilateral moratorium on testing 1996 Working with Japan on project to clean up chemical weapons left in China
Japan	Yes	Signed/ ratified 1997	Yes	Yes/Yes	Yes/Yes	Yes/Yes	Yes	Yes	BWC ratified 1982; CWC ratified 1995; founding member OPCW
DPRK	Yes	No	No	Yes/No	No/No	Yes/No	No	No	Threatened NPT withdrawal 1996
ROK	Yes	Signed/ not ratified	Yes	Yes/Yes	Yes/Yes	Yes/Yes	No	Yes	
ROC	(Yes)	No	(Yes)	No/No	(Yes)/ (Yes)	(Yes)/(No)	No	No	
India	No	No	Yes	Yes/Yes	Signed/ ratified	?/Yes	Yes	?	Vajpayee joint statement to forgo additional nuclear tests Tried to block CTBT draft treaty on grounds of NWS discrimination
Pakistan	No	No	Yes	Yes/Yes	Signed/ ratified	?	Signed	?	Refused to sign CTBT 1996 unless India did
Australia	Yes	Signed/ ratified	Yes	Yes/Yes	Signed/ ratified	?/Yes	Signed/ ratified ?	?	
NZ	Signed/ ratified	Signed/ ratified	Yes	Yes/Yes	Signed/ ratified	?	Signed/ ratified	?	

SOURCES: Compiled from CNS (1997); "Northeast Asian Participation in Arms Control/Nonproliferation Regimes" available on the CNS website at cns.miis.edu/cns/projects/eanp/fact/nearegms.htm; "Japanese Participation and Positions Regarding Various Arms Control and Nonproliferation Agreements, Organizations, and Regimes, July 1999" cns.miis.edu/cns/projects/eanp/fact/japan.htm.

INTERNATIONAL TREATIES:
   BWC/CWC: Convention on Prohibition of the Development, Production, and Stockpiling of Bacteriological (Biological) and Toxin Weapons (entered into force 1975); Convention on Prohibition of the Development, Production, Stockpiling, and Use of Chemical Weapons (opened for signature 1993). BWC: not to develop, produce, stockpile, or otherwise acquire or obtain microbial or other biological agents or toxins for nonpeaceful purposes and to destroy or divert to peaceful uses any such items within nine months of signing. CWC: same restrictions for chemical weapons. Signatories must destroy all weapons and production facilities within ten years.

CTBT: Comprehensive Test Ban Treaty (1996 opened for signature)—bans any nuclear weapon test explosion.

Geneva Protocol: Protocol for the Prohibition of the Use in War of Asphyxiating, Poisonous, or Other Gases and Bacteriological Methods of Warfare (1925)—signatories reserve right to exception if others resort to CW use.

IWC: Inhumane Weapons Convention (1983)—not to use weapons that create nondetectable fragments; not to mine or boobytrap against civilian populations; not to use incendiary weapons or air-delivered incendiaries against civilian populations.

NPT: Treaty on the Nonproliferation of Nuclear Weapons (est. 1970)—NWS do not transfer nuclear weapons; NNWS do not receive nuclear weapons; 187 member states of which 5 are NWS; only 4 states remain nonparties (Cuba, India, Pakistan, Israel).

Nuclear Material: Convention on the Physical Protection of Nuclear Material (1987)—for physical protection of nuclear materials during international transport (plutonium, uranium 235 and 233, irradiated fuel).

OPCW: Organization for the Prohibition of Chemical Weapons (1997): Came into being after entry into force of CWC. Implementing and verification body for CWC.

OST: Outer Space Treaty (1967)—prohibits use of outer space for military purposes; no weapons on objects that orbit the earth; promotes the use of outer space for peaceful purposes.

PTBT: Partial Test Ban Treaty (Banning Nuclear Weapon Tests in the Atmosphere, Outer Space, and Under Water) (1963)—bans nuclear weapon tests in atmosphere, outer space, underwater, and anywhere where fallout crosses territorial borders; precursor to CTBT; if states cannot ratify CTBT, they are still under obligations of PTBT.

SBT: Seabed Treaty (1972)—not to embed nuclear weapons, WMD, and installations for such purposes in seabed outside the 12-mile territorial limits.

Appendix E: Regional and Bilateral Institutions

Country	SEANWFZ	KEDO	NEA	SAARC	Rarotonga
United States	No	Yes	Yes	n/a	Accepts protocols
Russia	No	No	n/a	n/a	Accepts protocols
China	No	No	n/a	n/a	Accepts protocols
Japan	No	Yes; original board member	Yes	n/a	Dialogue partner
DPRK	No	No	n/a	n/a	No
ROK	No	Yes	Yes	n/a	Dialogue partner
ROC	No	No	n/a	n/a	No
India	No	No	n/a	Yes	No
Pakistan	No	No	n/a	Yes	No
Australia	No	Yes	Yes	n/a	Yes
NZ	No	Yes	No	n/a	Yes

SOURCES: Compiled from CNS (1997); "Northeast Asian Participation in Arms Control/Nonproliferation Regimes" available on the CNS website at cns.miis.edu/cns/projects/eanp/fact/nearegms.htm; "Japanese Participation and Positions Regarding Various Arms Control and Nonproliferation Agreements, Organizations, and Regimes, July 1999" cns.miis.edu/cns/projects/eanp/fact/japan.htm.

TREATIES AND INSTITUTIONS:

KEDO: Korea Energy Development Organization (1995)—meant to provide for financing and supply of LWRs and interim shipments of heavy fuel oil to DPRK.

NEA: Nuclear Energy Agency (1958)—semiautonomous body of OECD (formerly European Nuclear Energy Agency) to promote cooperation between members regarding safety and regulatory aspects of nuclear power and development of nuclear energy.

Rarotonga: South Pacific Nuclear-Free Zone Treaty (Rarotonga Treaty) (1986)—not to manufacture, acquire, possess, or control any nuclear explosive device anywhere within treaty zone; Protocol 1 obligates

France, the United Kingdom, and the United States not to manufacture, station, or test in the zone (3 states acceded in March 1996); Protocol 2 obligates China, France, Russia, the United States, and the United Kingdom not to use or threaten to use any nuclear explosive device against parties of the treaty (all acceded in March 1996); Protocol 3 obligates China, France, Russia, the United Kingdom, and the United States not to test any nuclear device in zone.

SAARC: South Asian Association for Regional Cooperation (1985)—meant to promote welfare of South Asia and ideals of collective self-reliance; past proposals for South Asian nuclear weapons ban have been raised in this venue (Pakistan in 1987).

SEANWFZ: South East Asia Nuclear Weapon Free Zone Treaty (Bangkok treaty) (1995)—precursor was 1971 ASEAN original five declaration of ZOPFAN (Zone of Peace, Freedom and Neutrality); no NWS have signed the protocols.

Works Cited

Abraham, Itty. 1998. *The Making of the Indian Atomic Bomb: Science, Secrecy, and the Postcolonial State*. New York: Zed Books.

Ahmed, Samina. 1999. "Pakistan's Nuclear Weapons Program: Turning Points and Nuclear Choices." *International Security* 23(4) (Spring): 178–204.

Alagappa, Muthiah. 1998. *International Response to Nuclear Tests in South Asia: The Need for a New Policy Framework*. Asia-Pacific Issues 38. Honolulu: East-West Center.

Aslam, Mohammad. 1989. *Dr. A. Q. Khan and Pakistan's Nuclear Programme*. Rawalpindi: Diplomat.

Betts, Richard. 1993–94. "Wealth, Power, and Instability: East Asia and the United States After the Cold War." *International Security* 18(3) (Winter): 34–77.

Blair, Bruce. 1993. *The Logic of Accidental Nuclear War*. Washington: Brookings Institution.

BMDO. 2000. "Theater Missile Defenses in the Asia-Pacific Region." *Ballistic Missile Defense Organization (BMDO) Fact Sheets*.

Bracken, Paul. 1999a. "Asia's Militaries and the New Nuclear Age." *Current History* (Dec.): 415–21.

———. 1999b. *Fire in the East*. New York: HarperCollins.

Bundy, McGeorge. 1984. "Existential Deterrence and Its Consequences." In Douglas MacLean, ed., *The Security Gamble: Deterrence Dilemmas in the Nuclear Age*. Totowa, N.J.: Rowman & Littlefield.

Calder, Kent. 1996. *Pacific Defense*. New York: Morrow.

Canberra Commission. 1996. *Report of the Canberra Commission on the Elimination of Nuclear Weapons*. Canberra: Department of Foreign Affairs and Trade.

Carpenter, William, and David Wiencek, eds., 1996. *Asian Security Handbook*. Armonk, N.Y.: M. E. Sharpe.

Cha, Victor D. 1999. *Alignment Despite Antagonism: The United States–Korea–Japan Security Triangle*. Stanford: Stanford University Press.

———. 2000. "Engaging North Korea Credibly." *Survival* 42(2) (Summer): 135–55.

———. 2001. "The Economic Crisis, Strategic Culture, and the Military Modernization of South Korea." *Armed Forces and Society* 28(1) (Fall): 99–128.

Chang, Gordon. 1988. "JFK, China, and the Bomb." *Journal of American History* 74(4) (Mar.): 1287.

———. 1990. *Friends and Enemies: The United States, China, and the Soviet Union, 1948–72*. Stanford: Stanford University Press.

Cirincione, Joseph. 2000. "Assessing the Assessment: The 1999 National Intelligence Estimates of the Ballistic Missile Threat." *Nonproliferation Review* (Spring): 125–32.

CNS (Center for Nonproliferation Studies). 1997. *Inventory of International Nonproliferation Organizations and Regimes 1996–1997*. Monterey: Center for Nonproliferation Studies.

Cochran, Thad. 2000. "Stubborn Things: A Decade of Facts About Ballistic Missile Defense." Report by Subcommittee on International Security, Proliferation, and Federal Services Committee on Governmental Affairs. Washington, D.C.: Government Printing Office.

Deutsch, John. 1992. "The New Nuclear Threat." *Foreign Affairs* 71(41) (Fall).

Dunn, Lewis. 1982. *Controlling the Bomb: Nuclear Proliferation in the 1980s*. New Haven: Yale University Press.

———. 1991. *Containing Nuclear Proliferation*. Adelphi Paper 263. London: IISS.

Evron, Yair. 1994. *Israel's Nuclear Dilemma*. Ithaca: Cornell University Press.

Feaver, Peter. 1992. *Guarding the Guardians: Civilian Control of Nuclear Weapons in the United States*. Ithaca: Cornell University Press.

———. 1995. "Optimists, Pessimists, and Theories of Nuclear Proliferation Management." *Security Studies* 4(4) (Summer): 159–91.

Friedberg, Aaron. 1993–94. "Ripe for Rivalry: Prospects for Peace in a Multipolar Asia." *International Security* 18(3) (Winter): 5–33.

Ganguly, Sumit. 1996. "Political Mobilization and Institutional Decay: Explaining the Crisis in Kashmir." *International Security* 21(2) (Fall): 76–107.

———. 1999a. "Explaining India's Nuclear Policy." *Current History* (Dec.): 438–40.

———. 1999b. "India's Pathway to Pokhran II." *International Security* 23(4) (Spring): 148–77.

Godwin, Paul. 1999. "China's Nuclear Forces: An Assessment." *Current History* (Sept.).

Goldblat, Jozef. n.d. "The State of Nuclear Arms Control and Disarmament: Reversing Negative Trends," Disarmament Diplomacy no. 44, www.acronym. org.uk/44neg.htm.

Goldstein, Avery. 2000. *Deterrence and Security in the 21st Century: China, Britain, France, and the Enduring Legacy of the Nuclear Revolution*. Stanford: Stanford University Press.

Gordon, Sandy. 1994. "Capping South Asia's Nuclear Programs." *Asian Survey* 34(7) (July): 662–73.

Green, Michael, and Toby Dalton. 2000. "Asian Reactions to US Missile Defense." *NBR Analysis* 11(3) (Nov.).

Gupta, Sisir. 1966. "The Indian Dilemma." In Alastair Buchan, ed., *A World of Nuclear Powers*. Englewood Cliffs: Prentice-Hall.

Hagerty, Devin. 1995–96. "Nuclear Deterrence in South Asia: The 1990 Indo-Pakistani Crisis." *International Security* 20(3) (Winter): 79–114.

———. 1998. *The Consequences of Nuclear Proliferation: Lessons from South Asia*. Cambridge, Mass.: MIT Press.

———. 1999. "South Asia's Big Bangs." *Australian Journal of International Affairs* 53(1).

Harrison, Selig, ed. 1996. *Japan's Nuclear Future*. Washington, D.C.: Carnegie Endowment for International Peace.

Hashim, Ahmed. 1995. "The State, Society, and the Evolution of Warfare in the Middle East." *Washington Quarterly* 18(4) (Autumn).

IGCC. 1998. "Energy and Security in Northeast Asia: Fueling Security." IGCC Policy Paper 35. La Jolla, Calif.: IGCC.

Jervis, Robert. 1984. *The Illogic of American Nuclear Strategy*. Ithaca: Cornell University Press.

————. 1989. *The Meaning of the Nuclear Revolution*. Ithaca: Cornell University Press.

Johnston, Alastair Iain, and Paul Evans. 1999. "China's Engagement with Multilateral Security Institutions." In Alastair Iain Johnston and Robert Ross, eds., *Engaging China*. London: Routledge.

Kaiser, Karl. 1989. "Non-Proliferation and Nuclear Deterrence." *Survival* 31(2) (Mar./Apr.): 123–36.

Kang, David. 1999. "Asian Bandwagons." Manuscript. Department of Government, Dartmouth College.

Karl, David. 1996–97. "Proliferation Pessimism and Emerging Nuclear Powers." *International Security* 21(3) (Winter): 87–119.

Katahara, Eiichi. 1997. "Japan's Plutonium Policy: Consequences for Nonproliferation." *Nonproliferation Review* 5(1) (Fall) http://cns.miis.edu/pubs/npr/katahara.htm.

Lewis, John, and Hua Di. 1992. "China's Ballistic Missile Programs." *International Security* 17(2) (Fall): 5–40.

Lewis, John, and Xue Litai. 1988. *China Builds the Bomb*. Stanford: Stanford University Press.

Lin, Chong-Pin. 1988. *China's Nuclear Weapons Strategy*. Lexington, Mass.: Lexington Books.

Manning, Robert, Ronald Montaperto, and Brad Roberts. 2000. *China, Nuclear Weapons, and Arms Control*. New York: Council on Foreign Relations.

May, Michael. 1998. "Energy and Security in East Asia." A/PARC Working Paper, Stanford University.

Medeiros, Evan. n.d. *Northeast Asia in 1999: Current Threats to Nonproliferation Regimes*. CNS Occasional Paper 3. Monterey, Calif.: Center for Nonproliferation Studies.

Miller, Steven. 1993. "The Case Against a Ukrainian Nuclear Deterrent." *Foreign Affairs* 72(3) (Summer): 67–80.

National Academy of Sciences. 1997. *The Future of US Nuclear Weapons Policy*. Washington, D.C.: National Academy Press.

O'Hanlon, Michael. 2000. "U.S. Missile Defense Programs." Nautilus Missile Defense Initiative Special Report 5. Available at http://www.nautilus.org/nukepolicy/TMD- Conference/ohanlonpaper.txt.

Paul, T. V. 1995. "Nuclear Taboo and War Initiation in Regional Conflicts." *Journal of Conflict Resolution* 39(4) (Dec.): 696–717.

Plesch, Daniel. 2000. "Anarchy in Action: Western Policy on Weapons of Mass Destruction." *Global Beat* (Apr.).

Pullinger, Stephen. 1994. "A Role for UK Nuclear Weapons After the Cold War?" *ISIS Briefing* 41 (Jan.).

Rauf, Tariq. 1999a. "Learning to Live with the Bomb in South Asia: Accommodation Not Confrontation." *Bulletin of Atomic Scientists* (Jan./Feb.): 14–16.

————. 1999b. "Successes of the Nuclear Non-Proliferation Regime." Monterey, Calif., Center for Nonproliferation Studies. cns.miis.edu/cns/projects/ionp/iaea.htm.

Richelson, Jeffrey. 2000–2001. "Whether to Strangle the Baby in the Cradle: The United States and the Chinese Nuclear Program, 1960–64." *International Security* 25(3) (Winter): 54–99.

Ruina, Jack. 2001. "46 Years, No Winners. Aim Elsewhere." *Washington Post (Outlook)*, 4 Mar.

Rumsfeld, Donald, et al. 1998. *Executive Summary of the Report of the Commission to Assess the Ballistic Missile Threat to the United States.* Washington, D.C.: USGPO.

Russett, Bruce. 1989. "The Real Decline in Nuclear Hegemony." In Ernst-Otto Czempiel and James Rosenau, eds., *Global Changes and Theoretical Challenges.* Lexington, Mass.: Heath.

Sagan, Scott. 1994. *The Limits of Safety: Organizations, Accidents, and Nuclear Weapons.* Princeton: Princeton University Press.

———. 1996–97. "Why Do States Build Nuclear Weapons?" *International Security* 21(3) (Winter): 54–86.

———, and Kenneth Waltz. 1995. *The Spread of Nuclear Weapons: A Debate.* New York: Norton.

Sands, Amy. n.d. *The Nonproliferation Regimes at Risk.* CNS Occasional Paper 3. Monterey, Calif., Center for Nonproliferation Studies.

Scheinman, Lawrence. n.d. "Challenges in South Asia to Nonproliferation Regimes." CNS Occasional Paper 3. Monterey, Calif., Center for Nonproliferation Studies.

Schelling, Thomas. 1960. *The Strategy of Conflict.* Cambridge, Mass.: Harvard University Press.

Singh, Jaswant. 1998. "Against Nuclear Apartheid." *Foreign Affairs* 77(5) (Sept./Oct.): 41–52.

Snyder, Glenn. 1965. "The Balance of Power and Balance of Terror." In Paul Seabury, ed., *The Balance of Power.* San Francisco: Chandler.

Stokes, Mark. 1999. *China's Strategic Modernization: Implications for the United States.* Carlisle, PA. U.S. Army Strategic Studies Institute.

Talbott, Strobe. 1999. "Dealing with the Bomb in South Asia." *Foreign Affairs* 88(2) (Mar./Apr.): 110–22.

Tannenwald, Nina. 1999. "The Nuclear Taboo: The United States and the Normative Basis of Nuclear Non-Use." *International Organization* 53(3) (Summer): 433–68.

Trachtenberg, Marc. 1985. "The Influence of Nuclear Weapons in the Cuban Missile Crisis." *International Security* 10(1) (Summer): 137–63.

Urayama, Kori J. 2000. "Chinese Perspectives on Theater Missile Defense." *Asian Survey* 40(4): 599–621.

Waltz, Kenneth. 1979. *Theory of International Politics.* Reading, Mass.: Addison-Wesley.

Wheeler, Nicholas J. 1990. "The Dual Imperative of Britain's Nuclear Deterrent: The Soviet Threat, Alliance Politics, and Arms Control." In Mark Hoffman, ed., *UK Arms Control in the 1990's.* New York: Manchester University Press.

Wilkening, Dean. 2000. *Ballistic-Missile Defence and Strategic Stability.* Adelphi Paper 334. London: IISS.

Yasmeen, Samina. 1999. "Pakistan's Nuclear Tests: Domestic Debate and International Determinants." *Australian Journal of International Affairs* 53(1): 43–56.

CHAPTER FOURTEEN

Managing Internal Conflicts

Dominance of the State

ARUN R. SWAMY AND JOHN GERSHMAN

Within months of declaring a "war against global terrorism," U.S. President George W. Bush found his administration engaged in trying to prevent a conventional war between two states armed with nuclear weapons, both of which ostensibly supported American goals. A suicide attack by Islamic militants against the Indian parliament in New Delhi, which followed an earlier attack on the legislative assembly of the Indian state of Jammu and Kashmir, brought India to the brink of war with Pakistan, the United States' principal ally against the Taliban regime in Afghanistan.

It has become common wisdom to suggest that internal conflicts now pose the gravest consequences for international security, and many have even argued for a new norm of "justifiable intervention" by external powers in civil wars. On the surface, the connection between the insurgency in Indian-held Kashmir and India's dispute with Pakistan over the status of Kashmir is a paradigmatic instance of this position. However, Kashmir is in many ways a departure from the norm, at least in Asia, except in demonstrating the obstacles to actually engaging in such intervention. In Asia, the trend is in the opposite direction from that suggested by common wisdom: the heyday for external intervention in internal conflict was during the Cold War. Since then Asian states have tended more toward mutual acknowledgment of territorial sovereignty. The shift in the priorities of the major western powers since September 11, 2001, will only strengthen this trend.

The central argument of this chapter is that in Asia the onus of managing internal conflict is on the states suffering conflict themselves. While external actors affected by these conflicts might press for policies that reduce their intensity, the policies will have to be consistent with the goals of the states suffering the internal conflict themselves. And the success of the policies in turn depends on taking into account the dynamic nature of the internal conflicts. Asian states are among the most militarized in the world, and most control the principal, if not the sole, means of coercion within their territories, making armed intervention a costly proposition. Maintaining and consolidating control over their territories remains the primary goal of these states, so that their willingness to adopt new management strategies will be conditioned by how they perceive these policies as likely to affect domestic control and stability. At least in the area of managing internal conflicts, then, Asia is unlikely to move toward a normative-contractual order as defined by Muthiah Alagappa in this volume, or if it does, such an order will be limited to defining states' reciprocal obligations in the area of preventing terrorism.

The chapter develops this argument in three sections. The first fleshes out the reasons why management of internal conflict is left to states by examining how three types of internal conflict—over national unity, national identity, and regime identity—interact with the regional environment. The second analyzes the overlapping sources of these conflicts in socioeconomic change and state policy. The third then identifies management strategies consistent with the sources identified. While the argument is made with illustrations from many cases in Asia and beyond, each section also includes relevant material on three case studies, each drawn from a different subregion of Asia and representing a different type of conflict. The cases have been chosen for their potential regional impact and in some particulars may represent exceptions to the general pattern. They are India's insurgency in Kashmir, Indonesia's struggle with Islamism, and China's response to its democratization challenge.

Internal Conflicts and the Regional Security Order

The term "internal conflicts" refers in this volume to sustained *violent* challenges to the state from within. From the perspective of their consequences for regional order, we identify three types, differentiated according to the type of change challengers seek to bring about in the afflicted state. The three types tend to overlap because they share similar causes. Over the last fifty years, Asia has experienced all three types, but the pattern varies across subregions and over time.

The most common internal struggles involve national unity, or separatist movements, which aim to change a country's borders. Here the consequences for regional order are the most direct but also, potentially, the most localized. Separatist violence is most common in South Asia, where it has affected every country except Nepal. It touches virtually every country in Southeast Asia, though not so

TABLE 14.1
Separatist Conflicts in the Asia Pacific

Conflict	Possible external actors	Outcome
China		
Tibet	India (passive)	Chronic/active but contained
Uighurs	Central Asia, Russia, Afghanistan	Chronic/active but contained
Inner Mongolia	Mongolia	Chronic/active but contained
India		
Kashmir	Pakistan, China, U.S., UN	Acute
Punjab (Sikhs)	Pakistan, expatriates	Dormant or resolved in favor of status quo
Northeast (several)	Bangladesh, Burma, China	Chronic/active but contained
Indonesia		
East Timor	Australia, UN	Victory by challenger
West Papua	Australia, Papua New Guinea	Acute
Aceh	Centre for Humanitarian Dialogue, Aceh diaspora	Acute
Pakistan		
Bangladesh	India	Victory by challenger
Sind	India	Chronic/active but contained
Pushtuns (not violent)	Afghanistan	Dormant or resolved in favor of status quo
Baluchistan	Afghanistan, Iran	Dormant or resolved in favor of status quo
Sri Lanka		
Tamils	India	Acute
Burma (Myanmar)		
Karen	Thailand	Acute with cease-fires
Shan	Thailand	
Mon	Thailand	
Arakanese	Bangladesh	
Philippines		
Moros (Muslims) on Mindanao	Malaysia, Indonesia, OIC	Acute
Bangladesh		
Chittagong Hills	India, Burma	Chronic/active but contained
Thailand		
Muslims (south)	Malaysia	Chronic/active but contained

Key for management approaches: see Table 14.4.

TABLE 14.2
National Identity Conflicts in the Asia Pacific

Nature of conflict	External actors	Outcome
India		
Religious identity: electoral, some violence	Pakistan; Islamic countries generally	Chronic/active but contained?: electoral victory led to dilution of ideology
Pakistan		
Role of Islam	India; Afghanistan	Chronic/active but contained or Acute
Sri Lanka		
Religious identity: violent	India (indirect)	Chronic/active but contained or Acute
Bangladesh		
Religious identity: electoral and violent	India (potential)	Chronic/active but contained
Taiwan		
Secession	China; U.S.	Chronic/active but contained or Acute
Indonesia		
Religious and communal: electoral and violent	International community; China	Acute
Malaysia		
Religious: electoral	International community; China	Chronic/active but contained

acutely, but is unknown in East Asia, except in the three non-Han regions of China: Tibet, Xinjiang, and Inner Mongolia. (See Table 14.1 for a summary of all separatist conflicts in Asia.)

Conflicts over national identity, the second type, challenge the cultural values embedded in a regime. Typically these are conflicts over the religious or secular character of a state but may also include challenges to the state's identification with a particular ethnic group that fall short of separatism.[1] Although conflicts over national identity are less frequent, they have become more prominent in recent years in South Asia and Southeast Asia. All states with an Islamic majority, two predominantly Buddhist countries (Burma and Sri Lanka), and Hindu-majority India are experiencing various degrees of conflicts over national iden-

[1]The most dramatic recent instance of the difference is Ethiopia where Tigrayan and Eritrean rebels joined forces to defeat the Amhara-dominated state but the Tigrayans chose to remain within Ethiopia. In Asia, communal conflicts between Malays and Chinese and Indians in Malaysia might be an example of a conflict over national identity.

TABLE 14.3
Regime Identity Conflicts in the Asia Pacific

Nature of conflict	Outcome
Pakistan	
Coups and democracy movements	Acute for both
Armed Islamist militias	
Nepal	
Democratization	Victory by challenger
Rural Maoist insurgency	Acute
China	
Democratization	Chronic/active but contained
Indonesia	
Democratization	Acute
Burma (Myanmar)	
Democratization	Chronic/active but contained
Cambodia	
Acute extended civil war with genocide over national identity and varieties of community ideology	Chronic/active but contained approaching Dormant or resolved in favor of status quo?
Philippines	
Communist	Chronic/active but contained
Coup threats	Dormant or resolved in favor of status quo
Thailand	
Alternating coup threats and democratization pressure	Chronic/active but contained

tity. Such conflicts can affect regional security by altering a state's foreign policy behavior, meshing with separatism or challenges to regime identity, or as in the case of Islamist movements, generating transnational challenges. (See Table 14.2 for details.)

The third type is conflicts over regime identity, which range from democratization movements to revolutionary challenges to a regime's class character. (See Table 14.3.) Conflicts over regime identity have been especially violent and protracted in East Asia and Southeast Asia: South Asia has experienced relatively stable democratic regimes (India and Sri Lanka) or relatively quick transitions between regime types without *sustained* violence (Bangladesh, Nepal, and Pakistan). Over the years, however, the type of regime conflict characteristic of the region has shifted. Through the 1970s, revolutionary communism was the most common type, often supported by China and opposed by the United States and associated in some Southeast Asian countries with overseas Chinese communities. Today only the Philippines and Nepal have sustained revolutionary communist challengers, but all three subregions have seen middle-class street protest bring about transitions to democratic regimes. It is the "unfinished business" of democratic transitions that causes the gravest concern for regional stability. In Burma (Myanmar) and China, which violently suppressed democratization movements in 1989 and 1990, popular resistance to authoritarian rule is presumed to continue, while the 1999 military coup in Pakistan and coup fears in Indonesia and the Philippines in 2001 underline the fragility of many new democracies.

Both the persistence of internal conflicts and their successful resolution can have implications for the regional security environment. Successful challenges to a state may have systemic effects, by altering the balance of power in a region, as the secession of Bangladesh did in South Asia, or by changing a major state's foreign policy through changes in regime type or the ideology underpinning national identity. The evidence here is at best ambiguous, though. More commonly, the implications for regional security stem from the externalities posed to neighboring states by the persistence of conflict. Here there are two types of threats—one to the internal stability of neighboring states, the other from the possibility of interstate war resulting from one state's decision to intervene.

These effects could be most pronounced when states collapse altogether as a result of conflict. However, it does not necessarily follow that the states whose collapse would pose the gravest threats to regional security are the largest states. In recent decades it is the collapse of small states, such as Cambodia and Afghanistan, acting as a buffer between larger powers, that caused severe problems by inviting intervention. While the breakup of China, Pakistan, or even Indonesia could still leave substantial forces capable of resisting aggression or controlling large areas, a collapse of the state in Nepal as a result of a protracted Maoist rebellion might involve both India and China.

Intervention as Problem and Solution

The causal relationship between internal conflict and regional security, though, runs in both directions. While the persistence of internal conflict in one state can present neighboring states with significant negative externalities, explored below, the neighbors' concerns are not limited to the benign interest in managing these externalities but may include efforts to promote their own interest by fueling internal conflict in the afflicted state. Moreover, interventions by external powers that appear benign—as a solution—to some, may seem a threat to others in the region. In other words, there is no clear line between the larger states' causing conflicts on the one hand and managing them on the other, and the regional consequences of internal conflict are not limited to destabilizing neighboring states, but may include interstate war.

These observations are especially important for Asia, which has a long history of external intervention in domestic conflict resulting in interstate war. The Vietnam and Korean wars both began as civil wars. India intervened in Pakistan's civil war in 1971 to create Bangladesh, supported a Tamil insurgency in Sri Lanka, and later sought to impose a settlement on the Sri Lankan civil war. Vietnam intervened in Cambodia in 1979 to overthrow the genocidal Pol Pot regime, which led to a conflict with China and excited fears of its expansionist designs in Southeast Asia. Malaysia, Indonesia, and the Philippines at various points have asserted an interest in each other's domestic troubles owing to territorial claims often linked to ethnic or religious ties. And, of course, Pakistan's claim to Indian Kashmir has raised the specter of nuclear war.

Although efforts to create a regional order may lead states to press an afflicted neighbor to solve its domestic disputes, common concerns over internal conflicts have led to a decline in external intervention even as the world moves in the other direction. The exceptions tend to involve disputes where existing United Nations resolutions legitimate the actions of the insurgents or the supporters: Pakistan's support of insurgency in Indian Kashmir, East Timor's secession, and pressure on Vietnam to withdraw support from the Heng Samrin regime in Cambodia (Berdal and Leifer 1996). Even when outsiders get involved in mediating disputes, they tend to be global rather than regional bodies. While Australia took the lead on East Timor, it was in the UN that the transfer of power was negotiated. Recent efforts to mediate the war in Sri Lanka have been left to the Norwegians; although India may get involved now that both parties have requested it, it is clearly reluctant to do so. Vietnam's withdrawal from Cambodia was overseen by the UN, not by regional organizations. The Organization of the Islamic Conference, not ASEAN, has been arranging negotiations between the Philippine government and the Moro National Liberation Front (MNLF) since the 1970s, although ASEAN has been involved in monitoring the 1996 Peace Agreement between them.[2] And while ASEAN has played a mediating role in Burma, it seems motivated primarily by a desire to gain Europe's acceptance of Burma's entry into ASEAN.

Externalities Posed by Internal Conflict.[3] Many internal conflicts pose direct consequences for neighboring states. The most obvious type of externality involves what some scholars have called "spillover effects." Civilian slaughter and a flow of refugees into neighboring states are the most common. The slaughter of civilians was cited by India when it intervened in Pakistan's civil war in 1971 and by Vietnam when it invaded Cambodia in 1979. Recent international action on

[2]Indonesia and Malaysia handled negotiations between the Philippine government and the Moro Islamic Liberation Front (MILF) in the 1990s, but this role derived as much from their status as Islamic states as from their location.

[3]The following discussion is adapted from Brown (1996: 1–31).

East Timor was stimulated by these concerns. Refugee flows from Bangladesh/ East Pakistan and from Sri Lanka were one reason why India intervened in these conflicts.

A second type of externality occurs when separatist movements in one country evoke sympathy or similar aspirations among ethnically related groups in another or when a separatist uprising marked by these characteristics occurs in an area adjoining one's own borders. Again the two covary. Uighur and Mongol nationalists in China have been encouraged by the creation of new Turkic-speaking states in Central Asia and by Mongolia's transition to democracy in 1996. Militant movements in Sri Lanka, India, Burma, and Kazakhstan have all used ethnically related areas in neighboring countries as a base of operations. Xinjiang, Tibet, Kashmir, Northeast India, and all of Burma's separatist movements fall in strategic areas where the potential for border clashes or interstate conflict is high.

These essentially bilateral consequences may acquire a wider regional impact for several reasons:

1. They may lead an outsider to intervene—causing concern about its broader intentions (Vietnam in Cambodia).
2. They may involve regionwide processes such as the spread of political Islam and narcotics trafficking associated with armed insurgencies.
3. They set precedents that may affect internal disputes in other states.
4. They tend to disrupt trade flows or other economic processes.
5. They may involve the potential collapse of a major regional player, such as China or Indonesia, with implications for the regional balance of power.
6. They sometimes involve states with weapons of mass destruction.

These various sources of regional concern, though, point to different sorts of potential regional responses. And in Asia, so far, they have mainly strengthened states' attachment to sovereignty norms.

Concerns over intervention by one state or transnational links among internal conflicts can elicit and have elicited collective actions by states to forestall the threatened outcome. In Asia, however, these have followed the balance-of-power and concert-of-powers pathways identified by Muthiah Alagappa in this volume, rather than a broader collective security approach. Vietnam's invasion of Cambodia led to the strengthening of ASEAN. Concerns over Islamic militancy from Afghanistan led to the formation of the Shanghai Cooperation Organization linking China, Russia, and several Central Asian states in an effort at regional security cooperation and have since, of course, led to a U.S.-led "war on terrorism." However, interstate politics have hitherto limited the scope of the latter efforts. The Shanghai Cooperation Organization has been unable to include two parties—India and Pakistan—crucial to the problem it addresses, while the United

States attempted initially to insulate its war against Afghanistan from any connection to the insurgency in Kashmir.

Concern over precedents—or the "demonstration effect" of successful regime
challenges—and the desire to improve regional trade links are in principle capable of promoting a broader normative-contractual order, as identified by Alagappa. However, in Asia they have strengthened mutual respect for sovereignty,
although they may have motivated informal mediation to reduce conflict while
preserving the status quo. In South Asia, even India has concluded a bilateral
trade agreement with Sri Lanka and sought to restore overland trade with Burma
and is now far less supportive of Tamil aspirations or Burma's democracy movement. While the expansion of ASEAN to include Burma, Cambodia, Laos, and
Vietnam—motivated by security concerns as much as trade—did lead to some
international initiatives toward ongoing conflicts in Cambodia and Burma,
ASEAN's role in such efforts was as much to insulate Burma as to pressure it
(Amer 1999; Nischalke 2000).

Nuclear weapons and concerns over the fate of major powers breed inaction at
the regional level. Both tend to globalize rather than regionalize conflicts and
cause all actors—including, in the case of nuclear weapons, the protagonists—to
proceed gingerly. These consequences were illustrated by the recent crises between India and Pakistan over militant activities in Indian Kashmir. In both 1999
and 2002, the United States, with support from other major powers, sought to
defuse the crises through diplomacy, but felt inhibited from actively intervening
to prevent war or resolve the two countries' dispute. Neither global nor regional
organizations played any role in these crises, although Russia did use the occasion
of the first Conference on Interaction and Confidence-Building Measures in Asia
(CICA), held at Almaty, Kazakhstan, to attempt to mediate between the two sides.

Regional Institutions and Internal Conflict. By now it is a commonplace observation that Asia has among the fewest and weakest regional intergovernmental
organizations. In most cases, multilateral security forums such as the ASEAN Regional Forum (ARF) or the ASEAN–Post Ministerial Conference limit their discussions to interstate conflict issues, while APEC and ASEAN have been unable
to respond effectively to the Asian economic crisis (Acharya 1993, 1998, 2001).
The South Asian Association for Regional Cooperation (SAARC) has been unable even to provide a forum to discuss any of the regional issues because of India's reluctance to internationalize its dispute with Pakistan. Even the nascent
efforts to create a South Asian Free Trade Area have largely proceeded bilaterally
between India and its smaller neighbors, excluding Pakistan. The powerful norm
of sovereignty has generally inhibited discussion of internal conflicts, whether the
issue is separatism or regime legitimacy. Exceptions include APEC's 1999 meeting
in Auckland, which followed the referendum and violence in East Timor, and

ASEAN's reluctant involvement in issues of regime legitimacy, which came about because of concerns expressed by ASEAN's dialogue partners, the EU and the United States (Dupont 2000a, 2000b).

Global institutions have been active in attempting to solve internal conflicts, but with mixed results. The World Bank and Asian Development Bank (ADB) have become increasingly involved in postconflict reconstruction efforts in the Moro areas of the Philippines. The UN was actively involved in the political settlement in Cambodia and reconstruction in East Timor. The International Labor Organization (ILO) and a special human rights rapporteur were involved in the recent negotiations between the Burmese military regime and dissident leader Aung San Suu Kyi. In only one of these instances, however, that of Cambodia, did military intervention occur, and even here UN forces had no mandate to pursue Khmer Rouge activists in the countryside (Berdal and Leifer 1996).

Hegemonic Order. Given the ineffectiveness of regional institutions, the reluctance of global organizations to use force, and a regional norm venerating sovereignty, a hegemonic order is a logical alternative. Yet this, too, has not been forthcoming except periodically in South Asia. India's overwhelming power and size and geographic centrality have allowed it to play a big brother role with respect to other countries in South Asia with the exception of Pakistan. In the past, India has indirectly supported popular movements bringing about regime changes in Nepal, intervened militarily to support the creation of Bangladesh, and, after first supporting the Tamil insurgency in Sri Lanka with weapons and training, sought to impose a peace agreement on the Sri Lankan civil war. In recent years, however, India has not played a serious role in resolving internal conflicts. One reason is that India's own interests are so involved in separatist conflicts in these countries that India is not always seen as a neutral party. Another is that India's own problems with separatism color what the central government is willing to do.

Similar factors have discouraged a hegemonic approach to regional order elsewhere and explain why there has been no sustained effort to create hegemonic order in East Asia or Southeast Asia by states in these regions since Japan's failed effort in the 1930s and 1940s. While it could be argued that the United States has been the de facto hegemon in Asia since the end of the Second World War, its influence is bounded in East Asia by China and constrained in South Asia by India. Moreover, American attention has been too fitful and limited in scope to sustain the costs and intrusive engagement required to manage internal conflict.

Case Studies

Our three case studies each illustrate several of the potential routes by which internal conflicts can come to have regional or even global implications. They are presented here in order from the most acute threat, that of the conflict in Kashmir, to the most speculative, that of challenges to regime identity in China.

Separatist Conflicts: Kashmir. India's insurgency in Kashmir is the clearest example of an internal conflict with serious implications for regional security. In this case, the most obvious consequence is the threat of interstate war between two large, nuclear-armed rivals, India and Pakistan. The presence of a third, China, which also borders on Kashmir and claims a part of it, had the further consequence of bringing in superpower interest during the Cold War, most obviously by motivating India to seek a friendship treaty with the Soviet Union.

However, there are other, less obvious consequences. By feeding the India-Pakistan rivalry, Kashmir has prevented the emergence of regional associations in South Asia. Through its support for the insurgency in Indian Kashmir, Pakistan has inadvertently helped to sustain a network of pan-Islamist militants based in Afghanistan that has fed insurgencies throughout Asia and produced terrorist attacks in the rest of the world as well. The Kashmir conflict has also contributed at least marginally to nuclear proliferation in the region and prevented the development of overland trade ties between the large Indian market and newly independent Central Asian countries. Most seriously, however, any conceivable *resolution* of the conflict could threaten the internal stability of either India or Pakistan, with potentially far-reaching spillover effects.

The Kashmir conflict stems from the conflicting principles on which the two states were founded. Pakistan claims to be a home for all South Asian Muslims seeking to avoid domination in a Hindu India; India claims to be a secular and pluralist democracy in which all ethnic and religious minorities are safe. The presence in India of a Muslim-majority region adjoining Pakistan has come to be viewed by each as a test of its national ideology, and each believes, with some reason, that giving up on its claim to Kashmir would spark separatist or sectarian violence. Moreover, sectarian violence in one country tends to harden the position of both. In early 2002 the massacres of Muslims in India's Gujarat state were followed by Pakistan's release of many Islamic militants even as India blamed Pakistani intelligence for an early attack by a Muslim mob that burned a train carriage carrying Hindu activists to a disputed religious site.

National Identity: Indonesia. The heightening of internal conflicts within Indonesia, combined with the ongoing economic crisis since 1997, has raised the question "Will Indonesia survive?" (Emmerson 2000). There are three different challenges to national identity in Indonesia. The first is territorially based, and has to do with contesting the legitimate (territorial) scope of the Indonesian state. The second is a challenge from radical Islamic groups relating to the pluralist nature of the Indonesian state. The third set of conflicts involves communal violence often with religious overtones. Communal violence with implications for regime legitimacy and regional order includes violence against the Sino-Indonesian community as well as violent communal conflicts in West and Central Kalimantan, Sulawesi, and the Malukus.

Taken separately, none of the conflicts is in itself a serious threat. Neither of the main secessionist movements (Aceh and West Papua) can win independence militarily. While there has been international concern over the possibility that Muslim violence in Indonesia might be associated with terrorist organizations such as al Qaeda, so far there is little firm public evidence of such links. Much of the violence in Indonesia involving Muslims can be adequately explained in domestic terms, although there is some evidence of limited involvement of foreigners (Gershman 2002).

The threat to regional security comes from the prospect that ongoing secessionist movements, economic and political crisis, and a sustained challenge to the secular identity of the Indonesian state could combine to produce a collapse of central authority or a restoration of authoritarian rule. Such a collapse or violent crackdown could have widespread effects in terms of economic dislocation, refugee flows (to Malaysia, Singapore, and Australia), and demonstration effects for other secessionist movements in the region (U.S. Committee for Refugees 2001). Moreover, as the increase in piracy in the region shows, a fragmenting or even weak Indonesia could also threaten the major shipping lanes and transportation of oil to East Asia (Morrison 2001: 73).

Even without a wholesale collapse, however, the ongoing economic crisis, internal conflicts, and unstable democratic transition have all lowered Indonesia's previously prominent roles in both ASEAN and the ARF, as well as reduced its ability to contribute to regional security by monitoring adjacent air and sea corridors (Simon 2001: 274). Indonesia played a key role in creating and supporting ASEAN and the ARF during the New Order regime. If Indonesia remains unable to resolve some of its more significant internal conflicts, it risks even greater inability to act on the regional stage, and as Australian security analyst Paul Dibb put it, "a disabled Indonesia means a disabled ASEAN" (2001: 840). Continued internal conflicts and a state collapse would weaken these organizations even further in a region where intergovernmental organizations are already few and the few that exist are weak.

Regime Identity: China. The questions concerning conflicts over regime identity in China stem, of course, from the failed democracy movement of the late 1980s, and from the perception of many scholars that social protest continues to grow without an effective outlet even as the ruling Chinese Communist Party's ability to incorporate new social forces remains weak. A democratic China could fundamentally alter the nature of interstate relations in the Asia Pacific, but concerns about the consequences of regime change in China have less to do with the possibility of a smooth transition to a democratic regime than with the potential for state collapse, with a return to the instability and fragmentation of the early twentieth century (Chang 2001) or the emergence of a more militarized, authoritarian, and assertively nationalistic regime (Fewsmith 1986; Friedman and McCormick 2000).

The speculation is that such changes could occur, given that the forces of decentralization accelerate as the Chinese Communist Party (CCP) leadership increases economic integration under its commitments to the World Trade Organization, continues to dismantle state enterprises, and exposes China's agricultural sector to international competition (but see Segal 1994, 1999; Wasserstrom 2000). China's political leadership has staked its legitimacy on the two pillars of economic growth and nationalism. An economic crisis, economic dislocation associated with China's entry into the WTO, grievances associated with corruption, and lack of accountability of party cadres could combine with anger at a perceived injury to nationalist sentiments to produce significant political mobilization. This could result in either a crumbling of state authority or the emergence of a more militarized regime.

Such an event, with China's size and location connecting it with all of the major subregions in Asia, would be of important regional significance. State collapse or widespread unrest would create significant economic dislocations, refugee flows and, by involving a nuclear power, be of significant concern outside the region as well. Moreover, as with all instances of state collapse, it could also create opportunities for neighboring states to expand their power and influence, creating interstate strife in the region.

Sources of Internal Conflict

Although the three types of internal conflict are distinct, their sources have common elements that need to be spelled out before each type is discussed in turn. State-building and nation-building policies provide the stimulus for all three: economic modernization, the spread of education, and the formation of middle classes create the constituencies, and specific events that undermine the state's moral authority frequently trigger full-scale conflict.

Most Asian countries inherited a state structure that left local authority in the hands of traditional leaders, as well as an economy with a large traditional sector. Most, therefore, sought to centralize administrative authority and chose to concentrate financial resources and economic decision-making power in the government's hands in order to promote industrialization. Frequently, however, this was achieved by erecting neopatrimonial structures that tied officeholders and business classes to a narrow ruling clique and required largesse from resource

extraction or other "rents" such as foreign aid. In most Asian states, the army became the most coherent and meritocratic organization, and army support became crucial for the regime's survival. Resentment at "corruption" is therefore a
frequent trigger for challenges both to regime identity and to national identity—
providing a rationale for army coups, democratization movements, and even religiously inspired challenges to national identity.

Similarly, most Asian states inherited an ethnically diverse society—though
unlike many African countries, they have a large core ethnic group—among
whom nationalist sentiment was articulated primarily in opposition to European
colonialism and limited largely to a middle class educated in the colonial language. Most were therefore faced with crucial decisions on cultural policy and institutional structure, including the official language and the role of religion in
government, and the degree of decentralization to adopt. With public employment frequently the principal avenue for upward mobility, these decisions critically affected the opportunities available to rising segments of different groups.
The emergence of educated middle-class groups, in particular, has proved a
catalyst for conflict and change in all these areas. Opposition to state policies is
often driven by relative deprivation (Gurr 1970)—when groups compare their
situation to others—and by economic competition engendered by the processes
of modernization and state building (Horowitz 1985: 96–135). The role played by
urban middle classes in pressing for democratization needs little elaboration.
Drawing on Deutsch's (1953) work on European nationalism, numerous scholars
have shown that uneven modernization across regions and groups and competition over jobs in the modern sector have caused ethnic competition and conflict
in much of Africa and Asia (Young 1976: 98–139). Less well known, perhaps, is the
common finding that religion-based challenges to regime identity often stem
from newly literate, upwardly mobile groups who have difficulty assimilating to a
Westernized elite.[4] Even radical challenges to regime identity based on class, especially those positing the superiority of rural values to urban ones, are often led
by culturally alienated elements of the middle class.[5]

These sociological explanations, however, only address why certain demands
arise—not why they become acute or why the movements pressing the demands
turn violent. Three broad sources of escalation seem to trigger full-scale conflict.
First, all these challenges may be stimulated by economic decline—which shrinks

---

[4]This point emerges from many case studies of "fundamentalism" in Marty and Appleby (1991,
1994).

[5]The Chinese, Philippine, and Indian communist movements all fit this pattern. The violent
Maoist Naxalite rebellion in parts of rural India in the 1960s, for example, was led entirely by middle-class intellectuals. The most notorious example, however, was Pol Pot, who returned from
failing to receive a degree in Paris to form the Khmer Rouge.

the resources available to purchase support—or by economic reform requiring cutbacks in social services. Resentment at elites for not curtailing their consumption can feed anticorruption sentiments; often the state's retreat presents insurgent movements with an opportunity to step into the vacuum.[6] Second, an action by the state in response to a lesser challenge may cross an invisible line in the public's mind. The assassination of Aquino in the Philippines and the Indian government's assault on the Golden Temple of the Sikhs are two among many such examples. And third, a dramatic event that demonstrates the state's weakness—such as defeat in war—may result in challenges to the regime (Skocpol 1979). In Pakistan, unsatisfactory outcomes in conflicts with India have led both to democratization and to military coups.

In addition to this broad set of common factors there are elements specific to each type of conflict.

Separatist Conflicts. Separatist conflicts often arise from the grievances of particular regions over migration or perceived economic exploitation. Conflicts between migrants and natives are especially prone to stimulate separatism when the migration is sponsored by the state in order to alter the ethnic balance of a region: for example, Tibet and Xinjiang in China; Kalimantan, Sulawesi, West Papua, and the Malukus in Indonesia; Tamil areas of Sri Lanka; and, covertly, Assam in India.[7] Charges of economic exploitation can arise from the displacement of traditional forest users (Indonesia, northeast India, southern Thailand, and the Philippines); from disputes over royalties for the extraction of mineral resources (Indonesia and India); or from broader trade and economic policies (Pakistan/East Pakistan, Indian Punjab). In most of these instances, the policy remedies are easy to identify, if difficult to implement.

A more important source of separatism involves state efforts to promote a uniform culture and especially language. As Deutsch showed, and Gellner (1983) has argued more recently, efforts to promote a uniform culture are historically part of economic modernization, but they become politicized when they alter the distribution of opportunities for upward mobility across ethnic groups. This suggests that resentments over *cultural* policy will be most marked among individuals seeking entry into modern occupations and will focus on those aspects of cultural policy that affect their prospects. One inference that has not been sufficiently considered is that language conflicts are sharper when minority groups have a literate culture of their own (India vs. Han China) or when educated

[6]Islamic fundamentalist movements, in particular, have expanded their base through the performance of social welfare functions abandoned by the state. See, for example, Roberts (1994) on Algeria and Ahmad (1991) on Pakistan.

[7]In Assam, migration from Bangladesh was tacitly encouraged by the Congress Party, which viewed Bengali Muslims as a more reliable vote bank than Assamese (Das Gupta 1990: 159–62).

members of minorities have already invested in learning the colonial language (Burma vs. Thailand).[8] Another, more common inference is that conflicts over cultural policy increase among groups experiencing rapidly *rising* literacy and urbanization. Examples include Tamil and Sikh nationalism in India, Moro separatism in the Philippines, and the Pattani Front in southern Thailand. (See Barnett 1976; Brass 1990; George 1980; Noble 1976; Suhrke and Noble 1977; Majul 1985; Man 1990; Vitug and Gloria 2000; McKenna 1998.)

Two other factors may make separatist conflicts more likely. When several attributes of cultural differentiation coincide, ethnic conflict is more likely. Kashmir, Punjab, Sri Lanka, Muslim areas in the Philippines and southern Thailand, India's northeast, Inner Mongolia, Xinjiang, and Borneo are differentiated from the majority in their countries by language and religion. Regime type, too, may make a difference. Electoral processes may promote the formation of cross-ethnic coalitions (as in Malaysia), or channel ethnic conflicts in nonviolent ways (as in India's linguistically homogeneous states), but can also stimulate vote seeking along ethnic lines, and may even, as in Sri Lanka, lead to competitive ethnic radicalism among parties seeking votes from the same ethnic group (Horowitz 1985: 342–48). Moreover, ethnic competition may be especially marked in the early years following an initial democratization (Snyder 2000).

National Identity. Economic rivalry and relative deprivation, as noted above, help to explain all three kinds of conflicts, not just those over national unity. One important difference between separatist disputes and conflicts over national or regime identity, however, is that the latter typically occur within a dominant cultural group.

Conflicts over a regime's religious or secular identity often represent a nativist reaction among newly educated groups or among new entrants to the middle class to a cosmopolitan westernized elite that led the nationalist movement and ruled for the first generation after independence. Frequently, concerns over the continued role of the colonial language in national life play a powerful role in motivating religiously tinged nationalism or even fundamentalism.[9] Alternatively, as in Indonesia and to some degree in Malaysia, they may represent the resentment of a native middle class about the economic dominance of a group (ethnic Chinese, for example) perceived to be alien. This nativist aspect of religious fundamentalism is found in Hindu nationalism and Sikh revivalism in India, in Buddhist revivalism in Sri Lanka and Burma, and in Islamic revivalism almost

[8]In countries such as Iran, Nepal, and Thailand, ethnic minorities seem more willing to assimilate to a core ethnic group than in similarly situated ex-colonies such as Burma (Keyes 1997; Brown 1994; Lande 1999).

[9]This has been true of Islamic fundamentalism in Algeria (Roberts 1994: 442) and Pakistan (Ahmad 1991: 496). Replacing English with Hindi was long part of the Hindu nationalist agenda.

everywhere.[10] In addition, of course, the role of Islamic schools, or *madrasas*, in spreading radical Islamist doctrines has now become widely known.

Relations among states also shape debates over religious identity. But there is a difference between Islamic and non-Islamic countries. In non-Islamic countries, movements aimed at linking a country's identity with its religious heritage are often tied to an assertive nationalist project of differentiating the country both from its neighbors and from its own minorities: Hindu revivalism in India, Buddhist revivalism in Sri Lanka, or Buddhist socialism in Burma. In Islamic countries, by contrast, identifying the country with a religious heritage blurs the boundaries between the nation and the religious community. Pan-Islamism has contributed to radical Islamist and separatist movements among Muslims throughout the Asia Pacific, especially since the Afghanistan war (International Crisis Group 2001a, 2001c; Rashid 2000). These regional Islamic currents have fed not only separatist conflicts—in India, the Philippines, and China—but conflicts over national identity as well—in Pakistan, Indonesia, and Malaysia.

Challenges to Regime Identity. The sources of communist insurgencies and democratization movements are quite distinct. Although frequently led by an alienated middle class, communist insurgencies were mainly rural and most successful in countries where landholding was particularly inequitable and there was a small middle class. Pressures for democratization, by contrast, have often emerged as the unintended consequence of successful industrialization strategies whereby educated urban middle classes are created and economic and political organizations emerge outside the direct control of the state. This was the case in Taiwan, China, the Philippines, Thailand, and South Korea. The international dimension is another significant difference. During the Cold War, communist challenges had the support of China and invited U.S. intervention in support of authoritarian regimes; the end of the Cold War, by contrast, has seen democratization emerge as an international norm. These considerations tie conflicts over regime identity to concerns over regional order.

One aspect common to all regime challenges is rising outrage at corruption. Yet here too there are differences. Like military coups, democratization frequently draws on this sentiment among the armed forces for support and is often a conservatizing reform in the face of massive popular mobilization: in the Philippines, South Korea, and Indonesia transitions were actively managed by segments of the elite. Anticorruption challenges may also influence another type of regime challenge, the one that most concerns the regional security order: the collapse of a state altogether, as in Afghanistan or Cambodia. Such collapses, though, are caused by the weakness of the preceding states and especially the

[10]Again, see the various case studies in Marty and Appleby (1991, 1994).

army's lack of coherence. If the armed forces of China, Indonesia, North Korea, and Pakistan, the favored candidates for state collapse, remain intact, there is little likelihood of this outcome. The only reason to fear otherwise is the danger that conflicts over national identity in Pakistan or Indonesia may divide the army against itself.

Case Studies

The case studies illustrate the convergence of many sources of internal conflict, including the international dimension, but they also highlight two factors that make management difficult: internal conflicts vary in intensity over time, and policies aimed at managing them that appear successful in one period may seem problematic in another.

Separatist Conflicts: Kashmir. Almost every potential source of separatist conflict converges in the insurgency in Indian Kashmir. Historical legacies and international legal precedents, socioeconomic grievances, interethnic rivalry, mismanagement by the central state, and external intervention by neighboring states all play a role.

The origins of the conflict are historical. The 1947 division of British India along religious lines to create two independent states, with Muslim majority areas going to Pakistan, and others—most of them Hindu majority—remaining with India, only affected the areas directly ruled by Britain. The subcontinent's many semi-independent princes were given the option of joining either state, subject to certain conditions. The Hindu Maharaja of Muslim-majority Jammu and Kashmir initially sought to remain independent, but the incursion of irregular troops from Pakistan led him to accede to India. A short war left Pakistan in possession of about a third of the state, almost entirely Muslim, and India with the other two-thirds, which became the Indian state of Jammu and Kashmir.

Both international law and great power rivalry contributed to the conflict. India's claim, based on the Maharaja's accession, was subsequently weakened by the UN Security Council, which passed a resolution calling for a plebiscite to determine the wishes of Kashmiris. This resolution has been especially important in legitimating both separatist sentiment within Kashmir and Pakistan's support for it. The Kashmir conflict eventually involved all the major powers in the Asia Pacific. China, which claims Ladakh, a Buddhist region within the state, as historically being a part of Tibet, occupied a portion of Ladakh in 1962, and has since signed agreements with Pakistan that recognize Chinese claims. The United States was a major military supplier of Pakistan both in the 1960s and in the 1980s, when Pakistan was the conduit for weapons to guerrillas fighting the Soviet occupation of Afghanistan. Finally, the Soviet Union in turn signed a long-term friendship treaty with India that provided India not only with weapons but also with a de facto deterrent against Chinese intervention and a proxy veto in the UN Security Council over resolutions having to do with Kashmir. Finally, U.S. support for Afghan rebels against Soviet domination eventually contributed to the current crisis by bringing into being a transnational movements—pan-Islamism—that, with the active support of Pakistan, fueled an insurgency in Indian Kashmir from 1989 onward.

However, the insurgency itself had domestic causes that stemmed from domestic mismanagement, the ethnic composition of Jammu and Kashmir, and social changes. Since the early 1950s, the Indian government's principal goal in Kashmir has been to quell voices calling for implementation of the UN call for a plebiscite. The state's electoral processes were consistently compromised from that point. Sheikh Abdullah, the state's most popular leader, was removed from office in 1953 and jailed or barred from the state for much of the next twenty years. The Congress Party, which ruled nationally, first split Abdullah's party, the National Conference, installing a pro-India chief minister and then absorbed a significant segment of the party and governed from 1964 to 1974. A constitutional ban on the contesting of elections by parties seeking secession prevented forces favoring a plebiscite from testing their strength, while the National Conference and state Congress Party were widely viewed as systematically rigging elections. These measures ensured that India's principal promise to restive minorities—sharing power through the electoral process—was never met (Ganguly 1997; Schofield 1996: 164–89).

Electoral politics within the state were also compromised by the ethnic diversity of Jammu and Kashmir itself. Composed of several distinct ethnic regions comprising the predominantly Muslim Kashmir and Kargil valleys, Hindu Jammu, and Buddhist Ladakh, this is one of the few states of the Indian Union that is not ethnically homogeneous. Although Muslim Kashmiris are a majority, they are only barely so, and divisions among them could prevent a Kashmiri party from governing. Abdullah's National Conference Party was avowedly secular and won wide support initially with a far-reaching land reform program—mainly at the expense of Hindu landowners and Buddhist monasteries. His party has remained essentially a vehicle of Kashmiri Muslim sentiment, leaving minority regions to be represented by the Congress party that governed nationally, and by Hindu nationalists (Ganguly 1997: 27–29, 39–40). Perceptions that the state government was discriminating against minority regions and seeking to alter their ethnic composition by encouraging Muslim migration made matters worse.

Finally, the central government's substantial development expenditures backfired. They succeeded in increasing literacy (often through Islamic schools) and exposure to modern communications (Kashmir was among the first states to receive television broadcasts) without creating new jobs. This led to an increase in the number of educated unemployed youth and a constituency for militancy (Ganguly 1997: 31–37).

National Identity: Indonesia. Indonesia illustrates the convergence among the various types of internal conflict discussed in this chapter. A major regime change from authoritarianism to an unconsolidated democracy unleashed separatist challenges, challenges to the secular character of the state, and communal conflicts both between ethnic Indonesians and ethnic Chinese and between Christian and Muslim indigenous Indonesians. These conflicts in turn challenge the survival of the regime. In some sense, all the conflicts stem from a conflict over national identity, specifically over the legitimate territorial and cultural basis for the Indonesian state. While conflicts over the exploitation of natural resources and state-sponsored migration have contributed to separatist challenges, the most significant of those challenges come from regions that were either not part of the Netherlands East Indies (East Timor) or weakly integrated into it (Aceh and West Papua). (For details see May 1986; Budiardjo and Liong 1988; Saltford 2000.) Cultural differences between these regions and what is perceived as "Indonesian"—Islamic and Malayo-Polynesian in language—contribute to the support for some armed separatist movements, although the absence of separatism in Hindu Bali and its existence in Muslim Aceh suggest a historical rather than a cultural explanation.

Challenges to regime identity by increasingly assertive radical Islamic groups are not unprecedented. But the particular form appears to be linked to their exclusion from politics under the New Order. The political liberalization since the fall of the Suharto regime has created new opportunities for Islamists to organize and challenge the secular nature of the Indonesian state. Indonesia's orthodox Muslims are conventionally divided into traditionalists, whose understanding of Islam includes traditions derived from Java itself, and modernists, who insist that the only true basis of Islam is the Koran and the example of the Prophet Mohammad. Political vehicles representing modernist Muslims were banned from the 1950s to the 1980s, and many of their leaders were imprisoned. Many contemporary radical Islamic organizations have their roots in modernist Islam (Hefner 2000).

Although political Islam is an increasingly prominent discourse and organizational force (represented most clearly by the Center Axis, a coalition of Muslim-based parties), radical Islam remains a small, albeit growing, political force. It is found mainly in large towns and cities where organizations were originally able to mobilize young people who had been excluded from the benefits of the New Order's economic growth and whose numbers have increased in the aftermath of the Asian economic crisis.

The assertiveness of Islamist groups has contributed to communal tension as well. Violence against ethnic Chinese has a long history in Indonesia, but was rare between the early 1980s and the mid-1990s (Mackie 1976; Coppel 1983). In 1994, attacks against Sino-Indonesians occurred, driven by a combination of factors. The booming economy was believed to disproportionately benefit urban Chinese business people. Further, there was growing dissatisfaction among modernist Muslims over what they perceived to be Suharto's favoring of ethnic Chinese and Christian Indonesians; when, in an effort to head off this dissatisfaction, Suharto offered the modernist Muslims greater access to political power, they, in turn, became more outspoken in their criticism of the Chinese (Hefner 1993, 2000; Liddle 1996).

In addition, four regions have experienced communal conflicts involving Muslims and local non-Muslims: West and Central Kalimantan, Sulawesi, and the Malukus. The conflicts have emerged at different times, and the role of national political actors varies across the cases, but all have involved areas where state-sponsored migration altered the original balance of power and where control over economic and natural resources was contested (International Crisis Group 2001d; Malley 2001). The conflicts in Kalimantan are more ethnic than religious: with Muslim Madurese immigrants being targeted for violence by both Muslim and non-Muslim Dayaks, while other Muslim migrant communities were left alone. Sulawesi and the Malukus, though, have attracted special international attention because of the involvement of Laskar Jihad, a radical Islamic paramilitary group. The conflict in Sulawesi is rooted in the collapse of informal local consociational practices that alternated power between Christian and Muslim leaders. The conflict in the Malukus began in January 1999 with economic and ethnic as well as religious undertones, and quickly polarized into Christian-Muslim conflict. Transmigration under Suharto was responsible for relocating Muslims to the Malukus from other parts of the country, altering the religious balance and displacing the Christian elite. The escalation of interreligious or interethnic violence has given rise to a sense that the conflicts indicate a broader deterioration in social cohesion throughout the country (Human Rights Watch 1997; van Klinken 1999; Mitchell 1999).

Regime Identity: China. The emergence of a contemporary democratic challenge to the CCP regime in China has its roots in two developments: the highly disruptive period of mass mobilization termed the Cultural Revolution during 1966–76, and the economic reform program that began in the late 1970s. The desire to forestall another Cultural Revolution and manage the social transformation begun by the economic reform program interacted with two additional processes. One was a debate between hard-liners and soft-liners in the elite over how much political reform (greater openness, accountability of the party, and dialogue with the public) should accompany economic reform. The second was the emergence of groups of party members and citizens that advocated a range of policies from democratization (a small group) to a Gorbachevist style glasnost to accompany the economic reform program (Pei 1998c; White 1998).

By the end of 1988, the actual achievements of officially sponsored political reform were limited. They included regularization and expansion of the role of people's congresses, direct elections of county-level people's congress deputies, limitations on terms of office for some party and state officials, establishment of employee councils in state-owned enterprises, and the enactment of several hundred laws conducive to procedural regularity. Legal reforms in China's constitutional, criminal, civil, and administrative laws contributed to an expansion of litigation in the 1980s and 1990s (with a slight downturn after Tiananmen) (Pei 1998a). However, political controls during this decade remained relatively relaxed, leading to the emergence of a range of autonomous and semiautonomous civic organizations, particularly in urban areas. The post-Tiananmen crackdown slowed this growth, as restrictive new government regulations made it more difficult for new groups to register (Pei 1998b). The emergence of such groups has created neither an ideal-typical autonomous civil society nor an entirely state-corporatist set of institutions, but rather, a "continuum of associational structures and experiences stretching from those relatively . . . state-dominated at one extreme, to those relatively . . . autonomous, at the other" (Shue 1994: 175).

During the 1980s, explicitly pro-democratic associations remained largely clandestine or semiclandestine but had begun to forge working relationships with each other. By 1989 they had grown slowly into a national force that had the participation or sympathy of many urban residents in China. In the process, the movement for Chinese democracy became more complicated in its social composition and in its mix of political goals and tactics. The rapid economic growth under the economic reform program had expanded the urban middle class. The economic reforms had also begun to lead to economic dislocation and growing inequalities (rural-urban as well as intra-urban inequalities) by the late 1980s, while the weakening of central state control also contributed to an increase in corruption. These factors were central to demands for further political reforms by younger party elites, students, and urban workers that culminated in mobilizations throughout major urban centers in China in 1989, the most famous of course being the protest in Tiananmen Square. Students were the driving force. However, they sought, not an overthrow of the regime, but a dialogue between student leaders and the party leadership on issues relating to greater openness and fighting corruption, as well as a recognition that the student mobilizations were a patriotic political force. More radical in their demands, and perceived by the party leadership as more threatening, were smaller organizations involving urban workers (Walder and Gong 1993).

The repression of the protests in Beijing and elsewhere in 1989 and the marginalization of soft-liners from the party leadership left the hard-liners clearly in charge and decimated the emerging pro-democratic movement. While associational life in China continued to diversify and expand in the 1990s, such associations were expected to forgo explicit political commitments and challenges to the CCP's monopoly on political representation. Groups such as the religious sect Falun Gong that appear to challenge the party's organizational hegemony are repressed, as was the one effort to formally register a political party in 1999.

While official data show an increase in protests since 1989, they are localized in nature—workers fighting for pay or peasants protesting corruption or taxation by local party officials. There has been a shift in some parts of rural China to framing demands and grievances in a rights discourse, and the practices of citizenship have emerged in some areas, even though the legal institutions for the exercise of citizenship rights do not exist (O'Brien 2001). Popular mobilization critical of the regime has occurred not only around broad political issues and in localized economic and environmental issues but also in nationalist responses to events such as the accidental bombing of the Chinese embassy in Belgrade and the spy plane imbroglio in April 2001. Neither nationalist nor economically motivated mobilization will be inherently democratic in character, and the CCP leadership's juggling act will only become more difficult as it tries to manage the continued transformation of China into a more market-oriented economy.

Managing Internal Conflicts

Internal conflicts are more easily avoided than resolved. In fact, internal armed conflict is more difficult to stop than conflict between states. Whereas the security dilemma between sovereign states can be attenuated by a truce that leaves each side with a secure border and armed forces intact, in internal conflicts this is impossible. And when armed conflict involves terrorism or guerrilla warfare rather than conventional warfare, even a conclusive military victory for one side may be elusive. States battling guerrilla warfare can win many battles without settling the war, and often they resort to indiscriminate repressive measures against noncombatants that only provide the insurgents with more recruits.[11]

However, the international relations metaphor can be overstretched: the constituencies involved in internal conflicts are not unitary actors. They contain actual or potential internal divisions that states can exploit. India contained both electoral Tamil nationalism (Swamy 1996a) and violent Sikh nationalism with the

[11]Fearon (1998) provides a widely used theoretical treatment in terms of the "commitment problems" facing ethnic antagonists. See also Lake and Rothschild (1998) and the various articles in Walter and Snyder (1999).

help of loyalist politicians and police, respectively, while divisions among Moro groups have helped the Philippine government find negotiating partners. In challenges to regime identity, the degree of violence often depends on the scope of splits within the ruling elites as well as on the strength of regime challengers. Divisions between hard-liners and soft-liners were critical for the transitions in the Philippines, South Korea, Taiwan, and Indonesia. Conflicts over national identity are perhaps the most irreconcilable, but even here religious parties are not equally militant in their demands. It is the transnational aspect of Islamic militancy that makes it difficult for a state to suppress or even negotiate with these movements. And, as recent experience has demonstrated, the most useful management strategy here may be a preventive one, in which the state takes the initiative in secularizing education instead of leaving it to religious groups. Other preventive and curative measures are discussed below.

Domestic Policy Responses

Despite the diverse sources of ethnic conflicts and challenges to regime or national identity, the policy responses available to elites share certain similarities. All have limitations. The responses fall into two broad categories: one set seeks to maintain an existing state-building or nation-building strategy; the other accepts alterations in order to preserve the state as a whole. The former can usefully be divided into coercion and co-optation—that is, providing material benefits as *side-payments* to disgruntled groups. The latter can also be subdivided into substantive policy concessions and changes in the rules of the game. Although scholars seldom recognize the difference, the responses have very different implications and encounter very different levels of resistance from state elites.[12] In the discussion below, which elaborates on these categories and discusses specific policies, we refer to the responses as accommodation and power sharing.

Both coercion and co-optation can be targeted at specific leaders, at certain insurgent organizations, at a particular region, or at society generally. (Economic growth is a general co-optive strategy.) Both variants have their limitations: coercive measures may increase resistance; co-optation fails when resources dry up or no longer satisfy the aspirations of the new middle-class groups who are the most important to placate. One sophisticated form of co-optation that may be exempt

[12]Sisk (1996) treats both as aspects of "power sharing" while Brown and Ganguly (1997) treat both as "accommodation." (Their other categories, "coercion" and "co-optation," have been adopted here.) However, the Indian experience suggests distinguishing between the two. The refusal of Congress elites to grant power sharing to Muslims in the form of separate electoral representation for Muslims and Hindus strengthened the movement for Pakistan while, in independent India, linguistic minorities who have been quiescent have enjoyed power sharing through the quasi-federal system, but religious minorities, who have not, have only been granted substantive concessions on cultural policy. See Swamy (1996b: chap. 7) for a fuller discussion of these points.

TABLE 14.4
Varieties of Domestic Response to Internal Conflicts

Response targeted at:	Policy		
	Repression		
Individual	Selective: ranging from arresting opponents to "disappearances"		
Organization	Banning membership in specific organizations		
Group/society	Substantial army, police presence, curfews		
	Co-optation		
Individual	Patronage resources aimed at traditional leaders or local community leaders		
Organization	Funds for language, religious, civic, or class-based organizations		
Group/region	Affirmative action programs, targeted development funds for region		
Society	Performance legitimation via growth		
	National unity conflict	National identity conflict	Regime identity conflict
	Accommodation		
	No or neutral official language; religious neutrality	Declaration of official religion without concessions to clergy	Local elections; promoting rule of law to fight corruption
	Power-sharing		
	Consociationalism or federalism	Consociationalism; distinct religious and secular spheres	Partial transition to elected or civilian authorities; corporatism

from the latter limitation is the use of affirmative action. Such policies can be used to contain conflicts over national unity or identity. China uses quotas for minorities to prevent separatist challenges; Malaysia uses them to deflect challenges to national identity among indigenous Malaysians; in India the key beneficiaries are members of traditionally low-status groups who might provide a constituency for class revolution.[13] Affirmative action policies have the benefit of being aimed directly at the upwardly mobile. They can spark a backlash from excluded groups, however, especially when these are in the majority. An intermediate strategy involves designing a discourse that creates a sense of inclusion without specific policy or institutional concessions. Both socialism and nationalism help to moderate conflicts over regime or national identity and have been especially prominent in China. Emphasizing a civic or territorial basis for nationhood rather than ethnic solidarity may moderate separatist sentiments and ease certain conflicts over national identity. But clearly there are tensions between, say, using nationalism to appease nonelite segments of the majority and using civic identity to placate minorities.

[13]Affirmative action policies are defined in a way to co-opt separatism in Sarawak and Sabah in Malaysia and in several of India's northeastern states.

When it comes to accommodation and power sharing, the varieties differ according to the type of conflict. In conflicts over national unity or identity, accommodation typically involves policies on language and religion. Regimes often face a conflict between the requirements for preventing separatist and nativist challenges to national identity. Accommodating linguistic coexistence means choosing an official language that allows minority groups to compete fairly with the largest linguistic group. But except in rare instances where the language of a small group is widely understood as a lingua franca by others,[14] this policy usually involves using the colonial language for official purposes and can lead to populist resentment of the elite's privileged access to the language of opportunity. In states that are more or less religiously homogeneous, like Pakistan, conflicts over the religious or secular nature of the state can be finessed by adopting an official religion but granting the clergy no real power. In multireligious states like India, however, such a strategy could spark separatism. A common compromise is to grant different religious communities the right to practice their own civil law—historically a practice of Islamic states—or to protect the rights of minorities to practice their own religion.

In the case of separatist movements, power sharing can be achieved by means of formal or informal consociationalism—assuring all ethnic groups a share of national powers—or by granting limited self-government through federalism or a measure of regional autonomy. In Asia the only real example of consociationalism is the informal alliance of ethnic parties that rules in Malaysia, where communal conflict has been defused (Case 1996; Winzeler 1998). Elsewhere the most common type of power-sharing arrangement is some form of federalism. Federal solutions imply granting a measure of self-governance to territorially concentrated ethnic groups. They require a democratic regime, the granting of genuine authority and financial autonomy to the regions, as well as a balance of (demographic) power among regions. In Burma and China, where provincial governors are centrally appointed, federal solutions solve little; the predominance of Punjab in terms of its large population compromises Pakistani federalism even during its democratic episodes. To contain separatism, federalism also requires that minorities must be territorially concentrated and that minority regions must be relatively homogeneous. Although modified federalism has prevented linguistic separatism in India, it has not worked in the more heterogeneous environments of Kashmir, Punjab, and the Northeast.

Capitalist regimes facing communist revolution and authoritarian regimes facing democratization inevitably choose different accommodative measures. For

---

[14]This was partly achieved by Indonesia's decision to adopt Malay (widely used in the country as a lingua franca and renamed Bahasa Indonesia) and, after 1971, by Pakistan's use of Urdu.

the former, land reform is the most common (if imperfectly implemented) policy. For the latter, the range of options includes efforts to strengthen the rule of law—in order to prevent anger over corruption from exploding into full-scale revolt—and the introduction of competitive elections at lower levels of government. Power-sharing approaches are essentially an extension of the accommodative measures. A frequent solution—not just in Asia—involves transferring power to elected civilian authorities with the military retaining institutional autonomy and an effective veto on issues considered crucial to national security broadly defined. This kind of solution is evolving in Iran—with the clergy taking the place of the military—to mediate the ongoing conflict over national identity, and it might also be envisioned as an outcome in states in Asia. Corporatist structures that grant class-based organizations formal representation in government are an extension of this principle to class-based challenges to regime identity, though in practice these structures seldom have enough autonomy to be thought of as anything more than accommodation.

Cases

With this broad survey of management techniques in mind, we turn to a brief consideration of how internal conflicts have been managed (or mismanaged) in our three case studies.

Separatist Conflicts: Kashmir. Over the fifty years that it has been in dispute, Kashmir has experienced the entire gamut of management strategies. These have included both the general power-sharing provisions accorded to all Indian states and special autonomy provisions; co-optation targeted at individuals, political parties, and the state; and coercion targeted at individuals, organizations and the state. Many appeared to work for a while, but none were able to address the international dimension.

To begin with, Kashmir was accorded a distinct status within India. Initially it drafted its own constitution, maintained customs barriers against the rest of India, retained authority over all matters except defense, foreign affairs, and communications, and titled its chief executive the prime minister, rather than the chief minister as is the practice in other states. A somewhat diluted set of special autonomy provisions was eventually incorporated in the Indian constitution as Article 370, which removed customs barriers but allowed Kashmir to prohibit the acquisition of landed property by non-Kashmiris. However, as noted previously, intra-ethnic conflicts in Kashmir weakened the prospects for self-governance, as did the manipulation of the electoral process by the Congress party. The two fed into each other, since it was the demands of minority regions for the abolition of Article 370 that sparked Sheikh Abdullah's decision to call for a plebiscite and led to his imprisonment. The subsequent steady dilution of Article 370—and the strident calls of Hindu nationalists to abolish it altogether—have been a steady source of friction (Schofield 1996: 165–89).

Until India defeated Pakistan in the 1971 Bangladesh war, the Indian government relied on a combination of co-optation and coercion to manage separatist sentiment in Kashmir. After 1971, Prime Minister Indira Gandhi was sufficiently confident in the strength of India's position to return to accommodative measures. Sheikh Abdullah was released and allowed to take charge as chief minister of the state. During extended negotiations, however, the government refused to allow a return even to the measure of autonomy envisioned at the time of accession. However, following the Sheikh's death, relations between the Congress Party and his son and successor, Farooq Abdullah, deteriorated. Farooq Abdullah was removed from office in 1985. The Congress Party's subsequent decision to compel the National Conference to ally with it in a 1987 election widely viewed as fraudulent completed the delegitimation of the electoral process and boosted support for militant activities (Ganguly 1997: 68–97; Schofield 1996: 221–30).

Since the onset of the insurgency, the Indian government's principal tool has been coercion accompanied by desperate attempts to restore meaningful electoral processes. Kashmir was placed under direct administrative rule from New Delhi for much of the 1990s and subjected to intense militant activity and an extraordinarily harsh military presence, reportedly accompanied by extensive human rights violations. The return of Farooq Abdullah as chief minister through an election with low turnout has not significantly helped matters (Schofield 1996: 237–83). Paradoxically, some hope arises from India's election of a Hindu nationalist government and its subsequent decision to test nuclear devices. The consequent nuclear standoff with Pakistan, and the fears of nuclear war raised by the Kargil conflict, have compelled a government dominated by hard-line positions on Kashmir to seek some negotiated way out. During 2000 and 2001 the government of the Bharatiya Janata Party (BJP) tried to find a negotiating partner domestically by releasing leaders of different civilian separatist organizations from jail and declaring unilateral cease-fires with various militant organizations. These measures failed, as most separatist organizations insisted on including Pakistan in negotiations. In June 2001, India issued a dramatic invitation to Pakistan's new military ruler, Gen. Pervez Musharaf, to visit India for discussions on all outstanding disputes. However, the talks failed, as India continued to deny that Pakistan had standing in the dispute.

Domestically, too, there has been something of a stalemate. The National Conference, back in power in Kashmir, is a member of the ruling national coalition and presumably able to press Kashmir's case. But the views of the BJP remain at odds not only with the National Conference, which passed a resolution calling for a restoration of autonomy to the state, but even with other Indian parties that have largely supported the resolution. The BJP remains committed to abolishing the special status of Kashmir and is willing to consider increased autonomy only in the context of granting broader powers to all Indian states. It is also unwilling to put the accession of Kashmir to India on the table, as are all Indian parties. The likelihood at present, therefore, is for a continuation of the present stalemate, barring significant international events. The escalation of India-Pakistan tensions to the brink of war in the months following September 11, 2001, and the subsequent pressure on Pakistan to crack down on Islamic militants have not pointed to a solution so far.

National Identity: Indonesia. Under Suharto, the New Order's "security approach" to regime challengers and separatist movements relied primarily on coercion, combined with a degree of shared economic growth, an ideology of tolerance and multiculturalism, a veto on discussion of racial, ethnic and religious issues (so-called "SARA" issues) and a form of corporatism through the political party Golkar.[15] This strategy enabled the regime to stay in power but ultimately repressed and deepened rather than managed the grievances underlying these conflicts, as the disruptions since Suharto's departure in 1998 suggest.

B. F. Habibie, Suharto's immediate successor, began the shift to strategies of accommodation (a referendum in East Timor and a human rights commission in Aceh) and co-optation (decentralization and competitive elections) (Usman 2001). These approaches continued in the early period of the Wahid administration. Opposition by legislators forced a return to a more coercive approach to the secessionist conflicts, an approach continued under Megawati when she assumed the presidency in July 2001, despite her signing of legislation for special autonomy for Aceh and West Papua that took effect in 2002. The laws provide the legal basis for the two provinces to have greater control over their economy, politics and security, as well as cultural and religious affairs, including the implementation of Islamic Sharia law in Aceh. Suspicion by citizens in these regions as to whether Jakarta is actually pursuing a co-optive or an accommodating strategy make the outcome of these efforts uncertain (International Crisis Group 2001b).

The more immediate challenges to regime identity come from Islamic groups, particularly as some have become involved in communal conflicts and in the post–September 11, 2001, environment in which the political mobilization of Islamic groups has become of regional and international concern (International Crisis Group 2001a).

[15]Golkar (acronym for *golongan karya* or "functional groups") was founded in 1964 as a counterbalance to growing PKI influence and was rooted in the state bureaucracy and the military during the New Order regime. SARA refers to Suku, Agama, Ras, and Antar-golongan—basically ethnicity, religion, race, and intergroup relations, public discussion of any of which was taboo during the New Order.

In contrast to his repression of secessionist, class, democratic, and other challenges to his regime, Suharto began to encourage Islamic participation in politics in the late 1980s to counter the influence of the army and to appease the increasingly restive modernist Muslim middle class. He allowed the formation of Muslim social and political associations and the growth of religious education. He also began to promote pro-Islamic "green" officers to senior positions in the military. As a result, Suharto parted ways with significant sections of the military leadership in the late 1980s, in particular the so-called *merah-putih* (red and white). This faction coalesced around the central tenets of nationalism and secularism, premised on a "professional" armed forces, and forged a de facto alliance with the current president Megawati Sukarnoputri in the early 1990s (Hefner 1993, 2000; Liddle 1996).

Communal conflict was relatively muted during the New Order regime, although it began to expand in the mid-1990s in Kalimantan. It increased dramatically following the Asian economic crisis and in the post-Suharto period. The three administrations since Suharto have failed to develop an effective management strategy for communal conflict, in part because of the security forces' recurring failure to prevent further conflicts or to take firm and early action to prevent its spread (Malley 2001).

The failure of the military to stop the violence has created openings for Islamist paramilitaries like the Laskar Jihad to intervene, as they have done in the Malukus and in Sulawesi. After Laskar Jihad sent militia forces to the Poso region in Sulawesi to attack Christian strongholds in November 2001, the Megawati administration sent military personnel and in late December 2001 negotiated a peace settlement between Muslim and Christian leaders. The settlement acknowledged traditional forms of dispute settlement and informal forms of consociationalism and represents a possible strategy for effective resolution of these types of communal conflict.

The shift to more accommodationist strategies, including decentralization and more local autonomy, will have the important unintended consequence of fueling the conditions that have led to communal conflicts. For example, while decentralization has been an initial step in responding to calls for greater autonomy, it has had ambivalent effects on managing resource-based conflicts, some of which have fed separatist and communal conflicts. In addition, the regional autonomy laws that went into effect in January 2001 transferred significant powers to Indonesia's 350-plus districts *(kabupaten)*, including the right to license small-scale logging concessions. In exchange for increased autonomy, the laws placed new obligations on districts to raise as much of their own revenues as possible. The easiest way to do so for districts in forest regions is to issue licenses. The desire to raise money fast is reinforced by corruption and patronage in local politics. The result tends to be rapid and damaging deforestation of the kind that has fed communal conflicts in Kalimantan (International Crisis Group 2001d).

The gravity of the Islamic challenges to regime identity in Indonesia is that they expose the weakness of the institutions of the state. Indonesia's democratic transition is being accompanied by a crisis of lawlessness that has allowed many groups—including radical Islamic groups—to engage in violent behavior with impunity (International Crisis Group 2000, 2001c).

Regime Identity: China. From 1949 to 1978, the CCP's dominant management strategy for challenges to the party's rule was coercion and an ideological appeal to legitimacy based on communist ideology. The CCP under Mao also utilized mobilization as a tool of both its development strategy (as during the Great Leap Forward) and its mass political campaigns to reinforce Mao's control over the party (as during the Cultural Revolution), but overall, coercion was the dominant strategy.

In parallel with its economic reform program, the party has gradually created new spaces for very limited political contestation, as a dual effort to co-opt and defuse political unrest and to channel it in ways that are at least not disruptive of sustained economic growth. These efforts have included ideological shifts in the basis of legitimacy that have gradually expanded the social base of the party, allowed for marginal autonomy between state and party institutions, and enabled the emergence of village elections, even while the party has simultaneously responded with coercion to any appearance of a sustained organizational challenge to its political monopoly.

The economic reforms that began in the late 1970s reflected a shift in the CCP's legitimating ideology, from socialism through class struggle to national economic development (Meisner 1996). During the period of economic reform, the party has gradually relaxed its membership criteria, slowly expanding the social base of the party. Although technical experts were brought into the party in large numbers to promote economic modernization in the Deng era, central policy forbade the recruitment of private entrepreneurs into the party. At the CCP's 80th anniversary in July 2001, President and CCP General Secretary Jiang Zemin's "Three Represents" Speech proposed allowing the entry of private entrepreneurs into the party, as part of an agenda for refashioning the party to represent the development needs of "advanced forces of production," advanced culture, and the interests of the overwhelming majority of the people. It is widely seen as sounding the death knell for a party ostensibly legitimated by its role as the vanguard of the working class, even though it ratifies current practice.

While the inclusion of private entrepreneurs in the CCP reflects a shift in the legitimation strategy of the party, it is also an effort to sustain rapid economic growth and modernization (thereby increasing reliance on performance legitimacy) (Alagappa 1995) as a means of ensuring that grievances do not translate into sustained political challenges to the party's dominance. The effects on democratization, in the short term at least, are ambiguous at best. As Pearson (1998) notes, the dependent nature of China's emerging bourgeoisie suggests that capital will not be a major force for democratization.

Localized disruptions and challenges to party officials, especially on issues of corruption, are tolerated and in some cases encouraged by the party leadership (O'Brien and Li 1995). But when such mobilizations threaten to become widespread, incorporate large numbers of urban workers, or seem to represent organizational challenges to the CCP's hegemony, then coercion remains the dominant management strategy to repress large-scale mobilization, whether of the secular variety (Tiananmen, attempting to register the China Democratic Party) or the religious variety (Falun Gong).

In the post-Tiananmen era, the CCP has maintained tight political control but has relaxed slightly the fusion between party and state, granting a small amount of autonomy for the latter, especially in legislative institutions like the National and Provincial Peoples Congresses. The latter have become an important vehicle in some localities as a check on corrupt and inefficient government action, becoming a force for more accountable, if not democratic, governance (Dickson 1998a; MacFarquhar 1998; O'Brien 1994a, 1994b; O'Brien and Luehrmann 1998). Legal reforms have also restructured state-society relations in ways that have constrained the arbitrary exercise of bureaucratic power. For example, Pei (1998a: 91–92) finds that the number of commercial disputes adjudicated by the courts rose from about 15,000 a year in the early 1980s to 1.5 million a year in the mid-1990s. Legislation allowing citizens to sue the government precipitated a rise in the number of lawsuits filed from approximately 600 in 1986 to nearly 80,000 in 1996 (O'Brien and Li 1995).

Finally, remarkably similar to what has been occurring under authoritarian regimes in Taiwan and Pakistan, among others, there has been a gradual trend toward establishing semicompetitive elections in villages (Cheng 1993; Dickson 1998b). As in Taiwan, the motivating factor in such elections was to contain organizational challenges to the party's rule. In China this new electoral system was necessitated by the return to family farming under the household responsibility system, which led to the dismantling of the village-level brigades and production teams that had previously maintained social order in the countryside (Oi 1996, 1999). Their disappearance led to a "governability crisis" reflected in higher crime rates and tax evasion that concerned party leaders. In some areas local coalitions of village elders, former CCP cadres and publicly minded villagers created informal elected village committees to fill the void (Li and O'Brien 1999; Manion 1996, 2000; Shi 1999). The initiative was picked up by some top party officials as a means of addressing the rise in what was perceived as "disorder" and maintaining a check and balance system against corruption, as well as advancing the party's organizational control. From 1990 onward, village elections occurred with varying degrees of competitiveness (Jennings 1997; O'Brien and Li 2000; O'Brien 2001; Oi and Rozelle 2000).

Given the probability of further economic dislocation following China's accession to the WTO, the relative balance between nationalism and economic growth as the centerpiece of the CCP's legitimating ideology is likely to become more contested. This dynamic is also affected by the status of Taiwan. (See Chap. 10 in this volume.) The party's concern over losing face on the Taiwan issue by allowing its permanent separation from the mainland centers on three related issues: sincere nationalism and the fear of national breakup; tactical nationalism and fears about CCP legitimacy; and individual leaders' concerns about surviving the succession process and preserving their historical legacies (Christensen 2001; Pei 1998d). Recent trends in unrest motivated by economic grievances will place the new channels for expressing dissatisfaction under pressure. The emerging use of a rights-based discourse (in contrast to democracy per se) as the basis for claim making will pose new challenges for the regime and offer no guarantee that the pressures for reform will be necessarily democratic in nature (O'Brien 2001).

Conclusion

In view of the analysis presented in this chapter, the conclusion has to be more predictive than prescriptive. The overriding *security* concern of most Asian states is, and will continue to be, the consolidation of their authority domestically. While internal challenges in one country do pose a threat to domestic stability in its neighbors, this is unlikely to result in regional efforts at managing internal conflicts, except in the rather weak sense that states will help and encourage each other to maintain domestic control. Asian countries in the past have used covert support of insurgencies in other countries as a way to weaken their adversaries, extend their jurisdictions, and strengthen national identity at home while circumventing the postwar norm of respecting "juridical sovereignty" (Jackson and Rosberg 1982). Today, Asian states increasingly fear that intervention in another state's conflict will legitimate internal conflicts within their own borders, and they are therefore moving toward a mutual recognition of territorial sovereignty.

The events following the attack on the World Trade Center on September 11, 2001, are only likely to strengthen this trend. Prior to September 11, Asian states faced international pressure to respect human rights and reduce the role of the state in the economy, a pressure that threatened to deprive them of the two principal methods used by nascent states to maintain control—coercion and material inducement (Ayoob 1995). Asia's emphasis on sovereignty appeared to be on a collision course with Western efforts to promote global norms. With international concern shifting to the suppression of terrorism—and the potential for "failed states" to became havens for terrorist networks—even the major Western powers have come to focus more on whether states are able and willing to eliminate terrorist cells than on how they achieve these aims. Concerns over human rights violations and excessive centralization of economic decision making will remain, but they will likely be couched more in terms of their potential for feeding internal conflict than for their intrinsic value.

External actors, moreover, will need to remember that internal conflicts are a moving target, their onset and progress the result of an interactive process between the internal and external environments of states and socioeconomic change. External actors have frequently been a source of the problem, both through deliberate mischief making and unintentionally through actions such as U.S. involvement in Afghanistan (for South Asia) and Vietnam (for Cambodia). The inevitable socioeconomic changes associated with development create new grievances and constituencies that did not exist previously, and these constituencies, moreover, are not unitary actors but may be internally divided or can be successfully divided by states. Policies that successfully manage change in one set of circumstances may fail in others, or may even come to be seen as part of the problem. And finally, for states facing multiple types of internal conflicts, policies that address one type of conflict may exacerbate others: it is difficult to accommodate majoritarian religious nationalism and the fears of ethnic minorities simultaneously, even though they may be espoused by similarly situated groups.

Works Cited

Acharya, Amitav. 1993. *A New Regional Order in Southeast Asia: ASEAN in the Post-Cold-War Era.* Adelphi Paper 279. London: Brassey's for the International Institute for Strategic Studies.

———. 1998. "Collective Identity and Conflict Management in Southeast Asia." In Emanuel Adler and Michael Barnett, eds., *Security Communities.* Cambridge: Cambridge University Press.

———. 2001. *Constructing a Security Community in Southeast Asia: ASEAN and the Problem of Regional Order.* New York: Routledge.

Ahmad, Mumtaz. 1991. "Islamic Fundamentalisms in South Asia: The Jamaat-I-Islami and the Tablighi Jamaat of South Asia." In Martin R. Marty and R. Scott Appleby, eds., *Fundamentalisms Observed.* Chicago: University of Chicago Press.

Alagappa, Muthiah, ed. 1995. *Political Legitimacy in Southeast Asia: The Quest for Moral Authority.* Stanford: Stanford University Press.

Amer, Ramses. 1999. "Conflict Management and Constructive Engagement in ASEAN's Expansion." *Third World Quarterly* 20(5): 1031–48.

Ayoob, Mohammed. 1995. *The Third World Security Predicament: Statemaking, Regional Conflict, and the International System.* Boulder, Colo.: Lynne Rienner.

Barnett, Marguerite Ross. 1976. *The Politics of Cultural Nationalism in South India.* Princeton: Princeton University Press.

Berdal, Mats, and Michael Leifer. 1996. "Cambodia." In James Mayall, ed., *The New Interventionism.* Cambridge: Cambridge University Press.

Brass, Paul R. 1990. "The Punjab Crisis and the Unity of India." In Atul Kohli, ed., *India's Democracy: An Analysis of Changing State-Society Relations.* Princeton: Princeton University Press.

Brown, David. 1988. "From Peripheral Communities to Ethnic Nations: Separatism in Southeast Asia." *Pacific Affairs* 61(1): 51–77.

———. 1994. *The State and Ethnic Politics in Southeast Asia.* New York: Routledge.

Brown, Michael E. 1996. *International Dimensions of Internal Conflict.* Cambridge, Mass.: MIT Press.

———, and Sumit Ganguly. 1997. *Government Policies and Ethnic Relations in Asia and the Pacific.* Cambridge, Mass.: MIT Press.

Budiarjo, Carmel, and Liem Soie Liong. 1988. *West Papua: The Obliteration of a People.* Surrey, U.K.: TAPOL.

Case, W. F. 1996. *Elites and Regime in Malaysia: Revisiting a Consociational Democracy.* Clayton, Australia: Monash Asia Institute.

Chang, Gordon G. 2001. *The Coming Collapse of China.* New York: Random House.

Cheng, Tun-jen. 1993. "Taiwan in Democratic Transition." In James Morley, ed., *Driven by Growth.* Armonk, N.Y.: M. E. Sharpe.

Christensen, Thomas J. 2001. "China." In Richard Ellings and Aaron Friedberg, eds., *Strategic Asia 2001–02: Power and Purpose.* Seattle: National Bureau of Asian Research.

Coppel, Charles A. 1983. *Indonesian Chinese in Crisis.* Kuala Lumpur and New York: Oxford University Press.

Das Gupta, Jyotirindra. 1990. "Ethnicity, Democracy, and Development in India: Assam in a General Perspective." In Atul Kohli, ed., *India's Democracy: An Analysis of Changing State-Society Relations.* Princeton: Princeton University Press.

Deutsch, Karl W. 1953. *Nationalism and Social Communication.* Cambridge, Mass.: MIT Press.

Dibb, Paul. 2001. "Indonesia: The Key to South-East Asia's Security." *International Affairs* 77(4): 829–42.

Dickson, Bruce. 1998a. *Democratization in China and Taiwan: The Adaptability of Leninist Parties.* New York: Oxford University Press.

———. 1998b. "China's Democratization and the Taiwan Experience." *Asian Survey* 38(4) (Apr.): 349–264.

Dupont, Alan. 2000a. "ASEAN's Response to the East Timor Crisis." *Australian Journal of International Affairs* 54(2): 163–70.

———. 2000b. "The Strategic Implications of an Independent East Timor." In James J. Fox and Dionisio Babo Soares, eds., *Out of the Ashes: The Destruction and Reconstruction of East Timor.* Adelaide: Crawford House.

Emmerson, Donald K. 2000. "Will Indonesia Survive?" *Foreign Affairs* 79(3) (May/June): 95–106.

Fearon, James. 1998. "Commitment Problems and the Spread of Ethnic Conflict." In

David A. Lake and Donald A. Rothschild, eds., *The International Spread of Ethnic Conflict: Fear, Diffusion and Escalation.* Princeton: Princeton University Press.

Fewsmith, Joseph. 1986. "China Among the Three Worlds." In Robert W. Clawson, ed., *East-West Rivalry in the Third World.* Wilmington, Del.: Scholarly Resources.

Friedman, Edward, and Barrett L. McCormick, eds. 2000. *What If China Doesn't Democratize? Implications for War and Peace.* Armonk, N.Y.: M. E. Sharpe.

Ganguly, Sumit. 1997. *The Crisis in Kashmir: Portents of War, Hopes for Peace.* Cambridge: Cambridge University Press; Washington, D.C.: Woodrow Wilson Center Press.

Gellner, Ernest. 1983. *Nations and Nationalism.* Ithaca: Cornell University Press.

George, T. J .S. 1980. *Revolt in Mindanao: The Rise of Islam in Philippine Politics.* Kuala Lumpur: Oxford University Press.

Gershman, John. 2002. "Is Southeast Asia the Second Front?" *Foreign Affairs* 81(4) (July/Aug.): 60–74.

Gurr, Ted Robert. 1970. *Why Men Rebel.* Princeton: Princeton University Press.

———. 1993. *Minorities at Risk: A Global View of Ethnopolitical Conflicts.* Washington, D.C.: United States Institute of Peace Press.

———. 2000. *Peoples Versus States.* Washington, D.C.: United States Institute of Peace Press.

———, Monty G. Marshall, and Deepa Khosla. 2000. *Peace and Conflict 2001: A Global Survey of Armed Conflicts, Self-Determination Movements, and Democracy.* College Park: CICDM, University of Maryland.

Hefner, Robert. 1993. "Islam, State, and Civil Society: ICMI and the Struggle for the Indonesian Middle Class." *Indonesia* 56 (Oct.): 1–35.

———. 2000. *Civil Islam: Muslims and Democratization in Indonesia.* Princeton: Princeton University Press.

Horowitz, Donald L. 1985. *Ethnic Groups in Conflict.* Berkeley: University of California Press.

Human Rights Watch. 1997. *Communal Violence in West Kalimantan.* New York: Human Rights Watch.

International Crisis Group. 2000. *Indonesia: Overcoming Murder and Chaos in Maluku.* ICG Asia Report 10, Jakarta/Brussels. Dec. 19.

———. 2001a. *Central Asia: Islamist Mobilization and Regional Security.* ICG Asia Report 14, Osh/Brussels. Mar. 1.

———. 2001b. *Aceh: Can Autonomy Stem the Conflict?* ICG Asia Report 18, Jakarta/Brussels, June 27.

———. 2001c. *Indonesia: Violence and Radical Muslims.* Indonesia Briefing Paper, Oct. 10.

———. 2001d. *Indonesia: Natural Resources and Law Enforcement.* ICG Asia Report 29, Jakarta/Brussels, Dec. 20.

Jackson, Robert H., and Carl G. Rosberg. 1982. "Why Africa's Weak States Persist: The Empirical and the Juridical in Statehood." *World Politics* 35(1): 1–24.

Jennings, M. Kent. 1997. "Political Participation in the Chinese Countryside." *American Political Science Review* 91(2): 361–72.

Keyes, Charles F. 1997. "Cultural Diversity and National Identity in Thailand." In Michael E. Brown and Sumit Ganguly, eds., *Government Policies and Ethnic Relations in Asia and the Pacific.* Cambridge, Mass.: MIT Press.

Lake, David A., and Donald Rothschild. 1998. "Spreading Fear: The Genesis of Transnational Ethnic Conflict." In David A. Lake and Donald Rothschild, eds., *The International Spread of Ethnic Conflict: Fear, Diffusion and Escalation*. Princeton: Princeton University Press.

Lande, Carl. 1999. "Ethnic Conflict, Ethnic Accommodation, and Nation-Building in Southeast Asia." *Studies in Comparative International Development* 33(4): 89–117.

Li, Lianjiang, and Kevin J. O'Brien. 1999. "The Struggle Over Village Elections." In Merle Goldman and Roderick MacFarquhar, eds., *The Paradox of China's Post-Mao Reforms*. Cambridge, Mass.: Harvard University Press.

Liddle, R. William. 1996. "The Islamic Turn in Indonesia: A Political Explanation." *Journal of Asian Studies* 55(3) (Aug.): 613–34.

MacFarquhar, Roderick. 1998. "Provincial Peoples' Congresses." *China Quarterly* 155: 656–67.

Mackie, J. A. C. 1976. "Anti-Chinese Outbreaks in Indonesia, 1959–68." In J. A. C. Mackie, ed., *The Chinese in Indonesia: Five Essays*. Honolulu: University Press of Hawaii in association with Australian Institute of International Affairs.

Majul, Cesar Adib. 1985. *The Contemporary Muslim Movement in the Philippines*. Berkeley: Mizan Press.

Malley, Michael. 2001. "Social Cohesion and Conflict Management in Indonesia." In Anita Kelles-Viitanen, Nat J. Colletta, and Teck Gee Lim, eds., *Social Cohesion and Conflict Prevention in Asia: Managing Diversity Through Development*. Washington, D.C.: World Bank.

Man, W. K. Che. 1990. *Muslim Separatism: The Moros of Southern Philippines and the Malays of Southern Thailand*. Singapore: Oxford University Press.

Manion, Melanie F. 1996. "The Electoral Connection in the Chinese Countryside." *American Political Science Review* 90(4): 736–48.

———. 2000. "Chinese Democratization in Perspective: Electorates and Selectorates at the Township Level." *China Quarterly* 163 (Sept.): 764–82.

Marty, Martin E., and R. Scott Appleby, eds. 1991. *Fundamentalisms Observed*. Chicago: Chicago University Press.

———, eds. 1994. *Accounting for Fundamentalisms*. Chicago: University of Chicago Press.

May, R. J. 1985. "Muslim and Tribal Filipinos." In R. J. May and Francisco Nemenzo, eds., *The Philippines After Marcos*. London: Croon Helm.

McKenna, Thomas M. 1998. *Muslim Rulers and Rebels: Everyday Politics and Armed Separatism in the Philippines*. Berkeley: University of California Press.

Meisner, Maurice. 1996. *The Deng Xiaoping Era: An Inquiry into the Fate of Chinese Socialism, 1978–1994*. New York: Hill & Wang.

Mitchell, David. 1999. "Tragedy in Sumba." *Inside Indonesia* 58 (Apr.–June): 18–22.

Morrison, Charles E. 2001. *East Asia and the International System*. New York: Trilateral Commission.

Nischalke, Tobias Ingo. 2000. "Insights from ASEAN's Foreign Policy Cooperation: The 'ASEAN Way,' A Real Spirit or Phantom?" *Contemporary Southeast Asia* 22(1): 89–112.

Noble, Lela Garner. 1976. "The Moro National Liberation Front in the Philippines." *Pacific Affairs* 49: 405–24.

O'Brien, Kevin. 1994a. "Agents and Remonstrators: Role Accumulation by Chinese People's Congress Deputies." *China Quarterly* 138 (June): 359–80.

———. 1994b. "Chinese People's Congresses and Legislative Embeddedness: Understanding Early Organizational Development." *Comparative Political Studies* 27(1) (Apr.): 80–107.

———. 2001. "Villagers, Elections, and Citizenship in Contemporary China." *Modern China* 27(4): 407–35.

———, and Lianjiang Li. 1995. "The Politics of Lodging Complaints in Rural China." *China Quarterly* 143 (Sept.): 756–83.

———. 2000. "Accommodating 'Democracy' in a One-Party State: Introducing Village Elections in China." *China Quarterly* 162 (June): 465–89.

O'Brien, Kevin, and Laura M. Luehrmann. 1998. "Institutionalizing Chinese Legislatures: Trade-Offs Between Autonomy and Capacity." *Legislative Studies Quarterly* 23(1) (Feb.): 91–108.

Oi, Jean C. 1996. "Economic Development, Stability, and Democratic Village Self-Government." In Maurice Brosseau, Suzanne Pepper, and Tsang Shu-ki, eds., *China Review 1996*. Hong Kong: Chinese University Press.

———. 1999. *Rural China Takes Off: Institutional Foundations of Economic Reform*. Berkeley: University of California Press.

———, and Scott Rozelle. 2000. "Elections and Power: The Locus of Decision-Making in Chinese Villages." *China Quarterly* 162 (June): 513–39.

Pearson, Margaret. 1998. "China's Emerging Business Class: Democracy's Harbinger?" *Current History* (Sept.): 268–72.

Pei, Minxin. 1998a. "U.S. Policy Options Toward China: Rule of Law and Democracy Programs." Testimony at the Hearing Before the House Subcommittee on Asia and the Pacific of the Committee on International Relations, 105th Congress, 2nd session, Apr. 30.

———. 1998b. "Chinese Civic Associations: An Empirical Analysis." *Modern China*, 24(3) (July): 285–318.

———. 1998c. "Democratization in the Greater China Region." *AccessAsia Review* 1: 2.

Rashid, Ahmed. 2000. *Taliban: Militant Islam, Oil, and Fundamentalism in Central Asia*. New Haven: Yale University Press.

Roberts, Hugh. 1994. "From Radical Mission to Equivocal Ambition: The Expansion and Manipulation of Algerian Islamism, 1979–1992." In Martin E. Marty and R. Scott Appleby, eds., *Accounting for Fundamentalisms*. Chicago: University of Chicago Press.

Saltford, John. 2000. "United Nations Involvement with the Act of Self-Determination in West Irian (Indonesian West New Guinea) 1968 to 1969." *Indonesia* 69 (Apr.): 71–92.

Schofield, Victoria. 1996. *Kashmir in the Crossfire*. London: I. B. Tauris.

Segal, Gerald. 1994. "China's Changing Shape." *Foreign Affairs* 73(3) (May/June): 43–59.

———. 1999. "Does China Matter?" *Foreign Affairs* 78(5) (Sept./Oct.): 24–36.

Shi, Tianjin. 1999. "Village Committee Elections in China: Institutionalist Tactics for Democracy." *World Politics* 51 (Apr.): 385–412.

Shue, Vivienne. 1994. "State Power and Social Organization in China." In Joel Migdal, Atul Kohli, and Vivienne Shue, eds., *State Power and Social Forces: Domination and Transformation in the Third World*. New York: Cambridge University Press.

Simon, Sheldon W. 2001. "Southeast Asia." In Richard Ellings and Aaron Friedberg, eds., *Strategic Asia 2001–02: Power and Purpose*. Seattle: National Bureau of Asian Research.

Sisk, Timothy. 1996. *Power Sharing and International Mediation in Ethnic Conflicts*. Washington D.C.: U.S. Institute of Peace.

Skocpol, Theda. 1979. *States and Social Revolutions*. Cambridge, Mass.: Harvard University Press.

Snyder, Jack. 2000. *From Voting to Violence: Democratization and Nationalist Conflict*. New York and London: W. W. Norton and Co.

Suhrke, Astri, and Lela Garner Noble. 1977. "Muslims in the Philippines and Thailand." In Astri Suhrke and Lela Garner Noble, eds., *Ethnic Conflict and International Relations*. New York: Praeger.

Swamy, Arun. 1996a. "Sense, Sentiment and Populist Coalitions: The Strange Career of Cultural Nationalism in Tamil Nadu." In Allison K. Lewis and Subrata K. Mitra, eds., *Subnational Movements in South Asia*. Boulder, Colo.: Westview.

———. 1996b. "The Nation, the People and the Poor: Sandwich Tactics in Party Competition and Policy Formation, India, 1931–96." Unpublished Ph.D. diss., University of California, Berkeley.

U.S. Committee for Refugees. 2001. *Shadow Plays: The Crisis of Refugees and Internally Displaced Persons in Indonesia*. Washington, D.C.: USCR.

Usman, Syaikhu. 2001. *Indonesia's Decentralization Policies: Initial Experiences and Emerging Problems*. SMERU Working Paper. Jakarta: Social Monitoring & Early Response Unit (September). Available online at http://www.smeru.or.id/report/workpaper/euroseasdecentral/euroseasexperience.pdf.

———. 2002. *Regional Autonomy in Indonesia: Field Experiences and Emerging Challenges*. SMERU Working Paper. Jakarta: Social Monitoring & Early Response Unit (September). Available online at http://www.smeru.or.id/report/workpaper/regautofieldexpchall/regautofieldexpchall.pdf.

van Klinken, Gerry. 1999. "What Caused the Ambon Violence?" *Inside Indonesia* 60 (Oct.–Dec.): 11–14.

Vitug, Marites Dañguilan, and Glenda M. Gloria. 2000. *Under the Crescent Moon: Rebellion in Mindanao*. Manila: Philippine Center for Investigative Journalism and Institute for Popular Democracy.

Walder, Andrew G., and Gong Xiaoxia. 1993. "Workers in the Tiananmen Protests: The Politics of the Beijing Workers' Autonomous Federation." *Australian Journal of Chinese Affairs* 29 (Jan.): 1–30.

Walter, Barbara F., and Jack Snyder, eds. 1999. *Civil Wars, Insecurity and Intervention*. New York: Columbia University Press.

Wasserstrom, Jeffrey N. 2000. "Big Bad China and the Good Chinese: An American Fairy Tale." In Timothy B. Weston and Lionel M. Jensen, eds., *China Beyond the Headlines*. Lanham, Md.: Rowman & Littlefield.

White, Lynn III. 1998. *Unstately Power: Local Causes of China's Economic Reforms*. Armonk, N.Y.: M. E. Sharpe.

Winzeler, Robert L., ed. 1998. *Indigenous Peoples and the State: Politics, Land, and Ethnicity in the Malayan Peninsula and Borneo*. New Haven: Yale University Press.

Young, Crawford. 1976. *The Politics of Cultural Pluralism*. Madison: University of Wisconsin Press.

CHAPTER FIFTEEN

Human Security

An Intractable Problem in Asia

DEWI FORTUNA ANWAR

Human security, a concept that focuses on the individual as the primary referent of security, encounters numerous challenges in Asia. For most countries in the region, concerns about security center almost exclusively on the state. Unlike the traditional realist conception of security, which focuses primarily on external military threats to security, many of these countries conceive of their security in a more comprehensive manner. Threats to security are seen to come not only from external military aggression but also from a myriad of internal challenges—separatist movements, social unrest, or collapse of the political system, all of which can challenge the nation-state's unity and sustainability. To most of the countries still undergoing a process of nation building and state building, in fact, domestic priorities define security. Though military security remains important, it is only one aspect of a multidimensional security problem, calling for a comprehensive approach that pays just as much attention to domestic economic, social, and political problems as to external threats to security.

Despite the widespread acceptance of comprehensive security and the recognition of the links between the various elements of security—a weakness in one part can weaken all the other parts—security concerns, as noted, focus almost exclusively on the state. All national efforts, such as the drives to achieve economic development, educational attainment, social harmony, and political stability, are ultimately aimed at preserving and promoting the security of the nation-state. Not only is the nation-state perceived as the ultimate good, in many Asian countries the rights of individuals must be subordinated to the rights of collectives. It is generally assumed that the individual's rights and security will be served if the nation-state prospers as a whole. But if these two interests should collide, the latter usually prevails.

This state-centered and community-oriented approach, combined with the predominantly inward-looking security preoccupation of many Asian countries, tends to relegate human rights and human security to secondary importance. Despite growing international concerns about human rights, the suppression of individual rights in the name of state security occurs with distressing frequency in a number of countries in the region. In many of these countries human rights are regarded as alien concepts that challenge the supremacy of the state—or, more precisely, the authority of the ruling regime—and are therefore viewed with suspicion, if not downright hostility.

Human security and human rights are two sides of the same coin. Human security can only be assured if human rights are guaranteed. Human rights are generally grouped into four major categories, namely civil, political, social, and economic rights. For years human rights activists have primarily focused on civil and political rights, such as the rights of free speech and assembly, a focus that often puts them in confrontation with state authorities who insist that social and economic rights must take precedence over civil and political rights. This argument is in most cases self-serving. It is aimed more at protecting the regime in power against its critics than protecting its citizens' social and economic rights.

This is not to say that human security has been totally neglected in Asia. Governments throughout the region have on the whole been active in trying to meet the basic human needs of their citizens, an important component of human security, by pursuing economic development. Many states have enjoyed considerable success in reducing the incidence of poverty and improving their human development index by means of various poverty alleviation programs, as well as by making education, health care, and housing more accessible to the poorer segments in society. A number of countries have also embraced democracy and professed commitments to protect and promote human rights, leading to some improvements in the civil and political rights of their citizens.

Moreover, the past two decades have witnessed the flourishing growth and activities of nongovernmental organizations (NGOs) that are aimed at empowering individuals and society, particularly vis-à-vis the state and big business. In many Asian countries nongovernmental organizations have been active in grass-roots community development efforts, helping disadvantaged groups that are often neglected by the state bureaucracies. Even more important, NGOs have also been at the forefront in promoting and defending the rights of individuals and communities against the arbitrary or unjust policies of the state.

Nevertheless, despite all these efforts and achievements, there is little doubt that the struggle in Asia to achieve human security in all its dimensions to ensure freedom from needs and freedom from fear remains daunting for at least six reasons. First, threats to human security are widespread and come from many sources: underdevelopment and chronic poverty, human rights abuses by the state apparatus, internecine communal conflicts, and environmental degradation. All of these problems affect men and women equally. At the same time, religions and traditions have also often been used by many groups in Asian societies to discriminate against women, at both the individual and the collective level. Second, the state's ability to address these problems is limited, even if it has the desire to do so, by lack of resources, skill, and institutional capacities. Third, in many cases there is little political will to address human security problems—and, more serious, the states themselves at times pose a major threat to human security. Fourth, it is not easy to shift the focus of security from the state to the individual in a region where the nation-states themselves are still undergoing consolidation. Fifth, with some important exceptions, civil society remains generally weak throughout Asia, so that it cannot yet fully counterbalance and control the power of the state. Sixth, although increasingly important, the ability of the international community to promote and protect human security behind national boundaries continues to be limited.

Defining Human Security

The current discourse on human security can be traced to the *Human Development Report 1994* produced by the United Nations Development Programme (UNDP). In its introduction the report looks at both the great advances and the major problems encountered by the world's communities over the past fifty years. On the one hand, most nations have won their freedom, the threat of nuclear war has diminished with the end of the Cold War, the improvement in human development has been unprecedented, the wealth of nations has multiplied, and there have been dramatic developments in technology. Moreover, global military spending has declined significantly and between one-half and three-quarters of the world's people live under relatively pluralistic and democratic regimes.

On the other hand, set against these undoubted achievements is a long list of miseries that continue to beset the people of the world. For all the technological breakthroughs, a fifth of the world's population goes hungry every night, a quarter lacks access to basic necessities such as clean drinking water, and a third lives in abject poverty. The world is characterized by a disturbing contrast between the few rich and the many poor. At the same time, rich and poor alike are faced with the growing problems of rising crime rates, drugs, AIDS, nuclear proliferation, terrorism, pollution, and other social problems that multiply the threats to personal security. Equally important, the threats to human security are no longer just personal or local or national but have become global. To quote the UN report: "Global poverty and environmental problems respect no national border. Their grim consequences travel the world" (UNDP 1994: 3). Concerns about environmental degradation and the rights of unborn generations have increased as well. And domestic conflicts caused by ethnonationalism and religious differences in many parts of the world have intensified, too, causing untold loss of life and destruction of property and transforming a great many people into refugees.

It was against this background of human achievement and human distress that the *Human Development Report* proposed a new concept of human security for the decades ahead. This new concept was intended to serve three purposes: to seek a paradigm for sustainable human development that can satisfy the expanding frontiers of human security; to seek a framework of development that brings nations together through a more equitable sharing of global economic opportunities and responsibilities; and finally to seek a new role for the United Nations so that it can begin to meet humanity's agenda not only for peace but also for development (UNDP 1994: 4).

For many in Asia, the multidimensional and interdependent nature of the human security concept is not necessarily novel. After all, the prevailing conceptions of security in many countries in the region, particularly within the ASEAN subregion, have always been comprehensive. These countries have always emphasized the multidimensional and interdependent nature of their security, encompassing military, political, economic, and social aspects. National security is not simply regarded as the absence of external military threats or the maintenance of independence and territorial integrity. Instead, comprehensive security envisages security in a holistic manner in the pursuit of national and regional resilience— defined as the ability of the nation or region to withstand any challenge. These conceptions of security have been well established in the ASEAN countries and formally adopted by ASEAN as an institution. Even in Northeast Asia, where preoccupations with external military threats have dominated the security concerns of such countries as Japan and China, equal attention has been given to nontraditional security issues, particularly to economic development as an important component of security (Anwar 1998: 477–512).

Human security, like comprehensive security, must be treated in all its dimensions. Unlike the traditional realist concern about the security of the state against external military threats, human security does not distinguish clearly between internal and external. Because of its emphasis on the individual instead of the state, however, the approaches to human security differ in several significant ways from those of comprehensive security. Whereas comprehensive security focuses on the state—and the state as well as society is privileged over the individual—human security focuses on the individual as the referent point of security. And while comprehensive security focuses on order and stability, human security is geared more to justice and emancipation (Acharya and Acharya 2000: 3). According to Acharya and Acharya, the salience of the "human person" sets human security apart from other notions of security that have emerged as an alternative to the traditional state-centered national security paradigm.

From the perspective of comprehensive security, the various people-oriented policies undertaken by the government, such as economic development, education, and health care, are primarily aimed at ensuring social order and support for the government, and hence the security of the state and the regime. In other words, human development is seen as a means for achieving state security or, more broadly, for attaining national resilience. According to the human security perspective, by contrast, human development is aimed at achieving human dignity. Instead of being regarded as the ultimate objective of national policies, state security is viewed as the handmaiden of human security.

Since the security of the state, though crucial, is not the ultimate end of national security objectives but rather a means for ensuring human dignity, the political approaches to security inevitably present the greatest contrast between comprehensive security and human security. While the state-centered security associated with comprehensive security in many cases follows the Machiavellian edict that the end justifies the means, human security approaches attach equal importance to processes. Whereas in the pursuit of state security several governments in Asia have followed a policy of repression to maintain regime security—often projected as synonymous with national security—the human security concept demands that every policy undertaken must not only have human dignity as its objective but must be carried out in a way that ensures the protection of human rights.

It is clear, therefore, that the human security concept not only challenges the traditional state-centered security of both realist and comprehensive security perspectives; for many countries in the region the concept implies a fundamental reordering of the relations between state and society as well as between the state and the outside world. The notion that there should be an emphasis on human security in Asia is still not generally accepted. This is of course not surprising given the heterogeneity of Asian societies, ranging from the more democratic to the most repressive and autocratic. Consequently there is no general consensus on how human security is to be achieved or managed in the region.

Human security broadly defined consists of two elements: freedom from needs and freedom from fear. Only when people enjoy both freedoms can they live in peace and with dignity. And both freedoms must be achieved simultaneously. Concern with threats to human needs has long dominated the agenda of the UNDP. These threats include hunger, lack of shelter, disease, lack of education, social inequality, and many other social shortcomings that should be the focus of national, regional, and global cooperative efforts. Freedom from fear entails removing or at the very least reducing the risks of violence against individuals or communities—particularly threats from organized violence either through wars between states, through state acts of repression, from insurgency groups, from terrorists, or from conflicts between different communal groups. In the past decade most of these violent threats to human security have come from within: either from the so-called predatory states or from failed states. Much of the recent debate about human security has, in fact, mostly focused on this dimension of human security, particularly in its relation to the security of the nation-state (Stohl 2000).

Given the extremely broad definition of human security, it is not surprising that critics have dismissed the concept as a useless analytic tool. Skeptics, for instance, have questioned the relevance of discussing developmental problems or problems of governance as security issues. The concept of human security is regarded as problematic for at least two reasons. As Barry Buzan has pointed out: "Versions of human security that seek to reduce all security to the level of the individual have somehow to confront the dilemma that bypassing the state takes away what seems to be the necessary agent through which individual security might be achieved" (Buzan 1991: chap. 1). Furthermore, Buzan argues that "attempts to securitise all of humankind have proved hard to sell. The referent object still seems too big and too vague to have popular appeal" (Buzan 2000: 8).

But it is precisely because of its broad definition and its stress on the well-being of humanity as a whole that the concept of human security has an important political appeal that can transcend national boundaries. Although the two dimensions of human security—freedom from needs and freedom from fear—have been emphasized equally in official documents, it is no secret that for most NGOs and observers in Asia the main focus of interest is freedom from fear. Although overcoming poverty is important, there has been very little debate about the subject at either the national or the regional level. In fact, many countries in the region have concentrated on achieving economic development. The problems of human security in Asia are mostly related to freedom from fear, given the difficulties encountered in advancing human rights—particularly civil and political rights—in the region. The usefulness of human security as an advocacy tool is in fact due to its vagueness and the interconnectedness of all its elements, making it possible to talk about human rights within a much broader context. In other words, the term "human security" is regarded as having greater political acceptability in the region than "human rights." While human rights are often perceived as being at odds with collective rights in a number of Asian countries, the pursuit of human security can be packaged as an integral part of national security.

Because human security can be used as an umbrella for other security issues at the national, regional, or global level, young scholars in ASEAN countries have been enthusiastic supporters of the human security concept. Frustrated at the inability of ASEAN to advance beyond maintaining friendly relations between member states—often by deliberately ignoring critical problems affecting the human conditions in these states—many have called for ASEAN to relax its noninterference principle. Instead of focusing on the debate about state rights versus human rights, which only puts ASEAN states on the defensive, the focus can be shifted to human security. That this need not be regarded as undermining state security can be seen from the tenor of all the papers presented at the ASEAN 2020 Conference organized by the ASEAN-ISIS in Bangkok in July 2000.

Herman Kraft of the Philippines advised that "ASEAN will have to be more strident in recognizing the needs for human security if it is to be true to its goal of creating a community of caring societies" (Kraft 2000). Simon SC Tay from Singapore argues that the ASEAN Regional Forum (ARF) should adopt the concept of human security: "Human security as a paradigm for the ARF would help strengthen the ARF's principles of comprehensive security, and of building a community, and give occasion to exercise its stated stages of confidence-building measures and preventive diplomacy. Human security can and should, for these reasons, be given greater attention" (Tay 2000). Drawing from the Indonesian experience of economic crisis and social upheaval in 1997–98 that led to the collapse of the Suharto regime, Rizal Sukma contends that human security and economic-political stability are mutually reinforcing. The former cannot be achieved without the latter, while the latter might not be sustainable without the fulfillment of the former in its comprehensive manner (Sukma 2000).

In the following pages I highlight the region's human security problems from both perspectives: freedom from needs and freedom from fear. Much of the discussion will focus on violent threats to security since this is the problem that has generated the most controversy. In many cases, however, the struggle to fulfill human needs is a major source of conflicts. Thus these two issues cannot really be separated.

Threats to Human Security in Asia

In Asia human security continues to face many threats that demand national, regional, and international attention. Ensuring the fulfillment of human needs and achieving a living environment free from fear are problematic challenges for many countries in the region. Underdevelopment and poverty have been at the root of many of the social ills facing humanity in this part of the world. Poverty has retarded human development and created activities that further threaten human security, such as increasingly violent criminal acts, prostitution and human trafficking, drug trafficking, and illegal immigration. In a number of Asian countries human security has also been endangered by political and social violence, resulting both from the general inability or will to solve conflicts by peaceful means and often from competition for scarce resources.

It is undeniable that in the past three decades until the onset of the 1997 financial crisis, several countries in the region achieved impressive economic growth that substantially improved people's living conditions. Beginning as some of the least developed economies, many countries in East Asia are now ranked as middle-income countries. Despite these undoubted advances, the incidence of absolute poverty remains high in a number of the countries, particularly in Southeast Asia, as can be seen from *Human Development Report 2000* (UNDP 2000: 169–71). In Vietnam between 1987 and 1997, for instance, 51 percent of the population lived below the national poverty line; in Indonesia during the same period, 15 percent of the population lived below the national poverty line and 26 percent lived on $1 a day. The life expectancy of a substantial portion of the populations in this region is also low as a result of poor living conditions. In Cambodia as much as 28 percent of the population was not expected to survive to age forty in 1998. In Laos the percentage was even higher: 29 percent of the population was expected to die before age forty. Laos ranks as one of the least developed countries in the world. The financial crisis of the late 1990s, which has reversed much of the development gain made in the previous two decades, has undoubtedly worsened the human security situation. Table 15.1 illustrates the poverty problems. Although there are no data on North Korea, economic mismanagement and famines are known to have caused mass starvation in that country, and a large number of children have died or suffer from serious malnutrition.

The magnitude of the underdevelopment and poverty problems is even greater in South Asia. The UNDP *Human Development Report 2000* revealed that in India 44.2 percent of the population lived on $1 a day, while in Pakistan and Bangladesh the percentage was 31.0 percent and 29.1 percent respectively between 1989 and 1998. People not expected to survive to age 40 made up about 15.8 percent of the population in India, 14.3 percent in Pakistan and 20.8 percent in Bangladesh (UNDP 2000: 170).

Education is one of the critical indicators of human development, since educational attainment enables people to improve their economic status and empowers them to fight for their rights. From this perspective the situation in South Asia is quite bleak. In 1998 adult illiteracy reached as high as 44.3 percent of the population in India, 56.0 percent in Pakistan, and 59.9 percent in Bangladesh, which has been ranked as one of the least developed countries in the world. In Southeast Asia only Laos has such a high incidence of adult illiteracy, about 53.9 percent of

TABLE 15.1

Poverty in Developing Countries in Asia and Progress in Survival

Country	People not expected to reach age 40 (1998) (%)	Adult illiteracy rate (1998) (%)	People living on $1 a day[a] (1987–98) (%)
Singapore	2.2	8.2	—
Malaysia	4.7	13.6	—
Thailand	10.4	5.6	28.2
Philippines	8.9	5.2	18.7
Sri Lanka	5.2	8.9	6.6
China	7.7	17.2	—
Vietnam	11.2	7.1	—
Indonesia	12.3	14.3	26.3
Burma (Myanmar)	17.6	15.9	7.5
India	15.8	44.3	44.2
Pakistan	14.3	56.0	31.0
Cambodia	27.7	—	—
Laos	28.9	53.9	—
Bangladesh	20.8	59.9	29.1

SOURCE: UNDP (2000: 169–71).

[a] $1 a day at 1993 PPP US$.

the population, while in the rest of East Asia the educational attainment is much better, with adult illiteracy rates of only 17.2 percent in China and 14.3 percent in Indonesia .

Poverty, illiteracy, and low educational attainment have trapped millions of Asians in a vicious circle of misery and despair. To escape their miserable conditions, parents have sometimes resorted to selling their children for prostitution or forced labor, and a great number of children cannot go to school because they must work. This situation creates further misery and human indignity. Moreover, thousands of low-skilled people have been forced to seek employment illegally in neighboring countries, often with disastrous consequences. Many illegal emigrants from Indonesia have been lost at sea, for instance, because they tried to enter Malaysia under cover of darkness in old and overcrowded fishing boats. Often those who succeed in entering Malaysia as illegal workers have been forced to work under harsh conditions and low pay and are forever fearful of being caught and deported. These illegal workers, many of whom become involved in criminal activities, have created major problems for the host countries as well. Thus poverty is not just a national problem. Inevitably its effects spill over into neighboring areas.

The inability of many countries to fulfill basic human needs is not only due to underdevelopment and lack of resources. Often it can be traced to poor policy, mismanagement, and corruption. Many of the poorest countries in Asia, such as Indonesia, are also known to be among the most corrupt. At the same time, a centralized and state-centered development policy in many of these countries has led to the marginalization of weaker segments in society. It was common practice in the fast-growing economies of East Asia to regard economic growth as an end in itself and the rights of the individuals as secondary. This could be seen, for instance, in policies regarding labor rights. In certain cases wages were kept low and strikes were often punishable by imprisonment—as in Indonesia under Suharto's New Order government. People were often forcibly evicted from their land to make way for real estate development, golf courses, or factories. Environmental concerns about ensuring sustainable development were neglected in the drive for rapid economic growth.

Democracy and democratization are key components of human security. Human dignity does not depend only on people's ability to secure a livelihood. Equally important is individuals' right to participate in the decision-making processes that determine their lives. Democracy goes hand in hand with the protection of human rights, particularly civil and political rights. A number of countries in East Asia, however, have been known to reject Western conceptions of human rights in favor of a relativist view. At the height of their economic success, a number of ASEAN countries—Singapore, Malaysia, and Indonesia—together with China, were proponents of "Asian Values." Asian cultures are distinctly different from Western ones, they argued, and the concept of human rights as espoused by the West is unsuitable or irrelevant for Asian societies with their unique traditions that regard the community as more important than the individual. While the newly democratizing Indonesia has abandoned this relativist approach to human rights, other countries in the region continue to adhere to it—notably China, Burma, and the other nondemocratic or semidemocratic regimes in Southeast Asia.

If democracy is still a contested issue in many countries in Asia, the second element of human security, freedom from fear, is even more problematic. Much of the violence that has taken place in recent years is violence within the states— either perpetrated by the state itself in pursuit of regime security or state security or caused by the state's failure to govern effectively and ensure law and order. Burma, for example, is a predatory state that pays almost no regard to human rights. The Burmese military regime has refused to hand over power to the democratically elected political leaders and has imprisoned opposition leaders without trial. In 1999, more than 1,200 political prisoners were arrested (AI 2000: Myanmar). Besides its suppression of democracy, the Burmese military regime has also carried out systematic repression of ethnic minorities who have been fighting the central government for greater autonomy or independence.

Human rights abuses are prevalent in China as well. Amnesty International reports that 1999 saw the most serious and wide-ranging crackdown on peaceful dissent in China in a decade. Thousands of people were arbitrarily detained for peacefully exercising their rights to freedom of expression, association, or religion. The Chinese government, for instance, has banned the Falun Gong spiritual movement: thousands of Falun Gong followers have been arbitrarily detained and forced to renounce their beliefs; some have been sentenced to long prison terms under draconian national security legislation and after unfair trials; and others have been assigned without trial up to three years' detention in "reeducation through labor" camps. Torture and ill treatment of prisoners have been widespread. Thousands of people have been sentenced to death and many executed. In the autonomous regions of Tibet and Xinjiang, those suspected of nationalist activities or sympathies are the target of harsh repression (AI 2000: China).

In recent years, Indonesia too has seen a series of humanitarian disasters. In the post-Suharto era, the violent threats to human security have resulted, not from a deliberate policy of state repression as in Burma and China, but mostly from the state's failure to stop mass violence and maintain law and order. The destruction of East Timor in September 1999—in the aftermath of a plebiscite that was overwhelmingly won by the pro-independence group—was largely blamed on the inability of the Indonesian government to rein in the pro-integration militia and rogue military elements. As a result, more than 250,000 people fled East Timor or were forcibly expelled.

The case of a state's failure to prevent massive violence has been clearly demonstrated by the two-year communal conflict in the Indonesian islands of Maluku, where open warfare between Christians and Muslims has resulted in thousands of deaths, wholesale destruction of property, and the displacement of tens of thousands of people. Similar communal conflicts have broken out between the native Dayaks and the Madurese settlers in Kalimantan, with hundreds of Madurese killed and thousands forcibly evicted from their homes. Muslim-Christian clashes have also occurred in Poso, Central Sulawesi. None of these conflicts has been fully resolved, and violent clashes continue to take place intermittently. Thus the numbers of internally displaced people throughout Indonesia have continued to swell. It is estimated that more than 1,300,000 people have been driven from their homes because of conflicts and other forms of violence scattered over nineteen of Indonesia's thirty provinces ("Aksara" 2001: 60). The largest number of displaced people can be found in North Maluku (212,000 persons) and Ambon (300,091 persons)—the two areas that have been engulfed in religious conflict for the past two years. The Indonesian government has not been able to deal with these internally displaced people effectively because of lack of resources and the unwillingness of many to be resettled elsewhere. The refugees' prolonged stay in camps, mostly without essential facilities, has further worsened their human security conditions and at the same time exacerbates the general security situation in these areas as a result of increased crime and tensions with surrounding communities.

Apart from its inability to prevent violent social conflict, the Indonesian government has often failed to enforce law and order. Because of past abuses of power, the Indonesian legal system has been discredited to the point where many people have taken the law in their own hands. The result has been a further deterioration of human security. Criminals (or suspected criminals) are summarily executed by mobs. At the same time, incidences of violent crime have gone up since the economic crisis. A general state of lawlessness has therefore beset the country over the past few years and caused people to feel insecure.

Elsewhere the Indonesian government's fight against an armed rebellion in Aceh has led to human insecurity in that troubled province as innocent civilians are caught in the middle of the insurgency and counterinsurgency operations. Often the rebels use civilians as human shields to protect themselves against army attacks; at times soldiers have indiscriminately killed villagers suspected of hiding rebels. According to the Aceh office of the Indonesian Legal Aid Institute, in the month of January 2000 alone over 100 people were tortured, 21 were unlawfully killed, over 400 homes, shops, and stalls were burned down, and 90 homes and shops were damaged (AI 2000: Indonesia).

In the Philippines, there has been an escalation of conflict in central Mindanao leading to the displacement of more than 400,000 civilians amid reports of indiscriminate bombings and human rights violations by the Armed Forces of the Philippines. Tensions and human insecurity in the region intensified after a series of kidnappings and killings of civilians by the Abu Sayyaf armed group in the Sulu archipelago (AI 2000: Philippines). Because Abu Sayyaf has especially targeted foreigners for kidnap and ransom, tourists and missionaries in the area are particularly vulnerable. Nuns and schoolchildren too have become victims of Abu Sayyaf terrorism, which is not just confined to Philippine territory but has crossed into neighboring countries. In May 1999, 21 tourists and hotel employees were abducted from their hotel on Sipadan, an island claimed by both Indonesia and Malaysia.

Singapore and Malaysia have both enjoyed a high level of economic development and a relatively equitable distribution of wealth among their citizens. Both governments, however, impose tight political control, particularly through the Internal Security Act. Anyone who dares to criticize the governments or oppose government policies can be arrested and imprisoned without trial.

Violent threats to human security in South Asia are equally serious. Although India is a well-established democracy, human rights violations continue to occur on a large scale, caused in part by the continuing existence of the highly undemocratic caste system. The socially and economically weaker sections of society continue to be particularly vulnerable to human rights abuses. Amnesty International reported in 2000 that attacks, often with the apparent connivance of police and local authorities, on "dalit" communities (disadvantaged groups determined by caste hierarchies) and tribal people were commonplace throughout 1999. Women are among the most vulnerable groups, while those engaged in protecting the rights of the disadvantaged groups also often become victims of abuses. Deaths in custody continued to be widespread throughout all states. Various forms of torture, including rape, continued to be used by the police and security forces. Besides abuses carried out by state authorities, armed groups operating in many Indian states have also continued to violate humanitarian law (AI 2000: India).

In Pakistan both civilian and military regimes have engaged in rampant human rights abuses. In 1999, law enforcement personnel carried out arbitrary arrests, torture, and extra-judicial executions with impunity. At least 258 people were sentenced to death, most by special courts after unfair trials. Persistent bias against the rights of women on the part of the government, the police, and the judiciary meant that abuses by private individuals, including the honor killings of hundreds of girls and women, were not investigated or punished (AI 2000: Pakistan). Political instability and competition have also been major threats to human security in Pakistan. Prominent political opponents are often jailed by the ruling regimes, while a number have been executed, sentenced to death, or exiled.

In Bangladesh, besides extreme poverty, chronic political instability and political violence have also continued to endanger human security. Clashes between the followers of the two major parties, the Awami League and the Bangladesh Nationalist Party, are frequent and often lead to hundreds of deaths. Party activists often engage in human rights abuses by beating political opponents to death. Nationwide strikes (hartals) are often used by the opposition to put pressure on the government, and the police have been known to use extreme violence to break up these strikes, causing many deaths and injuries. Violence against women is also a major problem in Bangladesh, as in the other two South Asian countries. The rape of women in police custody is not uncommon. In the wider community, hundreds of women and girls were scarred and maimed in acid attacks, and scores of others were murdered in dowry-related incidents in 1999 alone (AI 2000: Bangladesh).

Threats to human security are therefore serious and pervasive in Asia. The high incidence of poverty and violence has caused large-scale human suffering and death that is difficult to ignore. And the effects of human insecurity are not confined to the troubled countries. They have spread to neighboring countries as well—for example, through the spills of refugees and illegal emigrants—with negative consequences for interstate relations and regional security as a whole.

Managing Human Security

Although the human security concept has begun to gain currency in recent years, state security is still the primary focus of policymakers and security analysts in Asia. A recent report titled "Regional International Affairs Program in Asia," produced by the Colombo-based Regional Centre for Strategic Studies (RCSS 2000), reveals that "throughout Asia, concern about security seems to revolve essentially around the security of the state. In many places it was argued that basic state security is essential for consideration of other kinds of security concerns. Without state security there is no time, energy or resources to attend to other levels of security concern." Based on an extensive survey of countries in South Asia, Southeast Asia, and East Asia, the report adds: "Only a very few persons, mostly from the NGO community, emphasized societal or individual security as the basis for security policy, and almost none addressed global or human security insofar as these issues affected state security."

Nevertheless, some countries have begun to pay more attention to human security as a prerequisite for national security as a whole, since inequitable economic growth and human rights abuses could in the end lead to the collapse of seemingly powerful regimes, as happened with the Suharto regime in Indonesia. Despite the extended years of political stability and high economic growth, the financial crisis that hit Indonesia in 1997 quickly spread into a multi-dimensional crisis, which led to the collapse of the New Order structure and the emergence of various forms of violent conflicts throughout the country. Analysts argued that Indonesia's current predicament was caused, among other things, by the New Order's policy of repression and inequitable distribution of economic opportunities. Such policies marginalized and alienated large segments of communities, eventually causing them to revolt against the central authority. A single-minded pursuit of state security, with insufficient attention given to human security, can therefore in the end be counterproductive to the security of the nation-state as a whole. At the same time, a debilitated state also lacks the capacity to protect its citizens from violence from within societies, such as that which emanates from communal conflicts and the absence of law and order.

Satisfying Human Needs

Recently attempts have been made to deal with threats to human security in a number of Asian countries. Indonesia, which has faced some of the most serious human security problems in the region—and has undergone a fundamental transition from authoritarianism to democracy—undoubtedly represents one of the most interesting case studies for the management of human security. As we shall see, efforts to satisfy human needs by ensuring sustainable and equitable development no longer focus on high economic growth alone, but have also begun to emphasize good governance as well as a democratic and accountable political system. While most Asian countries would agree on the need for good governance, however, there is less consensus on the importance of democracy and a vibrant civil society. Differences are even greater on the issue of violent threats to human security. Many countries continue to insist on the inviolability of the principle of nonintervention in the domestic affairs of another country—a major obstacle to improving the human rights situation in many countries, particularly where the state itself poses the greatest threat to human security.

With a few exceptions such as Burma and North Korea, fulfilling human needs has always been the top priority of most governments in Asia, particularly in East and Southeast Asia. Most states have focused on economic development, therefore, with the immediate objective of achieving high and rapid economic growth. With the creation of greater wealth, states could finance various poverty alleviation measures, such as subsidies and credits for farmers and basic health care, education, and cheap housing for the poor. This policy succeeded for a while in improving the general living standards in most of the market-oriented East Asian economies and in greatly reducing the number of people living in absolute poverty.

Unfortunately, rapid economic growth without sufficient political accountability and transparency also led to massive corruption and abuses of power, causing a widening of the economic gaps in a number of East Asian countries. Reliance on market mechanisms to produce the "trickle down effect" did not work, as crony capitalism allowed a small business elite to capture most of the wealth through monopoly privileges. The onset of the 1997 financial crisis finally exposed the basic weakness of Indonesia's growth-oriented economic policy. Unequal development, a weak legal system, an unprofessional bureaucracy, pervasive corruption, collusion, and nepotism—all contributed to the collapse of the Indonesian economy and the ensuing social upheaval that finally brought down Suharto's New Order government, which had been in power for 32 years. Racial riots brought about by the indigenous community's envy of the Chinese minorities who had dominated the economy not only tore Indonesia's social fabric but also led to massive capital flight that has made economic recovery even more difficult.

Achieving good governance has therefore been one of the most important items on the reform agenda of the Indonesian government in the post-Suharto era, with particular emphasis on eradicating corruption, collusion, and nepotism (known locally as KKN). Other countries in the region—especially those that have suffered from the recent financial crisis—have also focused on good governance as a strategy for achieving economic recovery and preventing the occurrence of similar crises in the future.

The drive for governance reform has not been entirely internally driven, however. To a certain extent it has been forced upon the crisis-stricken countries by the international community, particularly by the International Monetary Fund (IMF) and the World Bank. These two powerful lending and donor agencies have attached stringent conditions before agreeing to bail out the economies of such countries as Indonesia, Thailand, South Korea, and the Philippines. Today the IMF and the World Bank are insisting on major structural reforms—not only in the economic domain but in the social and political dimensions as well, which they had studiously avoided in the past. There has been much unhappiness about the IMF's policies in the region. Many argue that they have worsened the plight of the poor because of their insistence on the closure of inefficient businesses. Yet there is also a recognition that such painful policies are necessary. The plight of the poor has been mitigated to a certain extent by the introduction of new social safety nets, a measure that has also received international assistance.

In promoting human security from the perspective of human needs, the main point is that there has been an emphasis on international cooperation, particularly in countries affected by the recent economic crisis. Most countries in Asia recognize that they lack the capacity to develop their economy or good governance entirely on their own. Many of them have therefore been willing to seek outside assistance for both financial and technical support. (Important exceptions include Burma and North Korea, which remain highly suspicious of the outside world.) In the case of Indonesia, for instance, the UNDP has taken the lead in a multilaterally funded program known as Partnership for Governance Reform aimed at both the state and civil society. The program provides funding and training for the bureaucracy, the national and local legislatures, the legal system, and various NGO groups. Japan has been the single largest donor for most Asian countries. In recent years Japan has also begun to allocate funds for the improvement of human security in the region, particularly for meeting human needs.

One of the most distinctive features of the approaches to human security is the importance attached to the role of civil society at the national, regional, and global levels. Not only is the state's ability to satisfy all elements of human security limited, thereby necessitating partnerships with NGO and business groups, but in many instances the state itself is a major cause of human insecurity and civil society's advocacy role becomes crucial for its mitigation. It becomes obvious, therefore, that human security can only be developed fully in places where there is a vibrant civil society to temper the exercise of state power.

In Indonesia, the need to rein in state power has led to the dismantling of the authoritarian New Order political structure and the beginning of democratization. A pluralistic democracy, which provides for a more transparent, participatory, and competitive decision-making process, is not only regarded as important for ensuring good governance. It is also seen as a key element of human security because it ensures inclusiveness and nondiscrimination against any groups in society. Support for democracy as a means of ensuring popular political control and a more people-oriented economic development has grown stronger in Asia over the past decade. More and more countries are now becoming democracies. A number of authoritarian regimes have now fully embraced democracy: South Korea, Taiwan, the Philippines, Thailand, and lately Indonesia.

The current emphasis on democracy as a means of ensuring good governance and sustainable development signifies a fundamental shift in a development paradigm, popular in the 1970s and 1980s, which argued that democracy is an unaffordable luxury for developing countries. In the earlier period, democracy was suppressed for the sake of economic efficiency; now it is recognized that transparency, accountability, and participation (not mobilization) are essential for long-term political stability and sustainable economic growth.

Nevertheless, this view of the importance of democracy is not yet fully shared by other countries in the region. Many countries, including China, Singapore, and Malaysia, continue to believe that popular participation is detrimental to political stability and economic development. These countries, moreover, have escaped the worst effects of the financial crisis and are again enjoying high economic growth. As a consequence, the argument opposing political liberalization has not entirely lost ground in the region.

Yet there is one thing that most of the countries in Asia do agree upon as a central strategy for fulfilling human needs: a market-oriented economy. Almost all the countries in the region, even those that retain their communist political systems, have adopted an open and market-driven economy. In South Asia, countries that in the past had pursued socialism, such as India, have also embraced the market economy in recent years. India's low level of economic development until recently was often used as a reason by many countries in East and Southeast Asia for not embracing democracy, on the ground that democracy hampers economic growth. India is the world's largest democracy. In fact, the obstacle to economic growth in India was not democracy but its socialist economic policy that had discouraged foreign investment.

Asian countries have also agreed on the importance of regional cooperation to their economic development. Besides intensifying their economic cooperation, the ASEAN countries and the three Northeast Asian countries, China, Japan, and South Korea, have established the ASEAN Plus Three forum to promote closer financial cooperation between the two subregions—a response to the region's sense of helplessness during the financial crisis. In South Asia, however, the development of SAARC (South Asian Association for Regional Cooperation) has been hampered by the open hostility between India and Pakistan over Kashmir.

At the same time, countries in Asia have increasingly focused on the development of small and medium scale enterprises (SMEs). Excessive reliance on a few big businesses or conglomerations has proved to be risky and costly for many Asian economies, since the collapse of these behemoths could bring the whole economy down. Moreover, as mentioned earlier, the unequal distribution of economic opportunities has kept most of the people relatively poor and created resentment against the conglomerates, which in Southeast Asia are mainly composed of ethnic Chinese. In the past, this had often led to racial tension and the occasional bloody riots in which many people of Chinese origin lost their property and lives. SMEs are viewed as a means of making the economies less vulnerable to external shocks, while at the same time ensuring a more equitable distribution of economic opportunities, which in turn would contribute to better relations among the different societal groups.

Nevertheless, given the magnitude of the problems, the various policies and approaches adopted to eradicate poverty and improve the livelihood of people in Asia only scratch the surface in many cases. Huge populations, limited natural resources, illiteracy and a shortage of skilled manpower, lack of infrastructure, lack of capital, lack of institutional capacity, and other problems associated with underdevelopment will continue to make the efforts to satisfy human needs an uphill struggle for many Asian countries for the foreseeable future.

Ensuring Freedom from Fear

Certain improvements have also been made with respect to freedom from fear. NGOs in a number of Asian countries, often with the support of regional and international NGOs, have taken the lead in advocating human rights. For instance, NGOs provide legal aid for indigent people who find themselves unjustly treated by the government or other powerful groups—forced off their land, for example, to make way for development. Moreover, several Asian countries are beginning to make serious efforts to improve their human rights practices. Human rights in general are obviously better protected under a democratic system of government than an authoritarian one. The transition to democracy of many formerly authoritarian regimes in Asia has been an important boost for human rights. These countries have abandoned their relativist attitude to human rights, that the concept of human rights is primarily Western and is incompatible with Asian values. Democratic and democratizing countries in Asia have generally accepted that human rights are universal values that must be protected universally.

In Indonesia, for example, protection of human rights is a key reform agenda. The old 1945 Constitution had no provisions for human rights and explicitly concentrated power in the hands of the executive, subordinating both the legislature and the judiciary. In the revised 1945 Constitution, articles guaranteeing human rights are included in the main body of the constitution, while the power of the three branches of government is clearly separated, making the legislature and the judiciary independent of executive control. Parliament has therefore become more responsive to the people's aspirations, while the courts have become less a tool of executive power.

Many Asian countries, such as Thailand, the Philippines, Indonesia, and Malaysia, have already established independent National Human Rights Commissions. As part of its reform agenda, Indonesia also produced a five-year National Human Rights Action Plan beginning in September 1998, which includes ratification of the various UN conventions on human rights. It has also passed a law for the establishment of a Human Rights Court to try future violators of human rights, and for the establishment of ad hoc human rights tribunals to try major human rights violations that took place in the past, including the crimes against humanity perpetrated in East Timor soon after the plebiscite in August 1999. Before this law was passed, military or police personnel accused of human rights crimes could only be tried in military courts that are not transparent and that have a tendency to protect their members.

Despite all these efforts, threats to human security have continued almost unabated. It is true that with the establishment of democracy and the recognition of human rights in Indonesia there has been a major reduction of state-sponsored violence against individuals. There are no more political prisoners or arbitrary arrests. Furthermore, the military is no longer primarily responsible for internal security. But as noted earlier, gross violations of human rights have continued unabated in different parts of the country since 1999, largely carried out by members of society. Both the government and elements of civil society, such as the NGOs, have been helpless in the face of these new social challenges—religious wars and ethnic feuds, for example, with their long and twisted roots. In fact, in a number of cases the military and the police sent to stop the violence have themselves been drawn into it.

As for Burma, little has changed in the past few years. Neither international economic sanctions nor the softer ASEAN approach of constructive engagement has succeeded in changing the ways of the Burmese military regime. On the one hand, the majority of the Burmese people continue to suffer economic deprivation because of the international economic sanctions; on the other, they live in fear of imprisonment, forced labor, or eviction from their land by the military. Efforts by pro-democracy activists to end military rule have so far resulted only in further suppression of democracy and human rights. It is true that in early 2002 the ruling junta released the pro-democracy leader, Aung San Sun Kyi, from house arrest, but it remains to be seen whether this development really presages an end to military domination in Burma. In China the power of the state has remained almost absolute in terms of its ability to control the activities of its citizens. Although China has carried out a certain degree of economic liberalization, civil society has remained weak and organizations that champion the cause of the ordinary people are almost nonexistent. Even in Malaysia—which enjoys a relatively high human development index and formally practices parliamentary democracy—suppression of civil and political rights has gone unchecked. The establishment of a National Human Rights Commission in 1999 has in no way softened the draconian Internal Security Act, which allows the government to arrest and imprison, without trial, political demonstrators or anyone suspected of criticizing the government.

In India, as noted earlier, a vibrant democratic political system has not been able to remove the pernicious discrimination caused by the caste system, which allows the lowest rank hardly any human rights. Women are also treated as secondary citizens with almost no rights in many Asian countries. In South Asia such discriminatory attitudes toward women have often allowed male relatives to commit violence against women and girls with impunity. Religions and traditions are often used to justify such actions, and anyone daring to challenge these pernicious practices often meets both official and communal wrath.

Ensuring human security from threats of violence has therefore remained an intractable problem—particularly when the state, which has primary responsibility for providing security for its citizens, is unwilling or unable to do so and there are gross violations of human rights. Should outsiders intervene in such cases, even against the wishes of the offending states, thereby violating the principles of national sovereignty and noninterference enshrined in the UN Charter? Most of the debate about human security has in fact centered on this crucial question regarding the appropriate role of the international community in preventing human rights abuses, particularly gross violations of human rights. The great number of human tragedies that have gone unabated in Asia in recent years testifies that the management of human security at the national, regional, and international levels has failed to meet the challenges.

Governments in Asia are deeply divided on the issue of allowing outsiders to intervene in internal humanitarian problems. Some people are strongly in favor of international intervention in cases of gross abuse of human rights. Others believe that the principle of national sovereignty should not be violated under any pretext and that outsiders should have no say in the domestic affairs of a sovereign nation-state. A third group takes a more moderate position. While accepting that in certain extreme cases the international community has a role to play in protecting human security within a state, it still must respect the principle of national sovereignty. These differences in attitude reflect the degree of importance attached by each group to the concept of human security vis-à-vis the security of the state.

To the proponents of human security, it is a matter of faith that human disasters such as violent conflict, refugee problems, hunger, or environmental degradation in one country affect human security in other countries—as highlighted in the 1994 UNDP report. As the focus shifts from the territorially bounded state to the human individual, measures for protecting human security cannot simply be left to the discretion of the nation-state or, more to the point, to the national government. Given the concept of human security and mutual vulnerability, there is a general assumption of collective responsibility among the world community for the well-being of the whole human race. When humanitarian disasters occur in some parts of the world, such as the recent gross violations of human rights in Kosovo and East Timor, the international community, according to this perspective, must take action to stop the violence and restore peace, even if this means infringing upon the sovereignty of the offending countries and disregarding their objections. Regional institutions such as ASEAN and international organizations such as the United Nations are expected to bear a certain responsibility for the human security conditions of their members.

The most vocal proponents for mobilizing external pressure or even intervention to protect human security behind the protective walls of the nation-state have been NGO groups, particularly human rights and environmental activists, as well as scholars and the media in the more democratic Asian countries. NGO groups in the region have long lobbied governments and ASEAN, as well as the international community, to pressure the military regime in Burma to relax its repressive policy. Groups such as the Alternative ASEAN Network, the International Network of Political Leaders Promoting Democracy in Burma, the Alternative Asia-Europe Meeting, and the Asian Network for Free Elections have coordinated national and international campaigns to improve the political situation in Burma (Sucharithanarugse 2000: 59).

Strong public pressure was instrumental in the Australian government's decision to take the lead in mounting a multilateral force for East Timor after the postballot violence. Indeed, elements in Australian society pushed the government to take unilateral action against Indonesia to protect the East Timorese even without Indonesia's consent or UN authorization.[1] International human rights watch groups such as Amnesty International and Asia Watch have long campaigned for international sanctions against states that commit human rights violations. Similarly, national, regional, and international NGOs campaigning for

---

[1]A casual reading of the Australian press in September 1999, as well as other Western media, would reveal the broad support for international intervention in East Timor—with or without the consent of the Indonesian government and with or without official UN authorization.

labor rights and environmental protection have coordinated their efforts to mobilize international opinion and action against various national transgressors.

Certain governments in Asia, such as Thailand and the Philippines, have also come out in favor of applying external pressure or taking collective regional and international action to protect human security, as well as adopting a more flexible attitude toward sovereignty and the principle of noninterference, including "humanitarian intervention." Because of its own internal constraints, Japan has mostly been silent on the issue of humanitarian intervention. By sending a UN Peacekeeping Operation overseas, Japan created as much controversy domestically as regionally.

In ASEAN, Thailand has been at the forefront of introducing the concept of "constructive intervention." Supported by the Philippines, this concept is designed to allow ASEAN members to comment on the problems of fellow members and take collective action if necessary. Thailand's suggestion is primarily intended to put collective regional pressure on Burma to improve its human rights practices—not least because they have had terrible repercussions for Thailand. The former Thai foreign minister, Surin Pitsuwan, also called on the United Nations to pay more attention to human security and to devise clear rules and mechanisms to enable this global body to act effectively to protect human security (Pitsuwan 1999, 2000).

The majority of countries in Asia, however, which include most members of ASEAN and China, have in principle opposed any outside interference in their domestic affairs—particularly their political or security affairs. Following the UN Charter, which protects the principles of national sovereignty and territorial integrity, ASEAN countries have made noninterference in each other's internal affairs a cardinal principle of intraregional relations. They have studiously avoided commenting on what happens inside the borders of their fellow ASEAN members. Not only has ASEAN tended to turn a blind eye to various internal transgressions against human rights, but the association has also campaigned vigorously to oppose any attempts by outside powers to intervene in internal ASEAN affairs. Burma, Vietnam, and lately Malaysia are among the ASEAN hard-liners opposing any moves to dilute the principle of noninterference in each other's internal affairs, whatever the pretext. In recent years, however, there has been some relaxation of ASEAN's rigid noninterference policy. This shift has been brought about by two factors: the democratization that has taken place in a number of ASEAN countries and the growing transnational problems that ASEAN members are facing—the air pollution caused by forest fires in Indonesia that covers a number of neighboring countries, for instance, or the problems of illegal migrants.

Thailand, as noted, proposed "constructive intervention" in the mid-1990s, a notion that was supported by the Malaysian deputy prime minister, Anwar Ibrahim, one of the liberal leaders in ASEAN, and backed by the Philippines. The proposal was strongly opposed by New Order Indonesia, however, as well as by Singapore and Vietnam. A compromise was reached by diluting the concept of constructive intervention to "enhanced interaction," which has not really produced any significant changes in the way ASEAN operates. Lately Thailand has come up with the idea of "flexible engagement" as a compromise between interference and noninterference.

Political and leadership changes in a number of ASEAN countries have reduced members' sensitivities toward each other. The imprisonment of Malaysian Deputy Prime Minister Anwar Ibrahim by Prime Minister Mahathir in September 1998, for instance, invited open criticism from the new Indonesian president, B. J. Habibie, and the new Philippine president, Joseph Estrada, when the two met on the Indonesian island of Batam on October 13, 1998, something that could not have happened in earlier times. Anwar Ibrahim was charged with sodomy, though many observers believe that his real crime was that he presented a threat to Mahathir's position. In the eyes of many, Anwar's arrest was politically motivated, and as such it was a clear infringement of human rights. Estrada was quoted as saying that Anwar Ibrahim should not be treated like a common criminal. Both Habibie and Estrada considered writing a joint letter to Prime Minister Mahathir urging that Anwar Ibrahim be put under house arrest instead of in prison during his trial. At their meeting Habibie and Estrada both expressed shock at the way their mutual friend, Anwar Ibrahim, one of the most respected young leaders in Asia, had been treated, particularly the solitary confinement and beatings.[2]

Although Mahathir reportedly said he regarded any outsider's comments about the happenings in Malaysia as interference, Anwar was moved to a regular prison after 24 days of solitary confinement in police headquarters, the very next day after the Habibie-Estrada meeting on Batam (Richardson 1998). The Indonesian press, which had avoided criticizing fellow ASEAN members during the New Order period, also strongly condemned Anwar Ibrahim's arrest, thereby drawing the ire of the new deputy prime minister of Malaysia, Gaffar Baba. In a press conference in Jakarta on September 27, 1998, Gaffar Baba criticized the Indonesian press for its support for Anwar Ibrahim, adding that Anwar was probably a suitable leader for Indonesia, where homosexuality is not illegal. Not surprisingly Gaffar Baba's slighting remark drew further fire from the Indonesian press. It is important to note that the Indonesian minister of information, Yunus Yosfiah,

---

[2]The writer was present at the meeting of the two presidents at the Melia Hotel in Batam on Tuesday, October 13, 1998. At the end of the meeting the foreign ministers of Indonesia and the Philippines made a joint statement before the press raising their common concerns about the ill treatment suffered by Anwar Ibrahim during his imprisonment, especially the beating he endured.

defended the Indonesian media's right to publish any news they wish so long as they are factually accurate, pointing out the differences between freedom of the press in Indonesia and Malaysia (*Kompas* 1998).

As mentioned earlier, Indonesia's views regarding human rights have undergone fundamental changes since the fall of Suharto and the onset of *reformasi* (reform). Besides democratic political reform, Indonesia has also put the protection and promotion of human rights on its reform agenda. To that end, Indonesia has abandoned its relativist attitude toward human rights and accepted that they are universal.

Nevertheless, while recognizing the legitimacy of international concerns over gross violations of human rights, either by state commission or omission, Indonesia has been concerned that the current emphasis on human security may be used as an excuse by more powerful states to intervene in the affairs of weaker states. The Indonesian government holds that any humanitarian intervention against a country must be based on clear and objective criteria, without discrimination, while fully respecting the national sovereignty and territorial integrity of the country concerned. In April 2000, Indonesia's foreign minister, Alwi Shihab, clearly stated Indonesia's position on this matter at the Nonaligned Summit in Cartagena, Colombia: "As to human rights, we maintain at the international level, human rights must be addressed with full respect for national and territorial integrity, while following the guiding principles of objectivity, impartiality and transparency as set down by the Vienna Conference on Human Rights."[3] Former Foreign Minister Ali Alatas recently pointed out that the increasing international focus on human security has inevitably led to "humanitarian intervention" in Rwanda, Somalia, Haiti, and Kosovo. Yet he also warns about the danger of this intervention if carried out without clear criteria accepted by the international community and without the legitimacy of UN authorization (Alatas 2000). Surin Pitsuwan of Thailand reminded the United Nations of the need for clear guidelines for intervention. In the 1999 address to the UN Assembly quoted earlier, Pitsuwan stated: "Unless and until we, as the foremost Assembly of Mankind, come up with criteria, objective and consensual, the international community will not be able to address the many lurking 'internal conflicts' effectively."

The secretary-general of ASEAN, Rodolfo C. Severino, has put his concerns about humanitarian intervention even more forcefully. While partly agreeing with UN Secretary-General Kofi Annan's statement that "no legal principle—not even sovereignty—can ever shield crimes against humanity," Severino insists that sovereignty remains vital: "Rogues and villains have used state sovereignty to shield themselves and their crimes. But in a world of nation states, a world without gov-

[3] http://www.indonesia.nl/database/200400_1.html.

ernment, the sovereignty of nations serves also as an essential and legitimate shield, a shield especially for weak states to protect themselves from domination of the strong." It is therefore, he says, absolutely essential that UN authorization be obtained before an intervention is carried out.

To ensure the acceptability and success of humanitarian intervention, Severino (2000) has outlined a threefold list of ASEAN objectives. One is to enhance the capacity of the UN and other legitimate international bodies, including regional organizations, to extend the scope of international humanitarian law and strengthen its application. The second is to cooperate as closely and as broadly as possible with the international institutions in this task, ensuring that "humanitarian intervention" is not carried out merely in the pursuit of national policy objectives. And the third is to make sure that the measures taken to apply international humanitarian law are effective and proportionate to their specific objective and that they result in an improvement in the lives of the great proportion of the people concerned and for the fairly long term. The intended cure must not be worse than the disease.

Because of the strong adherence to the principle of noninterference in each other's internal affairs, ASEAN members have so far shied away from developing a regional mechanism for dealing with issues regarded as purely domestic. ASEAN is still an essentially state-centered regional organization where important political decisions are made through consensus. Even during the haze pollution crisis, neighboring countries were reluctant to criticize Indonesia openly, and there was simply no ASEAN mechanism for dealing with the problem at the regional level. In the event, Indonesia requested help from Malaysia in putting out the fire. For fear of offending, such assistance would not have been offered unless requested. During the East Timor crisis, ASEAN countries were very careful not to push Indonesia into a corner. Unlike Australia, which tried to mobilize international pressure to force Indonesia to accept a multinational force for East Timor, no ASEAN country offered its services to the United Nations until Indonesia specifically requested ASEAN troops in East Timor. The concept of enhanced interaction or even flexible engagement had not been applied by the other ASEAN members toward Indonesia either in the air pollution issue or in the East Timor crisis.

If the regional constraints on involvement in members' internal affairs have been difficult to surmount in the small and relatively homogeneous ASEAN, the obstacles encountered in a larger regional grouping such as the ARF will be even harder to overcome. At this stage it is still difficult to envisage the ARF arriving at a consensus to develop a supraregional capacity to deal with domestic human security problems—particularly those relating to political and human rights. In fact, the ARF has not gone very far beyond confidence-building measures to promote peaceful relations between member states. Moreover, the ARF's proposal to include conflict resolution as part of its agenda has been strongly opposed by China, even though it is meant to resolve conflicts between states, not within states.

Unlike Europe, therefore, Asia is still poorly equipped with effective regional organizations, particularly in the political and security fields. The type of humanitarian intervention carried out by NATO to save the Muslim Albanians in Kosovo from the Serbs could not take place in this part of the world for obvious reasons. Above all, there is no regionwide collective security pact such as NATO; nor is there any likelihood that one will ever develop given the diversity of threat perceptions. In fact, while some of the more enthusiastic proponents of humanitarian intervention applauded NATO's intervention in Kosovo, debates about the desirability and efficacy of a Kosovo-style intervention continue to rage in Europe and the United States (Krauthammer 1999; Lane and Schwarz 1999).

So far as Asia is concerned, only the United Nations has the legitimacy to authorize and organize humanitarian intervention. Despite growing international pressure to shift the focus from state security to human security, particularly from NGO groups, humanitarian intervention remains highly problematic. The recent experience in East Timor is a case in point. The UN's ability to authorize the sending of multinational forces to East Timor was wholly dependent on the consent of the Indonesian government. As it happened, President B. J. Habibie agreed to accept an international peacekeeping force in East Timor because it was he who had given the right of self-determination to the East Timorese in the first place—not simply because of international pressure. This argument was in line with Habibie's general drive for democratization and improvement of Indonesia's human rights record. If Habibie had bowed to nationalistic pressure at home and refused to allow foreign troops in East Timor, however, it was unlikely that the United Nations or any of its members, least of all Australia, would have risked open conflict with Indonesia by sending troops there without Indonesia's consent—for that would certainly have created an even more serious security problem. In fact, it is debatable whether the UN Security Council would have been able to reach a consensus on sending a mission to East Timor if Indonesia had been violently opposed to it.

If Indonesia had been opposed, the most likely scenario would then have been the imposition of international economic sanctions against Indonesia. Yet the result would have been totally counterproductive for human security in Indonesia as a whole. Not only would the East Timorese continue to suffer violence from the pro-integration militia—maybe with more open support from the Indonesian military—but the worsening economic conditions in Indonesia would only cause further suffering to more than 200 million people, leading to even worse social and political upheavals than those created by the financial crisis in mid-1997. Economic sanctions would also have been likely to lead to a nationalistic backlash endangering not only Indonesia's economic recovery program under the tutelage of the IMF but, even more seriously, the democratization efforts that have been carried out with the active support of several Western governments, NGOs, and donor agencies.

This is the crux of the dilemma of the human security problematique: the means of enforcing human security forcefully from the outside is in fact quite limited. Moreover, despite the increasing concerns about human security, the broadening of the security agenda, and the proliferation of actors, it is hard to deny that in the final analysis it is the power relations among nation-states that determine international decisions and action—especially those that must pass through the UN Security Council. The problems for human security become even more acute in cases involving the interests of the permanent members of the UN Security Council with their veto power and nuclear arsenals. While moral outrage at Serbia's brutality in Kosovo prompted air strikes from NATO, no such action was forthcoming when Russia brutally crushed the Chechen rebellion. Indeed, the international community remained largely silent on the issue. China's repressive policy toward Tibet and toward its Muslim minorities may have excited criticism and protest from human rights activists, but there is little expectation that the international community will do anything about it. The repeated brutality of Israeli soldiers toward Palestinian civilians has never invited sanctions, let alone humanitarian intervention, from the United Nations because any such move would be blocked by the United States. It is difficult, therefore, to deny the accusation put forward by a number of developing countries that the application of humanitarian intervention and economic sanctions has so far been highly selective—and discriminatory toward the weaker states. It also means that building an international consensus and the will to take collective action to protect human security worldwide, particularly through humanitarian intervention, is no easy task.

At the same time, it is a Catch-22 situation. The countries with the worst record of human rights abuses are also the ones least likely to yield to international pressure for reform through, for example, economic sanctions. These repressive regimes are also the least likely to care about the harmful impact of international embargoes on their citizens. Imposing embargoes on such countries—such as those imposed by the West against Burma—has done little to effect a change in the behavior of their military regimes, but it has certainly added to the miseries of the long-suffering people of Burma. This is the main reason why ASEAN has criticized Western countries' sanctions against Burma. Instead ASEAN has adopted the policy of "enhanced interaction" and "flexible engagement" toward Burma, accepting that country as a full member in the hope that it will eventually reform itself through the organization's good influence. It has to be admitted, however, that ASEAN's soft approach toward Burma has not yielded the desired results in terms of improving the country's political and human rights conditions, though the opening of the Burmese economy has brought some benefits to the lives of the people there.

Prospects

Although threats to human security in Asia are numerous, there is only a limited political and intellectual commitment to attend to human security and shift the focus from preoccupation with state security. To some extent this is understandable. From the traditional realist security perspective, there are still many threats to national security and regional security in Asia. Throughout the region many overlapping territorial claims remain unresolved. These constitute potential—and in certain cases actual—conflicts between states, such as the dispute in the South China Sea between China, Taiwan, the Philippines, Malaysia, Vietnam, and Brunei. China's sovereignty claim over Taiwan remains a major source of regional conflict: despite a growing desire for independence in Taiwan, China has made it clear that it will not tolerate any such move and will not hesitate to use force if necessary. Whether the United States pursues a policy of rapprochement with China or provides greater military support for Taiwan is central to security across the Taiwan Strait. Similarly the situation in the Korean peninsula continues to focus on traditional concerns regarding the military (and nuclear) threat from the North. Any open conflicts in Northeast Asia will affect the security of Asia as a whole—given the tight economic links between Northeast and Southeast Asia and the importance of the sea-lanes of communication (SLOCs) linking these two subregions to the regional economy. Similarly, in South Asia the conflict between India and Pakistan over Kashmir has loomed large over the subcontinent, particularly as both countries now possess nuclear weapons.

From the perspective of comprehensive security as well, the importance attached to state security is difficult to dismiss. Many countries in the region, particularly in Southeast Asia and South Asia, are still struggling with the process of nation building and state building. For the people of these countries, the threats to their security continue to come from within—threats of territorial disintegration from secessionist movements, threats of communal conflict between different ethnic and religious groups, threats of social violence because of poverty, and the general threat of the state's incapacity to govern effectively because of underdevelopment. For these reasons, therefore, it is unrealistic to expect countries in the region to voluntarily shift the focus of security from the state to the individual. The difficulty becomes even greater if it is projected that human security must be pursued in spite of the state (or against the state). Arguments that the rights of the collective must always prevail over the rights of the individual—as put forward by the "Asian Values" school of thought—continue to hold sway to a greater or lesser degree in most Asian societies.

Yet as the UNDP's *Human Development Report 1994* has compellingly shown, it is no longer possible to ignore the reality of widespread human suffering caused by deprivation of basic needs or by violations of human rights. To focus only on the security of the state, particularly on the military threat to state security, is to miss the whole range of threats that make human existence unbearable. It makes no sense to talk of the security of a nation-state if its people lead lives of misery. In ancient and feudal times, it is true, the state was there to serve the rulers, who obtained their power by divine right or as a mandate from heaven, while the people existed only to work for the glory of their rulers. Such a relationship between rulers and ruled is no longer accepted in modern societies, where power is seen to derive from the people and the primary function of the state is to protect and serve its citizens.

A greater emphasis on human rights, which has characterized international politics in the past decade, has led to a fundamental shift in perceptions about the relations between state and society. More attention is now given to the rights of the individual and the community vis-à-vis the state. This shift is clearly reflected in the growing number of countries embracing democracy. For only a democratic form of government gives people the right to participate in decisions that affect their lives. Human rights are regarded as universal values that must be protected universally. The protection of human rights for the sake of ensuring human dignity has come to be seen as an end in itself, the raison d'être for every other aspect of human endeavor. But this view of the universality of human rights and the commitment to democracy, though increasing worldwide, is still resisted by a number of countries, including several notable states in Asia. It is no coincidence that most violations of human rights occur in nondemocratic states. To these countries the interests of the individual must always be subordinated to the interests of the state. Yet the sanctity of the nation-state in the international system has made it difficult, except in extraordinary circumstances, for the international community to intervene in the internal affairs of a country.

At the same time it must also be recognized that the existence of nation-states is critical for the protection of human security. After all, nation-states are created to defend and protect their land and population from external enemies, ensure law and order, and promote the general welfare of their citizens. The rights of self-determination, the pursuit to establish independent and sovereign nation-states free from foreign domination, are regarded as the most important means for ensuring human rights and human dignity by most nations, since colonized or conquered peoples are usually denied their rights. The sanctity of the nation-states, particularly for countries that have suffered colonialism and have had to fight hard to gain their independence from foreign domination, is therefore likely to remain inviolate for the foreseeable future.

The concept of human security has been offered as an intellectual and a practical means for transcending the impasse between state-centered security and the rights of the individuals living in the state. For the human security concept to gain ground in Asia, however, state security and human security must not be seen as antagonistic. Instead they should be regarded as a continuum—each reinforcing the other. There can be no real security for the state if its people are not secure, because this puts the state in permanent danger of disintegration or collapse. Conversely, human security cannot be ensured when the state is not secure and is thus unable to protect its citizens from external domination, lawlessness, and other forms of violence or to provide the basic goods and services necessary for a civilized existence. Together, human insecurity and state insecurity can also endanger regional security.

While the usefulness of human security as an analytic tool may be contested, the concept represents a powerful means for advocating the improvement of human rights and living conditions in general—particularly in places where infringement of sovereignty is a sensitive subject. As Gareth Evans, the former foreign minister of Australia, points out: "Even if 'human security' had no analytic utility at all, it would be worth employing as an advocacy tool" (Evans 1999). Evans argues that "addressing issues in human security terms helps to break down some of the barriers and inhibitions inhibiting discussion of 'internal' matters." At the same time, according to Evans, for those states that until recently were constrained to talk about security in the traditional terms of military defense, "human security is an umbrella term offering some comfortable shelter. Human security is a term comfortable at home in a domestic, regional or global multilateral context, and as such—with problems requiring solutions at all levels—it is an advocacy tool not to be ignored."

For Asia, the primary utility of the concept is undoubtedly its ability to overcome some of the barriers inhibiting discussion of domestic matters. Because human security emphasizes the links between the various domains of security and the mutual vulnerability of global societies, as well as the collective responsibility of the human community toward one another, it is no longer possible to draw a rigid line between internal and external matters. Moreover, many of the problems threatening nations today are transnational and can only be resolved through cooperative efforts at the regional or global level. As Evans points out: "It may well be easier to mobilize multilateral responses to a crisis if the issue can be seen and characterized in human rather than state v. state terms."

By approaching the problem in human security terms, for example, it would be possible for ASEAN members to deal with the air pollution caused by forest fires in Indonesia at the regional level without feeling they are interfering in a fellow member's internal affairs. Domestic conflicts, moreover, can sometimes spill over to neighboring countries. The flows of Burmese refugees entering Thailand, for example, are clearly a threat to human security in both countries. Thus the issue can legitimately be discussed in ASEAN forums and collective action can be taken to prevent further occurrences.

Given the urgency of dealing with violent threats to human security, whether the result of state commission or state omission, it is time for regional and international organizations to put human security at the top of their agenda. By now it is clear that states with a poor human rights record are unlikely to improve their practices without some form of external pressure. ASEAN and the ARF should play a bigger role in promoting human security in Asia. The credibility of ASEAN as a regional organization—one that has already suffered a beating because of its helplessness in the face of the Asian financial crisis—will be further damaged if it fails to deal with the continuing human tragedy in Burma and Indonesia. The need to protect human security is not only a moral obligation. It is a necessary precondition for the creation of national and regional stability.

The international community has already determined in principle that national sovereignty cannot be used as a shield to hide human rights abuses. The efficacy of this policy, however, has been undermined by the perception that this rule is applied only to weaker countries while major powers and their allies are exempted. Many Asian countries, seizing on this argument to resist international pressure to improve their human rights practices, insist that humanitarian intervention is being used by major powers as a political tool against developing countries. Until this problem is resolved, efforts to end violent threats to human security in Asia will continue to be hampered by suspicion.

Works Cited

Acharya, Amitav, and Arvind Acharya. 2000. "Human Security in the Asia Pacific: Puzzle, Panacea, or Peril?" Working Paper 1/2000. Bhubaneswar: Center for Peace and Development Studies.

AI (Amnesty International). 2000. *Amnesty International Report*. London: Amnesty International.

"Aksara." 2001. Special supplement to *Tempo*, June 11–17.

Alatas, Ali. 2000. "Dinamika perrkembangan situasi politik dan keamanan dunia serta perubahan konstelasi hubungan anta-negara menjelang akhir abad ke 20." Acara curah pendapat tentang perkembangan dunia dan kebijakan luar negeri. Jakarta, Nov. 20.

Anwar, Dewi Fortuna. 1998. "Indonesia: Domestic Priorities Define National Security." In

Muthiah Alagappa, ed., *Asian Security Practice: Material and Ideational Influences.* Stanford: Stanford University Press.

Buzan, Barry. 1991. *People, States and Fear: An Agenda for International Security Studies in the Post–Cold War Era.* 2nd ed. Hemel Hempstead, U.K.: Harvester Wheatsheaf.

———. 2000. "Human Security in International Perspectives." Paper presented at the 14th Asia Pacific Round Table, Kuala Lumpur, June 3–7.

Evans, Gareth. 1999. "Human Security and Society." Paper presented to Asia-Australia Institute Asia Leaders' Forum on Human Security in Development and Crisis, Sydney, Apr. 19.

Kompas. 1998. "Pernyataan Gaffar Baba mendapat reaksi keras." Selasa, Sept. 29.

Kraft, Herman Joseph S. 2000. "Human Security and ASEAN Mechanism." Paper presented to ASEAN 2020 Conference, Bangkok, July 21–22.

Krauthammer, Charles. 1999. "The Short, Unhappy Life of Humanitarian War (Kosovo I)." *National Interest* 57 (Fall): 5–10.

Lane, Christopher, and Benjamin Schwarz. 1999. "For the Record (Kosovo II)." *National Interest* 57 (Fall): 11–15.

Pitsuwan, Surin. 1999. Speech presented to 54th Session of the General Assembly, United Nations, Sept. 25.

———. 2000. Speech to 55th Session of the General Assembly, United Nations, Dec. 19.

RCSS (Regional Centre for Strategic Studies). 2000. "Regional International Affairs Program in Asia." Colombo.

Richardson, Michael. 1998. "US 'Horrified' About Anwar. In Protest, Clinton Downgrades Visit to Malaysia." *International Herald Tribune*, Oct. 15.

Severino, Rodolfo C. 2000. "Toward Expanding the Frontiers of International Humanitarian Law." Remarks made at opening of regional seminar on National Implementation of the Southeast Asian Countries, Jakarta, June 12.

Stohl, Michael. 2000. "Globalization and the Failed State: The Continuing Tensions Between National Security and Human Security: A Summing Up." Unpublished ms., Purdue University.

Sucharithanarugse, Withaya. 2000. "The Concept of Human Security Extended. Asianizing the Paradigm." In William T. Tow, Ramesh Thakur, and In-Tack Hyun, eds., *Asia's Emerging Regional Order.* Tokyo: United Nations University Press.

Sukma, Rizal. 2000. "Human Security and Political Security: Should There Be a Tension?" Paper presented to ASEAN 2020 Conference, Bangkok, July 21–22.

Tay, Simon SC. 2000. "Human Security and the ARF: Addressing Realities, Adopting Norms." Paper presented to ASEAN 2020 Conference, Bangkok, July 21–22.

UNDP. 1994. *Human Development Report 1994.* New York: United Nations Development Programme.

———. 2000. *Human Development Report 2000.* New York: United Nations Development Programme.

PART IV

Conclusion

CHAPTER SIXTEEN

Managing Asian Security

Competition, Cooperation, and Evolutionary Change

MUTHIAH ALAGAPPA

This final chapter returns to the five propositions advanced in the Introduction: Security order exists in Asia; it is of the instrumental type with certain normative-contractual features; multiple pathways sustain Asia's security order; the U.S. role is important, but order in Asia rests on certain other fundamental pillars as well; and Asia's present security order is likely to persist for some time and change only gradually, in incremental fashion. The preceding chapters support these propositions as well as highlight some of their limitations. Drawing on these chapters, on other published works, and on my own observation of the Asian security scene for over twenty years, this chapter further develops the five propositions. It also points out the challenges that must be overcome and the developments that must occur if today's largely instrumental order is to become a more robust and normative-contractual arrangement.

Proposition One: Security Order Exists in Asia

In Chapter 1 we defined international order as a formal or informal arrangement that sustains rule-governed interaction among sovereign states in their pursuit of private and public ends. The key criterion of order is whether interstate interaction is conducted in a systematic manner in observance of certain rules. Such rule-governed interaction creates a predictable and stable international environment: states can coexist, coordinate their interaction, or collaborate in their pursuit of national, common, and collective goals; differences and disputes are adjusted in a peaceful manner; and change is nonviolent. Order does not proscribe force and war, but it does limit their utility and prescribes rules to govern their use. Rules that govern international interaction may be formal or informal. They may be explicitly codified in global and regional instruments as principles, norms, and rules, including law, or they may be implicit and have to be inferred from practice. Irrespective of their form, rules must exist, they must be acknowledged, and much if not all international interaction should conform to them. Transgression of widely accepted rules should carry a cost—political, diplomatic, economic, legal, or military. If these conditions are present, then it is reasonable to infer that order exists.

In line with this reasoning, our contention that security order exists in Asia rests on the following elements: the existence of a widely shared normative framework; the salience of the principles and norms associated with this framework in easing the security dilemma and ensuring state survival; and their role in sustaining normal political and diplomatic interaction among all states that are part of the Asian security system and in facilitating coordination and cooperation among them in the pursuit of private and common security goals. The violation of these principles and norms carries a cost. Territorial disputes are being adjusted or managed in a peaceful manner. Even in the case of acute conflict management and limitation of force, certain basic understandings have been reached. At the same time, it is important to acknowledge that the extent and effectiveness of rules varies from issue to issue and from region to region and that certain rules are contested. Despite periodic crises, however, predictability and stability have characterized Asia for the better part of the last two decades. There has not been a major war since 1979, and international economic activity (trade, investment, production) has flourished. While the security order in Asia suffers certain weaknesses, it is not fragile.

A shared normative framework to govern the international political interaction of Asian states has been in the works since the early 1950s. Indeed, the core norms of the framework have been articulated in several declarations, agreements, and treaties. The Five Principles of Peaceful Coexistence articulated by India and China in 1953 set out the following axioms to guide interstate interaction: mutual respect for territorial integrity and sovereignty; mutual nonaggression; noninterference in each other's internal affairs; equality and mutual benefit; and peaceful coexistence. These principles were incorporated in the final communiqué of the twenty-nine-nation Asian-African Conference held in 1955 in Bandung. This communiqué set out ten axioms that would enable nations "to live in peace with one another as good neighbors and develop friendly relations." These principles also informed the Nonaligned Movement that was officially launched in 1961. Several Asian states, including India, Ceylon (Sri Lanka), and Indonesia, played key roles in promoting this movement. Although it does not make explicit reference to the Bandung conference or the Nonaligned Movement, the 1976 Treaty of Amity and Cooperation in Southeast Asia, which has since been signed and ratified by all ten Southeast Asian countries, reaffirms the foregoing principles. Interaction among the contracting parties, according to the treaty, is to be guided by these values: mutual respect for the independence, sovereignty, equality, territorial integrity, and national identity of all nations; the right of every state to lead its national existence free from external interference, subversion, or coercion; noninterference in the internal affairs of one another; settlement of differences or disputes by peaceful means; renunciation of the threat or use of force; and effective cooperation among parties to the treaty.

Although the ASEAN proposal that the non–Southeast Asian countries of the ASEAN Regional Forum (ARF) should accede to this treaty was not formally adopted, the treaty's axioms have been endorsed by the ARF. In 1998, ASEAN amended the treaty to make it possible for states outside Southeast Asia to accede to it. Similar principles of conduct are articulated in the charter of the South Asian Association for Regional Cooperation (SAARC). Cooperation within the SAARC framework, it states, "shall be based on respect for the principles of sovereign equality, territorial integrity, political independence, noninterference in the internal affairs of other states, and mutual benefit." The Shanghai Cooperation Organization (SCO), which is held up by Beijing and Moscow as the model institution for the post–Cold War era (in contrast to NATO and the U.S.-centered bilateral alliances in Asia), articulates similar values. China, India, and other Asian states have asserted that the Five Principles of Peaceful Coexistence and the UN Charter are still salient and should constitute the basis for a new political order in Asia and indeed the world. China has sought to include references to the UN Charter, the Five Principles of Peaceful Coexistence, and the ASEAN Treaty of Amity and Cooperation in its bilateral cooperation agreements with other Asian countries.

Observers, especially from the West, tend to view these declarations and treaties as merely pro forma echoes of the UN Charter with little meaning because Asian states have failed to translate the principles into binding rules of behavior and in fact have violated them frequently. This cynical view was in large part justified during the early postindependence period, which coincided with the Cold War. My argument here, however, is that although these norms may have been pro forma to begin with and were perhaps violated frequently, in time they have become deeply imprinted in the mindset of political elites across Asia— contributing to a shared normative framework that increasingly influences the behavior and interaction of states.

Sovereignty is the key idea informing the Asian normative framework. The recent liberation of Asian countries from colonial rule or a semicolonial situation, the aspiration of national political elites to build strong modern nation-states, and the internal and international challenges to the ongoing nation- and state-building processes are among the factors that underscore the high value attached to sovereignty and its associated norms. Chung-in Moon and Chaesung Chun (Chap. 3) contend that it is the Westphalian notion of sovereignty that holds sway in Asia. They observe, however, that Asian states do not have the capacity to enforce the writ of internal and external aspects of sovereignty—leading to frequent violation, contestation, and voluntary and involuntary compromise of state sovereignty. Zealous attachment to the Westphalian notion produces conflict in the domestic and international arenas, makes compromise and conflict management difficult, provides opportunities for external interference in domestic affairs, and creates an unstable international peace and an instrumental type of international security order in Asia. We will return to some of these observations later in the chapter.

For now it is important to clarify several points pertaining to sovereignty and the normative framework in Asia. First, despite challenges and weaknesses, sovereignty is still the operative principle in the interaction of Asian states. Second, except for a few countries, the political, economic, and legal-coercive capacity of Asian states to enforce internal and international aspects of sovereignty, as observed in the Introduction, has strengthened over the years. Third, compared with the early postindependence era, international contestation over the right to exist as a sovereign state is limited to very few cases. Although territorial disputes are numerous, few of them challenge sovereignty directly or significantly. And although one might argue that internal challenges to sovereignty are more numerous and more severe than international contestation, even here the challenges to sovereignty are fewer than before and increasingly limited to peripheral regions. Fourth, despite the formal attachment to a Westphalian notion, Asian states today are modifying their interpretation and practice of sovereignty. This process is most evident in the economic arena, where the benefits of participation in the global economy inform the greater willingness of Asian states to accept constraints and pool state sovereignty. Their vulnerability to international developments over which they have little control (heightened by the 1997 economic crisis) has tempered but not significantly altered such flexible notions of sovereignty in the economic arena. Even in the political arena, certain Asian states have become more flexible in the practice of sovereignty. China, for example, has ceded domestic jurisdiction and certain aspects of international sovereignty to Hong Kong and Macau and has been willing to concede a similar if not higher degree of control to Taiwan in the interest of achieving its goal of unification. It is not willing to grant such control to the minority regions of Tibet and Xinjiang, however. Nor is it willing to share international sovereignty in the political arena, as demonstrated by its steadfast refusal to accept a sovereign Taiwan or a confederal arrangement.

Although not much headway has been made, a confederal arrangement between North and South Korea has been advanced at various times as an option to resolve the conflict between them. Recently the Indian minister of home affairs, L. K. Advani, mooted the idea of a confederal arrangement between India and Pakistan. Islamabad quickly rejected this idea, however, on the grounds that it reflected Indian nonacceptance of an independent Pakistan and was simply a plot by the Bharatiya Janatha Party (BJP) to absorb Pakistan. In the internal domain, while rejecting secession and outright independence, several states—Indonesia, Sri Lanka, the Philippines, Burma (Myanmar)—have become more willing to explore options like federalism and autonomy that would devolve domestic jurisdiction in most matters to minorities. Such changes in the notions and practice of sovereignty are rooted in instrumental considerations. In the case of China, for example, the flexibility is connected to the desire to achieve the goals of unification and economic modernization. The willingness to devolve power to minorities in Sri Lanka, Indonesia, and the Philippines similarly derives from the desire to end the political and financial cost of fighting long-running insurgencies. In certain cases, of course, the articulated proposals may simply be tactical posturing. Nevertheless, the flexible notions are an indication of change, though they highlight the limits of such change as well—at least for now. As Stephen Krasner (1993) observes, ideas may often serve as hooks for practical ends but can subsequently assume a life of their own. For the resolution of many internal and international conflicts in Asia, more flexible interpretations of sovereignty are necessary. Such flexibility may emerge as states become more legitimate, stronger, and more confident.

As noted in Chapter 2, an intense debate was waged in the late 1980s and the better part of the 1990s between the proponents of Asian and Western values and models.[1] Focused on specific features (international interference and intervention in domestic affairs, protection of human and minority rights, and systems for political governance and economic management), this debate modified certain aspects of the Asian normative framework but did not alter it in any fundamental manner. Today there is greater recognition in Asia that human rights and human security must be protected (Anwar in Chap. 15) and that the principle of noninterference in internal affairs cannot be considered absolute. There is still contention over the appropriate system for political governance, but there is growing acceptance that sovereignty resides in the people and political participation has to be broadened. What form this participation will take remains a contentious issue. Although there is much less contention over the economic system, vulnerability

---

[1] On the Asian values debate, see Alagappa (1994), De Barry (1998), and the chapters in Bauer and Bell (1999).

to global economic developments has emerged as a new concern. Two points are worthy of note here. First, the debate over values, coupled with the 1997 financial crisis, has contributed to an evolution of the Asian normative framework, not a radical departure. Sovereignty and the associated principles still constitute the key pillars. Second, the modification was a consequence of debate, discussion, and pressure (political and economic), not force and imposition. Here the formal interstate multilateral forums, and the numerous nongovernmental organizations and processes, often denigrated as talk shops, have played important socializing and learning roles (Acharya in Chap. 6; Job in Chap. 7).

State practice has influenced—and been influenced by—the developing normative framework. In the early years, China violated the principles it was propounding as a matter of course. It frequently used force to settle disputes with other countries, propagated a revolutionary ideology, supported communist insurgency movements engaged in revolutionary wars in several Southeast Asian countries, and interfered at will in the internal affairs of other states. China's behavior has since altered substantially. Although force is still a key instrument of policy, Beijing now seeks to settle its many territorial disputes in a peaceful manner (Wang in Chap. 11). China is not a revolutionary state and does not seek the overthrow of regimes in other Asian states. Although concerned about the fate of overseas Chinese communities, it has accepted the notion that they are citizens of the countries in which they reside. Generally, then, Chinese interference in the internal affairs of other countries has declined dramatically. In the case of India, by contrast, there was a shift from relatively strict observance of the noninterference principle to extensive interference in the affairs of neighboring countries—interference that reached a peak in the Indira and Rajiv Gandhi eras when New Delhi intervened in Sri Lanka, the Maldives, Nepal, and Pakistan. Since the late 1980s, India has refrained from such behavior and today is reluctant to become involved in internal disputes and conflicts in neighboring countries even when invited. The Gujral Doctrine seeks to build close relationships with India's neighbors on the basis of certain principles, including noninterference in the internal affairs of other countries. (Pakistan is an exception because of its support for Pakistani and Kashmiri militant groups and their terrorist activities in India.) In an earlier era, Indonesia, Vietnam, Thailand, and several other Southeast Asian countries intervened in each other's internal affairs. Although breaches still occur, they are fewer today and much less significant than in the early years after independence. For the ASEAN states, then, it is not an exaggeration to say that noninterference has become a key principle which influences their thinking and practice in interactions with one another. Debates about noninterference have had to do with the absolute interpretation of the principle, not its abandonment.

In the early postindependence period, many Asian states contested each other's legitimacy, sought to overthrow incumbent regimes, and intervened freely in the internal affairs of fellow Asian countries. Today, with the exception of Taiwan and in certain ways North and South Korea, Asian states accord mutual recognition to each other. They do not seek the political demise of fellow Asian states; nor do they aspire to alter national and regime identity through political, diplomatic, and economic pressure or through force. The many territorial disputes on land and at sea today are a holdover from a previous era and also a consequence of the delimitation of maritime boundaries based on the UN Convention on the Law of the Sea (UNCLOS) (Wang in Chap. 11; Blanchard in Chap. 12). Except for these disputes, no Asian state seeks to annex the territory of another. Victorious China withdrew from much of the Indian territory it had occupied after the 1962 war, and victorious India did not annex East Pakistan after its successful intervention in 1971. The attempts to invade and occupy another country (Vietnam's invasion and occupation of Cambodia) or annex territory (Indonesia's annexation of East Timor) were opposed and the actions were eventually reversed.

Although the rules (respect for the political and territorial integrity of existing states and renunciation of force to settle differences) were important to ASEAN, geopolitical interest was perhaps the core reason for the opposition of major powers (China, United States) to Vietnam's occupation of Cambodia. Nevertheless, such opposition has helped to establish the principles that conquest and occupation are not acceptable behavior in contemporary Asia and that any violation of this norm will incur a cost. The relative robustness of the normative framework has eased the survival concerns of small states (Singapore and Brunei) and weak states (Cambodia, Laos, Bhutan, Nepal, Mongolia) alike. Survival as a distinct political entity is a problem for very few states. Even Taiwan and North Korea, whose survival is problematic, do not function in a context of constant danger and fear as posited by the proponents of a dangerous Asia thesis.

That the ideals of the Asian normative framework are the same as those in the UN Charter does not make them less significant. Certainly the extensiveness and intensiveness of rules in Europe exceed those in the UN Charter and in Asia. This indicates a high degree of order in Europe, however, not the absence of order in Asia. Specific rules based on the principles and norms noted earlier inform the routine interactions among Asian states—diplomatic intercourse, political negotiations, economic relations, travel, bilateral and multilateral coordination and cooperation, participation in regional and subregional forums—which taken together account for the bulk of international interactions. Observers often focus on the small number of cases where rules may not pertain. This criticism is reasonable if such cases dominate all interaction. But the potential of the Korean and Indo-Pakistani conflicts, for example, to disrupt order on a regionwide scale is limited. The Taiwan conflict has prevented cross-strait political and diplomatic relations but not economic and social interaction. Nor has it significantly affected the wide range of interaction between China and the United States, much of which is conducted on the basis of widely acknowledged rules.

Even in the difficult cases (Taiwan, Korea, Kashmir), an understanding has been reached among the conflicting parties on the basic rules of the game for conflict management. In the case of Taiwan, for example, there is an implicit understanding among the United States, the PRC, and Taiwan that unification, when it occurs, should be peaceful and that either forceful absorption by the PRC or unilateral declaration of independence by Taiwan will be opposed by the United States. Though it is not fully acceptable to China and Taiwan, both of which have periodically tested the waters to shift the boundary in their favor, the understanding—reinforced by the deployment of two U.S. carriers in 1996 and a firm statement by George W. Bush in April 2001—still holds. China will not give up the force option, but it has begun to reemphasize economic relations as the path to eventual unification. Beijing may be on the verge of resuming the cross-strait dialogue with the DPP government of Taiwan.

One might even argue that a basic understanding—that the conflict cannot be settled through war—has also been reached in the Korean case. Despite the rhetoric, no party has the political will or the military capacity to impose a settlement by force, and even if these could be mustered, the cost of war would undoubtedly be very high. Thus neither party wants war. When a crisis escalates and reaches a certain threshold, one or more parties back down, as in 1976 and 1994. The military clashes in the Korean peninsula have occurred on the margins, with no substantial consequence for the central balance or the critical interests of the conflicting parties. A similar case can be made, with reservations, with respect to the Kashmir conflict. Presuming that India would not escalate hostilities to the nuclear level, Pakistan pursued a strategy of supporting militant movements and infiltrating a small contingent of regular troops into Indian Kashmir. The weakness of this strategy became apparent in the wake of the international denunciation of the Pakistani infiltration that led to the Kargil conflict in 1998, and in the wake of the American-led war against international terrorism and the Indian mobilization in response to the October and December 2001 terrorist attacks on India. Pakistan backed down on both occasions.

Certain recent developments—the ban on militant Islamic liberation movements, the crackdown on terrorism, and the formation of a National Commission on Kashmir, for example—suggest that Islamabad may be concluding that the solution to the Kashmir issue does not lie in a military struggle with India or in supporting militant movements which engage in terrorist activities in that country. New Delhi too may be coming around to accepting the need to negotiate the issue with Pakistan. Certainly the two countries have thus far abided by an understanding not to attack each other's nuclear facilities. One observer has argued that as a consequence of the series of crises since 1998, a stable state of deterrence may be developing in Indo-Pakistani relations (Haider 2002). But in light of the vital interests at stake and the deep animosity that characterizes this bilateral relationship, there is no certainty that these developments will lead to a firm understanding on conflict management.

The other disputes in Asia are for the most part being settled or at least managed in a peaceful manner. The PRC's territorial disputes with Burma, Nepal, Mongolia, Afghanistan, Pakistan, Russia, Vietnam (land boundary), Kazakhstan, and Kyrgyzstan have been settled. The Sino-Indian, Thai-Burmese, Thai-Cambodian, Thai-Lao, Malaysia-Philippines, China-Bhutan, and Afghanistan-Pakistan border disputes and the Russo-Japanese dispute over the Northern Territories or Kuril Islands have still not been settled. And although the obstacles standing in the way of settlement of some of these conflicts are unlikely to be overcome any time soon, the probability of their precipitating war is low. Occasional military clashes cannot be ruled out, however. Similarly, little progress has been made in settling the conflicting claims in the East and South China Sea, and the prospects for their settlement in the near term are not good (Blanchard in Chap. 12). The East and South China Sea may also witness occasional military clashes, but here again the probability of war is low. There has not been a military clash in the South China Sea since 1998. Despite the lack of progress in actual settlement, several developments like the 1992 ASEAN Manila Declaration (which articulates a code of conduct for resolving the conflicting claims in the South China Sea), the ARF's endorsement of the declaration in 1995, Beijing's statement that the conflicting claims should be settled through friendly bilateral consultations and negotiations under international law (including the 1982 UNCLOS), and the China-ASEAN dialogue have ameliorated tension and may pave the way for eventual peaceful adjustment of the dispute. At their regular dialogue meeting in April 2000, China and the ASEAN countries discussed the code of conduct issue and agreed to speed up the drafting of a code. Malaysia, Singapore, and Indonesia have agreed to submit their conflicting claims over the Pedra Branca (or Pulau Batu Putih), Sipitan, and Ligitan islands to the International Court of Justice. Thailand and Malaysia, Malaysia and Vietnam, and Indonesia (East Timor) and Australia have agreed to undertake joint development of the maritime space in their overlapping claims. Territorial disputes on land and at sea that are not ripe for settlement—like those between China and India, Russia and Japan, and in the South China Sea—are being managed through bilateral or multilateral discussions. There is little likelihood that force will be used to resolve them or that they will lead to full-fledged wars.

TABLE 16.1
Defense Expenditures of Major Countries in the Asian Security System
(in billion US$)

Country	1989 expenditure	%GDP	1994 expenditure	%GDP[a]	1999 expenditure	%GDP[b]	Comments
USA	294.900	5.7	280.600	4.3	275.500	3.1	
USSR/ Russia	119.440	5.4	79.000	9.6	31.000	5.1	Western intelligence estimated 1989 expenditure to be twice as large as officially stated by the USSR government
China	6.600	1.6	6.400	5.6	39.500	5.4	PPP estimate for 1994 is $28.5 billion. (The officially stated expenditure is listed here.) The 1999 figure is based on PPP estimate. The percentage of GDP for 1989 is based on GNP (% GNP)
India	8.940	3.3	7.330	2.8	14.200	3.4	
Japan	30.090	1.0	45.800	1.0	40.800	0.9	
N. Korea	4.154	n/a	5.600	26.6	2.100	14.3	Estimates are listed for 1994 and 1999
S. Korea	9.886	4.7	12.500	3.6	12.000	3.0	
Mongolia	2.680	n/a	0.017	2.8	0.019	1.9	Estimates are listed for 1994 and 1999
Taiwan	8.180	5.4	11.300	5.0	15.000	5.2	
Burma	0.334	2.0	1.800	3.1	2.000	5.0	PPP estimate is listed for 1999
Malaysia	1.384	3.7	3.100	3.9	3.200	4.0	
Thailand	1.801	2.8	3.600	2.6	2.600	1.9	
Vietnam	2.320	16.0	0.900	5.7	0.890	3.1	Estimates are listed for 1989 and 1999
Indonesia	1.593	1.9	2.400	1.4	1.500	1.1	
Philippines	1.280	2.9	1.100	1.4	1.600	2.1	
Singapore	1.490	5.6	3.100	4.8	4.700	5.6	
Bangladesh	0.289	1.5	0.467	1.8	0.612	1.9	
Nepal	0.039	1.4	0.043	1.1	0.051	0.8	
Pakistan	2.470	7.0	3.500	4.7	3.500	6.6	
Sri Lanka	0.233	3.5	0.516	6.9	0.807	5.1	

NOTE: Expenditure data from *The Military Balance*, published by Brassey's for IISS, 1989–90 to 2000–2001. As far as possible, data for "military expenditures" are listed. In cases where "expenditure" data were not published, "military budget" figures are listed. Estimates, PPP (Purchasing Power Parity) approximations, GNP, off-year data, and intelligence-based revisions of official statements are noted here.

[a]IIIS 1996, "International Comparisons of Defense Expenditures and Military Manpower."
[b]IIIS, 2001, "International Comparisons of Defense Expenditures and Military Manpower."

Notwithstanding the low probability of war, force is still a key instrument of state policy in Asia. Not only does the threat of force remain the central component in the management of three acute conflicts (Kang in Chap. 10), but it is also important in defending land and sea boundaries, supporting maritime claims, patrolling to prevent piracy and smuggling, and in the management of internal conflicts (Chaps. 11, 12, 14). Nuclear weapons and ballistic missiles remain a tempting option and in some ways have become even more salient in the post–Cold War era (Cha in Chap. 13). Certainly defense consumes substantial state resources (see Table 16.1). Rather than declining, in fact, defense expenditures have remained steady or increased in the post–Cold War era. Nevertheless, several observations are in order. First, the utility of force has become more circumscribed. Its deployment to invade and occupy another country, or to annex territory that is internationally recognized as belonging to another state, is no longer legitimate in Asia. The utility of force has been circumscribed, too, by the inability of Asian states to marshal the requisite power to impose settlements by force. China, India, North and South Korea, Taiwan, and Pakistan do not have the military capability to impose the settlements they desire (Kang in Chap. 10). The political, diplomatic, economic, and military cost of using force has become high (but not yet prohibitive).

Second, the acquisition of nuclear weapons and ballistic missiles further circumscribes the utility of force. Nuclear weapons, especially those of the type possessed by Asian states, are not for fighting wars—and, moreover, they dramatically increase the cost of using force. The expensive technology needed to make nuclear weapons and missile systems more accurate, and therefore more usable, is beyond the reach of Asian states for now. Third, contrary to the widespread belief in the West, the nuclear threshold and the norm of no-first-use are as strong in the second-generation nuclear states as in the first (Cha in Chap. 13). In light of these considerations, the use of force has for the most part been limited to military skirmishes in peripheral areas on land and at sea and to low-intensity operations. Force has not been directed at core interests or central military assets. Fourth, even in cases of acute conflict, force is not the only, and not always the first, recourse in conflict management. The reasons noted earlier also apply to the observation that the role of force in Asian international politics is being transformed. Force is becoming more relevant in matters of defense, deterrence, and reassurance than in combat. In the Taiwan dispute, the key role of force is to dissuade Taiwan from declaring independence and to prevent the PRC from forcefully absorbing Taiwan. On the Korean peninsula, force is most relevant in deterring war and preserving the stalemate. And in the Indo-Pakistani conflict, deterrence is becoming the primary role of force.

Finally, the major Asian powers are becoming more positively disposed toward global arms and military technology control regimes. China's perspective has significantly altered from "accusation and suspicion to more participation and guarded endorsement of the international norms in arms control, disarmament, and nonproliferation" (Yuan 2000). Since the early 1990s, Beijing has acceded to the Treaty on the Nonproliferation of Nuclear Weapons (NPT), supported its indefinite extension in 1995, signed and ratified the Chemical Weapons Convention, and signed the Comprehensive Test Ban Treaty (CTBT). It has also pledged to abide by the Missile Technology Control Regime (MTCR) and is introducing domestic regulations governing export of nuclear, chemical, and dual-use material. Although its record on nonproliferation is still spotty and a number of questions remain on China's adherence to arms control regimes, these changes indicate a definite shift in attitude. India has been steadfastly opposed to the NPT, but since 1998 it has indicated its willingness to sign the CTBT and support the Fissile Material Cutoff treaty (FMCT). It has also pledged to abide by the MTCR. India is signatory to the chemical and biological weapons conventions. Like China, India has pledged no-first-use of nuclear weapons and has been willing to support nuclear-weapon-free zones in areas that do not directly affect its security. China's behavior with respect to arms control has been influenced by its concerns about national security, international image, commercial interests, and security and technological benefits to be gained from adopting a more positive attitude. India's change in attitude stems in large measure from its desire to be accepted as a nuclear power and roll back the damage arising from the sanctions imposed after the 1998 tests. Although instrumental considerations are the primary drivers of the changed perspectives of China and India, the change is not unimportant. As these countries become more status-quo-oriented, their support of arms control regimes is likely to increase.

The intensity of rules varies by issue and subregion. Rules are more extensive in the economic arena, and such rules cover dispute management too. Although for the most part these are global rules, limited regional rules exist as well. In the security arena, rules are less extensive, and they are essentially at the level of principles and norms. Specific rules are limited to the regulation of routine interstate interactions. Rules are less salient in managing disputes and controlling armaments and violence, where they are more implicit and based on the threat of force. The primary purpose of rules in the security arena is coordination in support of coexistence and limited cooperation to address common security problems. As common interest in mutual survival and economic development through regional and global arrangements has gained ground, rule-governed interaction has become more salient in Asia. Such development is most evident in Southeast Asia but has recently emerged in East Asia as well. Mutual interest in economic growth and modernization has created a higher level of economic cooperation and interdependence among most states in these two subregions with their growing desire to forge common values and distinctive identities. The development that began in Southeast Asia with the ASEAN Five has expanded to embrace all ten Southeast Asian countries and now East Asia through the ASEAN Plus Three (China, Japan, and South Korea) forum. Common visions and plans of actions have been formulated: ASEAN 20/20, the Hanoi Plan of Action (HPA), the ASEAN integration plan, the APEC trade liberalization goals, and the East Asian Vision. Although certain aspects of these plans are ambitious and not all their goals will be realized, they are nevertheless a political statement of the desire of governments in these subregions to construct a predictable, rule-based environment that is conducive to the attainment of their national goals—rather than simply to suffer the dictates of material structure or the policies of external powers.

Rule-governed interaction is least developed in South Asia, a subregion still beset by the weakness of Pakistan as a nation-state and by the Indo-Pakistani conflict. Over the years, however, this conflict has become less central to the area's international politics and economics. Apparently India and states other than Pakistan have decided to move beyond this conflict. India's predominance in the subregion appears to have been accepted by the other states, and New Delhi appears to be retreating from its coercive regional hegemonic tendencies. Economic cooperation, though still in a limited and tentative manner, is moving ahead. Sri Lanka has concluded a preferential trade agreement with India; Bangladesh is exploring exporting natural gas to India. Like the economic triangles and quadrangles in Southeast Asia, Bangladesh, India, Burma, and China are engaged in a preliminary investigation of economic cooperation in the area comprising northeastern India, Bangladesh, Burma, and Yunnan province in China. A shift in India's regional policy from the time of Prime Ministers Narasimha Rao and Inder Kumar Gujral, as well as shifts in the attitudes of the other South Asian states, appears to have facilitated these recent changes (which are still tentative). Some observers (such as Ayoob 2000) believe that South Asia, with the exception of Pakistan, may make quick and substantial progress toward a strong international society.

When viewed in a comprehensive manner, the existence of security order—a set of arrangements to sustain rule-governed behavior that makes for predictability and stability in the interaction of Asian states—is difficult to deny. While it is true that rules are less extensive in the security arena, that often they have their origins in expedient considerations, and that there are gaps and breaches, this is indicative of the degree and type of order, not its absence.

Proposition Two: An Instrumental Order with Normative-Contractual Features

International social life in Asia displays features of multiple paradigms. Although in several ways it resembles complex interdependence, realist features still dominate the security arena. Nevertheless the dominant security orientation of Asian states is defense and deterrence, not offense and aggression. Moreover, certain realist features, such as the struggle for power and influence, are tempered by normative constraints and by growing economic interdependence and cooperation. Reflecting this perspective, the largely instrumental security order in Asia has normative-contractual features as well. This combination is evident in the goals of order, in the principles that constitute the Asian normative framework, in the purpose and roles of regional institutions, and in the scope and domain of order.

The primary goals of order in Asia are national in character—survival and prosperity. The common goal of a stable and relatively peaceful international environment derives its significance from the contribution it can make to the attainment of national goals. As noted in the Introduction, sheer existence as a separate political entity is problematic only for a few states (although a number of small and weak states do not take their existence for granted). More widespread is the concern with preservation and enhancement of national identity and regime security. Concern with these aspects of national survival runs deep and is reflected in the intensity of internal and international identity conflicts and the unwillingness of Asian states to compromise on such issues. Economic growth and modernization, high-priority goals for nearly all Asian states, are viewed as a key means to further national identity, power, and influence in the international domain, as well as to sustain regime legitimacy and manage conflicts in the internal domain. This instrumentally driven goal, however, especially the chosen path (participation in the global capitalist economy), has tempered the pursuit of national survival and blurred the hierarchy of national goals (Wan in Chap. 8). Consideration of the high economic and political cost combined with the lack of military capability to impose a settlement by force, for example, has tempered the PRC's pursuit of its highly desired unification goal. It is not clear, though, whether such restraints will still prevail if Taiwan opts for a unilateral declaration of independence.

The pursuit of economic growth and modernization through participation in the global economy requires Asian states to act in accord with international agreements and rules. Their vulnerability to international pressure and unforeseen developments—especially downturns in the global economy—also emphasizes the need for regional cooperation. Such cooperation may not only mitigate their vulnerability and amplify their voice in global forums but also further the attainment of national economic goals. As a stable and peaceful environment is considered essential to national survival and prosperity, its promotion has become a key regional goal of security order in Asia. Although it is still subordinate to core national interests, this regional goal is beginning to temper the pursuit of national interests. Though the goals of regional security order in Asia (national survival, national prosperity, stable environment) are all basic, the complexity of these goals and the relationship among them support our proposition that the purpose of a regional security order in Asia is not simply survival as narrowly defined but also the pursuit of multiple goals that require regionwide collaboration.

And although national interest predominates in political and security matters, the definition of national interest is in large measure status-quo-oriented. Common interest in a peaceful and stable environment, the expectation that bigger countries must demonstrate good citizenship and provide material and ideational public goods in support of their claim to major power status, and the potential for mutual gain through cooperation—all are beginning to influence and broaden the definition of national interest. China's aspiration to take its rightful place in the region and the world, Beijing's policy of allaying neighbors' suspicions and fears of its growing power, and its pursuit of economic modernization through participation in the global capitalist economy have created a firm stake in a stable international environment and inform its good neighbor policy. They also restrain Chinese behavior regarding Taiwan, the South China Sea, and other territorial disputes. Though such a move would have been advantageous, China did not devalue the yuan in the wake of the 1997 financial crisis. Instead it sought to demonstrate that it is a good citizen and a responsible power that acts in the interest of the larger community. Modification of national interests based on the consideration of the larger public good, however, is still an incipient and tentative step that could be reversed by developments that affect China's core interests. Moreover, the belief that the status quo disadvantages them inhibits the major Asian powers from defining their national interests in a more enlightened manner to take account of the interests of other states.

The dominance of national autonomy and national interest is reflected in the emphasis on sovereignty (international autonomy and supreme domestic jurisdiction) in the Asian normative framework and in the nature of regional cooperation that has developed. The primary function of such cooperation is to facilitate peaceful coexistence and limited collaboration on issues where mutual gain can be realized rather than to transform identity and interest. Though several visions have been articulated by ASEAN, ASEAN Plus Three, and APEC, none of these proposals aspires to a collective political identity that will override national identity and interest. Even in the economic arena there is no desire to

move toward an integrated community. This orientation is reflected in the declared purposes of regional organizations, the principles that inform their constitution, the rules and procedures that govern their operation, and their limited
role in conflict management. Considerations of national autonomy have inhibited the adoption of binding goals and rules. Even in the few cases where such
goals have been projected, it has been difficult to realize them. The ASEAN
Way—consensus in decision making and the privileging of process over goals—
has guided the functioning of regional institutions. Although principles and
norms figure prominently, there is a tendency to shy away from specific measures
designed to govern dispute management and limit force. This explains the absence of regulatory regimes in Asia.

There is also great reluctance to accord authority and resources, as well as
conflict management roles, to regional institutions. Asian states have been hesi-
tant to create full-fledged secretariats for the various regional forums. It took
more than two decades for ASEAN to agree on the redesignation of the ASEAN
secretary-general and to redefine the status and functions of that position
(Alagappa 1987). The ARF and ASEAN Plus Three still do not have separate secretariats. Moreover, the human and financial resources available to all three institutions are modest. In the area of conflict management, member states have
been reluctant to assign a conflict prevention role, let alone a conflict settlement
role to the ARF—the premier multilateral security institution in Asia. The dispute settlement mechanism envisaged in the 1976 Treaty of Amity and Cooperation remains unrealized. Tentative steps (such as third-party mediation) have
been initiated to expand the conflict management role of ASEAN, and the ARF
may in due course take on a circumscribed conflict prevention role. But with
member states unwilling to relinquish control in key areas, regional institutions
like ASEAN (and to a lesser degree the ARF) are likely to be more useful in developing shared understandings and in preventing the escalation of disputes to
overt hostilities than in stopping disputes from arising in the first place or in
conflict containment and settlement. Self-help, bilateral negotiations, concerted
action by two or more major powers, or the actions of the premier world power,
the United States, are likely to be more important in the effort to contain and
settle conflicts.

Another noteworthy feature of the Asian security order is its confinement to
the international domain. Viewing domestic order as the preserve of the state,
Asian countries are unwilling to allow a role for global and regional institutions
in managing domestic conflicts. They do not support a role for regional institutions in the protection of human and minority rights, for example, and firmly
oppose international interference in domestic affairs (Swamy and Gershman in
Chap. 14; Anwar in Chap. 15). The role of regional institutions has been confined

to debate and discussion of the appropriate norms. In contrast to its position on the Cambodian conflict, ASEAN did not take the initiative in the East Timor situation, which was considered to be Indonesia's domestic affair. In fact, ASEAN states contributed peacekeeping troops only after Indonesia had consented and the UN Security Council had authorized the operation. There is no desire in ASEAN or the ARF to take on a regional peacekeeping role or to manage force in a collective manner on behalf of the community in either the internal or the international domain.

Proposition Three: Multiple Pathways to Security

The largely instrumental nature of the security order in Asia is also reflected in the predominantly competitive approach to security order. Self-help, alliances, balance of power, and hegemony are key pathways to security order. These pathways, however, are increasingly tempered by the growing significance of the cooperative approach. Although the competitive approach predominates, no single pathway has achieved paramount status. Security order in post–Cold War Asia rests on multiple pathways, each serving specific functions that cannot be performed by the others.

The preponderant power of the United States and the public goods it provides weigh heavily in the management of Asian security affairs (Mastanduno in Chap. 4). Washington plays key deterrence and reassurance roles that are crucial in stabilizing major power relations and preventing the outbreak of war across the Taiwan Strait and on the Korean peninsula. Japan and, to a lesser degree, India and certain Southeast Asian countries view the United States as critical in balancing the rising power of China. And China, South Korea, and several other Asian states view Japan's security dependence on the United States as slowing the emergence of Japan as a normal power. In addition to tempering major-power relations, Washington has played a key role in defusing crisis situations like that on the Korean peninsula in 1994, across the Taiwan Strait in 1996, and in Kashmir in 1998 and 2001–2. Even if they had so desired, none of the major Asian states could have defused these crises. Either they were a party to the conflict or they suffered a "legitimacy deficit." Only the United States had the legitimacy and resources to defuse these crises. Washington's support was also crucial in launching the UN peacekeeping and peace-building efforts in Cambodia and East Timor. American capital, technology, and markets continue to be critical to the prosperity of Asian states.

Security order in Asia has a number of hegemonic features, but as observed by Michael Mastanduno (Chap. 4), hegemony is incomplete in several respects. American security management in Asia has been more akin to a holding operation. Washington has been less interested (and has had less success) in settling conflicts, promoting stable relations among the major powers, and developing effective regional institutions. The transformation of American power into authority and the development of genuine hegemony confronts several challenges—including integrating China and India into the system while maintaining support for Japan, sustaining the domestic political support and vibrant economy that are necessary to sustain hegemony, and resisting "the temptations of arrogance, triumphalism, and unilateralism" (Mastanduno in Chap. 4). We will return to the limits of the American role in security management in the next section.

While the hegemonic pathway relies on the power and authority of a single state, the balance-of-power pathway arises from the efforts of states to improve their security by developing their national capability or augmenting it through alliance and alignment. Avery Goldstein (Chap. 5) asserts that power balancing is the fundamental pattern defining Asia's security order. States in Asia, as elsewhere, seek to preserve and improve their power position while balancing and constraining the power of countries they consider threatening (or likely to threaten) their core interests. The United States seeks to maintain its predominant position while constructing an Asian counterbalance to the rising power of China; China seeks to balance the United States while limiting the development of Japan's and India's power; Japan and India seek to augment their power and balance China; Taiwan, Vietnam, and the Philippines seek to balance China; Pakistan seeks to balance India; North and South Korea seek to balance each other and are also concerned about the rising power of China and Japan; North Korea is concerned with the preponderant position of the United States. Because of their weakness and their inability to match the conventional capabilities of rivals, many Asian countries rely on nuclear weapons to balance and deter them: China vis-à-vis the United States; India vis-à-vis China; Pakistan vis-à-vis India; and North Korea vis-à-vis the United States and South Korea. In situations where conventional capability cannot be matched and the nuclear option is not available, balancing takes the form of alliances and alignments: Japan with the United States to balance China; South Korea with the United States to deter North Korea; Taiwan with the United States to deter China; the Philippines with the United States to deter China in the South China Sea; Singapore with the United States to deter its immediate neighbors.

The primary contribution of power balancing to order in Asia is related to the goal of survival. It is crucial for the survival of Taiwan and that of North and South Korea. In other cases, power balancing is designed to improve status, strategic autonomy, and flexibility, to secure a favorable position in dispute management, and to increase negotiating power. While power balancing may enhance national security by deterring war and aggression, its potential for settling conflicts, creating a stable environment, and promoting national prosperity is questionable. As Goldstein observes (Chap. 5), power balancing in Asia is certainly evident, but its contribution to security order is less clear. And while balancing is a prominent feature, the security order in Asia cannot be characterized as a balance-of-power order. The distribution of power and the lines of amity and enmity in Asia do not support balance-of-power constructs like bipolarity and multipolarity. Neither do they support a concert of power in Asia. Although several analysts (Rosencrance 1992; Allison et al. 2001; Kupchan and Kupchan 1991; Shirk 1997) have advocated global and regional concerts, the conditions for such an arrangement in Asia do not exist (Acharya 1999; Goldstein in Chap. 5). Loose ad hoc coalitions of major powers have formed from time to time, however, to manage issues of common concern such as the 1994 crisis in the Korean peninsula. Regular dialogue among the major powers in a loose forum can be a useful component of Asia's security architecture.

Power is central to both the hegemony and the balance-of-power pathways. Because of the gross imbalance in the distribution of power vis-à-vis the United States and Asian states—as well as the belief among several Asian states that power-based pathways cannot produce a stable order—regional multilateral institutions commanded increasing attention in the post–Cold War era, leading to the formation of the ARF in 1994. Regional and subregional institutions initially were "weapons of the weak" who were seeking to increase their role in the regional system and construct a norm-based security order that would reduce the centrality of power and create a relatively peaceful and predictable environment. In time, however, regional institutions have begun to command the attention of the major powers, especially China. Overcoming its initial inhibitions, Beijing has begun to view the ARF and subregional organizations like the SCO as useful forums through which it can pursue its security objectives.

Judged on the basis of rationalist criteria, the contribution of multilateral institutions to security order in Asia has not been dramatic (Acharya in Chap. 6). In fact, their failure to manage conflict and provide material public goods appears to justify the realist claim that institutions matter only on the margins. Thus several observers have cast regional institutions as an adjunct to the hegemonic and balance-of-power pathways. Although the weakness of regional institutions in conflict management is difficult to deny, it is equally important to observe the limitations of the power-based pathways in this regard. They have been effective in preventing the outbreak of war but not in settling the region's many disputes and conflicts. Indeed, in certain cases they have aggravated conflict, making conflict resolution more difficult.

Despite their shortcomings, regional institutions have made significant contributions in specific areas. By creating regional awareness and a sense of common good, regional institutions have tempered the definition of national interest on certain issues and affected the means by which certain goals have been pursued. Interaction in the ARF context and with ASEAN, for example, has affected the way Beijing pursues its claims in the South China Sea. Regular interaction, awareness of each other's concerns, the opportunity to air misgivings and ameliorate tension—all are key contributions of regional institutions. Even more significant is the role of regional institutions in socialization. ASEAN has played a central role in shaping the normative framework for Southeast Asia, while SAARC has thus far failed on this score. Although ASEAN has not resolved the disputes among member states, it has prevented the outbreak of war among them by creating a sense of community. Because the ARF is of recent vintage and because it comprises a wider group of countries and has a much larger footprint, its record is difficult to evaluate. Nevertheless the opportunity it has provided for discussion of contested issues, as well as its impact on constraining the use of force in managing conflicts like that in the South China Sea, suggests its utility in this area.

Despite the controversy over their effectiveness, regional and subregional multilateral institutions are here to stay. No state has withdrawn. Indeed, several more states seek membership in the ARF, if only to secure recognition and protection and to influence the agenda and process of the only regionwide security forum in Asia. Such cooperative multilateral institutions have become a key feature of the Asian security architecture. Although their roles and contribution may be limited, their functions cannot be performed by the power-based pathways. Hence they are not an adjunct. It is more useful to view them as one of several pathways with specific functions in the management of security affairs. Much of the recent disillusionment with regional institutions arises from unrealistic expectations. The significant contributions of regional institutions so far have been in the realm of process and ideas, which are important but intangible. To fulfill their potential to address common and collective security problems, regional institutions must overcome certain obstacles that will be discussed in the final section of this chapter.

Global multilateral institutions—those that comprise the UN security system—have not played a major role in the management of regional security in Asia since 1945 (Foot in Chap. 9). The UN is not a player in the Taiwan, Korean, and Kashmir conflicts or in the numerous territorial disputes in Asia. And although the UN has undertaken two major peace-building operations in Asia in the post–Cold war era—in Cambodia and East Timor—it is not a player in the many ongoing internal conflicts in Asia. Several reasons account for this situation: the presence of several major players—the United States, China, Russia, and

India—three of whom wield veto power in the UN Security Council and their reluctance to submit disputes in their sphere of influence to the UN; widespread Asian suspicion of the UN as a vehicle for domination by the former imperial powers and the advanced Western countries; and the growing tension between the UN's expanded liberal agenda and the Westphalian norms and values that are still cherished in Asia.

Although the UN's role in conflict management is limited, like the regional institutions it does serve certain purposes in managing Asian security affairs. First, it is an important "teacher of norms." The principles articulated in the UN Charter provide the inspiration for regional and subregional normative frameworks in Asia. The UN's expanded liberal agenda creates tensions, but in Asia this is viewed as an imposition by the West through its control over the Secretary-General. Asian leaders hark back to the Charter's principles and contest the liberal concerns (human rights, democracy, justified or humanitarian intervention) that have come to dominate the UN's contemporary agenda. Second, the UN system is valued for its role in developing global arms control regimes like the NPT, CTBT, CWC, BWC, and FMCT and for supporting such initiatives as subregional nuclear-weapon-free zones (NWFZ). Except for the NWFZ, there is no regional arms control regime in Asia; regulation must rely on global regimes. Finally, there is no regional peacekeeping mechanism or force in Asia. Here again the UN becomes relevant when the circumstances are propitious. That the UN is on the sidelines does not imply irrelevance—only that its role is limited.

Economic cooperation is a key pathway to security in Asia. Economic interdependence among East Asian and Southeast Asian states has increased significantly over the last two or three decades as a consequence of the rise of economic development as a national priority and its pursuit through participation in the global capitalist economy (Wan in Chap. 8). In some cases, economic cooperation is a consequence of deliberate policy. Though national security defined in traditional terms is still a key concern, many Asian countries attach equal and in some cases higher value to economic growth and development, which has led to a comprehensive definition of national security (Alagappa 1998). Asian states are both realists and trading states. The emergence of a trading system in Asia that is part of a larger global arrangement has had several consequences for regional security. First, the growth of economic relations has contributed to more complex relationships among the United States, China, and Japan. Tension in one sector is often mitigated by benefits in another. Economic considerations, for example, have had a stabilizing effect on the roller-coaster political and security relationship between the United States and China. Similarly, security considerations tempered the tense economic relations between Japan and the United States in the 1980s. Second, economic cooperation and interdependence have had a mitigating effect on the management of disputes, including the acute conflict across the Taiwan Strait. In the case of the Taiwan conflict, economic relations have persisted despite crisis situations and have provided the building block for the resumption and further development of cross-strait relations in the postcrisis period. Where economic interdependence is weak or nonexistent—as, for example, between India and Pakistan—political and security considerations become all-consuming and make dialogue that much more difficult. Third, growing economic interdependence has made force irrelevant in the pursuit of economic goals. It has also increased the cost of using force and contributed to a change in the salience and role of force (for defense and deterrence) in Asian international relations. Fourth, economic cooperation and interdependence have made it imperative for Asian states to honor international agreements and abide by the rules of global and regional regimes, thus elevating the goal of national and regional stability. And fifth, economic growth through participation in the global capitalist economy has transformed the definition of national interest, has altered domestic interests and power configurations (which are becoming more diverse and complex), and in several cases has contributed to democratic transitions or the movement toward more participatory political systems.

This is not to say that economic cooperation and interdependence alone can resolve political disputes, make force irrelevant, or prevent war. But they do make for much greater complexity in defining national interest and, except in the most extreme cases, make the resort to outright use of force unlikely. Moreover, they promote rule-governed interaction and hence stability and predictability in interstate relations. They have had a modifying and in certain cases transforming effect (Wan in Chap. 8). But the effect of economic cooperation on security is not a one-way street. Political considerations weigh heavily in situations like Taiwan, Korea, and Kashmir. Political decisions have to be made before economic cooperation can occur and its effects take hold. Even after the initial decision, political considerations may inhibit further cooperation, although this is becoming more difficult as demonstrated by the cases of Taiwan and Japan. There is growing concern in Japan, for example, that Japanese economic assistance has contributed to a rising China that is now viewed as a security challenge. Nevertheless, it is difficult for Tokyo to terminate economic assistance and cooperation completely. There are still strong groups in Japan who argue that the best way to manage China is to increase its economic interdependence with Japan and the region. The link between economic interdependence and security is complex. It should be noted here that Asian states rely on several strategies. The failure to resolve disputes and prevent the outbreak of war is a shortcoming, not only of commercial liberal arguments but of realist strategies as well.

It is evident from the foregoing discussion that Asia's security order rests on multiple pathways, each performing specific functions. In some ways the pathways complement each other, but their interface (on the issue of the centrality and role of the American alliance system in the region, for example) also produces tension. Reflecting the competing aspirations and legitimacy problems experienced by the major powers, the existence of competing pathways may be an obstacle to the rise of a more coherent security order in the region. Multiple pathways to order are not unusual, however, and in some ways are a healthy feature. The failure of one pathway can be compensated for by another—thus avoiding complete collapse or all-out struggle.

Proposition Four: Multiple Pillars of Stability

Many analysts ascribe peace and stability in Asia to the deterrence and reassurance roles of the United States. Hence they argue that American disengagement will intensify the security dilemma and destabilize Asia (Christensen 1999, 2000; Kupchan 1998). This is a key element of the official Washington line, as well, and the rationale advanced to justify America's forward military presence in Asia. The U.S. security role is certainly a major ingredient, but it is not the sole or even the most important foundation for peace and stability in Asia. Indeed, America's involvement in Asia has not always been stabilizing. The extension of the Cold War to Asia escalated local conflicts, resulted in two hot wars, and polarized the continent. Today the United States plays a key deterrence role (in the Taiwan Strait, for example), but this role has been viewed by certain Asian countries as provocative and destabilizing. Similarly, the U.S. determination to move ahead with the national and theater missile defense systems is viewed by a number of Asian countries as a manifestation of American unilateralism with the potential to destabilize the region. In the 1980s, unilateral U.S. actions in the economic arena were perceived as predatory behavior holding the Asian states hostage to the American security role. The initial U.S. inattention—followed by the tough U.S.-supported IMF response to the Asian economic crisis—have also been criticized in the region. My intention here is not to minimize the importance of the U.S. role but to put it in proper perspective.

Three questions are crucial. Is the United States responsible for the transformation that has occurred in Asia? Are the present peace and stability predicated on America's forward military presence and security role? And can peace and stability be maintained in the future with a reduced American role or even U.S. disengagement from Asia? Short of a real-world experiment, it is difficult to answer the second and third questions definitively. Yet it is possible to offer a reasoned response based on recent (postwar) history and ongoing changes in the region. America's deterrence role during the Cold War and the access it provided to its market, capital, and technology certainly benefited the countries allied with Washington but had negative consequences for those in the other camp. Its confrontation with the Soviet Union polarized the region into two hostile camps, with certain states opting for nonalignment. This polarization and the reliance on superpowers not only exacerbated local conflicts but stunted the development of rule-governed interaction among Asian states. The key point is that the development of international society has made the greatest progress in a subregion—Southeast Asia—after American disengagement and has made much less progress in a subregion—Northeast Asia—where the United States has continued to be engaged most heavily. Contrary to the widespread expectation that Southeast Asia would fall apart after the American withdrawal (one domino after another), the indigenous states, beginning with the ASEAN Five and gradually expanding to encompass all ten countries of the subregion, have managed to avoid competition and war among themselves. The continuation of the Cold War and the Soviet-supported Vietnamese invasion of Cambodia did pose serious challenges. But instead of undermining ASEAN, such challenges stimulated regional cooperation and the rise of an indigenous framework for interaction among the Southeast Asian states.

Analysts often argue that Northeast Asia is different from Southeast Asia. The interests of four major powers intersect in the Northeast, and conflicts there are much more intense than in the Southeast. This much is indisputable. But this argument overlooks the fact that Southeast Asia was also the scene of an intense war involving the United States and another clash (the Cambodian conflict) that engaged China directly and the Soviet Union indirectly. The intersection of the major powers' interests and a greater intensity of conflicts do not necessarily imply that Northeast Asia will become destabilized without an American presence. The claim that stability in Northeast Asia is predicated on the U.S. role rests on several assertions (Zagoria 1993): the United States deters war on the Korean peninsula and across the Taiwan Strait; the United States reassures allies and friends, allowing them to maintain low defense budgets; nearly all countries trust and prefer the United States; the U.S.-Japan security alliance prevents the emergence of a remilitarized Japan that could spark an arms race in the region; and the United States checks China's growing power and influence, which are feared by other Asian states.

Although there is an element of truth to these assertions, there is much that is also controversial. The United States does play a key role on the Korean peninsula, but it is hard to argue that North Korea, which is clearly the weaker party in the conflict, would invade South Korea in the absence of U.S. support. Indeed, the American military deployment complicates settlement of the conflict. In the case of the Taiwan dispute, American support deters PRC military action, but it also perpetuates and may even aggravate the conflict, with no resolution in sight. While the American alliance network may reassure allies and friends (Japan, South Korea), it creates apprehension in nonallied states like China and Russia, forcing them to draw closer together to counter American predominance and policies. Such a rearrangement could polarize the region. The "cork in the bottle" rationale advanced by certain American officials and echoed by others (including some Japanese) does not give due weight to the changes that have occurred in Japan over the last fifty years. Instead it stresses the historic antagonism generated by Japanese colonialism and aggression. The antagonism is real, it is important, and it must be addressed. But it does not have to be the dominating factor in the interactions of Asian states. Perhaps the "American cork" is in fact retarding regional accommodation and development. Similarly, while there is concern with the growing power of China, containment of China does not appeal to many Asian states. They would prefer a comprehensive engagement policy, but one that also includes a military dimension. It is pertinent to observe here that Sino-Vietnamese suspicion and animosity run deep. But in the aftermath of the Cold War, Hanoi, with limited options, has reached out to Beijing—and not confronted it or embarked on a self-defeating military buildup. Thus while the U.S. role is certainly important, it is not without shortcomings and is not a universally accepted good. As we will see shortly, there are other factors as well that explain the transformation that has occurred and account for the relative peace and stability which prevail in the region.

Moreover, the United States is not always the central factor in major-power relations in Northeast Asia. The PRC and the USSR were allies, then enemies, and now the Russians and the Chinese have become friends again. The role of the United States in the amity and enmity between these two countries has shifted over the years. Although Beijing aligned with Washington from 1971 through the late 1980s, beginning in the early 1980s it entered into a rapprochement with Moscow. This rapprochement and the amicable relations between them today have little to do with the United States except possibly in a negative sense. Notwithstanding their different relationships with the United States—and without American help—the two countries came to terms with each other.

Likewise the Russo-Japanese and Sino-Japanese relationships have marched to their own tunes. Changes in Soviet-American and then Russian-American relations have not affected Russo-Japanese relations in any substantive way. Tokyo still views Moscow with suspicion; the Northern Territories dispute has not been settled; and a peace treaty has yet to be concluded. Japan has been allied with the United States for the past fifty years, but its relationship with China has altered over time—and not always in sync with U.S.-China relations. In the early years, when America's strategy in Asia was focused on containing the revolutionary

Chinese communist threat, Japan did not perceive a threat from China. The U.S.-Japan alliance became more relevant to Japan in the context of the Soviet threat in Asia. The 1997 revision of the guidelines for U.S.-Japan defense cooperation has a China focus. Although the alliance with the United States is important, it is not always the dictating factor in Japan's relations with the other major powers. Further, Japan's security policy is conditioned not only by system-level changes but also by domestic considerations, especially the strong pacifist orientation of its society.

This is not to say that the role of the United States in preserving stability is unimportant or that its withdrawal from Asia will have no consequences. But its security role, while important, is not the only or even the primary foundation for peace and stability in the region. Peace and stability rest on a number of pillars. The consolidation of Asian countries as modern nation-states is a crucial part of the explanation for Asia's transformation. It has reduced the domestic and international vulnerabilities of Asian countries and increased their ability to defend their internal and external sovereignty, resulting in mutual recognition of each other as like units. Combined with the imperatives of economic development, a key priority of nearly every Asian government, mutual recognition has fostered common interests in mutual survival, prosperity, and a stable, rule-governed, international environment. Relative peace and stability in Asia have been fostered as well by the rise of an international normative structure that has naturalized the notions of sovereignty, noninterference in domestic affairs, private economic activity, and restraint in the use of force. The assurance of survival (except in a few cases), the commitment to market-based economic growth, the growing salience of norms in international behavior, and the continued attention to positional power and development of military capabilities have created a complex international social life in Asia—one that combines competition and cooperation—and have paved the way for an order that has both instrumental and normative-contractual features. Stability in the region has been aided, too, by the termination of the Cold War, the shift in the distribution of power from bipolarity to unipolarity, and the public goods provided by the United States. Taken together, then, the consolidation of Asian states, the growing salience of norms, and the shift in the distribution of power to a structure in which the United States is the predominant force provide the answer to the puzzle of stability and prosperity, despite a context of serious security challenges.

Many of the early domestic and international conflicts in Asia had their origins in the decolonization process, the state-building processes under way in the newly independent Asian countries, and the imposition of the Cold War dynamics on these processes. The internal conflicts in Asia can be traced to the newness and weakness of most Asian countries as modern nation-states and the ensuing conflict among competing factions in constructing national identities and systems for political domination. The resulting secessionist challenges and legitimacy contests weakened the nascent (and in many cases debilitated) states and opened the way for competitive interference in their domestic conflicts. Many of the early international conflicts in Asia—the Indochina wars, the Korean War, the Taiwan conflict, the Indo-Pakistani wars, the Indonesian confrontation against Malaysia and Singapore—stemmed from the decolonization process and the extension of the Cold War to Asia.

Over the years the countries of Asia have matured as modern nation-states. Although only a few states are fully consolidated and several of them still confront serious problems, many have a come a long way since independence. National identities have become more established; political systems have become more widely accepted; state capacity has increased substantially. Several Asian states still confront secessionist challenges, as noted, but for the most part these challenges are now confined to the periphery. Despite the serious internal turmoil, even Indonesia is not in serious danger of a breakup except in the peripheral areas of Aceh and West Papua. And although political systems are still in transition in a large number of countries, contestation today is not over the legitimacy of political systems but over the actual exercise of state power by incumbent rulers. And much of this contestation is channeled through the ballot box or public protests. The legitimacy of the political system is in question only in China, Vietnam, Burma, North Korea, and Pakistan. Compared with the early independence era, the capacity of most Asian states to integrate, administer, develop, and protect themselves has grown substantially. They are now much better able to manage their domestic affairs, defend their external sovereignty, and fulfill their international obligations. They have come to accept and extend mutual recognition to each other. Except for the case of Taiwan, nearly all states accept the present political map of Asia.

State consolidation in Asia has also been facilitated by the focus on economic development since the mid-1960s. Here Japan's success in "catching up with the West" has been crucial. Seeking to emulate Japan, the other Asian states— beginning with the New Industrial Economies (South Korea, Taiwan, Hong Kong, Singapore), then the Newly Industrializing Countries (Malaysia, Thailand, the Philippines), followed by China and Vietnam, and now India and the other South Asian states—accord high priority to economic growth. The emphasis on economic development, as noted earlier, has blurred the traditional hierarchy of issues, created common interest in cooperation for mutual gain, and facilitated the rise of regional institutions and regional commercial and production networks (Katzenstein and Shiraishi 1996). Market-based economic development and participation in the global capitalist economy have created further convergence in national goals that bind the Asian states to specific international norms and rules. This is not to say that there are no differences and no disagreement. But today there is much greater convergence than when states embraced rival capitalist and socialist models of development. Convergence has become even more marked in the wake of the 1997 financial crisis, which appears to have discredited Asia's developmental state model. Concentration on economic development attaches a high premium to international stability and has tempered the pursuit of traditional security goals.

The consolidation of Asian states has both contributed to and been fostered by the growing salience of international norms associated with sovereignty, private economic activity, and restraint on the use of force. Such principles favor the survival even of small and weak Asian states. The Vietnamese invasion of Cambodia and the Indonesian annexation of East Timor, for example, were resisted by Asian states and the global community and were eventually reversed. With the exception of Taiwan (and possibly South and North Korea), no Asian state is in danger of disappearing from the political map in the near term. Territorial expansion and annexation are not the objectives of any Asian state.

As noted earlier, international social life in Asia today combines features of realism and commercial liberalism and closely approximates complex interdependence. Though power politics is not absent, international politics in Asia is not the law of the jungle. Nor is it mechanically driven by structural imperatives. For the most part, states interact in accord with a set of accepted principles: mutual respect for each other's sovereignty and territorial integrity, for instance, and respect for international agreements. Violations of these principles do occur, but they are deviations rather than the norm. Power politics is tempered not only by these principles but increasingly also by the desire to cooperate for mutual gain—especially in the economic arena. The imperatives of common interests and mutual gain operate side by side with competition and zero-sum behavior.

And, finally, relative peace and stability in Asia have been aided by the predominant position of the United States and the public goods it provides. Through its alliance network and forward deployment, the United States deters war on the Korean peninsula and across the Taiwan Strait, provides security for its allies and friends, keeps the sea lines of communication open, moderates the security dilemma, and generally contributes to stability in the region. American leadership and backing have been crucial to defusing crises and initiating confidence-building and conflict-settlement measures in key regional disputes. The security and stability afforded by the United States—combined with the access it provides to its market, capital, technology, and educational facilities—have been pillars of prosperity in the region. But the United States does not want to get involved in managing the entire range of security affairs. It looked to Australia and the ASEAN countries, for example, to shoulder the responsibility in East Timor. Further, Washington is not in a position to write and enforce the rules of the game alone. Recognizing this, the United States seeks to improve its position by reinvigorating its alliance network in the region, by engaging and socializing the major countries (China, Russia, India) outside this network and steering them toward a framework based on its global and regional vision, by supporting friendly regional and subregional multilateral institutions (but only as a supplement to its alliance network) while opposing those it deems hostile, and by relying on the threat of force against countries that challenge its interests and those of its allies and friends.

That the United States plays a critical regional security role is accepted by nearly every Asian state. But the notion advanced by Washington and certain analysts—that without the American security role and forward military presence Asia's security dilemma would become full-blown and lead to an unrestrained competition for power among Asian states which would undermine regional stability and prosperity—is at best controversial. It is rejected by certain Asian countries, especially China, which, with the support of Russia, views American hegemony as provocative and destabilizing. The Treaty of Friendship and Cooperation signed by China and Russia in July 2001 is meant to counter the growing American unilateralism through coordination of their policies. And the assertion that the American security role keeps the lid on the Asian security dilemma does not take into account the implications of the consolidation of Asian states, the development of international society, and the stabilizing impact of norms. When push comes to shove, the contention is that power and force will trump norms. Although it is impossible to substantiate or refute this assertion, clearly it overstates the significance of the American role. The consequences of a reduction in the U.S. security role—and, in the unlikely worst case, the consequences of total American disengagement—may not be as disastrous as posited.

American dominance, though criticized by China and Russia, is acknowledged (or at least not contested) by most Asian countries. Their acceptance, however, is grounded in instrumental considerations. The United States provides invaluable public goods for which there is no credible alternative at this juncture. There is also a fair measure of convergence among Asian countries and the United States on the basic goals, norms, and rules associated with international interactions involving survival. Growing convergence is discernible, too, in the model for economic development, although there is disagreement over the role of global and regional institutions in crisis management as well as the content and pace of reform of national economies. There are deeper disagreements over political and strategic visions—particularly the American proposition that its alliance network forms the bedrock of security and stability in the region, its claim that democracy and human rights are universal values, and its notion that domestic affairs are not the exclusive preserve of the state.

There is general discomfort in Asia with having to rely on one power—an outside power at that—to sustain order in the region. China, Russia, India, and in some ways also Japan are dissatisfied with the status quo. These major states strive for greater status and equality among themselves and with the United States; the smaller Asian states seek to avoid being pawns in a game among the major powers. Although the post–Cold War security order in Asia has hegemonic features, it is not a hegemonic order in the Gramscian sense. There is no common worldview and no ideological unity. Consequently, as observed earlier, other pathways also feature in Asia's post–Cold War security order: power balancing (through the development of national capabilities and through alignment) among the Asian countries and against and with the United States; bilateralism; concerted issue-specific action by a select group of states that sometimes includes the United States (as in Cambodia and Korea) and sometimes excludes it (ASEAN Plus Three); participation in global and regional multilateral institutions (the UN, WTO, APEC, ARF, ASEAN Plus Three, and SCO) in order to restrain the power and influence of the United States and other Asian powers; and Asian dialogue with Europe (ASEM) to dilute reliance on the United States. The multiple layers that make up the post–Cold War order are in some instances complementary, but they have also produced tension and conflict.

Proposition Five: Evolutionary Change

As observed in Chapter 1, change may be caused by alterations in the organizing principle of the system, in the distribution of power, or in the ideational content of order and its legitimacy. The high value attached to the sovereign nation-state in Asia and the United States—as well as the presence of several major powers—implies that the organizing principle of the Asian system is unlikely to change. It will continue to be anarchic, though a hierarchical distribution of power will persist. States may adopt more flexible notions of sovereignty. Economic growth and modernization may assume even greater prominence in national agendas. Economic interdependence is likely to grow. The freeing of controlled economies, combined with the technological and information revolution, is likely to erode state control in several sectors. Nongovernmental, transnational, and multinational actors may become more significant in domestic and international politics. The role of force will continue to decline. Domestic order is likely to become more subject to international scrutiny. Although such changes will be consequential for the distribution of power and the content of order, the sovereign state will continue to be the principal actor, and sovereignty will still be the operative principle of the Asian system. Empire, colonial domination, suzerainty, voluntary political integration and union—none of these scenarios is likely. Any changes in Asia's security order, if and when they occur, are likely to come about through shifts in the distribution of power or changes in the ideational structure.

Dramatic change in the distribution of power is unlikely. Earlier predictions that Japan would become the preeminent power and challenge the United States in Asia have not been borne out (Vogel 1979; Fingleton 1994). Given Japan's current political, economic, and social circumstances, as well as the rise of other Asian powers, particularly China, it is unlikely that Japan will become Asia's hegemon. China appears to have much greater potential in this regard. Projections based on purchasing power parity suggest that China may become the world's largest economy by 2015 or 2020. As in the case of Japan, however, there is no certainty that China will realize its full potential. It faces numerous political and economic challenges. The conflict between an open economic system and monopolization of political power by the CCP; development of a legitimate political system; high unemployment and widespread social protests; a vulnerable banking system; the difficulty of reforming the state enterprise sector—these are among the challenges Beijing must overcome. Although the PRC's dramatic economic growth is an inspiration for several Asian states, its political and economic systems are not models for emulation. In fact, Beijing itself is looking for suitable political and economic models to follow. Politically, a one-party-dominant system with limited competition on the margins—as in Singapore—has attracted the attention of some Chinese leaders like Jiang Zemin. Economically, Beijing is not likely to be in a position to provide public security and welfare goods on a scale comparable to the United States for some time to come, or to articulate a credible regional vision that major Asian states would find acceptable.

The irreversible decline of the United States and the unrelenting growth of the Asian states predicted by many analysts in the 1980s and 1990s has not materialized. Hegemonic struggle and succession are unlikely. The United States is likely to continue to be the preponderant power for at least another decade or two. Washington's lead in several key areas (economy, high technology, military assets, soft power) is unlikely to narrow substantially in the near term. Moreover, there is broad agreement in the U.S. political and policy communities that Washington must be engaged and play a leadership role in Asia.[2] This consensus has become even stronger in the context of the war against international terrorism. The continued American supply of public goods—as well as the mutual dis-

[2]The advocates for disengagement from Asia and Europe are in a minority and on the fringe of the U.S. policy community. For an articulation of the reasons for disengagement, see Gholz et al. (1997).

trust among the major Asian states, which does not seem likely to disappear soon—underscores our claim that the United States will continue to play a central role in managing Asian security affairs. In time, however, the power, influence, and role of the major Asian states—China, Japan, and India—are likely to increase while those of the United States suffer relative decline. Although it faces serious challenges and may encounter setbacks, in all likelihood the Chinese economy, which appears to have passed the take-off stage, is likely to grow at a fairly fast pace. Although India, facing enormous challenges, is still hovering around the take-off stage, there is consensus in India on the need to reform and grow the economy at a faster pace. Indeed, the Indian economy has sustained respectable growth rates over the past decade, and this pattern is likely to be sustained. It is unclear when Japan will overcome its economic stagnation, but it is still the second-largest economy in the world and is technologically advanced. The move toward becoming a "normal" country will elevate its status and role in Asia.

As the identity, power, influence, and roles of the major Asian states undergo change, they will begin to adjust their perceptions and expectations of each other. This process may already have begun in the Sino-Japanese relationship. Although Beijing has been critical of the revised guidelines for U.S.-Japan defense cooperation that expand Japan's regional security role, it has come to accept that Japan is destined to become a normal power and that it is in China's interest to channel this development. Beijing may also have concluded that an independent Japan is preferable to one that is a client of the United States. Adjustments in Sino-Russian relations were discussed earlier. Some adjustment is under way in Sino-India relations as well. Although Beijing and New Delhi still have misgivings about each other and their border dispute remains unresolved, they appear to be moving toward minimizing their differences and placing the bilateral relationship on a positive footing in the context of long-range considerations. While we should not read too much into these developments, we cannot simply dismiss them. So far I have focused on the major powers, but it is important to note that Asia has several second-tier powers (Indonesia, Pakistan, Vietnam, Thailand, South Korea and potentially a unified Korea) which in the context of other regions would be considered to have the potential to become major powers. In Asia these countries are consequential for security order at the subregional level.

The foregoing discussion suggests several conclusions. A hegemonic struggle is unlikely in the next decade or two. Among the Asian countries, China's power and influence are likely to increase rapidly, but the regionwide system is unlikely to become bipolar in the short to medium term. Bipolarity hinges not only on the distribution of power but also on clear lines of enmity and amity that are not visible in Asia. Though widely anticipated in the early post–Cold War years, a multipolar order is also not on the cards any time soon. But we may well see the development of a system comprising several spheres of influence in which major countries like China, India, and Russia play central management roles in their respective subregions. Such management roles may be undertaken in conjunction with—or with the exclusion of—the United States and the other Asian powers.

Turning to the ideational dimension, the Asian security order is likely to witness substantial incremental change in the years to come. Although sovereignty will continue to be the fundamental principle and the capacity of most states to enforce internal and international aspects of sovereignty is likely to increase, these states are also likely to exercise greater flexibility in the interpretation and practice of sovereignty. This is already the case in the economic sector. As private economic activity gains ground in countries like China and India, as states become more integrated into the global capitalist economy, and as regional and bilateral trade, investment, and production regimes take root, constraints on and the pooling of sovereignty for the national and common good will become more acceptable. Economic reform and development, moreover, are likely to make societies more pluralistic and alter the domestic power configuration, spurring devolution of power and authority to states, provinces, and minority groups. In the political sector, the demands of societies that are becoming more pluralistic and the imperative to terminate long-running domestic conflicts will make participatory political systems and the options of federalism and autonomy more tenable. These developments, if they materialize, will have several consequences. They will reinforce the flexible notion of sovereignty, blur the line between domestic and international politics, and expand the role of nonstate actors in domestic and international governance. Human rights and minority rights may assume greater significance as well, and states may become more willing to consider regional and international roles in protecting and promoting these rights. Such developments will modify the Asian normative framework.

A related development is the likelihood of forging a value consensus. As noted earlier, private economic activity and the pursuit of economic development through participation in the global capitalist system are now almost universally accepted in Asia, although the pendulum may have swung too far and may soon invite adjustments to correct the negative consequences of globalization. Today there is contention over the pace of reform and the distribution of the benefits and adjustment costs, not over the right model for development. In the political arena, too, there is growing acceptance that sovereignty resides in the people and that public participation and acknowledgment are necessary to establish regime and government legitimacy. In the last two decades, democratic transitions have occurred in the Philippines, South Korea, Taiwan, Mongolia, Russia, Bangladesh, Nepal, Thailand, and Indonesia. Some of these transitions are fragile, however, and may suffer reversal. And there are several determined holdouts, including China, Vietnam, Pakistan, Burma, and North Korea. The legitimacy of the incumbent political systems in nearly all these countries has eroded substantially, however, and the political leadership is groping for alternative political frameworks. In China, for example, there is growing recognition that the CCP cannot continue to monopolize political power (Dickson 2001). Some tentative steps—broadening the base of the Communist Party, for example, by admitting businessmen and organizing local elections—have been taken. But these may not be enough. The fourth generation of the CCP leadership might be forced to experiment with more far-reaching steps to bring about democracy with Chinese characteristics. Political developments in Taiwan and South Korea refute the claim that democracy is incompatible with Chinese Confucian values. The long-term trend in Asia is toward a market economy, democratization, and protection of individual and minority rights. Yet values in the political arena will be slow to change. And the process will be tension-prone and subject to setbacks. Taken together, however, the developments cited here—the rise of Asian powers, the consolidation of Asian states, and the strengthening of the Asian normative framework—will gradually reduce the centrality of American power in the Asian security order.

The pace and specific direction of this trajectory will be affected by several developments. A prolonged economic downturn in the United States (as in the middle to late 1980s), a war on the Korean peninsula, or a war across the Taiwan Strait in which the United States incurred high casualties would raise questions about the depth and cost of U.S. engagement in Asia—as would growing opposition in Korea and Japan to American forward deployment. A U.S. failure to attend to Asian concerns—or a tendency to extract more benefits than it provides—could also raise questions in Asia about relying on the United States as the cornerstone of order. The pursuit of expansionist foreign policies by China or Japan would also challenge American hegemony. Should one or more of these developments materialize, Asia could move rapidly in the direction of an uncontrived balance-of-power system in which instrumental considerations would weigh heavily in the management of international affairs. A negotiated settlement in Korea or Taiwan and continued economic growth in the Asian countries would lead to a contrived balance-of-power system in which there is common understanding among the major players. But severe and prolonged economic downturns and internal turmoil among the major Asian powers, especially in China, are likely to reinforce the dominant position of the United States.

If the evolutionary model does hold, features of the normative-contractual order are likely to become more prominent in Asia. Certain aspects of the solidarity order may also develop. As trade, investment, and other economic, political, and social interactions deepen, the remaining conflicts are likely to be managed without recourse to war. Rule-governed international interaction will become the norm. This cautiously optimistic scenario, which runs counter to the idea of Asia as a dangerous place, is based on an extrapolation of developments in the region over the last two or three decades. Cautious optimism does not imply that there are no challenges to be overcome. Indeed, there are many. In addressing the challenges highlighted throughout this book, the goal should not be to produce a brand-new blueprint. Such an approach is not feasible. After all, we are not writing on a blank slate. Moreover, the challenges cannot be dealt with quickly. Instead the goal must be to strengthen the relevant forces and features of the present framework gradually in order to make Asia's security order more robust.

Works Cited

Acharya, Amitav. 1999. "A Concert of Asia?" *Survival* 41(3): 84–101.

Alagappa, Muthiah. 1987. "ASEAN Institutional Framework and Modus Operandi: Recommendations for Change." In Noordin Sopiee, Chew Lay See, and Lim Siang Jin, eds., *ASEAN at the Crossroads*. Kuala Lumpur: ISIS Malaysia.

———. 1994. *Democratic Transition in Asia: The Role of the International Community*. Honolulu: East-West Center Special Report No. 3.

———. 1998. "Asian Practice of Security: Key Features and Explanations." In Muthiah Alagappa, ed., *Asian Security Practice: Material and Ideational Influences*. Stanford: Stanford University Press.

Allison, Graham, Karl Kaiser, and Sergei Karaganov. 2001. "The World Needs a Global Alliance for Security." *International Herald Tribune* (Paris), Nov. 21.

Ayoob, Mohammed. 2000. "From Regional System to Regional Security: Exploring Key Variables in the Construction of Regional Order." *Australian Journal of International Affairs* 53(3): 247–60.

Bauer, Joanne R. And Daniel A. Bell, eds. 1999. *The East Asian Challenge for Human Rights*. New York: Cambridge University Press.

Christensen, Thomas J. 1999. "China, the U.S.-Japan Alliance, and the Security Dilemma in East Asia." *International Security* 23(4): 49–80.

———. 2000. "Spirals, Security, and Stability in East Asia." *International Security* 24(4): 195–200.

De Barry, W. Theodore. 1998. *Asian Values and Human Rights: A Confucian Communitarian Perspective*. Cambridge, Mass.: Harvard University Press.

Dickson, Bruce. 2001. "Taiwan's Democratization: What Lessons for China?" In Muthiah Alagappa, ed., *Taiwan's Presidential Politics: Democratization and Cross-Strait Relations in the Twenty-first Century*. Armonk, N.Y.: M. E. Sharpe.

Fingleton, E. 1994. *Blindside: Why Japan Is Still on Track to Overtake the U.S. by the Year 2000*. Boston: Houghton Mifflin.

Gholz, Eugene, Daryl C. Press, and Harvey M. Sapolsky. 1997. "Come Home America: The Strategy of Restraint in the Face of Temptation." *International Security* 21(4): 5–48.

Haider, Ejaz. 2002. "Stable Deterrence and Flawed Pakistan Nuclear Strategy." *Friday Times*, Islamabad, Feb. 2.

IISS (International Institute for Strategic Studies). 1996. *The Military Balance 1995–1996*. London: Oxford University Press.

———. 2001. *The Military Balance 2000–2001*. London: Oxford University Press.

Katzenstein, Peter J., and Takashi Shiraishi, eds. 1996. *Network Power: Japan and Asia*. Ithaca: Cornell University Press.

Krasner, Stephen D. 1993. "Westphalia and All That." In Judith Goldstein and Robert O. Keohane, eds., *Ideas and Foreign Policy: Beliefs, Institutions, and Political Change*. Ithaca: Cornell University Press.

Kupchan, Charles A. 1998. "After Pax Americana: Benign Power, Regional Integration, and the Sources of a Stable Multipolarity." *International Security* 23(2): 40–79.

———, and Clifford A. Kupchan. 1991. "Concerts, Collective Security, and the Future of Europe." *International Security* 16(1): 114–61.

Rosencrance, Richard N. 1992. "A New Concert of Power." *Foreign Affairs* 71(2): 64–82.

Shirk, Susan L. 1997. "Asia-Pacific Regional Security: Balance of Power or Concert of Powers?" In David A. Lake and Patrick M. Morgan, eds., *Regional Orders*. University Park: Pennsylvania State University Press.

Vogel, Ezra F. 1979. *Japan as Number One: Lessons for America*. Cambridge, Mass.: Harvard University Press.

Yuan, Jing-Dong. 2000. "The Evolution of Chinese Nonproliferation Policy 1989–1999: Progress, Problems, and Prospects." Paper presented at the 41st Annual Convention of the International Studies Association in Los Angeles.

Zagoria, Donald S. 1993. "The Changing U.S. Role in Asian Security in the 1990s." In Sheldon W. Simon, ed., *East Asian Security in the Post–Cold War Era*. Armonk, N.Y.: M. E. Sharpe.

Index

Index

In this index an "f" after a number indicates a separate reference on the next page, and an "ff" indicates separate references on the next two pages. A continuous discussion over two or more pages is indicated by a span of page numbers, e.g., "57–59." *Passim* is used for a cluster of references in close but not consecutive sequence.